OF
CABBAGES
AND KINGS
COUNTY

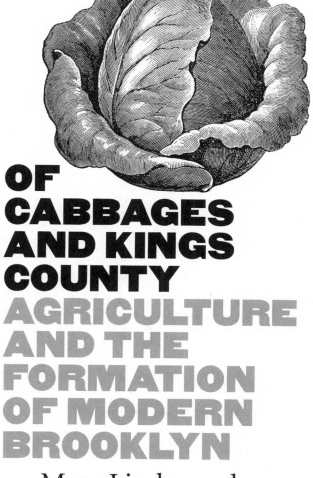

OF CABBAGES AND KINGS COUNTY

AGRICULTURE AND THE FORMATION OF MODERN BROOKLYN

Marc Linder and
Lawrence S. Zacharias

University of Iowa Press ♅ Iowa City

University of Iowa Press, Iowa City 52242
Printed in the United States of America
http://www.uiowa.edu/~uipress
Printed on acid-free paper

Library of Congress Cataloging-in-Publication Data
Linder, Marc.
    Of cabbages and Kings County: agriculture and the formation of
modern Brooklyn / by Marc Linder and Lawrence S. Zacharias.
        p.   cm.
    Includes bibliographical references and index.
    ISBN 0-87745-670-4
    1. Brooklyn (New York, N.Y.)—History.   2. Brooklyn (New York,
N.Y.)—Economic conditions.   3. Land use, Rural—New York
(State)—New York—History.   4. Urbanization—New York (State)—
New York—History.   5. Agriculture—Economic aspects—New York
(State)—New York—History.   6. Farms—New York (State)—New
York—History.   I. Zacharias, Lawrence.   II. Title.
    F129.B7L6   1999
    333.76'13'0974723—DC21   98-51779

99   00   01   02   03   C   5   4   3   2   1

Publication of this book was made possible in part by a grant from the
Iowa Law School Foundation.

Dere's no guy livin' dat knows Brooklyn t'roo an' t'roo

(only the dead know Brooklyn t'roo and t'roo). . . . He'll

neveh live long enough to know duh whole of Brooklyn.

It'd take a guy a lifetime to know Brooklyn t'roo and t'roo.

An' even den, yuh wouldn't know it all.

— Thomas Wolfe, "Only the Dead Know Brooklyn," 1935

CONTENTS

ACKNOWLEDGMENTS

Arthur Bonfield could not know that he was provoking this book when he idly reminisced about commercial vegetable gardens in the Bensonhurst of his childhood. Sylvia Linder, who lived in nearby Bath Beach in the 1930s and has lived in Flatbush during the last half of the twentieth century — on land once part of a large Flatlands farm owned by John A. Lott, a major agent of the suburbanization of rural Kings County — made signal contributions to this book. Despite her 81 years and failing eyesight, she meticulously read, on microfilm, a rare copy of the *Kings County Rural Gazette* at the Brooklyn Historical Society just before it shut down for five years, identifying and photocopying crucial sources. She also shamed the author-lawyers by showing how simple title searches at Brooklyn City Hall and finding wills at the Kings County Surrogate's Court can be.

Frank Allen, Dick Andress, Arthur Bankoff, Daniel Bluestone, John Celardo, Lola Schenck Cheney, Christopher Clark, Ken Cobb, David Cohen, Merle Davis, Carlotta De Fillo, Andrew Dolkart, Firth Fabend, Cynthia Fox, Charles Gehring, Joy Holland, Gail Hollander, Kenneth Jackson, Jeffrey Kroessler, Paul Mattingly, David Ment, Annette Mont, Stuart Mont, Delia Nelson, Eric Nooter, Judy Polumbaum, Tom Prendergast, Rev. Daniel Ramm, Debbie Randorf, Peter Rapelje, Eleanor Rapelje, Christopher Ricciardi, Eleanora Schoenebaum, Catharine Weber Scarborough, Vincent Seyfried, Steve Sullivan, Louis Tremante, Reginald Washington, Craig Wilder, and William Younger pointed the way to important sources or questions. Librarians, archivists, and others at the Brooklyn Historical Society, Brooklyn Public Library, Reformed Protestant Dutch Church of Flatbush, Holland Society of New York, Lefferts Homestead, Museum of the City of New York, National Archives (Washington, D.C., and Northeast Region), New-York Historical Society, New York City Department of Records and Municipal Archives, New York Public Library, New York State Archives, New York State Library, and Staten Island Historical Society made essential materials available.

Several custodians deserve special mention: Ken Cobb of the New York City Municipal Archives for sending scores of microfilm reels of Kings County documents; Joy Holland and Judith Walsh of the Brooklyn Division of the Brooklyn Public Library for facilitating the reproduction of that library's possibly unique microfilm copy of the entire run of the *Rural Gazette*, whose 706 issues proved to be the single richest source on daily life in rural Kings County in the 1870s and 1880s; and Annette Mont and Stuart

Mont, owners of the Wyckoff-Bennett Homestead, for photocopying unique farm ledgers (quickly and expertly performed by Laura Hlavin) and opening their Gravesend house and barn for strangers to rummage through the last written and material remains of the county's intensive agriculture.

Finally, to Judy Polumbaum goes the credit for relentlessly encouraging this book as well as discovering the heretofore unknown connection between Lewis Carroll and Brooklyn.

1. INTRODUCTION: URBAN REMOVAL OF AGRICULTURE

Brooklyn of all great cities . . . is provincial as a land of rich earth and of this earth an enormous farm, whose crop is . . . human flesh and being.
— James Agee, "Brooklyn Is," 1968

Someone standing on the highest hill in Flatbush in the 1860s, to the east and south of Prospect Park and to the southwest of a large primeval forest, would have taken in "a vista of the finest farmlands in America, almost tree-less for 6 miles and beyond, in full view of the Atlantic Ocean." To the south lay the village of Flatbush with its one thoroughfare, Brooklyn and Flatbush Turnpike, "winding its way through the most magnificent growth of orna-mental trees in the country, the dwellings of the comfortable Dutch owners peeping through an occasional opening in the trees, giving evidence of thrift and competency." [1]

Looking out from the same crest of the ridge in early 1873, the editor of the *Kings County Rural Gazette*, the new Flatbush weekly, rhapsodized about "one of the loveliest landscapes ever mortal vision was permitted to gaze upon . . . the rich farmlands of the southern slope with their ancient home-steads standing out here and there in quiet rural beauty." But H. J. Egleston's absorption in the "beauties of nature and art as displayed in the proximity of city and county" did not blind him to the fact that the "palatial residences of the merchant princes of the cities have now attained to the very sum-mit of our dividing ridge." In an editorial titled "Development," he pre-dicted that hundreds of dwellings would be built for the thousands of new residents following in the wake of rapid transit: "Already does the far-seeing eye of the speculator in real estate cast its keen penetrating gaze upon this beautiful southern slope, and soon with ruthless hand, the golden king will sway his potential scepter over our rural district, and perhaps entice our own staid citizens into a participation of the spoils which may accrue in a more full development of the advantages our village possesses as a place of abode."[2]

Egleston's vision of creeping development was prescient indeed. Because the process had been so gradual as to be "almost unawares" to contemporaries in the 1870s, while "the city of Brooklyn experienced a building boom . . . , some three miles away" the village of Flatbush seemed to remain "essentially the same, and eighteenth-century houses . . . evoked daily memories of the early Dutch settlers." Yet, being so "stunningly close to the nation's financial, commercial, and industrial center . . . created a kind of time warp" that was intolerable during the Gilded Age and called forth dramatic change. And so by the end of the 1890s, the fields had vanished and someone standing on that same hill in Flatbush would have seen mainly dense residential settlements.[3]

American urban history conventionally traces the growth of cities, focusing in particular on the internal dynamics of expansion. Rarely have historians paid attention to what was lost, treating the landscape surrounding the core settlement as merely a city-waiting-to-happen. The dichotomy between agriculture and cities (definitionally "made up of persons who do not cultivate the soil") was so self-explanatory to Adna Weber's turn-of-the-century international comparative study of urbanization that he declared it "conceivable that transportation . . . might be so perfected as to permit the cultivator of the soil to reside in a city, but . . . very unlikely." This book explores a question that has largely remained a black box of urban history: exactly how did a major city embrace, enclose, and finally obliterate its surrounding farms? This study considers what the city destroyed and the opportunities that were lost. By melding analysis of the rise and decline of intensive vegetable farming with the study of (sub)urbanization, this book seeks to add a new dimension to agricultural history and urban history instead of perpetuating their disciplinary separation or mutual ignorance.[4]

Kings County, New York, as the vegetable capital of America? If *The WPA Guide to New York City* found that people in 1939 were startled by Brooklyn's rank as the country's fifth largest manufacturing center, credulity today must snap under the revelation that as late as 1880, this icon of city life sustained enough farms to rank as the nation's biggest producer of vegetables after neighboring Queens County: "The numerous Flatbush farm trucks that rolled into the New York City markets in the 'Eighties' gave

FIGURE 1. *William Schenck (1839–1913) driving his market wagon in rural Kings County. Courtesy of Lola Schenck Cheney.*

ample proof of this." Kings County vegetable farmers in the 1880s were "doing a thriving business" and "reaping enormous crops." Flatbush and the other rural Dutch towns in Kings County were still known as the "Market Garden of America." An article on market gardens in the popular press in 1888 noted that while "all of arable Long Island" produced vegetables for New York and Brooklyn, it was particularly "on the cityward end" of the island, between Brooklyn and Jamaica Bay, that "'truck farming' is to be seen in all its picturesqueness." [5]

Yet already by 1905 the *New York Times* found it quaint that someone was "Teaching City Children How to Become Farmers." When the park commissioner permitted a park in Manhattan to be used to teach children to raise cabbage, lettuce, and spinach, the newspaper asked rhetorically: "Farms, farmhouses, and farmers in the heart of New York City seem an anomaly, don't they?" The same year, *A Home Geography of New York City*, a textbook for elementary schools, was indoctrinating in children the axiom that: "The inhabitants of New York are not miners, not farmers, not lumbermen, not quarrymen, not fishermen. They are manufacturers and distributers." And by 1913, the Brooklyn Botanic Garden in Flatbush found it necessary to initiate those too young to remember into what had become the mystery of where vegetables came from: "It would indeed seem absurd in a village or small city to offer the public as an educational exhibit, speci- mens of . . . cabbages, but in a city the size of Greater New York there are in- numerable children and young people who have never seen . . . beans and peas growing on the plants that produce them."[6]

This vanishing of the agrarian past is not limited to popular conscious- ness. The sudden disappearance of the agricultural sector of Kings County remains a missing page in urban historiography as well. Historians have paid scant attention to the fact that Kings County thrived as a leading agricul- tural center in the United States for 250 years and then, in the surprisingly short period of 20 years, semiarbitrarily registered between the decennial censuses of 1890 and 1910, was almost entirely converted into an urban res- idential community. This discontinuous development is also missing from the pages of the New York region's histories and the related historical liter- atures about Dutch Americans, the principal farming group during the ear- lier period. It is also absent from works on U.S. agricultural development in general. Even excellent social histories of urban growth either totally ignore the process of deagriculturalization or, where they discuss the incorpora- tion of the rural land base, treat the demise of farming as a quasi-natural process not in need of elucidation. This book is the first work to examine the historical formation of a major city in the United States from the per- spective of the economics of the disappearing agricultural sector while fully appreciating the political-economic agency of the (self-)displaced farmers.[7]

If, as the author of the only dissertation on nineteenth-century rural Kings County observed, "Brooklyn has been almost totally ignored by his- torians," such neglect has been even more intensely the fate of farming, the economic mainstay of the county's nonurban southern half. When the di- rector of the Long Island Historical Society said of a catalog of paintings that they "trac[e] the evolution of Brooklyn from a collection of rural agrarian villages to a modern industrial metropolis," he was speaking only meta- phorically. This agricultural amnesia has been widespread. The *Brooklyn Eagle* — itself destined to disappear a few years later as the borough's last re- maining daily newspaper — reported in 1949 on the "last farmer," who pro- duced such vegetables as broccoli, squash, and Italian dandelions on a three- acre rented farm, which was yielding to a housing project. Pictured against the frame of the rising apartment houses, the "weather-beaten toiler and his two helpers . . . looked like people in a stage setting." The only hint that agriculture had once been a way of life in this eastern section of Flatbush was the farmer's story that when he had begun vegetable farming 23 years earlier, "he could rent as much land as he could handle, and there were many other farmers around him."[8]

The inevitability of agricultural dissolution in the face of urban expansion was taken for granted for much of the nineteenth and twentieth centuries. This view surfaced in connection with the earlier history of Manhattan, then again just past midcentury when Brooklyn's population boomed, and once more when Queens, which as late as 1905 was still largely "a region of farms . . . mostly devoted to the production of vegetables for sale in the city markets," underwent urbanization. At the turn of the century, it seemed "certain" to a historian of Long Island that the future of this "purely agricultural community . . . where the ground [was] tilled by its owners" was "not to lie in agriculture. It will be by the growth of its manufactures," the prerequisite for which was "cheap and adequate communication with the rest of the continent," which was "promised in the fullest measure in the near future." It was no everyday event when in 1928 a front-page headline of the *New York Times* Sunday real-estate section waxed nostalgic: "Farms Disappear in Dyckman Area: Apartment Building Has Wiped Out Vestiges of Early Rural Life." Although the remaining farms in northern Manhattan were only miniature, they were "laid out with considerable artistic taste, and the crops of vegetables and succulent greens for tasty salads provided several hundred families in neighboring apartment houses with appetizing food and doubtless curtailed household expenses." This "partnership with nature," which included "the joy of seeing things worth while grow," reminded the *Times* of "the extensive market garden acres in Queens which seem to have disappeared from sight almost overnight."[9]

At almost the same time, the chief apologist for the expulsion of agriculture from Queens, dispensing with the nostalgia, could argue simply that the "home of six families has grown into the home of 2,000 families, or more than 6,000 persons." In a formal democracy, no matter how corrupt or dominated by "machines," numbers count; and when the relative numbers are as disproportional as these, the perseverance of the countermajority is not likely to find much favor. Another observer suggested that the merging of city and country was not "a compromise of equals. The original movement was, and the major movement is the city's. The suburb is a footnote to urban civilization affecting the countryside."[10]

Curiously, even late-nineteenth-century contemporaries — policymakers and urban planners among them — took little note of the rapid market-forced conversion into residential real estate of virtually the entire sector of profitable potato, vegetable, and dairy farms, which had been a vital component of the provisioning of the explosively growing populations of the cities of New York and Brooklyn. As late as 1884, Henry Stiles's history of Kings County could still call it "one immense garden" catering to the "vast and increasing demand of the city of New York for vegetables and fruits of a perishable nature." At this relatively early period in U.S. economic growth, when agriculture still accounted for half of total employment nationally and was adding one to two million persons to its rolls each decade, the disappearance of a territorially discrete way of life should have been a sufficiently uncommon experience to have merited comment. Yet if the largely completed process of deagriculturalization in Manhattan was viewed as the archetype, inevitabilist attitudes rendered discussion moot.[11]

In the event, within a few years of the formation of Greater New York in 1898, the second-largest city in the world (after London) was quickly becoming an international financial center without losing its status as the country's largest manufacturing center and entrepôt. These linked economic functions forged "a complex assemblage of building types set within a diversified metropolis: a vast array of skyscrapers, department stores, and hotels juxtaposed with residential quarters both lavish and squalid, warehouses and port facilities, factories and sweatshops" — but not an acre for farms.[12]

This story is not an uncommon one in the United States or other industrialized societies. Already by the beginning of the seventeenth century, "the relentless spread of building had pushed market gardens into the suburbs and surrounding countryside" of London, employing thousands and "contriv[ing] a minor revolution in the ordinary citizen's diet." Before the middle of the nineteenth century, Boston's growth had converted some close-in market gardens in Brookline, Roxbury, and Jamaica Plain into house lots, inducing vegetable farmers to push outward to Arlington, Watertown, and Newton. Chicago and other cities grew at even faster rates in the nineteenth century, displacing substantial and fertile farmlands with the signposts of urban geography. Now known as (sub)urban sprawl, the process has been repeated many times since the 1890s and on a much larger scale. In the northeastern United States, for example, 85 percent of rural land urbanized between 1950 and 1960 was converted to residential use. Socioeconomic and political conflicts over agricultural land are said to have been generally muted because: "With its abundance of high-quality farmland, the United

States has never had to work out a way for agriculture to coexist with metropolitan expansion. The sharp increase in land prices accompanying commercial or residential development, leaving the land much too expensive for farming, has never threatened the food supply; cheaper land has always been available elsewhere."[13]

The force of capitalist development can be so profound that it propels the conversion of farmland even where "the nightmare of food shortages" for hundreds of millions may result. In China in the 1990s, land in Guangdong province "is prized by farmers for its fertility, but real-estate developers say that its value to farmers cannot compare to its value as the site of" the luxury hotels or soda bottling plants that have ousted farmers. Despite orders from the central government to preserve the little remaining farmland, "the huge profits from land sales tend to overwhelm any fear of the central Government." Regarding the outskirts of the provincial capital, Guangzhou, a city of several million inhabitants, the New York Times finds it difficult to imagine how the farmers can survive — "the land is just too valuable to permit it to be used for farming much longer."[14]

The result of urban sprawl has been a renewed rigidification of the historical division of labor between city and countryside, dichotomizing farmers and urban residents in both geography and attitude: "The widening gap in physical distance between the point of production and the point of consumption has its counterpart in the attenuation and mutual understanding between producers and consumers." The physical deterioration associated with mutually reinforcing urban overcrowding and rural depopulation that early-twentieth-century planners identified as the legacy of industrialization has scarcely abated.[15]

All along, explanations and rationalizations for what took place have emphasized variations on the-market-knows-best theme. Many economists believe that "no process can take into account all of the relevant variables as fully as do bid and asked prices in a competitive market, since the market process harnesses nearly all available information. . . . [T]he only market failure that could justify social intervention in the land market is the provision of open space as a collective public good." With regard to all other uses, however, the "equilibrium market price for agricultural land" is allegedly so perfect that it even represents "the interests of future generations . . . since speculative bids are based on what future users are expected to be willing to pay." This unerring accuracy does not presuppose omniscience; on the contrary, even a short-sighted speculator in agricultural land can drive this machine — provided that he is "motivated by profits." For even if his view of the land's future value is wrong, "if potential bidders begin to realize this, he will suffer a loss as the land's value rises less rapidly than other assets that could have been purchased. Whatever happens, the farmland is preserved."[16]

Yet at the same time, troublesome questions linger that few have chosen to address. One way of formulating the question for discussion here is whether this apotheosis of the market fits the urbanization of rural Kings County at the end of the nineteenth century — that is, whether "the private market will normally guide developers to use land that is less suited for crops when it is in society's best interest to do so," or, conversely, whether the market made a mistake, as it were, because there were no institutional means by which the collective-good character of the land on which a diverse selection of local fresh vegetables could be produced for New York City's population could be reflected in land prices. Was the conversion of Kings County at the turn of the century, in other words, an early American illustration of "the irrational spread of cities into farmlands"? After all, even some who concede that utilization of "farmland by urbanization is often justifiable as the highest and best use of land at current land values," note that "the range of market values of farmlands does not reflect the long term value or the irreplaceable nature of these living soils."[17]

The nineteenth-century case study embodies crucial twentieth-century dilemmas, for these troublesome issues have come full circle in the context of land-use planning and urban environments. Perhaps the most spectacular recent site of irrational deagriculturalization is Los Angeles–Orange County, where as late as the postwar 1940s, farms within a fifty-mile radius of the Los Angeles civic center met most of the city population's demand for produce, dairy, and poultry and most of the nation's demand for citrus. Yet within fifteen years, even this "exceptionally scarce . . . land that can grow high quality citrus and other fruits and winter vegetables at high yields with a minimum amount of crop failure" had largely made way for metropolitan expansion: by 1960, the City of Los Angeles had taken over nine-tenths of Los Angeles County's best farmland. Unlike the transformation of Kings County in the 1890s, however, the conversion of California land has engendered a high-profile and contentious public dispute. In Los Angeles, the conflict erupted over the fact that private benefits created at public cost were not reflected in market transactions: "Perhaps it makes sense to pave over farmlands that are in production, and then spend millions to make arid lands suitable for farming. In somebody's reckoning it must pay off to build houses on orange groves in Los Angeles County, and then pump water down from Northern California to make oranges grow in Kern County."[18]

Some economic geographers believe that "population growth of urban nucleations, and the transport innovations accompanying the industrial revolution . . . precipitated and facilitated an orderly change of agricultural land-use patterns and the spatial extension of agricultural hinterlands." Yet others were still confirming the rationality of close-in vegetable farming as late as the 1960s: "For a radius of forty or fifty miles around New York City land not already occupied by urban functions frequently can best be used for truck crops. This intensive use helps satisfy the almost insatiable demand for these products by the city and at the same time results in enough production from a given acre to warrant the longest possible continuation of the land in agricultural use." The reasons for the demise of Kings County farming are, in any event, not adequately stated by those that geographers use to explain why almost two-thirds of all New York State farmers went out of business from 1875 to 1960: noncompetitiveness based on poor soil, small size, unfavorable location with respect to transportation and markets, and unenlightened management.[19]

On the other hand, a thoroughly plausible argument is that selling off farmland in the 1880s and 1890s and cutting coupons financed by the proceeds appeared more lucrative to Kings County Dutch farmers than continuing to cultivate cabbages or extracting rents from those who did. It is regrettable that archival research turned up no contemporaneous document — not even the back of an envelope — in which some ninth-generation Bergen, Kouwenhoven, or Vanderveer made the relevant calculations. But this book does present an analysis of a mass of unpublished data, distilled from manuscript schedules of the censuses of population and agriculture, assessment rolls, tax records, and newspapers, which not only quantifies how lucrative the sell-off was, but also explains why the abandonment of farming was not purely "market driven," if that term is taken to mean that Kings County vegetable producers could not compete with distant market gardeners who shipped their produce to New York.

An axiom of orthodox land economics that has been applied to understand the conversion of farmland to other economic uses in the New York City area is that: "Under urban regimes as various as the Dutch, British, Tammany Hall, and others . . . the real estate consistently followed two 'iron laws.' The first was that when strategic moments arrived and decisions had to be made, almost every owner put his land to whatever use would make him the most money. The second iron law was that, once committed, land remained in that use until the land by itself was worth more for other purposes than for any use the land could sustain in combination with the building on it." [20]

Although even "Times Square could be returned to farming," because "the expense is utterly beyond anything economically sustainable . . . the transfer of land away from agriculture has been irreversible." Two startling examples illustrate the laws of commercial highest use. Ground at the corner of Wall and Broad Streets in Manhattan was sold in 1882 for the equivalent of $14 million per acre. In 1916 the annual rental income from 22 square feet — the size of two desks — situated in Wall Street exceeded the annual income of the average farmer with a 100-acre farm. If that average farmer had owned 100 acres of land around Wall Street, his income would have been $6,000,000. [21]

Underlying these "laws" is the process by which a sphere of consumption (housing) can outbid agriculture for its land. This process is mediated by the "professional land dealer, who looks upon the land as a commodity to be traded in, rather than as a factor of production to be used in a production process." To be sure, it was true in Kings County in the nineteenth century, as it has been in the post–World War II period nationally, that: "With rare exceptions, undeveloped suburban land that conceivably could be developed within twenty years has a price far above its price for any alternative use. There are exceptions: good citrus-growing land in California and Florida, where the agricultural value may be several thousand dollars an acre. . . . But the vast majority of undeveloped suburban land with any prospect for development within two decades is held at prices ranging upward from ten times its agricultural income." [22]

Nevertheless, the overexpansion of the older cities and their eventual supersession by more modern, convenient versions — more manageable, better planned, and technologically more adaptable cities — seem as inevitable as the original impetus toward expansion, and are accompanied by endless cycles of poverty, intractable ghettoes, and a massive waste of social resources. The ultimate question thus becomes: Should these planlessly cumulated, market-registered profit aspirations of speculators, developers, and builders as well as individual consumer preferences for residential locations be considered an adequate proxy for a set of consciously articulated community preferences — let alone be taken for granted as the superior method of making quasi-irrevocable spatial realignment land-use decisions of massive proportions? Or are there reasons to seek and maintain a balance, where possible, to plan, allocate, and to set more manageable goals and boundaries for urbanization? [23]

Urban sprawl may have been a necessary condition of industrialization in the United States in the sense that the agricultural base that preceded and surrounded the city could not have survived the onrush of residential real-estate speculation without foresight and public policies that the politically outnumbered farmers could not have implemented on their own. As this book acknowledges, however, it would have been politically implausible in late-nineteenth-century New York to justify a public sector urban-planning process since municipal planning was minimalist and regional planning authorities nonexistent. Indeed, New York may have been in the worst possible position to carry out such planning: as late as 1913 the National Conference on City Planning heard that New York City had "less power . . . than any other city in the United States. In New York you cannot alter the plan of a single street . . . without having to go to Albany for an act of the legislature." Moreover, governmental authorities were so restrained in their provision of infrastructure of any kind that an interventionist location or preservation strategy on behalf of agricultural land would have been virtually unthinkable. Development in the New York region "occurred mostly through the accretive results of market forces or political deals." If opposition to the introduction of zoning (even without general planning) in New York City in 1916 was rooted in the laissez-faire notion that "if a man paid money for a piece of land he was entitled to use it as he saw fit," such anti-statist views were even more pronounced in the Gilded Age. After all, since the early nineteenth century the city had been "treated not as a public institution, but a private commercial venture to be carved up in any fashion that might increase the turnover and further the rise in land values." [24]

Even later on, in 1929, the Regional Plan of New York and Its Environs, predicting that to "acquire land for 'lung' space and to use it for farms might not be regarded by the courts as legitimate county or city uses and purposes," opined that legislative enactment would be required to legitimate such actions. Indeed, several generations later, the enormously expanded powers of the various New York City metropolitan area planning agencies were not used to bring country and city closer together. For example, the same "public [that] built the Verrazano-Narrows Bridge from Brooklyn to Staten Island . . . that has suddenly opened up the last rural part of New York City to massive residential development by private persons . . . neglected to regulate the planless, headlong rush to subdivide, to bulldoze and to build badly designed houses that are . . . scarring the Staten Island landscape." As a result, New Yorkers are no longer "permitted the refreshing contrast of escaping to . . . a swath of open country whose isolation from urban traffic makes it possible to still engage in farming." The contemporaneous dumping onto Long Island's potato fields of "a population the size of Philadelphia" without any provision for mass transit is another example of how undemocratically structured, publicly built infrastructure can perpetuate urban congestion.[25]

Nevertheless, historians and urban planners have noted counterexamples of public sector intervention, even for the earlier period. For example, Stockholm's turn-of-the-century acquisition of agricultural land outside of the city limits for eventual residential development was designed to avoid the unplanned sprawl of working-class suburbs. In the second half of the twentieth century, too, Stockholm has been credited with having preserved rural space for its metropolitan area.[26]

Commonly ignored in the free-market celebration of historically evolved urban configurations is that the claim that "Americans have 'voted with their feet' in favor of the great cities is . . . nonsense. . . . [F]reedom of individual choice . . . is largely an illusion. In the aggregate the nation's . . . workers must distribute themselves according to where the jobs are. And workers do not decide where jobs are located; employers do. . . . The United States, alone among advanced industrial democracies, has made it a matter of practice . . . to uphold the freedom of corporate choice." [27]

If governments in the United States in the latter half of the twentieth century have largely refrained from interfering with the industrial location decisions flowing from the anarchic demands of capital accumulation, their hands-off stance in the late nineteenth century is self-explanatory. The irreversible conversion of the bulk of Kings County farmland within the relatively short time from the middle 1880s to the end of the 1890s was facilitated by the inevitabilist attitude of landowners, policymakers, and commentators. As early as 1873, the *Kings County Rural Gazette* discerned that the "steady, onward, irresistable march of improvements . . . has fairly commenced to plow its way through the quiet meadows of the beautiful rural districts of our incomparable Southern slope." It did not hesitate to predict that within a few years the rural district's "manifest destiny" to become part of one of the world's largest cities would be realized. The newspaper even analogized the forces pushing toward (sub)urbanization of Flatbush to gravity: "when the rapid transit route shall have been completed the full tide of city emigration will flow onto our beautiful southern slope just as naturally as water flows down hill." To the extent that judgments about the destiny of farming may have been shortsighted, the decision process lacked the kinds of features that might have shielded an appropriate amount of land from conversion.[28]

Against this inevitabilism, the aim of this book is to identify the gray areas situated deep within what many contemporaries deemed a sphere of the inexorable, driven as it was by the supposed wisdom of market price. How, for example, did Kings County farmers come to recognize and confront changes in agricultural markets? How did real-estate developers come to understand at what point farmland became ripe for residential consumption? Furthermore, in light of these constraints, what conclusions can be reached regarding whether agriculture in Kings County had to disappear altogether? What might have been required by way of intervention to preserve more balanced land use in the area? In short, to address these questions it is necessary to know more about what actually did happen that caused farming to disappear and why.

Understanding the modern world by reference to the market has a certain appeal: without knowing why things changed it is impossible to speak of the "margins" that mark the moments at which actors changed course or of the "forces" that shaped individual choices into larger social movements. But economic analysis is necessarily static, concerned with specific constraints at specific times. And if markets make history, so, too, does history make markets, for history provides insight into the ways in which the margins materialized, into the ways individuals' choices were contoured and tempered over time.

Moreover, just as policymakers readily draw on economic analysis to rationalize what in fact has taken place, they also quickly forget the history that can serve as a repository of creative alternatives. Thus a principal objective of this book is historical — to retrieve a piece of the past. The richly detailed accounts of farms, farmers, farming, and farmworkers in part I and of the process by which those farms became suburbs in part II could stand alone, and many readers may find them absorbing in their own right. But the discussion progresses to analyze how these changes fit into larger patterns of urbanization, and to speculate on the meaning of the widely perceived inevitability of the disappearance of urban farming.[29]

How market gardening became such a dynamic and dominant political-economic phenomenon in the southern half of Kings County is the subject of part I. Chapter 2's description and analysis of the Kings County agricultural sector in the latter half of the nineteenth century reveals how Kings

County advanced to the pinnacle of national vegetable production. Special attention is given to the transition from extensive to intensive agriculture and to the interaction between the fuel inputs and excremental outputs of urban horse-drawn transportation of New York City and Brooklyn and the manure needs of fertilizer-intensive cultivation in Kings County. Chapter 3 describes vegetable markets in New York and Brooklyn and the consequences of the rise of southern competition in the last quarter of the nineteenth century. The farm sector's decline at the end of the nineteenth century is shown not to have resulted from a collapse of competitiveness or profitability. Chapter 4 provides an overview of the farm sector's labor requirements, laborers, and labor relations. It begins by examining the labor force that was available to mid-nineteenth-century farmers by virtue of the fact that Dutch farmers had made the county first-ranked in the North in terms of slaves and slaveowners as a proportion of the population well into the nineteenth century. The origins of agricultural labor in slavery left their imprint on labor relations in the sense that Dutch farmers continued to exercise paternalistic powers over their wage laborers. The streams of rural immigrants, especially from Germany and Ireland, to the New York City area from the 1840s on ensured an adequate supply of labor. Thus urbanization proved to be not an obstacle, but a boon to the growth of vegetable farming.[30]

Once the viability and profitability of Kings County market gardening has been established in part I, the focus in part II shifts to how, when, and why Dutch farmers closed out a quarter-millennium of agriculture in Kings County, and developers bought those farms in order to convert them into middle- and upper-middle-class residential suburbs. Chapter 5 contrasts the demographic and economic development of the city of Brooklyn and the rural towns to shed light on the difficulties standing in the way of and opportunities beckoning to annexation. Chapter 6 presents the prehistory of the conversion of farmland into real estate and an account of the private and public provision of the infrastructure that was a prerequisite of suburbanization. Dutch farmers' temporary success in thwarting the modernizers is the focus of chapter 7, which delves into the arguments that undergirded the rich annexation debate in 1873.

Chapter 8 subjects to empirical scrutiny the view that the imposition of higher, city-lot, taxes on farmland "forced" farmers to sell their farms because they were not sufficiently profitable to sustain a customary standard of living and to finance tax payments. A significant element in this account is the discovery that, contrary to the received wisdom, New York State, like a number of other states in the nineteenth century, enacted laws to protect Kings County farmers from such taxes in the wake of annexation. The trend toward tenancy and the associated ethnic heterogeneity that characterized the farm sector by the 1880s forms the germ of chapter 9, which investigates the consequences of this farm-tenure structure for the longevity of vegetable cultivation and the specific patterns shaping the eventual land sell-off. The intertwined "push-pull" processes of agricultural self-dissolution and developers' creation of middle-income residential suburbias are illustrated in chapters 10 and 11. Chapter 10 reconstructs the agricultural cost-profit calculations that undergirded farm owners' decision to abandon operating farms or taking rents from tenants who farmed. Chapter 11 shifts the focus to the mobilization of the land and environment for suburbanization, taking the perspective of developers, who enabled sellers to receive high enough prices to abandon cabbage-cultivating for coupon-clipping.

Finally, chapter 12 explores the effects of the disappearance of urban market-gardening for twentieth-century land-use patterns in Kings County and New York City. Based on the insights of New York City and regional planners in the years before the depression of the 1930s, who perceived the untoward consequences flowing from the complete loss of greenbelts and local fresh vegetables, as well as the more recent state and county initiatives to preserve agricultural land and production, the argument contrasts the inevitabilist, laissez-faire approach in the United States with the more flexible intervention of European societies in the twentieth century.

PART ONE
THE RISE AND FALL
OF KINGS COUNTY AS
VEGETABLE CAPITAL
OF THE UNITED STATES

If New York City is the active elephant's trunk which ministers to a whole nation, these five towns of Kings County lay comparatively supinely on the Bay and Harbor in the form of a huge turtle.

— Samuel McElroy, "Town Survey of Kings County," 1875

2. KINGS COUNTY FARMS

It is an odd yet logical coincidence that some of America's most efficient
and prosperous farms are those about to be liquidated by the city.
— Jean Gottmann, *Megalopolis*, 1961

Late-eighteenth-century travelers remarked on the picturesque juxtaposition of the rurality of the western end of Long Island, whose climate "is better suited to agricultural pursuits than that of the remainder of the State,"
and the great city of New York. Kings County had long been an agricultural
producer for New York City. Before the Revolution, farmers there, among
the first in the United States to develop intensive agriculture and to use fertilizer, "found that often the richest returns per acre were to be obtained by
growing crops for the tables of Manhattan." In the 1790s, a British visitor remarked on the "rustics chiefly of Dutch descent whose chief occupation
is . . . raising vegetables for the supply of the market of New-York." The towering importance of farming in rural Kings County in the mid-nineteenth
century was captured by Gertrude Lefferts Vanderbilt's observation in 1880
that: "The head of every family in Flatbush, with few exceptions, was a
farmer, until within the last thirty years. They cultivated their land in the
most careful manner, and were among the best farmers in the State." [1]

During the first three decades of the nineteenth century, Kings County as
a whole remained rural and sparsely populated. In addition to the towns of
Brooklyn and Bushwick, the county consisted, as shown in figure 2, of Flatlands, Flatbush, and New Utrecht, which had been settled by the Dutch in
1624, 1634, and 1652, respectively, and Gravesend, which an English woman,
Lady Deborah Moody, founded in 1643. Despite the Netherlands' surrender of its possessions to Britain in 1664, Dutch culture was of such overwhelming importance that the Dutch language remained dominant at least

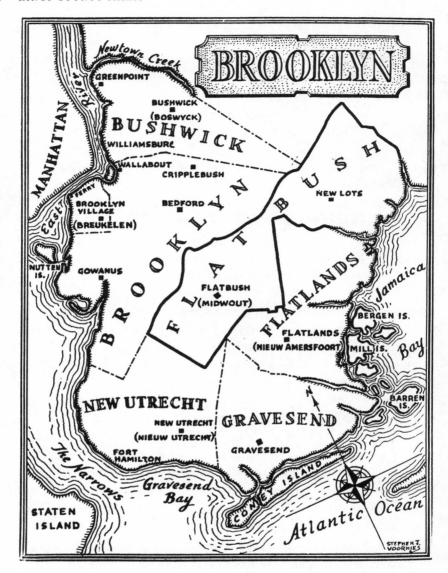

FIGURE 2. *Towns in Kings County. From Brooklyn Eagle,* The Towns That Became Brooklyn.

until the revolutionary period in the 1770s. The postrevolutionary New York State legislature recognized the division of Kings County into these six towns in 1788.[2]

Farming in the New York City area, which had been devoted largely to grains and livestock, was transformed by the opening of the Erie Canal in

1825. On the one hand, the canal made it possible to transport grain cheaply from the Ohio Valley and other interior lands, where the cost of production was lower, to the city. As a result, maintenance of the traditional extensively cultivated farms in Kings County became increasingly tenuous. On the other hand, the canal helped spur the transformation of New York into the country's leading port and most populous city. The explosion of population there and in Brooklyn meant, as it did elsewhere, that a much larger proportion of a much larger population was no longer able to produce its own food. As fewer and fewer people had access to home gardens, a market — initially weighted toward classes with higher incomes — arose for vegetables, which specialized farmers produced on a large commercial scale. By 1880, market garden production dominated Kings County agriculture.[3]

LONG-TERM INDICATORS

So many and so radical have been the changes in modern commercial gardening during the last twenty-five years that a practical market gardener, of a quarter of a century ago, who, like Rip Van Winkle, should have taken a sleep from 1870 until the present, on awaking would find his profession . . . had passed away, his old-fashioned and pet methods having been so altered that he would neither recognize nor understand the ways and means in practice by his scientific successors.

— Burnet Landreth, *Market Gardening and Farm Notes*, 1892

A statistical overview of the whole sweep of Kings County agriculture for as long as census data have been collected — from 1820 to 1992 — is presented in tables 1a and 1b. Table 1a shows that the number of farms, though fluctuating, began and ended the second half of the nineteenth century at almost exactly the same level — about 360. Why the number rose during the 1850s and early 1860s, fell sharply in the latter part of the 1860s, and then increased again in the 1870s, though not to the peak achieved in 1860, is not wholly clear. Shifts in the extent of tenancy or the potential pool of tenants among whom owners could divide farmland may account for some of the fluctuations; part of the fluctuation in the number of farms (and acreage and output) around 1870 may be the result of an official undercount.[4]

The 25 percent decline in the number of farms between 1880 and 1890 (from 409 to 307) was interpreted by the commissioner of the New York State Bureau of Statistics of Labor as a reflection of the fact that "many" farms that "were formerly occupied and cultivated . . . are now lying idle in the hands of real estate speculators." But the 17 percent rise in the number of farms between 1890 and 1900 (from 307 to 360) while acreage was halved and the average size shrank by more than half (from 41 to 18 acres) casts doubt on that explanation; it appears more likely that new owner-speculators rented out smaller sections while waiting for the most propitious moment to sell or develop. However, 1900 unmistakably marked the turning point, as the number of farms declined by 70 percent during the next decade and was halved again (to 54) by 1920. In 1930 a low of 11 was reached, which the self-help needs of the Depression and the national mobilization of World War II temporarily reversed; the 65 farms recorded in 1950 were the most at any time since 1910. The new trend bottomed in 1969 when farming reached its theoretical nadir of one (three-acre) farm. Although this endangered species did not become extinct, by 1992 three one-acre (nursery) farms were all that remained of the county's 350-year agricultural tradition.[5]

Total agricultural acreage, by contrast, declined almost continuously after the opening of the Erie Canal in 1825. Until the Civil War, Brooklyn accounted for most of this loss. This trend was reversed between 1870 and 1880, as acreage rose by about 12 percent during the decade of peak vegetable production. This increase may have been triggered by the steady profitability of vegetable farming, but it could also have been an artifact of the aforementioned possible undercount in 1870. During the 1880s, too, while Kings County remained a leading producer, the amount of farmland held relatively constant — total acreage increased slightly while improved acreage declined by 8 percent. Despite clear signs of suburbanization during the 1880s, the agricultural landmass was thus able to hold its own until 1890. Thereafter acreage plummeted until, by the beginning of the Great Depression, it had dwindled to fewer than one hundred acres.[6]

Average farm size generally followed the course of total acreage, although it rose more steeply between 1880 and 1890 and rose during the 1910s while acreage was in decline. At no point, however, did the average farm exceed the 57 acres recorded for 1850, the earliest year for which this figure can be calculated. Yet despite the completed transition from extensive grain cultivation and raising of livestock to vegetables and dairy by 1890, the average farm at 41 acres was marginally larger than its counterpart just before the Civil War (39 acres). In terms of improved acreage, it was slightly smaller.

The fragmentary series in table 1a show that the countywide value of farm products, first recorded in 1870, attained its high point of $1.2 million in 1879 before dipping to $1.1 million in 1889, at which point it held steady for another decade. From 1899 to 1929, however, total value declined by almost 90 percent. The Great Depression and World War II, again, boosted output, which by 1944 had almost regained its turn-of-the-century level (in current dollars). Thenceforward the value of farm products again declined sharply. Since farm prices declined throughout most of the last third of the nineteenth century, the dip in the last two decades should be treated with caution; after all, the total value of farm products in all of New York State also declined between 1870 and 1890. Similarly, the average value of farm products per farm in Kings County evolved as follows: 1870 — $3,683; 1875 — $3,044; 1880 — $2,961; 1890 — $3,531; 1900 — $3,054. Total and average value of vegetable production, the mainstay of Kings County farms in the latter part of the nineteenth century, are discussed below, as are trends in grain production.[7]

The data in table 1b make clear that although the output of potatoes, a leading crop, peaked in 1880 and total acreage was higher in 1890 than at any time since the Civil War, by 1910 all indicators pointed to demise. The census data on milk production fluctuate so wildly as to raise questions about their accuracy — apart, perhaps, from the strong increase during World War II. Nevertheless, some trends are evident. Production peaked in 1855, whereas the number of cows, which peaked in 1865, declined steadily if not linearly, especially after the turn of the century; the industry died out during the 1960s. The periodic increases in output were a function of increased yields. The number of horses, the chief nonhuman source of energy on farms during the nineteenth century, also registered inexplicable swings until, like the number of cows, it peaked in 1865. Yet the number of horses remained relatively constant at the three federal censuses of 1860, 1870, and 1880; after a dip in 1890, the number of horses remained constant in 1900, at which point the precipitous decline set in. The trend in the output of oats and hay, which should have been closely associated with the trend in the number of horses, fell more steadily throughout the nineteenth century, virtually disappearing by the turn of the century.[8]

In the peak year of vegetable production, 1879–80, the total number of farms, total acreage, and average acreage per farm were distributed among the towns as indicated in table 2. The fact that Flatbush lost about half of its agricultural acreage between 1850 and 1880 whereas New Utrecht, despite fluctuations, retained its intact, indicates that suburbanization in Flatbush had begun earlier and developed faster. Nevertheless, across the four rural towns the average farm size was almost identical; only in New Lots, which was characterized by many milk farms with little or no acreage, was the average significantly lower.

THE TRANSITION FROM EXTENSIVE TO INTENSIVE CULTIVATION: KINGS COUNTY'S RISE AND FALL AS A VEGETABLE PRODUCER

There are two great problems which the successful market gardener must solve, namely: first, to grow garden products; and second, to sell them. . . . There are always plenty of people who appreciate a good article and are willing to pay for it. The producers of trash must find sale in the Italian or Negro quarters of the cities, and accept any price that this class of purchasers are willing to pay.
— T. Greiner, *The Young Market Gardener*, 1896

The "logic of crop transition" from extensive grain production to intensive vegetable production in the vicinity of a large urban market has long been a staple of economic location theory. Its most prominent exponent was Johann Heinrich von Thünen, a North German junker, who first presented it in 1826. Positing a very large city located in the middle of a fertile plain, he sought to explain how distance from the city affected agriculture. He hypothesized that in the vicinity of the city farmers would have to grow products that were heavy in relation to their value, occupied a large space, and whose transportation costs were too great to justify being supplied from more remote areas. In addition, highly perishable products that had to be consumed fresh would also be produced close to the city. At greater distances from the city, products would be produced that required lower transportation costs in relation to their value.[9]

Von Thünen's scheme entailed the formation of sharply differentiated concentric circles around the city, each devoted to the production of a different set of agricultural products. Closest to the city would be grown the more delicate plants such as cauliflower, strawberries, and lettuce, which could not endure transport in wagons and therefore had to be carried to the city and sold in small quantities and very fresh. For reasons of perishability, milk was also assigned to this circle. Transportation costs meant that potatoes, cabbage, and root crops also had to be grown close-in.

The distinguishing characteristic of this circle was that manure was largely bought from the city and not, as in the remote areas, produced on the farms themselves. The possibility of securing manure from the city made it possible for the closest farms to sell products that more remote farms had to keep to maintain soil fertility. The two major products of this type were hay and straw. Von Thünen also imagined that, because close-in farms could have little competition for their products, rents would be high — so high that land would not be permitted to lie fallow; moreover, unlimited purchases of manure would confer such fertility on the soil that fallowing was unnecessary. The border between the first circle and the next was determined by the distance at which it was no longer advantageous to acquire urban manure.[10]

Von Thünen further assumed that within each ring land would be cultivated at its highest use as embodied in the highest land rent. No matter how high land prices rose in the vicinity of the city, von Thünen understood that land values in the city itself would rise even higher. Thus, even if someone who wanted to build a house in the first circle did not have to pay more for a construction site than vegetable farmers, the much higher residential land prices in the city center were a function of the labor savings, greater comfort, and reduction of loss of time in the conduct of business that such locations afforded residents.[11]

Some modern economic geographers have concluded that, because the prime mover of von Thünen's analysis, the cost of transportation, has been fundamentally changed by technological advances (such as cheapness in relation to other agricultural costs, refrigeration and air-conditioning, pretransportation processing, and large-scale production in distant, specialized regions), his predicted land-use patterns no longer conform to industrial realities. Whatever the validity of such conclusions for today, von Thünen's description bears an uncanny resemblance to the developmental phases of nineteenth-century Kings County agriculture.[12]

Contemporary observers were acutely aware of the economic and aesthetic-environmental consequences of the transition from grain to vegetables in Kings County. In the mid-1880s, the local historian Stiles made a von Thünen–like commentary on the "radical changes" that had been made "in the system of agriculture, in the crops produced, fertilizers applied, machinery employed" in living memory in Kings County: The growing population of New York and Brooklyn increased demand for articles (vegetables, milk, hay, straw) "of a perishable and bulky nature as cannot be profitably transported long distances." As a result, grain production declined "greatly" while stockraising was "mostly abandoned as a source of profit." Because hay production was much more profitable than livestock, "the farmer could afford to buy stable manure, street sweepings, lime and ashes from the city to apply to his land. Guano and artificial or manufactured fertilizers have been largely used with good results; but stable manure is the great staple manure for market gardeners, for they raise double crops each year, a draft no land can endure without constant manuring."[13]

Gertrude Lefferts Vanderbilt, writing of Flatbush in 1880, also noted that when the canals and railroads had made grain cultivation less remunerative on Long Island, the enlarged demand for market garden produce "by degrees changed the whole character of the farm work on this island. Flatbush farmers, being so near to the city, began to raise those vegetables which were to supply the markets of New York and Brooklyn. Where formerly wheat, rye, buckwheat, oats, corn, flax, and barley were the products of the farm, with only so much of cabbage, peas, potatoes, and turnips as were necessary for the family use, all this is now reversed; only so much hay and grain as the farmer needs are raised, while he depends upon his market produce for remunerative sales." The shift from extensive to intensive agriculture meant that "the farms are not so picturesque as they were when the fields were waving with the graceful growth of grain. The market gardens and the great fields of potatoes and cabbage show signs of industry and thrift, but the farms are not so beautiful as they were before this change took place."[14]

The New York State censuses for 1845 to 1874 and the manuscript schedules of the national Census of Agriculture for 1850, 1860, 1870, and 1880, which coincide with the transition period, corroborate Lefferts Vanderbilt's impressions. The decline in grain cultivation is striking. In Flatbush, for example, total corn, wheat, rye, and buckwheat acreage in 1845 amounted to 1,553; by the next state census a decade later, the total acreage (including oats) had fallen to 563; 20 years later, the total had declined further to 250 acres, almost all of which were planted to corn.[15]

Table 3 shows that yields in terms of bushels per acre continued to rise on Kings County potato farms in tandem with rising output until both peaked at the Tenth Census in 1879. In corn and wheat, which were smaller crops, yields rose even as output fell sharply. The transition from extensive to intensive cultivation is also clearly reflected in table 3. If the two major grains, corn and wheat, are taken to represent the old agriculture and potatoes the new, then the latter's predominance was secure by the early post–Civil War period. Total corn and wheat acreage declined almost as continuously as potato acreage rose. Whereas corn and wheat acreage (4,662) was almost triple that of potatoes in 1845, already by 1855 potato acreage was slightly greater; at the peak of potato production in 1879, its 4,172 acres were triple those of corn and wheat, and in 1890 almost ten times greater. If in 1845 the largest potato farmer in Flatbush harvested 2,500 bushels, by 1870

FIGURE 3. *Hauling hay, Vanderveer Farm, Flatbush, c. 1890. Courtesy of the New York Public Library, Astor, Lenox and Tilden Foundations, P. L. Sperr Collection, No. 1339 A-3, Photographic Views of New York City.*

four-fifths of Flatbush farmers produced that quantity or more, with one harvesting four times as much. Some of the larger and more efficient farmers achieved significantly higher potato yields than the countywide averages, which in turn exceeded the state average.[16]

Changes in farm size are further evidence of the transition from extensive to intensive culture. In the late eighteenth century, one of the members of the Bergen family owned a 300-acre farm in the Gowanus section of Brooklyn — a size far in excess of any nineteenth-century Kings County vegetable farm. Even as late as 1850, 19 Flatbush farms, or almost one-fourth of all 82, encompassed one hundred acres or more. Ranging as high as 208 acres (the largest farm in terms of improved acreage embraced 190 acres, while 11 others included one hundred or more acres of improved land), these farms were owned largely by the most prominent old-line Dutch families. These included no fewer than four Vanderveers and three Lotts in addition to the following families: Bergen, Cortelyou, Ditmas, Duryea, Lefferts, Martense, Wyckoff, Van Sinderen, and Williamson.[17]

Ten years later, only a single farm in Flatbush fell into this size category.

FIGURE 4. *Loading hay, Vanderveer farm, Flatbush, c. 1890. Courtesy of the New York Public Library, Astor, Lenox and Tilden Foundations, P. L. Sperr Collection, No. 1339 A-4, Photographic Views of New York City.*

To be sure, another seven farms in New Lots, which had been carved out of Flatbush in the interim, also reached or exceeded one hundred acres in 1860, although only three included that much improved acreage. In 1870 and 1880 there were no longer any Flatbush farms as large as one hundred acres, the 97- and 88-acre farm that William Allgeo rented from John A. Lott being the largest in 1870 and 1880, respectively. In New Lots, three farms in 1870 and two in 1880 reached one hundred acres, but only one (Stephen Vanderveer's 109-acre farm in 1880) included more than one hundred improved acres. The trend in farm size was similar in the other towns. Flatlands' eight farms of one hundred acres or more in 1850 (two each being owned by the Ditmas and Lott families) fell to only two (both owned by the Lotts) in 1870; by 1880, the 84-acre Lott farm was the town's largest. In New Utrecht, the eight farms of one hundred acres or more in 1850 (Nicholas Conover's 203-acre farm being the largest) fell to only one by 1870; of the two returned in 1880, one was operated by a tenant.[18]

   This long-term decline in large farms, which, as chapter 4 reveals, was not driven by a lack of workers to support intensive agriculture, can also be documented from the perspective of land ownership. According to the assessment rolls for New Utrecht, for example, the number of taxpayers owning one hundred or more acres of land also declined sharply during the nineteenth century: whereas in 1830, 1840, and 1850, 10, 14, and 9 persons respectively owned that much land, by 1860, 1870, and 1880 the number dropped to 2, 3, and 4, respectively.[19]

The transition from extensive to intensive cultivation is also evident on the production side. As late as 1842, the Kings County Agricultural Society appointed a Committee on Farms and Grain, whose members (Garrit Kouenhoven, Garrit Stryker, and Jeremiah Johnson, chairman and president of the society) inspected numerous farms. The committee report focused on the yields of the wheat, corn, oat, and hay fields, stressing the highly positive correlation between manure use and moneymaking. It made only one brief mention of potatoes — which were being grown on 16 acres of Dr. Adrian Vanderveer's 181-acre farm, 124 of which were planted to wheat, hay, oats, and corn.[20]

At the 1850 federal census, the enumerator returned only one farm in Flatbush as having produced $1,000 in market garden produce — Adrian Vanderveer's 198-acre farm. Ten years later, 23 Flatbush farms produced at least that much in vegetables; the largest producer, H. B. Van Wick, whose 140-acre farm was by far the town's largest, manifestly did not require its full extent to produce $5,000 worth of vegetables. As for the other towns in 1850, no farms in Gravesend, 1 in Flatlands, and 7 in New Utrecht produced at least $1,000 worth of vegetables. The largest producer, J. Remsen Bennett of New Utrecht, reported the market garden produce of his 82-acre farm to be worth $6,000. By 1860, 85 farms in the five towns produced $1,000 or more of vegetables. Bennett, whose farm had in the meantime shrunk to 33 acres, was still the county leader with $10,000 in produce. (In 1869, he was still prosperous enough to have the 30th highest income in rural Kings County.)[21]

These impressive figures — as well as the county's overall increase in market garden produce from $84,000 to $319,000 during the 1850s — nevertheless represent a significant understatement. The 1860 enumerator for Flatlands failed to collect data on the value of market produce; instead, crossing out the rubric for hops, he entered, "Cabbages." As a result, the fact, which would otherwise be lost to posterity, is preserved that Flatlands farmers produced 1,280,000 cabbages that year. The largest volume on any one farm was 60,000; four Remsen family farms alone (embracing 230 acres) produced 185,000 cabbages. The variety of vegetables produced in Kings

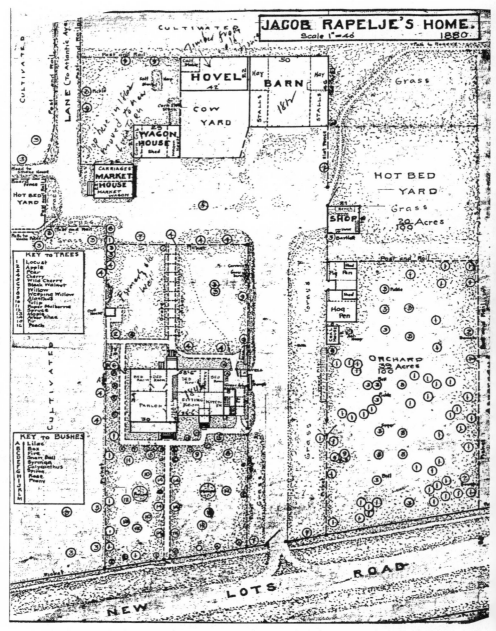

FIGURE 5. *New Lots farm of Jacob Rapelje (1846–1927), 1880. Prepared by his son Peter Rapelje (1873–1951), c. 1890. Courtesy of his great-grandson Peter Rapelje.*

County was amply on display at the Flatlands farm of John C. Bergen, who in 1865–66 sold several varieties of potatoes, cucumbers, tomatoes, cabbages, onions, pumpkins, and turnips. Flatlands farmers also grew asparagus and sweet corn — in 1875, for example, 13,000 bunches and 712,000 ears, respectively — carrots, parsnips, leeks, beans, peas, and celery. In the 1880s and 1890s, William Bennett and his son Edward marketed on their Gravesend farm tomatoes, sweet corn, squash, turnips, beans, sprouts, cucumbers, carrots, peas, pears, and cherries, in addition to their staples, potatoes and cabbages. New Utrecht farmers also produced large quantities of tomatoes and cauliflower.[22]

Market gardening had appeared as agricultural specialization in Kings and Queens counties as early as the 1820s. Adriance Van Brunt recorded in his diary from 1828 to 1829 that he had his "market truck" vegetables (peas, potatoes, corn, turnips, kidney beans, and cabbages) and fruits (cherries, raspberries, pears, and apples) transported from his farm in Yellow Hook (Bay Ridge) to market in New York daily during the season. By 1850, even before the transition to intensive farming was complete, one of the census enumerators inserted in a blank space at the bottom of one of the manuscript schedules these unique "Remarks — Most of the Lands of this County are very Fertile and Suitable for early Vegetables and eagerly Sought after by Gardeners and Marketmen." During the latter half of the century vegetable farms at the western end of Long Island "simply grew in size until they swallowed up all the fields."[23]

One influence that might have facilitated the transition to intensive market gardening among Dutch American farmers was its long tradition in the Netherlands: already highly developed in the seventeenth and eighteenth centuries as a result of urbanization and the presence of a relatively high-income stratum of consumers, market gardening became even more important there in the second half of the nineteenth century, eventually encompassing one-tenth of the agricultural labor force. Furthermore, like Holland's farmers, who were by then both the world's biggest users of artificial fertilizer per hectare of arable land and helping that country approach "the ideal of a 'recycling economy'" by reusing waste productively for manuring, Kings County farmers had access to one of the principal inputs, manure, in large quantities and at low prices.[24]

Kings County's transition from grain to vegetable production from about the 1850s was driven by advances in transportation, especially the opening of the Erie Canal, which shifted regional cost advantages and thus made commercially possible the importation to the growing urban population of the New York City area of cheaper grains grown in upstate New York and the upper Mississippi Valley. In neighboring Queens County, too, wheat and flour had been the staples until the canal was built. Although the apprehension was "almost universal" that the canal "would depreciate all the farms on Long Island," it in fact turned Queens "into a garden, and added two or three times, and perhaps more, to the value of every tillable acre." What the president of the Queens County Agricultural Society said of his county's farms in 1852 applied, mutatis mutandis, to Kings County (which was only one-fifth its size): "Queens county cannot be interfered with in its prosperity, as long as there are in that metropolis [New York and Brooklyn] hundreds of thousands of mouths to be daily supplied, and hundreds of thousands of dollars to be expended for . . . fruits and vegetables. . . . But then gardens will come to have the dimensions of farms." [25]

Market gardening on Long Island was powerfully aided by another advance in transportation: the opening of the Long Island Railroad in 1836 enabled truck farmers to ship to New York "in a few hours produce that by boat had taken as many days." Potatoes in particular became "immensely profitable." By the early 1860s, the Queens County Agricultural Society could not only record the striking progress of vegetable production — on a territorial scale that Kings County farmers were foreclosed from duplicating — but also foresee its inevitable ousting by nonagricultural activity. Just a few years earlier Queens farmers had already sent market garden produce worth more than half a million dollars to "the all-consuming adjacent city." Nevertheless, the expansion of market gardening, especially in western Queens, could be gauged by the fact that "one single proprietor, the produce of whose farm a dozen years ago averaged but two wagon loads per week, now devotes to asparagus alone one hundred acres, to cabbages eighty acres." Soon, the society predicted, that part of the county "will assume the appearance of one vast market garden, which will drive before it to the eastward all farms of grain and hay, itself to be driven back in turn when the march of improvement shall demand the surrender of the soil to purposes of building." [26]

The force of the midcentury drive toward vegetable production was also highlighted from the perspective of Staten Island, Kings County's neighbor across the Narrows. At the Richmond County Agricultural Society's 1852 annual fair, Congressman Obadiah Bowne observed that New York City's proximity "would seem to impose it upon us almost as a necessity, to convert our farms into gardens." The proof that vegetable production was "a most profitable system of farming" he saw in the fact that land in Kings County was "selling for gardening purposes at rates as high or higher than those obtained here in those localities best suited to the demands of taste or wealth." [27]

A startling interpretation of the transition stemmed from the New York State assessors. Created by the state legislature in 1859 to equalize taxes among counties, the assessors in their first annual report divided the counties into three "natural agricultural divisions" based on the "productiveness of . . . soil": those in which winter wheat was the staple crop; those adapted to spring grains and to grazing and dairy; and those devoted chiefly to grazing and dairy. Because location could make land "of inferior soil" more valuable than the best land, the assessors classified Kings County (together with Queens, Richmond, Suffolk, and Westchester) in the first group because of their "easy access to the great consuming market of the continent." The assessors excepted Kings and Queens from the subgroup of counties that did not "compare favorably" with those possessing the best soil, and characterized them as "among the most valuable in the State," but they nevertheless faulted the two counties for not being "the most productive and populous." Market-oriented modernizers who could abide no land use that did not generate the highest possible income and, derivatively, assessments, the assessors attributed the failing to "the proprietors or occupants. It is credible neither to the patriotism or [sic] intelligence of the people, who, refusing to sell, keep a large body of the most desirable lands in the State in a barren waste." [28]

In his 1863 *Report on the Agricultural and Other Resources of the State of New York*, senior assessor Theodore Peters informed the legislature that "Kings county can no longer be regarded as an agricultural county, being almost entirely occupied by a city, or urban and suburban population." To be sure, Peters' view was crucially shaped by the assessors' understanding that real farms raised winter wheat, other grains, and cattle: "Farming, as understood and practiced in other portions of the State, would be an unprofitable occupation" in the New York City area. Nevertheless, he was persuaded that: "The lands can be most profitably occupied as market gardens, and all its agriculture tends to that direction, and will be profitable." The requisite heavy manuring would have rendered this type of cultivation infeasible or unprofitable elsewhere in the state, but market garden farms maintained their prosperity by paying for the manure by selling back to New York and Brooklyn the vegetables that it made possible. But even given this bias, the assessor's prognosis was astonishing: Peters denied Kings

County agricultural status on the ground that "its available surface is occupied for city or village purposes, or as a market garden. It derives its principal value from this cause, and in a very few years will be occupied by only an urban population." Ironically, despite the nonagricultural position that the assessors accorded it, Flatbush in the 1870s was still plagued by "Street Cattle Nuisance," which allegedly caused injury to real estate valued at $100,000 in addition to compelling women to walk in the street to avoid cows on the sidewalk.[29]

Peters' assessment of Kings County's future is particularly ironic in light of his admonition that: "Our farmers should remember that there is only one law which admits of no exceptions, and which everywhere produces the same results, that is the law of markets." If market gardeners were obeying the ubiquitous law of markets by making a flawless transition to the currently and prospectively profitable production of vegetables — Peter's own figures showed that the value of agricultural products per acre in Kings County vastly exceeded that of any other county in the state — it is unclear why Peters was so certain that Kings County had to become urbanized (and even more rural Queens County suburbanized). Such a prediction in the midst of the Civil War, when Kings County had yet to complete its meteoric rise to the peak of national vegetable production, seems counterintuitive. If Peters's perspective was not merely idiosyncratic, it may have implied this reasoning: old-line Dutch farmers regarded profitable market gardening as a stopgap measure to tide them over until the inexorably spreading city of Brooklyn created enough demographic pressure to make any agriculture in Kings County either impossible or financially inferior to the prospective profits that conversion to residential real estate would generate.[30]

To other observers, however, it was apparent that market gardening would endure as a profitable business. By the late 1840s, the New York market could absorb "vast" amounts of vegetables "cultivated on a scale truly astonishing." In the aftermath of the Civil War, however, population, demand, and supply all jumped to considerably higher levels. Peter Henderson (1822–1890), a large New Jersey market gardener and the author of "the first and most valuable practical work . . . then available to the American market gardener," described the scope of vegetable farming in the New York area in 1865. Some might imagine that supplying "a population of a million inhabitants daily, throughout the year, with fresh vegetables would . . . require an immense tract of land." In fact, however, he doubted whether more than 4,000 acres were devoted to green vegetables, three-fourths of which was occupied with corn, peas, and beans. The finer early vegetable crops—asparagus, beet, cabbage, cauliflower, cucumber, lettuce, onion, radish, rhubarb, tomato, and turnip — were all raised on no more than 1,000 acres by market gardeners on farms of five to fifty acres, the average being about ten acres. Long Island, which became the country's most concentrated area of potato production — as well as "the cauliflower garden of the United States," an especially lucrative crop the supply of which never met demand — was the best example of intensive agricultural specialization.[31]

The Dutch farmers of Kings County did not falter when faced with the decision whether to leave behind "the great diversification of products characteristic of subsistence agriculture." An entrenched subsistence way of life did not become a serious obstacle to their determining "the relative advantages of producing or purchasing products for their own use, as well as the crops that might be advantageously produced for sale." They rationally accommodated larger national economic pressures to abandon grain production.[32]

Nevertheless, a farm newspaper editor who noted in 1861 that "any farmer having a proper soil, and being within the proper distance of the New York market, may raise large quantities of cabbage with great profit," also knew of many farms within ten miles of the city raising grains in competition with western farmers on land "the interest on the value of which is as great as the fee simple of western farms. In our own neighborhood . . . many farmers . . . do not realize two percent upon the value of their farms, while market gardeners in their midst are realizing comparative fortunes."[33]

The *Real Estate Record and Builders' Guide*, in an 1869 article on "Farms Near New York," commented that whereas grain farmers could not pay more than $80 per acre, "market gardeners in the immediate vicinity of the city can afford to pay over one hundred dollars for land, and, by dint of hard work, make out of it a fair living. . . . Hence we find that farming is falling into decay in all the country immediately adjacent to New York city, except, of course, where vegetables or choice fruit is raised." A horticulturist noted at the beginning of the 1870s that individual farmers were planting more cabbage than whole townships had fifteen to twenty years earlier: "It is no longer a rare sight to see, in the vicinity of large cities . . . fields of five, eight, or ten acres exclusively devoted to Cabbages." Two decades later, a New Jersey horticulturist added that: "In our large commercial and manufacturing cities where wealth has concentrated, and where abound families who live regardless of expenditures, fabulous prices are freely paid for vegetables and fruits to please the palate or adorn the table." By 1890 truck farmers were growing vegetables on more than 100,000 acres in the New York–Philadelphia area.[34]

Table 4, which presents the value of Kings County vegetable production, reveals the explosive growth in the fifteen years after the end of the Civil War followed by an even sharper reduction between 1879 and 1890, although some of this decline may be more an artifact of incomplete reporting. A deep plunge in vegetable production then took place during the 1920s, when the value of output fell from $263,000 to a mere $29,000 as the acreage planted to vegetables dropped by 84 percent. By the 1950s, commercial vegetable production disappeared as the handful of remaining agricultural entities had become nurseries.[35]

An examination of market-gardening acreage and output on the town level discloses a remarkable fact: until the mid-1850s and perhaps even as late as the 1860s, the city of Brooklyn was the biggest vegetable producer in Kings County. Although some uncertainty stems from radically different data generated by the state and federal censuses, both sets of data underscore how late the transition to intensive vegetable farming took place in the rural towns. Nevertheless, farmers undertook this transformation before significant land sales for residential suburbanization had occurred. This sequencing casts strong doubt on the possibility that the conversion was merely a conscious stopgap strategy to secure a continued livelihood for the old Dutch farming families until the most propitious moment arrived for selling off their land to developers and speculators.[36]

The manuscript schedules of the Census of Agriculture make it possible to observe changes in the individual towns during the crucial decade for Kings County agriculture, the 1870s. From 1870 to 1879, the value of market garden produce grown in Flatbush increased fourfold — from $32,360 to $137,882. Whereas market garden produce accounted for only 31 percent of the $104,854 of total output that 29 farmers produced on 1,472 acres in 1870, by 1879 market gardens contributed 85 percent of the $161,034 total output that 47 farmers produced on 1,666 acres. Whether the 31 percent decline in average farm size from 51 to 35 acres in association with the 62 percent rise in the number of farmers was a function of the spread of tenancy is unclear (the 1870 census did not collect data on tenants), but the almost exclusive reorientation toward the kinds of vegetables that were contributing to the growing urban population's more varied diets was underscored by the fact that while market garden production soared, potato output was almost unchanged in the two census years (133,200 and 135,350 bushels).[37]

In Flatlands, the value of market garden production rose almost fivefold to $203,200; whereas in 1870 it accounted for only 25 percent of total output, by 1879 this share had climbed to 80 percent. Farmland acreage also expanded by about one-fourth. New Lots, the largest and most urbanized of the towns as well as the one closest to being annexed to Brooklyn, offered a deviant course of development: its market gardening increased only 19 percent during the 1870s and actually declined as a proportion of total production from 91 percent to 68 percent. Not surprisingly, farm acreage also contracted. The censuses of 1870 and 1880 implausibly credited Gravesend (which had produced a small amount of vegetables in 1860) with no market garden production at all, but it was a significant potato producer — although low fertility in Gravesend "requires a great deal of enriching by manures to yield crops of any kind." During the 1870s, farm acreage there fell by more than a fourth. The gains in New Utrecht during the 1870s were outsized, though the data are methodologically suspect. Vegetable production increased 2.6-fold, reaching $287,035; market gardening had gained absolute dominance by 1879, accounting for 95 percent of all farm output compared with 52 percent in 1870. Farmland also doubled during the 1870s in New Utrecht, expanding from 1,680 acres in 1870 to 3,024 (or, including untilled land, 3,403) acres in 1880.[38]

The extraordinary achievement of Kings County vegetable producers in their peak year, 1879–80, merits closer scrutiny. That the vast majority of farmers produced vegetables that year is the clearest indicator that the transition to intensive farming had been effected. Bracketing the classification of potato cultivation, only 31 of Kings County's 409 farms did not report market garden production; almost all of these nonproducers were dairy units in New Lots. Market gardening would have been officially almost universal if the enumerators had not excluded potato production from the value of market garden produce sold. This definition especially affected Gravesend, where no farm reported vegetable cultivation, but 63 of 64 produced potatoes. As a share of the total value of production, market gardening doubled from 36 percent in 1869–70 to 70 percent in 1879–80.[39]

The national importance of Kings County vegetable or market garden production is quantified in table 5, which rank-orders counties at the federal censuses from 1850 to 1900. Kings County rose from 12th position in 1850 — "[o]wing to the prevalence of the Cholera of 1849 the early vegetables . . . were suffered to decay in the fields and necessarily showing a small account in market produce" — to 8th in 1860; after slipping to 9th in 1870, it catapulted in 1879 to 2nd place behind Queens, which was the first or second largest vegetable producer at every federal agricultural census from

1850 to 1900. After reaching its high point in 1879, Kings County's market garden output fell enough to displace it to 23rd in 1890; other counties were pushing forward so fast that even another significant increase in output in 1899 could not prevent Kings County from plummeting to 40th place. Vegetable production's demotion was forcefully signaled by the fact that in 1899 sales of flowers and ornamental plants in Kings County — at $518,733 the fifth highest after Cook, Philadelphia, Middlesex, and Hudson counties, four other large metropolitan vegetable producers — was twice as great as the value of market garden produce.[40]

The other leading market garden counties during this period were also largely located in the vicinity of the large eastern cities (Boston, New York, Philadelphia, and Baltimore). Despite its larger population, however, New York, cut off by water on three sides, was not surrounded by the largest agricultural hinterland. In 1850, the total improved acreage as well as the value of the land and improvements in the counties within a fifty-mile radius of New York City amounted to only two-thirds of those around Philadelphia; by 1900, the farmland near New York and the value of its products reached only about three-fifths of the levels around Philadelphia.[41]

The course of New York City's own position as a vegetable producer is also noteworthy because it underscores how late market gardeners were able to hold on even in the country's largest city. It ranked seventh in 1850 and, by more than tripling its output, rose to sixth place by 1860. Although New York disappeared from the list of the 12 leading counties by 1869–70, its output fell only marginally below that of the 12th to $256,530. Manhattan market gardening's demise occurred during the 1870s when output fell by more than 94 percent to a minuscule $14,350. Kings County did not register such a rapid descent for another half a century: not until the 1920s did the value of its market garden production plummet by 89 percent.

At the peak of their recorded vegetable production, in 1879–80, Kings County farmers could claim the leading position with respect to farm value, value of implements and machinery per farm, fertilizer per farm and acre, yield per acre, and output per farm. Tables 6a and 6b highlight these crucial variables. Kings County's status as the country's second biggest vegetable producer is, as seen in table 6a, all the more remarkable in light of the fact that (with the exception of Hudson County, discussed below) it had the fewest farms with the smallest acreage of the 12 leading counties. The value of Kings County farm output per acre was (again with the exception of Hudson) four times greater than that of its closest competitor; on a per farm basis, its output far exceeded that of the other leading counties.

Some of the factors explaining how Kings County farmers, despite their small numbers and acreage, attained their leading position are displayed in table 6b. First, Kings County farmers were the most specialized in market gardening, which accounted for 70 percent of their output by value. Only Hudson County, New Jersey, which was undergoing more explosive population growth in Jersey City and Hoboken and whose already small acreage was more than halved by the time of the 1890 census, was more specialized.[42]

Second, Kings County farmers used more implements and machinery than any of their competitors: the $549 per farm average was 40 percent higher than that of the next most capital-intensive county (Philadelphia) and about 170 percent higher than the average of the other 11 leading counties. These figures strikingly confirm the memoir that Daniel Tredwell wrote of Flatbush in 1879 without the benefit of census data: "The original farmers of Flatbush had large productive farms with all modern appliances through which they had attained to wealth. . . . [N]o farmers in the country were better equipped than they for obtaining the best results in their line of agriculture."[43]

A much better sense of the kinds and quantities of equipment that Kings County farmers maintained in the 1870s and 1880s can be gleaned from the notices published in the *Rural Gazette* in the 1870s and 1880s for auction sales of the farm stock of farmers who had died, retired, or gone into another business. An administrator's sale of the stock, utensils, and seeds of the late Henry T. Van Pelt, a member of one of New Utrecht's most eminent Dutch farm families, took place in November 1875. At the time of the 1870 census, Van Pelt, then 45 years old, produced $5,000 worth of products, $4,000 of which were market garden produce, on his 21-acre farm. Although his output was average, the $2,000 that he estimated his implements and machinery to be worth was considerably above average for all of Kings County. The auction notice listed, in addition to the "usual amount of Tools to carry on the business of Market Gardening": 1 bay colt, 3 horses, 2 cows, 2 market wagons, 2 farm wagons, 1 rockaway, 1 buggy, 1 wood sleigh, 1 cart, 300 hotbed sash and frames, 2 wheelbarrows, 3 sets double harnesses, 2 sets single harnesses, cart harness, 275 shutters, 100 baskets, lot straw mats, 3 barrels vinegar, lot pea seed, lot chickens, 2 straps bells, 3 wagons covers, 3 harrows, 1 hay cutter, 12 plows, 1 road scraper, 1 cider press, 1 roller, 1 grind stone, 75 loads manure, bone dust and guano, hotbed soil, corn stalks, 2 bushels cucumber seed, lot other seeds, early rose potatoes, blankets and robes.[44]

Third, despite its minuscule size, Kings County was the 12th largest user of fertilizers as measured by total expenditures of all counties in the United States. As a result, on a per acre and per farm basis, Kings County farmers used far more fertilizer than their counterparts elsewhere. They used more than four times as much per acre as their closest competitors (apart from those in Hudson County) in Queens; $519 worth of fertilizer per farm was 130 times more than farmers in Hamilton County (the seventh largest vegetable producers) used, and almost six times more than the average for all the other 11 leading counties. Although this gap is exaggerated by the fact that a much smaller proportion of farmers in the other counties produced vegetables or used any fertilizer at all, it is large and real. The extensive advertising for fertilizers, adapted to individual crops such as cabbages and potatoes, in publications that they were bound to read — in 1884, for example, issue after issue of the *Rural Gazette* contained large advertisements dominating the front page — strongly underscores that Kings County farmers were large and steady customers.[45]

Kings County's yield was more than three times higher than the next highest county's, but these ratios significantly understated market garden yields because the Tenth Census did not collect data on market garden acreage. The state censuses of 1855 and 1865, however, did publish the relevant data: Kings County farmers produced, on average, $193.46 worth of vegetables on each of 1,414 acres in the former year and $226.87 on 1,110 in the latter. In 1879, Kings County ranked far above all other counties in fertilizer expenditures per improved acre: $21.29 compared to $0.08 to $4.88 for the other counties (except Hudson County, which averaged $13.35). At the 1889–90 census (but without specific data on vegetable acreage), Kings County's per acre yield at $105.05 remained far above that of any other county (except Hudson). Its yield was almost three times higher than that of neighboring Queens, the second biggest producer ($38.41), while its per acre fertilizer use ($13.60) was not quite twice as high (Queens farmers used $7.31). The yield in the biggest producer, Middlesex County, was only one-fourth that of Kings County, but its fertilizer use was less than one-tenth as high. In terms of total value of farm productions per farm, Kings County farms in 1889 still recorded the largest output among the leading market garden counties. At $3,531 they produced more than twice as much as their leading competitor ($1,653 in Camden) and three times more than the average among the 12 biggest market garden counties.[46]

The census of 1900 also published data on vegetable acreage by county. Even at that late date, when Kings County farms were already in eclipse and had fallen to 40th place in total output, they yielded on average $135 worth of vegetables on 1,936 acres — only slightly behind the two leading producer-counties, Queens ($144) and Middlesex ($164), and 11th-ranked Philadelphia ($152), and considerably ahead of the other top 12 counties. In 1899, the surviving Kings County market gardeners still used far above average quantities of fertilizer per acre of vegetable, but they no longer led the country. They used $44.28 worth compared with the $29.11 required by their counterparts in Queens, who underwent an extraordinary shrinkage in total improved acres from 130,242 in 1880 to only 21,865 in 1900; farmers in Nassau County (the fifth largest producer), formerly the western part of Queens (created after Queens became part of New York City in 1898), used almost as much as Kings County farmers ($40.21) to produce $78.24 worth of vegetables per acre. Significantly, among the largest producers, Norfolk used fertilizer most intensively ($46.71 per acre); nevertheless its $106.71 per acre yield remained considerably below that of Kings County.[47]

The meaning of Kings County's persistent outlier status as fertilizer user is ambiguous. It does not necessarily indicate inferior fertility. Because Kings County farmers in 1879 cultivated the fourth most valuable farmland in the country, they may have had an incentive to farm more intensively. If Kings County market gardeners' transportation costs to market were lower than average, it may have been rational for them to use part of the savings to crop more intensively. The fact that the leading counties' per acre fertilizer use tended to converge over time — with Kings County's falling and the others' rising — suggests that diminishing fertility in Kings County was not a significant cause of the decline of agriculture there. Finally, although the precise quantitative proportions are unknown, the fact that "some vegetables require an enormous quantity of fertilizer, while others will thrive on much less," may, depending on the degree of regional crop specialization, have accounted for different levels of use.[48]

The labor intensity of Kings County vegetable farming is indicated by the fact that in 1879–80 its per farm average of $735 in wage payments was greater than the per farm value of total (including non-market garden) production in one of the other leading 12 market garden producing counties and not much inferior to that of five others. Of the 288 Kings County farms with market garden sales (excluding all farms producing only potatoes), 275 paid a total of $211,674 in wages to hired labor. Given the large number of sons and other family members working on the farms, wage-intensity is not, however, a wholly reliable indicator of labor-intensity. Indeed, variations in wage-intensity among Kings County towns suggests that the availability of unwaged family labor may have varied.[49]

The wage- and fertilizer-intensity of market gardening in Kings County may be compared with the cost structure given by Hudson County horticulturist Peter Henderson. In two editions of his *Gardening for Profit* published in the mid-1870s and mid-1880s, Henderson offered average cost and revenue figures for the previous ten years on his own farm in Jersey City Heights, which are reproduced in table 7. The total wage bill of Kings County's 288 market gardeners amounted to 25 percent of the total value of market garden production, while total fertilizer expenditures ($166,123) amounted to 20 percent. The combined total of 45 percent approximated the 47.5 percent that Henderson calculated. This almost identical proportion, however, conceals two widely deviant subshares: Henderson's wage and fertilizer bills amounted to 39 percent and 8 percent, respectively, of his receipts. The below-average wage bill and above-average expenditure on fertilizer in Kings County may in part be explained by the availability of more unwaged family labor and the use of much more fertilizer.

The low wage-fertilizer ratio on Kings County farms may mean that farmers either were heavily reliant on unpaid family labor or used a far above average amount of fertilizer. Although they did lead the nation in fertilizer expenditure, their $21 per acre outlay was only one-fifth of the amount mentioned by Henderson. The $29 per acre average wage cost, however, was barely one-twentieth of Henderson's figure. Alternatively, the discrepancy between census data and Henderson's reports may in large part be explained by the fact that Henderson was literally referring to a single acre, whereas the census figures are averages based on total acreage, some or most of which may not have been planted to vegetables (but rather to hay for the draft animals) or any crop at all. Inclusion of the other acres obviously lowers per acre yields as well as per acre expenditures. This alternative explanation is supported by other contemporaneous accounts of typical expenses, which reported that vegetable farmers spent $72 to $150 per acre on manure. Moreover, Henderson himself noted that market gardeners in the New York vicinity were so convinced of the adverse impact of continuously cropping land that, even on land worth $500 per acre, "when twenty acres are under cultivation at least five acres are continually kept in grain, clover, or grass." Because the market gardeners of Hudson County, whose land was limited and rented for $50 per acre, could not "well afford to let their lands lay thus comparatively idle," their crops became inferior to those on Long Island.[50]

The large differences in wage and fertilizer expenditures among Kings County towns are also worth examining. Since many market gardeners also produced output other than vegetables, total production will also be ex-

amined. New Utrecht was the largest vegetable producer. Of 103 farms returned at the 1880 census, 101 were market gardens (the other two produced
potatoes) accounting for 34 percent of total county market garden output.
New Utrecht farmers' position as the county's leading capitalist vegetable
producers was signaled by their wage payments: they accounted for 47 percent of all wages paid by market gardeners, and their per farm average of
$984 was also the highest. New Utrecht's wage bill, in turn, amounted to
35 percent of the total value of its output — almost one-half higher than the
next most wage-intensive town, Flatlands (23 percent). New Utrecht had
been the biggest user of fertilizer in 1874, when the state census first collected
data on the subject, accounting for 48.5 percent of all fertilizer purchased;
by 1879 its use was only average. Nevertheless, total wage and fertilizer costs
amounted to 54 percent of total market-garden value in New Utrecht, the
county's highest — only 2 percent higher than in Flatlands, the next biggest
producer, but fully 20 percent higher than in New Lots and Flatbush. Flatlands farmers, all of whom were market gardeners by 1879, were the biggest
users of fertilizer in 1879 both in absolute expenditure ($58,100) and as a pro-
portion of output (29 percent). That Flatlands' wage bill was much lower
than New Utrecht's may be linked to the fact that Flatlands had by far the
highest proportion of owner-farmers: Dutch farmers' sons and other relatives may have contributed enough unwaged labor to lower wage costs; the
tenants who operated many farms in New Utrecht may have faced greater
obstacles in persuading their families to forego industrial employment to
cultivate cabbage on rented land.[51]

The fact that wage and fertilizer costs bulked largest in the the two biggest
producing towns, New Utrecht and Flatlands, does not necessarily mean
that profits there were lowest. Because the Census did not collect data on
other costs such as rent, seeds, transportation, and marketing, it is possible
that the smaller producing towns' profits were unusually burdened by
them. Nevertheless, since wages and fertilizer made up 72.5 percent of Henderson's total market gardening costs, it is at least plausible that New
Utrecht's and Flatlands' total costs were higher too. Why the biggest producers would not have been the most profitable is unclear. Interestingly, in
1880 New Utrecht vegetable farmers on average used implements and machinery worth 30 percent more than their Flatlands competitors ($642 and
$492, respectively). Whether some technological relationship was embed-
ded in the negative correlation between the use of tools and fertilizer in the
two towns seems unlikely since New Lots market gardeners spent the most
on fertilizers ($817) and used the most expensive equipment ($822).[52]

Table 8 summarizes the crucial indicators collected by the Census of Agriculture for 1879–80 for the individual towns. New Utrecht and Flatlands produced the most vegetables, but the average farm there was on the small end of the spectrum, market gardeners in New Lots and Flatbush being the largest. New Utrecht farmers produced almost exclusively vegetables: 97 percent of the value of their output was market garden produce. All Flatlands farmers were market gardeners, their market garden produce being, on average, less than half as large as that of their counterparts in New Lots; in addition, only 80 percent of the value of their output was vegetables.[53]

THE URBAN-RURAL MANURE-FOOD CYCLE: THE CHANGING SIGNIFICANCE OF FARMING IN THE SHADOW OF THE METROPOLIS

The profit in agriculture comes from an abundance of manures.
— "Profit in Farming," *Kings County Rural Gazette*, Feb. 16, 1878

The transformation of agriculture in nineteenth-century Kings County was integrally linked to several central features of the period's urban history. The agricultural absorption of horse manure from city streets and stalls, for instance, was entwined with the emergence of municipal sanitation measures, which in turn contributed to the rise of professional urban planning. Also, changes in agricultural methods and crops paralleled shifts in urban strategies for preserving the benefits of country life for its citizens; as agriculture became increasingly labor- and manure-intensive, advocates of the city beautiful and healthy abandoned their love of the farm in favor of city parks and landscaping. In time, the role of agriculture itself became a distinguishing feature among campaigns for reshaping suburbanization, as planners and developers drew on competing visions to mend the social and cultural fissures between the ever-expanding city and the increasingly remote country.

Despite the ongoing creation of waste and its implications for fertilizing local agriculture well into the twentieth century, urban planners gradually dismissed local agriculture from their list of concerns. From the start of the nineteenth century, the city's immense collections of waste, supposed to be the incubator of epidemic disease, led to a variety of municipal sanitation measures. As New York City grew, pressing problems such as hazardous construction, dense traffic, and mass poverty multiplied; still, the waste problem remained very much in the forefront. Near the end of the century, urban sociologists addressed the problem of decongesting the city without turning the urban fringe into more of the same. Sanitation and the possibilities for preserving an urban-agricultural waste and production cycle receded from the forefront of urban problem solving in this context.[54]

A central feature of these changes is the farmer's role in relation to the city. During much of the nineteenth century, Kings County farmers performed a useful service to the city by absorbing the mountains of waste produced by the city's growing population of horses as well as persons. Manhattan, Brooklyn, and Long Island "became a huge recycling system. . . . Often, the very same boats, and later trains, which carried hay, produce, and fuel wood westbound to market, returned loaded with manure. Horse-drawn railroads during the 1870s and 1880s frequently placed advertisements — "Manure! Farmers, Attention!" — offering to sell their unwanted by-product on an annual or other basis. While Brooklynites, as the *Rural Gazette* noted in 1873, "are, no doubt, glad to get rid of their filth (and the Board of Health will compel them to do so) our farmers are glad to obtain means with which to enrich their lands, and to pay a fair price for such materials" — even if some farmers were too proud to think of being seen "seated on the top of a load of manure driving out the great city of churches."[55]

The sale of the Lefferts farm in Brooklyn's 21st Ward in 1873 shed interesting light on urban manure problems. From a practical real-estate perspective, the *Brooklyn Daily Eagle* reported that one of the greatest drawbacks to prosperity was the condition of vacant lots: "to the disgust of residents and visitors, the city railroad has accumulated an immense mountain of manure and built it up along the so-called sidewalk." Little wonder, then, that in the 1870s *Scientific American* pronounced "the problem of the conversion of the excremental waste of towns and people . . . into useful materials" as "engaging as much of the attention of intelligent minds throughout the world as any social question."[56]

Emblematic of the centrality of manure to Kings County farmers' operations is the scene that the *Rural Gazette* portrayed in January 1875 of the Bay Ridge section of New Utrecht: "All the farmers are hauling the manure for their lands from boats which land near the beach, and the carts are driven into the water (wagons could not be used) up to the boat and filled." The crucial role played by manure in maintaining market gardens' fertility and value is underscored by the provision commonly found in farm leases requiring tenants to "work in a good and thorough manner the said farm, putting on the necessary manure for the crops as is usual." John Lefferts, one of rural Kings County's richest residents and largest landowners, attested to manure's importance in his will as late as the 1890s by bequeathing to his son James "all manure on the farm at the time of my decease." [57]

If city residents sometimes forgot the salutary role played by market gardeners, they were forcefully reminded of it when farmers who had overloaded their wagons on bad roads had to leave part of their load on the roadside, "as no one desires a lot of manure dumped in front of their premises." By 1882 complaints grew more insistent that farmers were daily violating an ordinance requiring them to cover up their manure wagons. Flatbush residents were concerned that the heaping of manure on lots in Brooklyn near the city line would not only affect their health, but "depreciate the value of property . . . in every section of the town." Farmers' public health role continued through the end of the nineteenth century, but at the same time its significance receded from popular consciousness and the imagination of urban planners and sociologists. [58]

Meanwhile, new questions arose about farmers' usefulness along the city's urban fringe: If the use of horses in urban transportation would eventually be supplanted by electric and gasoline-powered vehicles, and if agricultural products of all kinds could be imported from distant sources without extraordinary cost, what point was there to low-density, agricultural land uses so close to the city? It was in this context that the farmer's significance in relation to the city became the subject of a search for new urban values.

The first part of this story grows out of the transformation of agriculture itself — discussed earlier in this chapter — from extensive grain production to more intensive land use for vegetable production. Kings County's wheat output, the hallmark of extensive agriculture, peaked in 1850. Long Island farmers, reputedly the first in the state to grow wheat, had turned to it because it was more remunerative than other crops. Yet in part because wheat also deprived the soil of nutrients and thus required huge amounts of fertilizer, farm voices throughout Long Island by the late 1840s complained of its relative unprofitableness. [59]

A major focus of discussion was the relative cost and availability of manure. In Suffolk County, for example, heavy outlays for manure made the wheat crop "by far the most expensive and least profitable of our whole system of agriculture." In the 1840s: "Long Island in all its length and breadth, particularly in its western counties, depends essentially upon a supply of manures, from the cities and towns on the North and East Rivers, which is brought by water and railway to the nearest points where it is required; and the farmers of this county . . . have proceeded for years, upon the principle, that it is better and more profitable to sell the corn, the straw and the hay, for cash in the market, and with it, to purchase the manures required for the growth of their crops." [60]

Even in the late 1820s, Adriance van Brunt, who produced vegetables for the New York market, devoted much of his attention to inspecting and buying large quantities of manure, which were often transported by boat and which his employees spent many days unloading, cutting, and spreading. Throughout Long Island, farmers, who probably spent more on manure than in any other part of New York State, by the 1840s no longer tried to increase their "home manufacture" of manure, but generally kept "as little stock to consume the produce of their farms as possible, selling their hay and grain at New-York and Brooklyn, and buying their manure in return." They took all the stable manure made in Brooklyn, "[a]lmost all" made in New York, and "a considerable portion" of Albany's. Farmers in the immediate vicinity of Brooklyn carted that city's street dirt to their farms in their own wagons. Little wonder that the Kings County Agricultural Society reported that the "farmer who uses the most manure and cultivates his land best, makes the most money." [61]

Indeed, the large city was rapidly becoming a "manure factory" in the service of nearby agriculture. As the city's population grew, so too did its horse traffic. The resulting growth in the supply of urban manure and night soil rendered the farming of vegetables, which were so crucially dependent on fertilizer, the more feasible. The fast growing cities on the East Coast experienced powerful incentives to expand their recycling relationship with their agricultural hinterland, of which that between New York–Brooklyn and rural Long Island was the most highly developed:

> The intense market gardening around these cities required far more manure than could be produced on the farm. The demand for hay, the principal energy source for urban transportation systems, created even more dramatic demands for manure. . . .
>   . . . Even if all the hay and produce had been fed to animals, there would not have been enough manure produced to maintain the fertility. . . . Moreover, the city's profitable market for hay and produce tempted most farmers within reach to keep as few animals as possible and to ship the maximum amount of their produce into the city. These two factors combined to create a demand for manures unequalled anywhere else in the country. . . .

For farmers on the western end of the island, the solution was to import the large quantities of manures produced in New York City, which was a veritable manure factory. The large number of horses that powered the city's transportation system provided immense quantities of dung. . . . [M]uch of it was deposited on the streets along with garbage and the excrement of numerous hogs that roamed New York's streets eating the garbage. Dairies located in the city produced still more, and the human population contributed its share. . . .

Removal of these wastes was essential for the cleanliness and health of nineteenth-century New York. Fortunately, the agricultural market for manure provided considerable incentive for the owners of dairies and stables to have their manure removed. Sometimes they sold it directly to farmers, but often they sold it to dealers who carted it to the outskirts of the city where they composted it . . . to produce a light, friable manure for which farmers were willing to pay premium prices.[62]

Just as the city required an outlet for its waste, so too did farmers require guarantees for a stable source of that waste. As was the case throughout Long Island, the various soil types of Kings County shared the geologically caused characteristic of relatively shallow soil. This shallowness had a two-fold impact on crop growth: first, it limited root development to horizontal spreading, thus leading to crowding among long-growth crops planted close together; and second, it also limited storage reserves for maintaining moisture. Although both effects tended to lower yields, for the shallow-rooted crops typical of market gardening in Kings County, the loams and sandy loams were sufficiently deep and moisture-retentive. To counteract such tendencies toward low yields, however, the intensive application of manure was required not only on Hempstead loam — which covered most of Flatbush and parts of Flatlands and New Utrecht — but also on the much deeper Miami stony loam, which covered the Fort Hamilton and Bay Ridge sections of New Utrecht for as far as two miles inland from the coast. Of this latter soil, which was usually classed as a general farming type producing grasses and grains, which the proximity of New York City had prompted farmers to appropriate for more intensive cultivation, the U.S. Bureau of Soils wrote: "The majority of the crops are produced by the fertilizer rather than by inherent fertility of the soil."[63]

As early as the 1840s, U.S. farmers had been made aware of the specific chemical compositions that rendered different fertilizers effective for various vegetable crops. Kings County farmers bought specialized commercial fertilizers for various crops such as potatoes, cabbage, and corn. One historian has gone so far as to argue that: "By purchasing large amounts of fertilizers, farmers had become businessmen, buying raw materials and selling finished products. . . . This transition from self-contained recycling to purchasing raw materials may have been a more important step toward the commercialization of agriculture than the decision to grow crops for the market."[64]

The large-scale supply of manure had become so vital to farmers in New York and its environs that in 1864 the state legislature enacted a statute incorporating the Farmers' Protective Union of Kings, Queens, Suffolk, Westchester, Richmond, and Rockland counties. With a capital stock of not less than $200,000, the association's object was "to protect and the better to promote the business and interests of those engaged in the pursuit of agriculture, and especially for the purpose of procuring, purchasing and selling manures, ashes and other fertilizers of the soil." By 1873, the organization was "practically confined" to Kings and Queens, where it was recognized that the "best producing land . . . is undoubtedly that which is manured the best." Kings County farmers continued to figure prominently among the organization's directors into the 1880s.[65]

That market gardeners around large cities annually used 100 tons of manure per acre was "appalling to the average farmer," who applied as much to 50 acres as a vegetable farmer did to one, "but every one who has had experience in growing vegetables or fruits knows that the only true way to make the business profitable is to use manure to the extent here advised." Little wonder that "[g]angs of men . . . hard at work hauling out manure and spreading it" were a common sight in Kings County. By 1903, the U.S. Bureau of Soils reported that throughout western Long Island nature was yielding to technique: "The influence of natural soil fertility upon crop production . . . is rapidly decreasing in effect through the employment of large amounts of commercial fertilizer and stable manure, and through increasing intensity of cultivation."[66]

Closer examination of Manhattan and Brooklyn as sources of supply and of the relative levels of consumption of fertilizers by the farmers in neighboring counties suggests the extent to which the farm-city supply cycle determined local agricultural patterns. Until the end of the century, Kings County farmers had access to horse and human manure from both cities. In Brooklyn, the U.S. Census Office observed in 1878, the city's 75,000 houses were associated with 25,000 privy vaults: "Night-soil to the amount of 20,000 cubic feet per annum is taken to farms and gardens outside the city, where it is utilized as fertilizer." In 1880, Brooklyn and New York counted

150,000 to 175,000 horses; ten years later, after the advent of the electric streetcar, 22,000 horses and mules still pulled streetcars in those two cities. With a horse estimated as dropping on average 15 to 30 pounds of manure daily, the aggregate amounts were prodigious.[67]

Meanwhile, market gardening in Kings County expanded and contracted with the use of manure. In analyzing the census results, the *Rural Gazette* opined in 1882 that Kings County should no longer be regarded as agricultural because farming there "is conducted under exceptional circumstances, and the product of the land would not afford a fair basis for comparison with that of ordinary farming lands. It would not be practicable, as a rule, to manure lands as heavily as is done in the farming portions of Kings County, because these lands are within easy reach of a great city, and its wastes are turned to account by the farmers adjoining the city."[68]

The shift to more manure-intensive vegetable farming overlapped with the expanded use of horse-drawn transportation in Brooklyn and New York City as the superabundance of cheap accessible horse manure became a foundation of post–Civil War market gardening. Some have linked the decline of market gardening to the disappearance of manure associated with the displacement of horses in cities, but Kings County's decline as a vegetable producer began before any loss of manure supplies could have become relevant. There is no evidence that decreasing availability of manure became problematic for Kings County farmers. The Brooklyn City Railroad, for example, recorded a tripling between 1864 and 1883 in its income from the sale of horse manure, from $4,430.99 to $11,135,40. As late as 1890, when Kings County farming was beginning its steep decline, animal power still accounted for 81 percent of rapid transit mileage in Brooklyn and 75 percent in New York City. Ultimately, electrification of transportation, construction of sewerage systems, and manufacture of cheap commercial fertilizers toward the end of the century reduced both the supply of and demand for urban manure.[69]

Rural Kings County itself was an East Coast center of fertilizer production from menhaden. In the 1870s Barren Island in Flatlands boasted four factories, which still earned the island the epithet "odoriferous" in the 1890s, and the smells of which were "as fragrant as ever" in the first decade of the twentieth century. The Barren Island fertilizer industry, which by the 1880s was capable of processing up to 1.5 million fish daily and employed 500 workers including those in the fleets, began in the 1840s when 2,000 tons of fertilizer were produced annually from dead animals carted there from Brooklyn and New York.[70]

Even as local transportation systems weaned themselves of animal power, manure suppliers apparently faced little market or other pressure to make the recycling process more efficient. In 1897 the USDA, in an effort to help city officials and make farms more productive, discovered that only 60 of 354 cities used street sweepings for fertilization. Despite pleas from sanitation experts, conservationists, and agrarians that cities were wasting a treasure, not until the 1920s did a few U.S. cities begin selling their sewage sludge as organic fertilizer materials.[71]

By 1910 the USDA confirmed that commercial fertilizers were "extensively used in the production of truck-crop potatoes, particularly on the Atlantic seaboard." This shift was not without risks: contemporary agronomists warned of the adverse impact on the soil of the continued use of commercial fertilizer, especially in connection with single-cropping designed "to get the greatest possible return in the shortest time, regardless of consequences." They stressed how fortunate it was that the cities consuming the products of intensive agriculture could amply supply the manure needed to restore proper soil conditions.[72]

3. COMPETITIVENESS AND THE "COURAGEOUS CAPITALIST"

There are plenty of people now living in Brooklyn who remember all
this part of the city, as it was laid out in farms, orchards, gardens, &c. It
used to help supply the New York market with garden vegetables, just as
Flatbush and other outer towns do now.
— Walt Whitman, "Brooklyniana," 1862

Producing large quantities of vegetables efficiently did not guarantee their
sale at profitable prices. Finding solvent consumers and establishing physically accessible markets for their cabbages and potatoes in the face of cheap
southern competition were also indispensable tasks confronting Kings
County farmers.

MARKETING VEGETABLES

For the past two or three weeks our village streets have nightly resounded with
the noise of farm-wagons loaded to the brim with potatoes on their way to
market, while the morning hours have been made resonant with the merry
rattle of their return, bespeaking ready sale and good prices.
— "Potatoes," *Kings County Rural Gazette*, July 27, 1872

In addition to the compelling economic consideration of the mass availability of cheap manure in the city, which von Thünen had emphasized,
many farmers preferred farming higher-priced land near the city to cheaper
land farther away because they were optimally located with regard to the
market for vegetables that the explosively growing urban population cre-

ated. For this reason, some Long Island and New Jersey market gardeners were willing to pay "large sums" to rent farmland near farmers' markets in Manhattan or Brooklyn. In the 1880s, three thousand to four thousand farmers' wagons entered Manhattan daily to sell market garden produce.[1]

Brooklyn lacked a public market for vegetables before 1826; prior to that time, farmers with "their immense carts" gathered on a commons. By the mid-1850s, 50 wagon loads of vegetables were delivered daily to the James Street Market during the season. The lack of an efficient infrastructure for vegetable marketing in Brooklyn had become so palpable to farmers by the early 1870s that the *Rural Gazette* used it as an argument for rejecting annexation: "We send you the great bulk of your produce, and yet you won't provide a suitable place for selling it; so we are often forced to cart it to New York and let your grocers cart it back again." Worse yet, Brooklyn authorities arrested farmers for selling without a license (which cost $3.00 for a team of horses and $1.00 for a single horse) or even traveling through the city to New York without a tag (costing 30 cents).[2]

Kings County farmers took their produce to Washington Market and West Washington Market in Manhattan for much of the nineteenth century. During the 1858 season, "when garden produce is sold by every man who raises it for the city, there are no less than sixteen hundred to two thousand wagons which pay daily for the privilege of selling their vegetables." Despite the large supplies of vegetables, complaints were voiced as early as the 1860s that, through the indifference or corruption of city officials, middlemen in New York were able to extract "enormous profits" from consumers. The city's industrial classes thus carried an almost intolerable burden in the form of prices 45 percent higher than in Philadelphia.[3]

Stiles described vegetable marketing in Manhattan at the end of the 1870s: "Nearly all the produce raised within twenty-five miles of New York is carted in with teams by the proprietors, in the night. The largest part is sold at wholesale to dealers or middle-men, between midnight and daylight, chiefly in the vicinity of Washington market, which until recently was the center of the retail as well as the wholesale trade." Those who failed to sell their produce wholesale stayed until morning to sell at retail. As a result of the "great throng of market wagons, which for years had greatly impeded business in the lower part of the city," another market was established near West 12th Street and 10th Avenue.[4]

Reacting to complaints from residents of congestion on the Lower West Side, the Board of Aldermen adopted a resolution on August 6, 1878, designating a part of the former Fort Gansevoort, situated farther uptown, as a market stand for farm wagons. The chief of police and superintendent of markets addressed the problem at Washington Market by extending the hours during which farm wagons were permitted to stand in the streets from 7 P.M. to 10 A.M. Queens County farmers were satisfied with this new arrangement, but their counterparts from Kings County, "who are in the habit of wholesaling their loads in the afternoon, found their business materially interfered with." When Kings County farmers sought the aid of their Queens competitors, the latter were tempted to refuse on the grounds that two years earlier the former had failed to assist in improving conditions at the market. But when Queens farmers realized that the streets would be even more crowded in the mornings if Kings County farmers were forced to stop wholesaling in the afternoon, they reached an agreement with the superintendent of markets that farmers would be privileged to wholesale in the wide parts of certain streets from 1 P.M. to 5 P.M. Soon thereafter, however, the Common Council of New York prohibited the farmers from selling their goods in the streets near Washington Market, requiring them instead to move uptown to Gansevoort Market.[5]

During their waning days at West Washington Market in 1879, farmers saw their conditions deteriorate because, in the words of the market's semi-official organ, the *Market Index and Journal*, "they have no recognized rights in the way of disposing of their produce. They are compelled to stand along the curbstones whenever they get a chance, all night long, and, if the market is poor, nearly the whole forenoon of the next day, and either dispose of their produce at a sacrifice, or else carry it back home with them. Grocers and hucksters are their only salvation."[6]

When Gansevoort Market opened, during a snowstorm, on December 22, 1879, farmers, who had to pay the same 25 cents daily fee that they had previously paid for the privilege of standing in certain streets with their wagons, immediately complained that it provided space for only 300 wagons, whereas more than 2,000 farmers daily brought produce to New York. By January, a representative of the Kings County farmers said that the prospect of the new market had so discouraged them that they were "really hesitating whether or not to plant their fields." The *Market Index and Journal* predicted that as a consequence Kings County farmers would sell their produce to grocers in Brooklyn. This possibility prompted the *Rural Gazette* to propose making a virtue of a necessity: if farmers just withheld their produce from New York markets, Gotham would let loose such an "unearthly howl" that buyers would be forced to accept higher prices. Queens and Kings County farmers' reactions to the forced move differed sharply. Whereas

Gansevoort required Kings County farmers, who landed at Manhattan on the lower ferries, to drive their wagons an additional four miles, the ferries from Queens, which docked farther uptown and thus had been inconvenient in relation to Washington Market, were closer to Gansevoort. Moreover, "coming so far as some of them do, they would lief as stay and sell to grocers, and not as our farmers, deliver two and three loads a day to shippers."[7]

One of the chief irrationalities of the distribution system as practiced at Washington Market continued to mar the operation of Gansevoort as well: with many more farmers than places to stand, those who arrived first each day could choose their stand, whereas others might find no stand at all. The farmers' grievance was also visited upon New York consumers: since farmers were obliged to drive to New York hours ahead of time merely to secure a place to stand, they were unable to offer vegetables as fresh as would otherwise have been possible.[8]

By January 1880, Kings County farmers began organizing in opposition to the forced move to Gansevoort. One hundred farmers enthusiastically convened in the New Utrecht town hall. The meeting was chaired by the well-known New Utrecht farmer and politician Adolph Gubner. Some complained that if Washington Market and West Washington Market were scarcely able to accommodate the 1,800 to 2,500 wagons that congregated there, the much smaller Gansevoort would be disastrous. One farmer charged that the more remote market would force farmers to "keep more horses, more help, and receive less" for their produce. Since shippers were located downtown, if farmers took in a load at midday, they would have to drive three miles uptown, wait until they sold it, and then drive three miles back downtown. Following such presentations, the assembled farmers voted to form the Farmers and Market Gardeners' Association of the Town of New Utrecht, and to confer with their counterparts in the four other rural towns to form similar organizations.[9]

That goal was exceeded a week later when, spurred on by the *Rural Gazette*, more than one hundred fifty farmers, representing all the towns, met to create the Kings County Farmers and Market Gardeners' Association — which outlived this immediate crisis — dedicated to protecting its members' rights and interests in the sale of market produce in New York City. A committee, consisting of one farmer from each of the five towns, was formed to meet with a committee of merchants, lessees, and owners to plan the opposition to Gansevoort. Wholesale grocers in the Washington Market area were also injured by the farmers' expulsion because farmers were wont to spend much of the money that they realized at the market on provisions that they bought from the grocers. To be sure, Kings County farmers insisted that, although they much preferred returning to Washington Market, it, too, needed to be expanded to accommodate them: "they would not consent to be driven from street to street, as they had been in the past." In addition, as they emphasized at yet another countywide meeting, they objected to being forced to leave the streets around Washington Market at 6 or 7 A.M., and desired to be permitted to remain until 9 A.M.[10]

The City of New York ended the farmers' uncertainty on February 12, when its comptroller issued an opinion upholding the decision to exclude farmers from Washington Market. He focused on the inevitability of disruptive change in an explosively growing metropolis beset with congestion: "With the immense increase in population of the city and the necesssity for greater supplies of vegetables and farm products the number of farmers' and gardeners' market wagons have also multiplied disproportionately, until from a few score of wagons occupying stands in the streets twenty five or thirty years ago, there are now frequently more than one thousand in a day . . . encumbering the main thoroughfares and side streets through the night and early in the morning." The shift to Gansevoort afforded farmers the advantage of concentrating the trade in one place: they could sell their produce promptly "without being obliged to close out at a sacrifice to middlemen and peddlers, as they were often obliged to do when required to leave their stands in the streets at fixed hours." The longer distance that Kings County farmers had to travel was more than compensated for by the ability "to get an eligible stand without the necessity of coming to the city in the afternoon or early in the evening before market days, as formerly, to get a good stand in the streets."[11]

Despite the enactment, three months later, by the state legislature of an act establishing the lands around Gansevoort as a public market place for farmers' wagons and authorizing New York City to buy whatever portions of the described land that were not already city property, Kings County farmers, who supported the bill, remained discontented. Gansevoort's failure to provide them with adequate space or a "paying location" prompted them to try to return to their old location. Farmers who continued selling downtown ran the risk of being fined $25 for letting their wagons stand in the street while they sought out customers. They were permitted, however, if they had sold their produce before they came to New York, to deliver it and drive away, but it was unlawful to sell from the wagon. But since farmers were increasingly marketing mixed loads, which required them to find a customer for each kind of produce, risk-free sales in Manhattan were becoming less likely. Consequently, many farmers began selling in Brooklyn. By late 1882, 300 farm wagons lined Fulton Street.[12]

Indeed, immediately after the comptroller had published his decision, agitation began for the creation of a vegetable market in Brooklyn. By 1883, farmers delivered more than one hundred loads at the new Fulton Street market. Midday loads to New York were also common. Public discussion of the need for a new public market in Brooklyn in 1883–84 was based on the large and potentially even larger output of Kings County farms, which produced about as big a harvest of peas and beans as Queens and Suffolk county farms combined in addition to a somewhat smaller volume of potatoes. More significant, however, was the contemporary claim that the gross farm sales of Kings County ($1,000,000), Queens ($3,125,000), and Suffolk ($1,600,000) could be increased sixfold. Such contemporary impressions strongly contradict an inevitabilist conception of the demise of urban agriculture, in spite of the *Rural Gazette*'s conviction that the county towns were "all destined to become one grand metropolitan commonwealth — one immense Brooklyn."[13]

Because the farmers were soon also prohibited from standing on Fulton Street near the ferry, their representatives urged the authorities in Brooklyn to provide them with appropriate market facilities. In the interim between the breakup of Washington Market in Manhattan and the opening in 1884 of Wallabout Market in Brooklyn, farmers complained that they, "like wandering Jews . . . had to drive all around a great city to sell a load of produce." Fulton Street in Brooklyn soon "was lined with farmers' wagons laden with products fresh from the gardens and farms of the suburbs."[14]

Progress toward opening a market gained momentum in 1883 when the public learned of the irrationality of a system that required Kings County farmers to sell their produce in Manhattan, where Brooklyn grocers then bought it to cart it back for sale in Brooklyn. The unnecessarily increased price and the loss of freshness — as one farmer explained to a large audience: "You eat on Sunday what was gathered three days before" — galvanized action to establish a large permanent market at Wallabout.[15]

To alleviate the impediments to other traffic, the Brooklyn Works Commissioner issued an order on September 20, 1884, requiring the farmers to stand on another street adjoining the wastelands of the U.S. Navy Yard. After that date farmers had to go to Wallabout to sell their produce because wagons were not permitted to stand elsewhere. This removal was linked to a promise by the city of Brooklyn to find a permanent location for a produce market. By October 13, the U.S. Navy leased over 400,000 square feet to the city, which then drained the land, built streets, sewers, and water mains, and installed gas and electric light for a 104,000 square foot market large enough for 400 farmers' wagons.[16]

To eliminate the uncertainties arising from an at-will lease, the city of Brooklyn persuaded the federal government in 1890 to sell 18 acres, to which it received title in 1891 for $700,000. The federal government sold the city an additional 27 acres in 1894 for $1,200,000, which was raised through special market bonds that New York and Brooklyn bankers and trust companies readily took at premiums ranging between 4 and 8 percent. These extensive measures and the enactment in 1894 by the state legislature of a statute regulating the administration of Wallabout market suggest that even as late as the mid-1890s, local, state, and national political authorities and financial circles were convinced that Long Island vegetable farming could look forward to a profitable future.[17]

Wallabout became the world's largest market, a middle-of-the-night wholesale market designed to eliminate the nuisances that plagued residents when farmers and their wagons — the latest models of which were deep enough to hide a standing man — and horses gathered on and near Fulton Street. By the early 1890s Wallabout Market, where market days were Tuesdays and Saturdays from April to November and Fridays the remainder of the year, was described as bustling with activity: hundreds of farmers, who began arriving at four o'clock in the afternoon from as far as twenty to thirty miles away, crowded the square with their produce-laden wagons. At the peak, one Saturday in the summer of 1896, 546 wagons of market gardeners' vegetables were sold at Wallabout. As late as 1903, the vitality of farming throughout the western third of Long Island was sufficient to prompt the U.S. Bureau of Soils to observe that "nearly every level acre not occupied for building purposes, or held in large country estates, is under intensive cultivation to market gardening and truck crops."[18]

At the turn of the century, market gardeners on the western end of Long Island were still using 1,800-pound horse-drawn wagons, costing $350, that hauled three tons of produce. Leaving their farms in the evening or night, they drove twenty or thirty miles on macadam roads to arrive at 2 A.M. at the New York City market, which opened at daybreak. In 1915, when intensive market gardening was still being practiced on the western end of Long Island on land worth $7,500 or more an acre, farmers personally took their market wagons to New York City markets, returning home as quickly as possible to do a day's work.[19]

FIGURE 6. *Marketman John Torborg ready to drive a market wagon loaded with celery to Wallabout market from the Rapalje-Hitchings farm, New Lots, c. 1900. Courtesy of Peter Rapelje.*

The importance that Dutch farmers attached to marketing can be gleaned from the actions of a market gardener who had the opportunity to shape one of the very few governmental interventions into agriculture. Teunis Garrett Bergen (1806–1881) was the scion of one of Kings County's oldest Dutch farm families. Although a surveyor, for decades he farmed in

New Utrecht. Bergen was elected to the 39th Congress as the representative from the Second Congressional District in New York from 1865 to 1867; his major legislative contributions to a Congress of monumental importance in reconfiguring post–Civil War relations between North and South and the future of the freed slaves focused on matters of pecuniary significance to himself and his fellow market gardeners. He proposed an amendment to the Civil War internal revenue law that farmers and gardeners who "travel through the cities and sell the produce of their farms and gardens" be exempt from a $10 peddler license. Despite Representative (and future President) Garfield's objection that if "a man goes peddling his own produce he ought to be considered a peddler and to pay a tax," the amendment was adopted. During House debate on a proposal to exempt from federal tax farmers' wagons costing up to $200, Bergen declared that farmers around New York used wagons for carting produce to market that cost $300 to $400: "I know this by experience." The House promptly agreed to his amendment to raise the ceiling.[20]

A striking description of the system of vegetable marketing at the very peak of Kings County's production has been preserved in the litigation between John Turner, an Irish farmworker and marketman, and his Dutch farm employer, William W. Kouwenhoven, of Flatlands, in the early 1880s. July through November were this typical vegetable farm's busiest months, during which loads were marketed daily; until October the marketman took three to five loads a day. Vegetables were marketed at least as late as Christmas. That Turner sold barrels of Kouwenhoven's lettuce as late as December 23, 1881, suggests either that the growing season extended into the winter or that the farmer held back produce to obtain premium prices in the winter. Alternatively, since Kouwenhoven owned a hothouse, he, like many northern metropolitan farmers, was equipped to produce beyond the natural growing season (although some of the lettuce was sold at a reduced price because it was "touched by frost"). Sending an average of four loads per day of potatoes and cabbages to market was common for market gardeners during the harvest season.[21]

From the $30 to $35 for which the farmer on average sold his load had to be deducted the direct marketing expenses. One reckoning for Kings County in 1872 stated that a farmer had to pay his marketman $3.00, the carrier $1.25 for the stand fee, 20 cents for the watchman, 50 cents for the ferry, and 12 cents for toll gates, for a total of $5.07. At times farmers could realize much higher amounts per load: W. H. Algeo, the long-term tenant on

John A. Lott's Flatbush farm, received upwards of $500 for four loads of potatoes that he sold on one day in Manhattan in July 1873. William Bennett of Gravesend, who regularly marketed more than $100 of produce daily, sold potatoes, tomatoes, sweet corn, and pears for $713.96 on August 19, 1893. And on one day in 1882 a New Utrecht farmer took $926 worth of peas off his farm.[22]

Kouwenhoven sold part of his produce directly to grocery stores in Brooklyn: Saturday "was market day, when we sent loads to New York; Fridays we sent goods to Brooklyn. . . . When we go to New York we go in the night, and when we go to Brooklyn it is in the day time. We sell a great deal of stuff in Brooklyn. The principal portion is sold in Kings County. In the market season some market in the night and some in the day time. I market both night and day." Selling was in part a chaotic, random, and desperate process driven by the need to dispose of all the produce that had been loaded at the farm onto the wagon at the best prices the marketman could get: "The sales are made almost entirely in open market for cash (hence no accounts kept and no book charges), and are made generally to strangers . . . , of whose very names the marketman is ignorant . . . , in quantities to suit the purchaser and at prices varying greatly even for the same goods and on the very same day." If the marketman could not sell it as a whole load, he generally had to take any price he could get. Consequently, he "might get so much for a barrel of sprouts of one man and at a later portion of the day would take considerably less from another."[23]

The travails of nocturnal marketing were manifold: "All the summer evening long . . . you may meet on the streets of lower New York the great wagons of the Long-Island farmers from Flatbush, Flatlands, Gravesend, and New Utrecht, trundling their slow way from the ferries to Washington Market. . . . Arrived there, and their place secured in the line, the drivers sleep for a few hours, in their wagons or in the neighboring taverns, until their wares are disposed of, and then make their way home, still in the gray of the morning." A Flatlander, mocking the supposed advantages of annexation to Brooklyn, urged his fellow townspeople in 1873 to "think of the gas lamps, which light you on your midnight tours to the market, and enable you to furnish a fresh supply of vegetables every morning to her [Brooklyn's] generous residents." To exacerbate matters, farmers were sometimes robbed on the way back from the market. Marketing, especially in the years before the opening of the Brooklyn Bridge, was also very time-consuming for the marketmen, who complained of being stopped by people "just for fun" at

2 A.M. as they congregated in a "big drove" of wagons in Manhattan all night until the grocers came.[24]

The obvious inefficiencies of this marketing mechanism suggest one weakness in the competitive position of Kings County producers that collective action might have remedied. Although farmers themselves despaired of effecting improvements in marketing conditions, their resistance to eviction from Washington Market, which ultimately led to the opening of Wallabout Market, demonstrated their capacity for self-organization. That Kings County farmers as late as the 1880s actively and collectively pursued new markets also emerges from a meeting that a group of New Utrecht farmers, including representatives of such old-line families as Cowenhoven, Van Pelt, and Bennett, attended in 1885. They met with the management of the Staten Island Rapid Transit Company, which operated the Bay Ridge Ferry and the Sea Beach Railroad, to "discuss the advisability of increasing the facilities of the Bay Ridge Ferry, so as to accommodate the truck farmers by opening a new wagon road to the ferry, building a new slip at Bay Ridge, and putting on boats which can be used for transporting teams." The transportation managers were pleased to hear the farmers report that at least three thousand teams carrying market garden produce would use the ferry during the season. Although the outcome of these plans is unknown, the fact that farmers at this late date sought new outlets for their produce outside of Brooklyn and New York suggests that they were dissatisfied with transportation to or conditions at Wallabout or that they perceived competition there as increasingly unfavorable. Alternatively, Kings County farmers may have been producing more and desirous of selling to a potential market of people whose per capita consumption of vegetables had been below average.[25]

As disruptive as the nightly trips to the urban markets may have been for the farmers and their marketmen, many residents were more concerned about disruptions to their own lives. For years the *Rural Gazette* functioned as a forum for such complaints. In 1873 it published a letter in which "We the people affected and annoyed humbly beg . . . the farmers from Flatbush, Flatlands and New Utrecht" to use the wooden pavement after 7 P.M. "as they wend their weary way to the ferries . . . to . . . dispose of their produce." Many farmers preferred to travel with their wagons over the horse-drawn rail tracks, but set their wheels too wide to fit them, the consequence being "a constant grating, screeching, howling noise, at all times of the night." Three years later, the newspaper editorialized on the subject. Sympathizing

with the Brooklyn residents, the *Rural Gazette* suspected that the real cul-
prits were newly employed drivers "stupidly ignorant of the annoyance."
The editorial at last elicited responses from farmers, who conceded the
justice of the complaints, but could see no remedy because riding on the
wooden Nicholson pavement "would send a three-deck load of potatoes or
vegetables all over the street," while horses would be severely injured at-
tempting to take a heavy load down on the smooth scrimshaw pavement.[26]

Such clashes between agrarian and urban ways of life would have become
an increasingly contentious issue, which would have tested the social viability of urban farming. The advent of the steam railroad and electric trolley and their adoption for transporting farm produce would have been a
relatively uncomplicated solution. In light of the unprecedented number
and kinds of horrible injuries and deaths that railroads inflicted in Kings
County as elsewhere, however, they would not have eliminated the injuries
and deaths that farmers caused by driving over pedestrians with farm wagons on the way to and from markets in Brooklyn and New York.[27]

The transformation of agriculture in the East in adjustment to western
competition prompted similar conversions to market gardening and truck
farming along the East Coast from Boston to Baltimore to meet rising demand from the burgeoning middle class in the cities for such semiluxuries
as vegetables and fruits. Indeed, by the end of the century, the taste and solvent demand for these products had reached into working-class families:
a survey of New York City from the mid-1890s revealed that they were eating fewer potatoes and more onions, beets, peas, beans, tomatoes, strawberries. A distinct source of demand for specialty vegetables was the new
European immigrants, who brought their culinary tastes with them. Kohl-
rabi, for example, was "highly appreciated in New York, especially amongst
the Germans." Adequate data on urban vegetable consumption did not become available until after World War I, but even New York's poor possessed
enough solvent demand for fresh vegetables to assure Kings County's farmers a market that they could not glut.[28]

The *New York Times* provided an amusing description of the extent to
which consumption of fresh vegetables and fruits had become customary even among the poor in New York City by 1884. Located in Lower
Manhattan, Union (or Houston) Market was open Saturday nights in the
spring, summer, and autumn; there largely non-English-speaking "foreigners" bought cabbages for 3 to 5 cents, onions for 4 cents a quart, potatoes for
15 cents a peck. There might be little satisfaction "in buying the freshest and

greenest vegetables from a . . . dirty-fingered peddler who probably never saw a fifty-acre farm in his life, and ten chances to one couldn't tell if he were asked whether asparagus grows in the sod or on bushes," but it was "the great green grocers' shop of economical buyers. Poor people get more for their money there than anywhere else in town."[29]

New York's marketing system was not optimally arranged to ensure vegetable prices that workers could afford. In 1882, according to the *New York Times*, after commission merchants, wholesale dealers, and green grocers had added their profits, consumers paid prices at least 50 percent higher than the wholesale price. The central problem was that whereas other cities provided markets where "truckers can take the products of their farms and sell them directly to the consumers," New York not only lacked such accommodations, but "compels those growers who do come here to carry their produce to some out-of-the-way place like the farmers' market at Gansevoort-street or sell it at wholesale to some dealer." Intermediaries whose livelihoods depended on this system sought to justify it on the grounds that direct marketing to consumers was good in theory, but impracticable because farmers lacked the time to peddle their crops. Some busy farmers — such as John L. Ryder of Flatlands, a longtime town supervisor, who could be seen driving his wagonload of vegetables to New York at three o'clock in the morning and at every supervisors board meeting — drove their own wagons, but their employment of marketmen was not necessarily an irrational division of labor.[30]

Those involved in the vegetable trade were acutely aware that the future lay with supplying a mass market at prices low enough for the expanding urban proletariat to afford. In 1881, the *New York Market Index-Journal* reported on intimations in the press that William Vanderbilt, the railroad magnate (who until the age of 45 had been relegated to a farm on Staten Island, for which he hauled manure from his father's stables in Manhattan), had devised a plan to establish a vegetable market at 34th Street in Manhattan to be supplied by a vegetable train that would run along the Hudson River. There thousands of farmers, unable to compete with western grain farmers, would be encouraged to convert to vegetable farms, the products of which Vanderbilt's train would get to New York as early as those of Long Island farmers. The plan hinged on the widely accepted claim that "Long Island, as a vegetable garden, is no longer capable of providing for the three million of people now drawing on it and the suburban New Jersey farmers for fresh vegetables." Although the *Market Index-Journal* was not prepared to accept that view, it recognized that "with a population ever increasing . . . the question of cheap vegetables must in the near future present itself, unless larger supplies are forthcoming." [31]

SOUTHERN COMPETITION

Up to about 1890 the great cities drew most of their fruits and vegetables from relatively high priced land . . . near the centers of population and industry. . . . Outside competition with the local product was almost unknown. Every producing area had its one, natural, nearby market and usually only one. The ice plant and refrigerator cars changed all this with tremendous rapidity.
— Wells Sherman, *Merchandising Fruits and Vegetables*, 1930

The greatest competitive threat to the viability of Kings County vegetable production, however, arose not among Vanderbilt's would-be customers in the Hudson Valley, but from the rise of low-cost truck farming in the post-Reconstruction South. As new transportation and refrigeration technologies made it possible for southern farmers to sell their vegetables in northern markets, a new set of cost pressures restricted the profitability of suburban New York agriculture. Even these intra-industry forces, however, did not suffice to drive Kings County farmers out of business. Southern vegetables "caused no little alarm among gardeners who depend upon New York and Philadelphia for their markets," but the force of this threat was much weakened by the fact that their "crops are, as a rule, about ended when ours commence," while northern consumers "are willing to pay a price for the fresh . . . products of home growth." [32]

Dr. Armenius Oemler, "the largest slave-owner previous to the war engaged in the business in the neighborhood of Savannah" and author of a book on southern truck farming that went through several editions, shed light on this interregional competition in his somewhat tendentious 1885 insider account. Thirty years earlier, Long Island and New Jersey market gardening had been "very profitable," often conferring "competency and wealth, notwithstanding the farm land was sometimes worth from $200 to $1,000 per acre." When the advent of fast and frequent steam transportation "revolutionized" the situation, "the higher prices of early produce accrue to gardeners of southern latitudes at a distance of hundreds of miles, who cultivate land averaging not more than one-fifth the value, and, in consequence of the warmer climate, at less expense. In fact, market gardening has recently become comparatively so unremunerative that many of those formerly pursuing that branch of husbandry have turned their attention to dairy farming." Norfolk became the first major point of production for supplying Eastern markets, but "within the last few years competition from more southern localities . . . subjected Norfolk . . . to similar experience."[33]

Several empirical defects mar Oemler's account. First, the thirty-year period during which market gardening had allegedly already been in decline saw its aggregate value in Kings and Queens counties increase 5.5-fold. Second, from 1850 to 1900, not only did the value of Norfolk County's market gardening also rise fivefold, but no other southern county was among the 25 top producing counties. As late as 1901, a treatise on vegetable growing in the South observed that truck farming there had "not yet become near so extensive as it is conducted in most of the Northern States." Norfolk's position as the national leader in per acre use of fertilizer in 1900 must be seen in connection with the fact that much of the southern soil "was long ago exhausted, or never had any great depth."[34]

Third, the reference to cheap southern land as an explanation of the rise to prominence of its truck farming made little sense with respect to at least one group. Dutch farmers in Kings County whose families had owned their land for a century or two presumably made no provision for the "cost" of their land in calculating prices for their vegetables since no one had paid anything for it for generations. Indeed, even at one-fifth the value, the relevant cost of southern farmland, if recently acquired, may have been higher than among Dutch farmers. To be sure, by the 1880s, relatively few old-line Dutch farmers were still personally farming, but even for recent farm buyers or tenants rent may not have played an important part; in contrast to general farming, where rent or interest on land purchase money amounted to almost half the cost of operating, in market gardening it was "usually only about 10 per cent. of the working expenses, so that an apparently cheap rent, or cheap purchase, does not very materially affect the result." In addition, practical horticulturists advised that it was "always better" to pay higher rent or interest in order to be closer to the market and to avoid the extra expenses of teaming and obtaining manure and labor farther out.[35]

Finally, the swift southern advance was contradicted by Oemler's own report on "the many difficulties of transportation," which included discriminatory freight rates. By the turn of the century, the USDA recognized not only that southern advantages had been offset to some extent by higher transport costs, but that "the far South can not compete with more northern localities at the same season with most crops."[36]

Kings County farmers were alert to all these advantages and disadvantages. In the early 1870s the *Rural Gazette* noted that although the soil might be better and the land cheaper in the West, demand and transportation costs were just as important. It used this comparative analysis to urge industrial urbanization on Long Island as the savior rather than the scourge of local farming: "if all over this Island, our villages should increase to towns, (especially manufacturing towns) the benefits would naturally accrue to the farmers, whose lands would increase in value, and who would also have an increased demand for their produce and could furnish the market without paying dearly for transportation, or subjecting themselves to the extortions of middlemen. Thus the secret of success is, not to go West, but encourage the growth of our own population."[37]

Whatever cost advantages southern vegetable farmers may have enjoyed vis-à-vis their Long Island competitors were in large part rooted in the vestiges of slavery. Oemler considered "emancipation . . . the birth of truck farming on an extensive scale. It was not an industry that could have recommended itself to rice planters, and these were the only agriculturists owning large forces of slaves in the vicinity of the large Atlantic coast cities, nor would any of them have for a moment entertained the proposal of hiring their hands to truck farmers." The farmer had to look to "the same God-given instrument, the negro, . . . for his labor. It is rarely, even in the vicinity of Norfolk, that recourse is had to any other race." Oemler did not reveal whether the sunrise to sunset working hours for 50 to 75 cents per day were also divinely ordained, but he gave an impression of the immense pool of labor required by noting that for the strawberry harvest at Norfolk alone "between 2,560 and 3,200 hands are indispensable."[38]

Oemler also explained the logic behind the apartheid labor policy: "The negro must be accepted as the only practical solution of the labor question, and, notwithstanding his instability, he is the best for many reasons. It would be impolitic, even were it possible, to trust to more intelligent and energetic laborers from abroad, and mix the two races as field laborers." Farm owners could not depend on "retaining the foreign help, as his greater energy and a praiseworthy desire for self-elevation would soon prompt the emigrant, or white laborer, to . . . better his condition."[39]

Nor were such frank racial views confined to pecuniarily interested ex-slaveholders. The author of a major turn-of-the-century history of the postbellum South went even further, virtually inverting causality and arguing that southern vegetable farming owed its existence to free blacks' "preference . . . for work that is not continuous. . . . [T]he labor is engaged for single jobs, which cover only a few days or a few weeks; the hands come and go according to the demands of each crop. . . . The negro is thus afforded numerous opportunities of earning wages sufficient for his wants without his whole time, throughout the year, being occupied." [40]

The census reported that in 1889 day wages on truck farms in the South were little more than 60 percent of those in the New York–Philadelphia area, and the cost of labor per acre in some crops such as string or snap beans was less than one-fourth that in the North. Although many truck farmers kept "little or no record of their business," the Census Office, based on "cheerful cooperation" by planters, marketmen, and transportation firms, recorded 70,342 laborers at some time during 1889 in the New York–Philadelphia area compared with 22,489 in the Norfolk district. To be sure, in some crops, for example, beets, sweet potatoes, and spinach, per acre labor costs were higher in Norfolk than in New York–Philadelphia. Despite these low wages, the census of 1900 asserted that: "At a distance from centers of population, this transient labor is hard to secure, and even fancy wages sometimes fail to attract a sufficient supply." As late as 1909, the major economic history of the postbellum South confirmed that cheap and abundant labor was such an essential element of southern truck farming that "on this account many trucking areas are located rather close to large cities." In the North, in contrast, observers emphasized: "Proximity to the large cities and manufacturing works draws labor away from the farms, and unfortunately for the agricultural industry it loses the most enterprising and intelligent." [41]

Advances in railroad transport, ice plants, and mechanical refrigeration made southern truck farmers competitors of market gardeners in and around the cities of the Northeast. In 1854, the first shipments of vegetables were sent by ship from Norfolk — where a decade earlier two farmers from New Jersey had introduced intensive agriculture — to New York, but such southern supplies did not become commercially significant until after the Civil War. Residents of New York and other cities as yet "had not acquired the taste for vegetables out of season, but were satisfied with the supply during the period of natural growth in their own immediate locality." With the labor "surplus" that the end of slavery created, southern planters began dedicating thousands of acres to vegetables and fruits for northern markets. Along the Atlantic seaboard, from Norfolk to southern Florida, "probably the finest trucking country in the world," owners of truck farms ranging from ten to one hundred acres saw the value of their land rise from as little as $2 to as much as $500 per acre. As late as 1882, the *Rural Gazette* still referred to the ability of Florida truck farms to supply northern markets with "an almost unlimited amount of early vegetables" as an event that would occur "bye and bye."[42]

Southern producers' greatest impact on Kings County farmers lay not in direct competition, but in their preemption of the early market and shortening the season during which local producers monopolized the market. Beginning in the 1830s and 1840s, in certain sections of the county such as New Utrecht, "almost all residents were engaged (owing to the peculiar quality of the soil) in raising early vegetables for the New York market. As there was no Southern competition (such as now [1894]) their products commanded high prices, and consequently by prudence, economy, energy and industry, they acquired wealth and independence." But by the last decade of the century, when market gardening had been "completely revolutionized," it was no longer possible for early Long Island vegetables to be sold profitably in New York. Although even contemporaries conceded that "very little can be said with absolute accuracy" about vegetable prices, they had no doubt that nationally "prices of fresh vegetables declined very greatly from 1890 to 1900" in no small part as a result of the pressure exerted by southern production.[43]

This South-North trade took on new dimensions in 1885 when Norfolk truck farmers made their first rail shipments to New York. The advent of long-distance refrigerated transport of perishable foodstuffs made it possible to move such large amounts so quickly that it facilitated "the greater growth of the city itself." This new technology "changed the whole face of the production map," but as late as 1929, an official of the Port of New York Authority, in writing about the city's food distribution system, could still observe that although railroad refrigeration cars "caused sources of supply which were most favored under the old transportation system to lose their former relative advantage, . . . in the main it has so expanded demand as to call merely for a shift in the type of production rather than visiting disaster even upon these former sources of supply." If, therefore, the disappearance of Kings County farmers was not inevitable as a matter of price competition with Florida and California farms, self-preservation would have required significant entrepreneurial reorganization. In particular, given the enormous and intricate continuous distribution system established in New York City from the 1880s on, direct marketing of perishables was "often a time-consuming and difficult proposition" for the farmer, who could "scarcely be a producer and salesman at the same time on account of the time spent in making trips to market and disposing of his product." Farmers' "lack of

organization and knowledge of the prospective supplies of shipped-in produce" also disadvantaged them in selling to dealers with such knowledge of
the "prospective railroad supply through passing reports." In the absence of
an intense process of concentration and centralization that might have enabled a few Kings County vegetable farmers to emerge as sufficiently large
producers to justify the creation of their own marketing departments, they
could have dealt with this structurally lopsided information disparity only
by forming sales cooperatives, which they failed to undertake.[44]

As New York City became the largest U.S. market for southern vegetables, "people of modest means" could do what a few decades earlier not
even the rich could manage — namely, buy vegetables out of season. Railroads, realizing how profitable the transport of vegetable and fruit crops
could be, provided crucial support for the development of the industry by
furnishing specialized rolling stock, sponsoring demonstrations for and
supplying plants to farmers, and transporting harvest workers. The railroads' self-interest was clear since it was "only at points where a sufficient
number of men are growing the same crop or crops that are marketed at the
same season to enable shipments to be made in car-lots, that good shipping
facilities" could arise. Consequently: "Often only one or two truck crops are
grown in a given locality."[45]

Burnet Landreth, a New Jersey vegetable farmer and horticultural author, writing shortly after the results of the 1890 agricultural census had
been published, noted that the "unprecedented development in the Caroli-
nas and Gulf States of the business of growing vegetables for autumn and
winter shipment to the cities of the North . . . has been one of the surprises
in modern agriculture." Whereas in the past vegetables "all had their seasons, and, when they were past, only those people who had greenhouses
could expect more until the return of the corresponding season the following year," Georgia and Florida, "with their evergreen productiveness, have
been able to revolutionize the old conditions, by sending to the northern
cities, even when snow clad and ice bound, the fruits of balmy summer."
Winter vegetable production in Georgia and Florida, still "in its infancy,"
was "certain to develop to an immense degree, as no competition can come
from a more southern district. The profits of the Norfolk truckers were cut
by the Charleston and Savannah market gardeners, and they, in turn, by the
Florida cultivators, but the Gulf is south of Florida, so the competition
stops."[46]

Landreth was alive to the fact that within "fifty to sixty hours of market
by rail or boat, delicate fruits and comparatively perishable culinary vege-

tables may be moved successfully, but beyond that distance danger of decay increases.... A shipment, eighty hours on its travels, may occasionally reach its destination and pay largely, but the loss of other shipments which may arrive at destination heated and decayed will more than absorb previous profits." Even international competition in vegetables was a reality, brought on, for example, by a drought in 1881 that reduced yields by half: "Bringing potatoes to this country from abroad seems very much like carrying coals to Newcastle; nevertheless, it is a fact that more than half a million bushels of imported potatoes will have found a market in the United States before this years domestic crop is available."[47]

Not even southern boosters denied that local farmers could offer freshness that distant competitors could never match. One of the "drawbacks of truck-farming," as Oemler himself conceded, was that "as soon as the same vegetable matures at a point farther North, it comes into market in a condition fresher and more acceptable to the trade, and, therefore, excludes from profitable sale all shipments of the article from the more southern and distant points." In the New York City area, "gathering of perishable vegetables and picking of fruit may be pursued till sunset, and the next morning find them in market." And more specifically, whereas the earlier season at which southern crops were harvested enabled farmers to sell them in the North despite the greater expense of transportation, "no Southern grower of tomatoes, cucumbers, egg plant or other garden products would expect to find a market for his goods in Northern cities when those markets were in receipt of the same class of garden truck from territory adjacent, the products of which would be fresher and cheaper than those from distant points." By June, shipments of southern produce fell away "before the local competition" on the New York vegetable market. Even in Florida, shipments "cease when the warm season advances beyond the northern boundary of the State."[48]

In some cases, seasonality also meant two-way trade. Northern growers, for example, supplied southern consumers with cabbages during the summer, whereas the North procured its cabbages from the South after exhausting its winter supply. Moreover, the distance- and transportation-related competitive disadvantages applied only to crops that were both bulky and perishable such as cabbage, celery, and lettuce. Low value per unit cost of transport remained an overriding factor in regional competition.[49]

There may have been no summertime demand for southern cucumbers in New York, but the mere existence of extensive shipments from Charleston and Norfolk depressed New York farmers' profits. Thus southern production always imposed some constraints on Kings County farmers by creating a ceiling on the prices they could charge and certain consumer price expectations. Nevertheless, as Henderson observed, although "Southern competition . . . seriously interferes with the forcing of cucumbers, as it does with nearly everything else in early vegetables and fruits . . . the bloom and fine appearance, together with the more delicate flavor, of the forced Cucumber, finds customers in all large cities who are willing to pay for the finer quality." Thus Long Island farmers could still average profits of $125 to $150 per acre for pickling cucumbers.[50]

Fortunately for Kings County market gardeners, cabbage — the "universal consumption" of which meant that its markets in the 1890s had "never yet been glutted" — was their principal crop. For example, in 1865, when Kings County produced 61 percent of all the cabbage in New York State, the crop accounted for 34 percent of the farmers' total market-garden production. In addition, celery, as a winter vegetable crop, was "never shipped from South to North, as it can be grown much cheaper North," and lettuce, because it was consumed in great quantities, was "likely to be one of the most profitable vegetables to force [in hot houses], for the reason that from its soft and bulky character it cannot be shipped from the South as many other kinds of vegetables."[51]

Heated forcing houses or cultivation under glass was an important method of competition to which northern vegetable farmers turned in response to the impact of southern produce on their markets. As early as 1860 one Queens County farmer had enclosed three and one-half acres under glass "to compete with Norfolk and Charleston in the production of early cucumbers, radishes and salad." In the decade and a half following the Civil War, growers in the Boston area, the center of forcing winter vegetables such as lettuce, cucumbers, and tomatoes — the prices of which were about five times higher than those grown as field crops — began using hot water to heat greenhouses as substitutes for hotbeds. New York market gardeners also adopted these methods. The USDA estimated in the 1890s (though the data may have been from a decade earlier) that nationwide 1,000 commercial establishments employing 2,250 workers were engaged in these practices: "Within 15 miles of Boston there are probably not less than 40 acres of glass . . . devoted to vegetables. . . . Two-thirds of this is in houses, the rest being in hotbeds and frames. . . . [T]he amount devoted to vegetable growing about New York, Chicago, and other cities will bring the total up to 100 acres." Using capital equipment of $2,250,000, these operations produced an annual product with a retail value of $4,500,000.[52]

In the early 1890s, when some market gardens on Long Island maintained acres under glass in hothouses and cold frames, one farmer netted $5,000 from vegetables in a single winter. Hothouses enabled Long Island farmers to deliver some vegetables to the New York market by Christmas — several months before their first shipments from the South. They also offered large Long Island farmers one additional competitive advantage: by making it possible to employ laborers all year round, they enabled employers "to get and keep the best workmen." [53]

Although little is known about the extent of hothouses in Kings County, they were common. The fact that farmers selling their products at the Manhattan farmers' market in a December snowstorm resembling a "Siberian desert" feared losses resulting from freezing suggests that they must have been growing vegetables in hothouses. In 1880 in New Utrecht alone "there were more hotbeds than on the whole of Long Island outside of it. Some farmers have as many as 800 hotbeds for furnishing early lettuce and other things" to the New York market. From the inclusion of hotbed sashes and shutters among the farm stock items sold at auction when Kings County farmers died or abandoned farming, it is clear that out-of-season cultivation was common in the 1870s and 1880s. The auction in 1875 of the utensils of Henry T. Van Pelt, a recently deceased large and "first-class" market gardener in New Utrecht, included 300 hotbed sashes and frames, 275 shutters, and hotbed soil. Nor was hotbed cultivation confined to New Utrecht. Farmers in Flatlands made raising lettuce under glass a specialty, "netting handsome profit." [54]

The Census of Agriculture in 1900 recorded a huge increase in agricultural land under glass, with Cook County alone reporting 125 acres. Kings County was not a leader in this specialty, but its 948,000 square feet (or more than 21 acres) still placed it 19th nationally. [55]

The comparative locational data that Landreth gathered on what he called capital per acre (including fertilizers, seed, tools, and rental) revealed a predictable differential. The figure ranged, along the eastern seaboard, from $95 in Florida, to $75 to $125 at Norfolk, to $75 on eastern Long Island, and $150 on western Long Island. Higher land prices may have accounted for Kings County's position at the high end. He also noted that expenses could swell "to an astonishing degree": $700 or more was not uncommon on five- to ten-acre farms on the outskirts of Philadelphia and other large cities that employed several men to the acre, intensely manured, and used expensive forcing-house methods. Late-nineteenth-century urban vegetable production could absorb considerable amounts of capital: $3,000 with the labor of

3 men and 2 horses was required for 2 acres; $5,000, 6 men, and 3 horses for 10 acres; and as much as $20,000, 40 men, and 20 horses for 100 acres. Alternatively, the annual expenses for running farms of these three sizes were $2,500, $8,000, and $25,000.[56]

Synthesizing the foregoing considerations, Peter Henderson concluded in 1886 that "the business of gardening in such large cities as New York, Philadelphia, Boston or Chicago, is by no means so profitable as formerly, mainly owing to the vast competition from the Southern States, but that it is yet far more profitable than farm operations for the labor and capital employed . . . cannot be doubted." And in 1895, Charles Baltet's compendious international study of horticulture stated that far from having been ruined by southern competition, northern urban market gardeners continued to prosper. The absence of any freight costs made it possible for New York City vegetable farmers, despite "the extremely high price of labor, the high value of land, and the enormous capital invested," to achieve the highest profit per acre of any open-air (nongreenhouse) operations in the country. Little wonder that as late as 1901 the USDA reported that the "western end of Long Island is so thickly occupied by this industry that it virtually presents to the eye the appearance of one great truck farm; and the vast output from this section is almost entirely consumed by the millions of people located within a few short miles of the base of supply."[57]

By 1901, when the ranks of Kings County vegetable producers had been thinned to perilously low levels, the Massachusetts Horticultural Society heard a quarter-century retrospective of the pressures to which New York City farmers would have been exposed had they not sold already out: "California, the great West, and the sunny South, are now getting the cream of prices by their early, and with us, unseasonable, productions, now that transportation is so cheap . . . connecting distant sections of this great country, constantly supplying their best fruits and vegetables to our market. All this tends to discourage many, and only the courageous capitalist, who can afford to purchase modern appliances, is now making any profit."[58]

Despite the advances achieved by southern producers, the late-nineteenth-century agricultural censuses failed to register any significant breakthrough by southern counties into the ranks of the largest vegetable producers. "Yet," a USDA horticulturist observed in 1913, "many of our largest and most important truck farms are situated in the South Atlantic States. The reason for this is that the climatic and soil conditions of these regions, together with the labor supply which is available, render the industry profitable in two respects — cheapness in the cost of production, and the ability to produce crops in advance of the normal season farther north." By cheap southern labor, the official meant "negro laborers" whose "large numbers make possible . . . harvesting . . . at moderate cost, and this means . . . at a satisfactory profit to the planter."[59]

In spite of the growth of southern truck farm shipments, northern market gardeners were able to maintain many of their local markets. By the turn of the century, they were, to be sure, "driven out of the race in many lines by competition of specialists at distant points, where conditions of growth are so unusually favorable as to overcome the expense of transportation. But," the Census of Agriculture continued, "to offset this they have redoubled their efforts in the production of those crops in the cultivation of which the advantage remained with them." In particular, better equipment "enabled them to cheapen the product without decreasing their margin of profit." Five- to ten-acre farmers located on high-rent land around the large northern cities and "employing several men to the acre and sometimes a larger force" had "everything new in the way of labor-saving appliances." Indeed, practical horticulturists had been advising market gardeners at least since the 1860s that since "the high price of farm-labor" was the "only drawback to a relative profit," it was critical to use "the best labor-saving instruments."[60]

One of the most prized devices "superseding the old methods" was the seed drill. In onion cultivation, it enabled "a smart boy of sixteen [to] seed more ground in a day, and do it better, than twenty men could." Even more effective than the hand drill was the horse drill: by the 1890s, it could furrow, plant, and cover root crops such as beets, carrots, onions, and turnips in one-forty-eighth the time that pure hand labor had required in the 1850s to 1870s. Similarly, horse-drawn planters reduced by 90 percent the amount of time needed to furrow the ground, and drop and cover potato seeds; digging machines reduced the required time by two-thirds in the latter part of the nineteenth century.[61]

As late as 1884, the New York City-area horticulturist Henderson wrote that: "It is safe to say that the average profits to the market gardener in the vicinity of our large cities, where he pays sometimes as high as $100 per acre annually for rent, is at least $300 per acre. The usual amount of ground cultivated by market gardeners is ten acres, and they think it is a poor year when their profits from that amount of land do not average $3,000" even when they sell wholesale to middlemen. The annual net profit of 30 percent at wholesale prices, Henderson had little doubt, could be doubled if the farmer could sell directly to the consumer.[62]

On well-cultivated New York City-area farms other than his own, Henderson estimated that profits had been only $200 per acre during the ten years prior to 1886 — half of their level during the Civil War, whose farm prices he expected never to see again, and two-thirds of the $300 per acre average profits that he estimated for "all well cultivated market gardens" in the New York area during the 1850s. To be sure, the "vast competition" made the New York profit level in the 1880s "a low average for the majority of towns and cities" nationally. In reprinting Henderson's figures in 1880, the *Rural Gazette* assured its readers that "such a grand result" was attainable in an average season.[63]

Other practical horticulturalists reported similar cost and profit structures in the latter half of the nineteenth century. According to one account from about 1890, on an acre worth $200, it cost $163 to grow 8,000 head of cabbage, which could be sold for $280, leaving a profit of $117. Another report stated that 6,000 head of cabbage that cost $240 to produce (including $140 for manure, $6 for applying the manure, $2 for plowing, $2 for furrowing, $5 for transplanting, $30 for the plants, $25 for rent, and $25 for marketing) could be sold for $360, leaving a profit of $120 per acre. Twenty years earlier, a horticulturist reported a $250 per acre profit for 6,500 to 7,000 cabbage that cost $100 to produce. For onions, one account referred to $600 to $800 of proceeds from an acre from which $300 of costs had to be deducted, leaving $300 to $500 of profit.[64]

Despite the pressure of southern competition, surviving Kings County farmers were able to hold their own. William Bennett's Gravesend farm, for example, was quite profitable in each of the 16 years covered by his surviving account books: from 1883 right up to the time he sold the farmland, Bennett's profits totaled $41,419.06 on $93,214.51 in sales. Such consistent profitability was largely a function of the fact that the price of potatoes — his chief crop — held steady except during the depth of the depression in 1895–96. As late as 1903, a history of Long Island, invidiously comparing Suffolk county, noted that largely because "the proximity of a great market makes a vast difference in the value of vegetable productions, . . . many an acre in Kings county . . . furnishes support to a whole family."[65]

Kings County farms' profitability could not hide one major disadvantge that they faced. Any given land area, which could produce only a limited number of crops and was economically useless the rest of the time, was competing with uses in the South producing year-round rents. Assuming that all farms had the same basic costs for equipment, labor, and supplies, the ability to spread costs over more months and crops would have reduced unit costs. Even if there had been no national market for vegetables and Kings County farmers would not necessarily have been driven out of business in precisely the same way that a small local steel company would have been bankrupted by the emergence of much more productive capital-intensive national firms, less-profitable farms might nevertheless have been exposed to heightened pressures in the sense that financial rationality could have constrained them to invest their capital in operations promising a higher rate of return.

If Kings County farmers adjusted microeconomically to keep up with their competitors, their achievement is the more remarkable for their failure to benefit from the external economies of collective institutions in which farmers elsewhere participated. Such institutions encompassed the educational apparatus that evolved in the nineteenth century to inculcate in farmers scientific as well as commercially viable practices. The growth of science in agricultural practice was manifested in the spread of agricultural societies at the state and local levels; the steadily growing circulation of the agricultural press; private support for experimental, educational, and marketing initiatives; and finally federal and state government subsidies, beginning with departments of agriculture and extending also to the state colleges, their extension programs, and experiment stations.[66]

Notwithstanding the spread of knowledge and collective action among farmers in general, many of these rationalization efforts — particularly those requiring collective enterprise — came to nought among truck farmers in the New York region, particularly in Kings County. The principal function of local agricultural societies was to organize meetings with knowledgeable speakers and to run local or county fairs and exhibits where information about the latest techniques and products could be exchanged. The Kings County Society for Promoting Agriculture and Domestic Manufactures was established early enough (1819), but soon languished with only occasional revivals. The New York State Agricultural Society never published another report from the Kings County Agricultural Society after it inexplicably failed to submit its annual report in 1843.[67]

Complaining in 1873 that "almost every county in our State has a farm club," the *Rural Gazette*, in vain, urged "our farmers to consider this subject and by union of effort make their lands and property much more productive." Observing later that year that "[e]ven our sister county of Queens is annually in the habit of holding" a fair, the newspaper lamented that "we of Kings county are trudging on in an oldfashioned way, each for himself without regard to his neighbor, and none striving to excel in their calling

except it be to get the crop to market first and obtain the highest price."
Kings County farmers visited the Queens County Agricultural Society annual exhibition, but not as exhibitors. In 1884 the *Rural Gazette* still viewed
Kings County farmers' failure to hold a county fair a "mystery, unless a
leader is lacking," especially since it would offer them the opportunity to
learn about the best methods of producing the best crops.[68]

The failure of Kings County farmers to commit themselves collectively
to spreading scientific methods or to marketing their products persisted to
the end of the century. Whether this attitude reflected an immunity born of
local circumstances — the abundance of inherited land, the steady supply
of manure, and the ready market demand that outstripped the local supply
of fresh produce — or resistance stemming from inbred habits is unclear.
But as late as 1912, the keynote speaker at the second annual meeting of the
New York State Vegetable Growers Association described his reluctant con-
stituency as isolated from the general large body of farmers and maintaining their individualistic and competitive method of work.[69]

4. LABOR SUPPLY: AGRICULTURAL WORKERS AND LABOR RELATIONS

Our laborers in the market gardens are generally an ignorant class with
very little ambition, and not one in a hundred of them is fit to manage.
— Peter Henderson, *Gardening for Profit*, 1890

The transition to intensive agriculture in Kings County would have been
impossible without the requisite labor force. The proximity of New York
City, instead of luring away farmworkers and driving up their wages, attracted a large supply of experienced immigrant agricultural laborers. Vegetable farms may not have been a major destination of the world-historical
waves of European emigration, which the advance of industrial capitalism
and the commercialization of agriculture triggered in the nineteenth century when they drove Irish and German peasants and farm laborers across
the Atlantic. Nevertheless, old-line Dutch market gardeners, as well as German and Irish farm owners and tenants, who employed laborers in Kings
County, benefited from the transformations wrought by the world economy
and, especially and ironically, by the successful penetration by U.S. grain of
European markets. As a result, the viability of urban vegetable farming was
never threatened by the lack of a labor force willing to work at the wage rates
that farmers could afford.[1]

Before turning to the nineteenth-century European immigrant labor
force, it is necessary to examine the much neglected role of slaves and former slaves in Kings County agriculture. The presence of this traditional labor force on the Dutch farms facilitated the transition to intensive cultivation at midcentury; indeed, premodern slave society in Kings County was
closely linked to the forces shaping modern Brooklyn. This startling juxta-

position is best illustrated by John A. Lott, one of New York State's highest judicial officers and the county's largest landowner. His extensive inherited wealth was in part created by agricultural slave labor, but he played a major role as a suburbanizer of Flatbush and Kings County in the 1860s and 1870s. Lott was born on a farm in Flatlands in 1806, the same year his father Abraham certified the birth of a child to one of his slaves. Lott grew up on the farm with enslaved persons, his father reporting the ownership of three slaves at the census of 1810 and seven at the census of 1820. That the memory of slavery, even in the immediate aftermath of the Civil War, was apparently not an embarrassment, is suggested by the fact that the *Brooklyn Daily Eagle* published excerpts from the late-eighteenth-century wills of the heads of such Dutch farm families as Lott and Lefferts in which the bequeathing of slaves was common.[2]

FARM SLAVES: THE FIRST SOURCE

"Well, I swear! Here is William Kouwenhoven, with his runaway slave Frank. This is the third time the negro has run away."
— Willis Boughton, "Old Flatbush," quoting unpublished diary of John Baxter, entry for May 25, 1790 [3]

Studying the role of Kings County's almost entirely forgotten large black slave agricultural labor force, who "did the most of the farm labor," is crucial not only with regard to the prehistory of market gardening, but also for understanding the presence of black farm laborers throughout the nineteenth century and the paternalistic matrix that continued to leave its imprint on farm labor relations.[4] The economic and legal bases of slavery were intimately interlinked. By upholding private enslavement of workers well into the nineteenth century, the New York State legislature empowered Dutch farmers to extend their exploitation of their labor force. When the legislature finally enacted "An Act for the gradual abolition of Slavery" in March 1799, it meant the modifier literally:

> That any child born of a slave within this state after the fourth day of July next shall be deemed and adjudged to be born free: *Provided nevertheless*, That such child shall be the servant of the legal proprietor of his or her mother until such servant, if a male, shall arrive at the age of twenty-eight years, and if a female, at the age of twenty-five years.[5]

In reenacting this provision in 1801, the legislature eliminated any doubts as to the status of existing slaves by condemning them to continued slavery unless their owners chose to manumit them.[6]

This scheme, common to the northern states, has been called "philanthropy at bargain prices" because it shifted to the slaves themselves almost the entire "direct financial cost of their freedom." Not until 1817 did New York decide to free the slaves, even then postponing emancipation another decade until July 4, 1827. Slaveowners could also shift the cost of manumission to taxpayers in general by taking advantage of the statutory provision permitting them to abandon their right to service within one year of the child's birth by notifying the town clerk; such children were then considered paupers and were bound out by the overseers of the poor. Adrian Martense, for example, availed himself of this opportunity on October 8, 1802, certifying that: "I abandon my right of Servitude of a Black male Child Named Frank Born the Eighth Day of July, which said Child you have got on record and I have now in my possession." Since the statute expressly characterized the service to which the slaveowner was entitled for 25 or 28 years as "in the same manner as if the child had been bound out to service by the overseers of the poor," it is unclear how this type of manumission differed from slavery — except that service ended at age 18 and 21 for females and males, respectively, at which time the master was obligated to give the servant a new bible.[7]

Other slaves continued to be traded. In 1802, Robert Benson, whose family's farmland eventually became the Bensonhurst section of New Utrecht, paid Martin Boerum of Kings County $75 for Jack, a slave, for the unexpired part of a five-year term lasting three years and fifty-seven days.[8]

Until the first decades of the nineteenth century, Dutch farmers in Kings County were so heavily reliant on black slave labor that the county exhibited the highest proportion of slaveholders and slaves in the North: "Nowhere was the commitment to slavery more apparent than in Kings County," where 59 percent of white households at the first national census in 1790 owned slaves; in the villages of Flatbush and New Utrecht the proportions rose to two-thirds and three-fourths. These extraordinary shares, which exceeded those of major slaveholding states such as South Carolina, were correlated with the predominance of the Dutch, who "wanted slaves not as servants but as agricultural laborers as they sought to profit from feeding the metropolis." As late as 1810, nine-tenths of households in rural Kings County using black labor still owned slaves compared to only one-half in

Queens County, where relatively few descendants of the Dutch lived. Kings County immigration patterns until the early nineteenth century resembled those in the South in the sense that slave labor made free wage labor so un-competitive that "immigrants avoided the county" and the population re-mained sparse.[9]

Because "Dutch boers . . . had been since colonial times by far the largest users of slave labor in New York," by 1790, 30 percent of all Dutch families in the state were slaveholding compared to 11 percent of English and Welsh families and 14 percent of all white families. Overall, there were 98 slaves per 100 Dutch families compared to only 39 for all white families in New York State. No wonder that in the New York State Assembly in the 1780s, repre-sentatives of Kings County, "where Dutch slaveowners were zealous of their property rights," were among the leading opponents of emancipation. Con-sequently, whereas slaveowners in New York City, realizing that slavery could not maintain itself, negotiated self-purchase agreements or freed their slaves, slaveowners "in the surrounding countryside . . . and particu-larly farmers of Dutch origin, maintained the institution of slavery to the bitter end." The Dutch farmers' mentality was well represented by Judge Nicholas Cowenhoven of New Utrecht, who owned 10 slaves in 1790 and used chains in the cellar of his house "for punishing refractory slaves."[10]

At the first U.S. census in 1790, slaves accounted for one-third of the to-tal population of Kings County and two-fifths in Flatbush. In the even more rural and remote counties of Richmond, Queens, and Suffolk, the propor-tions were only 20, 14, and 7 percent, respectively. In Kings County, 61 per-cent of all white families owned slaves, rising to 74 and 75 percent in Flatbush and New Utrecht, respectively. The agricultural orientation of slaveholding in Kings County emerges from its size distribution. In 1790, 34 percent of slaveholders owned 5 to 9 slaves, while 7.5 percent owned 10 to 19; in purely agricultural Flatbush, the shares were even higher — 41 percent and 12 per-cent, respectively. Overall, the average slaveowning family in Kings County owned 4.5 slaves, reaching its peak in Flatbush at 5.2.[11]

The largest slaveholding families in Flatbush in 1790, that of Laurence Voorhis and Johannes Lott, which owned 16 slaves each, were also the larg-est in Kings County. All families in the county with 10 or more slaves were, with one possible exception, Dutch. Among the Dutch farming dynasties owning slaves in 1755 that would still be prominent at the end of the nine-teenth century were Lefferts, Lott, Van Sicklen, Vanderveer, Voorhees, Dit-mars, Kouwenhoven, Wykof, Cortelyou, Van Brunt, Suydam, and Denyce.[12]

That emancipation did not effectively take place in Kings County until its statutorily prescribed date of 1827 can be seen in the population figures from the last census before that year. In 1820, the 689 slaves in the towns of Kings County other than Brooklyn accounted for 17 percent of the total population: at this late date, fully one-fifth of the entire population of Flatbush and Flatlands was still enslaved. Flatbush alone, with 9 percent of the county's population, accounted for 24 percent of all its slaves.[13]

The trends in the slave and/or black populations in the county as a whole and in Flatbush from the early colonial period through the end of the nineteenth century are shown in table 9. From 1738 to 1790, the slave population almost tripled in Kings County. Even after 1790, the number of slaves continued to expand in parts of the county, although some Dutch farmers also sold off their slaves. Johannes Lott, a Flatlands farmer who owned three slaves at the time of the 1790 census, "sold all his negroes" on August 12, 1791. The slave population stabilized in the county as a whole and declined somewhat in Flatbush, but in New Utrecht, Bushwick, and Gravesend the number of slaves actually rose by 4 percent, 10 percent, and 20 percent, respectively, between 1790 and 1800. Only thereafter did their numbers begin to fall significantly in all county towns. In Flatbush, between 1800 and 1810, the decline in the number of slaves and the increase in the number of free blacks were almost identical: 125 and 131, respectively. Between 1810 and 1820, however, the number of slaves rose slightly whereas the number of free blacks fell by 87. These relations suggest both that a core of slaveholders kept slaves to the end and that many former slaves left Flatbush or died. The proportion of families owning slaves declined only slightly between 1790 and 1800 — from 74 percent to 69 percent; at the next two censuses, 1810 and 1820, the proportions were still high — 61 percent and 50 percent, respectively. Voorhis's and Lott's slaveholdings fell only slightly between 1790 and 1800 — from 16 to 13 and 16 to 12, respectively. But Cornelius Vanderveer still reported 10 slaves, while new large slaveowners appeared in 1800 who had been absent from the list of family heads in 1790: Johannes J. Lott with 16 slaves and Garrett Martense with 10. Some slaveowners actually increased their human holdings during the last full decade of legal slavery as prices for slaves "plummeted" in the wake of the emancipation statute. John Lefferts, for example, owned 5 slaves in 1810 and 8 in 1820, while Teunis Schenck increased his ownership from 8 to 12, making him the largest slaveowner in Flatbush.[14]

The tenacity with which many slaveowners held on to their human property during the final decades can be gauged by their compliance with the formal requirements of the gradual abolition act of 1799. In order to be entitled to the compulsory 28-year service of their slaves' children born after July 4, 1799, slaveowners were required to submit to the town clerk such children's birth certificates so that the clerk could record their ages. The files of the town of Flatbush were replete with such certificates submitted by large Dutch farmers, including Johannes Lott, Jeremiah Lott, John Lott, John Lefferts, and John Vanderveer. They certified that the mother was "a Slave and my Property," or "belonging to me," or "belonging to the estate" of the self-characterized "Yeoman" who had in the meantime died. The records contain a certificate for a slave child born as late as February 13, 1826. John Lefferts and John Vanderbilt manumitted slaves in 1822, George and Adrian Martense in 1824, while farmer John Hegeman waited until March 4, 1825, to manumit "a certain Female Slave named Bet and her Son Sam, now or late the property of me." Similar patterns of the maintenance of slavery prevailed in the other Kings County towns. In Flatlands, for example, John Ditmars certified the birth of ten children to his slaves beginning in 1814 and ending in 1826.[15]

Slavery became unlawful and disappeared by 1830, but its demise did not proceed uniformly throughout the county. Between 1800 and 1820, the number of slaves fell by 57 percent in industrializing Brooklyn, but only by 19 percent in the most outlying and agricultural area, Flatlands. Contrary to the trend in New York State as a whole, where slaves as a share of the total population declined during the latter part of the eighteenth century, they stood at historic high points in Kings County and Flatbush in 1790. If it is true, therefore, that statutory emancipation in New York State merely codified the economic system's abandonment of slave labor as "uneconomic" as the increased availability of white workers lowered their wages sufficiently to make slavery obsolete, this generalization overlooks the fact that forced labor remained the norm on Kings County farms into the first decades of the nineteenth century.[16]

Evidence suggests that ex-slaves may have continued to work on the farms of their ex-masters for some years. The strongest piece of quantitative evidence stems from the 1830 census, the first conducted after the termination of slavery. In that year, 175, or 68 percent, of 258 "free colored persons" in Flatbush were returned as living in a family headed by a white person. Six or more "free colored persons" were returned as living with each of five white families — four of them leading Dutch farm families: Jeremiah Lott, John Bergen, Adrian Martense, and G. Martense. Twenty-five of the 35 "free colored persons" living in these five households were between the ages of 10 and 55 and thus probably at work. By 1840, relatively fewer blacks lived with

FIGURE 7. *Vanderveer farm, Flatbush, 1890. From Edmund Fisher,* Flatbush Past and Present *26.*

white families and those who did were more dispersed. Of 288 "free colored persons" living in Flatbush, only 53 percent were still living with whites. The farmers with the largest contingents of blacks returned as living in their families were John Antonides (4), Samuel G. Lott (4), John Ditmas (4), Jacob Snedecor (4), Garret L. Martense (4), John C. Vanderveer (5), Jeremiah Lott (9), and Abraham Lott (9). Of the 43 blacks in these eight families, 31 were between 10 and 55 years old. Although 35 members of these "mixed" white and black families were returned as employed in agriculture, not all prime-age blacks were employed in agriculture. Only three members of Jeremiah Lott's family, for example, were employed in agriculture, yet five prime-age blacks lived in his family. Presumably, then, Lott and other Dutch farm families were wealthy enough to retain servants who performed non-farm labor.[17]

By 1850, the dispersion of blacks in Flatbush had progressed to the point at which only 15 percent of the entire population of 257 lived in white households. Even within this small group, only 10 were returned by the census as laborers living in a farmer's household and thus presumptive farm laborers. Jeremiah Lott was still among this group of farmers, but only one black laborer lived with him, and only one farmer (William Stoothoff) was returned as employing two black laborers living in his family. Presumably many of the working-age blacks living with farmers' or nonfarmers' families who were listed as without occupation were servants, an occupational designation that the enumerator did not use in Flatbush. Indeed, the enumerator knew virtually no occupation for blacks other than "laborer," which covered every black Flatbush resident in 1850 with an occupation except for one lone peddler. By 1860, only 11 of 34 black farm laborers in Flatbush lived in their employer's household. In addition to such old-line Dutch farm families as Ditmas, Lott, Schenck, Suydam, and Vanderbilt in each of whose households one black farm laborer lived, William Story's household included four who were employed on his 55-acre farm.[18]

Perhaps the most useful extant contemporary evidence on the aftermath of slavery comes from Gertrude Lefferts Vanderbilt, who self-consciously wrote her memoir of Flatbush from "a different standpoint. As a woman, I have inclined to the social side of life, and have endeavored to record the changes which time has made among the people in their homes and at the fireside." Lefferts Vanderbilt, whose wealth and position derived from two influential Kings County Dutch families, "was a friend of the negroes, organizing a society for ameliorating the condition of the poor of that race in Brooklyn."[19] Looking back in 1880, she wove a few tantalizing facts into her nostalgic paternalism:

> It is probable that there were few, if any, foreigners employed as domestics in the family or as laborers on the farms in Flatbush previous to 1822, the year in which all traces of slavery ceased to exist.
>
> At that time those who were formerly slaves, and their descendants, still found employment in the families of which they had once formed a part. They felt a certain claim upon the master and mistress under whose roof they were born; this claim, if not legally recognized after this period, was at least so far acknowledged in the higher realm of duty that a kindly oversight was extended to the families of their former slaves, and they were provided for in cases of sickness and destitution. . . .
>
> In some instances colored families continued after their manumission in the employ of those to whom they had once belonged, and always found employment when well and assistance when sick from their old master and mistress.
>
> Scarcely twenty-five years ago [ca. 1855] traces of this, the only pleasant phase of that institution, still existed in Flatbush. . . .
>
> . . . The foreign element in our population which now preys so largely upon our pity and our purse had not then come to our gates. . . .

FIGURE 8. *Loading hay, Jacob Rapelje farm, New Lots, c. 1890.*
Courtesy of Peter Rapelje.

It was considered in times gone by rather a sign of a well-to-do farmer
to have a large family of colored people in his kitchen. . . .

This race for more than a century and a half formed part of the family of every Dutch inhabitant of Kings County. Speaking the same language, brought up to the same habits and customs, with many cares and
interests in common, there existed a sympathy with and an affection between them and the white members of the household such as could
scarcely be felt toward the strangers who now perform the same labor
under such different circumstances.[20]

Lefferts Vanderbilt's idealized reminiscences are difficult to reconcile
with other accounts that portray the postslave era in a much harsher light.
For decades, Dutch farmers continued to rehearse denigrating tales about
their families' slaves. Even the worldly Teunis Garrett Bergen, old-line
Dutch farmer in New Utrecht, surveyor, and member of the 39th Congress
(which was so instrumental in supporting emancipated slaves' civil rights),
reveled in stories about his ancestors' slaves in his family genealogy. A year
after the Civil War ended, he regaled readers with an account of Negroes'

proverbial fondness for pilfering neighbors' poultry, which often led to their arrest and sentencing to the whipping post, prompting their owner to "shed tears to serve them." [21]

The racial discrimination to which "The Last Flatbush Slave" was exposed decades after his enslavement had ended suggests what agricultural employment relations may have been like. "Uncle Sammy" Anderson, born a slave on Jeremiah Lott's farm in 1810, died in 1902. Appearing as the head of his own household at the 1840 census, he was returned a farm laborer at the 1870 census, and a laborer in 1880. After conversion to Christianity at the age of 19, Anderson attended the Flatbush Reformed Dutch Church, but was confined to the gallery, which was "reserved for colored people." He rarely had enough money to ride the stagecoach from Flatbush to Fulton Ferry, but "when so fortunate, he was required to ride on the top of the stage, as the inside seats were reserved for 'white folks.'" [22]

THE VEGETABLE PROLETARIAT: THE SIZE AND ETHNIC COMPOSITION OF THE LABOR FORCE

They composed a Dutch aristocracy as well as boers, their farm labor was performed by themselves, their sons and their negroes, under which they were rapidly attaining to wealth. New York, the greatest of American markets for their farm products, was at their doors, and the demand was limitless.
— Daniel Tredwell, "Kings County in Fact, Legend and Tradition," 1917

Because neither the contemporary press nor later scholars discussed the nature and source of labor on Kings County farms in the aftermath of slavery, information must be teased from sporadic and fragmentary evidence. From a rare surviving diary, for example, it is known that Adriance Van Brunt employed on his typical Dutch American farm in Yellow Hook in June 1828 two year-round hired men, three indentured servants, two hired women, four white men from New Jersey (including three hired by the month), two blacks hired by the month, one Virginian hired by the month, and five girls from New Jersey picking peas on a piece rate. [23]

Unlike the situation in the postbellum South, where the ex-slaveholder Oemler boasted that emancipation had made extensive truck farming possible, in Kings County the Dutch farmer could no longer look exclusively to "the same God-given instrument, the negro . . . for his labor." That slavery had come to an end decades before the Civil War and before Kings County farmers made the transition from extensive to intensive cultivation meant that the generation of ex-slaves that had continued to work on the farms had already died and some of their children had moved on (to the city of Brooklyn and elsewhere) before market gardening became the dominant form of agriculture.[24]

The transition to more intensive and seasonal market gardening may have necessitated the recruitment and employment of a transient work force: "The labor per acre that is required on a highly cultivated vegetable patch greatly exceeds that for a wheat or corn field, hence the size of the plot of ground in vegetables which one man can cultivate by himself, is correspondingly limited." Whether late-nineteenth-century Kings County vegetable farmers, like their counterparts elsewhere, employed transient harvesters is unclear. Whether the unemployed, and "especially" women and children, who had "an advantage over men" in harvest piecework, in the New York area "eagerly" sought out such "opportunities" as they had elsewhere is unknown.[25]

Local children did form a part of the agricultural labor force. For example, when potato bugs infested the plants in Flatlands in 1876, "boys were in quite a demand in town to help get rid of these pests, and find themselves with plenty of business." And a report in the late 1880s noted that in the late summer and autumn many a "thrifty modern husbandman" living in "quaint old Dutch mansion[s]" between Brooklyn and Jamaica Bay employed "scores of the poorer men, women and children of the neighborhood to dig his potatoes . . . and take care of his crops generally."[26]

Historical researchers have long complained of a paucity of precise census data on agricultural labor in the United States. However, the manuscript schedules of the federal population censuses for rural Kings County in 1860, 1870, and 1880, unlike those for 1850, which used only the category "laborer," do include returns for "farm laborer," which make it possible to gauge the size and ethnic background of the self-reported agricultural labor force in those three census years.[27]

To be sure, methodological inconsistencies and flaws in the census detract to some degree from the accuracy of the count of farm laborers. One major source of undercounting was the practice of labeling as "servant" all female employees living in farm households: even if engaged part-time in fieldwork, they were not included in the farm labor force. Since female servants lived in a very large number of Kings County farm households, the undercount is potentially large. In 1860, two-thirds of Flatbush farm households included at least one servant as did a majority in Gravesend and New Utrecht; in Flatlands and New Lots servants were returned as living in one-third of farm families. Since enumerators listed literally only a handful of women as working on farms, the census doubtless underestimated the contributions of wives and daughters.[28]

Another source of undercounting was omission of the occupation on the manuscript schedules. For example, Cato Oliver, a black man, was returned as a farm laborer in Flatbush in 1860, but his occupation was omitted in 1870. Yet his obituary in the *Rural Gazette*— extraordinary for a black person — in 1879 focused on his devoted work for 48 years on the John Vanderveer farm, which he performed virtually until the day he died. This obituarial vignette may well have been representative of master-servant relations between Dutch farmers and their black farm laborers: "No matter how tired he might be in the evening, if any of the family expressed a wish to have anything done, Cato would cheerfully exclaim 'All right, I'm here.'" Serendipitous discovery of this omitted occupation suggests that census omissions of farm laborers' occupation may have been common — especially among children who worked as farm laborers.[29]

The data on farm laborers may be misleading insofar as they include sons and other relatives of farmers. (This issue did not arise in 1860, when the enumerator returned no sons of farmers living in the household as farm laborers.) To be sure, the sons did not bulk nearly so large as in one midwestern study, which found well over half the farm laborers to be sons of operators in 1880, but they were significant enough to merit comment. Enumerators did not list all sons as "farm laborer," "working on farm," "works on farm," or "farm hand"; some were returned as "farmer." In Kings County, 87, or about one-seventh of all, farm laborers in 1880 were closely related to the farm operator; of this number, 76 were sons.[30]

Kings County was just one in the New York City environs in which "an untold number of immigrants swelled the shifting population of farm laborers ... on the prosperous market gardens." Given, for example, Irish immigrants' largely agrarian backgrounds, it is plausible that the two to five thousand Irish-born counted among the rural Kings County population by the census between 1855 and 1890 formed a source of late-nineteenth-century farm laborers. And indeed, the manuscript schedules reveal that although the Irish lost their status as the chief source of the farm labor force after the Civil War, they still constituted the largest group of farm laborers in 1870 and the second largest in 1880. That so many Irishmen became farm laborers must have reflected a lack of other employment opportunities; for their association of farming with "impoverished potato patches" and oppression in Ireland prompted few to seek such work in the United States.[31]

Table 10 records the ethnic breakdowns for farm laborers. In 1860, 63 percent of rural Kings County residents self-identifying as farm laborers had been born in Ireland, 11 percent in Germany, while another 12 percent were U.S. blacks. These three groups accounted for 85 percent of the work force. In 1870, the Irish share had fallen to 38 percent, while that of Germans and blacks had risen to 22 and 14 percent. Thus almost three-fourths of farm laborers still came from these three groups. The share of U.S.-born whites increased from 10 to 22 percent of those returned as farm laborers. Ten years later, a small shift had taken place toward U.S.-born whites (excluding second-generation Irish), who now accounted for 35 percent of farm laborers. Native Irish in 1880 constituted 27 percent of the labor force, rising to 32 percent with the inclusion of second-generation Irish. That year one-sixth of farm laborers were native-born Germans, while blacks formed another 12 percent.[32]

These relative shifts in the composition of the farm labor force between 1860 and 1880 are shown in table 11, which gives the absolute and percentage changes in the four major groups — Irish, Germans, and U.S. whites and blacks. Over the 20-year period, the decline in the overall size of the labor force in rural Kings County farming was controlled by opposite changes in two subgroups: whereas the number of Irish laborers fell by a total of 328, or 67 percent, the number of U.S.-born white workers rose by 134, or 170 percent. In contrast, Germans and U.S. blacks moved in and out of the farm labor force in much smaller numbers.

Irish, Germans, and blacks were significantly overrepresented in the farm labor force in relation to their numbers in the overall rural Kings County population. In 1870, the native-born Irish and Germans accounted for 18 percent and 14 percent, respectively, of the whole rural Kings County population, while blacks formed an additional 3 percent, for a total of 35 percent compared with 74 percent of farm laborers. In 1880, native-born Irish were 14 percent and native-born Germans 12 percent of the rural population, while blacks remained 3 percent for a total of 29 percent compared to a total of 55 percent of farm laborers.[33]

The aggregate data for Kings County obscure large differences in the size and ethnic makeup of the farm labor force in the five towns. Table 12 compares the towns for 1860, 1870, and 1880. Whereas Flatbush and New Utrecht experienced sharp decreases in the number of farm laborers from 1860 to 1880, the other towns saw increases. The 258 laborers in Flatlands in 1880 were the highest figure in any town for any of these census years. In rank order, the most concentrated farm labor populations resided in New Utrecht,

Flatlands, Flatbush, Gravesend, and New Lots in 1860, Flatlands, New Utrecht, Gravesend, New Lots, and Flatbush in 1870, and Flatlands, New Lots, Gravesend, New Utrecht, and Flatbush in 1880. Whereas Flatlands was the largest and Flatbush the smallest residential base in 1870 and 1880, New Utrecht was the largest and Gravesend and New Lots the smallest in 1860.[34]

In 1860 and 1870 the Irish were the largest ethnic contingent in all towns except New Lots, where Germans predominated; in 1880, non-Irish U.S. whites became the leading group in New Utrecht and New Lots. Black farm laborers formed an appreciable proportion of the work force in all towns (exceeding one-fifth in Gravesend in 1870) except New Utrecht, from which they were totally absent in 1880 — and where U.S. whites were much more heavily represented than anywhere else — and in New Lots in 1860 and 1870. The predominance of the Irish among farm laborers was paired with this occupation's predominance among the Irish. In Flatbush, for example, the category of laborer closely followed by that of farm laborer accounted for more than half of all employed Irish males in 1870. That predominance was of some vintage in Flatbush: as early as 1850, when the census did not use the term "farm laborer," 62 percent of the 89 laborers returned as living in farmers' households were Irish. In 1860, when the Irish made up 17 percent of the population of rural Kings County (excluding the institutionalized in Flatbush), ranging from 8 percent in New Lots to 25 percent in New Utrecht, Irish farm laborers accounted for 26 percent of the entire Irish population, ranging from 6 percent in New Lots to 56 percent in Flatlands.[35]

The decline in the total farm labor force by 17 percent during the 1860s and a further 6 percent during the 1870s, which coincided with the shift from extensive to intensive agriculture, is counterintuitive. One plausible explanation is that as farming became more seasonal, many who harvested vegetables did not work all year in agriculture and therefore did not report themselves to the census enumerator as farm laborers. Migratory farm laborers who were not residing in Kings County at the time of the enumeration in June or July would also have been excluded. How large this seasonal harvest force was is unknown. Because the principal crops, cabbage and potatoes — early potatoes can be dug as soon as they are large enough to eat, whereas late potatoes should remain in the ground as long as possible without freezing — unlike strawberries and other fruits, did not need to be urgently harvested within a very compressed time period, it is possible that the seasonal peak demand for harvesters in Kings County was much lower than in New Jersey, where many migrant workers picked fruits and vegetables in the late nineteenth century. The labor exchange established in 1850 at Castle Garden, the main entry point for immigrants, which undertook to supply agricultural laborers to employers anywhere in the United States, may have been a source of recruitment, but of "the immigrant farm-laborers, only a small number remained in New York." In addition to private employment bureaus in Brooklyn, the Free Employment Bureau in Manhattan, under the auspices of the Young Men's Christian Association, could supply farmers and other employers large numbers of men on one day's notice, requiring them to pay only the transportation cost to the workplace.[36]

Significantly, not a single Italian-born farm laborer was recorded at the 1860, 1870, or 1880 census. Large-scale immigration to the United States from Italy, where an agricultural crisis had erupted in the 1870s, did not begin, coincidentally, until 1880; at the time of enumeration in June of that year, only 25 Italian-born residents were returned for all of rural Kings County. The *Rural Gazette* was apparently describing an uncommon sight when it reported in 1873 that: "Large crowds of Italian laborers were seen on Wednesday morning last, on their way through Clarkson street en route for the Kings county sewer. They seemed to be all hearty fellows . . . though they are short in stature." Nevertheless, the next year many Italians were praised for doing good heavy landscaping and paving work at Washington Cemetery in Gravesend and New Utrecht. The extensive employment of Italians (who lived in Manhattan) by the mid-1870s to lay track for the steam railroads to Coney Island suggests that they were a potential source of seasonal harvest labor if Kings County had faced shortages.[37]

A large majority of pre-World War I Italian immigrants had been employed in agriculture in Italy, but only a very small proportion of them engaged in farmwork in the United States. Yet by the early 1890s, the USDA singled out Italian immigrants among the foreigners lacking "adaptation or intelligence" on whom — in addition to "incompetent" workers of native origins discharged by manufacturing enterprises — New Jersey farmers had to rely. Nevertheless, by the turn of the century, the Department called Italian immigrants at work on farms on Long Island and in New Jersey "good help." Beginning in the first decade of the twentieth century, many farms "abandoned by the Yankees who go west or enter business in the city" were taken over by Italians, who specialized in vegetable truck farms in southern New Jersey, the vicinity of Philadelphia, Pittsburgh, Cleveland, Cincinnati, and Chicago, and, later, on Long Island. At the turn of the century, too, entire families of Italians and Poles dominated market gardening on rented microplots within New York City. By World War I, Italians (together with Poles and Germans) formed the great proportion of market gardeners on the western end of Long Island. At this time an urban market gardening enthusiast recommended that for large weeding jobs, "you can hire Italians or Germans to do it better and cheaper than you can do it yourself." And the *Eagle* was touting "350,000 acres of fertile soil" on Long Island that were "standing idle, awaiting willing hands."[38]

As vegetable farming became more labor intensive, requiring more regular picking and pruning in season, and as Irish and German immigrants found employment more readily in industry, it is possible that farmers who wished to expand their operations might have experienced difficulty in recruiting a long-term workforce. In 1892, when Kings County agriculture was already beyond its peak, the Department of Agriculture reported a labor "scarcity, caused by abundance of work on public improvements. It is more difficult each year to get men to work. Large contracts are given out yearly, and men are in constant demand." Nevertheless, during the first decade of the twentieth century, day laborers were still "extensively employed" on market garden farms in Kings and Queens counties. Ironically, if vegetable farming had been able to resist suburbanization for another decade or two, sufficient Italian immigrants might have been available to work in the market gardens — if not as laborers, then as tenants or owners.[39]

Ethnic and racial historiographies have neglected the late-nineteenth-century agricultural employment of these groups in Kings County. Consequently, nothing is known of the working or living conditions of farm laborers such as Henry and Joshua Jackson, 62- and 22-year-old black father and son in Flatbush in 1880, or 27-year-old Irish-born John McGuire, living and working on William Kouwenhoven's Flatlands farm in 1870, or 48-year-old German-born Jacob Hammerschlag, living and working on Abraham Van Siclen's farm in New Lots in 1880, or U.S.-born Abraham Applegate, still a farm worker at 60 years of age, who felt obliged to report to the census enumerator in 1870 that he owned $200 worth of personal property. There is no evidence that black workers remained on or migrated to Kings County farms out of a conviction that "economic improvement could best be achieved by abandoning the cities for the simple and virtuous attractions of agrarian life," but it is plausible that the at times virulent and antagonistic competition between them and Irish immigrants for low-wage jobs spilled over into agricultural employment.[40]

This extraordinary reliance on immigrant workers becomes ambiguous when contrasted with the derisive remarks by Peter Henderson, a large vegetable farmer across the Hudson River in Hudson County:

> To such as require large numbers of hands, and look to such ports as New York for emigrants, let me caution my friends from the rural districts not to believe too implicitly in the promises of these prospective American citizens. Much vexatious experience has taught me that one out of every three men is either worthless, or will run away, so that for many years back, if I wanted four hands, I made one job of it and hired six, well knowing that before a week had passed, my force would be reduced to the required number.[41]

The virtually total silence with which the *Kings County Rural Gazette*, which was published from 1872 to 1885, enveloped the issue of the farm labor supply suggests that scarcity was not a general problem. Indeed, at times the newspaper reported that harvesters were plentiful — for example, to harvest the likewise plentiful strawberries in Flatlands in 1876.[42] The only direct light that the newspaper shed on the subject involved William Bennett, a large farmer in Gravesend, one-fourth of whose 100 acres were planted to potatoes. In the summer of 1872 it reported that:

> To manage these twenty-five acres, Mr. B. employs nine horses and six men, who work early and late. Much trouble is experienced in keeping hired help in digging season, as the usual monthly rate of $20 is small compared with 8 cents a bushel paid for digging by the job. Men who work by the month will dig 30 and 40 bushels a day, but when working by the job, the same men will often dig 100 bushels a day.[43]

Although the gist of Bennett's predicament — namely, how to retain year-round employees when they could earn as much in two and a half days on a piece rate as he paid them for an entire month — is clear enough, the consequences are not. Were those working by the job seasonal workers who migrated from elsewhere? Or were they other Kings County farmers' year-round laborers who abandoned those farmers to secure this sinecure? And, finally, if farmers could afford to pay harvesters the higher piece rate, why could they not offer the same wage to their year-round workers during the harvest season? The work itself could be brutal at the height of the summer, when workers were overcome by heat, narowly escaping death by sunstroke. Whatever potato farmers' predicament with their human employees in 1872, it soon paled beside that of their horses — which had to be used in

FIGURE 9. *Workers harvesting potatoes, Jacob Rapelje farm, New Lots, c. 1890. The smokestacks in the background reveal the advance of urbanization. Courtesy of Peter Rapelje.*

relays of teams for field and market work especially on days when several wagon loads were marketed — many of which died in an almost nation-wide epidemic.[44]

Bennett's productivity data also make it possible to estimate upper and lower limits of the harvest workforce. The total number of potato harvest-ers was a function of the length of the harvest. If the harvest lasted 30 days, the maximum would have been 858 workers (1879) and the minimum 140 (1874). Where the harvest lasted two months or longer, the required number of potato harvesters could have been fewer than half as many as this maximum and minimum. Despite concurrent and overlapping cabbage and other harvests, these numbers suggest that the rural Kings County population would not, under any plausible scenario, have been overwhelmed by a burgeoning migrant labor or dependent farm labor population if farmers had sought to continue their operations later in the century. These labor requirements must also be adjusted downward to take into account the considerable number of wives, children, relatives, and neighboring children who harvested crops without having been returned by the census as having any occupation.[45]

Despite their proximity to the third largest city in the United States, Kings County farms in the latter part of the nineteenth century were hardly commuter operations. In 1860, before the transition to market gardening had taken place, about two-thirds of farm workers lived in farmers' households. Some farmers built special separate structures for their farm laborers, sometimes above a wagon house; some lodged them in the former slaves' quarters. In 1870, after market gardening had become the mainstay of Kings County farming, 301, or 46 percent, of those returned as farmworkers lived on their employer's farm; this number declined to 194 by 1880, but still represented 32 percent of the enumerated farm laborers. The largest contingent of resident farm laborers worked on Williamson Rapalje's 51-acre market garden farm in New Lots in 1870: 10 Germans and 1 Swiss. This kind of ethnic homogeneity was widespread and aided by the fact that by 1870 the vast majority of black farm laborers no longer lived in their farm employers' household.[46]

The labor intensiveness as well as the degree of proletarianization of Kings County agriculture are reflected in the ratio of the number of farm laborers to the number of farms. In the five towns, this index rose from 2.1 (778/367) in 1860 to 2.6 (648/254) in 1870, before falling markedly to 1.6 (611/391) in 1880. As low as these ratios seem, they were considerably higher than for agriculture in general in an era when many farm laborers were both geographically and socioeconomically in transit. In 1860, for example, the ratio in the 15 principal northern states was only 0.4; the highest ratio in any state, neighboring New Jersey, amounted to only 0.66. The trend in the number of farm laborers per acre, a more accurate gauge of labor intensity, differed in that the decline during the 1870s did not bring about a lower value than at the starting point: the ratio rose from 0.06 laborers per improved acre (778/14,871) in 1860 to 0.07 (648/9,700) in 1870, and then declined to 0.06 (611/10,383) by 1880. The continued decline in farm laborers during the 1870s in tandem with the trend reversal in acreage suggests the possibility of rising productivity during the peak decade of vegetable production.[47]

Labor intensity can also be measured by farmers' payrolls. The quantitative significance of wage labor in Kings County agriculture can be gauged by unpublished data on wages collected by the census for 1879. Of the 406 farms, 372 (92 percent) reported that they had paid $284,063 in wages for farm labor (including board), the average farm paying $764. This sum amounted to about 23 percent of the value of all farm productions, 127 percent of the value of farm implements and machinery, and 134 percent of that year's expenditures on fertilizer.[48]

The data collected on wages (including board) by the census in 1869–70 also make it possible to compare Kings County with other counties with regard to average per farm expenditures. The average for Kings County farms, $1,035, was almost nine times the national average of $117, six and one-half times the New York State average of $159, and three times that of neighboring Queens County, whose total wage expenditures were more than three times higher.[49]

Table 13 displays the wage intensity of the 20 largest market garden-producing counties (arranged in descending order) in 1869–70. Per farm wage expenditures in Kings County were almost three times higher than the aggregate average for the other 19 counties ($391). In general, counties in which labor-intensive vegetable production bulked large also spent more on wages. With the exception of some even more labor-intensive cotton and rice producing counties in the ex-slave South, Kings County farms were the most wage-intensive in the United States. At least among counties whose aggregate farm wages were as large as Kings County's, only in 19 were per farm wage expenditures greater. These extraordinary outlays in Kings County bespeak — unless Dutch farmers paid wages to their own sons — a radical break with cultivation based on family labor and an impressive turn toward capitalist agriculture. Such wage expenditures would be consistent with the employment of large numbers of seasonal piece-rate harvesters, but there is no evidence that migrant farm laborers worked on Kings County farms in the later part of the nineteenth century.[50]

This degree of labor-intensity warranted the employment of a foreman on some farms. Abraham Linington, who owned the second-largest vegetable farm in Kings County in 1870, with $12,200 in sales from 82 acres, employed 31-year-old U.S.-born William Selover as a foreman, who also lived on the farm. Although the enumeration may not have been complete, all the foremen were young, U.S.-born, and worked on farms in New Lots.[51]

Proletarianization in Kings County agriculture was not permanent or lifelong in the sense that very few of the more than two thousand workers returned as farm laborers at the 1860, 1870, and 1880 censuses remained in that class, sectoral, and geographic location from one decade to the next. Not a single worker appeared in all three censuses as a farm laborer in rural Kings County. Nathaniel Vail (or Veil), who was 82 years old in 1880, came closest. This black resident of Gravesend was returned as a farm laborer in 1860 and 1880, while in 1870 he was a gardener.[52]

Rem Hegeman, who was a farm laborer in 1860 and 1870, was returned in 1880 as a laborer — whether he had really left agriculture or whether the enumerator merely used shorthand is unclear. His long-term status as a laborer is instructive. His like-named father had been a large farmer in Flatbush, but at the time of the 1850 census, when he was also returned as a farmer on his 72-year-old father's farm, his two older brothers, who were also returned as farmers there, presumably had greater claims to the farm. The 56-acre Hegeman farm appeared in the 1850 Census of Agriculture, but not again. Perhaps the farm, which reported no market garden production in 1850, failed to make the transition to intensive agriculture. Nor was any member of that Hegeman family returned as a farmer in Flatbush at the 1860 census; by 1860, both of Rem Hegeman's older brothers were returned as living in his household without occupations.

Table 14 presents the most important cross-tabulations, broken down for race, ethnicity, nativity, and town, relating to persistence among farm laborers at the three censuses of 1860, 1870, and 1880. Despite the long period between censuses and the happenstance of what kind of work a particular worker might have been performing at the time the census was conducted, the low degree of persistence from one census to the next is still striking. Overall, the rate was only 1 percent in 1860/1870 and 6 percent during the next decade. Even these low aggregate figures conceal large differences among groups, years, and towns. The black persistence rate was almost ten times as high as for whites in the 1860s and seven times higher in the 1870s, when it rose to 21 percent. In the 1870s, 28 percent of black farm laborers in Gravesend and fully one-third in Flatlands remained in this occupation; in contrast, not a single one in either town did during the 1860s. Especially in Flatlands, this black persistence rate in the 1870s was a function of the fact that men of ages varying from 16 to 70 in four families (Moore, Anderson, Johnson, and Thompson) remained on the farm.[53]

The overall white persistence rate, minimal as it was, also consisted of vastly different rates among subgroups. The rate among U.S.-born whites, surprisingly, was four to five times higher than among Irish immigrants, while only a single German farm laborer was returned as persisting in his position throughout either decade. The high rate among U.S.-born whites in New Utrecht derived largely from the fact that three sons of Dutch farmers had not yet taken over from their fathers and were still working on the farm. But much more remarkable than the proportions among U.S.-born whites, whose numbers were too small to be meaningful, was the virtual absence of persistence among Irish and German immigrants. This exit-mobility strongly suggests both that working in a subordinate position on a rural Kings County vegetable farm in the 1860s and 1870s did not appeal to these immigrants as a viable long-term occupation and that they had better job opportunities either elsewhere or in other industries. Of the more than one hundred Irish-born farm laborers in Flatbush in 1860, only four reappeared in the 1870 Census of Population for Flatbush in other occupations (all were nonagricultural laborers).[54]

For a few, upward mobility meant tenancy. In Flatbush, at least three Irish immigrants (James Bennett, Edward Kennedy, and James Leary) who had been farm laborers in 1870 reappeared 10 years later as tenants. As old-line Dutch farmers increasingly withdrew from active farming by the 1880s, tenancy became more common among Irish and German immigrants. Since revenues from farm rents by the late 1880s and early 1890s could not provide landowners with income flows remotely approaching the deals that real-estate developers and speculators could offer, it would have been very difficult for such tenants to induce their landlords to sell them the farms even if they had sufficient capital to finance the purchase.

STINGY BILL AND PRETTY JACK: WAGES AND WORKING AND LIVING CONDITIONS

Because no data on the wages and working conditions of farm laborers in Kings County were ever collected, some sense of farm labor conditions must be teased from census data as well as incidental and anecdotal sources. Unemployment among Kings County farm laborers was pervasive and extended. Although census officials concluded that the data on unemployment that the Census of Population collected for the first time in 1880 were too erratic and incomplete to justify tabulating and publishing, some Kings County enumerators took their charge seriously. No figures were entered for residents of Flatbush and those for New Lots and New Utrecht were scanty, but the entries for Flatlands and Gravesend, the towns with the largest and third largest farmworker populations, appear to be comprehensive. In Flatlands 29 percent of farm laborers reported having been unemployed during the census year, while 51 percent of those in Gravesend experienced unemployment; the modal duration was two to three months. The pervasiveness of unemployment showed an unmistakable racial skew: whereas 20 percent of Germans, 23 percent of U.S.-born whites, and 29 percent of Irish had been unemployed, fully 61 percent of black farm laborers in Flatlands had been out of employment. Whether this difference resulted from the more casual or seasonal farm employment of blacks or their difficulty in securing other employment is unknown.[55]

Such levels of unemployment are even more impressive because 1880 fell in the prosperity phase of the business cycle. Nevertheless, the New York *Irish-American* reported that year that discussion was taking place of the possibility of "utilizing the waste lands of Long Island by forming colonization societies and establishing villages for mechanics and laboring men in overcrowded cities." At $10 to $15 per acre, acquisition of such land was deemed financially manageable.[56]

Although there are no data on wage rates for Kings County farms, $1.50 per day and $20 per month with room and board were probably the prevailing rates. In 1883 William Bennett paid his laborers in Gravesend $1.00 per day in April and $1.50 per day once the harvest season began in June; in the 1890s he paid various workers between $16 and $30 per month. The Kings County highway commissioners paid $1.50 per day to (the mostly Irish) workers performing road labor in the 1870s and 1880s, and practical horticulturists indicated that in Manhattan in the 1870s as well as generally in the early 1890s, $40 per month or $1.50 per day was the average rate. Dividing the total wage bill of rural Kings County ($275,292) for 1879 by the 611 farm laborers returned for 1880 generates average annual wages per laborer of $451. With two months of unemployment factored in, this sum seems plausible. Total wages paid out in rural Kings County in 1870, $274,865, divided by that year's farm labor force of 648, work out to almost the same amount — $424.[57]

Little is known about labor relations on late-nineteenth-century Kings County farms, but scattered evidence suggests that not all was idyllic. The extremely antiunion editor of the *Rural Gazette* claimed in April 1877 that he was informed that "it is in contemplation by some farm laborers when our farmers get hurried with work along in June next, to inaugurate a strike and use means to prevent those who won't strike from doing any work." Though perhaps only anecdotal in isolation, the facts of one prominent lawsuit seem sufficiently realistic and familiar from the general run of labor relations to claim some representativity. The *Rural and Brighton Gazette* not only deemed it significant enough to report and editorialize on it at great length from the employer's point of view, but observed that, having "attracted great attention," the trial "was considered one of the most interesting that ever occurred in this country." Styled John Turner v. William W. Kouwenhoven, this suit for wages pitted a farm laborer against a member of one of the largest old-line Dutch farm families — or, in the words of the *Rural Gazette*, "an Irishman . . . against a well-known market gardener and respected citizen of Flatlands." The decisions in the case, together with the unpublished briefs and trial transcript and the unpublished manuscript schedules of the 1880 census, shed invaluable light on the day-to-day operations of a Kings County vegetable farm and the relations between the owner and his employees.[58]

In 1880 John Turner was a 25-year-old Irishman who lived on the 45-acre Flatlands farm of the 34-year-old Kouwenhoven. One other farm laborer also lived on the farm — 19-year-old U.S.-born Thomas Duley (or Dooley). The farm, which was valued at $10,000 in addition to $700 worth of farm implements and machinery and $1,000 of livestock, in 1879 produced $5,000 in products, $4,000 of which were market garden produce. On 23 of the acres 4,600 bushels of potatoes were harvested. Kouwenhoven spent $1,500 on fertilizer and $1,000 on wages for 100 weeks of hired labor, and had six horses at his disposal, for which he harvested six tons of hay. He had only one milk cow and three swine on hand in 1880, and bought and sold one head of cattle in 1879. His farm produced 150 pounds of butter and 200 dozen eggs in 1879. He also grew 150 bushels of Indian corn on six acres and 60 bushels of wheat on two acres. The farm was typical both in its size and in having made the transition from grain and livestock production to vegetable production while retaining small self-consumption capacities for certain basic foods.[59]

If, based on Henderson's data for the 1870s and 1880s, wages and fertilizer accounted for about 77 percent of total market-garden costs (abstracting from rent for farms that had been in the family for generations), adding 30 percent to those two cost components and subtracting the total from the value of productions should generate an approximation of the farmer's profit. In 1879, then, Kouwenhoven's profit should have amounted to about

$1,750 or 75 percent more than he paid all his laborers. It was also more than seven times greater than Turner's $240 annual wages.

At trial in 1882, Kouwenhoven testified that he had met Turner eleven years earlier at Castle Garden at the southern tip of Manhattan — the chief immigrant station in the United States from 1855 until Ellis Island replaced it in the early 1890s — where he had gone "to get" the 16-year-old. Thus from the moment Kouwenhoven "found the plaintiff — an emigrant boy just arrived from Ireland" — Turner was in his employ: "When he first came to work for me he did general farm work. I promoted him to be my market man since 1876." Kouwenhoven paid Turner $20 per month during the entire 11-year period. Turner received an additional $1 for each wagon-load of produce that he sold. Kouwenhoven generally paid Turner, who had a sleeping room in the farmer's carriage house, his annual wages at the beginning of the following year. The structure of this relationship implies that the laborer must have been receiving room and board throughout the year to make it possible for him to live until he received his entire annual wage at the end of the term. The terms of payment suggest either that the farmer had a cash-flow problem and could not pay out wages until he himself had sold his crops or that the labor market was favorable enough to workers that the farmer felt it necessary to impose a severe financial disincentive on laborers for departing from their service before the end of their term. That at least some workers acquiesced in such terms suggests, in turn, either that they were without less onerous employment opportunities or that the annual compensation included a premium sufficiently above the going monthly rate to justify the risk of total forfeiture — an empirically implausible possibility.[60]

The relationship between Kouwenhoven and his farm laborer was distinctly paternalistic. When asked at trial how he paid Turner, the farmer replied: "Whenever he needed any money during the year, I would give him whatever he called for; then at the end of the year I would deposit in the Brooklyn Savings Bank the balance coming to him." The dependency embedded in this system of dribbling out a few dollars now and then to the employee-supplicant when he made specific requests was highlighted by a story that Kouwenhoven recounted at trial about how Turner had given money to a Sunday school. One Sunday about dinner time, when Turner came to ask for $2, Kouwenhoven asked him why he had not come Saturday night when he was in the habit of paying the men. Later that day Turner gave 12 shillings of the $2 to the school: "He was a member of my class, and it was the habit, just before Christmas festival, to give money to the missionaries. If he had not borrowed the two dollars from me his contributing $1.50 would have caused me to make inquiry where he got it from, knowing that I had all his wages. I have been a farmer in Flatlands for quite a while." The account creates a mystery of how an Irishman came to support a Dutchman's missionaries, but it leaves no doubt as to the nature and source of the power relations: after Turner had worked for 11 years for Kouwenhoven and with but a few days left in 1881 before the lump-sum payment of his annual wages came due, Kouwenhoven not only jealously regarded every "shilling" of it as still his, but found it perfectly appropriate to demand to know where his employee had obtained as little as $1.50.[61]

The picture-book image of close family relations between the farmer and his "hands" was hardly applicable to this farm. Presumably the most reliable characterization of Kouwenhoven's reputation in the small Flatlands community came from his own defense witness, Jackson Ryder. A 41-year-old neighbor, who had known him for 20 years, Ryder farmed 30 rented acres at the time of the 1880 census. In addition to confirming that Turner was known as "Pretty Jack," Ryder testified that he and others called Kouwenhoven "Stingy Bill": "Yes: there are three William Kouwenhovens. One is called Big Will, one Dandy Will and another Stingy Bill." [62]

Other aspects of the relationship between this particular farmer and worker and other personal characteristics may not have been representative. Turner, who according to his own account could not read writing and did not keep any papers — Kouwenhoven testified that Turner could read and write, but was not certain that he could do more than sign his name — not only entrusted his employer with his annual wages and his savings bank book, but permitted Kouwenhoven to assist him in investing $2,000 of his savings in a mortgage and bond in March 1879. "With that exception," according to Kouwenhoven, "his wages have remained on deposit from the beginning." Turner appears to have had another savings account as well; the combined total of his deposits during his 11 years with Kouwenhoven, which included gifts and inheritance from relatives — he also inherited a farm from his father in Ireland — reached several thousand dollars. If Turner's nonproletarian financial status had in fact been typical for young Irish immigrants, it would explain why so few Irishmen remained in subordinate positions on Kings County farms from one census to the next.[63]

Turner's suit centered on the year 1881, during which Kouwenhoven marketed over $7,000 worth of produce — $2,000 more than the census year of 1879 and on five fewer acres. In 1881, the farm's vegetables, including potatoes, cabbage, sprouts, squash, turnips, carrots, and lettuce, went to market in 211 loads, 201 of which were taken by Turner and 10 by his coworker Dooley. Kouwenhoven had three farm wagons for such transports, the oldest of which was fifteen to twenty years old. Over the course of the year, the average load was worth $30 to $35. Ryder testified that for Kouwenhoven's 40-acre farm, 100 to 175 loads constituted a good annual crop and 211 an "extra crop"; Kouwenhoven's father, C. B. Kouwenhoven, as a 62-year-old farmer at the 1880 Census of Population, characterized 150 to 200 loads as good, whereas 211 "would be pretty heavy." [64]

Turner's complaint alleged that he had sold 398 loads for Kouwenhoven, who had not paid him the agreed-upon $1 for any of them; in addition he claimed that he was owed his wages of $240 for the year minus a $10 advance, for a grand total of $628. That Kouwenhoven delegated the task of marketing his key cash crops to a young semiliterate Irishman suggests that it did not require any significant special expertise and/or that Kouwenhoven's attention was fully occupied in managing the farm itself or perhaps even in some other business. Thus, just as Turner entrusted his entire wages and savings to his employer, Kouwenhoven may have let his entire cash flow pass through his employee's hands. Kouwenhoven testified that he had also gone to market himself and understood the business. Marketing manifestly required energy, patience, and perseverence. If, for example, Turner could not sell the entire load in Brooklyn, it was "his duty to go over to New York and sell the rest for less or whatever he could get." [65]

The legal proceedings and rulings in the case — the jury's award of $431 to Turner was upheld by the higher courts — are not pertinent here, but the rhetoric deployed by Kouwenhoven in his brief to the state's highest court recreating a context that underscored the vitality of Kings County vegetable production in the early 1880s is crucial to the overall argument here.[66] The defendant sought to explain why:

> The practical importance of the question of law here at issue can hardly be over-estimated when the number of farmers in our country towns is considered. . . . The question of supreme importance here is: What is to be the permanent and abiding rule of law which this Court is prepared to establish and apply for the protection of the respective rights of the numerous farmers and marketmen within this State?
>
> In the County of Kings alone hundreds of these marketmen are employed. They are all of them, as far as we can ascertain, employed upon yearly contracts, similar to the one on which this plaintiff sues. From the

very nature of the employment — the sales being for the most part to utter strangers in public market — but little check can be kept upon them by their employers, even were the latter far more skilful accountants than farmers are wont to be. On the other hand these marketmen have large opportunities and great temptations to dishonesty, since almost the entire capital of their employees [sic; should be "employers"] passes through their hands in the course of the year.[67]

Even discounting for inflationary advocacy, no lawyer would have expected such a plea to solve a burning social problem to resonate with judges if the public believed that urban market gardens in general and those of Kings County in particular were about to disappear. Even if the Dutch farmers' inability to implement a system of formal controls placed them "entirely at the mercy" of their Irish marketmen, the imminent or inexorable extinction of close-in vegetable farms would have made the verdict in Turner v. Kouwenhoven not "transitory" but conclusive and definitive.[68]

PART TWO
FROM FARMS TO SUBURBS: THE REAL ESTATE MARKET-INDUCED SELLOUT AND THE RESISTANCE

Rome was not built in one day, nor can Brooklyn be.

— "The Progress of the Consolidation Commission,"
Brooklyn Daily Eagle, August 28, 1873

5. COMPARATIVE DEMOGRAPHIC AND ECONOMIC DEVELOPMENT IN BROOKLYN AND RURAL KINGS COUNTY

If there ever existed a city whose resources were undeveloped . . . it is Brooklyn. No other place . . . that possesses a tithe of its natural advantages suffers them to lie unimproved, when such rich returns would assuredly wait upon the expenditure of capital and enterprise. . . . But perhaps, after all, profit and interest is the best awakener, and when it is clearly seen that great improvements may be made to pay, they will be forthcoming.

— Walt Whitman, "The Future of Brooklyn," July 14, 1858

As employment in the New York metropolitan region grew in tandem with the expansion of manufacturing and a variety of services, and as the region's potential for population growth increased through immigration from abroad and internal migration following the Civil War, the demand for affordable housing increased as well. As the urban transportation system was extended outward into rural Kings County, the spaces available for housing not only became more attractive, but were increasingly tied to the salaries and wages that could be earned in the more densely populated sections of Brooklyn and Manhattan. All these factors tending to push up the rents on rural Kings County land — the city's attraction as a population center, its growth as a labor market, and the expansion of urban and suburban transportation — were dynamically interrelated and linked to the potential residential sites' proximity to Brooklyn and Manhattan in time and convenience.

Early on in Manhattan's explosive development, elites expressed concern about where the multitudes would be housed that a dynamic capitalist economy had to have at its disposal in rapidly varying quantities. In 1873, a few days before the election that approved the annexation by New York City of parts of Westchester County, the *New York Times* editorialized that "New-York cannot be depopulated, and it must therefore be extended."[1]

The following year the newspaper devoted an entire page to the "very important" question for "every man, woman, and child of the City of New York," of the availability of the suburbs for this extension. A year after parts of what are now the Bronx were annexed from Westchester County to the city in the first of its acts of territorial self-aggrandizement, the newspaper pronounced the "occupation of . . . suburban homes" to be the subject "which next to her commerce most directly touches the welfare of the Metropolis." The issue, however, was distinctly defined along class axes. "To a man of large material resources, New York is good enough to-day, as it will afford him an aristocratic town residence . . . and a Summer residence wherever he chooses to place it, so that he reaches his counting-room before noon" and could arrive home by six o'clock after a three-hour express train trip:

> But New York is not made up of such men, nor does it altogether depend on them for its prosperity. That merchant would be powerless without the hundred clerks, porters, and messengers in his employ, and the important question is how are these, not merely of to-day, but of the next century, to be provided for. It is to the masses of the people, the tradesmen and the artisans that there is a particular interest in this question of suburban domiciliary occupation and facilitation.[2]

Given the existing "facilities of exit," the *Times* defined New York's suburbs as bounded by a fifteen- or twenty-mile radius from City Hall and extending to the north, east, south, and west to Yonkers, Flushing and Garden City, Staten Island, and Plainfield, New Jersey, respectively. Although Kings County was "almost as naturally within the suburban range as" Westchester, physically it was separated by a "considerable" water obstacle. Nevertheless, the "constant effort" of the county's "corporate Governmental capacities" and private enterprise had made it "more attractive and accessible than any part of New York City above Forty-second street." Indeed, the *Times*, viewing Kings and the other counties as "foreign local jurisdictions," worried over their stormy post–Civil War growth and the possibility that nearly all of the 400,000 people who had moved there during the previous ten years "might have been retained to swell the population and wealth of the Metropolis, had an energetic and business-like policy been adopted by New-York capitalists, real-estate owners, politicians, and railroad corporations." Instead, the building of the Brooklyn Bridge, the "only rapid transit project" which the city was really pushing, was "calculated to check its growth." Unwilling, apparently, to propose additional annexations in all directions, the *Times* contented itself with predicting that: "Having all the advantages of ocean, bays, and rivers, of fertile fields and picturesque hills and valleys within easy reach of the commercial heart of the City, it promises well, ere a quarter of a century has elapsed, to become the most charmingly varied place of residence in the world." The prophesy that within 25 years New York City would undergo transformation was stunningly accurate: 24 years later consolidation assured its preeminence. Just as stunningly inaccurate, however, was the speculation that "fertile fields" would remain part of the city's attractions.[3]

Ironically, at the same time, boosters in the rural towns of Kings County bemoaned that the lack of rapid transit meant that they could not absorb even 1 percent of the 100,000 people crowded out of Manhattan each year. While villages and towns had "sprung up as by magic" along the railroad lines fifty miles into New Jersey, and land could not be bought for $6,000 an acre in Westchester, land in New Utrecht could not be sold for $700 per acre: "Men will not build homes here with the view of living in them, if they have to spend as many hours in getting to and from the city as they live miles from it." The *Kings County Rural Gazette* conjured up the image of steam power as annihilating distance and liberating time (also in its alter ego as money) as "an article available in the upbuilding of large and wealthy communities."[4]

To contemporary writers the growth of nearby populations alone foreshadowed the eradication of rural life in Kings County by the 1880s, but the question as to how the inevitable would occur was more complex. The increasing pace of population growth in Brooklyn, beginning at the end of the eighteenth century, has been attributed largely to its location as the terminus of roads branching from the New York ferries to the Long Island settlements. The population of Brooklyn barely exceeded 20,000 when it was incorporated as a city in 1834; its rapid territorial and demographic expansion resulted from the same economic influences that were propelling New York to national preeminence: the advent of the Erie Canal and the "phenomenal development of domestic commerce." As manufacturing enterprises proliferated, "the wage earner was becoming a more important factor in Brooklyn, as in New York. The predominantly rural aspect of the place gave way, as large warehouses were built along the shore, and as factory buildings, extensive and costly for the period, appeared." Contrary to later notions that Brooklyn's growth was primarily due to its convenience as a "great dormitory, where thousands upon thousands of men doing business in New York sleep and keep their families," its advancing population resulted largely from the manifold forces of industrialization. Stiles was right in 1870 when he observed in his history of Brooklyn: "The oft-repeated saying that Brooklyn is only a large bedroom for the business men of New York, may pass for a joke, but as a fact it is not tenable, when we consider the immense amount of manufacturing which is here carried on."[5]

Brooklyn's inconvenience as a commuter suburb in the early part of the nineteenth century can be gauged by the observation of Nathaniel Prime, a historian of Long Island writing in 1845, that crossing the East River by ferry "was frequently more formidable than is now a voyage to Europe." The author himself had "waited from morning to night on the Brooklyn side, in a north-east storm, before any boat ventured to cross to the city. And frequently the passage was made with manifest hazard, and sometimes attended with serious disaster and loss of life." By the 1840s, however, the proliferation of steamboats had rendered the crossing, at any time of day or night, as safe as and faster than walking the same distance on land. Significantly, by midcentury farm wagons were the principal freight of the ferries between Williamsburgh and New York.[6]

Marked differentiation between the occupational structure of the populations of Brooklyn on the one hand and the rest of Kings County on the other appeared as early as the 1820 census, the first to publish data on this question. Whereas only 32 percent of Brooklyn's population was returned in agriculture and 60 percent in manufactures, the figures were reversed in the rest of Kings County: 71 percent were engaged in agriculture and only 27 percent in manufactures. In Flatbush and Gravesend, four to five times as many were engaged in agriculture as in manufactures.[7]

Brooklyn's incorporation as a city was itself emblematic of this shift toward industrial enterprise. Whereas a few years earlier "the interests of the urban and agricultural areas had seemed so diverse that a proposition to bisect the town into two separate jurisdictions had been seriously entertained . . . in the early thirties nothing was more certain than that the village streets would soon extend far into the countryside, and that the farms out-

side the corporation limits would shortly be divided into city lots."[8] Earlier
in the nineteenth century:

> Many of the Dutch landowners of the surrounding countryside, then
> comfortably living on rich farms, were in a position sooner or later to
> amass considerable fortunes through the appreciation of their proper-
> ties, although it is probable that few of them then foresaw it. For genera-
> tion after generation the acres which . . . surrounded the village in a wide
> half circle . . . had yielded their increase; and there was little in the appar-
> ent prospects of the time and place to cause the Boerums, the Remsens,
> the Schencks, the Vanderbilts, the Ryersons, the Bennets, and the Cor-
> telyous to stake out imaginary streets or to anticipate profits from the
> sale of city lots.[9]

By the 1830s, however: "Farsighted owners of land in Brooklyn, eager to
profit from this inevitable expansion, now comprehended that union with
the village, under an adequate charter of government, was a matter of necessity." Within months of Brooklyn's incorporation, Abraham Schermer-
horn sold his 170-acre farm in Gowanus, three miles from Brooklyn, for
$600 an acre. Speculation was so rampant that he regretted selling it so cheap
despite the fact that the $102,000 he received was more than five times as
much as he had been willing to accept four years earlier. Nor was he alone at
the time: others also became "immensely rich by the good fortune of owning farms of a few acres of this chosen land."[10]

The national census of 1840 published more detailed data on occupational structure, which underscore the progressive differentiation between
the cities of Brooklyn and Williamsburgh and the rural towns. Table 15 presents the number of persons employed in various sectors. In Brooklyn,
which encompassed virtually the county's entire commerce and ocean nav-
igation sectors, and Williamsburgh, which was even more heavily industrialized, manufactures accounted for 54 percent of the employed population,
whereas agriculture accounted for only 16 percent. Their favorable location
on the ice-free East River enabled these two harbor cities to secure considerable maritime commerce and helped propel their growth. Brooklyn's industrialization was accompanied by a further skewing of wealth and expansion of the class of "propertyless proletarians."[11]

In the rest of the county, the proportions were reversed: agriculture accounted for 70 percent and manufactures and trades only 17 percent. Abstracting from Bushwick, which underwent urbanization sooner than the

other rural towns, and the anomalous and inexplicably high figure for Flatbush, fewer than 10 percent of the employed population in Flatlands, Gravesend, and New Utrecht were engaged in manufactures or trades. Another facet of the pronounced differentiation between the city and the rural towns was recorded for 1845: in Brooklyn and Williamsburgh, 38 merchants, manufacturers, and mechanics were returned for every agriculturist. In contrast, in the four rural towns, there were almost twice as many agriculturists as merchants, manufacturers, and mechanics, reaching a high of six to one in Gravesend. Indeed, only 16 merchants and not a single manufacturer was returned as living in the rural towns.[12]

The overwhelmingly agrarian character of Flatbush — in 1840 "most" of its 7,000 acres were under cultivation, "furnishing abundance of produce to Brooklyn and New York markets" and wealth to the farmers — especially in the property-holding classes, in the first half of the nineteenth century is revealed by the town's juror lists. In 1815, 97 percent of those subject to serve were "yeomen." By the 1830s, yeomen (or, as they were called from 1833 on, farmers) constituted three-fourths of all those liable to jury duty or selected from among the assessed on the assessment rolls: 75 percent in 1830 and 1833 and 74 percent in 1837. Farmers' share of selected jurors fell to 58 percent in 1840, but by 1846 their share rose again to 66 percent. Since the farmers during these years were almost all Dutch, the homogeneity of the property-based political power was also striking.[13]

Gravesend's abiding agricultural character was highlighted by the occupations (which served as a basis for claiming an exemption) recorded in the enrollment list of all able-bodied male residents between the ages of 18 and 45 liable to military duty during the Civil War. Of 256 men, 29 percent were farmers and 32 percent laborers, in addition to 8 percent who were reported as fishermen or boatmen. Similarly, as late as the 1860 and 1870 Census of Population, 7 and 8 percent (114 and 184 persons), respectively, of the entire population of the most rural town, Flatlands, were returned as fishermen. In contrast, tailors were most frequently encountered in the most industrialized town, New Lots, in 1860.[14]

Some sectoral shift is also visible for New Utrecht by the early 1860s. The same Civil War enrollment list showed that of the 603 prime-age enrolled men in 1862, 106, or 18 percent, were listed as farmers. Although the category "laborer" did not distinguish between those working on farms and elsewhere, presumably the vast majority of these 224 men (or 37 percent of the total) were agricultural. Even if all of them were farm laborers, 191, or 32 percent, of all military-age men in New Utrecht worked in nonagricultural occupations such as merchant, storekeeper, clerk, shoemaker, coachman, lawyer, carpenter, bookkeeper, insurance, hotel, importer, wheelwright, barkeeper, waiter, physician, mason, and blacksmith. These occupations are not indicative of industrialization, but they point to a division of labor that had advanced beyond that of a closed agrarian economy. By 1874 New Utrecht boasted of a large steam-powered factory for manufacturing horse-drawn railroad cars.[15]

A sense of the spatial configurations of the Kings County towns can be gleaned from table 16, which reports on their area and population density in 1840. The urbanized towns, Williamsburgh and Brooklyn, had already achieved population densities 15 to 60 times greater than those of the rural towns. Even the latter were clearly differentiated: those most remote from New York City, Flatlands and Gravesend, were only one-third to one-fourth as densely populated as the other agricultural towns. As scarcely populated as most of the towns were, they were all so compact that Kings County's entire area of 76 square miles was smaller than several individual towns in the other Long Island counties, Queens and Suffolk.[16]

As late as 1845, more than 3,000 acres of improved agricultural land were located in the city of Brooklyn, amounting to 15 percent of the county total. Table 17 breaks out the acreage for all the cities and towns in Kings County. Flatbush accounted for more than one-fourth and New Utrecht one-fifth of the county total of almost 21,000 acres. Brooklyn farms were concentrated in the Eighth and Ninth Wards, which bordered on New Utrecht and Flatbush. In particular the Eighth Ward, Gowanus, had been an old area of settlement for Dutch farmers, who as late as the revolutionary period owned farms as large as 300 acres.[17] Indeed, Jeremiah Johnson (1827–1898), a towering figure in the post–Civil War real-estate business, recalled in the 1890s that in the 1830s "nearly all residents of the outer wards of Brooklyn were farmers and market gardeners. Their produce and vegetables found ready sale in New York. By industry, prudence, and economy, they accumulated wealth." In the 1840s much of the Ninth Ward

> was covered with forest trees, and owned in plots of from five to twenty acres by farmers who cut wood during idle times and carted it to their homes for winter use. . . .
>
> If the wood plots . . . which . . . were almost valueless, had been disposed of as a whole to some wealthy capitalist and properly improved, in accordance with the inimitable methods of James D. Lynch, as shown in his . . . Bensonhurst developments, the location would have been one of

the most beautiful in the city, and lots instead of selling for a song would have commanded high prices.[18]

As late as 1865, Brooklyn still reported more than 1,100 acres of improved farmland, or 8 percent of the total for Kings County. Five years later, the city's population had increased by another 100,000, reaching almost 400,000, while its agricultural acreage had shrunk to fewer than 400 acres, or 3 percent of the county's total.[19]

Despite the sharp absolute and relative decline of Brooklyn agriculture between 1820 and 1840, "[u]rban Brooklyn clearly still had much farm land in 1841" — the only year during the second quarter of the nineteenth century for which its tax assessment records are preserved. Even in that year, when Brooklyn was the seventh most populous city in the United States, 5 percent of its wealthiest persons were farmers. This figure becomes more impressive in contrast with the occupational structure of the rich in other northeastern cities: in New York, Philadelphia, and Boston, even earlier in the century, farmers failed to represent even 1 percent of the wealthiest.[20]

By the time Bushwick and the city of Williamsburgh (which had become a village in 1827 and a town formed from Bushwick in 1840) were consolidated with Brooklyn in 1854, its population was well over 200,000, and by 1860 Brooklyn was the third-largest city in the United States after New York (which then consisted only of Manhattan Island) and Philadelphia. The town of New Lots was formed from Flatbush in 1852 and annexed to Brooklyn in 1886. In 1894 Flatbush, Gravesend, and New Utrecht were also annexed to Brooklyn; and when, in 1896, Flatlands was annexed, the city of Brooklyn finally became coterminous with Kings County. The annexation of Flatbush (5.69 square miles), New Utrecht (7.96 square miles), Gravesend (10.96 square miles), and Flatlands (12.79 square miles) more than doubled the size of Brooklyn, which had been 28.99 square miles. But Brooklyn retained its independent status only briefly, already in 1898 becoming a borough within consolidated Greater New York.[21]

Much of the impetus for these consolidations came from a desire to eliminate the duplicative and inefficient governments of the county and individual towns. The officers of the town of Flatbush, for example, included a supervisor, town clerk, tax collector, three assessors, three auditors, five justices of the peace, a board of health, three excise commissioners, three commissioners of highways, and a sealer of weight and measures. The other towns boasted similar cadres. In the view of many, the almost comically crooked towns had, as the *New York Daily Tribune* put it, all "been governed by corrupt gangs and rings." The *Eagle* was even less restrained in characterizing Flatbush, Flatlands, Gravesend, and New Utrecht as "an expense, a confusion, a complication, a scandal and an abomination. . . . This double system of government . . . is a satire on civilization. It is a parody on justice. . . . It is an obstacle to order." Annexation of Gravesend, which was autocratically run by John Y. McKane, rescued from "barbarism" people who, according to the *Eagle*, had been governed by "a despotism of robbery, violence and lies meaner than captives ever experienced from Algerian pirates or from cannibals of darkest Africa, because exercised within the forms and sanctions of law." Much of the opposition to annexation stemmed from "Brooklyn's rascally politicians," who stood to lose many "profitable places and jobs," for widespread corruption also characterized Brooklyn city government for much of the nineteenth century.[22]

With Kings County, New York City finally had at the disposal of its overflow population an area, as the *New York Times* editorialized, "several times greater than that below Central Park, which is not crowded, and much of which is not occupied at all." In particular, the colonization of Brooklyn provided New York with material and ideological benefits in the struggle for the pacification of the working class — "land for manufacturing interests, with cheap homes for employees far from the tenement districts, that will develop a stronger, healthier, and more industrious manhood than it is possible to develop in the closely-packed sections of the city where cheap homes only are now obtainable."[23]

That the population of Brooklyn grew much faster than that of rural Kings County during the nineteenth century is obvious from table 18. Whereas Brooklyn at the first national census in 1790 accounted for only 36 percent of the population of Kings County and was only 70 percent larger than Flatbush, a century later the city of Brooklyn contributed 96 percent of the county's population and was 65 times more populous than Flatbush. The population of Flatbush, Flatlands, and Gravesend each took almost a half century to double; the next doubling after 1840 was not completed until after the Civil War. New Utrecht grew somewhat faster. The smaller absolute populations of Flatlands and Gravesend — these two outer towns were nowhere contiguous with the city of Brooklyn — were also reflected in considerably lower population densities. In 1850, the population per square mile in Gravesend and Flatlands was 93 and 81, respectively — lower than that prevailing in parts of Queens and barely higher than in western Suffolk

County. Population density in Flatbush and New Utrecht was several times higher.[24]

As modest as the population of Flatbush was in the nineteenth century, the census returns vastly overstated it. In 1870, the institutionalized population of the Kings County Lunatic Asylum, Alms House, Nursery, and Hospital, which were located in Flatbush, but the vast majority of whose inmates had doubtless been residents of Brooklyn, accounted for more than two-fifths of the entire population of Flatbush; without these extraterritorial expatriates the town would have numbered only about 3,600 inhabitants. Able-bodied pauper inmates of the "county farm" were required to break stones or cultivate the grounds; in 1860 the Kings County Farm produced 3,200 bushels of potatoes, $1,000 of market garden produce, and was the biggest producer of corn. The vast expansion of this exclave population is visible in the fact that in 1850 the Work House, Alms House, and Lunatic Asylum housed only 609 people, or about 19 percent of the town's population, which without them numbered a little over 2,500, while in 1860 the 1,248 residents of these institutions accounted for 36 percent of Flatbush, which without them numbered 2,223, or fewer than the noninstitutionalized in 1850.[25]

Flatbush boosters maintained that all county residents were acutely aware of the physical presence of these county buildings — on "the county farm is a Stygian pool, on the banks of which lie, festering in the summer sun, the excreta of Brooklyn's poor, filling the air with sickening malaria" — holding them responsible for deterring people from moving to the town and depressing property values. In the early 1880s, the *Rural Gazette* was still issuing recriminations against Brooklyn for making a "dumping ground" of portions of, and causing a "stigma" to attach to, Flatbush. Complaints were also frequently voiced that the institutionalized paupers were being used to vote unlawfully in local elections.[26]

The impact of deagriculturalization on Flatbush, Gravesend, and New Utrecht during the 1880s is manifest: while Brooklyn grew by 42 percent, their populations rose by 62, 89, and 87 percent, respectively. The 1890s, marked by annexation of the rural towns to Brooklyn in 1894 and 1896 and consolidation with New York City in 1898, witnessed even more explosive demographic growth: whereas the city of Brooklyn (within its pre-1894 borders) grew by an additional 35 percent, Flatbush, Flatlands, Gravesend, and New Utrecht recorded increases of 120, 102, 111, and 179 percent, respectively. The differential growth rates between the old wards of Brooklyn and the newly annexed towns continued after consolidation. Between 1900 and 1905, the population in the four towns increased 55 percent compared to only 13 percent in the rest of Kings County. At this early stage, however, the former farming regions were still uncongested. In Flatlands, which at the time of annexation the press called "a farming town" and an "agricultural district," the density was, despite a 60 percent population increase, still only one person per acre.[27]

A visually powerful reminder of the huge demographic and developmental gaps between Brooklyn and the rural towns jumps out from nineteenth-century maps. Figure 10 displays a county map from 1868 on which a thick street grid abruptly comes to an end where Brooklyn's borders meet those of New Lots, Flatbush, and New Utrecht. Instead of streets, farm lines mark off hundreds of farms, the names of whose owners are prominently displayed. Through these otherwise white spaces run only a few transportation arteries, such as the horse-drawn Coney Island Rail Road (from the brand-new Prospect Park to the Atlantic Ocean), dating from 1863; the Brooklyn, Bath and Coney Island Railroad from Greenwood Cemetery, opened in 1864, and the Brooklyn and Rockaway Beach Railroad, which opened in 1865 and ran through the village of Canarsie in Flatlands (the rural county's only two steam railroads); and a few unidentified farm roads. Two decades later, the street grid, at least on paper, has been extended even to the outer towns of Flatlands and Gravesend.[28]

The relative economic magnitudes are put in perspective by noting that Kings County's agricultural sector was dwarfed by Brooklyn's manufacturing. In 1880 the total value of all farm productions on the county's 406 farms was $1,211,000, whereas the products of the city's 5,201 manufacturing establishments were valued at $177,223,142. Table 19 compares manufactures in the city of Brooklyn and rural Kings County (i.e., Kings County without Brooklyn) in 1880 and 1890. The gap between Brooklyn, the country's fourth-largest manufacturing center, and rural Kings County was huge. In 1880, when Brooklyn's population was 17 times larger, its manufacturing establishments were 65 times as numerous, produced 90 times as much with 39 times as many employees to whom it paid 59 times as much in wages. By 1890, when Brooklyn's population was 25 times larger, the gaps had grown two- to fivefold: 265 times as many establishments produced 171 times as much with 209 times as many workers paid 200 times as much. The rural towns' manufacturing sector shrank by all indicators during the 1880s — largely because New Lots was annexed to Brooklyn in 1886 — to the point

FIGURE 10. *Farmline map of Kings County, 1868. From M. Dripps, "Map of Kings County N.Y."*

at which the value of its output only marginally exceeded that of the farms. Because the city generated so much more wealth per inhabitant than the rural towns, it became increasingly useful to have access to the areas of Brooklyn where the bulk of manufacturing and commerce was located. This relationship acted as a kind of centripetal force on the population until measures were taken to bring the outlying areas closer to the industrial centers.[29]

Similar orders of magnitude separated Brooklyn and rural Kings County with respect to assessed valuation of property taxed. Table 20 shows the major indicators for 1880 and 1890. The property valuations (the vast majority of which were of real estate) for Brooklyn not only overshadowed those for the rural towns, but also increased more rapidly during the 1880s. On a per capita basis, assessed valuations actually fell in three of the four towns. Regardless of the ratio between assessed valuation of real property and its "true valuation" — estimates reported to the Census Office ranged between 45 percent for Gravesend and 70 percent for Brooklyn — per capita taxable wealth in Brooklyn surged ahead of that in rural Kings County. Since Brooklyn occupied about one-half of the county, the relative densities of the urban and rural halves can be gauged by the fact that the city's assessment was 25 to 30 times greater.[30]

A longer series of the assessed valuation of real estate alone reveals a similar gap. In 1855, the assessed valuation of Brooklyn's real estate was $84.5 million, or 20 times greater than the $4.1 million valuation in the rural towns; 30 years later, the city's valuation had risen to $311.3 million, or 23 times greater than the towns' $13.5 million valuation. By the latter half of the 1880s, however, the rural towns, developing toward annexation, experienced a considerably steeper rise in the assessed valuation of their real estate than the city of Brooklyn. From 1886, the year in which New Lots was annexed and its valuation shifted to Brooklyn's, through 1893, the year before the other towns (except Flatlands) were annexed, real-estate valuation in the four towns rose almost 160 percent from $10.4 million to $27 million. In contrast, Brooklyn's real-estate valuation rose by only 43 percent.[31]

Differences in the capacity to produce values and accumulate capital of this magnitude were not merely quantitative: they were also reflected in the economic relationships between the farm towns and Brooklyn's nationally prominent industrial and financial firms. Emblematic of Flatbush's dependence, for example, was the fact that "during the two hundred and fifty years of its history Flatbush . . . had no banking institution until . . . 1899" because "while it was mainly a farming section, the great wagons of produce made frequent trips to Brooklyn, where most of the business was done." The vegetable farmers' failure to forge the kind of dynamic agricultural sector that could sustain its own credit institution in rural Kings County strongly suggests that the ultimate economic dominance there would flow from the city of Brooklyn, which, at the appropriate time, would finance residential development rather than modernization and expansion of farming.[32]

6. THE PREHISTORY OF THE CONVERSION OF RURAL KINGS COUNTY FARMS INTO SUBURBAN REAL ESTATE

As cities have expanded, rich fields have been planted with houses.
— Donald Bogue, *Metropolitan Growth and the Conversion of Land to Nonagricultural Uses*, 1956

OVERVIEW OF THE MOBILIZATION OF FARMS FOR REAL-ESTATE PURPOSES

A farm . . . furnishes a painful illustration of the unwholesome excitement attendant upon speculation. Here dwelt an honest, ignorant, peaceful old man, who inherited from his father a farm of little value. Its produce was, however, enough to supply his moderate wants. . . . Thus quietly lived the old-fashioned farmer and his family, and thus they might have gone home to their fathers, had not a band of speculators foreseen that the rapidly increasing city would soon take in Brooklyn, and stretch itself across the marshes of Gowanus. Full of these visions, they called upon the old man, and offered him $70,000 for a farm which had, originally, been bought for almost a song. $10,000 in silver and gold, were placed on the table before him; he looked at them, fingered them over, seemed bewildered, and agreed to give a decisive answer on the morrow. The next morning found him a raving maniac! And thus he now roams about, recklessly tearing up the flowers he once loved so dearly, and keeping his family in continual terror.
— L[ydia]. Maria Child, *Letters from New York*, 1844

A good sense of the agricultural land base available for conversion to residential housing in the various towns of Kings County can be gleaned from table 21, which presents the total farm acreage recorded at the agricultural censuses between 1820 and 1880 (see also figure 11). Abstracting from several methodological discontinuities, it is clear that in several towns farmland contracted almost continually. This pattern was characteristic of the most urbanized towns — Brooklyn, Bushwick (which on becoming part of Brooklyn in 1854 artificially inflated the latter's acreage in 1855), and New Lots. New Utrecht's farm acreage displayed remarkable constancy, remaining virtually fixed from 1820 to 1875, and then declining a modest 12 percent during the next five years. This development underscores the suddenness of the suburbanization of New Utrecht in the late 1880s. Flatlands, the most rural of the towns, held on to all its farmland from 1850 to 1860; after losing 1,200 acres between 1860 and 1870, it regained almost half by 1880. Thus during the whole period from 1850 to 1880, Flatlands lost about 650 acres, or 17 percent of its farmland. Gravesend added a marginal amount of land between 1850 and 1870, and then lost about 850 acres, or 29 percent, during the 1870s. This significant loss coincided with the acquisition of several large tracts devoted to horse-racing tracks, which soon "helped to build up Gravesend and aid in its financial prosperity." Finally, Flatbush, which progressed more quickly toward suburbia during the latter part of the nineteenth century than the other three rural towns, preserved its agricultural land base intact until about the Civil War (quantification is difficult because of the separation of New Lots). Then during the 1860s it lost almost 900 acres, or 37 percent of its farm acreage. Although it regained somewhat less than 200 acres during the 1870s, by 1880 farmland in Flatbush was probably only about half as extensive as it had been at the time that New Lots split off in 1852.[1]

The mass conversion of farms into residential lots in the 1890s was foreshadowed by developments decades earlier. Perhaps the earliest and most spectacular was John R. Pitkin's failed attempt in 1835 to found a great city, East New York, in New Lots. Until that time: "The prosperous and conservative Dutch and English farmers who tilled the land were content with their situations. The thought of dividing their land into building lots would never have entered their minds." But in that year, Pitkin, a Connecticut businessman, visited the village of New Lots and by 1836 began buying up farmland from the Van Siclen (54 acres and 16 parcels of land for about $25,000), Snediker (35 acres), Wycoff, Stoothoff, and Livingston families encompass-

FIGURE 11. *Kings County, 1865. From* Report of the Superintendent of the United States Coast Survey, Showing the Progress of the Survey During the Year 1865. *39th Cong., 1st Sess. H. Ex. Doc. 75, Coast Chart No. 20 (1867).*

ing a two-mile by one-mile area. Like many Easterners seeking "urban op-portunities rather than fertile soil," Pitkin and other "enterprising land speculators eyed those towns which they anticipated would grow into large cities." Pitkin's vision of transforming "farms and quiet villages" into "a vast transportation center along the shore of Jamaica Bay" was thwarted by the panic of 1837, which rendered him unable to meet his financial obligations; consequently, "much of the farm land he had bought reverted to its former owners."[2]

In Flatbush the conversion of farmland into residential real estate in the 1890s also had its prehistory. The *Brooklyn Daily Eagle*, looking back from the year of the consolidation of Greater New York in 1898, could discern "no changes of moment" in Flatbush from its founding in the seventeenth century until 1834, when "speculators began cutting up several of the old farms into building sites." Only then did "real estate speculation bec[o]me a prominent factor in the affairs of the town, the owners theretofore being too much interested in other pursuits to realize the possibilities of real estate ventures." In 1834 Gerrit Martense, whose ancestor, "Martin the Boor," had settled in Flatbush in the seventeenth century, laid out a tract as lots and opened two streets, but the project, which spawned the building of only a few houses, "was not a financial success."[3]

The underdeveloped state of transportation at this time meant that Flatbush remained too distant from New York and even downtown Brooklyn for commuting "to attract a massive influx of well-to-do suburban residents." No public transportation connected Flatbush to Brooklyn until 1830 when a once-daily stage line was instituted. Until that time the village had also been without a post office: letters to residents were addressed to Brooklyn and brought to Flatbush as a favor by a man who traveled there daily on business.[4]

Despite this impediment, by 1840 Flatbush had already revealed its potential as a residential suburb for the wealthy while retaining its character as an agricultural district of wealthy farmers furnishing an abundance of produce to markets in Brooklyn and New York. The village had, according to J. T. Bailey's *Historical Sketch of the City of Brooklyn and the Surrounding Neighborhood*, become such "a delightful spot" that "several splendid villas have been erected, all having the appearance of good taste, and conveying an impression of the wealth and opulence of these elegant mansions. A softer or more agreeable landscape than is here presented, is seldom met with, and can scarcely be wished for."[5]

Two years later, Thomas Strong, pastor of the Flatbush Reformed Dutch Church, could observe the embryonic mobilization of farmland for suburbanization in his town history:

> While in other sections of our country, the lands possessed by the original proprietors, have passed from their descendants; here, but few farms

comparatively, have changed hands; the spirit of roving not having been cherished. Most of the farms are still in the possession of the descendants of the first patentees and proprietors.

It no doubt will appear strange to some, that a village so contiguous to the great emporium of our country, and combining the advantages of health and means of education, with the absence of many temptations to the young should not have grown with more rapidity. But the reason is to be found in the fact that until within a very few years, not a building lot could be purchased in the town. The owners of property, living in comfort, and gradually adding to their estates, felt no inducement to part with their lands. But of late, some farms have been purchased, and Flatbush land is now in the market. Had the village been laid out regularly in streets and building lots, some thirty or forty years ago, it would we have no doubt by this time have rivalled some of our largest inland towns.[6]

In 1835 Dr. Adrian Vanderveer had his Flatbush farm surveyed into lots, "but little, if any, of the property was sold" for three decades; the next year, portions of the Michal Neufus and Schoonmacker farms were developed. In 1851 and 1852, another settlement, Greenfield (later called Parkville), was created from portions of the David Johnson and Henry S. Ditmas farms, the United Freeman's Association paying an average of $500 per acre for 114 acres. In 1867, Teunis J. Bergen bought a 14-acre farm from the heirs of Cornelius Antonides for development purposes, and soon buildings were constructed. Bergen, the son of a onetime New Utrecht farmer, moved to Flatbush and became the president of a Brooklyn insurance company and a real-estate broker.[7]

In a typical developmental pattern in Kings County, suburbanization of farming districts was preceded by a transitional phase in which "large landholders turned their farms into country estates." In the Bedford section of Brooklyn, for example, this process began about 1835 and lasted until the 1880s because the owner of the "choicest property," Leffert Lefferts, withheld his farm from the market. During these decades, and especially before the Civil War, speculators bought up farms and building cycles coincided with business cycles. A similar pattern repeated itself in Prospect Heights, Kensington, and Brownsville, where large realtors bought land for long-term speculative purposes during years of prosperity, but the selling of lots was curbed by the Civil War: "The actual settlement of these three suburbs was delayed from thirty to forty years following the breakup of the farms. . . . Brooklyn grew by spreading to land adjacent to settled locations. It did not, as in the case of Boston, develop from the filling of areas between various outlying areas." Because Flatbush lacked "the dramatic location desired by the wealthy, the upper class Brooklynite did not compete for the land, and it became the province of the middle class," whose influx, however, was slowed down by the "conscious policy on the part of speculators to hold their land until the demand for first class housing raised prices in the district." Even as late as the first half of the 1890s, at least until annexation by Brooklyn, development was impeded by the Flatbush town government's refusal to provide services such as paving and sewers: "As a result, Brooklyn banks were reluctant to give property loans to Flatbush residents, and those who could secure mortgage money paid higher interest rates than home owners living in Brooklyn." Overall, the building cycle governed development more than the extension of mass transportation lines.[8]

The upper class may not have competed with the middle class for Flatbush land once suburbanization gripped the town in the 1890s, but wealthy Manhattan and Brooklyn businessmen had resided in some of the choicest Flatbush locations for decades. Figure 12 maps the residences of the village of Flatbush in 1870: the prominence of wealthy nonfarmers is impressive. Moreover, not all who speculated on the future urbanization of rural Kings County let their investments lie fallow. Gertrude Lefferts Vanderbilt recounted how on one of the farms of the Flatbush Lott families, which was sold for division of property in 1865 and then cut into lots, "[h]eavy brick stores" soon "loom[ed] up upon the corner lots. They are the harbingers of the changes which in time must come, but which might have been for some time deferred. The owners of these stores have anticipated a future in which they may be needed rather than a present in which they are."[9]

THE PROVISION OF TRANSPORTATION AND OTHER INFRASTRUCTURE: LAYING THE BASIS FOR SUBURBANIZATION

One day, during my visit to New York, I paid a visit to the different public institutions on Long Island, or Rhode Island — I forget which.
— Charles Dickens, *American Notes*, 1842

The precondition for suburban growth and overcoming the "prevalent reluctance of the farmers to part with any of their acres" was improved transportation. The premodern character of transportation in rural Kings County just a few years earlier emerges distinctly from the state legislature's act in-

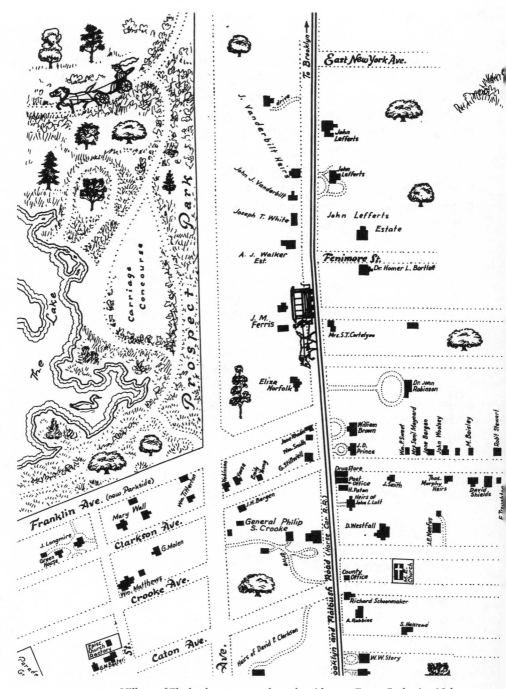

FIGURE 12. *Village of Flatbush, 1870, merchants' residences. From Catherine Nelson and E. Theo. Nelson, "The Village of Flatbush as It Was in the Year 1870."*

corporating the Bath and Coney Island Turnpike Road Company. Authorized to begin in Brooklyn and "thence continue over the hills" to the rural towns, the company was empowered in 1835 to exact tolls such as five cents "for every farm wagon or stage with four wheels and two horses or other animals." The commissioners appointed to lay out the road and to open the books included such prominent members of old-line Dutch farm families as James Bennett, Egbert Benson, and George Stillwell. In 1853, farm owners, including John Lefferts, Henry and John Ditmas, and Asher Hubbard, created the Flatbush Plank Road Company, whose road ran four miles from Brooklyn to Flatlands, and was macadamized by prisoners from the Kings County penitentiary. From the stockholders' perspective, the road's most vital feature was its toll gate, at which its toll gatherer was statutorily authorized to collect 1 cent per mile for each animal-drawn vehicle and one cent for each additional animal — except from farmers going to and from work on their farm.[10]

Until about 1857, Flatbush, which was "distinguished from the other villages only by its natural beauty, and the larger number of its inhabitants," had been able to preserve "its strictly rural character" despite its proximity to the city of Brooklyn. Symbolically, 1857 was also the year in which the state legislature enacted a statute to prevent horses, cattle, goat, sheep, ass, mule, or swine from running at large in the town of Flatbush. Because Flatbush residents opposed the opening of several avenues from Brooklyn, that city began growing toward its eastern, western, and northern suburbs, but not toward Flatbush to the south: "The long, tedious ride, by stage, over the hill, was a serious barrier to the growth of the city toward Flatbush. This had been, no doubt, in some measure, a benefit to the village; keeping back the tide of immigration which flooded the eastern section of the city, and preserving intact the woodlands which were afterwards purchased by the city for Prospect Park." It was only in 1860 that the Brooklyn City Railroad, aided by state legislative arrangement for opening Flatbush Avenue, extended a track so that the first horse-drawn streetcars could finally run to Flatbush. Significantly, this transit link had to overcome "the most bitter opposition on the part of local owners of farms and old estates, descendants of the early settlers, who justly feared that with these changes the quiet and exclusiveness of their communal life, which they had maintained for centuries . . . would be forever destroyed."[11]

If the advent of the streetcar spelled "the doom of Flatbush as a country place forever," the initiative may have rested with men "of prominence in

Brooklyn and New York circles," who lived in Flatbush and for whom "transit was not always convenient by private conveyance." In particular, the lawyer and judge John A. Lott (1806–1878), and the very wealthy farmer and capitalist John Lefferts (1826–1893) — at the 1870 census he listed no occupation, in 1880 "Gentleman" — were also responsible for establishing the infrastructural underpinnings of Flatbush suburbanization. Lott and Lefferts were linked in the traditional intertwined Dutch manner: the grandmother of Lott's wife, Catharine Lott, was a Lefferts, while Lefferts's mother was Maria Lott. The static quality of the political prominence of these two families — whose founders had settled in Flatbush in 1653 and 1660 — is underscored by the fact that John Lefferts and John Lott Jr. were elected Flatbush town clerk and supervisor, respectively, at the last Flatbush town meeting whose minutes were recorded in Dutch on April 4, 1775, and sheds interesting light on the inadvertently critical remark of Lott's son-in-law, Cornelius Wells, minister of the Flatbush Reformed Protestant Dutch Church, that Flatbush had "no aristocracy except the money power." [12]

Modernizers' authority was further supplemented in 1871 when the state legislature established a Board of Improvement of the Town of Flatbush with the power to open or improve streets with the consent of the owners of the land to be taken or who would be assessed for it. John A. Lott had prepared the statute, which he also induced the legislature to enact in order to prevent "scheming politicians" from "fleec[ing]" property owners. That the legislature in the statute itself named as board members representatives of major old-line Flatbush farm families such as Lott, Lefferts, Martense, Zabriskie, Vanderbilt, and Ditmas suggests that the agricultural powerholders occupied positions that could enable them to help accommodate and shape the changes in land-use patterns identified with suburbanization. [13]

Lott's appointment as president of the board by the other members underscored his pivotal role in the political-economic restructuring of the town. The board's choice of Lott's centrally located Flatbush residence as its sole meeting place for the first four years of its existence until it arranged for the building of a town hall — the $98 shortfall in the public financing of which the members made up for with their own money — reflected the ambience of cozy homogeneity that characterized the ruling class in Flatbush, almost all of whose members, for example, had attended and were trustees of Erasmus Hall Academy. [14] The absence on the board of any representative of the wealthy Manhattan or Brooklyn merchants residing in Flatbush could be interpreted as an indication either that they may have been too occupied with their businesses to attend to local civic matters or that the Dutch farm families retained the political-economic power, despite the much larger annual incomes of some of these mercantile neighbors, to shape the development of Flatbush. In fact, however, several of these businessmen, such as William Matthews (1822–1896), were intensely involved in the town's civic affairs. After having operated his own bindery in Manhattan for a few years, he became the head of the large D. Appleton bindery, moving to Flatbush in 1855. He devoted the greater part of his fortune to his house, and became one of the organizers of the Flatbush Water Works Company, of which he remained a director until his death.[15]

Lott and Lefferts were also the driving forces behind the creation of the Flatbush Telegraph Company in 1872. At the time of the transmission of the first telegraphic message from Flatbush to Brooklyn in 1873, the *Eagle*, noting how much progress had been achieved during the preceding decade, charged that the telegraph had been delayed so long "for reasons that can only be found expressed in the words 'old fogyism,' as ruling in the bosom of the gray haired and obstinate fossils who always stand in the way of material progress." Whereas a decade earlier the trip from Brooklyn to Flatbush was "a tedious ride through the country in some sort of a wagon," by 1873 it was only an hour in horse cars and soon it would be but 15 or 20 minutes "behind a screaming or bell ringing dummy . . . if indeed not behind a full fledged lightning express." In 1875, when a steamcar replaced horsecars on the Coney Island and Brooklyn Railroad running between the Brooklyn city line and Gravesend, the four-mile trip was reduced from 45 to 20 minutes.[16]

STREETS, PARKS, AND SEWERS

In 1869 the New York State legislature enhanced modernizers' capacity to galvanize change by enacting a statute that appointed the supervisors of the towns of Flatbush, Flatlands, Gravesend, New Lots, and New Utrecht to be commissioners to "plan and lay out streets, roads and avenues . . . conforming to the avenues and streets and plan of the city of Brooklyn, as now terminated at the city line, as nearly as may be practicable and judicious." By conferring exclusive power on the commissioners for this layout and prohibiting any street plan not in conformity with the officially prescribed seamlessness with the Brooklyn grid, the state legislature was either codifying what was manifest higher market-use destiny or preordaining that outcome. The inauguration of a town survey made it clear to the *Rural Gazette*, even before the commissioners submitted their report, that Flatbush was in a "transition state from town to city."[17]

The commercial far-sightedness of the commissioners, who recognized that the county was "destined . . . to contain a vast population," is reflected in their rejection of the view that "the lands should be treated as villa sites, with ample grounds between the streets and avenues," and adoption of the plan, in conformity with "the interests of the public," requiring "a regular city system of blocks, which would obviate any future trouble in subdivision." The commissioners demonstrated the seriousness with which they intended to "give the surplus population of New York access to Kings and Queens counties" by calculating that on the 23,336 acres (or 36.304 square miles) of Flatbush, Flatlands, Gravesend, and New Utrecht, assuming blocks 700 by 200 feet, streets 60 feet wide and avenues 80 feet wide, 4,992 blocks would be created. At 56 lots per block and seven residents per lot, the commissioners made provision for "a possible population of 1,956,836, at some future day" — a total in excess of the population that would ever live in those sections of Brooklyn.[18]

The commission itself apparently had no doubts since it touted the town plans as "a broad, comprehensive and uniform system of streets running toward the ocean or harbor, carefully connected with the city streets and avenues, and located without regard to farm lines or individual interests, so as to meet and develop the interest of the dense population destined in time to occupy this area; an area with which no other, within the same distance from New York, can be compared in advantages for suburban life." Indeed, the chief rationale behind the appointment of the commission was that "so many local plans of streets had been proposed, without any uniformity of interest, each owner cutting up his property as it suited him [that] the necessity for organized development was so generally felt."[19]

The commissioners were presumably influenced in their urbanizing policies by the annual report that Frederick Law Olmsted, the architect of Prospect Park, had recently issued to the Brooklyn Park Commission in which he addressed the introduction of a street plan. Olmsted's impact on urban planning in Kings County was profound enough to warrant a brief review.[20]

Urban agriculture had been central to earlier visions of the city. A succession of early nineteenth-century "urbtopians" envisioned the strong urban presence and democratizing influence of agriculture. By midcentury, however, a striking change of emphasis, from greenery that produced food to greenery that served to rest the eyes and refresh the air, could be de-

tected.[21] Not surprisingly, this reorientation of the urban future from production to aesthetics and residential health dominated changes in midcentury urban planning as well. In 1852, Olmsted joined with Calvert Vaux to
compete successfully for the commission to design New York's Central Park,
later forming the nation's leading landscape architecture firm. Olmsted concerned himself with bringing the pleasures and natural beauties of the country into town. His vision was not to bring the farm into the city, let alone to
preserve the farms as cities expanded, but to create parks and boulevards that
straddled residential city life with green, with beauty that imitated nature,
and with healthy space and air that would relieve urban residents, at least
temporarily, from the growing congestion and quickening pace of city life.

Olmsted's work accommodated late nineteenth-century American urbanization in several ways. In the case of rural Kings County, several possible futures presented themselves at midcentury. A village like Flatbush
might have developed into a discrete suburb or a subdivision that retained
the character of the village. Alternatively, Flatbush could have been wholly
integrated into an expanding Brooklyn, linked by a continuing street grid,
centralized planning, urban services and utilities, with newer, more densely
populated structures supplanting the old. In this regard, New Yorkers had
had some experience: as the century had worn on, New York City continually absorbed more northerly sections of Manhattan, eroding their local cultural and agricultural antecedents. Olmsted's Central Park design accommodated that expansion, taming upper Manhattan's wild landscape in
preparation for organized and attractive residential development.

Olmsted's participation in Brooklyn's expansion followed a similar pattern. At the point he was drawn into the discussions on the future of Kings
County, the city of Brooklyn was already planning a street grid that would
traverse and subsume all of the county's still rural, agricultural, and independent villages. Olmsted and Vaux had been hired in 1866 to design and
supervise construction of Prospect Park. Although Olmsted had by then begun to evolve a style of suburban development that retained a strong rural
presence, his ideas for Kings County ran parallel to those for Manhattan.[22]

In an 1868 essay on improving Brooklyn's street plans, Olmsted recommended that the street plan focus more closely on the possibilities offered
by the park. Given the rapid growth of Brooklyn's harbor and its proximity
to New York, Olmsted believed that urban spread into rural Kings County
could not be impeded, only shaped and regulated by street and park designs.
After noting the good port facilities and associated locational advantages for
mercantile and manufacturing purposes that the western end of Long Island

offered along a ten-mile-long shoreline, Olmsted mentioned that behind it lay a stretch of elevated ground, "the higher parts being at an average distance of more than a mile from any point to which merchandise can be brought by water. East of this elevation the ground slopes to the shore . . . of the ocean itself. A shore in the highest degree attractive to those seeking recreation or health, but offering no advantages for shipping, manufacturing or mercantile purposes."[23]

Olmsted seemed prepared to entrust future land-use decisions to the self-interest of the "gardeners and farmers" who occupied the slope, but he warned that suburban development was by no means a foregone conclusion. One or two streets had been laid out some years earlier, "but without intelligent regard to the alleged purpose in view." In the absence of direction, the land was at risk of being "given up in a few years almost exclusively to shanties, stables, breweries, distilleries, and swine-yards." If, however, Olmsted's plan for parks and parkways were adopted instead of a Manhattan-like street grid, then there would be "ample room for an extension of the habitation part of the metropolis upon a plan fully adapted to the most intelligent requirements of modern town life." He praised large parts of Kings County's "back country" as not only "open to sea breezes and . . . in full view of the ocean," but as sheltered by its geography from the total enclosure by commerce that would soon characterize the habitable part of Manhattan: "Thus it seems set apart and guarded by nature as a place for the tranquil habitation of those whom the business of the world requires should reside within convenient access of the waters of New York harbor."[24]

To the extent that the lands occupied by farms and country seats were susceptible to slumlike development, Olmsted was ready with the plan to preempt it. His principal recommendation was to give Prospect Park a more central presence by running boulevards and ribbons of green from the park to the outer reaches of the county, thus making Flatbush and neighboring communities spread along the green axes more attractive for residential development. His designs for Prospect Park's entrances incorporated elaborate street patterns to facilitate traffic flows toward the park.[25]

Olmsted's designs were intrinsically tied to the real-estate market, to what he thought would create not just social or aesthetic value, but actual financial gain: "Upon the manner in which there are good grounds for confidence that the elevated district which has been indicated will be occupied in the future, depends the valuation which can justly and sagaciously be now placed upon it, and upon this valuation mainly depends the financial prosperity of the city of Brooklyn." Accordingly, Olmsted paid no attention to the farmer's connection to the city. His vision of the urban fringe was tied quite narrowly to the interests of the city's affluent and middle classes, and his aim was to enhance their lifestyles by separating residences from places of business and by creating environments for each that would maximize convenience or pleasure. In this vein, Olmsted objected to the placement of a public (botanic) garden in Prospect Park; he argued that access to one side of the park itself would be obstructed, which, in turn, would diminish nearby land values for residential purposes.[26]

Olmsted's disregard for farming was a part of a particular strand of urban design in America, though one that would become increasingly dominant as new forms of transportation rendered the separation of work and home ever more attractive. Yet, the reliance on open space, parks, rural landscaping, wide, curvilinear streets and irregular lots to improve the air and relieve the emotions had some drawbacks on the financial side. Apart from the rather substantial public investments in construction that Olmsted's designs required, his greenery was unproductive — largely nontaxable, in other words — and costly to maintain.[27]

Olmsted's confidence in the self-interest that would impel Kings County farmers to sell off their farms for suburban residential construction may, in retrospect, have been justified. What neither he nor less sophisticated citizens of Kings County took into account was the societal consequences of the complete elimination of agriculture that suburbanization eventually required.

The creation of Prospect Park after the Civil War on what had been farms owned by John Lott, Helen Martense, Samuel Lott, Isaac Cortelyou, and the Vanderbilt family stimulated further residential real-estate activity. The necessity for locating this Brooklyn park in Flatbush and the state legislature's designation of the land as belonging to the city underscored "the probability that Brooklyn would eventually swallow up all the towns of Kings County." Indeed, spurred on by the park, "more advancement or progress, in the way of growth and development," according to the *Rural Gazette*, took place in the four years between 1869 and 1873 than ever before in the history of Flatbush. The newspaper measured that development by the construction of a hundred buildings costing more than half a million dollars, including "many . . . very fine and costly residences" owned by some of the village's richest "merchant princes."[28]

The *Rural Gazette* looked back at Flatbush during those years as a kind of Potemkin village — fabricated by Prospect Park, which had unleashed a speculative wave of investment "the result of which was to place the value of land at such ridiculous [sic] high prices that nobody wanted it especially when they found we had few or none of the improvements possessed in cities, and most other villages." Brooklyn residents doing business in Manhattan bought much of the land near the park. Certain that they would "reap fortunes on the rapid growth of the property, . . . when they found they could not get $2,000 quick, for every $1,000 they had invested, they turned around and cursed Flatbush, and its time-honored land holders." Land, for example, that the Reformed Protestant Dutch Church had sold for $4,000 per acre, was later sold for $2,000, and by 1875 could not have been sold again for even that much. The national depression of the mid-1870s affected no less a landed and moneyed potentate than John Lefferts, who, having sold land at very high prices in the town's most desirable location, by 1875 had to take it back under foreclosure of mortgage. By 1880, the *Rural Gazette* argued that real-estate prices had still not recovered from that speculative bull market, reaching only one-half of their level 10 years earlier.[29]

The real-estate boom could not be sustained in a suburb from which in 1873 the four-and-one-half-mile horsecar to the Fulton Ferry link to Manhattan still lasted an hour, especially when snow often blockaded the track, making it impossible for residents to return home for one or more nights. Such inconvenience may have prompted complaints from "mechanics and others who go at early hours," and may have "militate[d] greatly against the growth of the place," but the old farmers were not yet prepared to encourage an increase in the number of small lot owners who would be drawn to Flatbush by faster transportation. The *Rural Gazette*, perhaps reflecting the ambivalence of Flatbush's heterogeneous strata of "wealthy citizens" — some of whom in 1873 formed a stock company to finance the newspaper — explained their lack of interest in investing in rapid transit from Fulton Ferry to Flatbush on the grounds that "our citizens are most of them well located upon homesteads of their own which they do not wish to sell, and therefore cannot be benefited by the rise of property, which all admit will follow."[30]

Thus although the *North Side Herald* of Huntington, Long Island, praised the *Rural Gazette* in 1873 for its support of rapid transit to New York City "as a means of giving the working classes a breath of pure air, and a chance for cheap and comfortable homes," the propertied interests in the rural sections were not yet advocating development as a code word for proletarianization of their towns. And even the editor of the *Rural Gazette*, H. J. Egleston, who relentlessly promoted suburbanization of Flatbush, when alluding to the lure of "cheap living," meant that "some of our wealthy men [sh]ould erect the class of dwellings desired by the middle class of people, such as would rent for not over $400 a year." The *East New York Sentinel* thought that it had identified an inconsistency in its competitor's editorial standpoints: "With the inflowing tide into Flatbush of population and wealth, which the GAZETTE is doing so much to encourage, the newspaper, like the community, will readily merge into Metropolitan life — but what would become of the 'RURAL?' " But the *Rural Gazette* deemed itself relatively immune to such threats, believing that since it was inevitable that the towns would eventually be "Moving into the City" one way or another, annexation now "on a liberal plan of your own making" was preferable to "forced annexation" on less desirable principles later.[31]

The laying of sewers and the laying out, opening, and constructing of streets constituted the major role played by municipal government in guiding an urbanization process that was almost exclusively market driven.[32] The link between sewers and street openings was clear: since the number of streets was sufficiently great to interfere with natural water courses, failure to build sewers would result in the formation of stagnant pools of water. Apart from health concerns, advocates stressed that sewers would enhance real-estate prices. The *Rural Gazette*, ever attentive to the commercial advantages of modernization, demonstrated how the construction of sewers was closely linked to the preservation of a patrician Flatbush, which otherwise would be proletarianized:

> The time has gone by when men, who have our real good at heart, would hinder the influx of strangers, while the prices at which real estate is valued, and the burden of taxation, are both too great to allow longer the holding of large domains.
>
> If . . . the increase of population is inevitable, why not encourage the influx of *that class* which will add to us materially and socially, which we can only do by affording them the means of comfortable and luxurious living.
>
> . . . Like East New York, we may grow by the construction of cheap cottages and shanties, but if we want "brown stone blocks" and "palatial homes," we must not only have gas, but also water and sewerage.[33]

Ocean Avenue, running five miles from Prospect Park to the Atlantic Ocean, was opened in 1876, followed four years later by the 210-foot-wide Ocean Parkway, which ran a parallel course. Both promoted the development of Gravesend and New Utrecht as well as of Flatbush. Tensions between farm owners and modernizers were particularly sharp in relation to Ocean Parkway — one of the "octopian arms" by which Brooklyn was extending its power over the county towns — which was originally financed by considerable assessments on each parcel of land within the assessment district, which the Brooklyn park commissioners deemed benefited by the parkway. But as Flatbush town supervisor Peter Williamson observed in 1882, in urging that the county should pay for the parkway's construction since it was laid out in the interest of the city of Brooklyn: "No farmers wanted a highway 260 feet wide. They laid out narrow roads to save their land for agricultural purposes." To add insult to injury: "The farmer must pay for it but must not use it, for the smell of the vegetables or manure they cart would offend the nostrils of the Brooklyn aristocracy." Even after the state legislature amended the Ocean Parkway statute to impose two-thirds of the cost of improvement on all Kings County property taxpayers, Flatbush, Gravesend, and New Utrecht farmers remained outraged that the park commissioners denied them permission to use the parkway boulevard to drive their loaded market wagons on the way to New York.[34]

Street openings, to be sure, would "undoubtedly bring into the market and enhance the value of property which now cannot be sold at any price." By the height of the boom in 1873, real-estate prices had risen considerably, enabling Flatbush to attain to a certain pretentiousness: "Lots in the best portion of this place, 25 × 150, are held firmly at $3,000 in some instances which could have been bought a few years ago for $600." But the long depression that began later that year — and that continued to deter those who had made speculative purchases from improving their real estate as late as 1877 — also prompted some Flatbushers, who until then, according to the *Rural Gazette*, had been so sedentary and uninterested in selling that they "cannot be benefitted even if the [Prospect] park did enhance the value of their property," to "become anxious to realize." Typical of the "great bargains" that landowners offered were plats containing eight city lots "(which have been for a long time held at $4000) . . . now offered at $3000." One of the lures to potential buyers, in addition to lower prices, was the knowledge of "how very delightful it is to have . . . fresh vegetables at their command." When, as Jere Johnson Jr.'s auction notice in the *Rural Gazette*, put it, "the great panic of 1873" forced Robert Turner, a New York banker who would soon project a steam railroad to Coney Island, to sell off 1,000 Ocean Parkway lots formerly belonging to the Flatbush Dutch Church, the sale was trumpeted as the "most extraordinary chance for speculative investment that has ever been offered since the foundation of Brooklyn in 1642." That the lowest price for lots 20 by 125 feet was $525 — the equivalent of more than $9,000 per acre — suggests that, despite the depression and the recent defeat of annexation, many buyers must have speculated that "[n]o finer location exists for first class residences." [35]

RAILROADS

The superintendent of the street survey, Samuel McElroy, reporting on the commission's work in 1875, commented on the elements of the contradictory conceptions of land use without expressly concluding that agriculture and housing were mutually exclusive and thus unable to coexist. McElroy noted both that the fertility of Kings County's soil was "a proverb" and that "with broad and easy slopes delivering towards the bays on the south and east, admirably adapted to street and house construction; with an abundant supply of the purest and softest water; with fine roads, attractive boating, bathing, fishing and hunting; with a population intelligent, industrious, frugal, long associated with the land, and generally affluent; in the whole radius of forty miles [from New York City] . . . , this area, which represents about 15⅓ per cent in size, cannot be surpassed in advantages for suburban residence." In explaining why nevertheless from 1850 to 1870 New York's other suburbs had "accumulated a population of not less than 870,000, which should give this section 133,000 increase," whereas in fact rural Kings County's "41¾ square miles of unexceptional territory" recorded an increase of only 16,300, McElroy found "a reason, and a very simple one. Through this whole area there is no direct steam railway communication with New York; no way in which, with regularity, frequency, comfort and speed, a business man can be carried to and from the city, as he can be carried in any other direction; and in consequence of this an acre of building lots in the rocks or swamps or Harlem, six or seven miles from the Battery, is worth twenty-five times as much to-day as an acre in Kings County no further away!" McElroy noted, however, that: "Operators from Brooklyn or New York have here or there purchased farms for investment, and united with the farmers in urging local improvements." [36]

Ironically, in 1876, the New York, Bay Ridge, and Jamaica Railroad, of which McElroy was the chief engineer, included much of this language verbatim in its prospectus. How the railroad company intended to preserve such attractions as hunting and proverbially fertile soil while achieving its purpose of developing rural Kings County as a suburban residence by "di-vert[ing] to Long Island its legitimate proportion of the annual exodus from New York," it did not specify. But the mere fact that its owners expected the public to find the combination plausible suggests that neither regarded the extirpation of agriculture as inevitable.[37]

The prospect of railroad links between Brooklyn and the rural towns — the land for which appeared so valuable to the railway owners that they were willing to buy it from farmers at extraordinarily high prices — made it clear to boosters and detractors of the movement to consolidate with Brooklyn that the ridge of hills marking off the southern boundary of the city was only "an imaginary not a real barrier to the movement of population." The inaccessibility of the rural towns by steam railroads was, in the view of the *Eagle*, the chief impediment to Brooklyn's extension to the Atlantic Ocean and the answer to the vexatious questions as to the staying power of atavis-tic Dutch vegetable farms in the face of spreading modernity:

> Why is it that that portion of the County of Kings known as the county towns, has so long remained stationary, and, with the exception of the Town of New Lots, almost exclusively an agricultural district? Why is it that the city proper, with much the smaller ... territory contains a popu-lation of nearly half a million against $25,000 [sic] in the larger territo-rial divisions of the county? Why is it that cities as remote from the busi-ness centre of New York as Newark, Patterson, Elizabeth, etc., with populations ranging from 50,000 to 125,000, have grown up duplicat-ing their population every ten years, while the county towns of Kings County, with natural advantages greatly superior to the cities named, re-main stationary?[38]

Significantly for the perceived future of the rural sections, the *Eagle* em-phasized the industrial needs that metropolitan area railroads also had to serve: "It is the case with Brooklyn factories and nearly all manufacturing establishments in cities and suburbs tributary to New York, that their sales-rooms and warehouses are in that city. What manufacturers want is rapid and cheap communication between the salesroom and the factory."[39]

In the aftermath of the defeat of consolidation in 1873, the *Rural Gazette* explained that a railroad that enabled inhabitants of the rural towns both to reach the ferry to New York in 30 minutes and to travel from one town to the other without having to take a circuitous trip to Brooklyn would con-tribute more to increasing the county's population than any annexation plan. For years the *Rural Gazette* pleaded in vain for the construction of a steam railroad to connect Flatbush to Brooklyn and the ferries to New York. The chief obstacle was the "supreme selfishness of every property owner in Brooklyn" in refusing "to have a steam railroad near [their] property, be it on the surface or elevated." Ironically, when steam finally came, it headed in the opposite direction — from Flatbush south to Coney Island. In general, the development of steam railroads in Kings County was driven by entrepreneurs' aim of promoting the beach as a resort, initially for the affluent, and then for the masses from Manhattan and Brooklyn. The first steam railroad in the rural county was organized by Charles Gunther, the mayor of New York City from 1864 to 1866. Foreseeing the possibilities of Coney Island, then a relatively inaccessible site, Gunther organized the Brooklyn, Bath and Coney Island Railroad, which began near Greenwood Cemetery and was opened in 1864. This steam dummy road was without competition for a decade, but was eventually eclipsed because Gunther had been forced to build a "very roundabout" route to avoid landowners' opposition: "The slow going old Dutch farmers of New Utrecht and Gravesend fought him at every step." In 1865 a second steam railway, the Brooklyn and Rockaway Beach Railroad, running from East New York in New Lots to Canarsie in Flatlands, opened in order to make a connection with a steam ferry to the beach resort across Jamaica Bay.[40]

The first steam railroad through Flatbush was also a by-product of the transportation of the urban masses to the beach. In celebrating the advent of the steam railroad in Flatbush in June 1875, as the Prospect Park and Coney Island Railroad Company, organized by Andrew N. Culver, made the fastest trip ever between Greenwood Cemetery and Coney Island, the *Rural Gazette* also "congratulate[d] the Gravesenders that they will now be able to consider themselves as somebody and not as a peculiar people five miles from anywhere, bound to lock their doors at sundown and go to bed because they cannot reach civilization and return on the same day." Culver's steam railroad reinforced the marketability of residential real estate between the end points of the line by introducing hourly service during the off-season. The next year, after Gravesenders complained that the lack of spark-arresters had kindled fires putting them "constantly in peril of being burned out," the *Rural Gazette* admonished them not to doubt that "the few who are now annoyed . . . by the noise of trains shall . . . be a thousand fold profited by the growth of" Gravesend. The need for the rapid and cheap transit that would make it possible for a large population to live south of Prospect Park was so crucial to the *Rural Gazette* that five years later it rejected Brooklyn's renewed effort at annexation as a transparent attempt to force others to share its debt burden until the city was prepared to provide that railroad link.[41]

The next steam railroad through Flatbush also served as a link to Coney Island. The Brooklyn, Flatbush, and Coney Island Railway — itself the result of the consolidation of the Coney Island and East River Railroad, organized in 1876, and the Flatbush, Coney Island, Park and Concourse Railroad, organized in 1877 — was opened on July 1, 1878. The first train was pulled by a locomotive named for John A. Lott, who shortly before had resigned as the company's president as a result of infirmities. The Brooklyn, Flatbush, and Coney Island Railroad, which carried 602,662 passengers in its first, abbreviated, season was very profitable, recording profits of $59,000 on receipts of $135,000.[42]

This steam railroad, which was the most intimately connected with Flatbush territorially and in terms of management and ownership, provoked a sharp dispute within the town's political-economic elite over the route and the comparative injury that it would inflict on individual landowners. The construction of this below-street-level line, with its deep excavations, tree cutting, barn removal, and cutting away of the woods near the Flatlands town line, transformed the appearance of the section between Ocean Avenue and Flatbush Road. To be sure, the *Rural Gazette* counseled that: "Someone must be hurt, of course, but sensible men cannot fail to see that we must have *steam, steam, steam*." However, several landowners, most prominently William Matthews, the wealthy operator of the large D. Appleton bookbindery in Williamsburg, objected to the rail line's running along Ocean Avenue literally in their backyard. Matthews initiated judicial proceedings to shift the route to run along the town's main thoroughfare, Flatbush Avenue, instead. John A. Lott, president of the railroad and a resident of Flatbush Avenue, unsurprisingly represented the other property owners along that street in resisting that shift. In addition to his personal convenience, Lott preferred the other route because it would make the road "the shortest, quickest and best paying line from Brooklyn to Coney Island." Once the construction was underway, Lott's dual role as capitalist manager and landowner was even made the basis for praise: when he "liberally exchang[ed] land from which the timber had been cut for some on which it had not been cleared" in order to make way for track, the *Rural Gazette* observed that "[t]his is one of the advantages the public gain by having such a man as President of the road."[43]

FIGURE 13. *Flatbush Avenue, 1880. From John J. Snyder,* Tales of Old Flatbush *89.*

Three months after this line was opened, the *Real Estate Record* observed that:

> Charts of Brooklyn are already prepared and offered for sale which show the plotting of the whole region extending from the present corporate limits of Brooklyn down to and including the extremity of Coney Island. The many railroads which are now centering at Coney Island must supply most acceptable rapid transit for this intervening section. If these railroads are eventually continued to the ferries, or to the bridge, they must have the effect of attracting a large population to settlements on dry and wholesome lands between Coney Island and Brooklyn.[44]

Remarkably, however, several railroad companies did not immediately perceive the profitability of year-round train service to the section intervening between Coney Island and Prospect Park. They failed to take up the *Rural Gazette's* suggestion that "these wealthy corporations should take up sections of land . . . and build a number of neat cottages with garden plats about them, and lease them for reasonable prices, included in which should be the privilege of riding on the cars to town and back each day." Thus Flatbushers had to importune John Lefferts to intercede with the Brooklyn, Flatbush, and Coney Island Railroad to persuade his co-directors that it was in the company's own financial interest to base its business not on three months of beach traffic, but year-round local travel.[45]

Not only were the county towns "gridironed" with railroads, but by 1878

Flatbush, in particular, as the county's geographical center and "The Great Railroad Hub!" had "more steam railroad trains daily passing through it than almost any other town in the country and possibly more than any large city but Boston or Chicago." Figure 14 displays the railroad routes in 1879. The impact that the advent of steam railroads must have had on the traditional consciousness of the Dutch farmers can be gauged by the sudden explosion in the volume of traffic: already by the summer of 1878, on four railroads alone, 250 trains daily were transporting passengers to and from Coney Island. Suddenly experiencing the sight, sound, and smell of the world's most powerful machines racing through what until recently had been "a great stretch of unbroken farmland and pasture" extending from Flatbush Avenue to Coney Island Plank Road at 40 miles an hour must have given the farmers pause about the continued compatibility of their way of life with this inrush of urbanism. By the summer of 1882, no fewer than six steam railroads crossed the rural towns in various directions with trains every 15 minutes. Yet even following the opening of the Brooklyn Bridge in 1883, *Appleton's Dictionary of New York* was still calling Flatbush "a post-village."[46]

The steam railroad companies also directly promoted a significant increase in land prices in the process of buying up land needed for building the road and facilities. In 1877, the Brooklyn, Flatbush, and Coney Island Railroad paid $35,000 for a 106- by 513-foot strip of the Willink homestead for its depot. This price was equivalent to $28,000 per acre. Much more mundane property lying between Ocean Avenue and Flatbush Avenue was priced at $750 for lots 25 feet by 60 feet, which on a per acre basis worked out to $21,780.[47]

Arguably the only steam railroad in the 1870s that was not originally projected to transport passengers to Coney Island was the New York and Hempstead, which was to run from Bay Ridge to Queens and Suffolk. At its inception in 1870, it was designed to lower freight costs by creating a waterfront terminal in Bay Ridge, across the Bay from New Jersey terminals, in order to trans-ship freight by barge without breaking bulk, and on to Long Island. After some initial construction, the economic panic of 1873 brought work to a halt. Abraham Wakeman, a major investor in the defunct line, recreated it as the New York, Bay Ridge, and Jamaica Railroad, to run only as far as Queens. Significantly, it also added a passenger branch to Coney Island, which opened in 1876.[48]

In reporting on efforts begun in 1874 to rescue the failed New York and Hempstead, the *Rural Gazette* declared that it would "greatly benefit . . . the

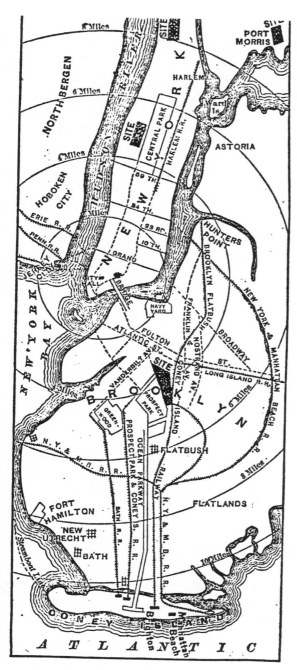

FIGURE 14. *Steam railroad lines in Kings County, 1879.*
From the New York Daily Tribune, *May 17, 1879.*

interests of property" in Flatbush and Flatlands by "facilitating the increase of population from the surplus of New York." Members of the modernizing landed elite such as John A. Lott manifested their agreement by donating right of way to the railroad as did many farmers in New Utrecht, Flatbush, and Flatlands. Indeed, in New Lots, such old-line Dutch farmers as the Rapaljeas, Wyckoffs, and Vansinderns even subscribed to stock in the railroad. The *Rural Gazette* counseled farmers that it was absurd to interfere with the railroad by demanding large sums for rights of way because within ten years the value of their land would quadruple.[49]

When Austin Corbin, a New York banker and future owner of the Long Island Railroad, bought the Bay Ridge line from Wakeman in 1876 and reorganized it as the New York and Manhattan Beach Railway Company, he changed its whole purpose: "Instead of running east to west as a commercial carrier with freight trans-shipment as the principal income, it was now to become largely a north-south road to serve purely as an adjunct to a beach resort hotel; passengers would form the overwhelming bulk of the travel and service would be seasonal only."[50]

That contemporaries did not perceive the focus on suburbanization as irreconcilable with the continued vitality of market gardening is underscored by the fact that farmers' needs were a significant factor in the construction of transportation facilities undertaken by private entrepreneurs. One of the selling points of the Brooklyn Bridge was its facilitation of transporting farmers' produce to New York. In 1872, the *Rural Gazette* advanced as one compelling reason for the construction of a railroad from Canarsie "through our rich plain" of Flatbush to Brooklyn that "our farmers might save much of their long night-work in going over to New York to market, by having a quick light draft steamer to take their produce from our own wharfs, directly around to the city, leaving say at 7 or 8 p.m. . . . . [O]nce begun no money would hire them to go back to the present system of market work." Two years later, the *Rural Gazette*, uncertain as to "whether capitalists and the people" would agree, suggested that a steam railroad be built to run from New Utrecht through Flatbush to a terminal at Wallabout, which had long been advocated as (and a decade later would become) a large market for farmers' produce. Nor did the promoters of the Bay Ridge Steam Railroad in 1875 forget to add that: "For the purposes of taking farm produce to Washington Market, there will be the most complete facilities, at lower rates than our farmers can go with their own teams, and in one-half the time." In 1878, farmers in Flatlands experimented with freighting manure on that railroad. The Prospect Park and Coney Island Railroad also offered to dispose of farmers' manure. When the New York and Manhattan Beach Railway sought permission from the Flatbush highway commissioners to run the Kings County Central Railroad from Prospect Park down Canarsie Lane to the Kings County institutional buildings, it supported its request with the rationale that the road would "be a great convenience to the farmers of Flatbush, Flatlands and Gravesend, in reaching Brooklyn, and will help to build up the section of country through which it passes."[51]

Finally, the environmental glories of market gardening even played a major part in projecting Flatbush's aspirations to independence, which attained their most palpable form in its unsuccessful effort in 1879 to become the site of the 1883 World's Fair. Farmland formed one of the chief attractions as boosters emphasized that "there spreads out before one's vision a broad expanse of living green — the garden farms of Long Island — fringed by the blue waters of the Atlantic."[52]

POLICE

Three weeks before the inauguration of service on the Brooklyn, Flatbush, and Coney Island Railroad in 1878, the New York State legislature passed "An Act for the preservation of the public peace, the protection of private property, and the maintenance of law and good order in the town of Flatbush," which required the town to appoint a board of police commissioners with the power to employ as many as ten policemen and required the Kings County board of supervisors to levy up to $5,000 annually on the town's assessed taxable real and personal estate to pay for the expenses. Burglaries throughout rural Kings County, especially repeated and often violent entries into the houses of some of the town's richest residents, created the perception that the local constables had been "utterly unable to protect the property of the residents of the village against the depredations of thieves who made frequent incursions into the village at night." Moreover, despite its constant flow of boosterist puffery extolling the virtues of Flatbush, the *Rural Gazette* had to concede that urban ills had already infiltrated the rural idyll. To attract new residents to a town that was running the risk of uniting the worst rather than the best of city and country, "we must make living here both safe and pleasant — which, in some parts of our town, it certainly is not. . . . Our whole Northern border is overrun by pigs, goats and cattle. Our streets are taken possession of, by day, by rapacious milk-producers to the detriment of life and limb, and at night by street-walkers and young roughs from the neighboring city. Houses of ill repute flourish in our very midst, without the fear of molestation, and ball-players and gin-mills make our Sabbaths a disgrace to modern civilization."[53]

Not surprisingly, John Lefferts and John Z. Lott, John A. Lott's son, stood behind the replacement of private watchmen with a public force and immediately served on the Police Board. Lefferts had had to pay his own watchman in any event to police his cornfields and arrest inebriated Irish interlopers. The *Rural Gazette* left no doubt that it was a "genuine Taxpayers Board": "It is superfluous to speak of Mr. Lefferts. He is, by far, the largest taxpayer in the town." John Z. Lott "represents a very large interest in the town." It was, indeed, fortunate for advocates of a police force that the town's chief taxpayer (who was also a trustee of the town fire department) was its preeminent modernizer, because many landowners, especially those residing in the town's southern portion farther removed from the Brooklyn city line, had opposed the bill on the ground that "farming lands are already over-burdened with taxes." The *Rural Gazette* criticized such opponents of the police bill, especially Henry S. Ditmas, "who represents a very large landed interest," for their short-sightedness. Although farmland, "at least at present," could not bear a large tax increase, the police force would cost only $1.25 for every $1,000 of assessed valuation. If the Ditmases and other more rural farm owners "would not give that amount for police protection," they might eventually find their property devalued by the cessation in the inflow of potential and especially wealthier residents, who alone could bid up real-estate prices. Instead, antimodernizers were apparently preoccupied with the rise in taxation: the total tax levied in Flatbush had increased from little more than $1,000 in 1837 to $75,000 by 1875.[54]

GAS AND WATER

The legislature promoted urbanization in 1864 by permitting Brooklyn gas companies to lay gas pipes in Flatbush and authorizing the Flatbush highway commissioners to contract with companies to supply gas for street lighting as well as to procure the requisite lamps and posts. Lott and Lefferts then organized the Flatbush Gas Company, of which they were president and treasurer, respectively. The motivation for introducing gas illumination was the "dense foliage" in Flatbush, which "rendered locomotion, upon moonless nights, not only difficult, but to a greater or less degree dangerous." These dangers were emphasized in the *Rural Gazette*, which used the occasions of street muggings to urge the necessity of gas lamps. Gas lighting enhanced the habitability of Flatbush, which was as close to the ferries to

Manhattan as were certain parts of the city of Brooklyn while, boosters claimed, offering refuge from "city noise and bustle as though fifty miles away." Moreover, the gas operations paid the company's owners "a fair profit even from the start." John Lefferts achieved that outcome by his hard bargaining with the highway commissioners over the price the town would pay; on at least one occasion, a stalemate led to the lights' being turned off for two nights in Flatbush.[55]

One of the improvements that the superintendent of the Kings County street survey, Samuel McElroy, had in mind was a water system. The supply of water may have been abundant, but until 1881 in Flatbush, "the methods of obtaining water for domestic and other purposes were as primitive as those that prevail in any little Western frontier town." Cisterns had been used to store rainwater for washing and cleaning as well as for the fire engine. Water for drinking and cooking came from wells, old-fashioned log pumps, or buckets, the installation of the former two often being shared by neighbors. Those who could not afford such private systems, used public pumps located throughout Flatbush. In 1881, a group of "capitalists and some of our largest landowners," led by John Lefferts — who after John A. Lott's death was "considered the leading man of our town" — John Z. Lott, and William Matthews, organized the private for-profit Flatbush Water Works Company, which pumped water through nine miles of pipes from artesian wells in part located in Flatlands. That year it sought permission to supply the residents of Flatbush with "pure and wholesome water," and entered into an agreement with the town of Flatbush to supply water for fire and household purposes. In 1885, the waterworks and the town entered into a 10-year agreement that authorized the company, in addition to laying a specified number of hydrants, to supply private consumers with water at agreed-upon rates.[56]

This new system vastly simplified the lives of Flatbush farmers — and especially of farmers' wives, for whom the lack of running water was a major source of "hours of back breaking drudgery" — but the leading old-line Dutch farm families-turned-modernizers such as Lott and Lefferts understood that provision of a modern water supply system, not least as the essential component of an urban fire-fighting organization, would sweep away a crucial obstacle to suburbanization. Indeed, their explicit purpose in undertaking this investment was to "benefit and render salable" the "large tracts of land" that they personally owned in Flatbush. Lefferts, the vice president of the waterworks, "owns miles of property in the town which he wants to develop." The *Rural Gazette* was gratified to report that the inception of work immediately "attracted the attention of capitalists" and sparked a real-estate boon, but it uncharacteristically warned of the potential for "extortion" and "monopoly" inherent in private ownership of such a necessity of life, and urged the town to take over the franchise.[57]

GROWTH

By the early 1880s, as the Brooklyn Bridge neared completion, the coming streams of commercial prosperity had become a foregone conclusion for modernizing boosters in Flatbush. Chief among them was the *Rural Gazette*, which did not expressly welcome or lament the demise of farming, but in an 1882 editorial aptly titled, "Growth," celebrated the unprecedented growth of the town's population and housing stock during the preceding ten years. The 50 percent increase in dwellings included some "costing even as high as $40,000." The editorial recognized that the "large increase of population which is continually coming among us from the neighboring metropolis . . . must continue to flow hitherward for many years to come. For as the great cities are continually growing and stretching out their borders, we must expect to see Brooklyn grasp our town and absorb it, just as every other town bordering on a great city is being absorbed in the insatiable maw of coming population. This result is inevitable."[58]

Despite the explicit analogy that the *Gazette* drew between the inevitability of New York's surpassing London and America's outstripping Britain, the period was sufficiently transitional that the newspaper could still take Kings County's agricultural vitality for granted. Thus while boasting in one editorial of the 25 first-class dwellings (costing at least $4,000) that had been built during the previous ten years on the John Lott farm, in the adjoining column it praised George B. Forrester, the inventor of the first complete chemical manures "used in our county towns," which did "wonders for the farmer." Until Forrester demonstrated that potatoes excelling those of former years could be raised on land treated exclusively with his chemicals seven years consecutively, it had been "a new idea to our farmers that chemicals could take the place of stable manure." Even though his office was located in lower Manhattan — his factory was in Brooklyn — farmers sought personal advice from Forrester, who advertised in the *Gazette* that his chemicals produced the "largest yield and best quality of potatoes, cabbage, onions." One advertisement in the newspaper even asserted that fertilizer had so far replaced manure that the custom of hauling it from the city had died out.[59]

FIGURE 15. *Flatbush farms from the steeple of the Reformed Protestant Dutch Church of Flatbush, looking east on Church Avenue from Ocean Avenue, ca. 1877–79. Courtesy of the Brooklyn Public Library, Brainerd Collection, No. 387.*

In 1882, in advance of the opening of the Brooklyn Bridge, which, when linked to a system of rapid transit, gave residents of interior Brooklyn as easy access to lower Manhattan as that of New Yorkers above 59th Street, the *Real Estate Record* knew that there "ought . . . to be money in well-located Brooklyn real estate." Since magnification of real-estate prices had long been one of the driving forces behind construction of the bridge, the *Record*'s insistence was scarcely surprising. In a jaundiced appreciation of the Brooklyn Bridge immediately after it opened, however, the *Railroad Gazette* warned that unless passengers were able to travel uninterruptedly by rapid transit from their homes in Brooklyn to Manhattan, the bridge would offer little advantage over ferries; but once such a link were established, "Brooklyn would truly be made a part of New York" and rents for houses near Prospect Park would double. In fact, annexation in the mid-1890s of the Kings County towns to Brooklyn followed in the wake of the development of a rapid transit system.[60]

In 1883, shortly after the Brooklyn Bridge opened, the *Rural Gazette* insistently proclaimed "The Real Estate Boom in Flatbush." Proudly announcing that: "Never before in the history of our town has there been a healthier tone regarding property," the paper declared that "the attention of a very large portion of dealers and purchasers in the great cities have [sic] been called to the fact that Flatbush has finally waked up from her slumbers. . . . If we can secure Rapid Transit, there can be no doubt of our population and wealth quadrupling in the next five years." The next year — marked by the inauguration of night-car service to Flatbush by the Brooklyn City Railroad — one of the authors of Stiles's history of Kings County finally made the prognosis explicit: the opening of streets in the wake of the commission's work and to "meet the pressing demand for building-lots" would "continue until all our farming-land is turned into building-lots, and we become a constituent part of what is destined to be the largest city in the world."[61]

The self-fulfilling glosses issued by McElroy and other inevitabilists proved correct not only for Flatbush. In the early to mid-1880s, market gardening in New Utrecht furnished "the best vegetables for the New York market of to-day" that were also "of far more value than any of the other towns of Kings County." At the end of the decade, just five years "before its annexation, New Utrecht had been little more than a farming town. But the arrival of the Second Avenue Trolley quickly revolutionized the neighborhood. Thousands of houses were constructed; streets were opened up; and the real-estate developers descended on the unsuspecting community." By the end of the 1890s, "Bay Ridge and Fort Hamilton ha[d] practically lost their rural flavor and . . . become thickly settled districts." Residential development and extension of the transportation systems reinforced each other as they both served to oust agriculture from its once dominant position.[62]

If in Flatbush, too, the trolley "marked the end of an era," "the destruction of its social life followed the same pattern as in New Utrecht, but the pace was more leisurely." The relatively prolonged transformation in Flatbush was a function of its longer developmental prehistory, but New Utrecht's course was not unique. Prior to its annexation to Brooklyn in 1886, Brownsville, too "had been a pastoral suburb given over to green fields, cow stables and barnyards." At midcentury it had been "purely a farmer's land."[63]

Growth in Gravesend also had to await rapid transportation and the dividing up of farmland into building lots. Prior to 1875, Coney Island had, from a commercial perspective, been "little more than a barren waste of sand." But the building of a steam railroad opened Coney Island to the masses and investors. If prior to 1875 the only land route from Brooklyn to Coney Island was unmacadamized, "wretchedly" maintained, and "fleeced" travelers by means of two tollgates, by 1879 eight steam railroads, nine steam-boat lines, and one streetcar transported as many as 150,000 visitors daily. The sale in 1877 of a 50-acre farm at public auction accelerated the dissolution. But more generally, the proliferation of horse racing (for example, at the Coney Island Jockey Club) and the development of Coney Island as a resort and amusement park were fostered by the advent of the trolley later in the century. Soon "the land-boomers got an eye on Gravesend and began to menace its rural life. . . . Old farms were abandoned to the builders . . . and the closer and more accessible an old farm was to the water front the more quickly was it staked out."[64]

In 1878 the *Rural Gazette* surmised that the run-up in the prices of Gravesend's Common lands "has no parallel unless it be in the mining regions of California." The next year, when "[a]lmost fabulous sums ha[d] already been spent in improvements" on Coney Island, the paper, which in 1880 signaled the growing commercial importance of the ocean beach by adding "Brighton" to its own name, observed that Gravesend "has been or is likely to become as much of a Utopia as was California in the palmy days of 1848–9." This new Atlantic bonanza was soon "attracting the attention of every species of speculator from the three card monte to the millionaire Presidents of Railroad corporations." The sky's-the-limit atmosphere prevailing in Gravesend was reflected in the *Rural Gazette*'s rhetorical question, on hearing that farmer John Voorhees had sold eight acres of meadowland at $1,000 per acre to Austin Corbin, the head of the Manhattan Beach Railroad: "Captain, why did you not ask two thousand dollars an acre?"[65]

7. MODERNIZERS THWARTED: THE GREAT ANNEXATION DEBATE OF 1873

"Will you walk into my limits?" said the city to the town,
"Tis the finest little city that can anywhere be found," . . .
"Oh no, no," said the country town, "to ask me would be vain,
For who goes into your limits can ne'er come out again." . . .
"Come hither, hither, pretty town, with your broad and gorgeous fields,
Your lands are rich and fertile, from every debt you're free,
And as for taxes and assessments they never trouble thee."
— Flatlands, "Brooklyn and the Country Town,"
    Kings County Rural Gazette, January 25, 1873

In 1873 a historically crucial debate took place around the campaign to annex all the rural towns to Brooklyn, by then the third most populous city in
the United States and intent on the territorial aggrandizement that would
make possible even greater growth. The resistance, led by old-line Dutch
farmers and overwhelmingly supported by other rural residents, sparked
sustained public controversy that shed considerably more light on the tensions and conflicts between farmers and (sub)urban modernizers as well as
among farmers over the future of market gardening than the successful annexation campaign two decades later. Farmers' ability to obstruct, at least
for a decade or two, plans to drive agriculture away from the city rested
on two strategies — some farmers being ideologically committed more to
one than the other — during the interim: to engage in profitable vegetable
production and to wait until demand for suburban housing space boosted
land prices to the point at which no cabbage crop could be more lucrative

than the coupon-clipping made possible by a mass sell-off of the farms. The difference between the 1870s and the 1890s lay in the fact that by 1893–94 developments had overtaken debate: regardless of whether the towns underwent formal administrative consolidation with Brooklyn, defenders of town autonomy no longer based their arguments on the long-term future of agriculture.

Despite the inevitabilists' propaganda, abandonment of the autonomy of rural Kings County was not unilinear. And although farm owners in Flatbush, a town that was more commercially developed and interlinked with the city of Brooklyn than Flatlands, Gravesend, or New Utrecht, more readily perceived the financial advantages of annexation in the short term, even a majority of them resisted the merger until the 1890s. The many-sided public debate on annexation in 1873, when inevitabilism had not yet become hegemonic, affords deep insights into the relationship between farming and general socioeconomic and political development.

The state legislature's creation in 1873 of a board of commissioners to devise a plan to consolidate the city of Brooklyn and the five towns of Kings County suggests that the wave of the market future was present to the governmental mind. But the ingathering of the rural parts of Kings County into the city of Brooklyn began much earlier. The pull of the largest and fastest growing manufacturing and mercantile area of Long Island on towns contiguous to it had been powerful for many years. As recently as 1854 it had resulted in annexing Williamsburgh and Bushwick.[1]

More importantly, discussion, reinforced by inauguration of work on the Brooklyn Bridge, had already turned to merging Brooklyn and New York. "It is 'manifest destiny,'" wrote one reader to the *Brooklyn Daily Eagle* in January of 1873, "that New York and Brooklyn must . . . become united as one great city. . . . The question will be . . . shall New York annex Brooklyn, or Brooklyn annex New York?" The reader, "H.," offered Brooklyn and "its extensive suburbs" as affording "ample space to accommodate all of New York's overcrowded population, who may desire to become possessed of homes in one of the most delightful and desirable localities to be found." H. believed that while New York, Long Island, and Westchester had procrastinated, New Jersey had busily built up railroads, "giving to the penned up denizens of New York the most liberal facilities for reaching her rural districts." Consequently, thousands of New Yorkers, investing millions of dollars, had "converted her miserably impoverished wilds into blooming parks, groves and elegant villas." H. correctly predicted that if Brooklyn built railroads to the various towns, "capital will flow in upon us so rapidly as to advance real estate fully one hundred per cent, on its present value and . . . ere long the beautiful hills, valleys and plains of Long Island will swarm with homes of thousands of New Yorkers."[2]

Others agreed that of the quarter-million people who had left New York City for Jersey City and other outlying districts, half might have gone to and enriched Kings County if only rapid transit had been introduced. An index of the impoverishment that had instead descended on the Kings County towns was comparative land prices: an acre of land within five miles of the center of Brooklyn was cheaper than a lot within many miles of Jersey City. In addition, in 1869 New Jersey exempted, in counties across the Hudson River from Manhattan, all mortgages from taxation, thus offering "a strong inducement to the inhabitants of . . . New York . . . to change their residences and become citizens of New Jersey."[3]

Even the more modest boosters of a Brooklyn encompassing all of Kings County gloried in the prospect that it would be, "territorially at least, the largest city on the American Continent," its 72 square miles being three times greater than New York. In this spirit, the Brooklyn Reform Committee, later known as the Committee of One Hundred, a body committed to municipal reform, at the end of 1872, prepared a bill annexing the county towns, which the Brooklyn authorities were reportedly prepared to support in the state legislature.[4]

Others, however, were just as certain that, as the Gravesend town supervisor put it, "creating a city out of a farming district" would injure many.[5] A reader of the *Rural Gazette*, argued:

> With the exception of a small area within the town of New Lots, and possibly a very small section of Flatbush, the whole territory . . . is purely agricultural; it consists entirely of farms cultivated for market produce, with a few country stores, blacksmith and wheelwright shops, auxiliar to and dependent upon the farming interests. There is not a territory anywhere of the same extent more purely agricultural, or which has less need of a city government.[6]

That the agrarian landlords of the commercially more highly developed town of Flatbush might have forged a different position on the advantages of annexation than the boers of Flatlands becomes plausible when it is realized that in the early 1870s the latter was "almost entirely an agricultural district" of 9,000 acres of good farmland on which owner-farmers produced vegetables for New York markets:

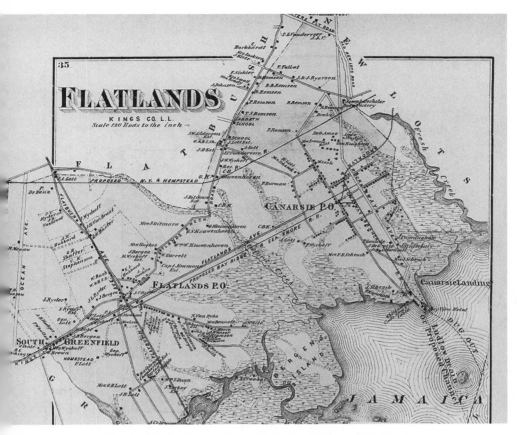

FIGURE 16. *Town of Flatlands, 1870. From Catherine Nelson and E. Theodore Nelson, "The Village of Flatlands As It Was in the Year 1870."*

The annexation question is not only new but startling to many of them. Their situation . . . is so remote and secluded that but few of the exciting events of the period disturb their serenity. Their [*sic*] is neither stage nor car line that penetrates most of this township, and a stranger that is set down on the highway in its central part, might easily imagine himself to be in one of the most obscure and old fashioned of far New England hamlets. On every side, as far as the eye can reach, is a broad expanse of well fenced, and well cultivated fertile flatlands.[7]

Flatlands' predominantly rural character is obvious from figure 16, which depicts its virtually uninhabited center situated between the small villages of Flatlands and Canarsie.

City government, in the words of Edgar Bergen, the 22-year-old lawyer son of Jeremiah Bergen, one of Flatlands' biggest potato farmers, was inappropriate to Flatlands, which had "four acres of land for every inhabitant, not a single block of houses nor any two houses adjoining." At the time of the next annexation struggle, twenty years later, the Brooklyn Corporation Counsel could still call Flatlands "one petty town . . . being smallest in assessed valuation and population." The agrarian underpinnings of Flatlands were readily visible in 1893, when, pursuant to a newly enacted state statute, 30 of its taxable inhabitants filed a petition with the Town Board requesting that it install electric lighting in all the streets. Two days later no fewer than 263 taxpayers signed counterpetitions protesting "against the lighting of the streets of the Town by electricity for the reason that the Town is largely composed of a farming community and public necessity does not demand it at the present time."[8]

Most of the Flatlands boers were, according to the *Eagle*, "descendants of the first settlers . . . and as a class . . . very wealthy, thrifty, and highly intelligent." But whereas the older farmers generally opposed annexation, the younger ones were rebelling against the idiocy of rural life:

> "We are shut up here from nearly all public progress, as though we were behind the walls of China. The old folks and some of the big landowners want to hold on to their lands and wait for a large and sudden advance in prices, and then to sell at enormous profits. We don't want that policy. Let the city government open up this country, run avenues through it, give us country seats, capitalists, railroad, quick time to New York. We can make it pay handsomely to ourselves."[9]

Edgar Bergen shared this position, believing that annexationists had put the cart before the steam railroad: what Flatlands needed was rapid communication, from which dense population and then annexation would follow.[10]

The battle lines seem clearly drawn here, but a slight haze befogs understanding when the *Eagle* quotes an antiannexationist as opining that: "The farms now pay moderately only, and not then unless very carefully worked." Annexation would, according to this farmer, withdraw land from market gardening for streets: "We want our farms let alone just as they are. When we want annexation, we'll ask for it." How Flatlands farmers became wealthy from only moderately profitable farms remains as puzzling as why farmers would tenaciously cling to them if they demanded such hard work for such modest returns — unless, as one of their sons charged, they were in fact slyly awaiting the right moment to sell at the highest developmental price.[11]

Flatlanders were especially worried about having to pay for superfluous city institutions — such as police and flagged sidewalks beside farms — and the tax consequences of annexation and development: "Instead of rating your farms at $500 per acre . . . you will then boast of lands worth $1,500 per acre, and instead of paying paltry tax of 50 or $100 per year, you will then have the privilege of paying more than your farms will rent for."[12]

The simplest way to defuse farmers' resistance to annexation — or at least to unmask the real basis of their opposition — was, as the *Eagle* noted, to condition annexation on a pledge that "the lands actually used for agricultural purposes shall be taxed even less than they are now." Annexation statutes and commission proposals failed to go quite that far in propitiating farmers, but they did offer significant tax preferences to them. In 1873, however, they did not suffice to accommodate the boers in Flatlands or elsewhere in rural Kings County, who recalled that when Bushwick had been annexed two decades earlier, it, too, "was at first taxed as an agricultural ward, but only for two years, and then was taxed as city lots, and to-day there are hundreds of vacant lots in that district many of which will not sell for sufficient to pay the taxes and assessments thereon." Moreover, annexation without representation — that is, mandated by the state legislature without approval by a majority of the annexees — would, in the words of Jacques J. Stilwell, a member of one of the oldest families and property owner in, and town supervisor of, Gravesend from 1861 to 1878, constitute "a revolutionary measure that would justify armed resistance." Although the legislature in 1873 ultimately decided not to compel annexation in the amended charter of the city of Brooklyn — and also abandoned the "spiteful" proposal to require the towns that refused annexation to form their own county or be joined to Queens — annexation in 1894 was prescribed by statute.[13]

Not coincidentally, then, the annexation proposals that resurfaced with ever greater frequency in 1872 and 1873 focused on New Lots, which by this time was almost as populous as the four other towns combined, although it also encompassed an important farming sector. On February 11, 1873, a bill was filed in the New York State Assembly to annex the town to Brooklyn. New Lots had originally been created by the overflow of the children of farmers in Flatbush and Flatlands: "In the rear of their farms lay the expanse of plain hill and forest, not then tilled or thought much of." The farmers opened roads to the area and apportioned lots to their sons, who "grew rich," and passed their possessions on to descendants, many of whom — such as the Van Siclens, Van Sinderens, Wyckoffs, Rapelyeas, Lotts, and Vanderveers — in the 1870s still owned the land. The town of New Lots consisted of the old farming village (population 500), and three larger towns, Brownsville (1,000), Cypress Hills (2,500), and, by far the largest and most industrialized, East New York (8,000). Annexationists' belief that inadequate police and fire protection and gas and water utilities had proved that economic and demographic growth had outrun the town's self-governing capacities formed, together with perceived necessity of rapid transit to the ferries, the focus of their testimony before the New York State Assembly Committee on Internal Affairs at its hearings on the New Lots bill. Opponents, largely but not exclusively old-line Dutch rural landowners, were actuated by a fear of higher taxes and "an undesirable inroad of new settlers who will be in unpleasant proximity." [14]

East New York in the 1860s was occupationally dominated by the German tailor and cigar maker, whose "rulers" were "the immortal descendants of the Dutch settlers, the Van Sicklens, Schencks, Cozines, Wyckoffs, who ruled him gently and did not try to rob him because their coffers were already full of yellow joy." Shortly before the annexation movement gained momentum, speculators approached the Dutch farmers, who "owned nearly all the property," some of whom "grasped at the prices offered," while "others twinkled curiously with their eyes and said they couldn't see it." By May, the *Rural Gazette* was urging "[c]apitalists" to invest in East New York property, which it predicted would double in value within three years.[15]

On February 18, 1873, another bill was filed in the New York State Assembly — this one to annex all the rural towns to Brooklyn. In June the state legislature enacted legislation directing the mayor of Brooklyn to appoint six commissioners, and each of the supervisors of the five rural towns to appoint one commissioner, to a board to "devise a general plan" to unite and consolidate all of them into a municipal corporation called the city of Brooklyn. Specifically, the board was to set forth "the relative rate of taxation . . . to be assessed upon the respective portions of the territory" as well as to provide for a consolidation with the Kings County government toward the end of reducing expenses. After a two-thirds majority of the board adopted the plan, it was to be submitted to the voters at the general election in November; if a majority of the votes cast in Brooklyn and a majority of the aggregate votes cast in the five towns favored consolidation, the commissioners were to prepare an act for consolidation for the legislature. The voting procedure in the rural areas was designed to deny any one of the small towns the power to veto annexation for the others by requiring all to come in or stay out together. From the outset it was deemed a foregone conclusion that the commissioners would favor consolidation and that voters in the three most rural towns, Flatlands, Gravesend, and New Utrecht, were "almost unanimously opposed to consolidation." [16]

MODERNIZERS VERSUS AGRARIANS:
JUDGE JOHN A. LOTT AND UNCLE TUNE BERGEN

It is in accordance with the natural order of things that the towns, already to a degree a practical part of the city, should become a political part. This natural tendency is sure to end in unification at no distant day, despite the present illogical attitude of some of the townsmen. The municipality is steadily creeping over the rural section of the County. . . . Streets are pushing out into the towns, paved thoroughfares are taking the place of country roads, town lots are commanding city prices, and as . . . the municipal line is a merely political one, practically disregarded by Brooklyn in her resistless development. [17]
— "City and County," *Brooklyn Daily Eagle*, April 8, 1873

Flatlands, Gravesend, and New Utrecht were represented by major farmers — Peter Lott, William Bennett, and Teunis G. Bergen, respectively. Flatbush's representative, John A. Lott (1806–1878), whom the members chose as their president, was the most eminent living member of the old-line Dutch farm families, "perhaps the wealthiest lawyer in Brooklyn" during the antebellum period, and the key political entrepreneur shaping the modernization of Flatbush. His centrality to Flatbush was symbolically on display spatially as well: as shown in figure 17, the Lott residence, located on Flatbush Road directly across from Erasmus Hall Academy and next to the Reformed Protestant Dutch Church, was at the center of Flatbush life. Lott became a judge on the Kings County Court of Common Pleas in 1838, a member of the New York State Assembly in 1842, of the Senate in 1843, a judge on the Supreme Court in 1858, and completed his career as a public official by serving on the state's highest court, the Court of Appeals, in 1869, and as Chief Commissioner of the Commission of Appeals from 1870 to 1875. A few months after the annexation election, the *Rural Gazette* and the *Eagle* suggested Lott as the Democratic candidate for governor of New York. [18]

Oliver Wendell Holmes Jr. called Lott the "ablest lawyer" in Brooklyn,

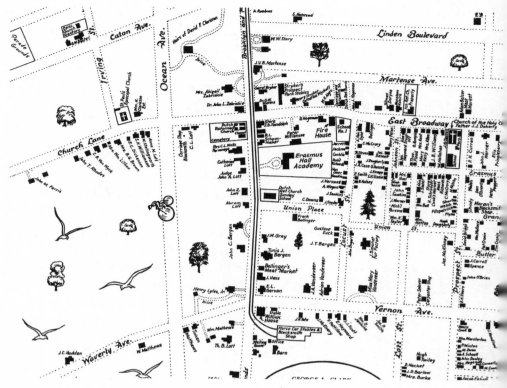

FIGURE 17. *Vicinity of John A. Lott residence, 1870. From Catherine Nelson and E. Theo. Nelson, "The Village of Flatbush as It Was in the Year 1870."*

while others regarded him as "the most distinguished member of Dutch lineage to occupy a judicial office in Kings County" in the nineteenth century. Though listed in federal population censuses as a lawyer or judge, Lott was not only a major farm owner in Flatbush (and other county towns), but also the central figure in an extended family of Lotts who owned considerable blocks of land throughout the rural towns. In 1850, for example, the Census of Population listed him as a lawyer owning real estate valued at $50,000, while in the Census of Agriculture he appeared as owning a 160-acre farm valued at $30,000, the output of which was, however, not great. By 1875, Lott owned, according to the *Rural Gazette*, "in acres, more property in Kings County than any other man in it. Of the Lott farms in Flatbush, not an acre has been parted with." Not all of this land had been owned by the Lott family for two centuries; for example, John A. Lott's father, Abraham, bought a section of prime farmland in Flatlands in 1821. At his death in 1878, John A. Lott left an estate valued at $500,000.[19]

FIGURE 18. *John A. Lott. Courtesy of the Reformed Protestant Dutch Church of Flatbush.*

Some old-line Dutch farm families' power derived from shrewdly diversifying their agricultural holdings to profit from the coming suburbanization:

The fat farm lands and their strategic position had brought wealth and independence to the old families, and they controlled the political power as well as the growing public utilities. . . .

The land of the Dutch settlers in "Vlacke Bos" had become valuable. By staying quietly at home the Dutch had located the gold the adventurous Scotch-Irish so often failed to find after suffering and hardship in . . . California. . . . [T]he descendants of the old settlers, the Lotts, Vanderbilts, Ditmases, Zabriskies, Leffertses, Wycoffs, Martenses and Snedekers held the offices and ran the Dutch Reformed Church. They owned the water works, the telegraph company, the toll road, the gas company; dictated the policy of the fire company, the excise commission, the law and order society and regulated all social affairs.

Consequently, the "most prestigious families in Brooklyn were those whose ancestors had received tracts of land and played active social and political roles" in the city itself and the outlying towns.[20]

John A. Lott was, together with John Lefferts, the most conspicuous example of such diversification. Through his long career as lawyer, politician, and judge, he amassed positions as president of the Long Island Safe Deposit Company, Flatbush Gas Company, Village Board of Improvement, and Brighton Beach Hotel and Railroad, and director of the Nassau Insurance Company and Long Island Insurance Company. He was also a trustee of the Flatbush fire company. His obituary in the New York Times characterized him as so "absolutely venerated" in rural Kings County, that when, in the final year of his life he became president of the Brooklyn, Flatbush, and Coney Island Railroad, which ran through "a rich farming district," the "farmers had such faith in Judge Lott that not a single lawsuit was brought against the company concerning the right of way."[21]

Lott, like John Willink and other rich residents of rural Kings County, maintained business interests extending well beyond local real-estate transactions. They financed land purchases in rural counties surrounding New York by means of mortgages, which were called indentures and could be foreclosed on if the farmers were unable to meet their payments. These relatively complicated financial arrangements suggest a high level of sophistication about land matters, which not only would have served Lott and others well in negotiating the sell-off of their own land, but also reveal that they may have undertaken the kinds of calculations about farming versus selling that are ascribed to market-rational farmers.[22]

The wealth that Lott accumulated through legal practice and his other enterprises may eventually have exceeded that generated on his farmlands, but the fact that as early as 1873 he was willing to promote annexation, which he must have known and hoped would mean the end of agricultural Flatbush — his commitment to "one city, one government and one destiny" was so firm that he was prepared even to abolish the names of the towns — suggests that the agricultural landowning class in Kings County was split along lines of diversification: those who had already begun shifting their assets into other productive forms were more eager to expedite suburbanization. This axis of differentiation undercuts the monolithic view that the "vast difference" between Brooklyn and Flatbush could be explained by the fact that the descendants of the original Dutch settlers in the rural town continued to hold "the landed ownership and administrative control."[23]

Lott, however, was no ruthless or mindless modernizer, bent on forcing Flatbush and the other towns into Brooklyn against their will. It did not escape contemporary observers such as the *Eagle* that the commissioners' success largely depended on Lott's ability to deploy his conservatism to bring along the country members while his (and Flatbush's) "spirit of progress" commended him to the Brooklynites. In this respect Lott's position resembled that of the *Rural Gazette*, which, while resisting annexation on terms set by Brooklyn politicians and taxpayers, steadfastly swore its advocacy of "progress": "We demand it; we must have it; Rapid Transit, both by Dummies on our surface road, and by more rapid means underground. Our location near you requires it; our property interests require it; our business men need it."[24]

Lott's urbanizing policies are particularly striking since his farmland, as seen in figure 19, extended into the much more rural towns of Flatlands and Gravesend as well as into New Utrecht. In 1870, for example, his aggregate holdings in the four towns amounted to 253 acres. Indeed, contemporaries assumed that he was the largest landowner in rural Kings County. It is uncertain whether large and wealthy landowning families such as Lott and Lefferts that had already diversified into nonagricultural assets understood the promotion of residential settlements as inconsistent with farming, but as land prices rose in the wake of the first successful suburbanization develop-

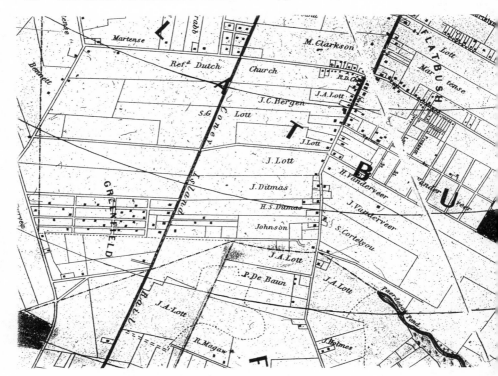

FIGURE 19. *John A. Lott's farmlands, 1868. From M. Dripps,*
"Map of Kings County N.Y."

ments, they presumably realized that a "privately" held agricultural greenbelt reflected a civic consciousness that not even they wished to afford.[25]

Judge Lott's backward-looking agrarian foil on the commission was the
New Utrecht representative, Teunis Garret Bergen, "a thorough Dutchman
of the old school in all things." He was not only a farmer, but an antiquarian genealogist of the Kings County Dutch, surveyor, the town supervisor
of New Utrecht continuously from 1836 to 1859, and former Congressman,
whose first language was Dutch. Bergen's unceasing rejection of annexation
throughout the commission's proceedings was at least as tenacious as Lott's
advocacy of modernity. Bergen's unyielding stance may have been rooted in
his knowledge that in February, when the New York State Assembly was
considering the annexation bill, nineteen-twentieths of the people of New
Utrecht had submitted a remonstrance to the legislature expressing their
opposition.[26]

Bergen's rejectionist reputation had preceded his advent on the commis-

sion in August: during the first several months of the year he had been instrumental in eliminating annexation from the proposed amendments to
the Brooklyn city charter. In April, the *Eagle*, weary of "the impenetrable
obstinacy of Uncle Tune Bergen" in the face of "pathos, entreaty and logic,"
published an anonymous satirical poem from New Lots, "The Wrath of
Bergen," which, as a unique document capturing the essence of the modernizers' caricature of the resisting Dutch farmers' mentality, deserves rescue from oblivion despite its length.[27]

"THE WRATH OF BERGEN"

The last Zebeck that came
   And moor'd within the mole,
Such tidings unto TUNIS brought,
   As stirred his very soul.

Uncle Tunis sat at Bay Ridge,
   The pipe within his lips,
And still at frequent intervals
   The Apple Jack he sips.
In spite of lulling vapor,
   From the soothing, brimming cup,
The spirit of our Uncle Tune
   Is fiercely kindling up.

For why? — He heard that Sam McLean,
   And "One Hundred" more,
Had journeyed up to Albany,
   A little time before;
And brought a bill, that brooded ill,
   To make the country towns
A part of Brooklyn's limits,
   And incorporate their Downs.

And so he jumped, and swore an oath,
   Like Stuyvesant of yore;
Then dashed his pipe and Apple Jack
   With fury on the floor.
Then, making three prodigious strides,
   He reached the outward door;

With every step his passion rose,
　　And burned within him more.

The marching over hill and moor,
　　O'er frozen swamps and swales,
Where the musquitoes loved to swarm,
　　But now the famished quails;
The timid quails before him flew,
　　O'er frozen roads, in flocks,
While furtive rabbits started up,
　　And scampered for the rocks.

Thus Uncle Tunis marched across
　　His patrimonial ground,
'Twas night time and the silver moon
　　Diffused its beams around.
Oh, shall these fields of bulrushes
　　Be turned to city lots?
Shall stately palaces be built
　　Where now the turnip rots?

"Forbid it, Heaven!" cried Uncle Tune,
　　"Such changes should take place."
Just then unclouded moonbeams fell,
　　And hit him in the face.
His breath rose on the frosty air
　　Like wreaths of silver lace.
Still Uncle Tune moved fiercely on,
　　Nor did he slack his pace
Till he met Martin Schoonmaker,
　　Who loves the "possum chase."

Now, Martin had a mystic turn,
　　With a discursive style,
That lengthened every sentence out,
　　Until it seemed a mile.
And Martin was amazed to see
　　His friend show so much bile,
For heretofore Tune Bergen's face
　　Had always worn a smile,

Which said, or almost seemed to say,
   "I've been striking *ile*."

His cheeks were like some dark ribbed cloud
   That holds the thunder in
Until a vivid lightning flash
   Let loose the storm within.
Says Tune, "*Trojani Fuimus*;"
   And Schoonmaker says "Eh?"
"The country towns," Tune Bergen cries
   Like Pantheus, "had their day."
And now he added with a sigh,
   "The appointed hour has come
When Brooklyn, Gravesend and Bay Ridge
   Are melted into one.
Even Flatbush, where Judge Lott resides,
   Is equally undone.

"No more we hear the bullfrogs sing,
   Nor bob for eels at night;
Our swamps will very soon be drained,
   And gas lamps give us light.
Adieu to clams and pollywogs
   And heaven defend the right."
With that he raised an old tin horn,
   And blew so long and loud,
That even the silent silver moon,
   Dodged in behind a cloud.

Then up came John C. Jacobs,
   And with him Dominick Roche,
And pledged that no city lot
   Should upon the swales encroach,
Nor any street surveyor
   The clams or eels approach.

Then Uncle Tunis simmered down,
   Resumed his former smile,
And Martin thanked these new found friends,
   In periods of a mile.

> So all things stand in *statu quo*,
>   The bull frogs still can sing,
> And night owls, o'er the stagnant beach,
>   Still flap their lazy wing,
> And Tunis from the neighboring marsh,
>   His eels at midnight bring.

The poem left no doubt as to whom the *Eagle* meant when, in commenting on the commission's first meeting on August 12, 1873, it cautioned the antiannexationist commissioners to consider "the ultimate destiny of the towns" while tempering their zeal with "a better appreciation of the real interests of the towns than fossiliferous leaders in them have sometimes exhibited." Despite his reputation, Bergen was practically involved in numerous modernizing projects: in his capacity as surveyor in the 1850s he had surveyed some of the main arteries in Flatbush such as the Flatbush Plank Road, which facilitated communication and transportation, and prepared the map for the Greenfield residential project in 1852, thus accelerating the drive for annexation. He was also surveyor for the railroad company, headed by John A. Lott, that operated the first steam railroad from Flatbush to Coney Island. Nevertheless, Bergen's premodern mentality was undeniable. Three years after the annexation debate, for example, in petitioning the Kings County board of supervisors to defer action on a vote in New Utrecht to build a new town hall there for $10,000, Bergen found it pertinent to dwell on his calculation that seven of his co-petitioners alone had paid more in taxes than all of the residents who voted in favor of construction.[28]

THE COMMISSIONERS DEBATE

[I]f the farmers . . . could see it, they'd make more money by consolidation
than they would by the cultivation of corn and cabbage all their lives.
— Edmund Driggs, Brooklyn Consolidation Commission,
    Brooklyn Daily Eagle, October 22, 1873

At the annexation commissioners' first meeting, a member from Brooklyn offered a resolution explaining the principles actuating the board, the pertinent point of which was: "That for purposes of taxation the property in the several towns shall be assessed as agricultural lands except when the same has been or may be divided and used as building lots."

Bergen, however objected to the annexation scheme per se:

The government of New Utrecht was the least expensive; it was only an agricultural village, a long way from Brooklyn, and not in need of being included in the expenses of municipal government, at least not for the present. The question of guarantees also arises. Brooklyn might make fair terms now, but what might be the future course? On the present basis of representation, the county towns would have only one Alderman among them. The great trouble . . . is the prevailing spirit of centralization. If the county towns do not desire annexation, it should not be forced on them.[29]

In response to Bergen's claim that Brooklyn's "sole object . . . was to lighten its own heavy taxes," A. B. Bayliss, a Brooklyn representative, observed that consolidation "could not be avoided, because of the great and increasing growth of the city, and the progress of the population toward and into the county towns. The county towns lying contiguous to the city needed police protection, lighted streets, and protection from fires, because of their nearness to the city." When Bayliss tried to force a vote on the issue of annexation itself to test the antiannexation faction's strength, Judge Lott decided that the commission's charge was not to discuss the question but to frame a plan. The members then adopted the resolution, the farmer-commissioners from the most rural towns, Flatlands and Gravesend, joining Bergen in the minority. The press correctly interpreted this eight to three test vote as indicative of the final outcome of the commission's deliberations.[30]

This debate suggests that some farmer representatives did not yet view (sub)urbanization as inevitable or at least as imminent. Resistance to Brooklynization need not, however, be interpreted as the boers' last hurrah: opponents' strategy could simply have been to continue farming while pent-up pressure for suburban housing forced up land prices without farmers' having to pay higher citylike taxes during the transition. Teunis Bergen, after all, was not some unreconstructed backwoodsman, but a highly literate surveyor and longtime politician, whom judges found acceptable as a commissioner to appraise the value of farmland to be taken for a railroad. Nor was his fear that after annexation the city of Brooklyn might impose higher taxes on the hopelessly outvoted farm towns outlandish.[31]

Bergen elaborated on these fears the next week at a meeting of the Committee on the Consolidation. When he "expressed apprehension that farm lands might be unjustly taxed" for the expense of introducing water into the towns, a Brooklyn commissioner replied: "The charter says that certain lands shall be assessed as agricultural lands, as was done in the Eighth ward here [Gowanus] for a long time. I mean that the city assessor shall not go down there and assess it as if it were laid out in city lots." But Bergen insisted: "The idea of valuing it as 'agricultural lands' is all humbug." He seemed mollified when two Brooklyn commissioners added that the agricultural portions of the county would not be taxed for fire protection or water connections until they asked to share such city services. But this concession taxed Bergen's credulity, prompting him to exclaim: "When I want to catch a fish, I bait the hook with good bait." Losing patience, his Brooklyn interlocutor then admonished him: "Look here, Bergen, you have got to have faith, you know. Faith, and plenty of it, will do a good deal." Bergen protested that although the commission "wants to do what is right," later politicians in the state legislature and on the Brooklyn Common Council might alter the policy. To persuade Bergen, Brooklyn commissioners related that when other farming districts such as Bushwick joined Brooklyn no farmers ever complained of being oppressed. When Bergen named one disgruntled farmer, a Brooklyn commissioner opened a line of argument that transcended Bergen's conceptual framework by observing laconically: "Well, he is a rich man to-day, and he was not then." In the end, even Bergen voted in favor of a motion to exempt the towns from taxes for the police, fire, and water departments until they requested such benefits. And later he also voted for the crucial tax preference for owners of agricultural land in the rural towns.[32]

Despite Bergen's skepticism, the commission's Committee on the Consolidation reported a few days later that the "county towns or agricultural wards" would not be taxed like the rest of Brooklyn with regard to street lighting, and the fire, police, water, and health departments. The report also proposed that: "In all levies of taxes or assessments on property in the several towns, real estate not divided up, or set apart, or used as building lots, shall be as now, as agricultural lands." As a further accommodation of agricultural interests, the commission's Committee on the Legislative Department, which Bergen chaired, reported that the new city's Common Council would "have no power to require licenses from farmers for selling the produce of their farms or gardens."[33]

Such concessions, particularly the agricultural tax preference, which John A. Lott repeated, as well as granting veto power over street openings in the new wards to the majority of property owners to be assessed, may have been designed to overcome the resistance of the farmers' representatives, but annexation to Brooklyn can hardly have seemed an unmixed blessing when virtually every day brought new headlines heralding the latest revelations of city officials' corruption. "Plundered Brooklyn" was just one of dozens of articles that adorned the front pages during the annexation commission's brief existence. Bergen's suspicions can hardly have been allayed when one of the Brooklyn representatives, Thomas Kinsella, the editor of the *Eagle*, expressed his resentment over granting the county towns agricultural tax preferences in addition to other advantages so that when the new wards were built up in a few years an "unfair disparity" would obtain between them and the old city. Kinsella's assertion that the towns "must be brought into the city, 'fairly if we can, but otherwise if we must,'" prompted even John A. Lott to voice his disapproval of a plan that would "force a section of county, against its wish, under the government of a municipality in which it had no voice." Lott predicted that such sentiments would exacerbate prejudice against consolidation and ensure its defeat in the towns.[34]

Despite conflicts that arose over equal rights to be accorded the towns, the future jurisdiction of the county government, and taxation of Flatbush residents for Prospect Park lands taken by the legislature from the town and transferred to Brooklyn, John A. Lott was able to fashion a resolution enabling the commissioners to present the annexation proposal to voters on November 4, 1873. Lott opposed any plan that would have burdened the county towns with the expenses that they had had no voice in creating and from which they derived no benefit. He therefore proposed that the towns as a whole not be charged with any of the interest on the loan for the construction of Prospect Park — but only that part of Flatbush directly benefiting from it. Lott's guiding principle was that the towns should "pay their share of the cost of the great improvement at some future time, but were relieved of the payment of the present accruing interest." Bergen's counterproposal that county towns, which had had nothing to do with the creation of the park, should be exempted from the payment of principal, interest, and maintenance "altogether and forever" gained the votes only of the commissioners of Gravesend and Flatlands, who also voted with him to reject Lott's proposal.[35]

But the state legislature had structured the commission and its voting procedure so that the Brooklyn commissioners required the agreement of only two rural towns in order to submit the proposal to the voters. Since Lott was committed to annexation and the three farmer-commissioners to rejection, success ultimately hinged on accommodating the demands of the most populous town, New Lots. An alliance between Flatbush and New Lots might have seemed preordained, but a certain tension between the towns had to be overcome. Despite its economic position as a primarily agricultural producer, Flatbush was being touted by Brooklyn boosters by the early 1870s as "destined to be the very centre of the future Brooklyn" — within fifty if not twenty years. The key role played by Flatbush was resented by some in New Lots, who called it "the spoiled child of the county," and resented the disproportionate share of wealth and resources that the town had been able to attract by virtue of its personal and political influence. In addition to needing the single vote of the commissioner from New Lots in order to forward the proposal, the annexationists also had to accommodate the New Lots electorate sufficiently to induce it to furnish a large enough proannexation majority to overcome a potential rejectionist majority in the other rural towns. Lott won over New Lots's representative by exempting the rural towns from responsibility for the outstanding interest on the loans for building Prospect Park on the grounds that, since most of the land in the towns was agricultural and used for agricultural purposes, "no immediate direct benefit or increase in value results to it from the Park."[36]

The agricultural land tax preference that ultimately lay before the voters provided that real estate within the new wards "shall be assessed . . . as agricultural land, on the value thereof for agricultural purposes only, unless the same has been, at the time of such union and consolidation, or may hereafter be divided up into building lots, and a map thereof filed in the office of the Register or the Clerk of the County of Kings, or in the office of the Assessors of the City of Brooklyn, and a sale or sales shall have been made, referring to such map, or unless the same shall have been otherwise sold as a building lot or lots, or used as such." The consolidation plan specified, however, that the tax rate itself for these different objects and purposes "shall be uniform, according to the assessed value of the property."[37]

Despite the final plan's provision prohibiting the Brooklyn Common Council from forbidding "the keeping of cattle or swine on lands used for agricultural purposes," the farmer-commissioners from Flatlands, Gravesend, and New Utrecht read a 12-point protest before voting against the plan. The profoundly agrarian mentality of their constituents was amply on display in their protests against: any charges for the city parks, which were "a luxury which a rural population does not desire and cannot afford"; charges for a police force, which would be "of little use, unless composed of an army, in consequence of our large and sparsely settled territory"; and the loss of their local fence viewers to settle disputes over stray cows and damages caused by cattle, "necessary in an agricultural community." (In New Utrecht, "the lives of women and children" were "in imminent peril, because droves of horses and cows" were "turned out to pasture in the streets.") The poignancy of this clash of rural and urban cultures and Weltanschauungen can be grasped only by keeping in mind that Teunis Bergen's New Utrecht, which he constructed here as a remote rural settlement, in fact shared a border with the third-largest city in the United States.[38]

The concluding paragraph of the dissenting farmer-commissioners' protest is perhaps the most eloquent defense ever mustered of the old agrarian way of life in the shadow of the metropolis. Bergen and his allies objected to the majority's report for

> unjustly subjecting an agricultural people to the heavy expenses of a city government necessary in a densely populated community, but unnecessary and burdensome in a rural district, and thus, probably, more than doubling their taxes, the effect of which in consequence of its unbearable and grievous burdens and the taxes for which, exceeding the rents of agricultural land can be let, or the profits which owners can obtain over the costs of cultivation will have a tendency to compel many of the farmers in our midst to dispose of their premises at such prices as they can obtain, abandon the homes of their ancestors and emigrate to more favored localities out of the reach of city burdens and oppressions, leaving their farms in the hands of speculators and non-cultivators and thrown out as common waste land, a pasture for goats, geese and stray cattle as is at present the case with most of the lands in the present outer wards of the city in place of the present smiling fields and highly cultivated farms and gardens yielding in abundance and ministering to the wants of the population of the city.[39]

Side by side with this vivid advocacy of a positive program of metropolitan agrarianism coexisted Bergen's parochial view of community best captured by the rhetorical query that he never wearied of repeating: "'Why should I contribute to pay for a dock or a school house which is four miles away from my property?'" Although such narrowmindedness was not a necessary attribute of a movement to sustain suburban vegetable farming, the fact that its leading proponent was such a self-caricature of possessive individualism made it an easy target of ridicule. The farmer-dissenters protested, for example, that after annexation they would not only be required to lose one day traveling to city hall to obtain a tax bill and another to pay it, but also "put to the annoyance of being compelled to enter into a line of those desiring to make payment, and of being jostled and kept standing for hours before arriving at the desk of the receiving office." After Bergen declared that Gravesend would not get water to attach to fire engines for at least the next half century, Commissioner Kinsella had an easy time countering that: "Mr. Bergen insists upon speaking of the towns as they now are. I hope to see them parts of opulent cities." When Bergen asserted that the Brooklyn Bridge, then under construction, would benefit the property that he owned in Brooklyn, but would be of "no earthly good in any way" to what he owned in New Utrecht, Kinsella adroitly responded that being able to ride a car from Bergen's farm to New York City Hall would surely benefit New Utrecht.[40]

Annexationists, however, could not rely on scoring such easy debaters' points. While hardly concealing that the whole point of annexation was sub-urbanization, they never confronted the structural-environmental consequences of deagriculturalization. They did not have to address this issue because they masked it by repeating: "We propose to assess their lands, when used for agricultural purposes, at their value for such purposes. This insures low valuation, and where there is such valuation there cannot be city taxation." Nevertheless, when the mayor of Brooklyn recommended annexation in 1879, some still believed it would mean "ruin for many farmers."[41]

The problem with this perspective was that the preservation of within-the-city farming required a political, not an economic or fiscal, solution. Although low assessments meant that high taxes might not render farming financially impossible, the much greater threat to which market gardening was exposed lay in the shrinkage of the land base that would inevitably result from lucrative sell-offs as some neighbors found it to their advantage to cut coupons rather than cultivate cabbage. That so many farmers had already become rent-takers as Irish and German tenants (and their laborers) increasingly performed the actual hard work of producing vegetables, made it easier both for farm owners to abandon their ancestral ties to the land and for annexationists to dismiss farmers as complaining all the way to the bank. As more and more of the surrounding land was converted into real estate for housing suburbanites, the greater would become the physical obstacles to farming and the interpersonal conflicts with neighbors. The only solution to this dilemma would have been some politically imposed protection such as the programs to purchase development rights that states did not create for a century. This form of state intervention was not ideologically available in the 1870s. But even if it had been available, urging such relief would have required Teunis Bergen and the other Dutch farmers to confess that what they really needed protection from was not rapacious tax assessors, but their own potential greed.[42]

Alternatively, a political solution would have presupposed the existence of a compromise vision between Bergen's rural idyll with local autonomy and the urban expansionists' drive to exterminate mosquitoes, bogs, and rotting turnips along with the farms that sustained them all. Yet no prominent public figure — let alone a movement — articulated such a compromise. Olmsted, with his cleaned-up countryside of landscaping and parks, perhaps came closest, but he had long lost interest in making or keeping the countryside productive. Urban boosters, however, were blind to such possibilities because their exclusive focus was the "close-fisted corporation" of Kings County farmers, whose "backward, antediluvian" policies against any and all "improvements" blocked the "flow of Brooklyn capital." The mere fact that the proceeds from the sale of a lot thirty miles from New York sufficed to buy a farm in New Lots was for them horrifying proof of the consequences of the stagnation that metropolitan agriculture necessarily left in its wake.[43]

Just how far the annexation proposal was from adopting a policy that would protect farmers from market and capital accumulation forces was readily visible in the commission's final plan empowering the "people of any ward of any town, or portion thereof [to] form a district, and upon the petition of a majority of property holders to be affected thereby, the Common Council shall include said district within the territory chargeable with the expense of the Police and Fire Department of the City of Brooklyn." This authority was tantamount to an invitation to new suburbanites to carve out colonies in which they could outvote farm owners and ultimately force on them the very city services that the farmer-commissioners had declared their constituents unable to afford, while annexationists assured them that any "talk of extending city expenditures over the towns" was "ridiculous, since it is specially provided that the real estate in the towns shall be valued as agricultural lands, so long as this real estate is used for no other than agricultural purposes."[44]

On the literal eve of the annexation vote, the *Eagle*, with the type of dispassion that only a conviction of manifest destiny could underwrite, editorially announced that regardless of "imaginary" lines of separation, the East River and Atlantic Ocean formed Brooklyn's "natural boundaries." Indeed, the newspaper attributed this conviction even to antiannexationists: "The friends and foes of present consolidation agree in this, that consolidation sooner or later is inevitable. Both sides admit that consolidation will be de-

sirable some time for both the towns and the city." Although Teunis Bergen
never offered such a concession, the *Eagle* insisted that the "hate and bitter-
ness" of the debate had been unnecessary because: "The question is a business question — one of dollars and cents, and of common interests to the
city and the towns." Yet money, from one publicly articulated point of view,
was precisely what the annexation debate was not about. Die-hard rejec-
tionists like Bergen were not posturing behind a hidden agenda of extracting a monetary offer they could not refuse. When annexationists implored
farmers to grasp that the increase in property values would "more than
compensate . . . owners . . . for any additional taxation which will follow
consolidation," they were disingenuously ignoring the whole point of annexation, which they simultaneously conceded with all imaginable clarity:
"the cheap lands of the towns will be bought for suburban homes rapidly,
as soon as those settling in the suburbs can be insured water, police, and fire
protection, and other advantages of city life, as soon as they require them."[45]
Farmers who were struggling for the preservation of a 200-year-old way of
life that they realized was incompatible with absorption by what might become the world's largest city could hardly be reassured by a program of suburbanization that would not stop until it had bought up the last cabbage
field.

The alternative interpretation, according to which farmers believed that
annexation in 1873 was merely "premature," had to be based on the assumption that they were simply waiting for a more propitious moment
in the development of the suburban real-estate market. All of Bergen's elo-
quence was, from this perspective, merely a rhetorical smokescreen for a
high-stakes game of land speculation. Without stating the point expressly,
annexationists sought to parry this thrust by warning the farmers that the
terms being offered in 1873 were as "fair" as they would ever be — in any
event, more favorable than they would be if the state legislature ever exercised its undeniably lawful power to impose annexation without consulta-
tion or a referendum. The chief flaw in this cynical interpretation was its
irreconcilability with the "anomalous condition" that the farmers were apparently content to live in towns some of which "are no richer than were a
quarter of a century ago" and one of which was allegedly losing population.
Regardless of the truth content of this annexationist claim — farm production was in fact increasing — their perception that farmers could live without the transformative impulses emanating from dynamic capital accumulation corroborated the argument that city boosters urgently sought to

deny: farmers were not holding out for more money, but were desperately trying to sustain a threatened traditional agrarian mode of existence.[46]

The contradictions inherent in annexation were palpable enough that on the eve of the election even the boosterist *Rural Gazette* had to concede that it was "beyond a question very damaging for Flatlands, Gravesend and New Utrecht (excepting the vicinity of Bay Ridge) to have to submit to the desires of the people of the more thickly populated towns." Once it was too late, the newspaper had second thoughts about the all-or-nothing procedure, which prevented New Lots and Flatbush from joining Brooklyn on their own.[47]

ANNEXATION DEFEATED

Since the consolidation scheme is defeated, the owner of a few hundred acres of land here, will not become a beggar just yet, or the laborer a millionaire.

— "New Utrecht," *Kings County Rural Gazette*, November 15, 1873

Even this belated insight was moot. On election day, November 4, 1873, 85 percent of Brooklynites favored annexation, whereas more than 70 percent of voters in the five rural towns opposed it, thus defeating the initiative. Large majorities favored the old regime in all the towns except New Lots, where, to some observers' surprise, the farmers' almost unanimous opposition led to its rejection by a small overall majority. In the four other towns, five-sixths of the voters rejected annexation.[48]

Table 22 shows the vote in the towns. Unsurprisingly, the electorate in the most rural towns, Flatlands and Gravesend, was almost unanimously opposed to union with Brooklyn, a minuscule 21 of 700 voters favoring consolidation. The main surprise to contemporaries was that a larger proportion of voters in New Utrecht, Teunis Bergen's "stronghold," supported annexation than in Flatbush, which was "more directly interested in its favor." Even to modernizers such as the *Rural Gazette*, the overwhelming majority meant that consolidation was "not likely to be accomplished in another decade."[49]

The *Eagle* interpreted the fact that on the same day, a large majority in the towns of lower Westchester voted to be annexed to New York City (forming part of what eventually became the Bronx) as an obvious consequence of their residents' having been the strongest annexationists. Nevertheless, on the long view, the setback in Kings County was trivial: although the towns in 1873 may have found "any real union of the rural and urban portions of the county" unacceptable, annexation was "inevitable" when the two sections "assimilate more nearly in condition and character than they do at present." And the *Eagle* knew exactly what had to bring about that assimilation: "With rapid transit, cheap and desirable homes can be provided for tens of thousands of the crowded people of New York, in the rural portions of Kings County, and the solution of the rapid transit problem will be found to be the solution of the question of consolidation." Annexationists could confidently await the completion of the Brooklyn Bridge, "a turning point in the history of Brooklyn," which would extend the city to its "natural" boundaries.[50]

A clear sign of the limited time left to the independence of the rural towns appeared in the very same column in which the *Rural Gazette* reported the election tally. Without detecting a connection to the contested visions of the future, the Flatbush-based weekly editorialized about one of "the greatest nuisances which towns laying [*sic*] adjacent to large cities are subjected to" — namely, "loafers" who took Sunday tramps into the suburbs, "with a perfect lawlessness, making common property of whatever they choose to lay their hands on." Worse still were trespassers out for a day's shooting with their guns and dogs: that very week "the villains actually murdered a quiet man on his own premises, because he ordered them off." Rather than viewing the incident as the occasion for creating an urban police force, the newspaper urged the townspeople to "take the matter in hand" themselves. The newspaper's vigilantism may have merely reflected its acquiescence in the election results: a few months earlier it had listed as the first reason to favor consolidation "a good effective police force" to combat "the rougher classes" and "crowds of lawless pleasure seekers" pouring out of the city who were wont to "desecrate" Sundays with their "ball playing and profanity . . . to say nothing of the drunken revelry in . . . our would be quiet localities."[51]

On November 25, 1873, after a spirited campaign, New Lots voted separately under authority of its own annexation statute, which the state legislature had passed the same day it established the commission. For New Lots, the most populous and developed of the towns, the legislators themselves created the terms and conditions of annexation, authorizing the electors to approve or disapprove. On the strength of farmer's numbers and virtually unanimous resistance, those opposing annexation prevailed 735 to 634, and again in 1875 by a larger margin of 773 to 510. Even some of those who favored annexation continued to concede that it was wrong to "coerce" farmers in New Lots under a city government, but annexationists there persisted, and kept the issue constantly before the legislature until they prevailed in 1886. And by 1895, "farming in the town of New Lots had become, practically, a thing of the past."[52]

Scarcely a week after the countywide election, the *New York Times* editorialized on the opportunities that Brooklyn's property owners had lost as "men of moderate incomes, having become tired of street-car blockades, high rents, and delusive schemes for securing rapid transit," had abandoned New York. But instead of moving to Brooklyn, they had preferred towns in New Jersey that were linked by railroads to the ferries to Manhattan. If during the years after the Civil War, the *Times* lectured, Brooklyn had introduced rapid transit in the form of steam railroads to its suburbs, "hundreds of acres overlooking New-York Bay . . . might to-day be thickly studded with workmen's cottages and handsome villas." A decade later, however, as a petition to reduce the fare on the Flatbush horsecar demonstrated, the $50 per year that the average workingman paid who patronized it for business purposes was still "a drawback to the improvement of the town."[53]

The town of Flatbush, emboldened by the defeat of annexation, asserted its independence by building a new town hall in 1874 and, for a few more years, by resisting seamless connection to the encroaching city street grid. Teunis Bergen continued to oppose annexation — at least until increased population compelled it. Yet even he remained acutely aware that time was running out. As he observed on the occasion of the opening of the Bay Ridge and Manhattan Railroad: "We are between two fires. Brooklyn tries to devour us, and New York tries to swallow us."[54]

Even when the Brooklyn Bridge and rapid transit were almost completed to expedite the bursting populations of New York and Brooklyn to a suburbanized Kings County, the *Rural Gazette* knew that the chief remaining question was whether the inevitable annexation would be carried out in a manner fair to agricultural landowners. No longer even hedging its bets, the newspaper, which on October 7, 1882, had changed its name to *Kings County Rural and Brooklyn Gazette*, declared a month before the bridge's opening that it would defend the rural towns' interests only "until the day when the city extends her authority over the agricultural districts."[55]

In 1894, a few months after the state legislature had annexed the rural towns to Brooklyn, a nonbinding referendum on consolidation with New York initiated by the region's "mercantile elite" to "promote the unified, comprehensive development of shipping, railroads, and related facilities" resulted in an almost equal number of ballots for and against in Kings County: 64,744 and 64,467. Without the votes of the newly annexed towns, a majority of Brooklynites voted against consolidation, but the majority in the new wards of Flatbush (57 percent), Gravesend (55 percent), and New Utrecht (76 percent) created a tiny countywide 50.1 percent majority.[56]

8. THE IMPACT OF PROPERTY TAX LAWS ON DEAGRICULTURALIZATION

The old Dutch farms, that have been so carefully tilled for over 250 years,
have at last given way to beautiful gardens and level lawns surrounding
palatial homes, the abode of some of Brooklyn's worthiest men.
— Charles Andrew Ditmas, *Brooklyn's Garden*, 1908

A commonplace of modern land-use planning is that as property-tax rates
rise, in the wake of (sub)urbanization, to reflect more intense and "higher"
economic uses, farmers, whose lower-order, market-evaluated activities are
not sufficiently profitable to support tax rates appropriate to industry and
housing, are "forced" to sell their land — to buy cheaper farmland in areas
farther removed from the urban housing frontier, to retire, or to move elsewhere to enter another occupation. In 1976, for example, the *New York Times*
quoted a farmer in Putnam County, north of New York City, who paid
$4,000 in taxes in the 1940s and $30,000 on his 700 acres three decades later:
"Farmers are being forced out." With such crucial socioeconomic processes
relegated to the status of "journal-fodder" in the self-help pages of the real-
estate section in the newspaper of record, disbelief once again prevails with
regard to farming's prosperity in other counties in and bordering on New
York City: "farms are nearly extinct in Westchester and Nassau Counties. . . .
It is difficult to believe today that Queens County as well as Nassau were,
until 20 years ago, major centers for dairy farming."[1]

Some local historians, applying the twentieth-century tax-coercion explanation to the nineteenth century, assert that the "new tax rates" in the
new city of Brooklyn following the annexation of Flatbush and the Kings

County villages in 1894, "forced farmers to sell to developers." However, unpublished census manuscript schedules, assessment rolls, and federal income tax assessors' lists suggest that such speculative assertions are unfounded. In fact, Kings County farmers had been selling out long before 1894; tax rates did not rise significantly following annexation; and rather than being "forced" by high taxes, farmland owners were motivated by the enormous rise in land prices to sell. Moreover, contrary to the received wisdom, agricultural property tax preferences did not begin in the 1950s: like their counterparts in other states in the nineteenth century, farmers in all the rural towns of Kings County (except Flatbush) enjoyed a statutorily conferred agricultural tax preference following annexation in the 1880s and 1890s.[2]

TAX BURDENS

Judge Lott said this was the first time he ever knew a Dutchman to refuse to take anything in the shape of property.
— "Consolidation: The Consideration of Judge Lott's Plan,"
    Brooklyn Daily Eagle, September 10, 1873[3]

The tax per acre of agricultural real estate in New York State did not rise during the 1890s, and the general tax rate for the city of Brooklyn as a whole actually declined in the wake of annexation. After consolidation into New York City in 1898, the tax rate in Brooklyn fell once again. From a post–Civil War high of $3.78 per $100 of assessed valuation in 1867, the Brooklyn tax rate fell to $2.31 in 1882; it rose again to a high of $2.94 in 1889, and then declined slightly to $2.85 in 1893; despite some fluctuations as Brooklyn underwent expansion and then consolidation as part of New York City, the tax rate as the century closed ($2.36 in 1899) was close to its lowest point in decades. The rates in the rural towns followed no uniform patterns, increasing in some instances more in the years immediately preceding annexation than afterward.[4]

Before exploring the tax data, it is necessary to understand how the total tax to be collected was determined and what the state tax encompassed. The state legislature fixed the amount of state tax to be raised from property assessments based on previous property valuations and apportioned it among the counties in accordance with their total assessed valuations; the county tax was similarly apportioned among the towns. The property tax in New York State was, seemingly, a comprehensive wealth tax, but the manner in which local assessors determined assessments for the state and county created "a rivalry among local assessing officers for advantage to their respective districts by low assessments of property, resulting in gross inequalities and discriminations." A legislative committee reported in 1863 that New York's tax laws, not having been materially changed in a half century, had become outdated since "the agricultural element was [no longer] the absorbent of almost the entire property." But the legislature failed to amend the law for many years to come.[5]

Significantly, property assessments and taxes were public information, widely disseminated, known, and discussed. Publicity was designed to help police the system by sustaining pressure to report and assess fully and accurately. The *Rural Gazette* frequently alluded to John Lefferts as the biggest taxpayer in Flatbush, and published a list of the largest taxpayers in Flatbush and Flatlands.[6]

The property subject to tax embraced both real and personal property. The tax on personalty included "all household furniture; monies; goods; chattels; debts due from solvent debtors, whether on account, contract, note, bond or mortgage; public stocks, and stocks in monied corporations." The statute also exempted from taxation all property exempted by law from execution. The various homestead exemptions would not have shielded much of the personal household property of very wealthy families such as Ditmas, Lott, Lefferts, or Vanderbilt. Rich families could, however, benefit from the statutorily provided-for deduction of their "just debts" from the value of their personal property. Taxpayers submitted affidavits attesting to the amount of these debts.[7]

Such tax avoidance was hardly confined to the landed rich among the Kings County Dutch. New York State revenue and tax officials repeatedly declared the treatment of personalty in general and the setoff for debts in particular to be a source of great inequality. In 1858 the comptroller charged: "It is a notorious fact, that practically a large portion of the personal property of the State escapes taxation. The devices and fraudulent practices of those owning personal property to escape taxation, are so generally resorted to that it has become almost impossible to procure assessment of such property." The next year the comptroller focused on the setoff: "When the assessors come, the 'just debts' are easily swelled to meet the exigency of the occasion; and not infrequently they are manufactured for the purpose of being used in that manner. The consequence is, that immense amounts of personal property liable to taxation, entirely escape." As soon as the state assessors office was created, these officials stated their agreement with the comptroller, calling the deduction of indebtedness "equivalent to a premium for perjury and fraud, and destructive of any just system for taxation." Again, in 1871, commissioners appointed to report on tax law revision confirmed that nothing is "more easy than to create debts for the purpose of diminishing valuation, which no investigation on the part of the assessors will suffice to prove fictitious." The assessed value of personal property in Flatbush fell so sharply during the 1870s (from $919,000 to $282,000) that the *Rural Gazette* conjectured that it would soon disappear there altogether.[8]

Kings County farmers, by and large, did not declare significant, or even any, personalty — William Williamson, whose taxes and farm profits are analyzed below, was one of the few exceptions. Taxpayers who did declare large amounts of taxable personalty were largely retired from farming, rented out land, or had not been involved in it such as the Ditmas and Cortelyou families, the Lefferts and Vanderbilt families, and the Willink and Ludlow sisters, respectively. Whereas John Lefferts always reported considerable personalty (in many years in excess of $100,000), John A. Lott often declared none at all. Although most farmers did not declare any personal estate, for those, like Williamson, who did, it is not possible to identify the components of the personal estates; it is therefore unclear whether their personalty represented savings, expensive furniture, or carriages. In Williamson's case it is also unknown why the value of his personal property fell so sharply in the 1860s — or whether, like many New York property owners, he was merely failing to disclose ever larger proportions of his personalty.[9]

The data on property taxation, which combined town, county, and state taxes, may shed important light on the forces propelling the decline of Kings County agriculture. In examining property taxes, it is important to note that whereas valuations remained relatively stable — the Kings County commissioners of taxes and assessments were, according to the state assessors, "careful and discreet men" — the rate of taxation and thus the total amount of tax paid by individuals and towns or counties fluctuated considerably from year to year. John A. Lott, for example, owned an 87-acre farm, which was valued at $53,810 from 1873 to 1877; his tax rose from $837.65 to $931.56 from 1873 to 1874 because the rate increased from 1.56 percent to 1.73 percent, whereas a fall in the rate from 1876 to 1877 caused the tax to drop from $830.75 to $740.42.[10]

Table 23 shows the rate of taxation in Flatbush and Brooklyn during the decades preceding the absorption of both into New York City. During the post–Civil War period, property situated outside of the gas district — which for the purposes of this study comprised the farming districts to the east of Flatbush Avenue, the heart of the village, where gas streetlighting was introduced — was subject to a tax rate that, despite fluctuations, did not permanently reach a significantly higher plateau until the early 1890s. The county's preeminent farmer-capitalist, John Lefferts, underscored the link between taxation and lighting even to farm residents of the gas district. In a letter to the Flatbush highway commissioners in 1880, Lefferts requested that two lamps be erected and lighted at specific locations on East New York Avenue: "As I pay gas tax on the whole of my farm I believe my request is a just one." Since Lefferts was not only treasurer of the Flatbush Gas Company but also the biggest individual taxpayer in Flatbush, paying almost $2,500 on his 90 acres — on which his son James harvested 7,500 bushels of potatoes — five houses, greenhouse, and $60,000 in personalty, and accounting in some years for one-fifteenth of the town's entire tax receipts, his justification cannot be denied a certain force.[11]

The rate as late as 1891, 1.31 percent, was actually lower than it had been in 1865 (1.45 percent). Tax payments by farm owners outside the gas district show little absolute increase during the intervening years. Although tax rates in the gas district were consistently higher, they, too, did not permanently reach a higher level until the advent of other urban services such as schools and sewers in the late 1880s and early 1890s. The gap in property-tax rates between the city of Brooklyn and Flatbush was large during the last third of the nineteenth century; often the Brooklyn rates were more than twice as high. By the 1880s, that is, more than a decade before annexation, the gap began to close; by the time of annexation in the mid-1890s, the Flatbush rate, as opponents had always feared, even exceeded Brooklyn's. But this phenomenon was short-lived: by 1899, the year after the formation of Greater New York, the tax rate for Brooklyn was lower than it had been since the Civil War (with the exception of 1882). Thus, rather than imposing Brooklyn rates on the suburbs, annexation effected a convergence between the two.

Since taxes can be raised by increasing tax rates and/or valuations, the product of both, the amount of tax paid (per farm acre), is the best measure of the trend in tax burdens. In 1853, when the Flatbush assessment rate was less than 0.5 percent: such a large farmland owner as Jeremiah Lott paid only $280.70 on 164 acres of farmland assessed at $31,444 (in addition to a $25,000 personal estate), and John C. Bergen paid only $90.16 on 90 acres assessed at $17,830. Such tax payments, however, are not meaningful until they are set in relation to enterprise-level microdata.[12]

Table 24 displays the course of assessments and tax payments for a large

Flatbush farmer, William Williamson, who farmed on his own land into the 1880s. The account begins with 1860, when he was 42 years old, and ends in 1893: in 1894 Williamson finally subdivided his farm. The key variable in table 24 is the tax on real estate. It has been separately calculated (as it is not in the assessment rolls) because the tax on personalty is largely irrelevant to the impact of taxes on the viability of farming. Even after this factor has been segregated out, the real-estate tax does not reflect exclusively the price of the farmland because the assessed value includes the value of the house — in Williamson's case, of several houses; between 1860 and 1890, the number of houses on his land increased from one to four. Despite the modest increase in assessed value between the census years of 1870 and 1890, the total and per acre real-estate tax actually dropped slightly. Indeed, between 1870 and 1880, while the assessed value of the real estate declined by 25 percent, the total and per acre real-estate tax plummeted by 57 and 61 percent, respectively. During this decade, the value of Williamson's total farm output almost doubled — from $5,500 to $10,000.[13]

That Williamson's enterprise was prospering during these years is confirmed by the taxable income that he reported for purposes of the income tax that the federal government imposed between 1862 and 1871. In this last year of the tax, he self-declared $838.78 of taxable income in excess of all his business expenses and a $2,000 exemption. This net income or profit was more than half the total value of his production the preceding year. Nor was that year's profitability a fluke. For the tax year 1869, he reported taxable income of $2,546.94 over and above the $1,000 exemption; and for the years 1863, 1864, and 1865 he reported taxable income, in addition to the $500 exemption, of $1,060.76, $1,902.79, and $1,781.85, respectively. Such magnitudes do not suggest that property taxes were interfering with Williamson's capacity to operate his farm profitably.[14]

The situation after 1890, however, changed significantly. From 1890 to 1893, the assessed value of Williamson's real estate rose by 63 percent while his property-tax bill jumped 117 percent even after he had stopped adding new houses. Although the loss of the manuscript schedules of the 1890 census makes it impossible to reconstruct the course of Williamson's operations after 1880, macrodevelopments in Flatbush farming during the 1880s suggest that Williamson probably did not continue to double his output. If his output did stagnate or decline by the early 1890s, the fact that he subdivided all his land in 1894 is hardly surprising.[15]

The higher tax rates in the gas district were not so much the cause of the earlier cessation of farming there as symbols of the intrusion of (sub)urban life, which was increasingly inconsistent with farming. Although by the 1880 Census of Agriculture all of the handful of surviving owner-farmers were concentrated east of Flatbush Road outside the gas district, much of the farmland in the gas district was rented out to tenants. Tenancy was not, however, correlated with the differential levels of taxation: it antedated the introduction of gas lighting, and many of the farms lying along or adjacent to Flatbush Road had been operated by tenants for decades.

If the ad valorem tax of 2.29 percent of Flatbush in 1890 had actually been applied to the full value of the average Kings County farm, which was 41 acres and worth $844 per acre in 1889 for a total of $34,604, the owner would have incurred a tax liability of $792. In New Utrecht the liability would have been $924. With assessed valuation running at only 60 percent of "true" valuation in Flatbush, the liability would have been limited to $475; the 45.1 percent ratio in New Utrecht would have limited the property tax bill there to $417. These sums presumably would have been significant for most farmers, but there is evidence that assessments of farmland were relatively even lower than the average. For nonwealthy farmers, and especially for immigrant owners with mortgages, however, even a few hundred dollars must have been an appreciable deduction from funds available for accumulation and family consumption at a time when the average farm produced products valued at $3,531 annually. Only 10 years earlier, before the land boom had erupted, when the 1880 census reported an average land value of $474 per acre and average farm size of 25 acres, the resulting total value of $11,850, or a third of the average in 1890, would have been subject to a much less burdensome tax liability — closer to $150 for a farm producing products worth, on average, $2,983.[16]

The trend in farmland taxes in the other rural Kings County towns was similar to Williamson's, although they remained at lower levels. In Flatlands, per acre real property taxes for a group of the largest farmers rose from $0.90 in 1860 to $2.47 in 1870 before declining to $1.85 in 1880. These amounts represented quite modest deductions from profitable operations. Even as late as 1890, the average per acre tax of $3.11 was only about one-third of Williamson's tax. Even in 1892, when the average exceeded $5, it still remained far below the more than $17 that Williamson was paying. In Gravesend, the course of agricultural land taxes between 1860 and 1880 closely tracked that in neighboring Flatlands, but thereafter, under the pressure of the relentless development of the beachfront resorts, taxes rose more sharply, reaching almost $9 per acre by 1893. However, as the surviving account books of William Bennett, a large Gravesend potato farmer, attest, even such taxes did not undermine profitable operations: of the more than $32,000 in profits that Bennett recorded between 1883 and 1893, his property taxes represented less than 10 percent.[17]

These quantitative studies for Kings County do not gainsay the reality of tax-induced pressures on market gardeners. At the turn of the century in the Boston area, even though rising land prices "laid the foundation of fortunes" for market gardeners,[18] complaints were voiced that:

> near-by market gardeners are now suffering from burdensome and often unjust taxation. Situated within the rapidly growing towns, and near large cities, they are compelled to carry their proportionate part of the expensive improvements in the central portions of those towns, often receiving but little or no direct benefit from them.
>
> The solution of this problem can only be found in the gradual absorption and cutting up into house lots, of those farms, thereby compelling those continuing in this line of business, to move back where lands are to be had cheaper, and where therefore taxation is lower. It is the opinion now of many that this condition should be adjusted, even by legislation if necessary, so as to give encouragement to those who are continuously doing so much for the advancement of agriculture.[19]

PROPERTY TAX PREFERENCES FOR FARMERS IN THE NINETEENTH CENTURY

Flatbush real estate has been the cause of much prosperity. One farm sold some eight or nine years ago [1899–1900] for the total valuation of 1817.
— Charles Andrew Ditmas, *Brooklyn's Garden*, 1908

In fact, several states did tailor tax adjustments to urban market-gardeners in the nineteenth century, and Kings County farmers were among the prime beneficiaries of such intervention. The manifold forces constraining farmers' decisions to keep farming or to sell out were complex, but one fallacy underlying the empirically unsupported claim that property taxes forced Kings County farmers out is the belief, held by many land-use planners and scholars, that no state enacted a preferential tax law for farmland until 1956, when Maryland required that: "Lands which are actively devoted to farm or agricultural use shall be assessed on the basis of such use, and shall not be assessed as if sub-divided or on any other basis." According to A. M. Woodruff, a land economist and planning commissioner: "Starting with Maryland in the 1960s, a movement spread throughout most states to tax fringe farmland not on market value but on usufruct."[20]

Such views, however, are amnesiac. Many states conferred various types of tax preferences on farmland owners in the nineteenth century in connection with the incorporation of such land into the burgeoning cities. One form in which states lightened the tax burden of urban farm districts was to relieve them of the obligation to contribute to the cost of supporting city services, such as police, fire, and lighting districts, which were deemed unnecessary for farmers. The New York State legislature treated the agricultural wards, such as Gowanus and Bushwick, that were incorporated into Brooklyn in 1834 and 1854 in this manner.[21]

In the wake of extending the corporate limits of its largest cities, Pennsylvania required assessors in Philadelphia in 1856 to assess and collect only two-thirds of the city tax rate on real estate used for agricultural purposes; in 1868 the legislature reduced this agricultural rate to one-half of the highest rate. Two years later, in extending the boundaries of the city of Erie, the legislature required the city government to "discriminate in laying the city taxes as not to impose on the rural portions those expenses which belong exclusively to the built up portions" such as those associated with lighting, paving, police, and water. In 1859 Connecticut limited the assessment of city tax on lands used exclusively for farming purposes within the territory annexed to Hartford that year.[22]

Nor were such special provisions for farms located within areas annexed to cities confined to the citified East. As early as 1833, and continuing for many years, Kentucky withheld from the city of Louisville the power to tax rural areas that the legislature permitted it to incorporate. Even rural Iowa enacted a city limits extension law in 1876 providing that no land within the new city limits that was not "laid off into lots of twenty acres or less . . . and which shall also in good faith be occupied and used for agricultural or horticultural purposes, shall be taxable for any city purpose." In upholding the statute in 1887, the Iowa Supreme Court opined: "Where the limits of a city are extended so as to take in what is used essentially as a farm, there is much reason for exempting it from city taxes." That court also explained the background to the intensively litigated disputes over the tax status of urban farmland in 1864: "the immigration to this State was heavy, and the growth and improvement of our river towns . . . were rapid, not to say marvelous, the population, in some instances, flowing over and beyond their chartered limits." When the legislature enlarged these cities' corporate boundaries, it took "very much more territory than was needed for immediate population and building purposes; in view, perhaps, of prospective enlargement of the same."[23]

From the mid-nineteenth century forward, farmers whose land had been incorporated into nearby cities challenged the constitutionality of any taxation on the grounds that they received no benefits from the urban services that their taxes financed. The details of these political-economic and constitutional-doctrinal struggles are not relevant here — in Kings County the issue was not whether in principle farmers in the towns annexed to Brooklyn could be taxed, but whether they would receive tax preferences. But the U.S. Supreme Court's rejection in 1881 of a Pennsylvania farmer's claim that the tax had violated his rights under the Fourteenth Amendment to the U.S. Constitution by depriving him of his property without due process of law is particularly illuminating because the facts that he alleged were so extreme that they lent strong support to the argument that city taxes "force" farmers out of business.[24]

James Kelly owned an 80-acre farm, which came within the consolidated city limits of Pittsburgh after the state legislature had extended them in 1867. He asserted that because the city had not filled in its orginal limits, not only did much vacant land separate the city's inhabited portions from his farm, but a generation or even fifty years would pass before the city would need his land for its growing population; in the meantime, Pittsburgh had failed to spend a dollar to enhance the farm's value. Under these circumstances, Kelly argued, the city lacked any right to interfere with his property — "until the natural growth and multiplication of numbers and extension, and reasonable business of the city shall require the use of his . . . farm for city purposes." This concession was significant for its acceptance of the "natural" character of the process by which cities absorbed farmland and converted it into an incompatible use. In the meantime, however, the city assessed Kelly's farm at $244,000 — this $3,050 per acre value far exceeded all other countywide farm values in the 1870s — and levied a tax of $2,672.48 for 1874. Since, according to Kelly, "the greatest productive income or value" of his farm was a mere $10 per acre or $800 for the whole farm, the tax was tantamount to "confiscation" — especially since he owed an additional $428.47 in state and county taxes.[25]

A tax bill that was almost four times the farm's net income was a spectacular illustration of every antiannexationist farmer's worst nightmare and thus the best imaginable propaganda. The master to whom the case was referred found that at least some of Kelly's allegations concerning the lack of city services were accurate, but he also reported that even before consolidation the value of Kelly's farm, which had been close to the city, had risen in tandem with Pittsburgh's growth and prosperity "until it became very great." Consequently, any interference with the city's development brought about by a reduction in tax revenues needed for providing services would "seriously affect the value" of the farmland. Therefore, Kelly's claim that he received no special benefits was misconceived and "the idea that taxing unproductive property according to its market value is confiscating it" was equally mistaken.[26]

Despite the impressive numbers pointing clearly toward bankruptcy or a forced sell-off and abandonment of farming, the Pennsylvania Supreme Court displayed even less sympathy, subtly suggesting that Kelly may have been a mere speculator. Without being able to divine the meaning of Kelly's argument that the city's tax power had to be suspended until the farmland was needed for city uses, the judges suspected that what Kelly really meant was that an annexed farmer could not be taxed "until the city is so nearly built up to his lands that they may be advantageously laid out and sold as city lots." Kelly's complaints about the disparity between burdens and benefits were hardly novel: "if direct personal benefit were to form a criterion for taxation we should have half the community clamoring at our doors for relief." After all, Kelly was not only no worse off than the childless who had to pay school taxes, but he had already received relief from the state legislature in the form of the statute mandating a 50 percent reduction in municipal tax rates for rural lands. The U.S. Supreme Court was also unable to muster much sympathy for Kelly's plight. His taxes might have borne "a very unjust relation" to the benefits he received: "But who can adjust with precise accuracy the amount which each individual in an organized civil community shall contribute to sustain it?" The Court consoled him with the prospect that even if the streets did not penetrate his farm, they at least led to it, and the waterworks "will probably reach him some day."[27]

When the New York State legislature, contingent on the approval by the electors, annexed the town of New Lots to Brooklyn in 1873, a compromise on levels of taxation for the new residents of the country's third-largest city facing large and expensive infrastructure projects was an essential component of the political process. The statute provided that: "The valuation for the purposes of taxation of lands actually used for agricultural purposes . . . shall be based upon the value of said lands . . . for agricultural purposes only." Farmers were able to mobilize a majority of voters against annexation

FIGURE 20. *New Lots farm of Jacob Rapelje, 1890s. The smokestacks in the background signal the city's encroachment. Courtesy of Peter Rapelje.*

at that time, but when it was finally implemented in 1886, the legislature provided that: "For the purposes of taxation the real estate included within the territory hereby annexed shall be assessed at the value of the land for agricultural purposes, unless the same shall have been, at the time this act shall take effect, or shall thereafter be divided up into building lots, and a map thereof filed in the office of the register of deeds of the county of Kings, or in the office of the board of assessors of the city of Brooklyn, and a sale or sales referring to such map made or unless the same shall have been otherwise sold as a building lot or used as such."[28]

The vitality of the 1886 New Lots provision was demonstrated by a decision of the state's highest court in 1891. Stephen L. Vanderveer owned a 109-acre farm located in Flatbush, Flatlands, and New Lots. In 1888, the Brooklyn assessors assessed Vanderveer, who resided on the 30-acre segment located within New Lots, on the whole farm including the parts lying outside of Brooklyn. Although the Court of Appeals decided the case against Vanderveer because another state statute specified that such farms were to be taxed in the county or ward where the occupant resided, no one contested the validity of the special assessment rate for agricultural purposes.[29]

When the New York State legislature at last gave effect to "the manifest destiny of the towns" to join Brooklyn by enacting annexation legislation in 1894, consolidating Kings County and the City of Brooklyn on January 1, 1896, it inserted provisions identical to the New Lots agricultural preference in the statutes for Gravesend and Flatlands, the two most rural towns. Flatlands in particular was a town that, according to the *Eagle*, in its more than 250-year existence "had never until after annexation risen much above the dignity of a farming settlement" because farming and market gardening were "extensively carried on" there on the eve of annexation.[30]

The accommodation for New Utrecht, in contrast, provided that: "The aggregate assessed valuation of the real estate . . . exclusive of the additional value caused by the erection of new buildings or other structures, shall not, during the five years commencing with the year eighteen hundred and ninety-four and ending with the year eighteen hundred and ninety-eight, be increased in any one year more than twenty per cent over and above such valuation for the year immediately preceding; and such valuation shall be deemed the 'full and fair market value' of such property for the purpose of taxation." New Utrecht residents argued for this provision on the grounds that town mismanagement had brought about such a high and unjust rate of taxation that it was difficult to borrow money on property; the tax exemption was designed to induce new property buyers to move to New Utrecht. In further negotiations, representatives of New Utrecht agreed to exclude new buildings from the 20 percent provision. The aforementioned bad government included "lines of costly lights strung along fields as destitute of cultivation as they are barren of settlement."[31] Speaking before the Society of Old Brooklynites in October 1894, Jere Johnson, a key county real-estate figure, vividly portrayed these developments:

> During the last few years the greatest extravagance has been practiced in the county towns which now form the Thirtieth [New Utrecht] and Thirty-first wards [Gravesend]. . . . [S]treets not needed for generations have been constructed at fabulous prices, and in the town of New Utrecht 4,000 gas lamps, erected principally to light grass, potato and cabbage fields, on a long contract, at an annual expense of $130,000. Wonderful for vegetables, attractive for night bugs, bankruptcy for owner! No wonder taxes in the now Thirtieth Ward have increased tenfold in eight years. I say shame on such useless prodigality.[32]

The Flatbush annexation statute alone lacked a corresponding provision. It is unclear why the legislature conferred such different levels of tax protection on the farmers of the five towns when they were annexed to Brooklyn. It is possible that the more advanced stage of deagriculturalization along with the more highly developed infrastructure in Flatbush — which was already constructing a sewer system — made it less necessary to accommodate its farmers, who were more clearly on the way out of business than were their counterparts in the other towns. If, as the *Eagle* editorialized, "Flatbush had more desire and less need of annexation than New Utrecht or Gravesend," then the other towns' greater need and less desire may have induced legislators to make the transition more appealing. Of New Utrecht *The Citizen Guide to Brooklyn and Long Island* noted in 1893: "Formerly the majority of its people were engaged in gardening, but it looks now as if all the farms were being cut up into streets and planted with the homes of the prosperous middle classes."[33]

This understanding of the differences among the towns that might have prompted the legislature to confer varying levels of tax protection on landowners receives strong support from the court submissions of a litigant defending the validity of the Gravesend annexation provision two decades later. The Coney Island Jockey Club argued that:

> The territory contained in the towns of New Utrecht and Flatbush was of a totally different character from that contained in the Towns of Gravesend and Flatland [*sic*].
>
> New Utrecht and Flatbush contained little farming land. Their real estate was mostly used for building lots.
>
> The Towns of Flatlands and Gravesend contained a great amount of farming lands, and a comparatively small amount of lots valuable for building lots.[34]

The New York press reported repeatedly on certain tax aspects of the annexation, but devoted scant attention to the favored agricultural treatment. Perhaps the most extensive discussion emerged in a statement by Brooklyn Corporation Counsel McDonald, at a hearing held by the New York State Senate Cities Committee on March 8, 1894. Emphasizing that the city of Brooklyn, which strongly advocated annexation of all the towns simultaneously or not at all, was caught in a fiscal predicament because it had almost reached its constitutional debt limit while having contracted for infrastructure projects in excess of the lawful limits of its bond issue, he noted the serious implications of annexing territories as large again as Brooklyn that were "to a certain extent rural, undeveloped and without such improvements as are customary to a city." By the same token, McDonald argued that the annexation bills embodied the town residents' self-regarding interests; among the measures "obnoxious to the city" was a restriction of

> the assessed valuation on a rural basis for a term of years and guaranteeing an increase of only a certain per cent. for the same term of years. This simply restricts the Brooklyn board of assessors by direct legislation from using the same liberty with the property in annexed districts that is used on property in the city. . . . I have the authority of our city treasurer that . . . the city cannot ignore one town at the expense of another. It must treat all with equal fairness.[35]

It was generally known or at least believed in real-estate circles of the time that: "Rural land is assessed . . . for only a proportion of its value, and what is worse, for a very varying proportion."[36] Dissatisfaction with unequal assessments had become widespread enough to prompt the *New York Daily Tribune* in 1896 to devote a long article to their excesses in Brooklyn. Purportedly reflecting "the unanimity of views" gathered from the borough's "leading real estate and business men," the piece repeatedly used farms in Flatbush (the new 29th Ward) as examples. Most prominent was a 45-acre farm mentioned by the counsel of the Brooklyn Taxpayers' Association, which was assessed at $136,400:

> The land has always been used for agricultural purposes, and is now being cultivated by a tenant, who pays $1,100 a year rent. There are no streets through the property. . . . The present use of this land is all that it is good for, as the Flatbush market is now overstocked with building lots, and no more lots are needed at present. The cash value of this farm is not more than $35,000. . . . Taking into consideration the sale of surrounding farms, and the asking price on any terms, what right has the Board of Assessors to value this property as city lots? When valuations are made, the property should be taken as it is, its use taken into consideration as well as the income. The Assessors should not judge as to how a man ought to improve his property.[37]

The *Tribune* reporter learned from the Assessors' office that "discrimination of the assessment in the various towns was caused by certain legislative enactments, being a part of the various annexation acts, which had to be treated in the nature of contracts with the residents of the respective localities, and that by reason of such acts the Assessors were compelled to assess the property in such towns according to its use, irrespective of value." After quoting the special tax provisions for agriculture in the New Lots, Gravesend, and Flatlands annexation statutes, the reporter observed that the "Assessors consider that their duties under this provision are to assess the land according to the amount of produce that can be raised on it. In other words, they become experts upon the value of land for raising crops, instead of its value as land in a residential community." In spite of the assessors' "clear" duty under the New Utrecht provision limiting increases in valuations to 20 percent annually through 1898, the land there had become "greatly undervalued" because valuations had not risen more than 10 percent. Another expert informant stated that residents of Flatbush had been "greatly surprised" by their tax bills for 1895 showing increases of almost 50 percent; in particular, "unimproved property or farm lands were in some instances assessed at the rate of $5,000 an acre." [38]

These examples suggest that the special provisions in the annexation statutes for the towns did in fact protect farm landowners from steep development-related tax increases in Kings County except in Flatbush, on which the legislature conferred no such benefit. But even in Flatbush, as another real-estate expert informed the reporter, an assessor valued vacant lots by figuring "the kind of 'crap' you can get out of it. Now, ''taters' is a pretty good 'crap' down there, and I think the value of those lots ought to be fixed by the amount of ''taters' you can raise on them." [39]

The precise longevity of the preferential agricultural assessment provisions of the Brooklyn annexation statutes is unclear. In 1897 a state intermediate appellate court construed the tax provision in the Gravesend annexation statute in favor of the landowner. It is unknown when the New York City tax authorities began administratively challenging the validity of the special provisions for farmers in the former Kings County towns, but the point was not judicially determined until 1912, when it was held that they had been repealed by implication by the Tax Law of 1898 or the Greater New York charter of 1898. The issue was still relevant in Gravesend where "[j]ust after the turn of century, the land still clung to its country character," and "prosperous farmers" owned fields and meadows. [40] In a case involving the assessment of 52 parcels of 430 acres of land in Gravesend owned by the Coney Island Jockey Club, the New York City Commissioners of Taxes and Assessments had assessed the land at a value in excess of its alleged value for agricultural purposes at $160,000. In explaining its decision, the court offered revealing detail about the purposes behind the original preferences:

The sentiment favoring urban enlargement resulted in the incorporation within the city of Brooklyn of the outlying and thinly populated territory, which had scant or infrequent need or capacities for the usual privileges, improvements and protections of the city, save as it should, from time to time, by subdivision into lots come into the uses of residence or business. To gather this outlying domain into the city and force upon it urban characteristics, which it did not have, appealed to the State as incongruous or undesirable. Hence it was included for what it was in its general extent, naked land, approximating more nearly to agricultural uses, and assessors were commanded to regard it as such, unless the owner would otherwise adapt his land in the manner indicated by the statute. Did the Legislature, after an intervening year, the territory having been brought in, capriciously reverse its policy and disappoint those who had abided by the promise that the rural quality of the land for taxation be preserved? That it could, by sheer force, have done so should not be doubted, but the act would have carried to the inhabitants of Gravesend some just sense of injury to them and of injustice on the part of the State. For in the meantime the nature of the locality could have little changed.

Although the court speculated that it was "contrary to the general policy of the State to limit for the purposes of taxation land to its value for agricultural purposes where its relation to population and the demand for it for other uses gave it a much greater value, which was its actual value irrespective of its incorporation into a city," it held that "justice" was subordinated to power: "The town of Gravesend did not voluntarily contribute its territory or yield rights. The Legislature had full power to incorporate it willingly or unwillingly, and if the State justly or unjustly made concession to the town in the matter of taxation, it could take away at any time what as an act of grace and without consideration it had given. The matter is purely political." [41]

9. WERE ALL KINGS COUNTY FARMERS DESCENDANTS OF THE ORIGINAL DUTCH SETTLERS? THE FARM-TENURE STRUCTURE

Farmers cannot pay more than twenty dollars per acre, rent, and make a living.
— Charles Andrew Ditmas, *Brooklyn's Garden*, 1908

The Dutch farmers successfully managed the transition from extensive to intensive farming, but many of them eventually removed themselves from actual farm operations. Although they continued to own much if not most of the farmland, Dutch farmers increasingly sold or rented their land to German and Irish immigrants. These trends toward tenancy and ethnic heterogeneity, which characterized the farm sector by the 1880s, are the focus of this chapter, which also explores the consequences of this peculiar farm-tenure structure for the longevity of vegetable cultivation and the specific patterns shaping the eventual land sell-off.

NOT ALL FARMERS WERE DUTCH OR OWNERS

As long as it was possible to do so, the landowners retained their farms as such; they were not anxious to cut up their beautiful fields into city lots, or to widen the green lanes and country roads into dusty avenues and wide boulevards.
— Gertrude Lefferts Vanderbilt, *The Social History of Flatbush*, 1880

The discussion of property taxes and other forces shaping Kings County farmers' decisions to sell their land conjures up the image of the prototypical farmer as a ninth-generation Dutch farm owner-operator, whose entire psychic and material inheritance and existence were inextricably interwoven with his farm. Such farmers did exist. Rulef van Brunt, a large New Utrecht farmer, died in 1883 on a farm that his family had owned for more than two centuries. The historian John A. Kouwenhoven in 1982 observed that his father, "born in 1870 on a Flatlands farm nine generations of his family had tilled, heard Dutch nursery rhymes from his mother and grandmother." And Gertrude Lefferts Vanderbilt poignantly reinforced this image in 1880: "Nearly all the landed proprietors in Flatbush are those to whom the titles of their farms have been transmitted for several generations, dating in many cases from the settlement of the Dutch on Long Island. Now the land is passing out of the hands of its former owners, the old names are disappearing, and the descendants of the first settlers are comparatively few." [1]

But not all late-nineteenth-century Kings County farm operators were owners of farms that had been in their families for two centuries. Nor were all farmers owners. Even in Lefferts Vanderbilt's Flatbush, the 1880 census revealed that literally only a handful of old-line Dutch owner-operators remained. A growing proportion were new immigrants, and slightly more than half of all farms were operated by tenants. Some tenancies were, to be sure, merely temporary expedients. For example, when Joris Lott, one of Flatlands' largest farm owners, died in 1835 at the age of 56, his wife Wilhelmina — "a most capable and energetic woman, possessing a mind of her own . . . showed much business tact and conducted her farm with exactness and profit" — leased the farm to various tenants until her sons Peter and George were old enough to operate it. [2]

But tenancy was not necessarily a transitional form: among the market gardeners to whom Peter Wyckoff rented 90 acres of his Brooklyn farm, one had leased for 41 years. Another factor promoting tenancy in Flatbush was that town's Reformed Protestant Dutch Church, which the *Eagle* in 1873 estimated as owning lands and houses valued at half a million dollars. Most of the land was retained in old farms, "generally let out to persons who usually are gardeners, who till the soil and devote all of its productive power to the yielding of market vegetables and fruits." Even if the Flatbush assessment roll for that year lists the church as owning only 50 acres valued at about $60,000, its centrally located lands clearly added to the stock available for tenancy. In the mid-1880s, the church was still letting considerable farmland to relatively large Irish and second-generation Irish and German vegetable growers: 56 acres to John Heaslip, 14 acres to William Garnin, and 13 acres to Edward Kennedy. [3]

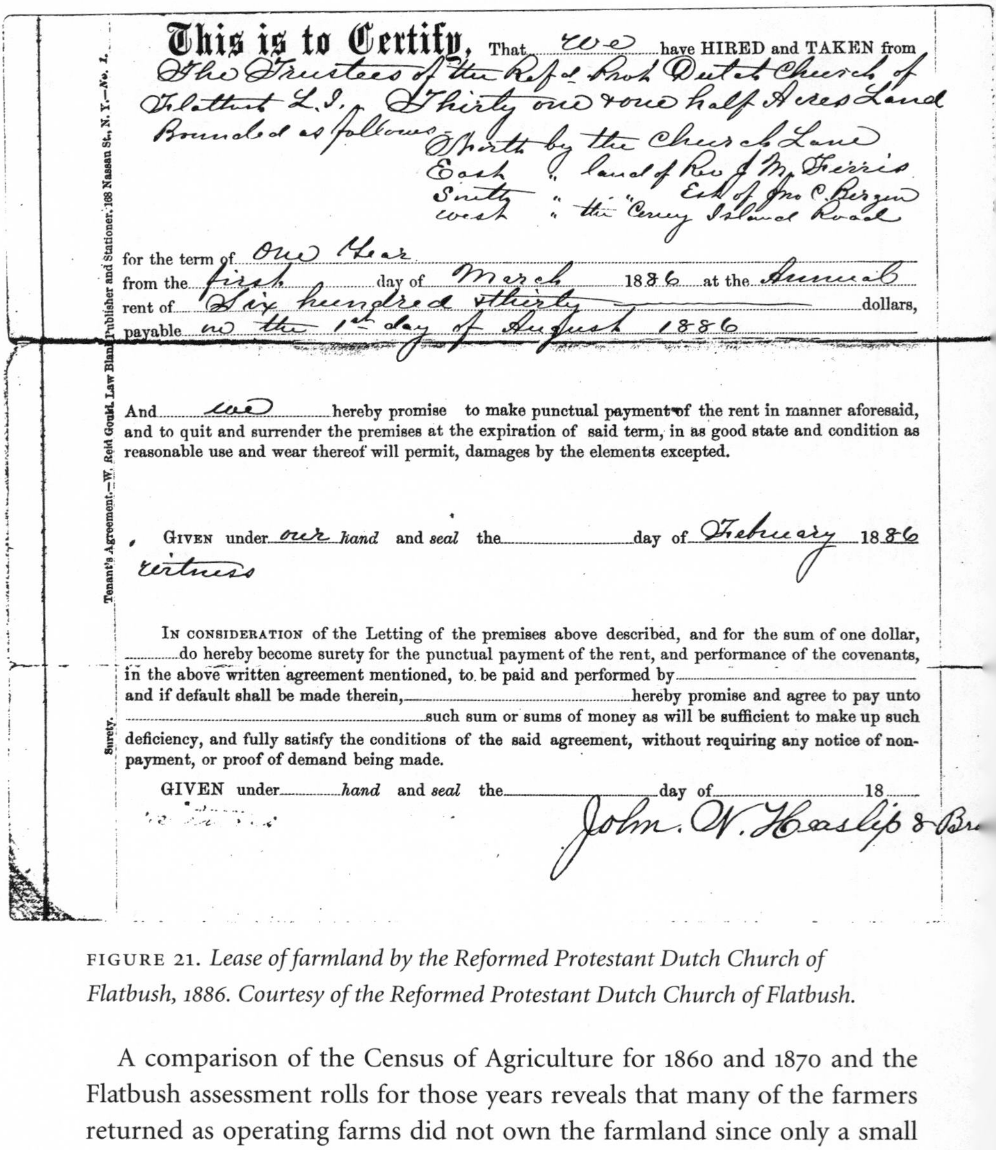
Tenant's Agreement.—W. Reid Gould, Law Blank Publisher and Stationer, 188 Nassau St., N. Y.—No. 1.

This is to Certify, That we have HIRED and TAKEN from The Trustees of the Ref'd Prot Dutch Church of Flatbush L.I. Thirty one & one half Acres Land Bounded as follows – North by the Church Lane
East " land of Rev J M Ferris
South " Est of Jno C Bergen
West " the Coney Island Road

for the term of One Year from the first day of March 1886 at the Annual rent of Six hundred & thirty dollars, payable on the 1st day of August 1886

And we hereby promise to make punctual payment of the rent in manner aforesaid, and to quit and surrender the premises at the expiration of said term, in as good state and condition as reasonable use and wear thereof will permit, damages by the elements excepted.

Given under our hand and seal the ____ day of February 1886
witness

Surety.

In consideration of the Letting of the premises above described, and for the sum of one dollar, ____ do hereby become surety for the punctual payment of the rent, and performance of the covenants, in the above written agreement mentioned, to be paid and performed by ____ and if default shall be made therein, ____ hereby promise and agree to pay unto ____ such sum or sums of money as will be sufficient to make up such deficiency, and fully satisfy the conditions of the said agreement, without requiring any notice of non-payment, or proof of demand being made.

GIVEN under ____ hand and seal the ____ day of ____ 18__

John W. Haslip & Bro

FIGURE 21. *Lease of farmland by the Reformed Protestant Dutch Church of Flatbush, 1886. Courtesy of the Reformed Protestant Dutch Church of Flatbush.*

A comparison of the Census of Agriculture for 1860 and 1870 and the Flatbush assessment rolls for those years reveals that many of the farmers returned as operating farms did not own the farmland since only a small proportion of the census farmers appear on the assessment rolls as owning any land, let alone the large acreage recorded by the census. The most intriguing possibility, at least for the 1880s, is that some landowners who were letting their farms to tenants may not have been (former) farmers themselves; instead, they may have been speculators who had bought up the farms and were at least obtaining rent (and taking advantage of the lower tax rate on agricultural land) while waiting for the most profitable moment for development.

Not even all Dutch farm families had owned their land since the beginning of Dutch settlement in the seventeenth century. Some acquired their farms in the late eighteeenth or even nineteenth century from other Dutch families. For example, Teunis G. Bergen, the militant traditionalist, occupied a farm that his father had not bought until 1828. By 1877, according to the *Rural Gazette*, John Lefferts, John Vanderveer, and Mrs. John Ditmas were the sole remaining landowners in Flatbush who held their titles from original grants that had never been transferred. And even in John Lefferts's case, the totality of land that he inherited had not been acquired all at once upon the arrival of his ancestor, Leffert Pietersen, in Flatbush in 1660, but had been assembled through purchases and marriage over several generations. Nor was all the land owned by Kings County Dutch farming families located in Kings County: John Lefferts's sister, Gertrude Lefferts Vanderbilt, inherited their father's lands in Jamaica, Queens.[4]

Another vivid illustration of long-term turns and twists in land acquisition is Rem Hegeman (1795–1867). In 1836 he bought a farm in Flatlands from Nicholas Van Dyke, whose family apparently had acquired it at some point from the Hogeland family, which, in turn, had purchased it in two parts in 1707 and 1722. This land was situated within the original 1636 patent to Andries Hudde and Wolfert Garretsen van Couwenhoven. Hegeman's ancestors had arrived in Kings County in 1650. Rem Hegeman, "a frequent purchaser of small plots of land and meadows," "evidently had a speculative tendency and his judgment seems to have been good, for he generally sold his purchases for more than he had given." (Hegeman was returned at the 1850 and 1860 Census of Agriculture as owning a farm of 48 acres and 10 acres, respectively.) The executors of his estate, in turn, sold it to the heirs of Jeffries Van Wyck in 1869. The land, at Flatbush Avenue and Kings Highway, had always been "the center of the village life of Flatlands."[5]

Even before the Civil War it was not at all out of the ordinary for large Dutch farm owners to rent out some of their land. For example, John A. Lott's uncle and father-in-law, Jeremiah Lott (1776–1861), whom the 1853 Flatbush assessment roll listed as owning 164 acres of farmland (in addition to 50 acres of woodland), and whom the 1860 Census of Agriculture returned as farming 80 acres, leased 10 acres to Thomas Bennet from 1858 to 1863 for $80 annually to be paid in two payments. Under the indenture, the tenant promised that he would "well and sufficiently plough, manure, plant, sow, employ, manage, cultivate and keep in tillage the . . . premises in a good, careful and husbandmanlike manner . . . and shall not . . . do or commit or permit, or suffer to be done any wilful or voluntary waste, spoil or destruc- tion . . . and furnish at his or their proper costs . . . all the necessary and re- quired manure, horses, cattles, carriages, wagons, tool and implements . . . and do . . . and cause . . . to be performed all the work and labor necessary for the proper cultivation." The $8 per acre rental that Lott received far ex- ceeded his $1.80 per acre property tax that year. Similarly, when descen- dants of the Martense family, one of Flatbush's most prominent, sold the old Martense Homestead in 1889, it, too, had already for many years been occupied by tenants.[6]

Contemporaries were well aware of the economically different positions of those in Kings County who owned their farms "free and clear of all in- cumbrance" and the larger class of renters. In a remarkable reflection on the need for "Local Emigration from Kings County," W. H. Stillwell in 1872 ex- empted to some extent farmers without mortgages from the forces of com- petition propelling tenants, who had to compete with distant farmers pro- ducing on cheaper land with cheaper labor and much less manure, "to newer and cheaper lands where they may reap the advantages of fertile soil and profitably contribute to supply the wants of Kings county, whose lands cannot supply a tithe of the wants of the city and suburban villages for agri- cultural products."[7]

Many different reasons impelled farmers to rent their farms to tenants. One unusual case can perhaps be understood as an illustration of the lack of capacity to operate or manage spatially separated farms. At the time of the 1880 census, the 27-year-old John Ditmas, scion of one of the oldest and land-richest families of rural Kings County, operated a 57-acre farm in Flat- lands, employing three farm laborers who lived on the farm, on which $5,000 worth of products were produced. Late that year he announced that since he was leaving for his new home in New Lots, a tenant would occupy the homestead farm and another would work 23 acres. Ditmas himself was "fully occupied in properly caring for the estate, without the extra labor nec- essary for farming." A few months later it was revealed that he had moved to New Lots into the house of his father-in-law. His wife's family, the Lin- ingtons, was one of the biggest farm operators in the county.[8]

Other farmers let out their farms because impairments of their health made it impossible for them personally to continue farming. Some land- owners were not farmers at all. William Langley, one of the richest New

York merchants living in rural Kings County, owned a 44-acre farm in addition to other land in New Utrecht. In 1876 he advertised in the *Rural Gazette* that those interested in letting his farm could inquire at 78 Worth Street in Manhattan or at his house in Bay Ridge after 6 P.M. John A. Lott, in a class by himself as a landowner, had never personally farmed; instead, he rented out his farmlands to various tenants in several of the rural towns. John C. Bergen, who in 1870 at age 44 owned a 145-acre farm in Flatlands (only 22 acres of which were improved) on which he produced only $1,500 worth of products, repeatedly advertised for tenants to occupy a 63-acre farm on Bergen's Island off Jamaica Bay in the 1870s, presumably because he had moved from Flatlands and perhaps entered into other business pursuits.[9]

WHO WERE THE KINGS COUNTY FARMERS?

Within the recollections of the author, there were three large farms in Bedford, one in Flatbush and two in New Utrecht cultivated by Leffertses, who were among the wealthy, respected and successful cultivators in Kings county: at present there is but one held by an individual of the name, that of Mr. John Lefferts of Flatbush, a worthy successor of his ancestors, occupying premises held by the family for at least five generations.

— Bergen, *Genealogy of the Lefferts Family 1650–1878*, 1878

As a first approach to gauging the trend to tenancy, the number and ethnic composition of the residents of the five Kings County towns returned as farmers at the 1860, 1870, and 1880 censuses are reported in table 25. U.S.-born farmers formed the large majority throughout this period, but the number and proportion of farmers who had been born in Ireland and Germany rose threefold — from 59, or 11 percent, in 1860 to 94, or 19 percent, in 1870 to 172, or 35 percent, in 1880. This shift toward foreign-born farmers suggests that some multigenerational Dutch farm families had either already sold their farms or were renting them to tenants. In fact, tenancy, especially by Irish immigrants, increased enormously by 1880, leading the *Rural Gazette* to acknowledge that they could be good market gardeners. The ethnic shift is underscored by a count of specific names. The number of farmers (including both those returned as "retired" and sons returned as "farmer" even though they were living in their parents' household) from 50 old-line Dutch farming families fell by almost one-half from the 1860 to the 1880 Census of Population. Whereas these 384 farmers accounted for 70 percent of all rural Kings County farmers in 1860, by 1870 their 300 counterparts made up 59 percent of farmers, and the 204 in 1880 accounted for only 42 percent. Similarly, the number of old-line Dutch family farmers returned at the 1850, 1860, 1870, and 1880 Census of Agriculture was 203, 194, 148, and 154; they accounted for 76, 51, 58, and 40 percent of all farmers enumerated in those years in rural Kings County.[10]

The full extent of concentration of wealth in the old-line Dutch families is obscured by the intense intermarriage, "a kind of extended clan" reminiscent of "the Hapsburg marital connections." This "rule of endogamy" included the following "Dutch patrician pairings":

> Judge John A. Lott and the daughter of his [uncle] Jeremiah Lott; Stephen Schenck and Maria Martense; Lucas J. Voorhees and Gertrude Suydam; John Lott Van Pelt and Anna Maria Cortelyou; Garret Co[u]wenhoven and Magdalen Van Nuyse; Theodore V. Bergen and Nettie Co[u]wenhoven; John C. Vanderveer and Elizabeth Van Brunt; Judge Garret L. Martense and Jane Vanderveer; Dr. Adrian Vanderveer and Elizabeth Lott; Rem Hegeman and Helen Wyckoff; Abraham Polhemus and Mary C. Gerritson; John Vanderbilt and Gertrude Lefferts; Garret Martense and Jane Ann Ditma[r]s; Teunis G. Bergen and Catherine Lott.[11]

This intermarriage extended also to families that were originally English, such as the Stillwells, who early on became so intertwined with Dutch families that they were well known for their unswerving allegiance to the Dutch government. This "unwritten, local social code that encouraged inter-marriage . . . and frowned severely on matrimonial alliances with 'outsiders,'" not only "caused the entire population to be intimately related," but also led to great confusion because there were "probably not more than twenty-five family names."[12]

The newly arrived Irish and German farmers could not have formed the same cultural-emotional attachment to their farms (if indeed they were owners at all) that long-term Dutch farmers had. To the extent that the newer immigrants developed short-term instrumental attitudes toward making a living in their new country of residence, this phenomenon would reinforce the argument that, despite the peak outputs achieved in 1880, the end of Kings County agriculture was already in sight. Even if the new immigrant farmers were owners, the fact that they had had to buy the farms implies mortgage payments that would have subjected them to cost and profitability pressures unknown to the old-line Dutch farmers. Unsurprisingly, they were also less likely to accumulate the great amounts of wealth that Dutch farmers had amassed. The late advent of non-Dutch farmers emerges clearly from the 1850 Flatbush census. Of 142 persons returned as farmers (including sons of farmers), only 6 were not U.S.-born (3 in Ireland, 2 in Germany, and 1 in Wales). Only 2 were also listed in the Census of Agriculture as owner, agent, or manager of a farm, and only 1, Thomas Murphy, owned a farm valued at an appreciable amount ($20,000). In 1870, 11 of the 13 farmers in Kings County who reported $100,000 or more in such property were members of old-line Dutch families; only 2 were Irish or second-generation Irish. One of these was William, the 38-year-old son of Thomas Murphy, who reported $120,000 worth of real estate, while 55-year-old Irish-born John Phillips reported $100,000.[13]

As with farm laborers, the countywide data conceal marked differences among the five towns. Table 26 breaks out the data by town. Whereas in 1860 and 1870 the predominance of U.S.-born farmers impressed all the towns with the same stamp, ethnic differences came to the fore by 1880: the Irish were clearly more important than the Germans in Flatbush and nonexistent in New Lots, whereas the Germans outnumbered the Irish in New Lots, Flatlands, and New Utrecht. The lopsidedness of the ethnic composition among farmers in Flatbush and New Lots conforms to that among farm laborers. The sudden advance of the Irish during the 1870s from 12 percent to 40 percent of all Flatbush farmers was particularly impressive when their historical disadvantages are recalled: few Irish (or for that matter few non-Dutch) settled in Flatbush or elsewhere in Kings County during the colonial period because the descendants of the original Dutch settlers monopolized the farmland. Even in the most homogeneous farming town, Gravesend, where in 1860 U.S.-born farmers accounted for 94 percent of all farmers, Germans and Irish increased their representation from only 4 percent in 1860 to 20 percent in 1870 and 34 percent in 1880.[14]

Unsurprisingly, only a single black farmer was recorded in 1860, 1870, or 1880. (In 1850, not only were no blacks returned as farmers in Flatbush, but every single black person whose occupation was entered was listed as a laborer.) This man, whom the Census of Population returned as 50-year-old F. Anderson of Flatbush in 1870 and 63-year-old Frank Anderson of Flatbush in 1880 (and may or may not have been the same person), was an example of a not uncommon census phenomenon — the "farmer" without a farm, who was not listed in the 1880 Census of Agriculture as a farm owner or tenant. Anderson was far from alone. In 1880, 481 persons (excluding retired farmers) were returned as farmers by the Census of Population in rural Kings County, whereas the Census of Agriculture returned only 388 persons as conducting a farm. This excess of 24 percent was considerably lower than the 88 percent in 1870, when the 478 farmers enumerated by the Census of Population exceeded the 254 agents, owners, or managers of farms returned in the Census of Agriculture, or the 46 percent for 1860.[15]

OWNERS AND TENANTS COMPARED

The old Dutch farmers somehow left their virtues in the soil, so that it has not been favorable to successors of ignoble breed.
—*Flatbush of To-Day: The Realm of Light and Air*, 1908

The tenure relations on Kings County farms by the late nineteenth century also no longer reflected a homogeneous Dutch yeomanry. Table 27 identifies Flatbush farmers by tenancy and ethnicity in 1880. It reveals that by 1880, of 47 farms returned by the Census of Agriculture for Flatbush, 38 were operated by tenants, only 7 by owners, and 2 included both owned and rented land. All six of the identifiable outright owners were old-line Dutch farmers (the seventh was not listed as a farmer in the Census of Population for that year): Neefus, George and John Schenck, Suydam, Vanderveer, and Williamson. Of the 33 tenants identifiable from the Census of Population, 18 had been born in Ireland (arguably all 5 unidentifiable tenants also had Irish names), 2 were second-generation Irish, 2 had been born in Germany, 2 were second-generation Germans, and 1 each had been born in England and Russia. Several of the seven U.S.-born tenants (Van Wyck, Eldert, Lefferts, and Schoonmaker) stemmed from old-line Dutch farm families and were presumably tenants of relatives. The most prominent Dutch tenant was James Lefferts, whose father John was one of the rural county's wealthiest landowners; in 1875, he started operating his father's farm "on his own hook."[16]

Thus already by 1880, when Kings County vegetable growers produced their peak output, tenants overwhelmingly conducted the farms and those tenants were largely immigrants, most of whom had been born in Ireland. Unfortunately, from the census records it is impossible to determine the identity of the owners of the tenant farms. The career-occupational paths of many of the tenants are also unknown. Some had been farm laborers, children of farmers, or nonfarm laborers in Kings County, but presumably other immigrant tenants had arrived in the United States during the 1870s and thus did not appear in the 1870 Census of Population.[17]

Table 28 shows the marked differences between three groups of farmers in Flatbush: the 6 old-line Dutch owner-operators, the 18 Irish-born tenants, and the 5 old-line Dutch tenants. The old Dutch tenants operated farms significantly larger than those of the Dutch owners, which in turn were much larger than the ones operated by the Irish tenants. The three groups accounted for roughly the same monetarized total production, while the Irish tenants produced somewhat more vegetables (in monetary terms) than the other two groups. On a per capita basis, however, the Irish tenant farms' output bore an even smaller proportion to that of the other groups than did their acreage. This smaller financial yield may be linked to the fact that the Irish tenants owned disproportionately less in the way of implements and machinery and spent disproportionately less on fertilizer and labor. The Irish tenants produced almost as big a potato crop as the Dutch owners and tenants combined, but their per acre yield was little more than three-fourths as high. Although the Dutch owners produced somewhat less than the Dutch tenants, they also spent considerably less on fertilizer and wages; since the latter, by definition, also paid rent, their operations appear to have been distinctly less profitable than those of the owners.

What is remarkable here is that the very same six Dutch owner-farmers were also the only Flatbush farmers who in 1870 owned all the land they farmed. The Census of Agriculture did not collect information on tenure relations in 1870, but a comparison of the census manuscript schedules with the Flatbush assessment roll for that year reveals that of the 29 people returned as agents, owners, or managers of farms, only these 6 also appeared on the assessment roll as owning acreage approaching the size of the farm they operated. Significantly, only very few of the other farmers were members of old-line Dutch farm families that owned large farms and from which they might have been renting the land that they cultivated. Chief among these were the Ditmas and Lott families. But many large landowning families (including Bergen, Cortelyou, Lefferts, Lott, and Martense) had ceased to operate their farms, which then became available to tenants. Several farmers were long-term tenants of certain families: Allgeo rented his 97 acres from the Lott family, while Berry rented from the Martense family. If turnover among tenants was high, those returned by the 1880 Census of Agriculture may not have represented long-term tenants. Such a possibility is embedded in an unusual qualitative comment inscribed by the enumerator of the Census of Agriculture for Flatbush, who wrote in explanation of the absence of production data for one Irish tenant that he had not farmed this land in 1879 and had informed the enumerator that "the party who had could not make it pay."[18]

Only when the search is taken back as far as 1860 — before the transition from extensive to intensive production had been completed — are farm owners found to be a large proportion among farmers in Flatbush. And although even then more than half of the farmers returned by the Census of Agriculture did not appear on the assessment roll as owning land at all or land approaching the acreage that they farmed, 1860 was the last census year in which several of the older farming families were still represented among active farmers. Prominent among them were the Bergen, Cortelyou, Ditmas, and Martense families, which during the last third of the nineteenth century figured only as landlords. The abandonment of direct farming by many of the old-line Dutch families, who began renting their land to tenants, coincided with the transition to vegetable production. The different and more intense managerial-organizational tasks associated with the new cultivation systems may have prompted them to relinquish day-to-day responsibility for their farms.[19]

A sense of tenure relations can be gleaned from a survey of the rural towns in the *Eagle* on the occasion of the annexation debate in 1873. The newspaper reported that "most of the farms" in Gravesend were "rented out to market gardeners at merely nominal rentals, the prevailing price being from fifteen to twenty dollars per acre. Much of the land is not fertile, and requires a great deal of enriching by manures to yield any crops of any kind." In New Utrecht, too, not "many of the farms are cultivated by their owners but are rented, either on shares or at the rate of twenty dollars per acre." Only in Flatlands did the farmers "for the most part" till their own land.[20]

The data collected by the Census of Agriculture in 1880 for the first time on tenure relations partially confirm the *Eagle*'s account. Table 29 shows the number and proportions of owners and tenants for all the county towns. The *Eagle* report may have exaggerated the preponderance of renting, but tenants still accounted for a majority of all farm operators. In the rural towns as a whole, renters slightly outnumbered owner-operators, but these proportions reflected the situation only in Gravesend, New Lots, and New Utrecht, whereas Flatbush and Flatlands deviated sharply from that pattern. In Flatbush, tenants outnumbered owner-operators by four to one; in Flatlands, tenants were in the distinct minority. Tenants by shares were everywhere a minuscule phenomenon.[21]

The *Eagle* did not venture a quantitative estimate for Flatbush, but it quoted, without identifying, one of "the most prominent of farm owners" as stating:

> all that we can rent the land for is (where there is a house upon it) about twenty dollars per acre yearly. Twenty-five dollars is very rarely paid, and I know that fifteen is not an unusual bargaining figure for it. Now, for instance, I rent a farm of thirty acres; its assessed value is $66,825. I get but twenty dollars per acre for it. The taxes and other costs last year ate up (within a few dollars) the entire rental. There are men I know who cannot advantageously sell now and who barely live off the small income they are able to command from the rents.[22]

Fortunately, this unique insider can be identified, and his biographical details deepen the understanding of his views. A property exactly fitting this description is found in the Flatbush assessment rolls for 1872: the heirs of Garrett L. Martense — who last appeared in the 1850 Census of Agriculture at the age of 57 as owning a 152-acre farm valued at $40,000, and was also an associate judge of the county courts — owned 30 acres on the west side of Coney Island Road assessed at $66,825; the tax assessed and paid was $930.27, which was more than 50 percent higher than the $600 annual rent that Martense presumably received.[23]

The farm owner quoted in the *Eagle* was 49-year-old Jacob Van Brunt Martense, who appeared in the 1850 and 1860 Census of Agriculture; his 70-acre farm, valued at $21,000, was one of the largest in Flatbush in 1860 in terms of number of horses and bushels of potatoes and value of market garden produce produced. In 1869, he declared $3,320.69 in net income for federal income tax purposes, while his mother, Helen (almost $8,000), and his sister's husband, John Prince ($6,500), were among the income-richest residents in rural Kings County.[24]

Why Jacob Martense, the last member of his family to operate the family farm and the Flatbush town supervisor from 1871 to 1874 (and thus a member of the Kings County Board of Supervisors), and dying in 1881 at age 57 "possessed of considerable estate," retired from farming at such a relatively early age and how he secured such a large income from such allegedly paltry rent collections is unclear; similarly odd is why he would have continued to rent land for a sum that fell so far short of the tax. But, if Kings County market gardening could easily generate profits of $100 to $300 per acre or several thousand dollars annually, it is unclear why rents would have been as low as $15 to $20. Conversely, if such large profits were achievable, why did farmers such as Martense pass them up for meager rent payments?[25]

The Berry family cultivated the Martense farm for many years. Richard Berry, who first appears in the Census of Agriculture in 1870, operated one of the largest farms in Flatbush. The 70 acres that he farmed in 1870 was exactly the size of Jacob Martense's farm, but it remains unclear who farmed Judge Garrett L. Martense's 152-acre farm. By 1880 Berry's output on 75 acres was valued at $9,500, almost all of it market garden produce. His combined fertilizer and labor costs ($4,200) amounted to a somewhat above-average 44 percent of total output, but the farm should nevertheless have been able to support rent of more than $20 per acre. Why would Martense not have caused the tenant to pay the tax or included the tax in the rent? Puzzling, finally, is why farm owners who could not live on such low rents allegedly spearheaded the resistance to annexation, which, rather than raising their taxes and thus plunging them into negative income, would have made — and eventually did make — it possible to sell out quite "advantageously."[26]

Some landed gentry did require their tenants to pay at least some taxes. For example, Egbert Benson, who owned more than two hundred acres in New Utrecht, included provisions in his leases requiring his lessees to pay school taxes and road assessments. In one of his leases, running from 1865 to 1868, Benson charged a rental of $15 per acre, in another running from 1863 to 1866, $11.25 per acre. As meager as these sums appear, they still far exceeded the Benson family's property taxes for these years, which ranged between $2.77 and $3.64 per acre.[27]

Jacob Martense presented his counterintuitive antiannexationist position not only with all imaginable clarity, but as typical of almost all of Flatbush's large landowners:

> We are almost unanimously opposed to annexation. We do not need it, we cannot afford it and we don't want it. We have our old homesteads and outlying farms just as they should remain, intact and undisturbed for years to come. . . . Some of us wish to keep our old family homes, the homes of several generations without alteration; we do not wish our old farms mutilated by being cut and hacked up into useless streets and unsalable lots. A few only can bear the increased burden of taxation, which the success of the project will surely bring. Some of the estates will entirely be eaten up in the expenses and taxes.[28]

That one of the county's richest landowning families, which by its own account reckoned its continuing agricultural ties a losing operation, really opposed the annexation that would predictably expand its wealth rapidly met with at least some skepticism. The *Eagle* quoted another (unnamed) "well to do lot owner" who was convinced that there was

> a great deal of sly underhand work going on about this annexation business among some of those who pretend to oppose it. Of course they must do so to "keep on the right side" of their old relatives and political friends, and there are some, undoubtedly, who are in a quandary, because they are without any resource except the rental or sale of their lands, and could not maintain their grasp on their landed possessions, if street and other assessments came upon them. I will wager that some of these large property owners who declaim against the proposition, when the truth is known, will be really in favor of it.[29]

In light of the fact that in the very year (1873) of the great annexation debate, 16 pages of the Flatbush assessment roll were taken up with listing the 548 lots into which the heirs of George Martense, the father of Jacob Martense, had divided his land — once one of Flatbush's largest farms — this anonymous skeptical neighbor appears to have correctly divined that urban development politics could be opaque. One reason might have rationally impelled some wealthy Dutch agricultural patriarchs: so long as they retained control over political-economic development in the town of Flatbush, the street, water, and gas lighting franchises remained under their control. Perhaps well-connected landlords like Martense sought to ensure that they would control all the franchises before annexation occurred. To be sure, this hypothesis fails to explain why a central figure like John A. Lott was such an early and stalwart advocate of annexation.[30]

A middle ground between modernizing annexationists and adherents of the status quo was also available and occupied. As late as 1883, a group of taxpayers in the rural towns supported economical improvements but opposed annexation.[31] The *Rural Gazette* to a large extent adopted this position although it believed that annexation was inevitable and imminent. In one of its most important editorials ever, the newspaper sought to dispel farm owners' fears that improvements would necessarily increase taxation. To this end it presented data for "some farm lands" in Flatbush showing that the assessed value per acre, tax rate, and tax per acre had all declined from 1870 to 1880. It explained this trend by reference to the improvements (such as gas and police) that had been introduced: by inducing neighbors to settle in Flatbush, they increased the total property base. To be sure, the per acre assessed value and tax figures were unrepresentative: most farmers' land was not assessed at $1,800 and taxed at $35 per acre in 1870 or $1,414 and $19 per acre in 1880. But the point that the *Rural Gazette* was trying to make was nevertheless crucial for understanding why farmers wanted to sell rather than rent out their land:

> It is unaccountable that the farm owners who value their acres at from $1,500 to $2,000 and let them at the low rate of fifteen to twenty dollars per acre, earning only one per cent, should be so blind to what these fig-ures should teach them, that they must encourage and help forward im-provements before they can expect to realize the value they place on their acres. If four houses, costing $2,500 each are built on the acre valued at $2,000 making houses and land worth $12,000, they will easily rent for $250, earning 8 per cent instead of one. But the land will not be bought nor houses built until those in search of homes can find in our town all the conveniences they can get in the city.[32]

Presumably the newspaper did not mean that the farmers would them-selves finance such housing construction at the rate of $10,000 per acre, but that only after an adequate suburban infrastructure was in place, would speculators or developers pay farmers as much as $2,000 per acre for their farmland. The close link between infrastructure and realizing high prices for the conversion of farmland into suburban real estate was manifest in the advocacy by Philip Crooke, a patrician powerholder in Flatbush, of the con-struction of sewers on the grounds that without them ten lots were needed for a residence, whereas with sewers one lot sufficed.[33]

A principal weakness of the *Rural Gazette*'s analysis lay in its assumption that the only choice for farmland owners was to rent to tenant farmers at $20 per acre or to sell to speculators. In fact, for real farmers the possibility still existed of cultivating vegetables for profits amounting to as much as $100 per acre. Here a closer look at the assessed value and real property taxes is necessary. The landowners assessed and taxed at the levels that the *Rural Gazette* mentioned were exceptional. The value of the principal holding of John Lefferts was assessed at $2,080 per acre and taxed at $41.51 in 1870 and at $1,468 and $19.59 in 1880. Significantly, Lefferts was both a farmer and a developer. The land of his sister, Gertrude Lefferts Vanderbilt, was assessed at much higher levels: $5,714 and $598.58 in 1870 and $5,600 and $74.67 in 1880, respectively. But her holding was too small for farming and her house was one of the most elegant in Flatbush. Even the per acre assessed value of the land of John A. Lott, the largest landowner in rural Kings County, was only $924 in 1870 and $764 in 1880, while his per acre tax amounted to $18.45

and $10.19, respectively. Scrutiny of Lott's individual holdings on the assessment roll reveals enormous differentials: on two small parcels, one-half and one-quarter acre, each of which included a house, the assessed value in 1870 was $16,000 per acre and the tax $319.24 per acre. In contrast, his large 90.5-acre farm (including a house), which was rented out for farming, was assessed at only $751 per acre and taxed only $14.99 per acre.[34]

The assessed value and tax of John A. Lott's farmland much more closely approximated those of the old-line Dutch families with large holdings, which they continued to farm. At the time of the 1880 census, the per acre assessed value of the land of the aforementioned six Dutch owner-operators (Neefus, George and John Schenck, Suydam, Vanderveer, and Williamson) ranged between $334 and $506, while the tax per acre ranged from $3.51 to $6.44. At such low levels, even annual rents of $15 to $20 per acre would have enabled the owners to obtain 4–5 percent. The taxes were so modest that they constituted only a small fraction of the net profit from farming. Nevertheless, and ironically, it was precisely such low valuations that enticed farm owners to sell in the late 1880s or 1890s when developers offered prices as much as ten times higher.[35]

The *Rural Gazette*'s analysis makes more sense as applied to one non-farming landowner — the Reformed Protestant Dutch Church of Flatbush. In the mid-1880s, the church's agreements uniformly charged tenant farmers $20 per acre for land that was assessed at as much as $1,600 per acre. The church's commercial behavior appeared all the less explicable in light of the fact that it was paying over 50 percent more per acre in property tax on some of this land than it was receiving in rents.[36]

The relatively large proportion of owners who rented out their farms in Flatbush raises the question as to the size of the group of old-line Dutch family heads who by the last third of the nineteenth century continued to call themselves farmers, but who were in fact landed aristocrats with other sources of income. Jacob Martense at the 1870 census listed himself as a government official (elected supervisor) and at the census of 1880, just a year before his death, revealingly called himself "Gentleman" — one of very few inhabitants of rural Kings County who did. His anonymous remarks in the *Eagle* would have made more sense if he had been identified as a member of the nonworking landed gentry, who insisted on financing a life of leisure or public service by extracting rents from the tenant farmers of their market garden farms. Some old-line Dutch farmers may have held their land in order to maintain a traditional way of life, while others used it as a key resource in outfitting their daughters with dowries for the complicated network of intermarriage and interbreeding that defined property transmission among the Dutch in rural Kings County. Others, finally, may simply have been holding on to their farmland for what they speculated would be an eventually highly remunerative sell-off.[37]

Table 30 records the ownership structure for the census years 1880 to 1910. The larger farms tended to be owner-operated in all years, and over time the relative importance of tenancy diminished — from 53 percent of all farms in 1880 to 38 percent in 1910. Once farming began to reach the vanishing point, however, tenancy unsurprisingly increased sharply: by 1925 tenants operated 78 percent of the 40 surviving farms. In 1910, 47 owners were U.S.-born whites and 16 foreign-born whites; 26 tenants were U.S.-born whites and 16 foreign-born whites. In 1910, of 46 owner-operated farms reporting, 34 were mortgage-free and 12 showed mortgage debt. These figures, however, fail to convey the peculiarities of Kings County farms. Table 31 shows how deviant the ownership structure was compared to that of farms in New York State as a whole. Of all counties in New York State, Kings County in 1880 had the smallest proportion of owner-operated farms, and in 1890 the lowest proportion of farm-owning families, the lowest proportion of farm families owning both with and without incumbrances, and the fourth highest proportion of owning families that owned without incumbrances. In other words, few families in Kings County owned (as opposed to rented) their farms, but among the owners a high proportion owned them free and clear. These unincumbered owners were presumably the last of the old-line Dutch farmers.[38]

Among the 40 Kings County families with incumbered farms in 1890, the average incumbrance amounted to $3,213, or 34.5 percent of the value of the farm; at an annual interest rate of 5.83 percent, the farm families paid on average an interest charge of $187. This sum amounted to about 40 percent of the average Kings County farm's expenditure on fertilizers in 1889.[39]

Deagriculturalization leads to urbanization through several economic routes. Landowners can convert their property from agricultural to urban uses by ceasing to farm, subdividing the land, and renting it out for housing or industrial-commercial purposes. Alternatively, owners may rent it out to others who in turn can convert parcels from agricultural to urban uses. Finally, the owner can sell the land to others who will undertake the conversion. The point is not only that land-use conversion can occur in various ways, but that the threshold at which owners decide that conversion is appropriate may also differ according to the mode of conversion.

By the end of the century, the groups that would have been in the best position to keep vegetable farming viable in Kings County were themselves not landed — German and Irish and, a little later, Italian tenants (and, secondarily, laborers). As rent payers, these tenants could hardly pay off old-line Dutch farm owners in the same way as real-estate speculators and developers. Moreover, it might have taken a generation of financial success before the new dominant ethnic groups would have achieved the requisite level of commercial independence. In the interim, more than a few Dutch owners would have had to remain supportive of these operations. Faced with a choice between financing their tenants/workers without any long-term assurances about the continued viability of market gardening and cashing out for amounts that would at least afford them a solid annuity, Dutch farm families, unsurprisingly, sold the land out from under the active tenant farmers.

10. WHAT WAS THE DUTCH FARMERS' PRICE? PROFITS, TAXES, LAND PRICES, AND INCOMES

Fate put it into the hands of Dutch farmers, old fashioned and conservative, and they clung to their land as a cripple clings to his crutches
or a drowning man to anything within his grasp. They had cabbages
and potatoes to sell, and sometimes horses and cattle, but real estate?
Not they!

— Henry Hazelton, *The Boroughs of Brooklyn and Queens*, 1925

Economists have traditionally examined farmers' land-sale decisions from
the perspective of pull and push forces. The chief pull force is the offer of a
high price, which the farmer is unable to resist. Farmers may also be pushed
into selling by low product prices, high input prices, or high property taxes,
which make farming unremunerative. In the 1960s and 1970s, when farmers reportedly received half of the $13.5 billion annual gain in land prices
from converting raw land to suburban residential use, land economists, in
explaining the supply side of suburban land conversion, argued that: "The
single most important cost of landownership is the interest which could be
earned by investing elsewhere the money that could be realized from the
sale of the land. Another cost of landownership is taxes." [1]

The question here is whether these forces were relevant to Dutch farmers in nineteenth-century rural Kings County. To the extent that farmers in
some of the Kings County towns were protected by annexation statutes that
prohibited taxing their land according to the value at its potentially highest
market use, property taxes may not have been so burdensome as to push

farmers out of agriculture. Since vegetable farming was not only still profitable but at its all-time peak in terms of output in the 1880s, when the great
land sell-off began, the claim that farmers were motivated to sell out in order to leave a dying or unprofitable industry is unconvincing.[2]

Similarly inapplicable to Kings County is the argument that it was rational for farmers to sell out because: "Between 1865 and 1896, the prices of
most commodities fell in real terms, as the American farmer paid more and
more and received less and less. This meant that the value of land was falling
for agricultural purposes, even as acreage within commuting range of a city
was becoming desirable for residential use."[3] The cumulative effect of a
handwriting-on-the-wall perception that has motivated some farmers in
the twentieth century to sell out is a more plausible argument:

> Once started, a decline in farming can perpetuate itself. When too few
> farms remain, local dealers for feeds, fertilizers, and seeds cannot sup-
> port themselves. Farmers will then have to spend more of their valuable
> time getting needed supplies.
>
> An even more insidious threat is the "impermanence syndrome" —
> the idea that the mere expectation of a decline brings about an actual de-
> cline. If farmers believe the end is at hand, they will not make long-term
> investments in . . . buildings, fences, and irrigation systems.[4]

But before any of these perspectives can bring their explanatory powers to
bear on farming in Kings County, the basis for the initial sell-off has to be
understood.

PREMODERN AND MONETIZED MENTALITIES

[T]he spirit of improvement resulting from our proximity to a vast and rapidly
growing city . . . levels hills, fills up valleys, sweeps away forests, swallows farms,
and forces the descendants of the founders of this portion of New Netherlands who desire to continue and enjoy that independence and contentment
which the cultivators of the soil possess in a greater measure than those in the
other pursuits of life, to abandon the homes of their fatherland and seek other
more favorable localities removed from the turmoil of cities, where they can
peaceably and quietly continue the occupation of cultivators without fear of
disturbance.
— Teunis G. Bergen, *Genealogy of the Lefferts Family 1650–1878*, 1878

It is not intuitively obvious that Dutch farmers descended from families
that had worked the same land for almost 250 years and were embedded in

a distinct regional, socioeconomic, ethnic, cultural, and religious tradition which, despite the early market orientation, may still have regarded the land as a use value for subsistence, would constantly have been looking over their shoulders to compare its capitalized value. If, toward the end of the twentieth century, culturally much less homogeneous farmers continue to mention their emotional attachment to their land and the noneconomic benefits of doing "something worthwhile" and "work[ing] close to nature" as reasons for resisting the sale of their farms, the prevalence of similar sentiments among nineteenth-century farmers is not implausible.[5]

The traditionalist mentality of the Dutch farmers was captured by Timothy Dwight, the president of Yale, in letters he wrote during a journey to Long Island in the early nineteenth century:

> Young men, even of wealthy families, are usually taught scarcely anything more than to read, write, and keep accounts. . . . Intelligence is . . . disregarded by the body of the inhabitants, except as it aids them to the acquisition of property. . . .
>
> *The insular situation* of these three counties has a very perceptible influence upon the inhabitants as a body. . . . Few objects can be presented to them, and few events can occur, of sufficient magnitude to expand thought. . . . Almost all of their concerns are absolutely confined to the house, or to the neighborhood. . . . Habitually bounded by these confines, the mind is neither very much inclined, nor very able to look beyond them. Its . . . pursuits will break through only to reach the market. . . .
>
> [C]omparatively few persons of talents and information reside here. There is nothing sufficiently inviting in the circumstances of the island itself to allure persons of this character hither from the continent. . . . Such, it would seem, must through an indefinite period be the situation of Long Island.[6]

In the early 1880s, Brooklyn boosters were still attacking this mentality of Long Island farmers, "[c]ontent to be in a wilderness," who "tilled the same few acres year after year . . . and never thought of making a change." By then, however, "the strong hand of an enterprising and large brained capitalist ha[d] overthrown the Chinese wall of stupid conservatism which excluded the world from this insular Eden."[7]

Despite these stigmata of inbred provincialism, the census data and land-sale records reveal that many old-line Dutch farmers had sold off or rented out their farms long before farming became (or would have become) unremunerative in Kings County. Presumably, therefore, either land prices had become so high that it was possible for farmers to live on the interest from the proceeds, or they foresaw that, regardless of the continued profitability of their agricultural operations, the encroachment of suburbanization was inexorable. Both possibilities, however, presuppose that their deepening integration into capitalist economic structures had detached the Dutch farmers sufficiently from their premodern ideological context to enable them socially and psychologically to abandon their economic base altogether. Especially where former farmers rented out their land to tenants, who in turn hired wage laborers, the land, for the participants in this transaction, became merely one field among many for the investment of their capital. Since the rent paid by the tenant, when capitalized, determined the land price, a farmer who based his decision to sell on whether he could live on the interest from the sale price was, in reality, merely going through the same calculation he had already undertaken in deciding to become a landlord: it was not a qualitatively new thought process.[8]

Toward the end of the nineteenth century, some observers formed the impression that the Dutch farmers' focus was coldly commercial. In the judgment of one of the Flatbush farmers' neighbors, Daniel Tredwell, there was nothing curious about their nourishing little sentimental attachment to their farms. He delighted in recounting the response that one of them had ventured to his inquiry as to "what he did with his vast accumulation of wealth. 'Oh,' said he, 'we count it.'"[9]

This kind of cost-benefit model, which reduces all dimensions of life to monetary commensurability, can be contrasted with the ideal-typical "premodern" model of incommensurability, in which no amount of money can induce a farmer to part with his land. Kings County Dutch farmers were not bereft of such premodern perspectives. Already in the 1790s, a French visitor commented that land was expensive in rural Kings County because New York assured the farmers a market for their produce and because the majority Dutch population did not wish to sell its land.[10] A century later, Jeremiah Johnson Jr., one of the county's leading post–Civil War real-estate figures, described the attitude of his grandfather, General Jeremiah Johnson (1765–1852), a farmer whose Dutch ancestors were among the earliest Long Island settlers and one of the county's richest men:

To the writer who more than once made overtures for the purchase of a portion of his land his reply was uniformly, "As my father left the land to me, so will I leave it to my children. They can do as they please, I expect them to sell it off for city lots, but I shall not." This tenacity of possession of inherited estates is not more characteristic of the old English families than of our Dutch nobility. Instances have come within the personal observation of the writer of the endurance of privations, but little short of poverty by Dutch families of large and immensely valuable estates, in order to retain them. At almost an hour[']s notice the plutonic money bags would have been dropped into their hands, to obtain a title to the lands which yielded by the most painful exertions barely enough to pay the rapidly increasing city taxes, and furnish them of bread.[11]

CASE STUDIES OF THE MICROECONOMICS OF SELLOUTS

It has long been an iron law of the real estate market that if farmland stands in the path of urban expansion, no crop is valuable enough to keep it out of developers' hands.

— Barnaby Feder, "Sowing Preservation: Towns Are Slowing Invasion of Farms by Bulldozers," *New York Times*, March 20, 1997

The question here is whether the kind of (opportunity) cost-benefit analysis that economists customarily apply to the micro-decision-making processes behind exits from farming is appropriate to the premodern mentality and habitus that Dwight described and are reminiscent of the "idiocy of rural life," from which, according to the *Communist Manifesto*, the triumphant bourgeoisie had rescued a part of the population. An economic geographer in the 1960s, for example, illustrated this process by reference to a New York State dairy farmer with a $30,000 investment and a $3,000 annual net profit which, together with some in-kind self-provisioning, permitted a livable if not spectacular country living. If he were offered a factory job at $2 an hour and the chance to liquidate his investment: "What would he do? If Jones looks at the money angle only, he would probably leave the farm, for he could invest his $30,000 at 5 per cent (producing $1,500 per year) and earn $4,160 in wages. This is a total of $5,660 as compared to $3,000 earned on the farm. Even if housing, food, and other costs run $1,800 higher per year in the city, he would still have $3,860, or $860 more than the farm provided." And even if higher income taxes take a part of this sum, "he has two days off each week, perhaps does not have to get up so early or work so hard; and maybe his wife and children are glad to get off the farm."[12]

Data are available to make similar calculations for Kings County farmers. A good sense of the potential financial inducement open to Kings County farmers can be gleaned from a tiny article that appeared in the *Real Estate Record* at the end of 1889. Declaring that New Utrecht was "just at present enjoying a sort of Western land boom," it listed the land sales reported in the previous few weeks, which are reproduced in table 32.

At a time when the agricultural census of 1889–90 reported that the value of farmland in Kings County, the third highest in the United States, averaged $844 per acre (almost double the value at the 1880 census), these sales, averaging $1,300 to $1,525 per acre, offered sellers 60 to 80 percent higher prices. In fact, the per acre valuation that many of these particular farmers reported at the 1880 census were below average, thus reinforcing the incentive to sell. Since the yields on U.S. railroad bonds and municipal bonds in the first half of the 1890s were about 3.6 percent, farmers could reasonably have anticipated annual interest income of $50 per acre from the investment of the proceeds from the sale of their land. Thus a farmer with 20 acres could have received about one thousand dollars annually. This figure was a little more than twice as high as nonfarm employees' average annual wages. No representative profit or net income data are available, but the average value of farm products per acre in Kings County was $121.50 in 1879 and $105 in 1889 (the second highest nationally). It might seem implausible that of these amounts $50 per acre could have remained available for the farm family's consumption, but these yields are significant understatements since only part of the total acreage was planted to crops in any given year.[13]

Data on individual named farmers from the 1880 Census of Agriculture make it possible to explore the micro-decision-making process in greater detail. The census did not collect comprehensive cost data, but it did secure information on the cost of fertilizer and hired labor as well as the value of the farm and of production. According to Peter Henderson's figures for the New York area during this period, wages and manure accounted for 72.5 percent of total costs. If rent is omitted as irrelevant to longtime Dutch owners, the proportion rises to 77 percent. Thus for individual farmers enumerated in the census, estimated profits can be calculated by adding 38 percent and 30 percent to the total wage and manure costs of renters and owners, respectively, and subtracting the total from the total value of production. This maximum net income can then be compared to the capitalized value of the farm.[14]

Such a calculation can be made for some of the aforementioned New Utrecht landboomers. By the time of sale in 1889, some of these farms were no longer operating or, if still producing, may merely have retained a name associated with a onetime owner. The wealthy Cortelyou family — Jacques Cortelyou established New Utrecht in the seventeenth century — was the prime example of this phenomenon. Jacques, Simon, and Peter Cortelyou were major slaveholders in 1800, owning 10, 9, and 5 slaves, respectively. Thirty years later, Ann Cortelyou still owned 186 acres, while Peter Cortelyou owned 125; but by 1837, the latter acreage had already passed into other hands, while the former was sold off a decade later. By the late 1850s, both holdings had been splintered, and no Cortelyou appeared as a farmer in New Utrecht in the Census of Agriculture for 1850, 1860, 1870, or 1880, or in the Census of Population for 1860, 1870, or 1880.[15]

Alternatively, tenants, who were particularly numerous in New Utrecht, may have been operating some of the farms. George Gelston, for example, appeared in the 1850 Census of Agriculture as operating a 170-acre farm, but disappeared from later agricultural censuses. The enormous discrepancy between the value of property that the 45-year-old Gelston reported at the 1850 Census of Agriculture ($32,000) and Census of Population ($135,000) and the large taxable income ($3,238.61) that he reported to the federal tax assessor in 1866, makes it likely that the man who designated his occupation as "gentleman" at the 1860 Census of Population, at which time he owned $105,000 of real and personal property, had other income sources.[16]

Tables 33a and 33b show the relevant variables for the landboom farmers who could be identified with reasonable certainty. If these farm owners had actually sold their farms for the amounts that they themselves stated them to be worth in 1880 and invested the proceeds, only one would have received even $500 annually at the aforementioned 3.6 percent interest rate: Andrew Cropsey's annual interest on $14,000 would have been $504. With one exception, however, the per acre values were all considerably lower than the average for Kings County even in 1880. Moreover, several of these farms did not appear to be flourishing. In terms of production and profit, only Andrew Cropsey, Martin, and Gubner were operating farms that might have sustained a family.

Adolphus Gubner, who in 1850 had immigrated from Prussia at the age of 21, had two sons, Friedrich and Stephen, ages 19 and 21, whom the census returned as "farming" in 1880, but who presumably could not both have supported families on the income that this one farm was generating. In the case of several farms, the output was so low or the relationship of costs to output so unfavorable that the owners may have been in the process of winding them down. In Gubner's case, the family's income was significantly supplemented by the $1,200 salary that he received as an interpreter at the county court; in addition, as a member of the New Utrecht Democratic General Committee, president of the ward association, and New Utrecht justice of session, Gubner had access to other political sources of income. Gubner was also the New Utrecht town supervisor from 1873 to 1878 and in 1880 became an associate justice on the Brooklyn Court of Sessions.[17]

Gubner, as the 1889 land-sale table suggests and farmline maps indicate, farmed jointly with Sieger. The net income before property taxes of 65-year-old German immigrant William Sieger — who in the mid-1870s "has one of the finest side-hills to raise hot-bed truck that we have seen for some time" — was only $562. It must also be borne in mind that Sieger and Gubner, as immigrants, unlike the old-line Dutch families, may have had mortgage payments as well that had to be financed from the farm's revenues; on the other hand, given the long period that they had been farming, it is also possible that their farms were already fully paid for. Even Sieger's low outlier profit exceeded the (national) average industrial worker's annual wages and was more than twice as great as the average farm laborer's $20 per month wage. Sieger's annual income would, however, have been lower than that of many skilled workers in Brooklyn — if they were not unemployed more than three months. Farmers whose profits fit in the $2,500 to $4,000 range fell "squarely within the ranks of the metropolitan upper middle class."[18]

The key indicator with regard to vindicating market rationality is profit per acre from farm operations (shown in the next-to-last column of table 33b) in contrast with the sale price. If the rate of interest on safe bond investments in the 1880s was about 3.6 per cent, farm owners should have sold when a buyer offered them a per acre price for their land more than 27.7 times (100/3.6) the profit per acre that they obtained from their farms. These thresholds amounted to the following per acre prices for the New Utrecht landboomers: Andrew G. Cropsey ($1,080), Andrew J. Cropsey ($1,773), William Cropsey ($1,607), Sieger ($388), Gubner ($1,191), Suydam ($1,967), Martin ($2,438), and Lott ($609). In relation to the narrow range of per acre prices at which these farmers actually sold their farms ($1,300 to $1,525), only one, 64-year-old Isaac Martin, had recorded per acre profits far in excess of the sale price — and significantly he sold a smaller share of his holdings than anyone else in this group (16 of 45 acres). Sieger and 52-year-old Aaron Lott clearly had the greatest financial incentives to sell out since their net incomes were far below the interest that they could receive from investing the proceeds from the sale.[19]

Since the per acre prices that these owners received in 1889 were as much as nine times higher than the self-valuations of 1880, it is no surprise that they agreed to sell. The total $67,500 that Aaron Lott was paid, for example, was 59 times the profit he received from farming a decade earlier. Because the profit data were from 1879 and the value of productions per acre for the whole county fell somewhat from 1879 to 1889, it is possible that the per acre profits for these potential sellers were even lower by the end of the 1880s, thus enhancing the rationality of departure from the dirty-hands world of farming for the loftier status of rentier. These transactions confirm the prediction that the *Rural Gazette* made in 1873 in support of annexation: "who among us will be the poorer 10 years hence for having sold our land now producing us $20 an acre for an amount the interest of which will bring without labor $35 or $40." [20]

Further light is shed on the microeconomics of the New Utrecht landboomers' farms by their property tax assessments. For the year (1879) for which the Census of Agriculture of 1880 collected production data, table 33b shows the amount of tax that five of the farmers paid. For the five farmers, property taxes in 1879 ranged between 1 percent (Martin) and 19 percent (Suydam) of their profits. For Martin and Gubner (5 percent), these tax payments did not significantly reduce their profits, but for the other three farmers taxes may have played a part in the decision to sell. Corroborating this causality is difficult, however, since the small size of their farming operations could also mean that they were being wound down for other reasons. In particular, Suydam's meager output, especially in relation to the acreage on which he was paying tax, but which he was apparently not farming, strongly suggests this possibility, since the farm had been shrinking since 1850 when it had encompassed 100 acres. [21]

For the years immediately before and after the sales, 1880–1890, table 34 shows the acreage, value, and taxes. The purchaser of much of this boomer land was the Bay Ridge Park Improvement Company, which was incorporated in November 1890. Its president, Daniel Lewis, represented the Brooklyn City Railroad Company, of which he was also president. The formation of the Bay Ridge Park Improvement Company was, in the words of the *New York Times*, "the first step in what promises to be a steady development of all the suburban resorts lying south of Brooklyn." The most pressing need for increasing the value of the company's property, which consisted largely of old farms situated between Brooklyn and Bath Beach and had cost it $500,000, was to extend electrified surface lines of the Brooklyn City Road through New Utrecht. The Improvement Company's contribution to sub-urbanizing the Bay Ridge section of New Utrecht lay in offering 3,000 build-ing sites from 69th Street to 86th Street and crossing 8th through 14th Ave-nue. That the boom was no onetime event was dramatized just days after the incorporation when the *Times* reported that at an auction of more than 300 lots in Bay Ridge single lots had been sold for as much as $745 — half of the very high price that the farmers had received for an entire acre just two years earlier. And by March 1891 the *Times* reported that a corner lot in Bay Ridge had been "run up to $1,800." [22]

The acreage subject to assessment during these years was, at least for Gubner-Sieger and Martin, almost identical with the amount sold in 1889; Lott's estate sold somewhat more than his assessed acreage and Suydam's heirs somewhat less. The value per acre of the land in the assessment rolls rose, as shown in table 34, from 33 percent to 100 percent between 1888 and 1890; vis-à-vis the self-valuation in 1880, the changes in per acre values var-ied wildly from farm to farm: Suydam's land was valued at far less in 1888 than in 1880, whereas Lott's more than doubled in value. The ratio of the per acre purchase price in 1889 to the assessed value of the same year ranged be-tween 6 to 1 for Martin's land to 1.8 to 1.0 for Lott's. The property tax per acre was rather low, varying from $3.19 for Gubner to an outlier of $12.10 for Lott. For most of the farmers such deductions from their per acre profits would have been far from fatal, but for Lott and Sieger, who already had the greatest financial incentives to sell out, this additional cost item would surely have operated to push them out of farming.

A prime reason for the sell-off was doubtless the death of the farmer-patriarchs. Gubner, Lott, and Suydam, for example, all died before 1889, and Andrew G. Cropsey would have been 86. Presumably, their male chil-dren, as the city grew nearer, were either more attracted to other, urban, pursuits, or decided that living from the proceeds of the sale was superior to cultivating cabbages. Ill health also may have contributed to the decision to abandon farming, as was the case with a number of farmers in Kings County.[23]

These accounts should not, however, lead to the hasty conclusion that economic conditions structurally precluded New Utrecht farmers across the board from achieving high levels of profitability. Another member of the Lott family did so: in 1879, James B. Lott, all of whose $6,500 in production stemmed from market gardening, produced $217 per acre in output and should have received (according to Henderson's ratio) $126 in profits from each of his 30 acres, which he valued at only $6,000. A member of another old-line Dutch farm family, William Bennett, all of whose $9,000 of output was likewise in vegetables, produced on his 25 tilled acres and 5 acres of meadow $300 per acre, of which $118 was profit.[24]

A comparison with the 1860 agricultural census confirms that the New Utrecht landboomers had successfully effected the transition to intensive agriculture. Sieger's 40-acre farm purportedly lost half its value while market garden output increased sevenfold; Aaron Lott's farm, almost unchanged in acreage, lost one-third its value while vegetable production rose 11-fold; Martin's farm, in contrast, almost quadrupled in size and vegetable production while losing half its per acre value. (Even in 1860, the per acre values of Sieger's and Lott's farms were below the Kings County average.) Similarly, Gubner reported to the census enumerator in 1870 that his 98 acres were worth $50,000, or more than $500 per acre — three times their reported value a decade later when Gubner farmed only 60 percent as much land but produced almost 40 percent more in terms of the value of his market garden produce.[25]

Similar calculations can be made for the other towns. In Flatbush, six old-line Dutch farmers were returned by the 1880 agricultural census as owning the farms they operated. The value of market garden produce as a proportion of the total value of these farmers' production ranged between 67 and 85 percent. Table 35 presents estimates of the economic variables underlying a decision to sell. The ratio of the value of the farm (including buildings) to profit can roughly serve as an indicator of the number of years the owner could live on the proceeds from the sale — not on the interest from the proceeds (which even in the case of the most valuable farm, Vanderveer's, would have amounted to only $1,800 at 3.6 percent). Only one of these farmers, Peter Neefus, could have lived longer than a few years on the proceeds in this manner. To be sure, John Vanderveer and Cornelius Suydam were both old men and might have wanted to sell their farms, but neither was listed in the population as retired (as were many other farmers), and both had farming sons: Suydam's 35-year-old son John lived in his household, while 49-year-old Jacob Vanderveer was John Vanderveer's son. Vanderveer, one of the largest market gardeners in Kings County, should have obtained $92.5 profit for each of his 80 acres. William Williamson's per acre profit was even higher — $137. The estimated per acre profits of three of the other four farmers were also high: $87 for Suydam, $98 for George Schenck, and $91.50 for John Schenck. Even Neefus's $38 per acre profit was considerable compared with his per acre property tax of little more than five dollars. Once Flatbush developers, however, began paying several thousand dollars per acre, even these quite high yields may have seemed scarcely worth the hard work of farming (if in fact these owners worked).[26]

That these farms, like the typical Flatbush farm, were expanding rather than contracting as intensive market-garden operations can be shown for at least the three of the six farms that were also enumerated in the 1860 agricultural census. In that year, Suydam reported no market garden production, John Schenck only $120, and the two John Vanderveers $500 and $1,000 compared with $5,000, $2,000, and $8,000, respectively, in 1879; similarly, the number of bushels of Irish potatoes they produced rose: Suydam's output from 1,300 to 6,000, and Vanderveer's from 2,000 or 1,000 to 5,000. Schenck's rose only from 1,300 to 1,600, but his acreage also declined from 45 to 20. The per acre value of the whole group of farms rose about 60 percent from 1860 to 1880.[27]

The $500 to $600 per acre farm values that these farmers reported in 1880 may not have induced them to sell regardless of how low their operating profits were. But the $2,000 to $8,000 per acre that developers paid them in the early 1890s, when compared with per acre profits only one-twentieth to one-eightieth the size, must have made the decision to close out a quarter-millennium of Dutch-American agrarian history much less painful. Significantly, all six of these farmers were located to the east of Flatbush Avenue, away from the urbanizing sections of Flatbush and toward the more rural parts of Flatlands and New Lots; all but Vanderveer were outside of the gas district and thus subject to lower tax rates.

It was not coincidental, then, that none of these six farms was cut up into lots until the 1890s. The Vanderveers sold much of their farmland to a large developer, Germania Real Estate and Improvement Company, in 1892, while the other owner-operators all subdivided their land in 1894. Williamson, who still owned 56 acres valued at $52,500 in 1893, was taxed on 117 lots in 1894, the year that Flatbush was annexed by Brooklyn. The Neefus family, to be sure, had been dividing its land into lots since 1874 — John Neefus, who had spent his entire life on the extensive farm, died in 1875 in his eighty-third year — but its 81-acre farm valued at $75,790 on the 1893 Flatbush assessment roll was completely subdivided by the next year. That year, 1894, was also the year in which the Suydam family subdivided its 50-acre farm, and the Schencks all cut their smaller acreage. Significantly, at the end of 1892, when owners of land fronting on East Broadway or Church Lane informed the Flatbush Board of Improvement that they favored granting a franchise or privilege to any responsible railroad that could give a satisfactory guarantee of the speedy completion of a proposed railroad along those streets, the first four signatories were Williamson, Neefus, and George and John Schenck.[28]

That these six Dutch farmers were "pulled" out of farming by very high land prices rather than "pushed" out by high taxes is underscored by the 1879 tax and profit data in table 36. All the farmers, with the exception of Neefus, were required to pay only a very small percentage of their profits to the town, county, and state, and even Neefus was left with a large profit. Even these shares represent a significant overstatement of the tax burden because an indeterminable proportion of the assessment was accounted for by the farmer's house (or, in Williamson's case, two houses), which was neither an imposition peculiar to farming nor one that the farmer could escape by abandoning agriculture. Thus since the tax on the income-generating enterprise itself was even lower than the aforementioned amounts, it is implausible that taxes "forced" these old-line Dutch farmers out of business.[29]

The irresistible pressures to convert farmland to urban uses can be illustrated, in the extreme, by using contemporaneous data from New York City, where the process of deagriculturalization was several decades in advance of Kings County's. The horticulturist Peter Henderson reported in 1886 that an elevated railroad passenger traveling from 60th Street to Harlem could see between June and October

> little patches of vegetation of different shades of green, ranged in uniform and regular lines. These are the "salad patches," cultivated mainly by German market gardeners; they range from two acres down to an acre in area. It seems a wonder that the cultivation of such a small plot of earth should give an able-bodied man a living; but a living it does give in nearly all cases, and some have quite a respectable surplus for a "rainy day." . . .
>
> Four crops of Lettuce are usually taken from June to October. . . .
>
> The plants are set about a foot apart each way, and will average one cent per head, so that the four crops give a return of nearly $2,000 per acre. This seems like an immense return for an acre, but though the net profits are respectable, there are some serious disadvantages attending the cultivation. Few, or none, of these men are owners of land in New York City, nor in hardly any instance have they a lease. They are tenants at will, and pay a yearly rental, in some instances, of $250 per acre. Many of our country readers may think that an extra cipher has been added to

the amount, but they must recollect that the value of some of these "salad patches" ... is $8,000 per city lot, or over $100,000 per acre, so that the paltry rental of $250 per acre hardly pays the interest on the amount of taxes.[30]

The owners of such land were, presumably, merely biding their time until they sold it to developers.[31]

HOW RICH WERE THE DUTCH FARMERS?

[W]e are quite certain no farmer in Kings County can get as much money from his farm to use it for agricultural purposes as he can to sell it off to people who want rural homes; invest the money so received and count his interest without laboring so hard as many of them do.

— "The Reason Why," *Kings County Rural Gazette*, October 11, 1873

One important source for gauging the progress of income and wealth formation within (and outside of) Kings County agriculture that has never been made use of is the surviving Internal Revenue Assessment Lists from the Civil War-era federal income tax (1862–1871). Lost to memory in many ways, the Civil War-era tax regime, which included the first national income tax, was extraordinarily invasive by today's standards. In addition to a progressive tax on income and legacies and distributive shares of personal property, the statutes imposed annual license fees for all trades and occupations (including doctors and lawyers), annual duties on carriages, yachts, billiard tables, gold watches, and silver plate, and monthly duties on manufactures, articles, and a broad variety of products, and monthly taxes on bond interest. All persons with income were required to fill out and submit a Form 24 akin to today's Form 1040, showing their income together with allowable deductions. Most startling to late-twentieth-century citizens accustomed to promises of tax secrecy, the lists that the assessors compiled from these forms setting forth the taxable income and tax due were advertised as publicly available for review.[32]

One possible side effect of the introduction of a federal income tax is that it prompted Kings County farmers to begin keeping account books. For example, in 1865 John C. Bergen of Flatlands, who in 1854 had taken charge of the farm of his father, who had apparently stopped keeping his account book in 1835, began keeping accounts, a focus of which was the preparation of his federal tax returns.[33]

The value of the assessment lists, which today would be inaccessible to scholars for identifiable persons, is considerably enhanced by the availability of the manuscript schedules of the 1870 Census of Population and Census of Agriculture, which reveal occupations and microeconomic data for farms. Such administrative record matching for 1869 — the year from which the Census of Agriculture collected most of its harvest data — makes it possible to estimate the profitability of individual named farm operations.

Table 37 displays the income and occupation of the 38 taxpayers in rural Kings County whose taxable incomes in 1869 exceeded $4,000. With the $1,000 exemption applicable that year, the incomes of all these taxpayers exceeded $5,000. The presence as early as the 1860s of numerous wealthy nonfarmers in rural Kings County, especially in Flatbush and New Utrecht, underscores the need to visualize these towns as much more than farming communities. The fact that so many large merchants and other businessmen with firms in New York or Brooklyn monopolized the highest reaches of the income hierarchy suggest that landed property was already losing its status as the dominant economic basis, although several of these rich non-agrarians (such as Hope, Langley, and Murphy) also appeared as significant landowners on the farmline maps of the late 1860s and early 1870s, and others (such as Lefferts, John A. Lott and his wife Catharine Lott, and Martense) derived some of their current income from agricultural rents or land sales. The robust contingent of dry goods merchants among the rich residents of Flatbush and New Utrecht reflected the fact that in the 1860s they constituted "the largest business interest of New York." Of the 38 richest taxpayers listed for 1869, at least 15 were listed in that year's *Trow's New York City Directory*. In the other years in which federal income tax was assessed, between five and nine of the ten richest rural Kings County residents operated businesses in New York City.[34]

Remarkably, only one person who was returned as an active farmer at the 1870 census was among the residents of the rural areas reporting more than $4,000 of taxable income. And even that farmer, 43-year-old Jacob Ryerson of Flatlands, the very last in rank, was presumably a part-time farmer or had other sources of income: according to the 1870 census, the total value of his agricultural production on his 21-acre potato farm was only $500, or less than one-eighth of his taxable income. A number of other active or retired taxpaying farmers fit the same description. The highest income of any farmer whose entire income could plausibly have derived exclusively from his farming operation in 1869 was the $1,167.68 (to which must be added the $1,000 exemption) of Abraham Linington of New Lots, the second-largest market gardener in the county. Bernard Larzelere of New Utrecht, another large market gardener, the farmer occupying this leading position in 1870, reported a taxable income of only $2,126.02 (in addition to the $2,000 exemption).[35]

Many other farmers also appeared in the Internal Revenue Assessment Lists. Of the 278 residents of the rural towns listed as having paid income tax for 1869, 56 appeared in the 1870 Census of Population or Agriculture as operating farms or as retired farmers. Viewed from the other perspective, about 13 percent of farmers returned by the Census of Agriculture and 10 percent of those returned by the Census of Population as farmers or retired farmers paid federal income taxes. By 1870, when as a result of the increase in the exemption to $2,000, the total number of federal taxpayers fell to 96, only 22 farmers were included among them. Many more paid federal taxes on their gold watches ($1 per watch) and carriages. But many larger farmers paid no income tax at all.

Several reasons may explain the failure to pay federal income tax. The statutory $1,000 or $2,000 exemption and business expense deductions (for wages, rent, interest, repairs, etc.) made it possible for farmers to produce considerable amounts before meeting the net-income threshold. Except for a few very large farmers, most farmers' gross output was low enough plausibly to preclude a net income in excess of the exemption. Widespread non-compliance with the filing requirements may also explain why so few large farmers paid any, or any significant, income tax.[36]

An examination of the accounts of several farmers reveals that their declared net income for federal income tax purposes appears implausibly low. Abraham Linington, for example, was the second-largest market garden producer according to the 1870 census, having produced $12,800 worth of products on his 110-acre farm, the second biggest in New Lots, which he valued at $100,000. Production values this large should, based on the typical cost structures of the period, have generated a considerable profit. Wages, according to Peter Henderson's contemporaneous calculations, made up 50 to 60 percent of total costs (table 7). Linington's $4,300 wage bill, even if doubled to arrive at total costs, should have left him with more than $4,000 in profit. Yet he declared only $1,167.68 in taxable income — to which the $1,000 exemption must be added to gauge his real income. The Henderson rule-of-thumb is supported by Linington's self-reported taxable income for 1870, which overlapped with the census year, amounting to $1,678.65 —

over and above the $2,000 exemption for that year. (For 1871, the last year of the federal tax, Linington's taxable income rose to $3,223.01 in addition to the $2,000 exemption.)

In 1869–70, William H. Allgeo produced $8,500 worth of output on 97 acres in Flatbush, the town's largest farm, which he valued at $90,000; despite having paid only $2,000 in wages (including board), which should also have left him with more than $4,000 in profit, he declared himself subject to federal taxation only with respect to two gold watches. Since Allgeo rented his farm (from John A. Lott), he may have paid $20 per acre, which at almost $2,000 should still have left him with taxable income. Similarly, George Lott produced $7,000 worth of produce on his 131-acre farm, the largest in Flatlands; his $2,000 wage bill should have left him with a $3,000 profit, but he declared net income of only $143.52. The output of the 88-acre farm of his older brother, Peter Lott, was valued at $7,720, so that his $2,300 wage bill should also have left him with more than $3,000 in profit; at least he declared a taxable income of $1,145.05 taxed at $57.25. In Gravesend, Henry R. Wyckoff produced $3,000 worth of output on his 50-acre farm while paying only $800 in wages; he could have been expected to have achieved profits of almost $1,500, but he reported a net income of only $12. Abraham Barre, operator of Gravesend's biggest farm in terms of acreage, produced $8,000 worth of produce including 6,000 bushels of potatoes on 100 acres, paying out $2,500 in wages; he should have obtained profits of about $3,000, but all that he declared was a gold watch, for which he was taxed $1. Gravesend's biggest farmer in terms of value of output, William Bennett, produced $9,000 worth of produce on 97 acres; despite paying only $2,310 in wages, he does not appear on the assessor's list even as the owner of a gold watch.

The largest New Utrecht farm in terms of acreage was owned by 77-year-old Daniel Roberts, who was also one of the income-richest residents of the town. The 1870 Census of Population returned him as a lawyer, while at the 1860 and 1850 census he had been listed as a farmer.[37] The approximately $10,000 incomes that he reported for 1869 and 1870 could obviously not have been derived from his 119-acre farm, the gross output of which was valued at only $4,000 and toward the production of which he paid $2,000 in wages. Similarly, John L. Van Pelt was taxed on a net income of $2,908.69 for 1869, although his farm's total output for 1869–70 was valued at only $3,000.[38]

David Bennett's 70-acre New Utrecht farm, which he valued at $70,000, showed the county's second-highest value of farming implements and machines ($3,500) and by far the county's highest payroll ($8,000). This extraordinary outlay for wages may have meant that total costs equaled the farm's total value produced ($15,000) — especially since its minimal $1,400 market garden output makes a puzzle of the farm's specialty. And, indeed, Bennett declared nothing but a carriage and a gold watch to the federal assessor. Bernard Larzelere reported to the census enumerator that he had produced $11,000 worth of output, $9,000 of which was market garden produce, yet paid out only $1,600 in wages to the one German and four Irish farm laborers living in his household; despite this very favorable cost-revenue structure on his 66-acre farm, he did not appear on the assessor's list at all for 1869, but did report net income of $2,126.02 for 1870, on which he paid $53.15 in taxes. Even the notional profit of more than $4,000 resulting from inclusion of the $2,000 exemption seems modest. Garret Cowenhoven reported $801.89 in net income (beyond his $1,000 exemption) for 1869, although his gross farm output amounted to only $2,500 and he paid out $1,000 in wages alone. More plausibly, Teunis Bergen, the surveyor and ex-Congressman, reported $968 in net income for 1869; his gross farm product for the year was $7,000 and his payroll $1,500. A number of New Utrecht farmers whose cost-revenue structures indicated that their operations were quite profitable for 1869–70 are not found on the assessors lists for those years. An example is Theodore Bergen whose output was valued at $8,000 and who paid wages totalling only $2,000.[39]

Kings County farmers' behavior is strikingly at odds with the taxpaying behavior of their prosperous contemporaries in Brookline, Massachusetts, a rural town developmentally comparable to Flatbush. More of Brookline's residents (357) paid federal income tax in 1867 than in all five rural Kings County towns in 1869 (239), which were about four times as populous. If nationally almost 7 percent of the population was assessed for income in 1869, in rural Kings County the proportion was only about 1 percent. To be sure, no matter how spectacularly Kings County farmers may have understated their incomes for federal tax purposes, even if they had been able to produce without incurring any costs whatsoever, the value of their gross output would not have ranked them among the richest residents.[40]

Only one active farmer appeared among the income-richest residents of rural Kings County, but several others were members of old-line Dutch families whose wealth originated in agriculture. These residents included Lefferts, Bergen, Schoonmaker, and the Lotts and Martenses. The predominance of non-Dutch nonfarm families at the highest income levels is, nevertheless, striking. The concentration of such nonagricultural rich, especially in Flatbush and New Utrecht, suggests that by the 1860s these two towns had already become suburban residential centers for capitalists operating in New York and Brooklyn. To be sure, a certain fusion of non-Dutch merchants with rural Dutch families took place through marriage: for example, in 1866 Henry Lyles Jr., who later also became president of the gas company, married Mary Lott, the daughter of Ann Bergen and Samuel Lott, who had bought his farm from Abraham Vanderbilt.[41]

FROM CABBAGE-CULTIVATORS TO COUPON-CLIPPERS? DUTCH FARMERS AFTER THE SELL-OFF

The males of the family in this vicinity . . . appear to be decreasing . . . so that there is a probability that the day is not far distant when the family name of Lefferts will disappear from our midst. . . . There is another family among us, that of the Martenses, once numerous, whose males have dwindled down to a single household.

— Teunis G. Bergen, *Genealogy of the Lefferts Family*, 1878

Did Kings County Dutch farmers who sold out become wealthy enough to participate in the Gilded Age as latter-day farmers are reputed to do? What did the Dutch farmers do with the proceeds from the sales of their farms? Did they retire to Brooklyn, Manhattan, or perhaps the Dutch settlements in Putnam and Dutchess counties north of New York City, or Bucks County, Pennsylvania, as did their early-eighteenth-century ancestors when Kings County farming land became occupied? Or did they go east to Nassau and Suffolk in the literal footsteps of their counterparts in the latter part of the seventeenth century and later too? "As the land in the older section of Flatbush became covered with farms and families increased in size, the new generation began to move out toward Queens." Although it was no less true then than now that "it does not bode well for the area's agricultural future if a farmer can sell out at a price that will allow immediate retirement," some of the traditionalist Dutch farmers must have asked themselves, as their late-twentieth-century counterparts do: "But then what would I do?"[42]

That a source of farmers on the move was available in Kings County must have seemed plausible to the Union Pacific Railroad, which as early as 1873 advertised in the *Rural Gazette* and *Eagle*: "12,000,000 Acres cheap farms." Advertisements for Maryland fruit farms at $10 to $25 per acre also suggest the presence of a pool of geographically mobile farmers. And although the local news columns of the *Rural Gazette* in the 1870s and 1880s were far from overflowing with items about residents departing for farms elsewhere, it did register a few such moves. Several involved buying farms to the east on Long Island that were larger than those in Kings County. Only one Dutch family operating a large farm was reported as leaving: in auctioning off their implements in 1885, the Van Wycks of Flatlands intended to move to New Jersey to raise livestock.[43]

Genealogies of some of the leading Kings County Dutch families reveal similar patterns of sporadic agriculturally driven out-migration. For example, in 1870, 40-year-old Tunis and 28-year-old John Bergen of Gravesend bought a farm at Mattituck in Suffolk County. Both carpenters, they were the sons of John Bergen, whose father was the owner of Bergen Island in Flatlands; since his older brothers had inherited the family farm, he moved to Gravesend, where he operated a country store and was postmaster. Martenus Bergen (born 1811), who took over his father's 120-acre farm in Gowanus in the 1830s, first moved to New Jersey to farm; then in 1873 he moved to Virginia, where he had bought 3,000 acres. His abandonment of farming in Gowanus may well have been driven by urbanization of this part of the newly incorporated city of Brooklyn.[44]

Only two items during the *Rural Gazette*'s 13-year run suggested that a more generalized migration took place before the mid-1880s. In connection with a report in 1878 that a resident of Bay Ridge had bought 20 acres in Mattituck, at the eastern end of the north shore of Long Island, for $5,000 — at $250 per acre the price was low by rural Kings County standards, but certainly not dirt cheap — the paper observed: "There is quite a settlement there now from Kings County, and all say they are pleased with the change." Three years later an unsigned piece by one who had moved to the north shore of Long Island from Kings County 14 years earlier revealed that neighbors of small means had followed him. What they all had in common was an inability to buy a farm in Kings County and the cultivation of cauliflower on Long Island. Further explaining the move, the writer asserted that "of all men that have a hard lot of it, who have to toil early and late, through sunshine and storm, through heat and cold, it is the market gardener of small means on the west end of Long Island."[45] Allowing for the rhetorical overload, these brief pieces hold out the possibility that Long Island, and especially the more remote Suffolk County, did offer some small or would-be farmers an opportunity to farm that they lacked in Kings County. These reports do not, however, support the speculation that larger established farmers, prior to the 1890s, moved there after either lucratively selling out or failing to make an acceptable living.

By the end of the 1890s, however, an eastward movement of farmers from Kings County was in full swing. In early 1899, the *Long Island Farmer* reported that the "migration of farmers from Gravesend and New Utrecht to eastern Jamaica and Flushing and more generally, to points in Nassau Co. is attracting attention. The movement is caused by the large sales of farmlands in Kings County at high prices to building syndicates." Alone in the preceding one year, at least forty Kings County farmers — "all skilled truck farmers and . . . nearly all wealthy and a desirable class of citizens" — had bought farms in eastern Jamaica, Flushing, and North Hempstead. Contemporaries were acutely aware that the "large purchase of farms between Brooklyn and Coney Island" and "filling up" of Kings County had prompted this unprecedented "general exodus of farmers" from Kings to Nassau County and thus a shift of the truck farming district 20 miles eastward. Intriguingly, when one well-informed local resident named three of the Gravesend farmers who had recently secured fifteen or twenty farms near Hyde Park and moved there, they all bore Irish names. This fact takes on added significance in connection with the statement that: "While the high city assessments have tended to drive the farmers out of the Kings County towns, the land owners have been assisted by the fact that there was an active demand for building lots and have let their farms go for that purpose." Gertrude Ryder Bennett's report that Irishmen who settled in Gravesend after having fled the famine "worked for farmers until they could purchase farms of their own" may therefore have been referring to farms on western Long Island.[46]

This distinction between farmers and landowners suggests the possibility that those moving eastward had been tenant farmers, whereas the enriched owners remained in Brooklyn. How the Irish tenants had accumulated sufficient resources to become "wealthy" and to buy farms is not clear. To be sure, if it was possible for Kings County market gardeners to achieve profits of $100 per acre while paying rents of only $20 per acre, then the tenants' accumulation of wealth would be understandable. The puzzle would then be owners' failure to extract higher rents. The fact that land prices were lower in Nassau County would have facilitated tenants' geographic and social mobility as would have the strategy of buying small truck farms, but that very surge of demand triggered a rise in prices — from $150 to $400 an acre within one year in some localities — that may have impeded the migration of tenants, but presumably not that of owners who might have realized $2,000 to $3,000 per acre for the farms that they had sold.

In Flatbush, several old-line Dutch farmers remained after selling their farms to become members of the new nonagricultural business elite; in an alternative interpretation, they were merely consummating a program of economic diversification that they had been pursuing for decades. As early as the second quarter of the nineteenth century, such rich men as Adrian Van Sinderen and Adrian Hegeman were officers of the Brooklyn Savings Bank, and "such other eminences" as Losee Van Nostrand, Leffert Lefferts, Jacob Bergen, and John C. Vanderveer had been prominent owners of Brooklyn's corporate wealth. The head of the Lott family at the turn of the century and son of John A. Lott, John Z. Lott (1838–1914), was an attorney, president of the Flatbush Trust Co. and the Flatbush Water Works Co., an organizer of the Flatbush Gas Co., and commissioner of the Flatbush Police Department. With such links, it is hardly surprising that "no important real estate movement has occurred in the last twenty-five years [1883–1908] in which the Lotts were not a prominent factor." Equally unsurprising is that he left an estate of $281,000. Significantly, not only did none of Flatlands farmer Rem Hegeman's sons become a farmer, but his grandson John Rogers Hegeman, symbolizing the Dutch farmers' diversification, was already president of the Metropolitan Life Insurance Company in 1891, five years before Flatlands was annexed to Brooklyn.[47]

Cornelius Schoonmaker, who was born on his father's Flatbush farm in 1823 and devoted his life to it, was still living there at 85. Like many Dutch farmers, he married into another Dutch farming family (that of Jacques Denyse); one of his daughters married into the Stilwell family, another farming family. William Allgeo, who farmed his family's acreage, remained in Flatbush after the land was cut into lots and houses built on it. Peter Remsen, a descendant of one of the early Dutch colonialists, after having devoted the greater part of his life to farming, built a modern home in Flatbush shortly after the turn of the century. Jerome Lott, who, after brief stints in a Brooklyn law office and a New York customs house brokerage, farmed at his family's homestead in Flatlands, disposed of the property in 1899, "making many investments in Flatbush, where he subsequently erected a modern home."[48]

The head of the Lefferts family, John Lefferts (1826–1893), despite having "devoted himself to agricultural pursuits all his life" on his large Flatbush tract, which had been "deeded to his ancestors by Gov. Stuyvesant in 1661," was also treasurer of the Flatbush Gas Company, president of the Flatbush Water Works Company, president of the Flatbush Plank Road Company, a director of the Brooklyn Bank and Long Island Safe Deposit Company, and a trustee of the Dime Savings Bank of Brooklyn. At the time of his death, with "the growth of the city toward Flatbush," his son, James Lefferts (1855–1915), "abandoned farming and began the development of the estate by opening streets and avenues through it and erecting many buildings." Little wonder that he, too, died "one of the very wealthy men of the borough." That the Lefferts family had diversified early is evident from the fact that Leffert Lefferts was the president of the first bank in Brooklyn, the Long Island Bank, from its incorporation in 1824 until his death in 1847. In addition to having owned a very large potato farm in Flatbush, John Lefferts also owned a 31-acre farm along Lefferts Avenue and numerous lots in New Utrecht, which he presumably sold during the real-estate boom in the 1880s. The houses that he built in Flatbush in the 1880s reputedly reflected "his usual earnest desire for the growth and prosperity of our town." Further diversification occurred in 1876 when John Lefferts Jr. married the daughter of Joseph W. Gray, a tobacco merchant and one of the income-richest residents of Flatbush.[49]

The Ditmas family, which had also settled in Flatbush in the mid-seventeenth century and several members of which farmed until the end of the nineteenth century, also branched out into other fields of enterprise. Henry Clay Ditmas, an intimate friend of the political boss of Gravesend, John Y. McKane, "made a fortune by transmitting by telegraph to the poolrooms throughout the country the news from the race tracks" in the New York area, and left an estate estimated at between $200,000 and $1 million at his death in 1893. John H. Ditmas, who inherited a part of the farm of his father, Henry Suydam Ditmas, in 1884, was a director of the Flatbush Trust Company, who at his death in 1914 left $177,000. An exemplar of the interbred Dutch family, John Ditmas married a Kouwenhoven, while his sister Jane married Judge Gerret Martense's son Gerret and Maria married John Z. Lott. Abraham I. Ditmas was secretary of the Flatbush Gas Company and of the Midwood Electric Light-, Heat-, and Power Company, and a principal of the Knickerbocker Electric Light and Power Company of Flatbush in the early 1890s.[50]

New Utrecht, too, could boast of its newly enriched Dutch farmers. Consider Garret Peter Cowenhoven (1846–1927), the son of Peter Cowenhoven (1816–1888). The father at age 64 appeared in the 1880 census as owner of an 80-acre farm, which he valued at $12,500 and produced $5,000 worth of market garden produce in 1879. The son, then already 33 years old, was still returned by the census as farming on his father's farm, which was located between 15th and 18th Avenues. The New Utrecht assessment roll for 1889 listed Garret Cowenhoven as owning 35.75 acres (located at 17th Avenue and

62nd Street) valued at $10,435 ($292 per acre), for which he paid $161.30 in tax. Peter Cowenhoven appeared on the New Utrecht assessment rolls for 1888 as owning two properties, 23.83 and 19.00 acres (at 18th Avenue and 51st to 52nd Street), which were valued at $7,850 and $4,750 ($329 and $250 per acre), respectively. Their assessed value, which remained virtually un-changed in 1889, rose by 45 percent and 60 percent, respectively, from 1889 to 1890. By 1892, just four years after the father's death, Jere Johnson Jr., a leading real-estate figure in Kings County, announced in the *Eagle* the "Grand Closing Out Sale of all the remaining 300 lots on the famous Cowenhoven Farm, New Utrecht, on Labor Day." Johnson advertised: "splendidly located," "[g]rade level, every lot ready to be built upon."[51]

Already six years later, barely 50 years old, Garret Peter Cowenhoven, "known as a retired farmer," was a "reputed millionaire." The circum-stances under which his fortune came to be reported in the *Eagle* themselves cast a fascinating light on one possibly representative career-ending trajec-tory of those Dutch farmers who made the rapid transition from cabbage cultivators to rentiers. Apparently having retained after the land sale his family's old farmhouse "in a lovely section of the suburbs," Cowenhoven in the mid-1890s "in order to entertain his friends . . . transformed his old barn into a club house. He fitted it up with gymnastic apparatus and included among the other fittings a pool table." Indeed, the barn's "modern design" made it appear "very much like a club house." All these details became pub-lic knowledge not because the *Eagle* was interested in Dutch farmers' in-terior decorating, but because a police captain raided the barn one rainy Saturday evening, arresting Cowenhoven and seven others as common gamblers. In 1926, a year before he died, Cowenhoven finally moved from his family New Utrecht farm homestead to the more sedate suburban Dit-mas Park section of Flatbush.[52]

Not all old-line Dutch farmers, however, transmogrified themselves into financially diversified and worldly sophisticates or led a life of ease made possible by the fruits of their quondam cabbage fields. Before another mem-ber of the huge and ramified Cowenhoven family, Randall Gordon Cowen-hoven, "about the last direct descendant of one of the oldest families on Long Island, dropped dead" in 1890, neighbors frequently saw "the old man plowing up the earth with an antiquated wooden plow, or planting seed." At one point the Cowenhoven family had owned land in Kings County "now worth millions, but by alienation and legal squabbles it passed into other hands" and Randall Cowenhoven had fallen into "financial difficulties."[53]

Perhaps the most prominent example of the unreconstructed was Abram

Van Sicklen, who died in 1898 at 79, the oldest resident of Coney Island. According to his obituary in the *New York Times*, his father had owned the oldest farm on Coney Island, which the son ran until two years before his death. At the time of the 1870 Census of Agriculture, he produced $3,500 worth of produce, including 2,000 bushels of potatoes, on the farm's 28 acres. Van Sicklen's most endearing characteristic was that after having arrived in Coney Island at four months of age, he "spent all his life there" — not just in the usual sense, but by virtue of never having remained away overnight and never having crossed the Brooklyn Bridge: "He used to say that there was plenty to see on Coney Island." [54] So struck was the *Times* by this sedentary provinciality, that the next day it devoted an editorial to Van Sicklen, which can also be interpreted as a valedictory to the literal agrarian insularity that might have shocked even Timothy Dwight if not Karl Marx. Finding it "practically impossible" to imagine Coney Island as anyone's residence, the newspaper opined that:

> It is obvious that nobody would live there permanently except under compulsion, and, as there is no compulsion, the conclusion is inevitable that nobody does or ever has. Unfortunately, Mr. ABRAM VAN SICKLEN has been doing just this thing for full eighty years, and only changed his habits this week at the persuasive entreaty of — death. . . . [N]ever in all his long life did curiosity or any other motive lead him so far away from home as the Borough of Manhattan. . . . Mr. VAN SICKLEN must have been a remarkable man, with vast mental resources and much philosophy of a sort which, if it were more common, would probably add to the sum total of human happiness. It would not accelerate the world's progress, however, so perhaps there is no reason to regret that he monopolized the whole American supply. [55]

Finally, there is Daniel Tredwell's description of what the Flatbush Dutch farmers did once they realized the capitalized value of their cabbage farms-turned-real estate: "Vast tracts were sold and the former owners retired independent, eschewed hard labor and went about dressed in their Sunday clothes every day in the week." [56]

11. CASE STUDIES IN SUBURBANIZATION

Fresh and green the fields, with an almost imperceptible slope, rolled southward, and from this, the dividing line between Flatbush and Brooklyn, the Flatbush farmers had an unbroken and beautifully cultivated expanse of farming land to the limits southward of the village. Upon this northern border of the town, which was once so fair a picture of agricultural prosperity, the change into a city suburb has begun. To the northeast fences are thrown down, the old stone wall is leveled, the sickly-looking cows of the city milkmen endeavor to graze upon the short and dried grass; pigs and dogs and goats, rough men and dirty women, scold and scream and bark in mingled confusion from the shanties of the squatters that have taken possession of the open commons. It is sad for us who have been so fond of this country life to think that this may be a precursor of the change which shall slowly creep onward in advance of the city growth.

— Gertrude Lefferts Vanderbilt, *The Social History of Flatbush*, 1880

The sadness that Gertrude Lefferts Vanderbilt felt in 1880 for the agrarian life that she suspected would soon be swept away by the Brooklynization of the county towns highlights an important factor in the sell-off of Kings County farms: once urban encroachment began to undermine the traditional benefits of rural life such as hunting and homogeneous social surroundings, the younger, inheriting, generation's resistance to abandoning agricultural pursuits and embracing the city's cultural advantages must have been severely weakened. By the end of the 1870s, as "[c]apitalists . . . awakened to the advantages offered for investment" in rural Kings County, the Dutch farmers must have recognized that rurality and nature were "no longer within the domain of nature. The city has stretched out its hand, and the mark of the beast can usually be seen." The outstretched hands of fruit and vegetable thieves were just one of many troubling signs of urban intrusion.[1]

Closer examination of the transition reveals a gradual crumbling of the farmers' ancestral or communal culture that in turn made rural Kings County lands more vulnerable to a complete takeover by urban-minded users. Lefferts Vanderbilt was reflecting on the outward signs of this cultural erosion in Flatbush and its eventual consequences. Reduced to a mere "incongruity . . . found in all our modern, legally enlarged cities," rural Kings County could be viewed as the comic or tragic result of "the contending forces of city and country."[2]

This process had begun much earlier in Kings County. Indeed, Lefferts Vanderbilt's families by birth and marriage figured prominently among the Dutch farm owners whose attachment to the land had made the transition from traditional to speculative, even if their willingness to treat their land as a commodity was not associated with the kind of geographic mobility observed elsewhere in the United States. But commercial modernization had, until the last two decades of the nineteenth century, only limped along because it both met with resistance by the entrenched farming community and its governmental representatives, and had been undercut by the advantages that real-estate developers and their clientele had found elsewhere in the New York metropolitan region.[3]

Lefferts Vanderbilt's nostalgia for the green fields of her youth was only one aspect of the complex process of transition: no matter how much she and her Dutch farming neighbors may have regretted the passing of country life, as astute investors they were determined not only to profit passively from the transformation, but to promote it themselves. In 1875, five years before she wrote her *Social History of Flatbush*, Lefferts Vanderbilt herself submitted a petition to the Flatbush Board of Improvement — which was presided over by John A. Lott and staffed by other scions of Dutch farming families, including her husband and her brother, whom the state legislature had appointed — to grade, improve, and open for public travel at her own expense East New York Avenue between Ocean and Flatbush Avenue, all the land for which she owned. Yet five years later she bemoaned the loss at this very location of the "noble hickories, gum-trees, and oaks, with an undergrowth of dogwood and clumps of hazel." In 1842, she exclaimed, it had been "the very picture of rural and pastoral life! . . . [A]s yet there was no possible sign from which the busy future could have been predicted." But by 1880, "the shrieking locomotives" and troops of "pleasure-seekers" created the greatest imaginable contrast to the seclusion and tranquility of her youth. Bulldozing their way to modernity, as it were, while lamenting the inexorable destruction of the past coexisted as two modes of thought and action for premodern agrarians who were eager to exploit opportunities — until they had converted the last cabbage field into suburban real estate.[4]

THE MERCANTILE GENTRIFICATION OF RURAL KINGS COUNTY

There have always been those who saw Brooklyn as a "banana republic" open for colonialist exploitation.

— Elliott Willensky, *When Brooklyn Was the World*, 1986

As they did in other parts of Long Island, wealthy New York businessmen selected certain desirable localities in southern Kings County as their "non-agricultural country seats." The chief property-based and spatial difference between settlement by these rich merchants in New Utrecht and Flatbush was that those in New Utrecht owned considerable acreage, whereas those in Flatbush owned only a small amount of land surrounding their expensive and stately residences. The difference is striking on farmline maps, which show large chunks of land in amongst the farms of Bay Ridge owned by William Langley, John Bullocke, George Hope, and others. Figure 22 shows the numerous Van Brunt, Bennett, and Bergen family farms in a row along Shore Road overlooking New York Bay and behind them the estates of several of the mercantile elite. In New Utrecht's Northern Drainage District alone, 14 such residents owned 277 acres in 1871, the largest holdings (51 acres) being assessed to William Langley. Langley's land formed half of a 109-acre farm at Yellow Hook (later Bay Ridge) that Tunis J. Bergen (1759–1826) had bought from the Cropsey family in 1807. Langley owned more than 92 acres in New Utrecht in 1870; a decade later, when his holdings had declined to 71 acres, those of clothing manufacturer Archibald Young had climbed to 158 acres.[5]

The gentrification of Flatbush and New Utrecht had been underway for several decades, attracting many well-to-do merchants from New York, who may have initially viewed their houses in those towns or Gravesend as summer homes. New York merchants also began buying acreage in New

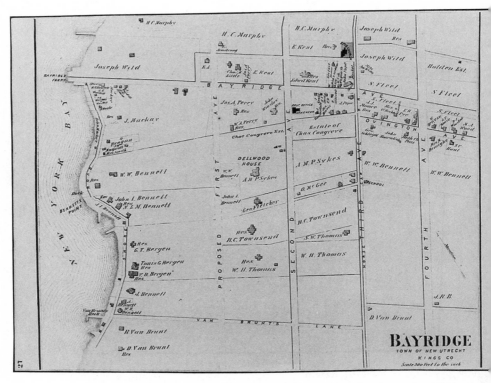

FIGURE 22. *Bay Ridge, 1870. From Catherine Nelson and E. Theodore Nelson, "The Villages of Fort Hamilton and Bay Ridge As They Were in the Year 1870."*

Utrecht earlier than in Flatbush. William Langley, for example, appeared on the New Utrecht assessment roll in 1846 as owner of a 45-acre farm, followed in 1852 by Hope and Henry C. Murphy.[6]

This developmental difference between the two towns finds a parallel in the fact that by the 1850s scores of New Utrecht nonresidents owned lots, whereas no such ownership pattern had yet emerged in Flatbush. William C. Langley, for example, who died at the age of 91 in 1890 one of the "richest dry goods commission merchants in the city," bequeathing his son $1,000,000, "owned a country place at Bay Ridge." As early as 1860, when his household included a black cook, black coachman, and five black servants in addition to one Irish and two English gardeners, he reported to the Census of Population that he owned real estate worth $300,000 and personalty worth $100,000. Robert Fox, who moved from Brooklyn after the middle of the century, bought a farm and farmhouse from a widow, before selling it and buying Fisher's Island in Long Island Sound. Jonathan Long-mire, a jobber and importer in the linen trade, married a granddaughter of Henry S. Ditmas and spent $100,000 on his house in Flatbush, which, together with its greenhouse, was located across the street from Prospect Park.[7]

The business career of Archibald Young, one of the rural towns' richest residents during the period of the Civil War income tax, described a much different path before his death at 78 in 1895. From upstate New York, he became a partner in his father's clothing manufacture business, retiring with a "fortune" by 1870. But a quarter-century earlier he had embarked on a land-buying venture that helped transform New Utrecht as he unleashed a latter-day enclosure movement in the course of gaining ownership of more than one-half of the Bath Beach section of the township:[8]

> he went with his father-in-law to Bath Beach. In order to make a village out of the little settlement he bought the old Lott farm and cut it up into lots, which he sold cheaply. While engaged in real estate speculation he opened a public park on the water front. . . . Later he purchased a part of the Bennett farm and also a portion of the Benson farm, upon which is Bensonhurst. In 1872 Mr. Young . . . bought the commons west of the Dycker Meadows. This tract for years had been used as a public pasture ground, and when Mr. Young fenced it in there was great indignation for a time.[9]

Young, who in 1879 became a director of the Brooklyn, Bath, and Coney Island Railroad, still owned 187 acres in 1886 in addition to numerous lots. When he bought 40 acres of the old Cropsey farm in 1885, the *Rural Gazette* suggested that Bath Beach "might very properly be called Youngstown."[10]

That three people who had been born in Paris and Milan and whose occupation was "opera singer" were returned by the 1860 Census of Population as residing in New Utrecht suggests that it was no longer an insular community of boers. Cultural aspirations culminated in the incorporation in 1871 of the Bay Ridge Atheneum "for the purpose of encouraging and cultivating literature, music, and the arts." The 30 incorporators included almost the entire Manhattan-based urban business elite, such as Edward Armstrong, John Bullocke, George Hope, Joseph Perry, and William C. Langley, as well as the wealthy retired farmer J. Remsen Bennett and the ubiquitous Teunis G. Bergen. The town's heterogeneity was, nevertheless, underscored by the fact that as early as the Civil War one-fourth of males between the ages of 18 and 45 were aliens.[11]

Businesses, such as William Matthews's large (D. Appleton & Company) bookbindery in Williamsburgh, Henry Johnson's bookstore, and Edward Hincken's ship brokerage, also required their owners — all British — to commute from the rural towns, which were too sparsely populated to support such large undertakings, to Brooklyn or Manhattan. Several of the other richest residents of Kings County were also English, including the gum manufacturer Davies.[12]

The 1869 Internal Revenue Assessment Lists — chosen for scrutiny in chapter 10 because they supplemented the 1869–70 Census of Agriculture — were not atypical. Table 38 shows the incomes and occupations of the 10 taxpayers reporting the highest incomes in rural Kings County in the years 1863 through 1871. The tax data for the years 1862–1865 and 1870–71 reinforce the pattern that prevailed in 1869–70: not a single one of the 10 highest-income taxpayers in any year was a farmer. The highest-income farmer in each of these years was ranked: 28th in 1862 (J. Remsen Bennett, New Utrecht, $3,061.22); tied for 19th in 1863 (Teunis Bergen, New Utrecht, $5,000); 21st in 1864 (Robert Magaw, Flatlands, $7,475.70); 23rd in 1865 (J. Remsen Bennett, $6,484.62); 19th in 1870 (John Ryerson, $2,387.36); and 17th in 1871 (Jacob Ryerson, Flatlands, $3,279.16).[13]

The income-richest resident of rural Kings County in 1869, Edward Ridley, was a 54-year-old Englishman whose income that year was almost $44,000 (including the exemption). At the 1870 Census of Population, he valued his personal estate at $350,000 — almost three times greater than that of the very wealthy John Lefferts — and his real estate at $70,000. Ridley, whose large and famous fancy and millinery goods store had been located in Grand Street in Manhattan since 1849, maintained a "beautiful homestead" in Gravesend, which he had bought from an old-line farm family there, but most of the land that he owned was in the Parkville section of Flatbush. Ridley's store employed almost as many people (1,700) as the total population of Gravesend.[14]

That so many wealthy merchants whose income derived from urban enterprises resided in the county's rural sections as early as the 1860s suggests that the lack of rapid transit was not an insuperable barrier to suburban commuters. After all, Edward Ridley, even after the opening of the Brooklyn Bridge, drove his carriage home seven miles to Gravesend every evening — despite the dangers of horse-drawn transportation and the serious injuries that he and his wife had once sustained. Nevertheless, even Ridley was alive to the barriers to residing in rural Kings County for those who worked in

Manhattan: in 1881 he proposed to build 50 cottages on the 40 acres he owned near Kings Highway in Gravesend to rent to his employees at moderate prices — but only after he completed arrangements with the Brooklyn, Flatbush, and Coney Island Railroad to operate trains all year round.[15]

MAKING THE ENVIRONMENT SAFE FOR SUBURBANIZATION: FIGHTING THE IRISH PIGGERIES

It was fortunate for Flatbush that wise men with long vision came and bought the farms, rather than greedy and short-sighted speculators.
—*Flatbush of To-Day: Realm of Air and Light*, 1908

The disamenities of living amongst densely packed working farms apparently did not deter wealthy city businessmen from preferring the rural towns to more conveniently located Brooklyn or Manhattan, any more than they prompted John A. Lott or John Lefferts, rich scions of farm families who continued to own land while they focused their attention on urban business affairs, to abandon Flatbush. At a time when these cities were themselves plagued with stenches and diseases emanating from manure-strewn streets, residents may not have perceived farm odors as posing any special unpleasantness or hazard. Nevertheless, both the agricultural and mercantile wings of the elite devoted some of their influence to combating health hazards not related to vegetable farming. Despite their wealth and power, some of their efforts seem laughably ineffectual. For example, in 1879, five years after the Flatbush Board of Health had been established and had issued a Sanitary Code forbidding owners to allow cattle to go at large, the board conceded owners were violating it in some sections of town. Throughout the 1870s, contractors and others continued to be "in the habit of" dumping night soil on empty lots and unloading wagons with manure and heaping it within the town limits.[16]

A related environmental battle lasted even longer and absorbed more of the political-economic elite's resources. Before it succumbed to or welcomed the city, the elite was preoccupied with Sisyphean struggles to dam the alien influences of an ever-approaching Brooklyn in general and the inrushing Irish in particular. As early as 1873, John A. Lott, John Lefferts, Abraham Ditmas, and "a very large number of our oldest, best, most influential and wealthy citizens" stepped forward to prevent the sale of intoxicating liquors in Flatbush on the sabbath. Their mission would last into the

1880s and demand much of their time. The success with which Lefferts, John Z. Lott (taking his deceased father's place), five members of the Ditmas family, and others remonstrated with the town excise board to deny the application for a hotel in the beginning of 1880 proved to be only one small victory. A few months later, "A Delegation of the Principal Property Owners," including Lott, Lefferts, Ditmas, and William Matthews, personally waited on the excise board to urge it to grant liquor licenses only under the strict letter of the law. Perceiving that achievement of their objective would require organizational continuity, 15 of Flatbush's largest taxpayers met at Matthews's residence to form the Law and Order Association of the Town of Flatbush. They appointed as counsel the politically well connected lawyer, William Gaynor, who then managed their dealings with the excise board.[17]

In addition to preventing liquor sales on Sundays and all liquor sales without a license, the association's object was combating houses of ill repute. Although John Lefferts held so many positions in so many private and public bodies that he was constrained to resign from some (such as the Brooklyn, Flatbush, and Coney Island Railroad) for sheer lack of time, he frequently attended hearings and trials pertaining to alcohol and prostitution. In 1880, for example, Gaynor, on behalf of the association, represented a resident of Flatbush who successfully sued a neighboring tenant to have him removed for running a brothel. Present in court were Lefferts (just returned from visiting his Vermont farm), his potato farming son James, John Z. Lott, Abraham Ditmas, William Matthews, Henry Lyles, and other wealthy association members.[18]

Despite their wealth, the political power of the diversifying Dutch farmers and their mercantile allies was far from absolute. And, in at least one environmentally significant conflict, upstart Irish businessmen held the elite at bay. The goal of eliminating the piggeries near the Brooklyn city line stymied the leading citizens of Flatbush for more than a decade — despite the early declaration by Philip Crooke, counsel of the Board of Health and himself one of the town's powerholders, that "the removal of this stigma from the gateway of our town, was the most important thing which could claim our attention at present." On September 9, 1874, the newly appointed town health officer, Dr. H. Bartlett, himself a Flatbush landowner, reported to the Board of Health on his inspection tour through "the stench infected and pig inflicted district" lying between Flatbush Avenue and the New Lots line. There he found "piles on piles of manure, mixed with the contents of privy vaults, distilled hops, decayed meats, and vegetables." This manure business was run largely by nonresidents who came to Flatbush "only to make money irrespective of consequences." The piggeries and bone-boiling establishments so reeked with filth that by contrast the Augean stables were "a paragon of neatness." The piggeries, where the pigs were fed garbage and swill transported from Brooklyn, were also operated by nonresidents and "of course, non-taxpayers; many of them squatters and not even paying rent." Whereas Brooklyn and New Lots had suppressed piggeries, the entire northern border of Flatbush, three miles long and one-third mile wide, was used "for purposes detrimental to health, to the exclusion of more desirable residents." Bartlett, equally attuned to property and health interests, found it a "burning shame" that such men had been allowed to take possession of a square mile which, "from its proximity to the city, should be valuable, not only destroying its material value but rendering it actually dangerous to life and health." [19]

The following week, Bartlett reported to the board that as a result of patrols by his sanitary police inspectors, the feeding of garbage had been entirely stopped, the dumping of manure effectively prevented, and most of the pigs "removed to more salubrious climes." He added that although some proprietors had been defiant, other larger operators had expressed a willingness to comply, but requested initial leniency "as they would suffer great pecuniary loss." When Bartlett not only supported their plea, but also recommended reducing the number of sanitary officers, board counsel Crooke, who took a dim view of the piggery operators' credibility, replied: "As a man averse to heavy stinks, let me tell you that within three nights from the time you took off these extra men, the nuisance would be as bad as ever." Crooke's interventionist approach uncovered tensions within the town's political-economic elite. Jacob V. B. Martense, the Flatbush town supervisor and a retired farmer who still rented his farmland out to tenants, and the board's only farmer-member, urged a decidedly more cautious fiscal approach: "Well, we should consider the expense. We don't want to spend too much." Crooke, obviously speaking on behalf of himself, Lefferts, John A. Lott, and other rich property owners, saw what was at stake for the drive toward suburbanization: "Those who pay the most taxes are the most willing to bear any extra expense. The largest taxpayer in the town is willing to pay any additional tax which may be incurred by action of this board." The elite appeared to suffer its first defeat when the board empowered Bartlett "to do as he thought best." [20]

At a special meeting on September 23, 1874, Dr. Bartlett instructed the board that a distinction had to be drawn between District No. 1, the area between Flatbush Avenue and Clove Road, and District No. 2, lying between

Clove Road and the New Lots town line, farther away from the village. Whereas the great majority of operators in District No. 1 paid neither taxes nor rent and were "consequently not worthy of much consideration," most operators in District No. 2 owned property, some of them considerable amounts, and had occupied it for a long time. Bartlett impressed on the board the need to deal with what he called the most important question that it would ever be asked to decide — how to maintain the town's "material growth and prosperity" and to guard the inhabitants' health in the face of special interests who profited from the piggeries and knew how to influence politicians. A considerable number of men, many "honorable and law-abiding citizens," according to Bartlett, were "largely interested pecuniarily in the perpetuation [of] this evil." It was only "natural" that they spent money freely on the "powers that be." They had offered their support, and the not inconsiderable support of their "fellows" "to any aspirant, no matter what his character or fitness, so long as he can further their cause." Their success had been so great that "those men are made to believe" that the board's regulations were "only a dead letter." [21]

Bartlett's remarks seem odd since the (largely Irish) group that he singled out lacked the wealth and political power of Flatbush's landed and mercantile elites.[22] Nevertheless, the board again avoided taking the hard-line approach that Crooke had proposed earlier. Instead, it resolved that no permits be granted for keeping swine or cattle to be fed on city garbage or swill between Flatbush Avenue and Clove Road and north of East New York Avenue, and that no one be allowed to dump manure there "except for strictly agricultural purposes." A motion proposed by Martense was also adopted that because a "large amount of capital is invested" in the piggeries and a "large pecuniary loss" would result from their sudden suspension, they would be given until April 1, 1875, to remove all such animals provided that they operated in the interim under the board's supervision. Tongue in cheek, the *Rural Gazette* suggested accommodating Brooklyn's desired enlargement by letting it annex the "exhilerating [sic] piggeries" along with the county institutions.[23]

By May 1875, however, the board received a petition from a number of the town's Dutch political-economic leaders, including John Vanderbilt, John Lefferts, and Martense (who was no longer town supervisor or a board member), asking the board to take summary proceedings to remove the piggeries east of Flatbush Avenue. But even these luminaries could not assert their will summarily. A report to the board the next month found that because of the great distance from the populated part of the town, the effluvia were not so great as to be detrimental. In 1877, residents, including P. L. Schenck, the medical supervisor of the county hospital and himself a scion of one of the county's Dutch farming families, requested that the board take measures against epidemics that the piggeries might cause once the weather became warm. At the same time, a standing committee appointed by the board to examine the piggeries reported that several of them were not fit to continue. Significantly, virtually all the owners of these piggeries had Irish surnames. Later that year the board of health raided some piggeries, ordering nonresidents to remove them, while residents were merely required to put their operations in "proper sanitary condition."[24]

In 1878, the elite once again urged the board to act. This time William Matthews, Jonathan Longmire, and John Prince (three of the town's income-richest mercantile businessmen), Lefferts Vanderbilt, John Lefferts, and William Williamson and George Schenck (two of the very few Dutch farmers in Flatbush still operating their own farms, which were on the less populated side of town near the piggeries) asked that the piggeries between Clarkson Avenue and the Brooklyn city line be removed. When the health officer reported that the 82 piggeries in Flatbush exceeded the previous year's count by 20 and contained 5,000 hogs, the board merely moved to enforce the sanitary code's prohibition of transporting garbage. In a transparent delaying tactic, Supervisor Peter Williamson and one of the other members unsuccessfully moved to appoint a committee to inspect the piggeries. The *Rural Gazette*, losing patience, both found it mysterious that Williamson could put himself on record as favoring these pestilences and solved the mystery: Williamson might have political friends who did "not favor catering to the lowest element of society," but the supervisor himself apparently found it "necessary to become surety for those who are not considered law abiding in order that his political supremacy may be sustained."[25]

In 1881, the elite — including, once again, Lefferts, Vanderbilt, Lott, and Matthews — were still remonstrating in vain to cause the board to abate the nuisance. On September 12, John Lefferts himself attended the board meeting, this time expressly abjuring any appeal to property values. Instead, he stressed that Flatbush was "eminently a place of homes and residences," that the odors should not be tolerated, and that the board should use its power to suppress the piggeries. Two days later, Dr. John Zabriskie, the new health officer and member of a large landowning family, read his report detailing the "disgusting business" of boiling garbage in immense vats to a "seething mass," which was allowed to run to waste on the premises, which then became the pigs' favorite wallowing ground. Appended was a list of the names of the occupants of the establishments, fifty of sixty of which appear to have been Irish. After taking a number of partial measures, the board — which now included members of such prominent landed elite families as Van-derveer, Lott, and Zabriskie — on September 22, 1881, ordered the piggeries declared nuisances to be discontinued by January 1, 1882. It also adopted a regulation prohibiting the keeping of "more than two animals of the species hog" on any premises without the board's permission.[26]

To no one's surprise, "Pigtown" continued to thrive. The *Rural Gazette* explained the failure of the health board's "[s]pasmodic efforts" against operators — whose names identified them as Irish — by reference to "politics . . . and as the piggery men held the balance of power they were simply warned not to keep nuisances." By "politics" the newspaper meant that the votes of "that section have always been purchasable." By the summer of 1884, the newspaper disclosed that some piggeries kept thousands of pigs. Late that year, under deceptively hopeful headlines, the *Rural Gazette* reported that thenceforward no swine, dead or alive, could be brought into or taken out of Flatbush without a permit. Pressing its credibility, it reported the next spring that the piggery nuisance was "very nearly exterminated." In fact, however, the *Rural Gazette* expired before the piggeries: in its last word on the subject before it ceased publication, the newspaper was constrained to concede in 1885, 11 years after it began documenting the fight against them, that the piggeries had grown bold once again.[27]

SUBURBANIZING FORCES

[I]t has only been within a few years that the farms have been cut up into building lots and the New Flatbush has come into existence. It was most fortunate that the farms were held intact until this period. . . . Had the farmers sold their land thirty or forty years ago, and the tide of city expansion been in this direction, Flatbush, to-day, would not be the beauty spot that it is.
—*Flatbush of To-Day: The Realm of Air and Light*, 1908

Frederick Law Olmsted knew in 1879 that Brooklyn was an essential part of New York as a metropolis, but only in the same speculative sense as Newark, Bridgeport, and Yale College. Because Kings County had not yet become a real part of New York, the city had experienced the recent urban tendency toward compact and vertical business and social concentration but not the concomitant broad and open residential dispersion. New York thus largely lacked residences "combining urban and rural advantages, neither solitary . . . nor a mere slice of a block," which were found in "healthy and pleasing localities, with quick and frequent transit to business, social, artistic, literary and scholarly centres," and were "springing up in hundreds of charming neighborhoods about London and Paris," and from which Boston and cities in the West were formed. New Yorkers made much less use of such areas than the inhabitants of any other large city because

> hitherto there have been no thoroughly healthy suburban neighborhoods sufficiently accessible about New York. In time such neighborhoods will be formed. Whenever they are, the metropolitan advantages of New-York and the profits of its local trade must be greatly increased by constantly increasing accessions to its population of men who have accumulated means elsewhere, and who wish to engage in other than purely money-making occupations. Such men, living under favorable circumstances and with capital and energies economically directed to matters of general interest, are the most valuable constituents of a city; and it is by their numbers, wealth and influence, more than anything else, that a city takes the rank in the world of a metropolis.[28]

The opening of the Brooklyn Bridge four years later made that incorporation much less metaphorical: Brooklyn "offered its broad expanse of uncovered acres within the city for the easy occupation of those who wish homes, either modest or splendid. The capital and the sea were henceforth also nearer to neighborhood." Although Kings County would make dispersion possible, residential concentration would soon replicate itself there. But before any of these forces could make themselves felt, the territorially dominant farming sector had to be eliminated. Once that impediment had been removed, Brooklyn would, as Abraham Abraham of Abraham and Straus, told the New York State legislature on behalf of Brooklyn's mercantile sector, offer a consolidated Greater New York "a city naturally endowed, and not exceeded by any other in the land, with a boundless territory for a large population, washed by the waves of the ocean and its numerous bays thus insuring healthfulness and salubrious air."[29]

The seeming inexorability of the suburbanization of Kings County was rooted in Manhattan's constricted geography: "The city was like a growing potato enclosed in a narrow tube. It wanted to expand in all directions, but the only line of growth was northward."[30] Brooklyn's advantage was twofold: not only could its residents reach Manhattan's business district more quickly than could Manhattanites north of 59th Street or Central Park, but it was also favored by an "enormous and inexplicable difference in the market values of real estate." Whereas

> [i]ndependent homes on Manhattan Island are already beyond the reach of any but the wealthy, . . . land is . . . so much cheaper . . . in Brooklyn, that a residence property can be purchased outright in Brooklyn, for what would pay only two years' rent of it in many parts of New York. . . . Upon this important fact is the prospect for a new era of prosperity for Brooklyn founded. . . . To the individual . . . it means, first, a home with all the advantages of residence in New York at from a tenth to a fifth of the original cost, and, second, a vastly larger annual increase in the value of his property and, consequently, a larger income upon his investment. . . . Brooklyn borders are wide enough for four times as many people as she now contains. . . . These are facts upon which the home-seeker and investor may depend.[31]

In spite of their unceasing promotion of the unique residential opportunities that Kings County's formerly rural sections offered, "New York's real estate developers were unable to take a clear position on consolidation" with Brooklyn. The authoritative *Record Estate Record and Builders' Guide* was ambivalent. On the one hand, it advocated development of the northern part of the existing New York City rather than "extending ourselves promiscuously over all the adjacent territory . . . of not very easily assimilated material." Although the magazine was willing to "regard Brooklyn as a possible rival in the not distant future, provided always that its clapboard domiciles do not get burned to the ground some day," a Greater New York "means the promotion of the interests of Kings county . . . [m]erely that we may surpass Paris in population and keep ahead of Chicago." This resistance was based in part on the argument that since Brooklyn taxes were much heavier on a higher valuation of property, taxes for New Yorkers would inevitably have to be raised. On the other hand, the *Record* simultaneously perceived an identity of interest rooted in the fact that Wall Street real estate ultimately benefited from the growth of the periphery, and opined that equalization of taxes would "naturally" come about. The press generally supported railway construction in Kings County, which "should soon be filled with fine houses," while "the adjacent territory in Queens county will increase in value so rapidly that the men who own property there will be made rich in a few years."[32]

Although the advent of large-scale speculators and developers by the late

1880s meant that suburbanization no longer proceeded haphazardly, individual real-estate firms' profit considerations did not amount to planning. The *Brooklyn Daily Eagle* limned the new state of affairs in 1893:

> The days of unmethodical suburban settlement have passed. Outlying villages and towns which derive their sustenance and owe their existence to the enterprise and needs of greater communities are no longer suffered to grow to maturity in whatever manner chance or caprice suggest. Where the prospective suburbanite once bought his building site from a farmer who half reluctantly parted with a portion of his ancestral acres, and gave for the purchaser's money no other equivalent than a piece of ground of questionable value, there can be purchased to-day property . . . supplied with all the modern conveniences calculated to enhance its value in the future. The wealth of a number of millionaires is attributable to judicious operations in suburban realty, and to the enterprise of such men is due the existence of the several beautiful villages just beyond the confines of Brooklyn.[33]

Exactly how these enterprising men implemented their precept that outlying villages, which have "never, except in name, risen above the dignity and measurement of a farming community," could not be suffered to grow to maturity unless subordinated to the urban property interests' conception of the proper function of farmland, will be explored by reference to Flatbush and Bensonhurst in New Utrecht.[34]

FLATBUSH BOUGHT AND SOLD

Meeting an old resident of Flatbush — a Mr. Fitzpatrick — he inquired if it was true that we had purchased the Cortelyou farm. I told him it was.

"Well, thin," said he, "yez'll niver sell thot farm in all yer loife."

I inquired on what grounds he based his prediction. Fitzpatrick's reasons were quite terrifying:

"Why, there's more schnakes on the Cortelyou farm than was iver druv out of Oireland by Saint Pathrick. Oi've seen mosquitoes so t'ick in Flatbush thot when yez opened yer mouth you'd almost shpit mosquitoes, and Oi'll warrant ye thot there's more schnakes in the Cortelyou woods than that there's mosquitoes in Flatbush."

— Henry A. Meyer, *Looking Through Life's Window*, 1930

Just as Kings County farmers were achieving their historic peak output at the time of the Tenth Census in 1880, Gertrude Lefferts Vanderbilt, the

56-year-old daughter of Senator John Lefferts, sister of the like-named pre-eminent political-economic manager of modernizing Flatbush, and widow of Judge John Vanderbilt, was writing her reminiscences about Flatbush with unmistakable nostalgia for a rural way of life doomed to extinction:

> The southern borders of Flatbush bound the towns on which the ocean waves measure the rise and fall of the tides; toward the north lies the ridge of hills that long kept back the ebb and flow of the tide of human life in the adjoining city. In past years Flatbush slept as quietly between the two as if the waves of the one could no more reach it than could the waves of the other. But the separating hills have been leveled, and the village has been awakened by the noise of approaching voices. The tide of increasing population within the city boundary has risen higher and higher, and has swept hitherward in larger and ever-increasing circles. The first ripple of this rising tide has touched our borders, and before long the sudden rush of some great wave will sweep away every trace of village life.[35]

Fifteen years earlier Lefferts Vanderbilt had already glimpsed the alien incursions when she was compelled to warn her even wealthier neighbor Elizabeth Ludlow that vagrants had been setting fires in the fields, necessitating a neighborhood watch association.[36] That the rural Dutch-American idyll was on the verge of collapse as modern transportation brought urbanity ever closer was underscored by an 1874 report in the *New York Times*, which paid scant attention to the rural Kings County towns:

> For some weeks past a large number of Brooklyn roughs have been in the habit of going to Flatbush every Sunday, and gathering . . . ostensibly to play ball and other games. Many complaints have been made of them by the residents to the Police. They are said to be a regular band of marauders, who have made themselves a terror to the citizens by entering saloons, and private dwellings even and demanding food, and liquor, which they took by force when refused. Yesterday Superintendent Folk sent a detachment of thirty policemen . . . to Flatbush with orders to arrest all whom he might find acting in a disorderly manner. They arrived at Flatbush about 2 P.M., and surrounded the gang, and succeeded in arresting forty of them, who were brought to Brooklyn and locked up.[37]

Nor were such incursions peculiar to Flatbush. A few months later 15 "roughs" from Brooklyn and New York who had been annoying people in the vicinity of the estate of William Langley, one of New Utrecht's richest merchant princes, were arrested, while the neighboring residence of the family of the deceased farmer-lawyer, Daniel Roberts, was burglarized. Ninth-generation Dutch farmers might well have asked themselves what overarching cultural virtues they continued to enjoy in raising cabbages in a backwater vulnerable to depredations by aliens. After all, just three weeks after this marauding, the state legislature prohibited the killing of robins, brown thrashers, or starlings during nine months of the year — three years after it had enacted a five-year ban on deer hunting in Kings County. Such pessimism must have been powerfully reinforced by yet another sign of urban propinquity: petty thieves had become so bold during harvest time that farmers had to put watchmen in the fields. Nostalgia was an understandable mode of relating to the past among these "direct descendants of the first settlers," who, into the 1890s, made it a part of "the delightful social life in the old Dutch town" to "get together and talk about the Indians which their ancestors killed."[38]

Yet as late as the 1880s "many large tracts of purely agricultural land and even much wild wood land" still covered central Kings County. In 1884, the *New York Daily Tribune* published a travelogue of Flatbush touting it as "the only pleasant suburb of New-York or Brooklyn" that the author, a new resident, had ever found. Unlike the others, it was not filled with rubbish-strewn vacant lots and pigpens and cow stables that "are rank and smell to heaven and . . . the abomination of desolation."[39] An even more "quaint and ancient" picture emerged from a piece on New York's suburbs in *Lippincott's Magazine* the same year:

> [Y]ou have only to drive half a mile away on either side [of Flatbush Avenue] to forget that you are in a world where horse-cars exist. There are long and leafy lanes which look very much as they must have looked when British riflemen marched through them a hundred and eight years ago this August, past farm houses which even then were old, and of which many are still standing. . . .
>
> It seems strange that these relics of colonial times should be lying in the path of yearly-broadening Brooklyn. . . . It all comes of the Batavian inertia. The houses are still inhabited by the descendants of their builders, who follow as nearly as practicable the ancient ways.[40]

Flatbush's antediluvian character was symbolized by the fact that as late as 1889, its main thoroughfare, Flatbush Avenue, was in the "unique position" of not belonging to the town, but being owned by the Flatbush Plank Road Company, which, under the presidency of John Lefferts had long paid good dividends and "exacts toll from all vehicles which pass over it." Lefferts was, by the 1880s, the premier modernizer of Flatbush, but his long-term and short-term material interests were apparently in conflict in connection with the town's efforts to abolish the toll. (In 1878 the company had objected to routing a steam railroad along Flatbush Avenue because steam engines might drive away wagons and thus reduce the company's revenues.) When the company's original 30-year legal existence was about to come to an end in 1883, it reorganized and extended its duration by another 30 years. By this point, Lefferts, who at the time of the original incorporation had been the company's largest shareholder with one-sixth of its shares, had secured almost a majority (44 percent) of them. When the committee established by a town meeting in 1883 to examine the issue of the toll gate requested that the shareholders, acting "for the best interests of the town," present the road to the town "for nothing or for a moderate figure," Lefferts, while demurring that he and the other directors lacked authority to act on behalf of the shareholders, was merely willing to state his belief that the road "could be bought at a fair valuation." In the event, it took six years and authorization by the state legislature for the town to spend up to $10,000 to purchase the road.[41]

It was precisely these remnants of the Dutch agricultural past that prompted modernizers to insist that Flatbush's "streets must be opened and large tracts of farm land yielded up to the demand for suburban homes." Once real estate had been mobilized, the *Rural Gazette* argued in 1883, "there can be no doubt of our population and wealth quadrupling in the next five years" if only rapid transit were introduced.[42]

One of the most trenchant contemporary analyses of deagriculturalization was offered by a local historian and longtime resident of Flatbush, Daniel Tredwell, who had been chief clerk of the Supreme Court of Kings County from 1850 to 1895. In a 1914 address to the Kings County Historical Society, the 88-year-old Tredwell provided an account that referred back to events that had taken place when he moved to Flatbush 35 years earlier. The choice of years is fortunate, since Tredwell's reference year, 1879, coincides with the year for which the 1880 Census of Agriculture collected harvest data.[43] About the time of his arrival,

> Flatbush farming lands were becoming no longer remunerative as such — land had become too valuable for truck farming and was now classified real estate. The owners, successors of the Dutch pioneers, were just preparing to close out the period of farming which had been suc-

cessful as a money making industry beyond all precedents in this country and convert their acres into building lots. Simultaneously with this determination all the farms in the town were on the market for sale and the issue was no longer cabbages and potatoes, but real estate and lots for construction purposes. Speculators jumped at the opportunity. . . .

The original farmers of Flatbush had large productive farms with all modern appliances through which they had attained to wealth — but the earliest method of farming was primitive and crude and followed in general that of the fatherland. But when we came to Flatbush no farmers in the country were better equipped than they for obtaining the best results in their line of agriculture. . . . John Lefferts, our nearest neighbor, raised on his farm that year 11,000 bushels of potatoes which he sold to relieve the famishing population of Manhattan at $2.50 per barrell. On that potato patch of Mr. Lefferts' now stands [sic] 320 dwellings and apartment houses with a population probably of 2,000 to whom the entertaining grocers of Flatbush are retailing potatoes at $2.50 a peck — a masterly adaptation of constructive larceny.[44]

Tredwell's account supports the argument that market gardening in Kings County was the most advanced and profitable of its kind in the United States, and that the Dutch farmers, who amassed "a greater average amount of wealth . . . than any other class in the county," dismantled their productive apparatuses not because property taxes exceeded the financial capacities of their farms, but because suburbanization promised even greater profits. This view accords with an anonymous manuscript from 1920, which emphasized the tenacity of the Dutch farmers' attachment to their land: "They had many opportunities to sell at tempting prices, but it was not until after the annexation of Flatbush to Brooklyn in 1894, that they gave a willing ear to such offers, and then only because they realized that the rural character of the town was gone forever."[45]

According to Charles Andrew Ditmas, the 22-year-old scion of one of the most illustrious Dutch families, it was the "historic sale" of the Martense homestead on February 20, 1889, that marked "the beginning of that great real estate movement." Nostalgically noting in 1909 that "the last semblance of farm life is being removed from this rural section," young Ditmas saw Greenwood Cemetery as "a reminder of the time when all this land was open country and when this farm included a part of the cemetery." The turning point took place in the early 1890s.[46]

Henry Adolph Meyer, one of the developers chiefly responsible for the

FIGURE 23. *Henry A. Meyer. From* Flatbush of To-day: The Realm of Light and Air *98*.

conversion of Flatbush farms into residential real estate, had been the un-successful Republican candidate for mayor of Brooklyn in 1891, later unsuc-cessfully sought to develop Jamaica Bay, and, as a Democrat, was Deputy Dock Commissioner of New York City from 1918 to 1934. Born in 1860, Meyer, after attending a German Lutheran theological seminary in Indiana, returned to Brooklyn to join his father's retail grocery business. By 1886,

Meyer, who was already in the grocery business for himself, became president of the Retail Merchants' Association. "In business he amassed considerable money, and has it invested largely in city property." His business acumen was informed by his belief that the "crowded conditions of the cities makes [sic] it almost compulsory for the masses to seek the suburbs as a solution of the problem as to the betterment of their surroundings and conditions."[47]

Meyer devoted a privately published turn-of-the-century memoir, which he incorporated almost intact as a chapter ("A Farm Today — A City Tomorrow") of his 1930 autobiography, to his role in transforming Flatbush. This memoir is useful because Meyer specified the per acre prices that he and his enterprise, Germania Real Estate Company, which he, Henry Dreyer, John F. Dreyer, and A. W. Schmidt incorporated in May 1892, paid for various farms. For example, the Vanderveer farm of 65 acres — "It seemed as if nature had intended the property as a place for homes, for it was as level as a floor" — was originally offered to Meyer at $2,200 per acre in 1892; smaller segments were offered at $3,250 (and eight months later at $4,500) and $1,500 per acre. Germania paid 40 percent down for this first purchase of 43 acres at $1,500 per acre in 1892, arranging a 5 percent mortgage for the balance.[48] In spite of nature's favor, however, Meyer's partners were apprehensive lest the proximity of a cemetery and of the Kings County hospital and asylums undermine the salability of the lots. Nor did all members of the community appreciate the drive to mobilize farmland for the real-estate market. Meyer himself described his reception

> at the hands of the old settlers of Flatbush in the Fall of 1892. We were looked upon as intruders and trespassers. They were of the opinion we had come to Flatbush to make a sort of goat-town of our Vanderveer Park property. Some members of the Vanderveer family were openly scored by their neighbors for committing such an unpardonable sin as to sell us a part of their farm.[49]

Because Flatbush in 1892 was still dotted with "spreading farms" and numerous salt and fresh water ponds, the "Flatbush people, both in the village and among the rich landowners, had a prejudice against the real estate men. But Meyer and his associates kept on."[50]

In 1893, Germania bought another 182 acres for $388,000 ($2,132 per acre); Meyer bought another, six-acre, Vanderveer farm, including "its immense barns and outbuildings," for $8,300 per acre, a price that according to Meyer "did much toward establishing a basis for values in the future."

That year, when "there was much talk of annexing Flatbush to Brooklyn" and rumors circulated of the opening of a new avenue, Meyer and his associates, realizing "what a vast benefit this meant to Flatbush, . . . took immediate steps" to buy the Cortelyou farm. Meyer viewed this transaction as "another vivid illustration of the very little confidence placed by the old citizens of Flatbush in the future of their town" — in spite of the fact that John A. Lott's son, John Z. Lott, a leading political-economic architect of a suburbanized Flatbush and "one of the most prominent lawyers of Flatbush," who prepared the contract, told Meyer that "he never expected to see the Cortelyou farm sold for the next fifty years." But the 1893 Flatbush assessment roll crossed out the holdings of the Cortelyou family, replacing them with an entry signaling Germania's ownership of 71.212 acres valued at $63,700 and taxed $1,406.45 — almost twice the amounts stated in 1892. This new assessed value of $659 per acre, in turn, was about half of the $1,250 Germania paid. Another important signpost on the way from agriculture to suburbia was the petition, written on March 20, 1893, to the Flatbush Town Board from Meyer on behalf of Germania requesting gas lighting on Avenue C between Rogers and Albany Avenues.[51]

The deed to one 15-acre section of the Vanderveer farm included one tantalizing provision: it was subject to a year's lease. Meyer offered the farmer using the land $1,500 for his unexpired term (of ten months), but when the farmer demanded twice as much, Germania decided to take its chances on selling the land subject to the lease. This failed negotiation suggests that the tenant farmer expected to earn at least $3,000 for the year. In April 1893, Germania bought a 17-acre farm for $2,750 per acre. That real-estate prices were rapidly rising in Flatbush was signaled by the fact that Hans Von Westering, who was farming this land at the time, assured Meyer that the previous year the farm could have been bought for $900 per acre. Soon, the Flatbush assessment rolls were filled with page after page of lots owned by Germania.[52]

In 1893, Germania also bought land in Flatlands for $2,500 per acre from Abrahams, McNulty, Dunne, and Taylor, who in turn had bought it from the original owners (the Lott estate) nine months earlier at $1,500 per acre with $20,000 down and a mortgage for the balance, enabling them to realize $74,000 on a nine-month investment of $20,000. In December 1894 and June 1895, Germania bought the Van Brunt–Ditmas farm and part of the Antonides farm, a total of 47 acres — "without exception . . . the most fertile farming land in the entire town of Flatlands" — at about $2,850 per acre. In 1896, Germania bought another 122 acres including a 30-acre farm (the

Percy Pyne tract) for $3,600 per acre. The same year, Meyer and associates made their largest single acquisition, the 92-acre farms of Elias and J. P. Hubbard, at $2,500 per acre, "a very high price at the time." This farm, owned by the Hubbard family since 1652, was the best part of the 1,000-acre Flower syndicate, which "collapsed in 1896 on account of its immensity." In 1897, Germania bought the 36-acre Wyckoff and Voorhees farm mapped into 633 lots. The next year Meyer and his partners bought the 51.5-acre Timothy I. Hubbard farm, the 59.5-acre Kouwenhoven farm, and the 100-acre Lott farm in South Midwood, "the largest in area and financial consideration ever consummated in Kings County." In order to focus on its development, Germania sold at auction 826 lots from 56.5 acres of two farms, all of which were disposed of in five hours on May 30, 1899.[53] In evaluating the role played by Meyer and Germania in the 1890s in transforming Flatbush from a community of vegetable farms into a fashionable residential suburb, it is crucial to remember not only that Flatbush had, on a limited scale, been a suburb for wealthy merchants for decades, but that subdivision into lots had also been going for years. By facilitating the dissolution of several large prominent farms, such as those owned by the Vanderveer, Cortelyou, Ditmas, and Lott families, Meyer accelerated the demise of farming in Flatbush in the sense that the abandonment of agriculture by these elite families was the clearest signal that 250 years of Dutch farming had come to an end before the twentieth century opened. Nevertheless, scrutiny of the Flatbush assessment rolls makes it plain that, since at least the late 1860s, lots, not farms, were Flatbush's future. Such insight is not merely hindsight: both residents and town and county tax and government officials were well aware of the proliferation of lots.

The 1867 assessment roll illustrates the state of encroachment by subdivisions. After recording the large and highly assessed farms owned by the Bergen, Cortelyou, Lefferts, Lott, Martense, and Vanderveer families, the roll listed numerous "maps" of land filling page after page with sections and lots assessed at as little as $50. For example, on land formerly belonging to Henry V. Vanderveer, the map of which had been filed in the county register's office in 1864, 13 owners were recorded as owning 18 sections valued at $50 to $400. In 1867, Tunis J. Bergen filed a map listing numerous sections with similar assessed values; 104 lots were listed on what had been the Clarkson farm before the map was filed in 1853; the Crooke farm's subdivision into lots was filed in 1855. In addition, the map of Greenfield, the development of the United Freeman's Land Association, was filed in 1852, while Pleasant Cottage Sites belonging to Windsor Terrace Land Association was subdivided in 1860. Eighteen sixty-seven also marked the year in which the heirs of Isaac Cortelyou filed a map of what until then had been the family's 81-acre farm in order to effect a division of the estate. By 1870, the Flatbush assessment roll listed no fewer than 23 such maps, including land that had once formed the farms of the Martense and Bergen families.[54]

Like other owners of extensive properties in Flatbush, Meyer enthusiastically welcomed the town's annexation to Brooklyn: "Flatbush will now . . . wake up from its sleep of a hundred years and begin to be what it ought to be." As early as 1890, when Democratic politicians and officeholders from Flatbush appeared before the state legislature to oppose annexation: "The business interests appeared for the bill, led by the old families, the Lefferts, the Lotts and the Vanderbilts."[55]

John Lefferts, for example, was not only president of the Flatbush Water Works Company, treasurer of the Flatbush Gas Company, director of the Brooklyn Bank, trustee of the Long Island Loan and Trust Company, and president of the Long Island Safe Deposit Company, but also "a warm advocate of the project of annexing Flatbush to Brooklyn." His personal financial interest was manifest: "He owns a large tract of land in Flatbush, and is doing much to add to the attractiveness of that suburb by building a number of handsome cottages on Lincoln road and other streets, a number of which he has opened, and also he has abetted the introduction of water and gas. The nearness of Mr. Lefferts' land to the city renders his cottages among the most desirable in the town of Flatbush." In the year of his death, 1893, Lefferts was listed in the Flatbush assessments rolls as owning only 47.75 acres of land with nine houses valued at $178,800. At that time, James Lefferts was still managing his father's farmlands, portions of which John Lefferts had advertised for use by market gardeners. Eighteen ninety-three also marked the beginning of the subdivision of his land for building hundreds of row houses in Lefferts Manor, although as early as 1887 the assessment roll reveals that Lefferts had begun dividing his onetime farmland into lots, reducing his 86-acre property to 55 acres. In the assessments for 1880, which was also a census year, Lefferts had been taxed on about 90 acres of land including four houses and greenhouses, valued at $135,975.[56]

In the run-up to and after the legislature's vote on annexation on April 25, 1894, Meyer's Germania Real Estate Company published escalatingly exuberant advertisements for building lots ("$200 and up, $5 and $10 monthly") in its Vanderveer Park subdivision in Flatbush in the Brooklyn Daily Eagle. On February 21, 1894, it stated that the trolley fare to the bridge and ferries was only 5 cents. By March 17, Germania announced: "Future 29th ward of

FIGURE 24. *Vanderveer Park. From Edmund Fisher,* Flatbush Past and Present *83.*

Brooklyn 'grand old Flatbush!' The ideal spot for homes or investment." By April 24, once the legislature had passed the Flatbush annexation bill, Germania proclaimed: "Finest residential or investment property ever offered." A few days later, Germania expostulated: "That this property is the most desirable in the ward has been demonstrated in the sale of 3,000 lots, at a time when other properties have been idle. Success of the past and present a guarantee for the future." [57]

Underlying this promotional hyperbole was a real point: speculators and residents achieved significant savings by building on farmland that was ready for construction rather than on hilly or rocky soil, which would have required considerable preparatory work. Two years later, Germania was still offering lots in Vanderveer Park, starting at $275 on $5 and $10 monthly installments. Meyer now also advertised "fine detached houses, with $500 first payment, balance same as rent you are now paying." These prices suggest that unlike financially exclusionary projects (such as Bensonhurst in New Utrecht), Vanderveer Park was designed for those with incomes superior to those typical of the working class who, however, could not afford lavish houses. [58]

Germania was not the only firm selling lots in Flatbush at the time of annexation. One competitor was Jere Johnson Jr. Born in 1827 into an old-line Dutch family, Johnson was the grandson of one of Brooklyn's elite — "the very rich" large farmer and mayor, General Jeremiah Johnson. On becoming a real-estate broker and auctioneer in 1866, Johnson "at once saw what great possibilities there were in suburban property, owing to the phenomenal growth of New York and Brooklyn." During the next quarter-century, through private sales and auctions, he disposed of at least 200,000 suburban lots, more than 20,000 of them on the monthly installment plan between 1886 and 1891. If in 1866 Johnson "saw at once that a fortune could be made in the selling of suburban property," by the early 1890s he had in fact "acquired a fortune," conducting "one of the most comprehensive real estate businesses in the state." The scope of his operations can be gauged by the fact that on newspaper advertising alone he spent $75,000 annually.[59]

In February 1894, Johnson advertised lots supplied with water mains and stone sidewalks starting at $250 and only 25 minutes from the Brooklyn Bridge. In March, Johnson, president of the Brooklyn Real Estate Exchange and a strong advocate of consolidation of Brooklyn and New York, touted his Kensington-in-Flatbush "suburban property" as "perfectly level and yet by far the highest and most healthful in the neighborhood" and "surrounded by beautiful houses, costing from $6,000 to $15,000, and in close to splendid churches, stores and schools." Immediately after annexation, Johnson advertised that "prices not yet raised . . . will soon double in value." Proving that Irishmen could profit from the demise of Dutch farming, James McGowan and Peter McNulty (of Wechsler & McNulty, Dry Goods) announced that by "this single stroke of annexation the lucky purchasers here in Kensington (by our advice) of some 2,400 superb dwelling plots during the past 18 months have doubled their money!"[60]

Some old-line propertied families did not sell off their land through speculators and developers, but sold their land as lots and plots themselves. Meyer seemed less than pleased that the Vanderveer family, for example, held back part of their farmland and sold it directly in 1897. As early as 1891, the Zabriskie homestead, an old farm that had been in the family's possession for more than two centuries, was auctioned off in lots. The advertisement in the Real Estate Record announced that the location, "the most desirable in Flatbush," was "surrounded by desirable modern-built dwellings, villas and Queen Anne cottages." It was "easy of access" because the Flatbush Avenue horsecars ran within one block and three electric cars passed the property.[61]

By the 1890s Flatbush had become "one of the most aristocratic suburbs of the city. Since the annexation many old-time Brooklynites have moved within its borders and land values have enormously increased." Flatbush had "shown the most remarkable development. . . . The property . . . has grown past the purely speculative stage and values are firm and steady." Within five years, Vanderveer Park became one of "the greatest real estate developments in Brooklyn," in which 10,000 lots were sold and 500 houses built. Even Meyer purported to have "adopted an iron-clad rule never to sell to one who seemed to us to be an objectionable person." In the long run, the deal that Meyer struck with the Brooklyn Heights Railroad to extend its Nostrand Avenue trolley line to Vanderveer Park in 1895 must have worked against socioeconomic exclusiveness. Such "restricted" Flatbush districts as Ditmas Park (which had been part of the farm of John and Henry S. Ditmas) and Midwood (created from John A. Lott's farm) retained this affluent character into the twentieth century as "substantial citizens" bought new houses there: "Flatbush is a city of homes, and its business is one that begins and ends with ministering to these. The land, fortunately, has been too high for factory sites." In 1900, Holmes V. B. Ditmas, architect and builder, advertised the "Famous Flatbush Water" and his houses and lots as "country homes for city people."[62]

Whether "the biggest gainers" from the conversion process were the farmers themselves or "real estate speculators and lawyers who had advanced information about street openings [and] bought such property at bargain prices" is unclear. The financial webs that made development possible are unexplored, but it is clear that both sellers and buyers realized sizable gains. One possible resolution of this issue was offered by Tredwell, who, looking back at his life among the Dutch farmers in Flatbush in the 1880s, asserted that in the wake of a "crisis" among real-estate operators — lot prices rose 400 percent and were "sold on all kinds of wild cat terms" such as $10 down and $5 per month — the Dutch farmers "entrenched themselves behind bonds and mortgages and became capitalists, bided their time and much of their land came back to them."[63]

This account is corroborated by the anonymous author of "Old Flatbush," who from the vantage point of 1920 noted:

Direct descendants of the early settlers are living in Flatbush today and they make false the theory that "from shirt sleeves to shirt sleeves is a matter of not more than three generations." The lineal heirs of the Dutch pioneers held on to the land acquired by their forefathers which in each succeeding generation became more valuable, until it became entirely too valuable for agricultural purposes. Then they cut it up or sold it to syndicates. The land was a gold mine. . . . Even now, though not a few of them are very wealthy, their style of living remains simple. Until a dozen years ago there were some who still occupied the old homesteads.[64]

BENSONHURST IS BORN

Why do not some of our large capitalists form land improvement societies, with a view to buying up whole streets and sections of the city, so as to improve them properly? It would pay enormously. We have no Emperor here to will the rebuilding of the metropolis. . . . What say our capitalists?
—*Real Estate Record and Builders' Guide*, September 25, 1869[65]

Deagriculturalization of New Utrecht differed from that in Flatbush. Even neighboring areas within New Utrecht developed in different ways. Like Flatbush, some parts of the town, such as Bay Ridge, whose high ground fronting on New York Bay made it "one of the pleasantest [localities] that can be found in the vicinity of New York as a place of residence during the summer and fall months," had long been colonized by "many of the professional men and merchants of New York and Brooklyn" whose great wealth enabled them to buy large acreages for estates.[66] By the same token, in the 1880s, according to Hazelton, the county's historian: "No country town could boast a more picturesque or inspiring site" than Bath Beach, "throned upon a grassy plateau backed by woodlands, twenty feet higher than the surrounding country" and overlooking the Atlantic Ocean and the Narrows:

> The plain on which Bath Beach was built, so high, so breezy, so level and so easy to drain, appeared to be set apart by Nature for the populous suburb of a great city. . . .
>
> Old Robert Benson stood on his farm east of the village and swore: "Bath Beach shall come so far and no farther!" He held to his word and the growth of Bath Beach was stunted for years, kept in farms and potato patches while the surrounding country grew. At length taxes mounted to a point where farming did not pay and the situation took another aspect. When the land was sold there was a wild scramble to possess it.
>
> James D. Lynch . . . flung himself into the struggle, a bright, stirring, energetic real estate dealer in New York. With millions behind him he could buy right and left. . . . He bought the hog wallows and . . . the sunken lots that stretched between Fourth and Fifth Avenues. He levelled the land and sold it, and improved his fortune.

When he entered the Bath Beach field, nothing less than a square mile would suit him, and he obtained what he wanted, after a struggle. In three years ending with the summer of 1889, Lynch owned the farms of Robert Benson, Egbert Benson, Margaret Benson, Richard V. Benson, Samuel Smith, an ex-mayor, Erhardt Schmidt, Ella Wyckoff, Robert McGaw, and Rebecca Van Sicklen. Robert Benson's farm was held out to the last.[67]

That some Dutch families had owned their farmland for more than two centuries did nothing to mitigate Hazelton's perception that clinging to land in the face of offers to buy it for sums far in excess of the monetary income that farming on it could generate was irrational. To be sure, Hazelton's account is marred by the fact that neither the 1870 nor 1880 population census for Kings County returned any farmer or retired farmer named Benson; nor was any farmer by that name listed in the 1870 or 1880 agricultural census. The last Benson to farm in New Utrecht was 33-year-old George Benson, whose 85-acre farm was recorded at the 1860 census. Indeed, other than Harmon Benson and his family in 1810, and Egbert Benson and his family in 1830, no Benson was even returned by any federal census as living in New Utrecht before 1860.[68]

The Bensons, who traced their lineage to one of the first Dutch settlers of New Amsterdam, did not even acquire their large farm before the nineteenth century, let alone farm it continuously. The turning point in the family's landed fortunes was 1820, when Egbert Benson (1789–1866) married Maria Cowenhoven (1803–1867), whose grandfather Judge Nicholas Cowenhoven (d. 1793) in the 1780s had bought more than 200 acres in New Utrecht (and Gravesend) from the Van Brunt, Wyckoff, Voorhees, and Gifford families. Egbert Benson acquired this land through a partitioning in 1826 at the request of Maria and her sister Jane, who received a separate 157 acres of land. Egbert Benson, whose heirs were recorded as the owners beginning in 1866, was listed as early as 1830 as owning a 207-acre farm, the town's largest holding. Yet by the 1840s, he appears to have sold off most of the farm. In 1842, Jacobus Voorhees owned 194 acres of it; in 1849, Voorhees was replaced by Jacobus Van Siclen, who owned 100 acres, while Egbert Benson was listed as owning 63 acres. By the latter part of the 1850s, however, Benson's holdings rose again toward 200 acres, but for several of these years he was listed as a nonresident of New Utrecht.[69]

Rather than farming themselves, the Bensons rented their farmland to some of the many tenant farmers in New Utrecht. In 1875, for example, Mrs. Margaret Benson advertised "farm to let" in the *Rural Gazette*. Surviv-

ing leases in the Benson family papers document some of these tenant relationships. In 1864, for example, Egbert Benson, who lived in New York City,
leased 18 acres, straddling New Utrecht and Gravesend — which at the time
was occupied by another tenant, W. Verity — to Garret Wyckoff of Gravesend, from March 1, 1865, to March 1, 1868, for $15 per acre per year. Inter-
estingly, the tenant was also liable for any school taxes and road assessments. Similar concurrent and overlapping leases demonstrate that the
Bensons rented out their extensive farmland to several tenants.[70]

Moreover, whatever antimarket oaths "old" Robert Benson (Egbert's
brother) may have sworn must have last occurred many years before Lynch
conceived Bensonhurst, since he was already 86 years old at the 1870 census,
and died two years later. At the time, he was living with his nephew Robert,
who at 48 already designated himself "retired," and his niece Susan together
with two domestic servants and a gardener. By 1880, the brother (who in the
meantime had become a director of the Brooklyn, Bath, and Coney Island
Railroad) and sister continued to live without occupations but with servants. In 1870, the heirs of Egbert Benson owned 190 acres of farm and
meadow land; by 1880, Susan, Margaret, Egbert, George, Richard, and Robert Benson had increased their holdings to a total of 234 acres. By the time of
the New Utrecht land boom in 1887, Susan Benson sold Lynch 36.85 acres of
a farm at the corner of Cropsey Avenue and 21st Avenue assessed at $16,585;
the next year Richard H. Benson sold Lynch 13 acres of a 48.5-acre farm (valued at $350/acre), leaving Benson with 35.5 acres (valued at $397/acre) in addition to 26.7 acres of meadowland (valued at $100/acre), while Egbert Ben-
son sold Lynch 14.7 of 15.7 acres he owned. All of these tracts were taxed at
the uniform rate of 1.56 percent in 1887 and 2.02 percent in 1888.[71]

Thus in 1887 Lynch succeeded in buying "nearly a square mile of ground
from those whom it was more difficult to buy than from any other class of
men around New York City — the historic Long Island families."[72]

> As soon as he owned a tract large enough for his purposes, Lynch began
> to develop the land. . . . [H]e set two hundred men with ninety wagons
> and carts at work to perform a task which looked interminable. This
> force "skinned" the land and levelled it off like a lawn. . . . The name of
> Bensonhurst was given to the territory in 1887, and it began to grow like
> a fairyland.[73]

Despite a setback in 1891, when "bear talk about Bensonhurst values and
prospects" caused many properties to be withdrawn from sale, the *Eagle*
praised Lynch's entrepreneurial prescience in 1893: "The modern idea of

mapping out an entire residential locality, arranging for streets, walks, houses, sewers, gas, etc., all before the first shovelful of earth is turned has inaugurated a new tendency, which promises some Utopian results in the future. . . . Bensonhurst-by-the-Sea . . . stands as a model for future creators of suburban settlements." [74]

Bensonhurst was heavily promoted. A month after the *Real Estate Record* had printed an advertisement (barely distinguishable from an article) calling it "the most perfectly developed suburb ever laid out around New York" and touting it to "the better half of the world" as filled with properties that "can at any time be sold at a profit," the magazine published an even more fulsome advertorial. It proceeded from the proposition that within a decade or two residential areas would have to be found for the surplus population unable to find housing south of 125th Street in Manhattan. Long Island had already attracted many who worked in New York City who could not afford to pay the annual rentals in excess of $500 that were common there. Because land could be bought "for almost a bagatelle" in the suburbs, where "frame cottages which cannot be built within the fire limits of New York, can . . . be erected, and homes consequently built, for a few thousands of dollars, rents being proportionately low," the population of the suburbs would increase. The *Record* therefore advised investors to think about the "immense wealth" and "fortunes" that had been made in places such as Bath Beach. [75]

Having praised Bensonhurst as part of this "immense stretch of territory which is geographically situated so close to the very heart and the business centre of New York" available for those unable to pay Manhattan-level rents, the *Record* then about-faced and described the development as a "model settlement, where some of the most refined, intelligent and cultured of New York and Brooklyn's citizens have built their homes." Rather than catering to the masses, Bensonhurst was suitable for financial and social elites such as a brother of Mrs. Vanderbilt, an architect, a physician, an assemblyman, and Samuel McElroy, who had supervised the portentous survey of Kings County two decades earlier. That the "evidently well-to-do people" figured so prominently was no coincidence since Lynch's "idea is to eventually settle the place with a thousand such families, cultivated and well-to-do, without displaying wealth or extravagance. . . . The secret of the rapid success of Bensonhurst is . . . found . . . in the restrictions which have been placed on the property. On the greater part no house must stand on less than three lots, and in some place five lots, while in several cases an entire block is occupied by a single residence. . . . The owner of Bensonhurst has wisely laid out . . . a plan to keep each class of property in its own neighborhood, so that any purchaser who builds on a plot might not fear that his neighbor would build an inferior home." Despite this elite orientation, the *Record* concluded by returning to its other theme — that New Utrecht was an investor's paradise: "When it is considered that the price of lots in New York City, within forty-five minutes' journey from Wall street, varies from about $3,500 to $40,000, and that at Bensonhurst, which takes only about the same time in reaching, lots can be bought for a few hundreds of dollars," real-estate operators were well advised "to look outside of New York City for their fortune." [76]

The *Eagle* contributed its share to the promotion in language appropriate to the stilted aristocratism that Lynch seemed to prefer for his development. The paper noted that for the 40-minute trip from the Brooklyn, Bath, and West End Railroad station in Bensonhurst to the southern tip of Manhattan, "the distance intervening may be covered at a pecuniary expenditure of ten cents." For just a dime there was "no more attractive journey after a hard day's work than that which carries the wearied business man from the turmoil of New York and Brooklyn to the cool and quiet fields that overlook the waters of the lower bay." No wonder that such "ready access to metropolitan centres" had "greatly developed that tendency which [was] continually moving the more desirable portion of an urban population towards the freer and less confined surroundings of the suburbs." [77]

In 1890, the *Record* was again promoting Bensonhurst-by-the-Sea as part of a series on suburbs within twenty miles of downtown Manhattan: "The growth of this region on every count has been scarcely less wonderful than of the metropolis itself. Millions of capital have been invested in factories; indeed it would not be in the spirit of wild prophesy to say this district is destined to be the greatest manufacturing centre of the country; farm lands have passed into villages; villages into towns and well ordered cities, and vacant places possessing hitherto unappreciated . . . advantages of site or surroundings, as though Nature in her work had not been blind to the commercial side of things, have been seized upon by capitalists and 'developed' with quite modern rapidity." Stressing that "within a distance of seven miles from New York . . . a quantity of farm land was being cultivated, it may be said, until yesterday, by the Bensons," the *Record* observed that after Lynch had had 500 men "turning the farm lands into streets and avenues," 90 to 100 houses were built from 1888 to 1890, "in every case of an ornate character." Lots 20 by 100 feet, which cost from $200 to $750, were assessed at $50; the property tax rate was 1.3 percent, or 65 cents per lot annually; the houses themselves, which cost $3,000 to $10,000, were assessed at one-third to one-half of their actual value.[78]

The cunning of history ultimately intervened to divert Bensonhurst from its intended purpose as sanctuary for a suburban elite. Like other farming sections on the outskirts of this outer borough, it eventually served the more pressing task of providing shelter for the Jewish and Italian proletariat. So far had Bensonhurst strayed from its patrician origins that by 1952 it could plausibly serve as the home of such archplebeians as Ralph Kramden and Ed Norton.

12. CONCLUSION: IS URBAN AGRICULTURE OXYMORONIC?

> From the story of Bushwick every town on Long Island may draw a valuable lesson. . . . Nassau County is today as near a neighbor to New York City as Kings County was a century ago and who can tell how soon Suffolk County will be in precisely the same position? Distance is today not as great a factor, as it was a century ago and the Long Island farmers of our days are not quite as unwilling to have their farms converted into city lots as the Bushwick farmers of old were.
> — Eugene Armbruster, *Brooklyn's Eastern District*, 1928

This final chapter examines twentieth-century land-use patterns in New York City to evaluate the consequences of the loss of market gardening in southern Kings County as farmers were "gradually pushed farther and farther . . . eastward" and rural Kings County was made available to mass residential settlement. Questions as to the appropriate relationship between city and countryside have assumed renewed importance: as urban and regional planners, ecologists, and agricultural developers all over the world reevaluate urban sprawl and the need for greenbelts or urban-agricultural balance, the lost opportunities of the past loom larger.[1]

THE DEBATE BEGINS

> But for one displaced farmer there are going to be those thousands of happy families finding homes.
> — Jane Corby, "Impact Is Widespread When a Housing Project Rises," *Brooklyn Eagle*, December 4, 1949

The point of questioning the market-knows-best equation of the existing pattern of land use with rationality is not to lend credence to some Khmer Rouge–like challenge to the notion that it "would be a tragic waste to turn Times Square into a potato patch." Nor is the purpose to portray Henry Meyer and other Kings County developers and speculators as the functional equivalents of the executors of Stalinist dekulakization. Nevertheless, although these pioneers of suburbanization hardly expropriated a boer yeomanry, it is worth recalling the admonition that the *Real Estate Record and Builders' Guide* issued in 1869 concerning the socioeconomic impact of the laws of capital accumulation on agriculture, which resulted in "the large farmer . . . buying up all the small ones." If economic forces prompted the typical Kings County vegetable farmer to abandon production in the realization of his "hopes that the elevations of his farm may be taken for building sites," while he "in imagination marks out city lots all over his broad acres," his place was indeed eventually taken by more capital intensive large plantations in the South and West.[2]

The *Real Estate Record* had anticipated by a decade some of the deeply held populist complaints to which Henry George gave eloquent voice in the 1880s. These tendencies toward centralization of agricultural holdings meant "the extirpation of the typical American farmer," who was being replaced by "the capitalist farmer and the farm-laborer. The former does not work with his own hands, but with the hands of other men. . . . The latter is a proletarian, a nomad — part of the year a laborer and part of the year a tramp, migrating from farm to farm." But George did not formulate his views of farming in isolation from the larger problems of capitalist development. For George, the concentration of population in the cities was as harmful to farmers as to urban dwellers: the "unnatural life of the great cities means an equally unnatural life in the country." The impoverishment born of overcrowding was reflected in "the barrenness of the isolated farmer's life. . . . Consider, what is still worse, the monotonous existence to which his wife is condemned." Regardless of whether George's panacea — taxing away all land rent and eliminating all taxation except on land — would have brought about his proposed reconfiguration of town and country, he envisioned a dispersal of urban populations and a denser countryside giving both "breathing space and neighborhood. . . . Agriculture would cease to be destructive, and would become more intense, obtaining more from the soil and returning what it borrowed. Closer settlement would give rise to economies of all kinds."[3]

In his 1886 New York City mayoralty campaign, George returned to his proposal that "the masses now festering in the tenement-houses of our cities . . . should each family have its healthful home, set in its garden." Nominated by the labor and socialist movements, George focused on an issue that political-economic elites had also targeted — the overcrowding of the working masses in Manhattan. Despite "miles and miles and miles of land all around this nucleus," it was not available for housing "because it is held by dogs in the manger who will not use it themselves, nor allow anybody else to use it, unless they pay an enormous price for it." George called this fetter "a blackmail levied on the city's growth. Here is a man who buys from the heirs of some dead Dutchman . . . a piece of land . . . and says: '. . . nobody else shall use it until he pays me my price.' And he adds to that price as the city grows, and the demand for the land becomes greater and greater."[4]

But the movement toward denser Greater New York settlement was so relentless that by the beginning of the century proposals to relieve congestion by removing people from the more crowded parts of the city to smaller towns and farms were rejected as a "Utopian scheme . . . involv[ing] the artificial resistance of a strong, almost irresistible, economic movement of population towards New York City." As early as 1907, the Jamaica Bay Improvement Commission bemoaned that large parts of the Bronx, "by nature the most beautiful" of New York City's possessions, had been "turned into a congested apartment house district."[5]

Even as the deagriculturalization of the southern half of Kings County made overall urban decongestion possible, the inexorability of concentrated demographic growth was so self-explanatory that in 1914 a plan for Brooklyn commissioned by the Brooklyn Committee on City Plan, a private group of businessmen, blithely assumed that within forty to fifty years Brooklyn "would have to support a population of about 5,000,000 people" — three times its then population. This planned inevitability was all the more startling because the report acknowledged that Brooklyn already had by far the highest ratio of population to park acreage of all large cities in the United States. How quickly antiquated became the New York Times's turn-of-the-century declaration that one of the little noticed characteristics that the new boroughs had conferred on Greater New York was "the opportunity afforded for people of moderate means but steady habits to make homes for themselves within easy reach of the great metropolitan mart, and yet not out of the sight of green fields and trees in summer, or deprived of pure, health-giving air all the year around."[6]

The *Brooklyn Daily Eagle*, which published part of the report, editorially surpassed the City Plan in asserting: "Nothing in the future can be more certain than that Brooklyn will have a population of 5,000,000 in from twenty-five to thirty years. . . . [I]ts growth will not be checked until all the land in this borough now vacant has been built up." To be sure, the *Eagle* also asked: "How are they to be supplied with food without excessive charges for trucking and profits for a long succession of middlemen?" But like the City Plan itself, it had to leave the "problem of markets" for the future to solve.[7]

FEEDING THE URBAN MASSES CHEAPLY: VEGETABLE MARKETS AND INTERURBAN FREIGHT TRANSPORTATION

"A radish tastes infinitely better if eaten the very day it is picked."
— "The Garden's Fruit," *Economist*, February 22, 1997[8]

The president of the Brooklyn Committee on City Plan, Frederic Pratt, conceding that the plan failed to address the fact that distributing markets were not accessible to everyone in Brooklyn, argued for decentralization: "A large proportion of our vegetables and farm produce comes from Long Island. . . . [T]hat stuff is carted into the Wallabout and then brought back again into other parts of the city. There is an immense duplication of steps. All that could be done away with if, for instance, a market was located in East New York where the produce for that territory could be deposited without having to be recarted and redistributed." Unsurprisingly, neither Pratt in 1914 nor anyone else in the city plan movement dwelt on the origins of the distribution problem: the elimination of Kings County market gardens. Intriguingly, in the same year, another supporter of the development of Jamaica Bay, which bordered on Flatlands, pointed to the proximity of "extensive truck gardens" as satisfying the criterion of "readily and always obtainable food supplies with economical facilities for distribution," one of the essentials of an "ideal community."[9]

The apprehensions expressed by Pratt and others were rooted in long-perceived deep flaws in New York City's food distribution system, which formed as distant producers provided more and more of the city's perishable food, and the municipal government gradually abandoned its control over the produce markets. Writing shortly after World War I, the Federal Trade Commission observed: "Relatively to their actual needs and standards of life, the early New Yorkers and their markets were more 'modern'

than they have been since. New York City was well served when all its perishable food came from the neighboring farms." But in the intervening century: "The territory made tributary to the demand of the perishable produce market of the New York zone reaches from ocean to ocean. It even
extends overseas to Belgium and Germany for Brussels sprouts, ... cabbages;
... to Great Britain for potatoes." But as locally grown produce shrank to as
little as 5 percent of consumption: "The supplying of the needs of a great
city is no longer the casual affair of farmers with their market wagons. . . .
The whole industrial efficiency of the city is involved in this question of
cheap food, and because New York is the great Atlantic gateway of the country the problem of the efficient feeding of New York City widens to a national problem." [10]

   Such warnings did not originate in the wake of postwar dislocations and
were not confined to New York City. In the first decade of the century, observers had urgently pointed to the need for urban reforms to check increases in the cost of living for the millions of workers concentrated in the
newly industrializing large cities. James Sullivan, a reformer who had been
associated with the National Civic Federation, an organization dedicated to
class collaboration for promoting the peaceful development of industrial
capitalism, understood that a "reduction in the cost of food, evidently, was
of pressing interest to the masses, even more than lower street-car fares
or reduced rates for gas, water, or electric light." With 45 to 60 percent of
the typical working-class family's income spent on food, he concluded that
"the most widespread reductions in the cost of living can come from
cheaper prices for food." But since "only a small area of market gardens" remained within a twenty-mile radius of New York City, the vast bulk of produce, which had to be transported from afar, was subject to "the chaotic
method of buying and selling" associated with multitiered intermediaries
such as commission men, speculators, wholesalers, jobbers, lesser dealers,
and retailers. He called "the hauling of the goods to and fro and back and
forth from one set of dealers to another" a "part of the waste in a planless
development." [11]

   Despite the exaggerated assertion that the development of freight and
cold storage facilities had "placed the city nearer to the farm a thousand
miles away then [sic] was the farm within the sight of the city's buildings a
quarter of a century ago," proponents of spatial specialization had to admit
that food costs rose with the distance between the city and its rural supply
sites. The source of this increase was not higher transportation charges, but
the more complex system for organizing distant shipments, which required

the compensation of more workers and greater risks. As early as 1912, food distribution inefficiencies were estimated to "cost the community between fifty and one hundred million dollars a year." A few years later, a study revealed that New Yorkers' daily consumption of fresh fruits and vegetables was materially lower than in other large cities. This reduced level, at a time (1923) when locally grown produce accounted for only one-tenth of the city's consumption, was a consequence of higher food costs. Moreover, a contemporaneous study of land planning noted with respect to vegetables and other crops that "planning on a national scale would render a service to producers and consumers" in eliminating "a great deal of unnecessary shipping." [12]

Some contributors to the debate over inefficient long-distance markets and unnecessarily high food prices did advocate increased local production. In 1913 the chief of the federal Bureau of Soils saw grounds for hope for lowering prices in New York City in the possibility of cultivating tens of thousands of acres of uncultivated agricultural land within a nearby radius. Such truck farms "could be made to supply to a great extent the New York markets with perishable foodstuffs which . . . would . . . not only relieve the question of the food supply of Greater New York but . . . to a large extent reduce the prevailing high prices for vegetables." [13]

Sullivan's proposal was even more specific. Pointing to outlying districts of Greater New York such as Bath Beach, Bay Ridge, Brownsville, Flatbush, and Flushing, as offering the same opportunities for local public retail markets as smaller cities, he suggested raising intensive crops on uncultivated land in these districts for the local market once sales were assured: "A beginning might be made in establishing any one of these markets by giving free scope to . . . market-gardeners . . . to hold open-air markets on two or three days of the week in the streets, or in open spaces owned either by the city or transportation companies, at points where the stream of travelers or other probable customers pass on their way." What made this plan all the more breathtaking is that less than two decades after these very communities had lost their position as vegetable capital of the United States, Sullivan — himself a resident of Gravesend — made no reference to the fact that this "vacant land" had, until very recently, been teeming with market gardeners. [14]

The rationality of extreme geographic specialization of vegetable production was by no means a foregone conclusion even as late as the mid-1920s. The USDA reported that "the same quantity of coal burned in locomotives is required to haul vegetables grown on an acre in southern Texas to the eastern markets as is necessary to heat an acre of vegetable-forcing houses located near the markets." This macroeconomic consideration was matched by microeconomic competitiveness. Greenhouse production of vegetables had been relatively unimportant in 1890, but by the 1920s, the quality of greenhouse-grown tomatoes, cucumbers, radishes, and cauliflower created an increased demand that made it possible to compete with producers in warmer areas who shipped to distant markets: "Although it requires from 200 to 500 tons of coal to maintain an acre of greenhouse space . . . for the season, and other heavy expenditures are also involved, . . . the gross return per acre is several times that obtained from the most intensive outdoor-vegetable production." These expenditures were largely offset by heavy transport costs and by the greenhouse grower's ability to "place a severe handicap on shipped material through the production of a high-quality food product which can be marketed within a few hours from the time it is harvested." Late-twentieth-century concern with the extravagant squandering of finite fossil fuels associated with transcontinental trucking of vegetables underscores the prescience of such analyses.[15]

At the end of the 1920s, Wells Sherman, the chief marketing specialist, in charge of fruits and vegetables, of the USDA's Bureau of Agricultural Economics, impressively documented the fact that the reduced presence of nearby farmers did not mean that they could not compete with distant truck farms with regard to price and quality. Part of the underestimation of the vitality of local farming was a perception problem. He ascribed public ignorance of the extent of local vegetable production to consumers' having become so accustomed to the availability of perishables from a distance that "we thoughtlessly assume that they have displaced the home-grown. . . . Therefore, we hardly notice . . . that many distant products almost disappear from many of our markets for the few weeks when the surrounding country is at the height of its season." The transportation and packaging costs of getting distant vegetables to urban markets were so considerable that "many local products do sell for less during their season." To illustrate the handicap of California competitors, Sherman cited celery growers near Boston, who "have continued in business until their lands actually went into use as suburban homes. These celery lands have not gone into nonproducing, speculative holdings. Competition . . . did not put them out of business."[16]

With regard to quality, too, Sherman noted that freshness and maturity ensured that radishes, peas, green beans, sweet corn, and tomatoes "from a distance are among the products which practically disappear from most of our large city markets during the season of the local crop." Because refrigeration and transportation had not yet been "so perfected as to bring any of these products over journeys of several days in midsummer and deliver them to the consumer in as attractive condition as the home-grown," consumers preferred the latter "simply because they are better." On the basis of these "fundamental advantages," Sherman concluded that a farmer located close to a large eastern market could "remain a market gardener . . . indefinitely." Indeed, rather than harming the local farmer, long-distance shippers actually promoted his interests by accustoming consumers to prices that included cost components that were barely borne by local market gardeners. These prices to which consumers are "educated" during the longer nonlocal seasons were frequently "decidedly higher than the producer got for any considerable part of his crop in the days when distant competition was unknown." That local farmers nevertheless often sold certain vegetables at lower prices than distant suppliers demonstrated their viability and profitability to Sherman.[17]

The real-estatization of New York City farms and their replacement by distant competitors freed up space for additional population while necessitating the importation of additional food for those new millions. From 1900, when the southern sections of Kings County, encompassing Bay Ridge, Bath Beach, Bensonhurst, Midwood, Sheepshead Bay, and Coney Island, were still the new city's outskirts, until the Great Depression, land values rose more than tenfold in the course of a relentless struggle against "vacant," "undeveloped," and "unimproved" land. As the Mayor's Market Commission of New York City noted in 1913: "The farming district around the city is not great enough or varied enough in its productivity or producing in long enough seasons to supply the needs of the city in any line. Suburban developments are all the time pushing the farm lands farther and farther away. It is impossible to alleviate conditions by establishing markets for producers to sell to consumers." Because new modes of transportation had "brought the farms of South Carolina and Kansas as near New York City as were those of Long Island and Westchester County" a century earlier, the commission argued that they had "removed any limitations on the growth of the city imposed by the difficulty of getting an adequate food supply, and, as a consequence, the city has grown until it is dependent upon the production of a very wide area for its continued existence."[18]

Local farms may not have been able to supply all the food needs of all of New York City's inhabitants, and could supply only minimal amounts of any crop during certain months of the year, but these limitations constituted no compelling reason to eliminate their contributions altogether and to crowd onto the former farmland even more inhabitants, who in turn, required even heavier reliance on transcontinental agricultural sources. The number of farmers' wagons unloaded annually at Wallabout increased almost unabated; by 1895 it had already exceeded 50,000, two and one-half times more than the number in the market's first full year of operation in 1885. During the busiest season, approximately one thousand farm wagons from farms within a forty-mile radius came daily to New York's three biggest markets, Gansevoort and Harlem in Manhattan and Wallabout in Brooklyn; the peak volume was 445 wagons at Wallabout in 1912. In contrast, one railroad alone averaged 100 carloads a day of food products all year round and 300 to 400 during the producing season.[19]

Even those who in the late 1920s ridiculed the intimation that it was "foolish for . . . New York City to use celery raised around Kalamazoo, Michigan," had to concede that vegetables such as asparagus, beans, cabbage, cucumbers, potatoes, sweet corn, and turnips were an exception to the rule that "only an infinitesimal part of the food supply of a large city can be produced within hauling distance." Despite his disdain for those who ignored the inexorability of "agricultural specialization according to conditions of soil and climate," agricultural economist Louis Weld was constrained to agree that interurban electric transport offered "great possibilities in extending the truck-garden area to distances of from twenty-five to fifty miles from our great cities, thus . . . enabling city consumers to draw a greater supply of fresh vegetables at some reduction in cost." Although Philadelphia, Cleveland, and Indianapolis had succeeded in improving transportation of farm produce in this manner, he saw the preexisting congestion of transportation facilities in New York City as a limitation on the development of trolley freight service there.[20]

Here Weld echoed the findings of the Mayor's Market Commission, which had found trolley freight to be a "promising agency for local distribution." By shipping on trolleys, farmers could market their produce in fresher condition to parts of the city that railroad terminals did not reach. In particular, trolleys enabled farmers to market their produce directly to consumers at higher returns without having to neglect their production activities. In 1913, a farmer fifteen to twenty miles from Philadelphia, for example, required one day to drive to the market, a second day to sell, and a third day to drive home, thus losing half his week. Trolley freight would make it possible to load his produce at 6 P.M., take the train early the next morning, sell to consumers along the way or at the market, and to return early the next afternoon, thus "using but half a day instead of three, and keeping his invested capital at home at productive work." Freight trolleys' dual advantage was their ability to stop from farm to farm in the country and to make possible the creation of numerous freight terminals in the city. Under such optimal conditions, market gardeners could, according to a contemporary reckoning, "support a family in comfortable circumstances" on two- to five-acre intensively cultivated farms located near large urban centers.[21]

Despite the unrealized potential for interurban electric farm freight transportation in the New York City area, transportation capital subverted the maintenance of urban agriculture. Wanting trunk lines to move freight in box cars, railroad owners encouraged the distant shipping of agricultural commodities. As late as 1905, the president of the New Jersey State Board of Agriculture complained that transportation cost was a major cause of agricultural depression in the urban eastern states: "It is not possible to have perishable products transported in such a way as to enable them to reach the consumer at a cost and in a condition that would allow the producer to compete with" distant producers. Urban railways, in contrast, wanted to increase local population in order to increase passenger traffic. Thus a politically imposed ceiling on population density to preserve agricultural production would have been a self-limiting way to develop more freight-oriented urban transit. But short-haul freight transportation was not feasible without subsidies, and these had already been preempted by a rapid transit system, which, in turn, had been the prerequisite for dumping the masses who were overcrowding New York City in what planners regarded as the the relatively "free space" that farms were occupying. In the event, interurban electric railways or the "farmers' street car" succumbed to the automobile after World War I.[22]

THE REGIONAL PLAN OF NEW YORK

The area of New York and its environs may be likened to the floor space of a factory. Regional planning designates the best use of this floor space.
— Robert Haig and Roswell McCrea, *Major Economic Factors in Metropolitan Growth and Arrangement*, 1927

Not all early-twentieth-century planners were mesmerized by the inexorability of dichotomous urban-rural development. In 1917, Thomas Adams, a Scotsman who was then a town planning adviser in Canada and later the intellectual leader of the Regional Plan of New York, told the National Conference on City Planning that although the growth of big cities could not be artificially restricted, it was possible to plan their expansion so as to preserve agricultural land for intensive culture around each population of 300,000–400,000. Cities growing beyond that size would be required "to leap over an area of open country, which should be protected by law from any form of building development. . . . This question of zoning cities so as to include agricultural zones . . . is not in the least fantastic, and in principle it has unconsciously been applied to many communities."[23]

At the time the most elaborate and extensive such urban survey ever conducted, the Plan's *Regional Survey of New York* "remains the most thorough and ambitious single project carried out in the history of American planning." Organized by financiers and businessmen, it was carried out under the auspices of the Russell Sage Foundation by the Committee on the Regional Plan of New York and Its Environs, which regarded congestion as large cities' "most defective condition," and conceded that the "restoration of a balance between agriculture and manufacture is of interest to New York." Its preferred solution was merely "bringing more of the quality of the country into the city and more of the organized efficiencies of the city into the country."[24]

Despite the fact that farming was on the verge of vanishing in Brooklyn, Manhattan, and the Bronx by 1925, the *Regional Survey* conceded that in "Queens and Richmond there is still time for some land to be reserved for open forms of development including horticulture and truck gardens, if it were considered desirable, and a practical method could be devised for doing it." One of the impediments to the articulation of a corresponding public policy was the perception by "the average city dweller [of] the existence of a farm or at least of any large acreage used for horticulture or agriculture within the environs of a city [a]s an anachronism." In contrast, contemporary European attitudes toward urban farming were far more welcoming; for example, it was "accepted as practicable to keep large areas of farm lands within the borders of English cities. Taxation is adjusted to encourage cultivation of suburban areas."[25]

The *Regional Survey*, while denying that the "question of maintaining agricultural production near to New York in order to keep down the cost of food by saving in cost of transportation from distant sources of supply" was "of any immediate importance," left open the possibility that further demographic centralization would become disadvantageous. At a certain point in its growth, the additional cost associated with transporting perishable food long distances "will become a serious factor in industrial competition between the cities in the region and the smaller communities that are more accessible to the sources of food supply. Then this would be an important reason for giving more encouragement than is now given to the use of land for intensive cultivation in the neighborhood of New York."[26]

Even without pursuing the flaws in the city's distribution system, the staff of the Regional Plan of New York and Its Environs was able to find an economic reason for reserving areas for cultivation within urban environs: it "would break up building masses into economically desirable units. It would bring city and country into frequent juxtaposition — with advantage to both." The Regional Plan was optimistic enough to assume that, under proper management, land that a public authority acquired for the public welfare at a reasonable price to rent for farming could yield a rent greater than it could raise in taxes from the same land operated privately by a farmer. The Plan even identified plausible localities for such intervention where urbanization and speculation had not already made it "too expensive" for the City of New York "to acquire for profitable cultivation": "Opportunities are still available in the boroughs of Queens and Richmond for reserving areas that are suitable for cultivation and are comparatively isolated from means of transit." The Regional Plan's realism, however, forced it to recognize that since "the needs of the potential population of these two boroughs, in the matter of recreation space, are such that the cost of acquiring park space will probably be as much as the city can reasonably afford, there is little prospect of any open areas being acquired within the city in addition to those needed for pleasure parks and active recreation." In a memorandum prepared for the Plan, Frederick Law Olmsted Jr. even raised the possibility of subsidizing "some types of agriculture . . . to remain there [in "open" regional districts] for reasons of public policy."[27]

In a similar vein, at the end of the 1930s, the New Deal National Resources Board still emphasized that because "probably no region on earth possesses such an enormous and immediate city market for its products . . . it has . . . been profitable to fertilize relatively infertile lands and to expand the production of crop specialties" in the vicinity of New York, Boston, and Philadelphia. The possibilities that still existed at this time (1934) are underscored by the fact that 9 percent of Brooklyn was still vacant land — the lowest proportion among all the outer boroughs and far below that of Queens (23 percent) and Richmond (41 percent).[28]

Not even the Regional Plan, however, fully recognized that city farms had not been mere productive havens, but, like the Cortelyou farm in Flatbush, also habitats for otter, fox, opossum, raccoon, muskrat, wild duck, high-holders, woodcock, snipe, and quail. After recounting this fact, the developer Henry Meyer, as responsible as anyone for destroying their niches, had felt it necessary to add as early as 1901: "One can hardly imagine such a condition of wildness existing in the very heart of Greater New York, but I beg to assure you that these are facts."[29]

STATE POWER AND URBAN LAND-USE PLANNING

Exclusive farm use zoning . . . justifies incentives and privileges offered
to encourage owners of rural lands to hold such lands in exclusive farm
use zones.
— Oregon Revised Statutes, sect. 215.243(3) & (4) (1996)

Given the favorable natural and market conditions for intensive vegetable farming in the New York City area — Long Island's "exceptionally fine climate" gave it a seven-month growing season compared to five months on the mainland — the *Regional Survey* found it "extraordinary that a higher percentage of rural population has not been maintained." It found the causes in special counteracting forces in the Greater New York region: a tax system based on urban land uses that made farming unprofitable, and "a sense of instability resulting from the expectation that the land will be required for building . . . or . . . speculative purposes." The kinds of agricultural tax preferences, districts, and development rights that New York State and other states have enacted in the latter part of the twentieth century can deal with these obstacles to close-in farming.[30]

Collective action to protect farmland on behalf of urban communities may seem to have been outside the realm of political discourse available to nineteenth-century New York, but the state was capable of intervening to block capital's access to certain types of land. For example, the legislature passed an act to prevent the sale of lands used for cemetery purposes, and the 474 acres of Greenwood Cemetery, which, lying between the farming area of Gowanus and Flatbush, at the end of the twentieth century still pre-empts an enormous parcel of Kings County, have been withheld from commercial exploitation since 1840, when it was more extensive than any similar institution in the United States or Europe. If the state could clog the real-estate market for huge blocks of urban land locked up in cemeteries so that "land, once devoted to burial purposes, becomes sacrosanct in its nature, the subject of taboo, and is excluded from the purposes and traffic of the living," why not for profitable and food-producing farms? After all, Greenwood Cemetery itself was once farmland. The force of the taboo is readily visible in the fact that although urban cemeteries, which in some cities such as Queens occupy most of the open space, are "the most frustrating" for planners, they have only "toyed with the thought of all the good things that could be done" if the cemeteries could be relocated: "Those who are wise have kept the idea to themselves."[31]

Ironically, in the 1870s, even cemetery promoters were such forceful urban boosters that they could not imagine that their own creations would remain undisturbed forever. Robert Criswell, the general agent of Washington Cemetery and the son-in-law of James A. Bennett, a New Utrecht farmer who in 1853 had conveyed 100 acres to the cemetery, predicted that the removal of Greenwood Cemetery "some time before the year 2,000 is about as certain, as that the sun will rise to-morrow." But then within another century, according to Criswell, the dead in Washington Cemetery, too, would have to be dug up to make way for New York City as it inexorably expanded "until it meets the waves on Coney Island Shore."[32]

While Swedish and German cities were "buying great tracts of land both within and without their borders and . . . holding them for the citizens," public shaping of real estate remained taboo in New York. As Florence Kelley, the leading advocate of state intervention on behalf of sweated laborers, observed in 1908: "[W]henever it is suggested that the city might well buy large tracts of land to mitigate the hardships inflicted by the landowners, it is assumed that this is impossible. . . . It is honestly believed by persons of sound mind, that . . . enough wise and honest citizens cannot be found to administer tracts of municipal land as disinterestedly and as wisely as our schools and our water supply are administered."[33]

New York City, like most U.S. cities, was severely handicapped by its ownership of meager amounts of land: "In America most cities were and are forbidden by statute and state constitution to enter the private land market freely." An alternative to the dominant American plan had emerged in Europe, where the exercise of public control and cooperative forms of investment were less unusual. Municipalities in Scandinavia, Germany, Austria, and the Netherlands in the nineteenth and twentieth centuries owned huge areas both within and outside the city limits. By the beginning of the twentieth century, progressives chafing under the powerlessness of U.S. municipalities to engage in comprehensive planning pointed to German cities as models. Frederic Howe, perhaps the leading reformer to advocate a planned urban democracy, traced the fecklessness of the city planning movement to "our unwillingness to face . . . the unchecked license of the landowner, the unrestrained freedom of property in all its forms. Thus far, city planning in America has limited its vision to those sides of the question which do not conflict with the claims or abuses of private property." In contrast, German cities, recognizing that city planning was "fundamentally a land question," based their planning "on a thorough control of the land within" and outside of their limits. The transition to municipal land-ownership was facilitated by the venerable tradition of German villages' owning "forests and other land in common, and . . . us[ing] it for . . . forestry and agriculture." Indeed, one of the first acts of a German town upon receiving official urban status was "to buy as much land as possible for the purpose of meeting all conceivable public needs, present and future."[34]

Berlin was the leading practitioner at the beginning of the twentieth century: it owned land amounting to 240.8 percent of its total area including large tracts outside its boundaries. Other German cities were also large landowners: in 1901–2, for example, Frankfurt owned 57.8 percent of the land within its limits. As a result of such ownership, German cities could "anticipate their future needs in a far-sighted intelligent way. Before a new territory is opened up for residence, the city authorities acquire land for playgrounds, gardens, and sites for . . . public buildings. The purchase of these lands, far in advance of the city's growth, saves the city from prohibitive prices and . . . makes possible the most generous provision for recreation and open spaces."[35]

Stockholm was perhaps the most prominent example of municipal planning. Beginning in 1904, the city assembly bought large areas of farm and forest lands outside the city to build garden city suburbs. It also extended its boundaries so that the city limits encompassed the new suburbs. "Some of these areas lay idle for as long as 20 years before they were developed, but the city reaped the benefit of having acquired them at very low cost." Stockholm was thus able to enlarge the supply of good but cheap dwellings by making cheap building sites available. In the 1930s, Manchester, England, created a unique satellite garden town within the corporate limits of an industrial city by buying several thousand acres of rural land at agricultural land prices and incorporating Wythenshawe. The municipality was driven by the need to construct housing for families from overcrowded sections of the city, yet its first town planning measure was to establish a 1,000-acre agricultural belt within the 5,500-acre ward.[36]

By the 1930s, too, Copenhagen owned one-third of the total land area for building; Oslo owned a suburb twice as large as the city; The Hague owned 45 percent of the city area; Vienna owned more than one-fourth of the city area; Berlin owned both one-third of the city and another 75,000 acres of forest and farmland outside the city. Larger German cities (with more than 50,000 inhabitants) owned on average almost one-fourth of their municipal territory (not including streets) in contrast with less than one-tenth among similar-sized U.S. cities. In addition to such purposes as parks and public buildings, which were common in the United States, large German cities held extensive agricultural estates and forest; indeed, 40 percent — 50 percent in Berlin and the cities with more than 200,000 inhabitants — of the land that they owned in the mid-1930s was agricultural. In the United States, in contrast, even during the New Deal, proposals that the national government help fund metropolitan housing authorities' acquisition of outlying land were decried as socialistic.[37]

Garden city movements, which originated in England and Germany at the end of the nineteenth century, also confronted the urban displacement of agriculture in the nearby country, rendering the farmer a conservator of the greenbelt, rather than a recycler of wastes. Ebenezer Howard's basic idea "was to combine the advantages and eliminate the disadvantages of living either in the city or the country in an entirely new entity." Garden cities would absorb the city's population overflows in smaller, self-sustaining communities consisting of a 6,000-acre municipally owned estate, the inner core of which would be occupied by a 1,000-acre city of 30,000 inhabitants. Designed to combat urban congestion and rural depopulation by integrating agriculture into the city and preventing sprawl of the urban core, garden cities were linked to one another and to the metropolis by convenient rail lines. In seeking to demonstrate that the prevailing rigid division of agriculture and industry and town and country was unnecessary, Howard imagined that on the outer 5,000 acres farmers engaged in vegetable and other production would benefit from urban demand for their products and the city's supply of its own waste products for fertilizer.[38]

Howard's innovative financial plans for the garden city undermined the spread of his ideas to the United States. His conception of the city was one of cooperative ownership: the developers would acquire the land "on behalf of the municipality, at agricultural prices. . . . The local community therefore had control of land in the green belt and could determine the nature and extent of urban growth." Howard developed this idea in the form of a land bank that would ensure "that the benefits of enhanced value . . . went to the community as a whole. In the United States, recognition of the value enhancement phenomenon encouraged real estate developers to agglomerate masses of land surrounding the original planned community." This tension between the community's future and the developer's profit subverted the introduction of Howard's ideas in the United States. Despite influential backers among urban planners and sociologists, by the First World War, garden city "advocates began to recognize what Edward Bellamy's followers had learned somewhat earlier — that communal ownership of real estate cut against a very tough American grain" because it "smacked of socialistic or communist conspiracies."[39]

Because the farmer was not part of the urban vision in America, farming as a meaningful urban-fringe activity receded from serious consideration among city and regional planners. To the extent that Howard's garden city movement — with its vision of the urban farmer as the guardian of the greenbelt — became influential in America, it did so too late to save the farmers in Kings County, or even in neighboring Queens. Thomas Adams continued to hold out hope for urban farmers as late as 1922: "The control of the development of land is essential to this solution of the problem of congestion. Large areas of land near and within cities can be more economically used for agricultural production than for building, because their levels are such as to make the cost of conversion into building land and construction of local improvements excessive in comparison with the values they create for building purposes." But Adams's expectations were not realized despite the intervention of the federal government's greenbelt town program during the New Deal. The federal initiative failed because of the political and ideological animus against publicly controlled enterprise and "the program's radical challenge to fundamental patterns of urban growth and real estate practice."[40]

Instead, under the pressure of mass misery and discontent, a phenomenon akin to the settlement house approach emerged: fragmented mini-farming inside the boundaries of the metropolis. For example, just as the dissolution of Kings County agriculture was intensifying and reaching its peak during the panic and depression of 1893–95, a community gardens movement sprang up in cities such as New York and Detroit to employ and feed the unemployed on vacant city lot farms. The mayor of Brooklyn appointed a Committee on the Tillage of Vacant Lands, whose work was carried out by the Brooklyn Bureau of Charities, while the German American Improvement Company granted use of its land in New Lots. In addition to the Bureau's four-acre common garden, 91 one-eighth-acre plots were assigned to as many gardeners, who, with fertilizer, seed, and tools supplied by the Bureau, grew vegetables.[41]

BEYOND THE REAL ESTATE MARKET

If market value at a given time is the criterion, . . . parks . . . might lose out. Home sites could give way to industry.

Through the postwar years of sprawl, farms often seemed to be worth more growing a crop of houses than a crop of strawberries. . . .

But looking at the long-term economic impact, land may contribute more to the economy left in agriculture than subdivided for homes.

— Jerry Tippens, "What's Highest and Best in Long Run?"
Portland Oregonian, June 11, 1990

It has taken most of the twentieth century to bury and disinter the insight that the market does not always know best, and that, as a real-estate man noted, "highest and best use" might need to be qualitatively redefined to incorporate "the overall economic scheme of things, rather than the use which will produce the highest monetary return." In 1971, for example, the New York State legislature created local structures "to assure farmers who wish to remain in farming that many of their neighbors will do likewise." Two years after the state constitution had been amended to make it the "policy of the state . . . to . . . encourage the development and improvement of its agricultural lands for the production of food and other agricultural products," and to direct the legislature to "include adequate provision for . . . the protection of agricultural lands," the legislature amended its Agriculture and Markets Law to create agricultural districts.[42] In explaining its intent, the legislature declared that:

Agriculture in many parts of the state is under urban pressure from expanding metropolitan areas. This urban pressure . . . brings conflicting land uses into juxtaposition . . . and stimulates land speculation. When this scattered development extends into good farm areas, ordinances inhibiting farming tend to follow, farm taxes rise, and hopes for speculative gains discourage investments in farm improvements. Many of the agricultural lands in New York state are in jeopardy of being lost for any agricultural purposes. Certain of these lands constitute unique and irreplaceable land resources of statewide importance. It is the purpose of this article to provide a means by which agricultural land may be protected and enhanced as a viable segment of the state's economy and as an economic and environmental resource of major importance.[43]

The legislature defined "[u]nique and irreplaceable agricultural land" as "uniquely suited for the production of high value crops, including, but not limited to fruits, vegetables and horticultural specialties." Such land located in agricultural districts created pursuant to the statute became eligible for assessment only on the value of the land as used for agricultural production. By 1987 8 million acres, or one-fourth of the state's total land area, had been included within such districts. The program arrived almost a century too late to preserve the locationally unique Kings County vegetable farms, but revealed that the market may not know best after all. That the pull of the market is not inevitable continues to be demonstrated by metropolitan-area farmers who farm in spite of knowing that "I could make a lot more if I sold the farm and lived off the interest."[44]

In 1975 Suffolk become the first county in the United States to implement a nationally recognized purchase of development rights program, under which farmers are compensated for restrictions placed on the use of their land with an amount of money equal to the value of the foregone development potential. On the 6,000 acres that have become part of the program, the county has acquired nonagricultural development rights, which are valued as the difference between the market value of the land at its "highest and best use" and the value of the agricultural rights.[45]

Elsewhere, too, governments have intervened to preserve metropolitan farming. Maryland combines the purchase of development rights from farmers with government assistance of metropolitan farming. The Howard County agricultural marketer encourages farmers to convert from cattle, soybeans, and hay production to fruit and vegetable cultivation for the local fresh market. By 1996, 15 chiefly northeastern and mid-Atlantic states had paid farmers to keep their land in agricultural use. At a cost of about $1,750 per acre, these programs had sheltered 420,000 acres, thus proving that "an iron law of the real estate market . . . can be bent a bit."[46]

This retrospective of the inevitabilist interpretation of the displacement of urban farming also coincides with the resurgence of a late-twentieth-century worldwide movement toward urban agriculture that confounds planners' dichotomous conceptualization of land-use boundaries. Especially as environmental interest in methods of sustainable agriculture has become linked to communitarian concerns with fresh fruits and vegetables grown locally and harvested on site by consumers or sold face to face at farmers markets, urban farming has found a new resonance.[47]

A brief survey of a few of these recent initiatives will be useful. Some implement one of the central purposes of the turn-of-the-century garden city movement — preserving a permanent agricultural belt around the city in order to limit its growth. In a pioneering struggle against urban sprawl, the state of Oregon, from the late 1970s on, created urban growth boundaries to separate urban and rural land. The city of Portland "drew a line around the metropolitan area" on one side of which the city and on the other farms, forests, and open space were located. Many firms moving to Portland explain their decision by reference to the presence of fruit orchards "just across the street from contained urban areas." Thus far the city has refused to "give in to industry demands to open up forests and farms to sprawl."[48]

The declining population of many of the largest U.S. cities toward the end of the twentieth century and the appearance of thousands of vacant lots have reawakened interest in urban farming as ecologists have pointed out that transcontinental transport of fruits and vegetables uses considerable quantities of fossil fuels while reducing their nutritional value.[49] In the 1960s, the major geographic study of the Boston-Washington corridor underscored close-in farming's vitality:

> Horticultural specialties are grown on the most expensive farm real estate. They are commonly produced on the very edge of the largest cities, sometimes within the cities themselves. . . .
>
> To some extent this same principle applies to that kind of market gardening that is not easily mechanized or otherwise subject to cheap mass production. Many growers of melons, bush fruits, squash, peas, beans, lettuce, and tomatoes rent land within city limits, land that is waiting development. . . . Staten Island . . . still has 60 commercial farms that together produced specialty crops worth nearly $1 million in 1956. Some of the more popular Chinese and Italian restaurants in New York City operate their own vegetable farms on near-by Long Island.[50]

In 1964 60 percent of U.S. vegetable production was concentrated in Standard Metropolitan Statistical Areas. The USDA offers this explanation of the persistence: "Some types of agriculture tend to be carried out near centers of population. This is particularly true of bulky or perishable products that have few climatic or soil constraints, such as . . . vegetables. When fruit and vegetable farms are sold for nonagricultural uses, the operator often moves just a little farther out and resumes production. Thus, fruit and vegetable production tends to remain concentrated in urban areas even as cities expand."[51]

The fragility of a food system based on the principle that distance and durability can overcome place and time has given new life to the conviction that it may not, after all, be rational to produce 40 percent of the country's fresh produce in California "while agricultural land around some cities falls into disuse," and led to a recrudescence of metropolitan food production and big-city farmers markets. The establishment of a Greenmarkets program in New York City in 1976, resulting in the creation of numerous farmers markets in the Bronx, Brooklyn, and Manhattan at which farmers from upwards of one hundred miles away sell directly to consumers, highlights the latter's concern with the freshness and unimpaired nutritional value of their produce. Rising energy costs in the late 1970s and early 1980s — when transportation and direct energy use alone accounted for 14 percent of the price of food — also prompted some large firms to undertake to produce lettuce indoors close to large cities more economically than it can be produced in California, Texas, and Florida and trucked to distant consumers.[52]

Recent years have also witnessed efforts by environmentalists to spare the eastern part of Long Island the relentless but unplanned encroachment of suburban sprawl that engulfed its western end a century earlier. In 1982 the ecologist Barry Commoner and associates at the Center for the Biology of Natural Systems at Queens College issued a study proposing that farmers in Suffolk County shift production from potato monocropping to certain vegetables (broccoli, carrots, cauliflower, celery, lettuce, green peppers, and tomatoes) that they could market more cheaply in the New York City area than the dominant California and Florida producers, whose prices reflected significant costs of environmentally damaging long-distance transportation. In addition to offering greater freshness, locally grown crops avoid the reduction in nutritional value (particularly regarding vitamins) associated with long transport routes.[53]

And finally, offering the faintest glimmer of the agro-urban past, the late 1970s also witnessed the rise of Green Thumb community gardens in New York City. The thousands of gardeners who cultivate the 75 acres that make Brooklyn the leading borough are motivated by the dual objectives of community improvement and fresh vegetable harvests.[54]

Kings County agriculture successfully adapted to one set of economic pressures by making the transition in the post–Civil War period from extensive grain and cattle farming to intensive vegetable production. By the

1880s, however, those adjustments came under attack from distant producers whose vegetables, thanks to new transportation and refrigeration technologies, streamed into New York markets during seasons when outdoor production was not possible in Kings County. Under the best of circumstances, Kings County farmers might have been able to weather this competition. Survival would have required urban planning and control initiatives such as tailored tax policies and land-use restrictions. Such state intervention would have had to include centralization of population controls, railway construction, and promotion of less odoriferous and noisy technologies more congenial to residential settlement. Finally, government financial assistance might have been needed to make it possible for low-income (especially immigrant) workers to operate farms as tenants or farmers at a time when the traditional farming groups no longer wished to devote their lives to market gardening.

But what happened to farming was not the best of circumstances. The process was rigged in favor of congested land development and its quasi-universal effects. This form of urbanization foreclosed the possibility of creating an urban lifestyle that proponents of urban farming today and even in the 1910s and 1920s recommended. New York and other cities thus forfeited numerous other possibilities for balanced population growth, more diverse and integrated self-sufficient urban economies, interurban public transportation, and less costly environmental pollution controls. To be sure, the inevitabilist thesis of the market-driven demise of close-in farming is not baseless. However, a broader interpretation shows that considerations neglected by the market were weighty enough to have justified policy initiatives to avoid the macrosocial irrationalities generated by thousands of self-regarding microeconomic decisions. In Central Europe, where governments applied greater controls and the population was spread more rationally, cities have proved to be more livable. In the United States, where "there is a huge vested interest in raising hell with nature, and there is very little money — in fact none at all — in letting well enough alone," mobilizing state intervention to preserve urban agriculture lacked adequate political-economic constituencies.[55]

TABLES

TABLE 1A. *Farms in Kings County, Selected Indicators, 1820–1992*

Year	Number	Acres (Improved)	Average Number of Acres (Improved)	Number Employed	Hired Laborers	Hired Labor ($)	Value of Farm Products ($)
1820		(22,530)		840			
1825		(24,426)					
1835		(22,535)					
1840				3,234			
1845		(20,720)					
1850	363	20,862	57				
		(17,419)	(48)				
1855	398	21,465	54				
		(15,874)	(40)				
1860	436	17,037	39				
		(16,006)	(37)				
1865	433	18,949	44				
		(14,297)	(33)				
1870	298	11,029	37			308,475	1,097,392
		(10,031)	(34)				
1875	282	11,090	39				858,511
		(9,110)	(32)				
1879	409	12,359	30				1,211,000
		(11,199)	(27)				
1890	307	12,496	41				1,084,080
		(10,320)	(34)				
1899	360	6,480	18	(2,540)		254,560	1,099,305
		(5,989)	(17)				
1909	110	1,443	13			180,762	547,617
		(1,259)	(11)				
1919	54	1,080	20				449,485
		(1,006)	(19)				
1924	40	300	7.5			43,010	52,769
		(275)	(7)				
1929	11	87	8	(1,497)	1,177	23,410	124,267
		(79)	(7)				
1934	42	117	3		88		
1939	39	229	6	(1,070)	118	128,143	364,865
		(184)	(5)				
1944	41	211	5		188	253,855	973,867
		(185)	(5)				
1949	65	219	3	(667)	76	178,300	660,160
		(180)	(3)		(373)		

TABLE 1A. (*continued*)

Year	Number	Acres (Improved)	Average Number of Acres (Improved)	Number Employed	Hired Laborers	Hired Labor ($)	Value of Farm Products ($)
1954	43	113	3		80	139,350	622,178
		(63)	(1)				
1959	14	15	1	(406)	8	39,000	306,210
		(6)	(0.4)		(214)		
1964	14	17	1		36	126,250	395,257
		(5)	(0.4)				
1969	1	3	3	(890)	(545)		n.a.
1974	3	21	7		—	—	30,000
1978	5	30	6		11	16,000	160,000
1982	5	5	1	(1,864)	(1,726)	D	110,000
1987	4	4	1			D	220,000
1992	3	4	1	(2,239)	2	D	139,000
					(1962)		

TABLE 1B. *Farms in Kings County, Selected Outputs and Livestock, 1821–1992*

Year	Corn (bu.)	Potatoes (bu.)	Wheat (bu.)	Milk (gal.)	Milch Cows	Oats (bu.)	Hay (tons)	Horses
1820								1,814
1825								2,291
1835								3,355
1840	81,824	95,805	24,964			72,460	5,437	3,019
1845	124,688	178,434	26,992			64,786		4,360
1850	91,949	208,452	29,926		2,794	29,538	6,804	3,034
1855	54,179	368,243	18,086	3,033,291		16,701		6,314
1860	84,782	607,182	21,927		1,411	9,835	7,086	1,543
1865	56,351	464,887	15,803	444,530	4,023	13,657		8,463
1870	44,600	547,403	5,355	497,040	1,148	3,375	2,057	1,941
1875	35,010	420,060	2,604	25,970	315	1,580		1,068
1879	52,990	772,246	3,240	554,951	1,254	3,158	1,493	1,623
1890	29,389	611,272	925	377,514	587	1,705	1,902	1,275
1899	6,020	197,216	0	1,007,450	2,439	310	332	1,150
1909	1,682	57,728	0	78,130	113	0	90	221
1919	540	35,421	0	353,400	590	0	0	133
1924	154	11,870		81,700	149	0	23	32
1929		($100)	0	269,200	209	0	0	7
1934	0	0	0	475,842	426	0	0	16
1939	0	0	0	327,035	328	0	0	24
1944	0	0	0	520,329	395	0	0	4

TABLE 1B. (*continued*)

Year	Corn (bu.)	Potatoes (bu.)	Wheat (bu.)	Milk (gal.)	Milch Cows	Oats (bu.)	Hay (tons)	Horses
1949	0	0	0	341,655	264	0	0	11
1954	0	0	0	342,829	226	0	0	2
1959				325,324	147	0	0	0
1964	0	0	0	D	126	0	0	
1969	—	D	—					
1974	0	0	0	—		0	0	
1978	0	0	0	0		0	0	
1982	0	0	0	0		0	0	
1987	0	0	0	0	0	0	0	
1992	0	0	0	0	0	0	0	

D = Data withheld by USBC to avoid revealing information on individual farms. Employment data in parentheses are based on residence in KC at nearest decennial census. An enumerator's tabulating error at the 1870 CA was overlooked by the national office: the total improved acreage for Flatbush of 2,472 should have been 1,472; the published totals for improved and all acreage for the whole county are too high by 1,000 and have been corrected in table 1a. In 1880, the published totals for all and improved acres, 10,287 and 9,967, were undercounts of 2,072 and 1,232, respectively; the published total number of farms was 406, an undercount of 3. Table 1a contains the corrected figures.

Sources: Census for 1820; JSSNY . . . Forty-Fifth Session; JSSNY . . . Forty-Ninth Session; CSNY, for 1835; DS, Sixth Census . . . 1840 at 119; DS, Compendium . . . Sixth Census 131–33; CSNY, for 1845; SUSC, Seventh Census . . . 1850 at 121–24; SC, CSNY, for 1855 at 272–76; SI, Agriculture of the United States in 1860 at 100–103, 209; SC, CSNY, for 1865 at 322–29, 394–409; SI, Ninth Census, vol. III: 210–12, 315, 359; SC, CSNY for 1875 at 324–31, 415, 421; DI, CO, Report on . . . Agriculture . . . Tenth Census 77, 127, 164, 199, 299; DI, CO, Report on . . . Agriculture . . . Eleventh Census 166–67, 220–21, 259, 299, 340, 377, 443, 482, 522; USCO, Twelfth Census, vol. V, pt. I at 106–7, 290, 462–63, 612–13; USCO, Twelfth Census, vol. VI, pt. II at 176, 252, 383; USBC, Thirteenth Census, vol. V at 738–39, vol. VII at 200, 206, 212; USBC, Fourteenth Census, vol. VI, pt. 1 at 212, 218, 224; USBC, United States Census of Agriculture 1925, pt. I at 193, 202, 211, 219; USBC, Fifteenth Census, vol. II, pt. 1 at 243, 249, 253, 258, 263, 269, 273, 289, 293; USBC, Fifteenth Census: 1930, vol. III, pt. 1 at 157, 169, 177, 199; USBC, United States Census of Agriculture: 1935, vol. I, pt. 1 at 54, 58, 63, 65; USBC, United States Census of Agriculture: 1935, vol. II, sec. ser., pt. 1 at 70, 72; USBC, Sixteenth Census: 1940, Agriculture, vol. I: first and sec. series, pt 1 at 222, 228, 234, 240, 244, 283; USBC, Sixteenth Census: 1940, Agriculture, vol. II, third ser., pt 1 at 96, 102; USBC, United States Census of Agriculture: 1945, vol. 1, pt. 2 at 34–35, 44, 54, 80; USBC, United States Census of Agriculture: 1950, vol. 1, pt. 2 at 40–41, 46–47, 50–51, 57, 68, 74, 82–83, 92–93, 106; USBC, United States Census of Agriculture: 1954, vol. 1, pt. 2 at 62, 79, 100, 106; USBC, U.S. Census of Agriculture: 1959, Final Report— vol. I, pt. 7 at 132, 172, 194, 200; USBC, Census of Agriculture, 1964, vol. I, pt. 7 at 260, 264, 270, 280–81, 288–89, 296–97, 304–5, 312, 318, 330–31, 352–53, 376, 382; USBC, 1969 Census of Agriculture, vol. I, pt. 7, sect. 1 at 284–85; USBC, 1974 Census of Agriculture, vol. 1, pt. 32 at II-9; USBC, 1978 Census of Agriculture, vol. 1, pt. 32 at 118–19, 131, 133; USBC, 1982 Census of Agriculture, vol. 1, pt. 32 at 123, 139, 202; USBC, 1987 Census of Agriculture, vol. 1, pt. 32 at 145; USBC, 1992 Census of Agriculture, vol. 1, pt. 32 at 67, 210, 408.

TABLE 2. *Number of Farms and Farm Size in Kings County, by Town, 1880*

Town	Number of Farms	Total Acreage	Average Acreage per Farm
Brooklyn	18	440	24
Flatbush	47	1,672	36
Flatlands	97	3,229	33
Gravesend	64	2,038	32
New Lots	80	1,563	20
New Utrecht	103	3,403	33

Source: U.S. Census, 1880, Agriculture, reel 18, KC, MS.

TABLE 3. *Potato, Corn, and Wheat Output in Kings County, 1845–1924*

Year	Potatoes			Corn			Wheat		
	Bushels	Acres	B/A	Bushels	Acres	B/A	Bushels	Acres	B/A
1845	178,434	1,630	109	124,688	3,242	38	26,992	1,420	19
1855	368,243	3,089	119	54,179	1,948	28	18,086	887	20
1864	464,887	3,500	133	56,351	1,636	34	15,803	819	19
1874	420,060	2,734	154	35,010	756	46	2,604	108	24
1879	772,246	4,172	185	52,900	1,256	42	3,240	139	23
1890	611,272	3,926	156	29,389	370	79	925	54	17
1899	197,216	2,285	86	6,020	178	34			
1909	57,728	591	98	1,682	35	48			
1919	35,421	418	85	540	13	42			
1924	11,870	80	148						

Sources: Same as table 1.

TABLE 4. *Market Garden/Vegetable Production
in Kings County, 1840–1974*

Year	Value ($)	Acres	Value/Acre ($)
1840	84,050		
1850	88,086		
1854	273,552	1,414	193
1860	319,134		
1864	251,830	1,110	227
1870	398,648		
1879	842,617		
1890	195,161		
1899	260,930	1,936	135
1909	133,448	848	157
1919	262,747	497	529
1924		88	
1929	28,845	81	356
1934		79	
1939	27,332	165	166
1944	24,700	65	380
1949	41,900	89	471
1954	17,430		
1959	50		
1964	0		
1974	0		

Sources: Same as table 1.

TABLE 5. *Value (in $) of Market Garden Production in Leading Counties, 1850–99*

1850		1860		1869–70	
County	Value	County	Value	County	Value
Philadelphia	436,813	Queens	886,934	Queens	1,059,17(
Queens	308,957	Middlesex MA	798,261	Middlesex MA	973,52(
Middlesex MA	220,982	Philadelphia	715,836	Burlington NJ	660,57
Norfolk VA	136,796	Monroe NY	476,158	Philadelphia	645,50(
Essex MA	132,431	Hamilton OH	459,196	Camden	514,07(
Hartford	123,535	New York	392,828	Hamilton OH	447,39(
New York	121,335	Albany	386,241	Anne Arundel	434,54(
Anne Arundel	115,690	*Kings*	*319,134*	Baltimore	430,7
Owen KY	107,211	Bergen NJ	295,540	*Kings*	*398,6*
Hudson NJ	91,619	Norfolk	292,968	Essex MA	376,1
Hamilton OH	91,186	Burlington NJ	267,217	Monmouth NJ	362,2
Kings	*88,086*	Baltimore	236,365	Fairfield CT	263,9(
Total	5,280,030	Total	16,159,498	Total	20,719,2(

1879		1890		1899	
County	Value	County	Value	County	Value
Queens	1,315,934	Middlesex	873,016	Queens	1,596,4
Kings	*842,617*	Queens	528,433	Middlesex MA	1,421,9
Middlesex MA	698,986	Anne Arundel	426,246	Baltimore	918,3
Baltimore	533,197	Allegheny	375,357	Cook	874,0
Allegheny	463,799	Berrien MI	368,350	Nassau	859,0
Philadelphia	403,786	Los Angeles	326,381	Allegheny	801,
Hamilton OH	397,550	Burlington	325,136	Burlington	734,
Norfolk	387,789	Bristol MA	301,145	Norfolk	705,
Camden	368,369	St. Louis	289,741	Harford MD	619,
Essex MA	321,239	Gloucester NJ	279,990	Anne Arundel	618,
Hudson NJ	282,050	Camden	263,859	Philadelphia	614,
St. Louis (city)	257,387	Monmouth NJ	253,195	Monmouth NJ	593,
Cuyahoga OH	246,060	*Kings (23d)*	*195,161*	*Kings (40th)*	*260*
Total	21,761,250	Total	29,033,080	Total	67,399

Sources: SUSC, *Seventh Census of the United States*, tab. XI at 60–866; SI, *Agriculture of the United States in 1*
at 32–160; SI, *Ninth Census: Statistics of the Wealth and Industry of the United States* 110–270; CO, *Report . . .
Agriculture . . . Tenth Census*, tab. VII at 104–40; CO, *Report on . . . Agriculture . . . Eleventh Census*, tab. 24 a*
500–37; USCO, *Twelfth Census*, vol. VI, pt. II at 293, 383.

TABLE 6A. *Indicators of Market Garden Production in the 12 Leading Counties, 1879*

County	Number of Farms	Improved Acres	Value of Farm per Acre ($)	Value of Total Farm Productions ($)	Value of Total Farm Productions per Acre ($)	Value of Total Farm Productions per Farm ($)
Queens	2,966	130,242	125	3,999,402	30.71	1,348
Kings	409	9,967	474	1,211,000	121.50	2,961
Middlesex	5,092	265,077	76	4,657,145	17.57	915
Baltimore	4,080	262,781	76	3,094,712	11.78	759
Allegheny	5,530	333,277	97	3,666,167	11.00	663
Philadelphia	780	35,902	357	1,434,240	39.95	1,839
Hamilton	4,064	182,051	108	3,276,550	18.00	806
Norfolk	1,569	63,239	20	1,393,693	22.04	888
Camden	950	56,985	70	1,321,849	23.20	1,391
Essex	2,847	141,426	76	2,257,114	15.96	793
Hudson	145	2,728	815	334,989	122.80	2,310
St. Louis (city)	423	10,818	280	543,147	50.21	1,284

TABLE 6B. *Indicators of Market Garden Production in the 12 Leading Counties, 1879*

County	Value of Market Garden Products ($)	Market Garden Products as % of Total Value of Farm Productions	Value of Implements & Machinery per Farm ($)	Cost of Fertilizers Purchased ($)	Fertilizer per Farm ($)	Fertilizer per Acre ($)
Queens	1,315,934	33	308.77	636,058	214	4.88
Kings	842,617	70	549.02	212,173	519	21.29
Middlesex	698,986	15	196.99	195,919	38	0.74
Baltimore	533,197	17	178.11	251,754	62	0.96
Allegheny	463,799	13	166.68	43,134	8	0.13
Philadelphia	403,786	28	393.66	105,994	136	2.95
Hamilton	397,550	12	143.20	15,367	4	0.08
Norfolk	387,789	28	57.05	168,367	107	2.66
Camden	368,369	28	262.52	155,923	164	2.74
Essex	321,239	14	175.39	80,106	28	0.57
Hudson	282,050	84	269.13	36,409	251	13.35
St. Louis (city)	257,387	47	96.04	5,332	13	0.49

Data on acres, value of farm production/acre, and fertilizer/acre refer to improved acres; data on value of farms/acre refer to total acres. Market garden products excluded potatoes and orchard products. *Source*: CO, *Report on . . . Agriculture . . . Tenth Census*, tab. VII at 104–40, tab. XIV at 250–309.

TABLE 7. *Average Expenditures and Receipts (in $) on 1 Acre of Peter Henderson's Jersey City Heights Vegetable Farm from 1860s to 1880s*

Expenditures	1864–1874	1876–1886
Labor	300	480
Horse-Labor	35	50
Manure, 75 tons	100	100
Rent	50	50
Seeds	10	10
Wear and Tear of Tools	10	10
Cost of Carriage to Market & Selling	100	100
Total	605	800
Receipts		
12,000 Early Cabbages @ 5¢/4¢	600	480
14,000 Lettuce @ 1¢	140	140
30,000 Celery @ 2¢	600	600
Total	1,340	1,220
Costs	−605	−800
Profit	735	420

Source: Peter Henderson, *Gardening for Profit* 20 (1874); Henderson, *Gardening for Profit* at 22 (1890).

TABLE 8. *Average Production Inputs and Outputs (in $) for Market Garden Farms in Kings County, by Town, 1879–80*

Town	Value of All Productions	Value of Market Garden Produce	Value of Market Garden Produce as % of Value of All Production	Value of Implements and Machinery	Wages	Fertilizer	Wages Fertilizer % of Value of All Product
Brooklyn	2,850	2,850	100	442	475	330	28
Flatbush	3,716	3,363	91	570	677	442	30
Flatlands	2,613	2,095	80	492	483	599	41
New Lots	4,429	4,677	106	822	827	817	37
New Utrecht	2,922	2,842	97	642	984	571	53
Total	3,144	2,926	93	601	735	577	42

Source: U.S. Census, 1880, Agriculture, reel 18, KC, MS.

TABLE 9. *Slave and Black Population of Kings County and Flatbush, 1698–1900*

	Kings County					Flatbush				
Year	Total	Slave	% Slave	Free Colored /Negro	% Free Colored /Negro	Total	Slave	% Slave	Free Colored /Negro	% Free Colored /Negro
1698	2,013	293	15	n.a.	n.a.	476	71	15	n.a.	n.a.
1723	2,218	444	20	n.a.	n.a.	n.a.	n.a.	n.a.	n.a.	n.a.
1731	2,150	492	23	n.a.	n.a.	n.a.	n.a.	n.a.	n.a.	n.a.
1738	2,348	564	24	n.a.	n.a.	540	134	25	n.a.	n.a.
1746	2,331	645	28	n.a.	n.a.	n.a.	n.a.	n.a.	n.a.	n.a.
1749	2,283	783	34	n.a.	n.a.	n.a.	n.a.	n.a.	n.a.	n.a.
1756	2,707	845	31	n.a.	n.a.	n.a.	n.a.	n.a.	n.a.	n.a.
1771	3,623	1,162	32	n.a.	n.a.	n.a.	n.a.	n.a.	n.a.	n.a.
1786	3,986	1,317	33	n.a.	n.a.	n.a.	n.a.	n.a.	n.a.	n.a.
1790	4,549	1,482	33	46	1	941	378	40	12	1
1800	5,740	1,479	26	332	6	946	341	36	39	4
1810	8,303	1,118	13	735	9	1,159	216	19	170	15
1814	7,655	943	12	832	11	1,062	179	17	205	19
1820	11,371	879	8	882	8	1,041	211	20	83	8
1830	20,535	0	0	2,007	10	1,143	0	0	258	23
1840	47,613	3	0	2,843	6	2,099	0	0	288	14
1850	138,882	0	0	4,065	3	3,177	0	0	258	8
1860	279,122	0	0	4,999	2	3,471	0	0	289	8
1870	419,921	0	0	5,653	1	6,309	0	0	203	3
1880	599,495	0	0	9,153	2	7,634	0	0	222	3
1890	838,547	0	0	11,992	1	12,338	0	0	n.a.	n.a.
1900	1,166,582	0	0	18,367	2	n.a.	n.a.	n.a.	n.a.	n.a.

Sources: 1698: E. B. O'Callaghan, *The Documentary History of the State of New-York* 3:138; 1723, 1731, 1738, 1746, 1749, 1756, 1771: O'Callaghan, *Documentary History of the State of New-York* 1:693–97; 1738: O'Callaghan, *Documentary History of the State of New-York* 4:186; 1786: Evarts Greene and Virginia Harrington, *American Population Before the Federal Census of 1790*; 1790: BC, *A Century of Population Growth*, tab. 104 at 194; 1800: DS, *Return of the Whole Number of Persons Within the Several Districts of the United States* 27; 1810: *Aggregate Amount of . . . Persons Within the United States* 28; CP, 1810, Schedules, NYS, KC, roll 28; 1814: *JSSNY* 133; 1820: *Census for 1820* [no pagination]; 1830: *Fifth Census . . . of the United States* 50–51; 1840: DS, *Sixth Census* 118–19; 1850: U.S. Census, *Seventh Census of the United States* 99–100; 1860: DI, *Population of the United States in 1860* at 335; 1870: DI, *A Compendium of the Ninth Census* 270; 1880: 10th Census, NY, vol. 38, Kings, pt. 10, MS; CO, *Statistics of the Population . . . at the Tenth Census*, tab. V at 402, tab. VI at 422; CO, *Compendium of the Tenth Census*, tab. XIX at 229; 1890: CO, *Report on the Population of the United States at the Eleventh Census*, pt. I, tab. 5 at 247, tab. 22 at 509, tab. 23 at 543; 1900: BC, *Century of Population Growth*, tab. 105 at 202.

TABLE 10. *Farm Laborers in Rural Kings County, by Nativity and Race, 1860, 1870, and 1880*

1860			1870			1880		
Group	Number	%	Group	Number	%	Group	Number	%
Irish	490	63	Irish	249	38	U.S. white	213	3!
U.S. black	93	12	U.S. white	143	22	Irish	162	2'
German	89	11	German	143	22	German	97	1(
U.S. white	79	10	U.S. black	89	14	U.S. black	74	1:
English	18	2	English	9	1	2d-generation Irish	35	(
Scots	5	1	Swiss	3		Swiss	7	
French	2		French	3		English	7	
Swiss	1		Swedish	2		Polish	5	
Danish	1		Dutch	2		Scots	3	
			Norwegian	2		Austrian	3	
			Scots	1		Swedish	3	
			Welsh	1		French	1	
			Danish	1		Dutch	1	
Total	778	100	Total	648	100	Total	611	10(

Sources: PS of the Eighth Census, 1860, NY, KC; PS of the Ninth Census, 1870, NY, vol. 30 (1–306), KC; 10th Census, NY, vol. 37, Kings, pt. 9.

TABLE 11. *Changes in the Rural Kings County Farm Labor Force, by Nativity and Race, 1860–80*

Group	1860–1870		1870–1880		1860–1880	
	Number	%	Number	%	Number	%
Irish	−241	−49	−87	−35	−328	−67
U.S. white	64	81	70	49	134	170
German	54	61	−46	−32	8	9
U.S. black	−4	−4	−15	−17	−19	−20
Total	−130	−17	−37	−6	−167	−21

Sources: Same as table 10.

TABLE 12. *Farm Laborers in Kings County Towns,*
by Nativity and Race, 1860, 1870 and 1880 (and in %)

Year	Total	Irish	U.S. White	German	Black	2d-Generation Irish
			Flatbush			
1860	173	102 (59)	15 (9)	10 (6)	38 (22)	
1870	70	41 (59)	13 (19)	6 (9)	9 (13)	
1880	19	8 (42)	1 (5)	0	3 (16)	7 (37)
			Flatlands			
1860	180	127 (71)	28 (16)	4 (2)	18 (10)	
1870	178	79 (44)	39 (22)	15 (8)	33 (19)	
1880	258	82 (32)	94 (36)	30 (12)	38 (15)	3 (1)
			Gravesend			
1860	93	72 (77)	4 (4)	2 (2)	11 (12)	
1870	121	55 (45)	15 (12)	24 (20)	25 (21)	
1880	121	61 (50)	15 (12)	6 (5)	17 (14)	13 (11)
			New Lots			
1860	93	16 (17)	13 (14)	53 (57)	6 (6)	
1870	121	3 (2)	28 (23)	75 (62)	10 (8)	
1880	139	3 (2)	54 (39)	51 (37)	16 (12)	4 (3)
			New Utrecht			
1860	239	173 (72)	19 (8)	20 (8)	20 (8)	
1870	158	71 (45)	48 (30)	23 (15)	12 (8)	
1880	74	8 (11)	47 (64)	10 (14)	0	8 (11)

Sources: Same as table 10.

TABLE 13. *Wage Intensity of the 20 Largest Market Garden-Producing Counties, 1869–70*

County	Total Wages ($)	Number of Farms	Wages/ Farm ($)	Value of Market Garden Produce as % of Total Value of Production
Queens	1,002,440	2,764	363	23
Middlesex MA	1,166,103	3,351	348	18
Burlington NJ	1,197,113	2,024	591	13
Philadelphia	608,910	898	678	29
Camden	480,066	1,234	389	25
Hamilton	709,837	3,310	214	10
Anne Arundel	526,928	1,228	429	24
Baltimore	1,093,706	2,840	385	12
Kings	*308,475*	*298*	*1,035*	*36*
Essex MA	617,942	2,242	276	15
Monmouth NJ	969,043	1,971	492	10
Fairfield CT	707,478	3,836	184	7
Allegheny	770,916	4,881	158	6
New York	155,300	198	784	69
Gloucester NJ	441,759	1,336	331	8
Bergen NJ	313,114	1,743	180	5
Norfolk VA	218,617	772	283	33
Hudson NJ	91,825	122	753	68
St. Louis	1,072,601	2,846	377	5
Albany	713,778	3,209	222	5

Source: SI, *Ninth Census*, vol. III, 94–284, 345–66.

TABLE 14. *Persistence Rates Among Persons Returned as Farm Laborers at the 1860 and 1870 or the 1870 and 1880 Censuses in Rural Kings County*

Group	1860 and 1870			1870 and 1880		
	Repeat Farm Laborers in 1860 & 1870	Total Farm Laborers in Group in 1860	Repeat Farm Laborers as % of Total Group in 1860	Repeat Farm Laborers in 1870 & 1880	Total Farm Laborers in Group in 1870	Repeat Farm Laborers as % of Total Group in 1870
All	9	778	1	36	648	6
White	4	685	1	17	559	3
Irish	1	490	0.2	6	249	2
German	1	89	1	0	143	0
U.S. white	2	79	2.5	11	143	8
Black	5	93	5	19	89	21
Blacks in Flatbush	4	38	11	0	9	0
Blacks in Flatlands	0	18	0	11	33	33
Blacks in Gravesend	0	11	0	7	25	28
Irish in Gravesend	0	72	0	4	55	7
U.S. whites in Flatlands	1	28	4	4	39	10
U.S. whites in New Utrecht	0	19	0	5	48	10

Source: CP, 1860, 1870, 1880, MS.

TABLE 15. *Persons Employed in Various Sectors in Kings County, 1840*

Place	Total	Mining	Agriculture	%	Commerce	Manufactures /Trades	%	Ocean Navigation	Canal/River Navigation	Learned Professions
Kings County	12,984	2	3,234	25	1,770	6,160	47	995	448	375
Brooklyn	9,525	2	1,597	17	1,673	4,666	49	978	302	307
Williamsburgh	1,281		120	9	22	1,118	87	9		12
Rural Kings County	2,178		1,517	70	75	376	17	8	146	56
Bushwick	369		249	67	7	92	25	6		15
Flatbush	788		533	68	35	187	24	1	8	24
Flatlands	286		190	66	3	32	11		60	1
Gravesend	281		198	70	7	22	8		50	4
New Utrecht	454		347	76	23	43	9	1	28	12

Source: DS, Sixth Census . . . of the Inhabitants of the United States in 1840 at 119.

TABLE 16. *Dimensions, Area, and Population*
Density of Kings County Towns, 1840

Town	Greatest Length	Greatest Breadth	Area in Sq. Miles	Population per Sq. Mile
Williamsburgh	1.5	1.5	1.67	3,050
Brooklyn	6.5	3.5	14.33	2,528
Bushwick	5	1.5	6.33	205
New Utrecht	3.5	3	8.33	154
Flatbush	7.25	4.5	16.33	129
Flatlands	5	3.5	14	58
Gravesend	4	4	15	53
Kings County	12	9	76	626

Sources: Dimensions and area: Prime, *History of Long Island* 67–68; population: DS, *Sixth Census . . . of the United States* 119.

TABLE 17. *Acres of Improved Farmland*
in Kings County, by Town, 1845

Town	Number of Acres	Percentage of Total Acres
Brooklyn	3,066.25	15
Williamsburgh	88.5	1
Bushwick	2,112.5	10
Flatbush	5,682.5	27
Flatlands	3,167.5	15
Gravesend	2,516	12
New Utrecht	4,086.75	20
Total	20,720	100

Source: *CSNY* for 1845.

TABLE 18. *Population of Kings County, by Town, 1790–1900*

Year	Kings County	Brooklyn	Bushwick	Flatbush	Flatlands	Gravesend	New Lots	New Utrecht	Williamsburg
1790	4,495	1,603	540	941	423	426		562	
1800	5,740	2,378	656	946	493	489		778	
1810	8,303	4,402	798	1,159	517	520		907	
1820	11,187	7,175	930	1,027	512	534		1,009	
1830	20,535	15,394	1,620	1,143	596	565		1,217	
1840	47,613	36,223	1,295	2,099	810	799		1,283	5,094
1845	78,691	59,574	1,857	2,255	936	898		1,863	11,338
1850	138,882	96,838	3,739	3,177	1,155	1,064		2,129	30,780
1855	216,355	205,250		3,280	1,578	1,256	2,261	2,730	
1860	279,122	266,661		3,471	1,652	1,286	3,271	2,781	
1865	311,090	296,378		2,778	1,904	1,627	5,009	3,394	
1870	419,921	396,099		6,309	2,286	2,131	9,800	3,296	
1875	509,154	482,493		6,940	2,651	2,180	11,047	3,843	
1880	599,495	566,663		7,634	3,127	3,674	13,655	4,742	
1890	838,547	806,343		12,338	4,075	6,937		8,854	
1900	1,166,582	1,166,582		27,188	8,243	14,609		24,700	

Sources: 1790–1890: Ira Rosenwaike, *Population History of New York City*, tab. 4 at 31, tab. 15 at 59; 1900: *BDEA: 1902* at 139.

TABLE 19. *Manufacturing in Brooklyn and Rural Kings County, 1880 and 1890*

	1880		1890	
	Brooklyn	Rural Kings County	Brooklyn	Rural Kings County
Establishments	5,201	80	10,583	40
Value of products	$177,223,142	$1,965,543	$269,244,147	$1,579,607
Employees	47,587	1,211	109,292	522
Wages	$22,487,457	$379,719	$65,247,119	$326,290

The data for rural KC were calculated by subtracting the data for Brooklyn from those for KC. *Sources*: CO, *Compendium of the Tenth Census*, pt. II, tab. LII at 998–99, tab. LIII at 1038–39; CO, *Compendium of the Eleventh Census*, pt. II, tab. 2 at 744–45; CO, *Report on Manufacturing Industries . . . Eleventh Census*, pt. I, tab. 6 at 536–37.

TABLE 20. *Assessed Valuation of Property Taxed in Brooklyn and Rural Kings County, 1880 and 1890*

	Assessed Valuation of Property Taxed ($)				Ad Valorem Taxation			
	Total		Per capita		Rate per $100		Per capita	
Place	1880	1890	1880	1890	1880	1890	1880	1890
Brooklyn	232,925,699	445,038,201	411.05	551.92	2.61	2.62	10.71	14.47
Rural Kings County	9,111,313	14,702,809	475.12	456.55				
Flatbush	4,260,827	6,271,765	558.14	508.33		2.29		11.64
Flatlands	1,099,080	1,381,936	351.48	339.13		2.31		7.83
Gravesend	1,566,576	3,059,140	426.40	440.99		3.99		17.58
New Utrecht	2,184,830	3,989,968	460.74	450.64		2.67		12.03

The per capita figure for rural Kings County in 1880 was calculated without regard to New Lots, which was annexed to Brooklyn in 1886. *Source*: CO, *Report on Wealth, Debt, and Taxation at the Eleventh Census*, pt. II at 390–94.

TABLE 21. *Total Farm Acreage in Kings County, by Town, 1820–80*

Year	Flatbush	Flatlands	Gravesend	New Lots	New Utrecht	Brooklyn	Bushwick
1820	5,653	2,883	2,402		3,835	5,222	2,535
1825	5,826	3,261	3,145		3,795	5,806	2,593
1835	5,777	2,881.75	2,587.5		4,009.75	4,624	2,655
1845	5,682.5	3,167.5	2,516		4,086.75	3,066.25	2,112.5
1850	6,337	3,875.5	2,862.5		3,880	2,321	1,384
1855	2,795	5,185.5	3,201	2,845	4,590.5	2,848.5	
1860	2,358	3,858	2,749	2,902	3,967	1,195	
1865	2,710.5	6,005.5	3,254	2,100	3,532	1,347.5	
1870	1,490	2,672	2,883	1,928	1,680	384	
1875	1,649	2,335	1,513	1,698	3,895	n.a.	
1880	1,672	3,229	2,038	1,563	3,417	439	

Sources: Table 1a; U.S. CA, 1850–80, MS.

TABLE 22. *Vote on Consolidation in Rural Kings County, 1873*

Town	For	%	Against	%	Total
Flatbush	125	16.6	626	83.4	751
Flatlands	13	3.4	365	96.6	378
Gravesend	8	2.5	314	97.5	322
New Lots	596	46.2	695	53.8	1,291
New Utrecht	222	33.4	442	66.6	664
Total	964	28.3	2,442	71.7	3,406

Source: "The Election," *KCRG*, Nov. 8, 1873, 4:1, 2.

TABLE 23. *Property Tax Rates (in %) in Flatbush and Brooklyn, 1863–99*

	Flatbush				Flatbush		
Year	In Gas District	Not in Gas District	Brooklyn	Year	In Gas District	Not in Gas District	Brooklyn
1863		0.92	1.58	1882	1.34	1.07	2.31
1864		1.89	3.21	1883	1.50	1.24	2.58
1865		1.45	3.06	1884	1.40	1.24	2.62
1866		1.66	3.41	1885	1.97	1.53	2.89
1867	2.07	1.62	3.78	1886	1.43	1.43	2.65
1868	1.73	1.60	3.76	1887	1.92	1.33	2.76
1869	1.78	1.62	3.26	1888	1.93	1.50	2.74
1870	2.00	1.82	3.77	1889	2.47	1.88	2.94
1871	1.79	1.53	2.74	1890	2.20	1.54	2.58
1872	1.60	1.39	3.50	1891	1.79	1.31	2.57
1873	1.56	1.36	3.47	1892	2.44	1.79	2.77
1874	1.73	1.45	3.53	1893	2.42	2.04	2.85
1875	1.62	1.35	3.41	1894	2.39	2.44	2.63
1876	1.54	1.28	3.24	1895	3.12		2.74
1877	1.38	1.14	3.15	1896	2.64		2.90
1878	1.61	1.27	2.68	1897	2.79		2.83
1879	1.27	0.99	2.53	1898			none
1880	1.33	1.05	2.67	1899			2.36
1881	1.15	0.86	2.36				

No taxes were levied for state and county purposes in 1898; *Annual Report of the State Board of Tax Commissioners of the State of New York, 1898* at 183. *Sources*: Flatbush, 1863–1894: ARTF, 1858–1894; Flatbush, 1895: *BDEA: 1896* at 250; Flatbush, 1896: *BDEA: 1897* at 352; Flatbush, 1897: *BDEA: 1898* at 413; Brooklyn, 1863–1886: *BDEA: 1887* at 103 ; Brooklyn, 1887–1899: *BDEA: 1900* at 448.

TABLE 24. *Assessments and Taxes of Flatbush Farmer William Williamson, 1860–93*

		Assessment ($)			Tax ($)		
						Real Estate	
Year	Acres	Real Estate ($)	Personal Estate	Rate (%)	Total	Total	Per Acre
1860	45	8,250	18,500	0.72	192.87	59.48	1.32
1865	45	10,875	14,500	1.45	367.56	157.53	3.50
1870	45	25,500	6,700	1.82	585.93	464.01	10.31
1875	49	20,860	6,700	1.35	371.03	280.83	5.73
1880	49.75	19,000	5,000	1.05	252.23	199.68	4.01
1885	50	19,300	5,000	1.53	372.07	295.51	5.91
1890	50	30,000	5,000	1.54	539.83	462.71	9.25
1891	50	45,000	5,000	1.31	652.52	587.26	11.74
1892	50	48,000	5,000	1.79	948.62	859.13	17.18
1893	50	49,000	5,000	2.04	1,104.14	1,001.90	20.04

Source: ARTF, 1860–93.

TABLE 25. *Farmers in Rural Kings County, by Nativity, 1860, 1870, and 1880*

Total	U.S.	German	Irish	English
		1860		
552	473	40	19	9
%	86	7	3	2
		1870		
505	395	62	32	9
%	78	12	6	2
		1880		
491	305	91	81	4
%	62	19	16	1

Sources: CP, 1860, 1870, and 1880, MS.

TABLE 26. *Farmers in Kings County Towns, by Nativity, 1860, 1870, and 1880 (in %)*

	1860				1870				1880		
Total	U.S.	German	Irish	Total	U.S.	German	Irish	Total	U.S.	German	Irish
					Flatbush						
67	49	5	9	50	38	3	6	65	34	2	26
	(73)	(7)	(13)		(76)	(6)	(12)		(52)	(3)	(40)
					Flatlands						
143	126	8	5	112	94	10	6	94	64	19	9
	(88)	(6)	(3)		(84)	(9)	(5)		(68)	(20)	(10)
					Gravesend						
108	102	2	2	140	108	12	16	131	84	17	28
	(94)	(2)	(2)		(77)	(9)	(11)		(64)	(13)	(21)
					New Lots						
90	77	8	1	87	64	18	0	78	59	15	0
	(86)	(9)	(1)		(74)	(21)			(76)	(19)	
					New Utrecht						
144	119	17	2	116	91	19	4	123	64	38	18
	(83)	(12)	(1)		(78)	(16)	(3)		(52)	(31)	(15)

Sources: CP, 1860, 1870, & 1880, MS.

TABLE 27. *Farm Owners and Tenants in Flatbush, 1880*

Name	Owner or Tenant	Nativity	Age	Tilled Acres	Farm Value ($)	Implements Value ($)	Fertilizer Cost 1879 ($)	Wages 1879 ($)	Productions Value 1879 ($)	Potato Acres 1879	Potato Bu. 1879	Market Garden Value 1879 ($)
Derby, Andrew	T	I	39	10	540	20			200	7	500	
Schenck, William	O/T	US	42	11	5000	400	150	150		6	700	
Cramer, Peter	T	G	32	19		300	130	12	1200	8	950	850
Farrell, Thomas	T			22		300	1000	600	2000	14	2100	1200
Suydam, Cornelius	O	US	77	46	25000	1000	700	1000	6200	25	6000	5000
Van Wyck, George	T	US	43	75		1000	800	1300	6000	25	4000	4000
Eldert, John	T	US	33	61		1000	750	1000	5500	22	5500	5000
Neefus, Peter	O	US	50	81	42000	600	400	700	4500	14	3000	3200
Williamson, William	O	US	62	56	28000	1000	800	1000	10000	24	4900	8500
Schenck, George	O	US	35	20	10000	500	300	500	3000	10	2000	2200
Schenck, John	O	US	53	20	10000	500	400	500	3000	8	1600	2000
Siglogh, Frederick	O/T	G	59	14		200	150	150	1250	3	600	1000
Lefferts, James	T	US	25	82		1300	1100	1600	8384	31	7500	
Bennett, James	T	I	48	50		200	150	200	2000	25	1500	1500
Vanderveer, John	O	US	78	80	50000	1500	800	1200	10000	25	5000	8000
O'Brien, Kennedy	T	I	43	10		100	150	50	1000	8	1600	800
Miller, Herman	T	G	31	13		500	300	10	1000	10	1500	850
Whalen, John	T	I	57	20		150	250		1200	12	1800	800
Welsh, Thomas	T	I	51	8		200	175	120	600	5	600	500
Connors, William	T			25		150	500	400	1600	13	1800	1500
Fitzpatrick, Patrick	T	I	50	43		400	550	800	3500	21	3200	3100
Connors, James	T	I	41	60		1000	800	800	4000	33	4900	5000

Parsons, Michael	T	I	40	29		1000	600	500	2800	18	2700	2300
Hogan, Edward	T	I	34	39	19500	400	600	600	3200	18	3600	2000
Boland, John	T	I	39	12	6000	400	20		3100	2	300	3000
Allgeo, William	T	US	50	88	44000	1400	1325	3000	10400	33	6600	10000
Schoonmaker, Cornelius	T	US	58	38	19000	560	1000	1200	6100	18	3600	6000
Maher, Patrick	T	I	48	24	16000	350	250	350	2000	15	3000	1600
O'Donnell, John	T	I	26	18	9000	200						
Heaslip, John	T	US/I	24	43	30000	800	500	300	4600	18	4000	4500
Reynolds, Herbert	T			6	6000	200	100	300	1600			
McGivney, Thomas	T	US/I	34	16	11000	450		600				6500 for milk
Kennedy, Edward	T	I	50	30	15000	200	350	450	4000	17	3200	3600
Garnin, John	T	US/G	32	70	35000	1400	2000	2000	9000	34	6800	8000
Garnin, William	T	US/G	30	15	7500	500	300	600	3250	6	1200	3000
Berry, Richard	T	US	43	75	37500	850	1500	2700	9500	30	6000	9000
Cooper, John	T	US	53	42	21000	550	550	650	4500	11	1700	4200
Keenan, John	T	I	44	60	45000	400	700	800	3900	25	5000	3600
Miller, Charles	T	R	58	14	7000	150						
Fox, Thomas	T	I	34	20	10000	400	200	300	1600	12	2400	850
Leary, James	T	I	40	40	20000	600	500	500	2000	25	5000	1500
Busby, James	T			45	25000	600	500	600	3000	30	6000	2500
Keenan, Patrick	T	I	37	40	20000	400	300	550	3500	25	5000	3200
Keenan, Charles	T	I	35	15	8000	200	150	100	1300	10	2000	1100
Staite, William	T	E	49	37	18000	700	650	800	4000	22	4000	3682
Wilder, James	O			12	10000	200	250	300	1200	4	700	550
Pierce, Michael	T			12	6000	400	250	200	1150	8	1300	1000

Sources: U.S. CA, 1880, MS; U.S. CP, 1870 & 1880, MS. O = owner; T = tenant; E = English; G = German; I = Irish; R = Russian.

TABLE 28. *Farm Owners and Tenants in Flatbush, 1880*

Economic Indicator	6 Old-Line Dutch Owners	5 Old-Line Dutch Tenants	18 Irish-Born Tenants
Acres	303	344	528
Acres/farm	51	69	29
Implements & machinery ($)	5,100	5,260	6,620
Implements & machinery/farm ($)	850	1,052	368
Value of productions ($)	36,700	36,384	39,900
Value of productions/ farm ($)	6,117	7,277	2,217
Fertilizer cost ($)	3,400	4,975	5,745
Fertilizer cost/farm ($)	567	995	319
Wages ($)	4,900	8,100	6,120
Wages/farm ($)	817	1,620	340
Fertilizer cost + wages as % of value of productions	23	36	30
Value of market garden produce sold ($)	28,900	25,000	34,450
Value of market garden produce sold/farm ($)	4,817	5,000	1,914
Irish potatoes (bu.)	22,500	27,200	46,300
Irish potatoes/farm (bu.)	3,750	5,440	2,572
Acres of potatoes	106	129	278
Acres of potatoes/farm	18	26	15
Bushels of potatoes/acre	212	211	167

Sources: U.S. CA, 1880, KC, Town of Flatbush, MS.

TABLE 29. *Tenure Relations on Kings County Farms, 1880*

Town	Number of Farm Operators	Owners Number	%	Tenants for Fixed Money Rental Number	%	Tenants for Shares of Products Number	%	Owners & Tenants Number	%
Flatbush	47	8	17	37	79	0	0	2	4
Flatlands	97	62	64	35	36	0	0	0	0
Gravesend	64	31	48	32	50	1	2	0	0
New Lots	80	37	46	36	45	0	0	7	9
New Utrecht	103	42	41	58	56	3	3	0	0
Total Rural Kings County	391	180	46	198	51	4	1	9	2
Brooklyn	18	1	6	16	89	1	6	0	0
Total Kings County	409	181	44	214	52	5	1	9	2

Source: CA, 1880, MS.

TABLE 30. *Kings County Farms by Tenure and Size, 1880–1910*

Total/% of column	<3 Acres	3–10 Acres	10–20 Acres	20–50 Acres	50–100 Acres	100–500 Acres
			1880 Cultivated by Owner			
189/47%	6/37.5%	16/50%	35/37%	90/46%	37/60%	5/71%
			Rented			
217/53%	10/62.5%	16/50%	60/63%	104/54%	25/40%	2/29%
			1890 Cultivated by Owner			
141/46%		20/61%	28/47%	43/32%	33/53%	17/89%
			Rented			
166/54%		13/39%	32/53%	90/68%	29/47%	2/11%
			1900 Cultivated by Owner			
188/52%						
			Rented			
172/48%						
			1910 Cultivated by Owner			
68/62%						
			Rented			
42/38%						

Sources: DI, CO, *Report on . . . Agriculture . . . Tenth Census*, tab. V at 76–77; DI, CO, *Report on . . . Agriculture . . . Eleventh Census*, tab. 5 at 166–67; USCO, *Twelfth Census*, vol. 5, pt. I at 106–7; USBC, *Thirteenth Census*, vol. VII, tab. 2 at 206.

TABLE 31. *Structure of Farm Proprietorship, 1880 and 1890*

| Indicator | Kings County | | New York State % |
	%	Rank by County	
Owned farms as % of all, 1880	47	lowest	83
Farm-owning families as % of all farming families, 1890	45	2nd lowest	77
% of all farming families owning unincumbered, 1890	32	2nd lowest	43
% of all farming families owning incumbered, 1890	13	lowest	34
% of owning families owning unincumbered, 1890	71	4th highest	56

Source: CO, *Report on Farms and Homes: Proprietorship and Indebtedness . . . Eleventh Census*, tab. 94 at 270, tab. 96 at 309.

TABLE 32. *Sales of Farms in New Utrecht, 1889*

Farm	Acreage	Price ($)	Price/Acre ($)
Cortelyou	130	182,000	1,400
Sharp	11	15,400	1,400
Cropsey	30	42,000	1,400
Gelston	9	12,600	1,400
Stevenson	40	56,000	1,400
Gubner-Sieger	60	91,500	1,525
Suydam	47	63,450	1,350
Du Bois	12	16,200	1,350
Martin	16	24,000	1,500
Aaron Lott	47.5	61,750	1,300
Total	402.5	564,900	1,403

The price per acre figures were calculated based on the other data in the article.
Source: "A Land Boom in New Utrecht," *RERBG*, 44 (1136): 1700 (Dec. 21, 1889).

TABLE 33A. *Costs of Farms of 1889 New Utrecht Landboomers in 1879–80*

Name	Age	Improved Acres	Value of Farm	Value per Acre	Fertilizer Cost 1879	Wages 1879	Total Costs (= Fertilizer + Wages × 1.3)
Andrew G. Cropsey	77	67	14,000	209	1,700	3,600	6,890
Andrew J. Cropsey	52	15	4,500	300	350	300	845
William Cropsey	53	15	4,500	300	370	500	1,131
William Sieger	65	40	8,000	200	550	1,710	2,938
Adolph Gubner	57	58	9,700	167	800	1,500	2,990
Evart Suydam	21	12	6,000	500	100	400	650
Isaac Martin	64	46	11,000	239	500	1,000	1950
Aaron Lott	52	51	11,500	225	900	1,300	2,860

TABLE 33B. *Profits of Farms of 1889 New Utrecht Landboomers in 1879–80*

Name	Value of Productions ($) 1879	Profit (= Value of Productions − Total Costs) ($) 1879	Ratio of Farm Value to Profit	Value of Productions per Acre ($)	Profit per Acre ($)	Tax Assessment ($) 1879
Andrew G. Cropsey	9,506	2,616	5	142	39	n.a.
Andrew J. Cropsey	1,800	955	5	120	64	n.a.
William Cropsey	2,000	869	5	133	58	n.a.
William Sieger	3,500	562	14	88	14	47.44
Adolph Gubner	5,500	2,510	4	95	43	118.13
Evart Suydam	1,500	850	7	125	71	163.05
Isaac Martin	6,000	4,050	3	130	88	37.39
Aaron Lott	4,000	1,140	10	78	22	137.73

Since it is not clear which Cropsey farm was sold, Andrew J. and William Cropsey are included in the table although only Andrew G.'s acreage was large enough to have encompassed the 30 acres sold. *Sources*: U.S. CP, 1880, KC, NU, MS; U.S. CA, 1880, KC, NU, MS; ARTNU, 1880.

TABLE 34. *Tax Assessments for New Utrecht Landboom Farmers, 1888–90*

Name/Year	Acres	Valuation ($)	Valuation per Acre ($)	Tax ($)	Tax Rate (%)	Tax per Acre ($)	Location	Buyer
Gubner (estate of)								
1888	43	11,550	269	233.77	2.02	5.44	13th Ave. & 75th St.	
	0.75	1,500	2,000	30.36	2.02			
1889	38.65	10,460	271	123.26	1.18	3.19	13th Ave. & 75th St.	
	0.75	1,500	2,000	17.68	1.18			
	4.35	1,090	251	15.38	1.41	3.54		
	1.90	765	403	13.25	1.73			Bay Ridge Park Improvement Co.
	2.45	1,075	439	18.66	1.74			Bay Ridge Park Improvement Co.
1890	38.65	16,260	421	258.18	1.59	6.68	13th Ave. & 75th St.	Bay Ridge Park Improvement Co.
Sieger								
1888	16.43	5,135	313	103.93	2.02	6.33	13th Ave.	
	16.43	4,710	287	55.50	1.18	3.38	13th Ave.	
	16.43	7,050	429	111.94	1.59	6.81	13th Ave.	Bay Ridge Park Improvement Co.

Year							Location	Company
Martin								
1888	5.62	1,405	250	29.38	2.09	5.23	10th Ave. & 72d St.	
	0.82	205	250	4.65	2.27			
	10.87	3,515	323	79.78	2.27	7.34	10th Ave. & 70th St.	
1889	5.62	1,405	250	19.82	1.41	3.53		
1890	5.62	2,810	500	48.77	1.74	8.68	10th Ave. & 72d St.	Bay Ridge Park Improvement Co.
Lott, A. (estate of)								
1888	30.00	16,000	533	363.15	2.27	12.10	20th Ave. & 65th St.	
1889	4.38	1,095	250	12.90	1.18	2.95	20th Ave. & 66th St.	
	23.62	16,665	706	235.08	1.41	9.95	20th Ave. & 55th St.	
1890	4.38	1,750	400	27.79	1.59	6.34		Murphy & McCormick
Suydam (heirs of)								
1889	57.06	16,265	285	191.66	1.18	3.36	20th Ave. & 75th St.	

Blank squares indicate that the datum was not identifiable. *Source:* ARTNU, 1888 at 74, 75, 140, 191, 322; ARTNU, 1889 at 1, 84, 253, 368; ARTNU, 1890 at 1:1, 154, 430.

TABLE 35. *Old-Line Dutch Farm Owners in Flatbush, 1879–80*

Name	Age	Tilled Acres	Value of Farm	Value per Acre	Fertilizer Cost 1879	Wages 1879	Total Costs (= Fertilizer + Wages × 1.3)	Value of Productions 1879	Profit (= Value of Production − Total Costs)	Ratio of Farm Value to Profit
Cornelius Suydam	77	46	25,000	543	700	1,000	2,210	6,200	3,990	6
Peter Neefus	50	81	42,000	519	400	700	1,430	4,500	3,070	14
William Williamson	62	56	28,000	500	800	1,000	2,340	10,000	7,660	4
George Schenck	35	20	10,000	500	300	500	1,040	3,000	1,960	5
John Schenck	53	20	10,000	500	400	500	1,170	3,000	1,830	5
John Vanderveer	78	80	50,000	625	800	1,200	2,600	10,000	7,400	7

Source: U.S. CP, 1880, KC, Flatbush, MS; U.S. CA, 1880, KC, Flatbush, MS.

TABLE 36. *Taxes and Profits of Old-Line Dutch Farmers in Flatbush, 1879*

Farmer	Tax Rate (%)	Tax ($)	Profit ($)	Tax/Profit (%)
Suydam	0.99	152.46	3,990	3.8
Neefus	0.99	408.91	3,070	13.3
Williamson	0.99	211.14	7,660	2.8
G. Schenck	0.99	77.78	1,960	4.0
J. Schenck	0.99	93.17	1,830	5.1
Vanderveer	1.27	490.68	7,400	6.6

Source: ARTF, 1879 at 13, 46; table 35.

TABLE 37. *Taxpayers with Taxable Incomes in Excess of $4,000 in Rural Kings County, 1869*

Taxable Income	Name	Occupation	Town
42,708.23	Ridley, Edward	Fancy & millinery goods	Gravesend
36,610.73	Gray, Joseph W.	Tobacconist	Flatbush
17,490.43	Hope, George T.	Insurance firm president	New Utrecht
16,909.50	Ludlow, Elizabeth (estate of)	Heiress	Flatbush
15,068.57	Murphy, Henry C.	Lawyer	New Utrecht
14,181.04	Armstrong, Edward	Linen merchant	New Utrecht
14,118.21	Lefferts, John	None (capitalist)	Flatbush
13,841.54	McNell, Thomas	Hotelkeeper	Flatlands
12,276.32	Matthews, William	Bookbindery operator	Flatbush
12,057.16	Wade, William	Retired merchant	Flatbush
10,761.47	Brown, William	Hops dealer	Flatbush
10,713.81	Lott, John A.	Lawyer and landlord	Flatbush
10,531.90	Hincken, Edward	Ship broker	Flatbush
10,346.94	Bullocke, John	Linen importer	New Utrecht
10,178.41	Shaffer, George H.	Hotelkeeper	Flatbush
10,030.06	Johnson, Henry	Bookstore owner	Gravesend
9,906.24	Roberts, Daniel	Lawyer and farmer	New Utrecht
8,817.05	Garvin, Edwin	Custom broker	Flatbush
8,441.37	Story, Martense	Clerk	Flatbush
7,962.16	Martense, Helen	Heiress	Flatbush
7,711.45	Lyles, Henry, Jr.	Merchant	Flatbush
7,454.77	Story, Joseph S.	None	Flatbush
6,944.63	Bergen, Tunnis J.	None	Flatbush
6,502.32	Prince, John D.	Paint dealer	Flatbush
6,232.30	Lott, Catharine L.	Housekeeper	Flatbush
6,119.02	Perry, Joseph	Greenwood cemetery controller	New Utrecht
5,543.97	Lott, Abraham	Lawyer	Flatbush
5,375.60	Kent, Edward	Stockbroker	New Utrecht
5,051.40	Wyckoff, T. S. (Estate of)	(Dead)	New Lots
4,757.30	Bennett, J. Remsen	Retired farmer	New Utrecht
4,641.89	Davies, James	Gum manufacturer	New Lots
4,427.89	Mackay, J. S.	Broker	New Utrecht
4,380.01	Schoonmaker, Richard	Grocer	Flatbush
4,294.81	Birkner, Joachim	Lithographic tool importer	New Lots
4,237.52	Thomas, S. W.	Cigar importer	New Utrecht
4,206.83	Winslow, David	Lawyer	New Utrecht
4,200.00	Mays, John	Machinist	Flatbush
4,194.90	Ryerson, Jacob	Farmer	Flatlands

Source: ALFBIR, 1869–70.

TABLE 38. *Taxpayers with the 10 Highest Taxable Incomes in Rural Kings County, 1862–65, 1870–71*

	1862				1863		
Name	Income	Occupation	Town	Name	Income	Occupation	Town
Fox, Robert R.	102,287.52	Merchant	Flatbush	Keyser, Samuel	50,000	Dry goods merchant	New Utrecht
Keyser, Samuel	32,180.11	Dry goods merchant	New Utrecht	Longmire, Jonathan	38,781.08	Dry goods merchant	Flatbush
Langley, William	20,850	Dry goods merchant	New Utrecht	Langley, William	27,300	Dry goods merchant	New Utrecht
Young, Archibald	14,560.92	Clothing mfr	New Utrecht	Hoag, Harvey	15,052.53	Wool buyer	New Lots
Spedding, Robert	13,130	Dry goods merchant	New Utrecht	Fox, Robert R.	14,332.31	Merchant	Flatbush
Sykes, John	9,000	Hotel owner	New Utrecht	Matthews, William	13,858	Bookbindery operator	Flatbush
Lyles, Henry	8,131.70	Merchant	Flatbush	Johnson, Henry	13,550	Book dealer	Gravesend
Lynch, Peter	7,900	Wholesale grocer	New Utrecht	Spedding, Robert	12,649	Merchant	New Utrecht
Hope, George	7,660.74	Insurance firm president	New Utrecht	Lyles, Henry	12,322.21	Merchant	Flatbush
Brown, William	7,400	Hops dealer	Flatbush	Sykes, John	9,877.29	Hotel owner	New Utrecht

(*continued*)

TABLE 38. (*continued*)

	1864				1865		
Name	Income	Occupation	Town	Name	Income	Occupation	Town
Langley, William C.	33,350	Dry goods merchant	New Utrecht	Longmire, Jonathan	48,683.78	Dry goods merchant	Flatbush
Keyser, Samuel	30,000	Dry goods merchant	New Utrecht	Wild, Joseph	35,228.40	Carpet importer	New Utrecht
Longmire, Johnathan	27,726.43	Dry goods merchant	Flatbush	Keyser, Samuel	33,712	Dry goods merchant	New Utrecht
Wild, Joseph	23,616	Carpet importer	New Utrecht	Langley, William C.	33,400	Dry goods merchant	New Utrecht
Kattenhorn, H. H.	21,729	Refiner	New Lots	Young, Archibald	23,956.80	Clothing mfr	New Utrecht
Ridley, Edward	16,826.30	Dry goods merchant	Gravesend	Ludlow, Elizabeth	20,761.24	Heiress	Flatbush
Matthews, William	16,337.75	Bookbindery operator	Flatbush	Lyles, Henry	20,449	Merchant	Flatbush
Thomas, William H.	12,945	Cigar importer	New Utrecht	Kattenhorn, Herman H.	18,503.10	Refiner	New Lots
Perry, J. A.	12,403.68	Greenwood cemetery controller	New Utrecht	Ridley, Edward	17,994.57	Dry goods merchant	Gravesend
Johnson, Henry	12,000	Book dealer	Flatbush	Bullocke, John	14,271.79	Linen importer	New Utrecht

1870

Name	Income	Occupation	Town
Ridley, Edward	27,520	Dry goods merchant	Gravesend
Gray, Joseph	21,056.64	Tobacconist	Flatbush
McNell, Thomas	18,718	Hotel owner	Flatlands
Murphy, Henry C.	17,408.26	Lawyer	New Utrecht
Lefferts, John	14,506.65	Capitalist	Flatbush
Johnson, Henry	12,000	Book dealer	Gravesend
Matthews, William	11,023.36	Bookbinder	Flatbush
Roberts, Daniel	10,509.95	Lawyer	New Utrecht
Lott, Abraham	9,040.21	Lawyer	Flatbush
Garvin, Edwin	8,678	Custom broker	Flatbush

1871

Name	Income	Occupation	Town
McNell, Thomas	24,142.05	Hotel owner	Flatlands
Lefferts, John	16,806.44	Capitalist	Flatbush
Westfall, Diedrich	16,804.08	Merchant	Flatbush
Hincken, Edward	14,325.73	Ship broker	Flatbush
Prince, John	13,458.87	Paint dealer	Flatbush
Gray, Joseph	12,317.80	Tobacconist	Flatbush
Matthews, William	10,197.89	Bookbinder	Flatbush
Johnson, Henry	9,000	Book dealer	Gravesend
Garvin, Edwin	7,888.25	Custom broker	Flatbush
Longmire, Jonathan	7,476.37	Dry goods dealer	Flatbush

Sources: ALFBIR, 1863–71.

ABBREVIATIONS

AAAPSS	*Annals of the American Academy of Political and Social Science*
AH	*Agricultural History*
ALFBIR	Assessment Lists of the Federal Bureau of Internal Revenue
AR	Assessment Roll
ARSESSNY	*Annual Report of the State Engineer and Surveyor of the State of New York*
ARTF	Assessment Roll of the Town of Flatbush
ARTFl	Assessment Roll of the Town of Flatlands
ARTNU	Assessment Roll of the Town of New Utrecht
BBGR	*Brooklyn Botanic Garden Record*
BC	Bureau of the Census
BDE	*Brooklyn Daily Eagle*
BDEA	*Brooklyn Daily Eagle Almanac*
BDU	*Brooklyn Daily Union*
BE	*Brooklyn Eagle*
BEA	Bureau of Economic Analysis
BHS	Brooklyn Historical Society
CA	Census of Agriculture
CD	Collection District
CG	*Congressional Globe*
CO	Census Office
CP	Census of Population
CSNY	*Census of the State of New York*
DA	Department of Agriculture
DAB	*Dictionary of American Biography*
DI	Department of the Interior
DS	Department of State
ED	Enumeration District
EG	*Economic Geography*
EHR	*Economic History Review*
ERS	Economic Research Service
FTC	Federal Trade Commission
GR	*Geography Review*
HJRART	*Horticulturist and Journal of Rural Art and Rural Taste*
HNMM	*Harper's New Monthly Magazine*
IA	*Irish-American*
IR	Internal Revenue
IRS	Internal Revenue Service
JASNY	*Journal of the Assembly of the State of New York*
JLIH	*Journal of Long Island History*
JSSNY	*Journal of the Senate of the State of New York*
KC	Kings County
KCG	*Kings County Gazette*

KCRBG	*Kings County Rural and Brighton Gazette/Brooklyn Gazette*
KCRG	*Kings County Rural Gazette*
LBDBKC	*Lain's Business Directory of Brooklyn, Kings County*
LDLI	*Lain's Directory of Long Island*
LIHJ	*Long Island Historical Journal*
LIHSQ	*Long Island Historical Society Quarterly*
MR	Microfilm Roll
MS	Manuscript Schedules
NA	National Archives
NL	New Lots
NLAR	New Lots Assessment Roll
NU	New Utrecht
NUAR	New Utrecht Assessment Roll
NY	New York
NYCMA	New York City Municipal Archives
NYDT	*New York Daily Tribune*
NYGBR	*New York Genealogical and Biographical Record*
NYH	*New York Herald*
NYHS	New-York Historical Society
NYPL	New York Public Library
NYRO	New York Regional Office
NYS	New York State
NYSDA	New York State Department of Agriculture
NYT	*New York Times*
NYTrib	*New York Tribune*
PS	Population Schedules
RERBG	*Real Estate Record and Builders' Guide*
RG	Record Group
RO	Regional Office
SC	Superintendent of the Census
SD	Supervisor's District
SI	Secretary of the Interior
SM	*Scribner's Monthly*
SUSC	Superintendent of the United States Census
TMHS	*Transactions of the Massachusetts Horticultural Society*
TNYCD	*Trow's New York City Directory*
TNYSAS	*Transactions of the New York State Agricultural Society*
TRKC	Town Records of Kings County
UD	Unbound Documents
USBC	United States Bureau of the Census
USBEA	United States Bureau of Economic Analysis
USBS	United States Bureau of Soils
USCO	United States Census Office
USDA	United States Department of Agriculture

NOTES

1. Introduction: Urban Removal of Agriculture

1. Daniel M. Tredwell, "Kings County in Fact, Legend and Tradition," ch. 2 at 7–8 (BHS). The rough draft of these reminiscences goes back to 1890. Ibid. at 4.
2. "Development," *KCRG*, Feb. 22, 1873, 4:1–2 (editorial). The particular rapid transit project alluded to, that of the Brooklyn Steam Transit Company, did not come to fruition. James Walker, *Fifty Years of Rapid Transit 1864–1917* at 274–75.
3. "Development" 4:2 (quote); William Younger, *Old Brooklyn in Early Photographs, 1865–1929* at 90 (quote); Elizabeth Johns, "The Farmer in the Works of William Sidney Mount" 276 (referring to Long Island in 1830) (quote); U.S. Geological Survey, Topographic Sheet: New York, Brooklyn Quadrant.
4. Adna Weber, *Growth of Cities in the Nineteenth Century* 162, 223 (quotes); Carl Bridenbaugh, *Cities in the Wilderness* 174.
5. *The WPA Guide to New York City* 432; Green Point Savings Bank, *Historic Flatbush* 18 (quote); "Parkville," *KCRBG*, July 22, 1882, 2:3 (quote); "New Utrecht," *KCRBG*, Sept. 9, 1882, 2:6 (quote); G. Warren Hamilton, "History of the Town of New Lots," in Henry Stiles, *The Civil . . . History* 306 (quote); "The 'Truck' Gardens and Market," *Frank Leslie's Illustrated Newspaper*, Nov. 17, 1888, at 218–19 (quotes).
6. "Teaching City Children How to Become Farmers," *NYT*, July 28, 1905, pt. 3 (Mag.), 5:1; Gustave Straubenmüller, *A Home Geography of New York City* 65; "The Economic Garden," *BBGR*, 2:101 (1913).
7. Illustrative of such urban histories are Sam Bass Warner Jr., *The Private City*; Robert Fogelson, *The Fragmented Metropolis*. An historian of Gravesend who fails to devote a single word to farming gratuitously writes of the 1930s: "Where once corn stalks grew, iron and cement were now taking over as the Industrial Revolution seized the once tranquil community." Eric Ierardi, *Gravesend: The Home of Coney Island* 143. For a study of a transformation not dealing with the economics of farming, see Vincent Seyfried, *Corona*. Wendy Futterman, "Which Came First" 99, overlooks Kings County's massively agrarian character by supposing that in the absence of mass transit, Brooklyn "might be the same as it was in 1860, a series of unsold lots."
8. Eleonora Schoenebaum, "Emerging Neighborhoods" ii; Russell Bastedo, "Introduction" 7; Jane Corby, "Impact Is Widespread When a Housing Project Rises," *BE*, Dec. 4, 1949, sect. 2 at 25:1, 3.
9. Edwin Spengler, *Land Values in New York in Relation to Transit Facilities* 109 (quote); Peter Ross, *History of Long Island* 1:523 (quotes); "Farms Disappear in Dyckman Area," *NYT*, Nov. 11, 1928, sect. 12 at 1:1 (quotes).
10. Franklin J. Sherman, *Building Up Greater Queens Borough* 64; Harlan Douglass, *The Suburban Trend* 3.
11. Henry Stiles, *Civil . . . History* 1:38 (quotes); USBC, *Historical Statistics of the United States*, pt. 1, ser. D167–81 at 139. Nevertheless, as late as 1837, only one-sixth of Manhattan was covered with buildings and paved streets, the remainder

being farms and gardens. Edward Bergman and Thomas Pohl, *A Geography of the New York Metropolitan Region* 39. On market gardening in Manhattan, especially as carried on by German immigrants, see Robert Ernst, *Immigrant Life in New York City 1825–1863* at 70.

12. David Ward and Olivier Zunz, "Between Rationalism and Pluralism" 3.

13. Malcolm Thick, "Market Gardening in England and Wales" 503 (quote); F. J. Fisher, "The Development of the London Food Market, 1540–1640" at 54 (quote); Ronald Webber, *Market Gardening* 29–48; Howard Russell, *A Long, Deep Furrow* 374–76; Ronald Karr, "The Transformation of Agriculture in Brookline, 1770–1885"; USDA, ERS, *Urbanization of Land in the Northeastern United States;* William Lockeretz, "New Life for Metro Farming" 81 (quote).

14. Philip Shenon, "Good Earth Is Squandered: Who'll Feed China?" *NYT*, Sept. 21, 1994, sect. 4 at 4:3 (Lexis).

15. W. P. Hedden, *How Great Cities Are Fed* xv (quote); Karl Marx and Friedrich Engels, *Die deutsche Ideologie* 50; Thomas Adams, *Outline of Town and City Planning* 151.

16. John Baden, "Regulating Agricultural Land Use" 149–50, 147–48 (quote).

17. William Fischel, "Urban Development and Agricultural Land Markets" 83 (quote); Raymond Dasmann, *The Destruction of California* 126 (quote); David Wallace et al., *Metropolitan Open Space and Natural Process* 38 (quotes). Fischel reveals that an ideological construction of human nature underlies the claim that profit seeking creates the closest approximation to complete knowledge: "The only advantage that speculators have over anyone else, including planning officials, is that if they guess right, they make money. If they guess wrong, they lose money. I submit that it is difficult to overestimate the power of the prospect of making or losing money in focusing the energies of people on gathering market information." Fischel, "Urban Development and Agricultural Land Markets" 89.

18. Donald Bogue, *Metropolitan Growth and the Conversion of Land to Nonagricultural Uses* 18 (quote); *Politics of Land* 27–32; Paul Relis, "Land Disputes and the Urban-Rural Border" 173; M. Reynells, "Urban Sprawl as It Affects the Southern California Poultry Industry" 65–74; Dasmann, *Destruction of California* 135 (quote).

19. Allan Pred, *The External Relations of Cities During 'Industrial Revolution'* 44–45 (quote); John Thompson, "The Primary Sector" 217 (quote), 203.

20. A. M. Woodruff and Charles Frink, "Introduction" 1–2.

21. C. Lowell Harriss, "Free Market Allocation of Resources" 129 (quote); "Editorial Notes," *KCRBG*, June 3, 1882, 2:1; Ellsworth Huntington, "The Water Barriers of New York City" 179, 181.

22. Marion Clawson and Peter Hall, *Planning and Urban Growth* 20, 28–29 (quote). For a sketch of the profitability of the early years of citrus plantations in Southern California, see Carey McWilliams, *Southern California Country* 205–26. The consumption of housing in certain locations can help reproduce labor power by enabling workers to get to work more quickly or conveniently. Thus demand for housing land is partly determined by how many people want to reside at what

distance (time and space) from workplaces and other amenities at what price(s). The time spent getting to possible workplaces is related to income per hour; this variable can, in turn, be expressed as a proportion of income, which would translate into different rents for each social-income class. In advocating rapid transit in 1873, the *KCRG* noted that "'if time is money,' (we might even save by it)." "Bonding the Town,"*KCRG*, Feb. 1, 1873, 4:1 (editorial).

23. For discussion of the expansion process in the New York Metropolitan Region, see Edgar Hoover and Raymond Vernon, *Anatomy of a Metropolis* 183–255.

24. Ernst Freund, "Discussion" (quote); David Johnson, *Planning the Great Metropolis* 26 (quote); Mel Scott, *American City Planning Since 1890* at 152; S. Makielski Jr., *The Politics of Zoning* 11 (quote); Lewis Mumford, *The City in History* 426 (quote). The city planning movement dates from 1905. R. D. McKenzie, "The Rise of Metropolitan Communities" 481–82. The state legislature amended the Greater New York charter in 1914 to authorize the Board of Estimate to regulate and restrict the location of trades and industries. 1914 N.Y. Laws, ch. 470 at 1943, 1944.

25. Staff of the Regional Plan of New York and Its Environs, vol. 1, *Regional Plan: The Graphic Regional Plan: Atlas and Description* 383–84 (quote); Benjamin Chinitz, "New York" 114 (quote); Lewis Mumford, *The Highway and the City* 227 (quote); Robert Caro, *The Power Broker* 943 (quote).

26. Ella Ödman and Gun-Britt Dahlberg, *Urbanization in Sweden* 58–60, 81–84; Mumford, *The Highway and the City* 237.

27. James Sundquist, *Dispersing Population* 256, 258.

28. "The March of Improvements," *KCRG*, May 24, 1873, 4:1, 2 (editorial); "A New County," *KCRG*, Apr. 12, 1873, 4:1, 2 (editorial). A few years later, however, the *Rural Gazette* was constrained to adopt a less mechanistic view of development, conceding a need "to encourage Capital to line our streets with cosy cottages and handsome dwellings" and a place to human agency: "the time is approaching when our town must either take a leap forward toward prosperity, or sink backward into 'stagnation.'" "Public Enterprise vs. Private Advantage," *KCRG*, Feb. 15, 1879, 2:1, 2 (editorial).

29. A Brooklyn-born historian of Brooklyn attributed historical amnesia in part to an educational bias: "As far as school was concerned, history was . . . not anything that might have been made by people like you or me or anyone we knew or were descended from. History was . . . memorizing names and dates, battles and places, kings and queens — but not the boroughs, thank you." Elliott Wilensky, *When Brooklyn Was the World* 41.

30. Late-nineteenth- and early-twentieth-century publications did not follow a uniform nomenclature, but the following distinction made by a USDA horticulturist is useful: whereas market gardening is "the production of large quantities of a great variety of standard vegetables and small fruits to supply the demands of a local market," "[t]ruck farming is more restricted in its scope, is usually more extensive, and has chiefly to do with a few standard crops which yield large returns per acre and which can be shipped to distant markets." He mentioned among truck crops: cabbage, spinach, potatoes, eggplant, cucumbers, lettuce,

beets, and cauliflower. Lee Corbett, *Garden Farming* 1. By World War II, standard works still emphasized that market gardening was intensive culture on high-priced land compelling farmers to maximize returns per square foot. Ralph Watts and Gilbert Watts, *The Vegetable Growing Business* 1. Others regarded truck farming as "simply market gardening on a large scale." F. Earle, "Development of the Trucking Interests" 437. Although the majority of Kings County farmers were market gardeners, only the enumerator for the 1870 CP for New Lots used the term, designating 12 farmers as "market gardener" or "farm gardener," most of whom were German-born; in 1880, the description was also used for one German farmer in New Lots.

2. Kings County Farms

1. Jay Bonsteel et al., "Soil Survey of the Long Island Area" 95 (quote); Moreau de Saint-Méry, *Voyage aux États-Unis de l'Amérique, 1793–1798* at 188–89. Robert Albion, *The Rise of New York Port* 125 (quote); William Strickland, *Journal of a Tour in the United States of America 1794–1795* at 41 (quote); Gertrude Lefferts Vanderbilt, *The Social History of Flatbush* 269 (quote).

2. 1813 N.Y. Laws, ch. 101 at 46, 47–48; Benjamin Thompson, *History of Long Island* 3:81–273; Linda Biemer, "Lady Deborah Moody and the Founding of Gravesend"; John A. Kouwenhoven, "Brooklyn Before the Bridge" 12; 1788 N.Y. Laws, ch. 64 at 151, 152–53. "Flatbush" was an Anglicization of "'t Vlacke Bos," an alternative name for "Midwout," which survives as the name of neighborhood's southern section. Charles Andrews, *The Colonial Period of American History* 3:79, erroneously referred to them as two different villages. "Flatlands" was the later English name for the Dutch "Nieuw Amersfoort." Maud Dilliard, "A Village Called Midwout." The last Flatbush town meeting minutes recorded in Dutch took place April 4, 1775. TRKC, Translations/Transliterations, Flatbush, Court Minutes, 1679–1681, Town Meeting Minutes, 1762–1818, vol. 107 at 108, 112. Cornelius B. Couwenhoven, a descendant of one of the original settlers, spoke no English until he attended school and still spoke Dutch with his family as late as 1865. Thompson, *History of Long Island* 3:146.

3. Albion, *The Rise of New York Port*; Wells Sherman, *Merchandising Fruits and Vegetables* 14–15.

4. For part of the nineteenth century, data are available at five-year intervals because the NYS census, which was conducted at mid-decade, included an agricultural component from 1825 to 1875. Methodological or other differences between the federal and state censuses may have rendered data series from the two sources not strictly comparable, but generally trends within each census appear similar. For an account of the growth in the details into which the federal agricultural censuses inquired from 1840 to 1890, see Carroll Wright, *The History and Growth of the United States Census* 99–106, 233–304. From the Tenth Census (1880) forward, production, harvest, and expense data were collected for the full year preceding the census (e.g., 1879), whereas data on acreage and land val-

ues referred to the year in which the enumeration was actually conducted. This procedure eliminated the confusion that had tainted previous census data:

> The schedule annexed to and made a part of the law of 1850 requires the products of each farm in the United States "for the year ending June 1." But there is no agricultural year ending June 1. The division made by the law is a purely artificial one, and cuts the agricultural year in twain.
>
> As a matter of fact, as the census under existing laws always has been and always will be taken, the production returned is not the production of any one year distinctly, but is made up, without any determinable proportion, indifferently from the production of two years.
>
> The enumeration at the Ninth Census, for example, beginning upon the 1st of June, assistant marshals obtain for a month or two the production of 1869 in the main, although in some sections many of the crops . . . are already so far advanced that the farmer is quite as likely to estimate his annual production (it must be remembered that few of the statistics of production are obtained as transcripts from actual accounts) from his impressions in regard to the growing crop, as by recalling the experience of the previous year. As the enumeration progresses through September and October, the crop of 1870 is returned in increasing proportion, earlier in some parts of the country than in others. . . . As the work is protracted through November and December, and through the utter want of control at the central office, is allowed to drag, in some counties, through January and February, the crop of 1870 becomes the only one that is in contemplation of either the farmer of the assistant marshal in filling up the agricultural schedule.

SC, *Ninth Census*, vol. III:71–72. The 1870 CA was conducted between June and September in Kings County.

The 1860 CA did not expressly state the number of farms in Kings County, but it provided a table of farms with three or more acres by size, which totalled 517. SI, *Agriculture of the United States in 1860* at 209. A count of the farms in the MS for that year revealed only 436. The published tabulation included 118 farms of between 100 and 500 acres and 1 of more than 500 acres; in the MS the latter was not enumerated at all and many fewer of the former were recorded. There is a discrepancy between the published CA figure for 1870 of 298 farms and a count of the farms in the MS, which is 297. The mistake in the tabulation may have resulted from the fact that although each full sheet contained space for 40 names, the enumerator actually filled only 39 lines on the first sheet for Brooklyn. The census rubric was "name of owner, agent, or manager of the farm."

The suspicion of an undercount derives from the fact that only 46 farms in New Utrecht were returned in 1870 compared with 96 in 1860 and 103 in 1880; moreover, a number of major farmers (including Peter Cowenhoven, Andrus Monfort, and William Sieger) who were returned as farming in 1860 and 1880 were missing in 1870, although they were listed as farmers in that year's CP. If many farm(er)s were omitted in 1870, total New Utrecht production (including market garden output, the value of which fell from $127,000 to $108,000 from

1860 to 1870 while that of Kings County overall increased by 25 percent) for that year may be significantly understated. Since the enumerator of both the CP (Schedule 1) and the CA (Schedule 3) in 1870 was George Self, a well-known grocer in New Utrecht, it is unlikely that he would have overlooked his own neighbors and customers. It seems more plausible that a sheet from the manuscript schedules was lost. The published tabulations are consistent with the manuscript schedules as preserved by the National Archives on microfilm.

5. *Tenth Annual Report of the Bureau of Statistics of Labor of the State of New York, for the Year 1892*, pt. I at 208 (quote). The Federal Writers' Project noted during the Depression that a few Italian families in Bensonhurst cultivated small truck farms. *The WPA Guide to New York City* 470.

6. Table 21 below. Deagriculturalization of Kings County in the 1890s was not completely synchronized with the pattern throughout the New York–Northeastern New Jersey Standard Metropolitan Area, which overall gained 9,616 acres of harvested cropland in the 1890s but lost 56,941 acres during the 1880s — the second greatest decrement in any area in the United States. Donald Bogue, *Metropolitan Growth and the Conversion of Land to Nonagricultural Uses*, tab. III at 29. Cropland losses were even greater during the following three decades. On the much slower demise of farming in Philadelphia from a much larger base, see Regine Levitan, "Urban Agriculture" 30–31 (M.A. thesis).

7. Fred Shannon, *The Farmer's Last Frontier* 291–95 (on prices). The value of farm products for 1870 was probably overestimated because it included "betterments and additions to stock." SI, *Ninth Census*, vol. III:210. The USBC did not attempt to estimate the total value of farm products for 1909; the figure in the table is the sum of the totals for crops, livestock products, and sales and slaughter of animals. USBC, *Thirteenth Census*, vol. V:738–39; USBC, *Thirteenth Census*, vol. VII at 12. The gross value of farm products for 1919 was also not published; as a surrogate, the value of all crops and livestock products is calculated in the table. USBC, *Fourteenth Census*, vol. VI, pt. 1, county tab. I at 212, county tab. II at 218. The total value of production was withheld in 1969 to avoid disclosing this information for the one and only farm enumerated that year. BC, *1969 Census of Agriculture*, vol. 1, pt. 7, sect. 2 at 176.

8. Elliott Willensky, *When Brooklyn Was the World* 69, 77, confuses his account by stating that by the 1920s "truck farms and small orchards had largely disappeared," and then noting that "an astonishing amount of land in Brooklyn's southern tier was still being used as farms." Beginning with the 1945 CA, the USBC used pounds rather than gallons as a production standard. In order to avoid confusion, the published data for 1944, 1949, 1954, and 1959 (4,478,364, 2,940,560, 2,950,660, and 2,800,000 lb., respectively) have been converted to gallons using a conversion ratio of one gallon of whole milk = 8.6068 pounds. The total number of horses and cows in New York State did not fluctuate wildly: both rose steadily throughout the latter half of the nineteenth century. The scattered data on numbers employed, hired laborers, and wages paid to hired labor are also difficult to interpret, but the 17 percent decline in total wages from 1870

to 1900 seems plausible. These labor-related data will be supplemented in chapter 4 with data drawn from the CP.

9. Edgar Dunn Jr., *The Location of Agricultural Production* 12 (quote). For comparisons with developments in New York State, see NYS College of Agriculture, *Changes in New York State Agriculture*. For background on von Thünen, see the otherwise dogmatic work by Herbert Luck, *Zur ökonomischen Lehre des J. J. Von Thünen*.

10. Johann Heinrich von Thünen, *Der isolierte Staat* 11–15, 206–10. Von Thünen regarded manure as a substance sui generis — neither commodity nor product, because it was produced involuntarily — whose quantity could not be altered by changes in demand, and which had a negative value for its owner. He deduced that where the city's manure exceeded the needs of the nearby farms, it would give its manure to all farmers even though close-in farmers would be willing to pay for it because price differentiation would require arbitrary compulsory means inconsistent with a market.

11. Von Thünen, *Der isolierte Staat* 199, 212–13.

12. Robert Sinclair, "Von Thünen and Urban Sprawl" 76–77.

13. Stiles, *The Civil . . . History* 1:39a.

14. Vanderbilt, *Social History of Flatbush* 271.

15. The sources are the state censuses cited in tab. 1a–1b.

16. U.S. Census, 1870, Agriculture, KC, Flatbush. Jeremiah Lott was reported as having produced 35,000 bushels in 1870, but this outlier quantity is not consistent with the total value of his output. In 1872, for example, Asher Hubbard of Flatlands and William Bennett of Gravesend both averaged 200 bushels per acre on 30 to 40 and 25 acres, respectively, while two years later J. J. Ryder of Flatlands averaged 225. "Flatlands," *KCRG*, May 11, 1872, 5:2; "Potatoes," *KCRG*, July 27, 1872, 6:1; "Flatlands," *KCRG*, July 4, 1874, 8:4.

17. Teunis G. Bergen, *The Bergen Family* 108. In 1845, 12 farms of one hundred or more improved acres were returned for Flatbush, the largest being John Vanderveer's of 180 acres. State of New York, Census for the Year 1845, Flatbush, in TRKC. In Queens, German-born Ascan Backus (1814–1880) acquired seven farms totaling 460 acres; his 50 year-round employees and as many as 300 other workers produced more market garden produce (valued in some years at $100,000) than any other farm in New York State. *Long Island Times* (Flushing), Nov. 12, 1863, 2:3 (reprinted from *Rural American*); Vincent Seyfried, "Truck Gardening" 3 (unpub.). According to Lefferts Vanderbilt, *Social History of Flatbush* 230, John Lefferts's farm encompassed 300 acres in 1840; it is unclear whether it was operated as one farm. For the sake of simplicity, the term "old-line Dutch" encompasses descendants of the original English settlers in Gravesend such as the Hubbard, Lake, and Stillwell families, many of whom intermarried with members of Dutch farm families. Thompson, *History of Long Island* 3:117. The Allgeo family was originally English, but married into the Antonidas family. *The Eagle and Brooklyn* 83.

18. U.S. Census, 1850, Agriculture, reel 4; U.S. Census, 1860, Agriculture, reel 4; U.S.

Census, 1870, Agriculture, reel 5; U.S. Census, 1880, Agriculture, reel 18. The census of 1840 did not collect data on the number of farms, and farm size and the MS for the census of 1890 burned. The seven farms in New Lots in 1860 were owned by three Vanderveers, two Rapeljes, one Conover (Kouwenhoven), and one Duryea. Gravesend reported only seven farms of one hundred acres or more in 1850; the one remaining such farm in 1880 was tenant operated. According to William Fausser, *The Brooklyn and Rockaway Beach Railroad* n. p. [1], 100 acres of the Vanderveer farm were still under cultivation as late as 1899. Although the Vanderveer farms were primarily situated in New Lots, in 1884 Abram Vanderveer bought Jerome L. Bergen's 60-acre farm in Flatlands, which was intended for Vanderveer's son to operate. The $400 per acre price was at the time the highest price that had been paid for any land in that town for many years. "Flatlands," *KCRBG*, Mar. 8, 1884, 2:3.

19. NUAR, 1830, TRKC, vol. 2043, roll 43; NUAR, 1840, TRKC, vol. 2050, roll 43; NUAR, 1850, TRKC, vol. 2124, roll 43; NUAR, 1860, TRKC, vol. 2133, roll 44; NUAR, 1870, TRKC, vol. 2143, roll 45; NUAR, 1880, TRKC, vol. 2153, roll 48.

20. "Kings County Agricultural Society: Report of the Committee on Farms and Grain" 345–46.

21. That the census of 1840 found only 10 men employed in all of Kings County horticulture, in which farmers had invested only $9,400, may have been a function of the rudimentary state of both data collection and horticulture. DS, *Compendium of the Enumeration . . . of the Sixth Census* at 133. On Bennett's income, see chapter 11 below.

22. U.S. Census, 1850, Agriculture, reel 4; U.S. Census, 1860, Agriculture, reel 4; John C. Bergen Papers, Account Book; "Census," *KCRG*, Aug. 21, 1875, 2:1 (amounts of Flatlands crops); "Flatlands," *KCRG*, Oct. 16, 1875, 2:5; "Flatlands," *KCRBG*, Oct. 16, 1880, 2:5; William Bennett & Son, Farm Accounts; "Bay Ridge," *KCRG*, Sept. 4, 1875, 2:7; "New Utrecht, Bath and Unionville," *KCRG*, Oct. 28, 1876, 2:5. The 1865 state census (with data for 1864) reported that all of Kings County harvested fewer cabbages (1,205,000 valued at $86,395) than Flatlands alone in 1860; *CSNY, for 1865* at 405. Even if the figure for the later year is an underestimate, Kings County nevertheless produced more than three-fifths of the state's entire crop. John C. Bergen (born 1826) inherited Bergen's Island, which included 90 acres of upland in the salt marshes of Flatlands, from his father, Cornelius (1798–1865), who, in turn, had inherited half from his father and bought the other half from his brother's heirs. Shortly after his father's death, he bought a 15-acre farm for $10,000 from his uncle Garret Bergen. Teunis G. Bergen, *The Bergen Family* 355–57, 364. It is unclear how the *Rural Gazette* obtained the New York State CA data so far in advance of their publication; even more puzzling is how it secured data on individual crops that were never published. Since enumerators were instructed to enter information on unenumerated farm produce, including asparagus and sweet corn, but such data were not published, presumably the newspaper had access to the enumerator's census schedules. Secretary of State, *Instructions for the Taking of the Census of the State of New York in the Year 1875* at 41–42. For an advertisement of sweet corn for sale by a Flatlands

farmer, see *KCRG*, July 10, 1880, 2:8. Tunis Kouwenhoven, a Flatlands farmer, sold asparagus to groceries in the city. "Flatlands," *KCRG*, June 7, 1884, 2:3.

23. D. W. Meinig, "Geography of Expansion" 166; Adriance Van Brunt, Diary; U.S. Census, 1850, Agriculture, reel 4, Ninth Ward, Brooklyn City (quote); Ralph Gabriel, *The Evolution of Long Island* 59 (quote).

24. J. L. Van Zanden, *The Tranformation of European Agriculture* 151–57, 113, 92 (quote).

25. *TNYSAS*, 12 (1852):535–36 (speech of John King) (quotes). See also Jeffrey Kroessler, "Building Queens: The Urbanization of New York's Largest Borough" 97–98, 93 (Ph.D. diss.). On the railway's extension of New York City's milkshed to as far away as Rutland, Vermont, see *Report of the Commissioner of Agriculture for the Year 1872* at 332. An *Eagle* editorial suggesting that, because it was more profitable to grow wheat near to the market with fertilizer than two thousand miles away on lands that cost next to nothing and need no manure, Long Island could or perhaps should produce as much wheat as then cultivated in all New York State, must have been fantastic even at the time. "The Future of Long Island Farm Lands," *BDE*, Nov. 15, 1873, 2:3.

26. U. P. Hedrick, *A History of Horticulture in America to 1860* at 241 (quotes); L. Bradford Prince, "Sketch of the Agricultural History of Queens County" 278 (quotes).

27. *TNYSAS*, 12 (1852):545–46.

28. 1859 N.Y. Laws, ch. 312 at 702; *First Annual Report of the State Assessors* 6–7 (quotes).

29. Theodore Peters, *A Report on the Agricultural and Other Resources of the State of New York* 262–63, 269 (quotes); "Street Cattle Nuisance," *KCRG*, Aug. 2, 1873, 4:2; "Street Cattle Nuisance," *KCRG*, July 26, 1873, 8:2; "Street Cattle Nuisance," *KCRG*, Aug. 9, 1873, 4:3; "Cows on the Sidewalk," *KCRG*, Aug. 22, 1874, 4:3.

30. Peters, *Report on the Agricultural and Other Resources of the State of New York* 260 (quote); *Fourth Annual Report of State Assessors*, tab. A at 87. Peters' perspective received an interesting confirmation from the fact that the same year a group of Brooklyn citizens, many of whom were descendants of Dutch settlers, founded the Long Island (today Brooklyn) Historical Society because they feared that rapid urban growth would destroy the area's past. Bastedo, "Introduction" 7.

31. H. Cleveland, "Notes on the Market Gardening of New Jersey" 403 (quotes); Michael Sullivan, "The Advancement of Market Gardening in the Past Twenty-Five Years" 65 (quote); Peter Henderson, "Market Gardening in the Vicinity of New York" 243 (quote); A. Oemler, *Truck-Farming at the South* 163–65 (quote at 165); Percy Bidwell and John Falconer, *History of Agriculture in the Northern United States* 260–61, 450; Paul Gates, *The Farmer's Age* 256, 269; Shannon, *The Farmer's Last Frontier* 259. As late as 1915, special railroad trains to New York City ran daily during the season collecting cauliflower from Long Island. W. Nissley, "Vegetable Growing on Long Island" 1229.

32. Clarence Danhof, *Change in Agriculture* 147–48.

33. "Farming and Market Gardening"

34. "Farms Near New York," *RERBG*, 3 (15):4 (June 26, 1869) (quote); P. T. Quinn,

Money in the Garden 72 (quote); Landreth, *Market Gardening and Farm Notes* 9; CO, *Report on the Statistics of Agriculture in the United States at the Eleventh Census* 595.

35. CO, *Twelfth Census*, vol. VI, pt. II at 300–302. The value per acre figures were not published and are calculated here for the sake of completeness. Acreage data on market gardening were not collected for the crucial last third of the nineteenth century, thus making it impossible to know how value per acre developed. The extraordinary fall in the value of market garden production between 1879 and 1890 is curious. Market garden production amounted to only 18 percent of the value of total production in 1890 compared with 70 percent in 1879; it is unclear what other production could have made up the difference. The cost of fertilizer amounted to 71 percent of the value of market garden production in 1890 compared with only 25 percent in 1879. In Queens County, which also suffered a very large drop in production, fertilizer cost even exceeded the value of market garden production. In fact, blight and rot in 1889–90 created the most serious and general loss of potatoes in New York State since 1849–50. *Forty-Ninth Annual Report of the New York State Agricultural Society* 9–11; *Fiftieth Annual Report of the New York State Agricultural Society* 9–11. The sharp decline in the 1920s may be overstated because the value of vegetable production in 1929 (and 1939) excluded that of potatoes. The value of vegetable production inferentially or definitely excluded potatoes in 1854, 1860, 1864, 1879, and 1899, but included it in 1919; for other years it is not clear, but the various rubrics seem to suggest that potatoes' value may have been excluded. The 1875 state census instructed enumerators to collect data on the acreage and value of market gardens but failed to publish them. Secretary of State, *Instructions for Taking the Census* 40–41. The reference point is not clear, but the 1924 CA confirmed the decline by reporting that the value of the same crops fell from $184,000 in 1919 to $10,808 in 1924. USBC, *United States Census of Agriculture: 1925*, county tab. IV at 219. According to Sam Bass Warner Jr., *To Dwell Is to Garden* 19, 20 million victory gardeners produced 44 percent of the fresh vegetables in the United States in 1944; it is unclear whether such gardens were included in the CA.

36. The following figures are based on the total calculated from the MS rather than the published data. According to the 1850 CA, the first to include town-level data, Brooklyn accounted for 31 percent of total market garden output, slightly more than New Utrecht. In 1860, when Brooklyn's share had fallen to 18 percent, its $58,464 worth of production (which had risen because the city in the meantime had annexed Bushwick) still exceeded that of Flatbush, which rose eightfold during the 1850s, while its offshoot, new town of New Lots, produced even more than Flatbush. By 1870, Brooklyn's production had declined to $46,000, but it still exceeded that of Flatbush and Flatlands. Not until 1879–80 did Brooklyn's vegetable production sink to an insignificant $17,800, or about 2 percent of the county total. At this point of peak recorded output, the towns were rank-ordered as follows: New Utrecht ($287,035, or 34 percent); Flatlands ($203,200, or 24 percent); New Lots ($191,750, or 23 percent); Flatbush ($137,882, or 16 percent); Brooklyn ($22,800, or 3 percent); and Gravesend (0). New York State cen-

suses reveal an even more pronounced and longer-lasting domination of market gardening by Brooklyn. In 1854, the city (including Bushwick) accounted for 30 percent of total acreage and 44 percent of total output; by 1864, these shares had risen to 65 percent and 69 percent, respectively. The minuscule acreage and production recorded for Flatbush and Flatlands in both years are not reconcilable with the federal census data for 1860. Regardless of whether the state census figures for the other towns are credible, Brooklyn's $120,078 and $173,950 worth of output for 1854 and 1864, respectively, are impressive. They suggest that farmers in Brooklyn underwent a temporally more compressed version of the market gardening that those in the rest of the county were about to adopt.

37. U.S. CA, 1870, KC, Flatbush, MS; U.S. CA, 1880, KC, Flatbush, MS.

38. "Annexation: City and County Union," *BDE*, Mar. 3, 1873, 2:6, 7 (quote); *KCRG*, May 17, 1873, 4:4 (reporting that N. Feltman was putting in tomatoes and had peas in very forward condition); "Gravesend Neck," ibid., 5:1 (J. Kouwenhoven had already cut 720 bunches of asparagus); "Gravesend," *KCRBG*, July 22, 1882, 2:4 (Daniel Barre planted celery and Stephen Wyckoff had cabbage as good as anyone's in town); U.S. CA, 1860, MS; U.S. CA, 1870, MS; U.S. CA, 1880, MS. William Bennett's Gravesend farm produced a large volume of cabbages and other vegetables in the 1880s and 1890s. William Bennett & Son, Farm Accounts. The development in New Lots would be even more deviant if what appear to be two large enumeration errors were corrected: the town's total market garden output would then have fallen by almost one-fifth and its share of total production would have fallen below one-half. Some of the differences in output and productivity among the towns may be explained by differences in soil quality. The Miami stony loam covering much of New Utrecht was the deepest soil in the county, permitting production of three or even more crops from the same field each year. A typical market garden rotation on this soil type included: early spring spinach, kale, and rhubarb; lettuce, radishes, and early peas; and later cabbage, parsnips, carrots, beets, turnips, onions, and potatoes. The well-drained and moisture-retaining Hempstead loam covering almost all of Flatbush, much of Flatlands, and the eastern part of New Utrecht offered good yields of potatoes, cabbages, tomatoes, and corn, being second in value only to Miami stony loams. Bonsteel et al., "Soil Survey of the Long Island Area" 99–100, 108–10. Some of the soil types in Gravesend, such as Galveston sand and Galveston sandy loam, were not valuable for agriculture, but others, in particular Norfolk sand and Sassafras sandy loam, were the sites of potato, pea, lettuce, and onion cultivation. Ibid. at 101, 103, 105, 115–18.

39. U.S. Census, 1880, Agriculture, reel 18, MS.

40. U.S. Census, 1850, Agriculture, reel 4, KC, Ninth Ward, Brooklyn (remark of enumerator) (quote); U.S. Bureau of the Census, *Twelfth Census*, vol. VI, pt. 2 at 785–88 (flowers). As late as 1893 Queens "for a distance of twenty miles from the city of Brooklyn is filled with market gardens, in which are grown in large quantities every conceivable vegetable that has any place in the culinary arts and can be grown in this latitude." *BDEA: 1893* at 46. The claim that "the struggle for agricultural survival which took place in Brooklyn at the turn of the century . . .

brought intensive and efficient cultivation of the most profitable market crops available" is set several decades too late. Harvey Mandel, "The Sequent Pattern of Agriculture on Long Island, New York" 5 (typescript). Kings County's absolute output and relative position at various censuses may have been artificially depressed by errors committed by enumerators. The tabulations published in the 1850 CA credited the county with $88,086 in market garden produce. However, the individual amounts recorded in the MS add up to $109,605, which would have lifted Kings County from 12th to 9th place. In 1860, Flatlands was credited with no market garden production because the enumerator, instead of filling in this column, recorded the number of cabbages harvested. Had these 1,280,400 head of cabbage been monetized together with the rest of the town's vegetable output, Kings County might have risen as high as 6th place. In 1870 one whole sheet from the CA covering 40 New Utrecht farms appears to have been omitted from the published tabulations. Since New Utrecht was the biggest vegetable producer in 1860 and 1880, inclusion of these "lost" farms might have brought Kings County as high as 5th place in 1870. The implausibility of census enumerators' failure to record any market garden production in Gravesend has been noted. These speculative upward adjustments of Kings County's position in these four census years presuppose that similar errors did not generate similar undercounts in other counties. On the other hand, the enumerator for the third election district of the town of New Lots in 1880 credited Nicholas Linington and U. Van Sinderen with $25,000 and $50,000 worth of market garden production, respectively. These sums were not only much higher than that of the next highest Kings County producer (which was $10,000, with one exception to be mentioned), but far in excess of the two farmers' total production, which was $5,000 and $10,000, respectively. The tabulators in Washington apparently did not notice this discrepancy. Even if their combined market garden figure of $75,000 were deleted, however, Kings County would still remain far ahead of third-place Middlesex. The enumerator for New Lots introduced another possible error by crediting Williamson Glover with $19,000 worth of market garden production; Glover's total production, which was crossed out several times and written over, appears to have been $23,000. Both of these figures were the highest in Kings County. Yet Glover was apparently a tenant, who paid $1,800 in rent for 12 acres of pasture and no tilled acreage and spent nothing on fertilizer. U.S. CA, 1880, KC, NL, SD no. 2, ED no. 261 at 2, and ED no. 258 at 1. Even if its total for market garden production in 1879 was erroneous, Kings County would still retain its second-place position.

41. Calculated according to Frederick Emerson, "A Geographic Interpretation of New York City" 20 (Ph.D. diss.).

42. The population of Jersey City rose by almost 4,000 percent between 1840 and 1880 from 3,000 to 120,000. Edward Bergman and Thomas Pohl, *A Geography of the New York Metropolitan Region* 37, 52.

43. Daniel Tredwell, "Flatbush" at 41–42.

44. *KCRG*, Nov. 27, 1875, 3:6. Other farmers owned more or different implements. Benjamin Hitchings, a lawyer who in 1879 auctioned the stock of his Gravesend

farm after the death of his son who had farmed it, offered not only five market wagons, but also a mowing machine, two cultivators, one gang-plow, five-beam harrows, steel plows, and a furrowing machine. *KCRG*, Dec. 20, 1879, 2:8. Although Hitchings advertised for a tenant after his son's death, the 1880 CA still returned Hitchings as operating the farm, which produced $6,000 worth of product. Ibid., Nov. 29, 1879, 3:5. Among the items that Jerome L. Bergen, who sold his Flatlands farm, offered in 1884 were a hay rack, potato marker, potato coverer, shovel plow (which was used for digging potatoes), potato harrow, corn harrow, cultivator, corn drill, Collins plow, Peekskill sod plow, seven-beam harrow, Fisher wheel plow, fan mill and corn sheller, fertilizer distributor, two cabbage plows, two six-beam harrows, and four other plows. *KCRBG*, Mar. 22, 1884, 3:3. Jerome L. Bergen was returned at the 1870 CP and CA as 29-year-old farmer who produced $3,125 worth of products on his 45-acre farm. He did not appear in either census for 1880 in Flatlands. Other auction notices included similar items. E.g., *KCG*, Oct. 3, 1885, 3:2 (George Ryerson of Flatlands); *KCG*, Oct. 31, 1885, 2:6 (W. J. and A. J. Cropsey of New Utrecht). On the shovel plow, see Arthur Gilbert, *The Potato* 230.

45. The eleven counties with the largest fertilizer expenditures were: Queens ($636,058), York, Pa. ($489,576), Lancaster, Pa. ($349,684), Montgomery, Md. ($335,175), Chester, Pa. ($319,948), Frederick, Md. ($305,038), Harford, Md. ($274,346), Suffolk, N.Y. ($272,134), Burlington, N.J. ($260,522), Bucks, Pa. ($259,887), and Baltimore ($251,754). The data on commercial fertilizer, which presumably included animal manures and chemical fertilizers, did not attain a "high degree of accuracy." CO, *Report on . . . Agriculture . . . Tenth Census* xxv. Forrester's complete manures was a major advertiser; e.g., *KCRG*, Jan. 4, 1879, 1:6.

46. SC, *CSNY for 1855* at 275; SC, *CSNY for 1865* at 326–27; CO, *Report on . . . Agriculture . . . Eleventh Census*, tab. 6 at 198–235, tab. 24 at 500–537.

47. USCO, *Twelfth Census*, vol. V, pt. I, tab. 19 at 266–307; USCO, *Twelfth Census*, vol. VI, pt. II, tab. 22 at 360–99. According to alternative data, Kings County farmers harvested vegetables on 1,191 acres with an average yield of $219, while average yields in Queens and Middlesex counties were $223 and $244 respectively. Ibid. at 316–18.

48. USCO, *Twelfth Census*, vol. V, pt. I at 306 (quote). The highest-valued farmland was found in Baltimore (city) ($1,258), Hudson, N.J. ($815), and Suffolk, Mass. ($528). Census authorities defined the cash value of farms as the price they would ordinarily bring if sold without reference to cost or assessed value. Secretary of State, *Instructions for Taking the Census of State of New York in the Year 1875* at 36.

49. U.S. Census, 1880, Agriculture, reel 18, KC, MS. Because the 1880 Census of Agriculture collected but did not publish wage data, a comparison with other counties cannot be made.

50. Rawson, *Success in Market Gardening* 99 (20 cords of manure at $7 per cord used per acre of cabbage); Landreth, *Market Gardening and Farm Notes* 124 ($80 per acre of celery); Henderson, *Gardening for Profit* 250 ($72 per acre of onions);

Henderson, *Gardening for Profit* 37, 158, 110–11 (1890) (quotes). Henderson stated that manure and guano together costing $100 to $150 per acre were used on vegetable crops in the vicinity of New York. Ibid. at 39. Kings County farmers did not always let a large proportion of their land lie fallow. In 1872, for example, Robert Magaw, a large Flatlands market gardener, cultivated 70 of his 80 acres. "Flatlands," *KCRG*, May 11, 1872, 5:2.

51. Calculated according to SC, *CSNY for 1875*, tab. 55 at 324. Why wage costs amounted to only 20 percent of the value of market garden production in Flatbush, which had the lowest proportion of owner-operators, is unclear. In Gravesend, where farmers produced chiefly potatoes, fertilizer and labor costs amounted to 20 percent and 29 percent, respectively, of the total value of production. Over the years from 1883 through 1898, William Bennett's fertilizer and labor costs — which in 1879–80 were a below-average 12.5 percent and 20 percent — amounted to 15 percent and 20 percent, respectively, of his total sales. William Bennett & Son, Farm Accounts.

52. Calculated according to data in U.S. Census, 1880, Agriculture, reel 18, KC, MS. The cost of seeds may, at least for potatoes, have been significant. In the spring of 1877, for example, high seed prices prompted farmers in New Utrecht not to plant as many potatoes as usual and small farmers not to plant at all. "New Utrecht, Bath and Unionville," *KCRG*, Apr. 21, 1877, 2:6. William Bennett spent considerable sums on seed potatoes: in 1884 he spent $138.25 on 79 barrels in addition to $21.25 on various vegetable seeds; in 1891 he spent $220 on seed potatoes and $10 on cabbage seeds. William Bennett & Son, Farm Accounts.

53. Compared with the value of total production, wage and fertilizer costs were highest in New Utrecht at 52 percent, and lowest in Flatbush at 30 percent. Table 8 reveals that the New Lots data are defective: the value of market garden produce exceeds that of all productions. The reason for this logical impossibility is that for a few farms the census enumerator inserted values for huge market garden produce that exceeded the value of the corresponding total production. The other New Lots indicators do not appear to be similarly flawed.

54. Frederick Law Olmsted [, Jr.], "Introductory Address on City Planning"; Joseph L. Arnold, *The New Deal in the Suburbs* 3–4.

55. Richard Wines, *Fertilizer in America* 11 (quote); *KCRBG*, Jan. 29, 1881, 3:4 (Atlantic Ave. R.R.) (quote); *KCRBG*, Sept. 22, 1883, 3:1 (Dekalb Ave. R.R. advertising manure from 400 horses for a year); *KCRBG*, Nov. 17, 1883, 3:4 (Franklin Ave. Railroad selling stable manure); *KCRBG*, Aug. 2, 1884, 3:3 (Nostrand Ave. R.R. selling cheap manure of 300 horses for a year or more); "Injustice to Our Farmers," *KCRG*, Dec. 20, 1873, 4:1 (editorial) (the injustice lay in applying an ordinance fining those who carted manure uncovered to several of "our well-to-do farmers" without having given them fair notice); Robert Criswell, "Economy in Farming," *KCRG*, Feb. 27, 1875, 1:1, 2 (quote). In the 1880s and 1890s, the Long Island R.R. operated twice-weekly piggyback market trains from Suffolk County to Brooklyn; farmers wagons were loaded onto flat cars, while the horses stood in box cars, and the farmers rode in passengers coaches; on return trips farmers could transport manure. Vincent Seyfried, "Truck Gardening" 2–3.

56. "The Lefferts Property," *BDE*, Mar. 6, 1873, 2:8; "Sanitary Notes — Sewerage and Sewage."

57. "Bay Ridge," *KCRG*, Jan. 16, 1875, 8:2 (quote); "An Agreement of Lease," Oct. 14, 1864, in Benson Family Papers, box V, first folder (quote); Last Will and Testament of John Lefferts, Dec. 17, 1892, KC Surrogate's Court (quote). Wintertime unloading of manure could be dangerous: Benjamin Lincoln, a black employee of Ditmas Denyse of Gravesend, "had his hands badly frozen while unloading a manure boat." "Gravesend," *KCRG*, Dec. 16, 1876, 2:4.

58. "Manure Heaps," *KCRG*, Dec. 18, 1875, 2:3 (quote); *KCRG*, Sept. 23, 1876, 2:3; "Local," *KCRBG*, Mar. 10, 1883, 3:1; "Brooklyn Garbage," *KCRG*, Sept. 5, 1874, 4:1 (editorial) (quote).

59. Elizabeth Johns, "The Farmer in the Works of William Sidney Mount" 269–70, 278.

60. *TNYSAS* 6:632–36 (1847), reprinted in James Bunce and Richard Harmond, *Long Island as America* 115 (quote); *TNYSAS* 8:527–29 (1849), reprinted in Bunce and Harmond, *Long Island as America* 116–17 (quote).

61. Adriance Van Brunt, Diary; William Ketcham, "The Manures Used Upon Long Island" 462–65 (quote); Jeremiah Johnson, "Kings County Agricultural Society: Report of the Committee on Farms and Grain" 346 (quote).

62. Wines, *Fertilizer in America* 9–11. The manure-vegetable recycling system was not confined to Long Island. Soon after the Civil War, Connecticut farmers imported horse manure from New York City to spread on their onion fields; much of the onion crop was then marketed in New York City. Russell, *A Long, Deep Furrow* 449. Nor was the urban market gardening-manure complex unique to the United States. In late nineteenth-century France, the "agricultural preoccupations of the urban periphery . . . were accentuated . . . with the development of garden or truck farming in response to the demands of the increased urban population." John Merriman, *The Margins of City Life* 36. One-sixth of the area of Paris was devoted to small-scale marais or market gardening; as many as 9,000 *maraîchers* not only supplied the city with more fresh vegetables than current consumption levels while exporting much to London as well, but also helped abate the transportation pollution problem by transforming enormous volumes of horse manure into fertile soil. On as few as one to four acres, market gardeners, using abundant manure and hotbed frames and hot-water pipes throughout the winter, and paying rents as high as $125 per acre, took as many as eight successive crops per season. Yet another heavy user of manure in the late nineteenth century were the 200 or more mushroom growers, who year-round produced tremendous quantities in the miles of caves or galleries that traversed Paris at depths of 10 to 20 meters. So heavy was the Paris vegetable growers' reliance on the city's horse manure that motorization of transport was a prime cause of the demise of this cultivation in the first quarter of the twentieth century. G. Stanhill, "An Urban Agro-Ecosystem"; George Campbell, "Horticulture" 389–91, 393–98; Petr Kropotkin, *Fields, Factories and Workshops* 73–86, 127–53. Paris, however, exercised greater control over sanitation and waste recycling. The city began to deal with its street sewage after it was recognized

that discharging it into the Seine polluted the water, poisoned and killed the fish, and rendered neighborhoods along the river unhealthful and unaesthetic. Experiments began in 1868 to use the sewage as fertilizer for horticultural products in nearby Asnières. Pumps controlled by steam engines, conduit pipes, drains, and trenches were built to direct the fertilizing streams at the rows of crops. Yields soon doubled and quadrupled on theretofore poor and infertile land, from which by the 1870s 140,000 kilos of cabbage per hectare were harvested. Campbell, "Horticulture" 414–18. Sewage farming was also widely practiced in Britain and near continental European cities such as Berlin. M. Baker, "The Utilization of City Wastes on the Farm."

63. Jay Bonsteel et al., "Soil Survey of the Long Island Area" 97–98, 108–9, 110 (quote); Soil Map No. 5, "New York: Hempstead Sheet," accompanying the volume.

64. *HJRAT* 3 (1): 487–89 (July 1848); *History of the Massachusetts Horticultural Society, 1829–1878*; Wines, *Fertilizer in America* 12 (quote). William Schenck, the Flatbush farmer pictured in figure 1, bought $33.25 worth of potato fertilizer and $10.00 worth of cabbage fertilizer from H. J. Baker & Co., Importers, Dealers and Manufacturers, in New York, on March 22, 1880. Copy of invoice furnished by Lola Schenck Cheney. William Bennett of Gravesend bought $523.80 worth of potato manure and corn manure on May 15 and 17, and July 5 and 8, 1893, from Baker. Invoice at Wyckoff-Bennett Homestead.

65. 1864 N.Y. Laws, ch. 310, sect. 2, at 743, 744 (quote); *KCRG*, Jan. 25, 1873, 6:2 (quote); "Farm Notes," *KCRG*, Feb. 22, 1873, 6:1 (quote); "Long Island Items," *KCRG*, Jan. 24, 1880, 4:2. At its meeting in Long Island City in 1880, farmers from New Lots and Flatlands, which were closest to that town, were especially well represented and included C. B. Kowenhoven, Abraham Van Siclen, and Simon Rapelye.

66. William Crozier and Peter Henderson, *How the Farm Pays* 302, 303 (quote); "The Fields," *KCRG*, Apr. 27, 1872, 2:3 (quote); Bonsteel et al., "Soil Survey of the Long Island Area" 123 (quote).

67. USCO, *Tenth Census*, vol. 18, *Report on the Social Statistics of Cities*, pt. I at 484 (quote); Joel Tarr, "Urban Pollution" 65–66.

68. "Long Island as a Farming Country," *KCRBG*, Aug. 26, 1882, 2:7 (quote). This article casts doubt on the accuracy of a fertilizer infomercial asserting that the "old fashioned custom of our farmers hauling manure, from the city for two or three months, every spring has to a large extent died out" as they recognized that chemical manures were superior and required only two or three days' hauling. "Manures," *KCRBG*, Apr. 12, 1884, 2:2. A previous infomercial for Forrester's Potato Fertilizer asserted that commercial fertilizer could save Kings County farmers "the labor of their teams in carting manure, and the labor of their help in cutting down and turning manure in the heap." *KCRG*, Mar. 23, 1878, 2:2.

69. Ralph Watts and Gilbert Watts, *The Vegetable Growing Business* 3 (disappearance of manure); *ARSESSNY 1863* at 164 (Brooklyn City R.R.); *Second Annual Report of the Board of Railroad Commissioners, 1884* at 2:962 (Brooklyn City R.R.); *BDEA: 1891* at 47 (animal power); Joel Tarr, "From City to Farm." Kings County's

position as an outlier with respect to fertilizer costs was not positively correlated with its livestock holdings (and thus with access to farm-generated manure), which at 0.38 livestock per acre was the second highest among the 12 largest spenders on fertilizer in 1879. CO, *Report on the Productions of Agriculture*, tab. VII at 104−40, tab. IX at 142−76. As late as 1916, 12,000 motor vehicles crossed the four East River bridges in a single day compared with 7,500 one-horse, 5,000 two-horse, and 500 three-horse vehicles. Ellsworth Huntington, "The Water Barriers of New York City" 174. William Bennett's account books shed light on the comparative use of chemical fertilizer and manure: although he spent much more (never less than 2.7 times as much) money on the former, he also bought many loads of the latter until the final years of the farm in the late 1890s. For example, in 1884, he spent $1,132.50 on fertilizer and $64.50 on 47 loads of manure. Manure became cheaper over time: in 1883 Bennett never paid less than $1.50 per load; by 1893, he often paid less than 60 cents and at times as little as 12.5 cents. William Bennett & Son, Farm Accounts.

70. G. Brown Goode, "The Sea Fisheries (A History of the Menhaden)" 168, 175, 189; Gabriel, *Evolution of Long Island* 76−88; *The Eagle and Brooklyn* 1137 (quote); Ross, *History of Long Island* 1:316 (quote); Stiles, *Civil . . . History* 1:78−79. In the 1930s, Barren Island still resembled "an isolated village in some remote country-side." *The WPA Guide to New York City* 504. The 1880 CP for Flatlands included a special subsection for Barren Island, listing 309 inhabitants; the occupation column of several pages of the manuscript schedules was headed, "Fisch Oil and Guano Factory" and "For Fertilizing Crops." Many of the factory laborers were black. Tenth Census, 1880, NY, vol. 38, Kings, pt. 10, Flatlands 60−66.

71. USDA, *The Fertilizing Value of Street Sweepings* 8; Edward Spann, *The New Metropolis* 130−31; USDA, *Yearbook of Agriculture 1931* at 362−64.

72. L. C. Corbett, *The Potato as a Truck Crop* 15 (quote); L. C. Corbett, *Intensive Farming* 129−34 (quote at 133); Corbett, *Garden Farming* 165. Although horse manure contains less nitrogen and less overall nutritive value than cow manure, there is no evidence that Kings County farmers' principal competitors had such greater access to the latter that it would have explained their vastly lower expenditures on fertilizer.

3. Competitiveness and the "Courageous Capitalist"

1. "Proposed Action of New Jersey Farmers," *KCRBG*, Sept. 17, 1881, 1:3 (quote); "Both Sides of a Question: Washington Market or Gansevoort Market?" *NYT*, Jan. 27, 1880, 8:3.

2. Stiles, *Civil . . . History* 2:972 (quote); "Facts," *KCRG*, Mar. 8, 1873, 4:1, (editorial) (quote); "Farmers Arrested," *KCRBG*, May 28, 1881, 3:1.

3. Thomas F. De Voe, *The Market Book* 1:448 (quote); "City Markets," *HJRART* 19:377−79 (1864) (quote). De Voe, a market merchant, focused his description on meat marketing. His account appears more reliable than later newspaper stories. He stated that Washington Market was opened in 1813, nine years before Fulton Market, and mentioned nothing about farmers' having been driven

from the latter to the former. Ibid. at 406−407, 488−96. According to "The Big Market Wagons," *NYT*, Jan. 24, 1880, 8:1, farmers began congregating at Fulton Market fifty years earlier and were then driven away. The Common Council authorized the establishment of West Washington Market in 1861; four years earlier, the clerk of the market had been directed to assign farmers certain streets for selling market garden produce. "Where Shall the Market Be?" *NYT*, Jan. 16, 1880, 8:4.

4. Stiles, *Civil . . . History* 1:39a.

5. "A New Vegetable Market," *NYT*, Dec. 14, 1879, 5:3; "Farmer's Rights in New York Market," *KCRG*, Aug. 3, 1878, 3:2 (quote); "Long Island Items," *KCRG*, Apr. 5, 1879, 4:2; "The Farmers' Wagons," *NYH*, Feb. 13, 1880, 9:1.

6. "West Washington Market," *KCRG*, Oct. 11, 1879, 3:1 (reprinting article). The *Market Index* suggested that West Washington Market would enable farmers to bring their produce directly to the market's dealers and return home, thus saving time and eliminating one set of middlemen.

7. "A New Vegetable Market," *NYT*, Dec. 14, 1879, 5:3; "The New Market Stand," *NYT*, Dec. 25, 1879, 8:1; "The Marketmen Protest," *NYT*, Jan. 13, 1880, 8:3 (quoting Andrew C. Cropsey); "The Farmers' Market in New York City," *KCRG*, Jan. 3, 1880, 2:2 (reprinting article); "The New Market for Farmers," *KCRG*, Jan. 10, 1880, 2:1 (editorial) (quote); "Farmers' Rights," *KCRG*, Jan. 24, 1880, 2:1 (editorial) (quote).

8. "A New Vegetable Market," *NYT*, Dec. 14, 1879, 5:3; "The New Market Stand," *NYT*, Dec. 23, 1879, 3:4. By World War II, Washington Market, though no longer a farmers' market, was both "the world's largest market for fresh fruits and vegetables" and also the most "cramped, inadequate, and obsolete." W. Calhoun, "The World's Largest Produce Market" 24.

9. "Market Men Agitated," *NYH*, Jan. 18, 1880, 12:1, 2; "New Utrecht Farmers," *KCRG*, Jan. 24, 1880, 2:7 (quote).

10. "Farmers Turn Out! Turn Out!" *KCRG*, Jan. 24, 1880, 2:1; "New Utrecht, Bath and Unionville," *KCRG*, Jan. 31, 1880, 2:7; *KCRBG*, Mar. 14, 1885, 2:7 (on the association's continued work on the market question); "The Big Market Wagons," *NYT*, Jan. 24, 1880, 8:1; "Both Sides of a Question," *NYT*, Jan. 27, 1880, 8:3 (quote); "The Long Island Farmers," *NYT*, Feb. 1, 1880, 2:7. See also "New Utrecht, Bath and Unionville," *KCRG*, Feb. 7, 1880, 2:7.

11. "The Farmers' Wagons," *NYH*, Feb. 13, 1880, 3:1.

12. 1880 N.Y. Laws, ch. 191 at 306; "New Utrecht, Bath and Unionville," *KCRG*, Feb. 14, 1880, 2:4; "Gansevoort Market," *KCRBG*, Dec. 18, 1880, 2:1 (editorial); "Gansevoort Market and the Farmers," *KCRBG*, Nov. 27, 1880, 2:4 (quote); "Farmers to Be Fined," *KCRBG*, July 30, 1881, 2:2 (reprinted from N.Y. *Market Index and Journal*); "Gansevoort Market," *KCRBG*, Jan. 14, 1882, 2:1; "Brooklyn Killing Washington and Gansevoort Markets," *KCRBG*, Oct. 7, 1882, 2:2.

13. "The Market Question," *KCRG*, Feb. 21, 1880, 2:3; Stiles, *Civil . . . History* 2:972 (quoting an identified issue of the *Brooklyn Daily Eagle* from 1883 or 1884); *KCRG*, Oct. 20, 1878 (on efforts to compel Kings County farmers to cease taking midday loads to New York); "Facts" 4:1 (quote).

14. "The Market Question," *KCRBG*, Aug. 4, 1883, 2:1; "Are Our Farmers Wandering Jews?" *KCRBG*, Jan. 12, 1884, 2:1 (quote). See also "Farmers' Rights in New York Market," *KCRG*, Aug. 3, 1878, 3:2; "Gansevoort Market," *KCRBG*, Jan. 14, 1882, 2:1; "Injustice to Our Farmers," *KCRBG*, Mar. 17, 1883, 2:2; "West Washington Market," *KCRBG*, Apr. 14, 1883, 2:1. For a description of Washington Market and other public markets in New York City, see "How New York Is Fed." *Washington Market Index and Journal*, which began publication in 1879, issued every Saturday morning for marketmen, stand-holders, their customers and friends, and copyright by Garret Bergen, listed prices for vegetables and included an index to the stands. It is unclear how long it was published. The only issue located was volume I, number 11, for July 26, 1879, held by the NYHS.

15. "The Brooklyn Market Project," *KCRBG*, Sept. 29, 1883, 2:1 (editorial).

16. "Editorial Notes," *KCRBG*, Sept. 20, 1884, 2:2; *BDEA: 1889* at 123.

17. Act of July 2, 1890, ch. 654, 26 Stat. 213; Act of Dec. 22, 1892, ch. 9, 27 Stat. 407; 1894 N.Y. Laws, ch. 569 at 1313; *BDEA: 1896* at 127.

18. "Flatlands," *KCRG*, May 13, 1876, 2:4; Fredk. Bartlett, *The History of Wallabout Market Established in 1884* at 6–11; "The Market at Wallabout," *KCRBG*, Sept. 20, 1884, 1:2; *BDEA: 1893* at 151; *BDEA: 1897* at 155; Bonsteel et al., "Soil Survey of the Long Island Area" 93 (quote). Kings County farmers themselves also took great care of their market wagons, building sheds to shelter them while standing in the fields loaded for market. Farmers also built shelters for their workers to watch the truck. "Bay Ridge," *KCRG*, May 1, 1875, 3:2.

19. L. H. Bailey, *The Principles of Vegetable-Gardening* 223; Nissley, "Vegetable Growing on Long Island" 1222, 1224; A. Wilkinson, "Market Gardening in New York State" 1215, 1217. Three-ton market wagons were in use in the 1870s. "Flatlands," *KCRG*, July 7, 1877, 2:5.

20. *CG*, 39th Cong., 1st Sess. 2656 (1866) (quote); Act of July 13, 1866, ch. 184, sect. 9, 14 Stat. 93, 119 (quote); *CG*, 39th Cong., 2d Sess. 1480 (1867) (quote); Act of Mar. 2, 1867, ch. 169, sect. 11, 14 Stat. 471, 477. In 1863 the Commissioner of Internal Revenue had already ruled that: "A person who sells the products of his farm by travelling from house to house and disposing of the same wherever he finds a purchaser is not, under the law, considered a peddler." Although farmers whose sales by means of a store or stall exceeded $1,000 were liable to license as dealers, this liability "when above a certain amount does not extend to their sales as peddlers." Office of Internal Revenue, Ruling No. 102, printed in George Boutwell, *A Manual of the Direct and Excise Tax System of the United States* 318. On Bergen, see *Biographical Directory of the American Congress* 654; Stiles, *Civil . . . History* 1:268; CP, 1870, KC, NU, MS, at 11; CP, 1880, KC, NU, MS, SD no. 2, ED no. 262, at 57. The course of Bergen's operations reflected the overall trend from extensive to intensive farming. In 1850 he produced $1,500 worth of market garden produce on his 53-acre farm; by 1860, his farm encompassed only 25 acres but the value of his market garden produce had doubled to $3,000; by 1870, his even smaller 16-acre farm yielded another doubling to $6,000. On Bergen's sale of part of his farm, see Bergen, *Bergen Family* (2d ed.) 366. As late as 1879, Bergen bought six acres of woodland from the Van Brunt heirs. "New Utrecht, Bath and

Unionville," *KCRG*, May 10, 1879, 2:2. Even in 1880, a year before his death, his 24-acre farm produced $2,740 worth of vegetables. 1850, 1860, 1870, and 1880 CA, KC, NU, MS.

21. Turner v. Kouwenhoven, Testimony of John Parker (Turner's brother-in-law, who worked for Kouwenhoven in 1881), William Kouwenhoven, and C. B. Kouwenhoven, in New York Court of Appeals, *Appeal Book* 10−11, 24−25 (quote), 51; "West Flatbush," *KCRBG*, July 17, 1880, 3:2 (J. A. Garnin); "Flatlands," *KCRBG*, Aug. 1, 1885, 2:4 (Jeffrey Van Wyck). In 1877 W. W. Kouwenhoven in Flatlands (three Flatlands farmers were named William W. Kouwenhoven) also ran four to five loads of potatoes to market daily. "Flatlands," *KCRG*, July 14, 1877, 2:5.

22. *Appeal Book* 42 (testimony of William Kouwenhoven); A.H.B., "'What I Know about' Tomato Catsup," *KCRG*, Sept. 7, 1872, 6:1; "Local," *KCRG*, July 12, 1873, 1:3; William Bennett & Son, Farm Accounts; "Bay Ridge," *KCRBG*, July 22, 1882, 2:4 (W. W. Bennett). On $75 to $100 license fees in 1880s, presumably at Gansevoort Market, see "Injustice to Our Farmers," *KCRBG*, Mar. 17, 1883, 2:2. Some Queens and Suffolk farmers, who had much longer distances to travel, spent one night on the road at an inn. Seyfried, "Truck Gardening" 2.

23. Turner v. Kouwenhoven (testimony of W. Kouwenhoven), in *Appeal Book* 34, 43 (quote); Turner v. Kouwenhoven, Brief for Appellant 3−4, in *Appeal Book* (quote); testimony of William Harrison, grocer (for defendant), in *Appeal Book* 16 (quote).

24. "Some Suburbs of New York" 125 (quote); A Flatlander, "Plea For (?) Annexation," *KCRG*, Jan. 11, 1873, 1:2 (quote); "Flatlands," *KCRBG*, Aug. 22, 1885, 2:4; *KCRG*, July 28, 1877, 2:4 (untitled) (quote); Turner v. Kouwenhoven, Testimony by John Turner, Mar. 17, 1882, at 90, in *Appeal Book* (quote). Turner was presumably referring to Manhattan Market on West 34th Street, which opened in 1880. "Manhattan Market," *KCRBG*, July 3, 1880, 2:4. It is unclear when farmers began using the Brooklyn Bridge, which users in the nineteenth century had to pay to cross. Initially, one horse and vehicle cost 10 cents, two horses and vehicle 20 cents; by 1889, one horse and vehicle cost 5 cents. By the end of 1889, after six and a half years of operation, 166 million passengers had paid almost $5 million in tolls. "The Bridge Toll," *KCRBG*, May 19, 1883, 2:1−2; *BDEA: 1890* at 86−87. On the danger to which a "rough" could expose a marketman, see "Gravesend," *KCRG*, Sept. 19, 1874, 1:1. Flatlands farmers had either to use extra horses to drive loads on the Flatlands town roads at night or to drive their wagons to Flatbush during the day and let them stand there until evening before proceeding to market. "Flatlands," *KCRG*, Sept. 15, 1877, 2:4.

25. J. D. M., letter to editor, *KCRG*, Apr. 22, 1876, 2:5 (complaining about carriers' exorbitant $1 wage at Washington Market); "New Utrecht, Bath and Unionville," *KCRBG*, Sept. 12, 1885, 2:5 (quote).

26. "Plaza Hill: Sleep and Music," *KCRG*, Aug. 9, 1873, 1:2 (quote); "To Farmers," *KCRG*, Aug. 8, 1874, 4:3; "'Now I Lay Me Down to Sleep,' But Cannot," *KCRG*, 4:4; C. Spence, letter to editor, *KCRG*, Aug. 22, 1874, 2:1; "Squealers," *KCRG*, July 29, 1876, 2:1 (editorial) (quote); *KCRG*, Aug. 12, 1876, 2:5 (untitled) (quote).

Farmers may have chosen this route because it was easy to follow after dark and/or enabled them to avoid the Flatbush toll road. Horse-car railroad companies apparently did not object. "Flatlands," *KCRG*, Nov. 6, 1875, 2:4. Nicholson pavement, which was patented in 1848, was laid extensively during the decade after the Civil War. U.S. Forest Service, *Wood Paving in the United States* 6. At least one large farmer, Rulef van Brunt, sent his vegetables to New York by boat from his own docks on the shore below his house in Bay Ridge. Younger, *Old Brooklyn in Early Photographs* 102.

27. See, e.g., "Gravesend," *KCRG*, July 18, 1874, 1:2 (a Gravesend farmer killed a girl in Brooklyn); "East New York," *KCRG*, Sept. 12, 1874, 1:2 (farmer's wagon severely injured boy).

28. USDA, Office of Experiment Stations, *Dietary Studies in New York City in 1895 and 1896*; Richard Cummings, *The American and His Food* 77–78; W. W. Rawson, *Success in Market Gardening* 143 (quote); Land Planning Committee of the National Resources Board, *Agricultural Land Requirements and Resources* 7.

29. "The Multitude at Market: Peculiarities of a Peddlers' Public Auction: An Outdoor Bedlam Where Vendors Most Do Congregate and Housewives Get Vegetables for a Song," *NYT*, Oct. 5, 1884, 5:3.

30. "Summer in the Markets," *NYT*, May 8, 1882, 8:2 (quote); G. Lawton, "Middle Men in the New York Markets," *KCRBG*, May 13, 1882, 2:2; "Flatlands," *KCRBG*, Jan. 20, 1883, 2:3.

31. "A Mammoth Market Enterprise," *KCRBG*, Mar. 12, 1881, 2:6–7 (quote) (reprinting article); Matthew Josephson, *The Robber Barons* 184. For an earlier discussion of the possibilities of Manhattan Market, situated at the terminus of the New York Central and Hudson River and Harlem railroads, for enabling farmers south of Albany to send vegetables to New York and to compete with Long Island farmers, see "Market Men Agitated," *NYH*, Jan. 18, 1880, 12:1, 2. On later developments, see *KCRBG*, June 26, 1880, 3:5 (advertisement); "Manhattan Market," *KCRBG*, July 3, 1880, 2:4.

32. Theodore Baker, "Market Gardening" 223. The *Rural Gazette* published some data on yields, costs, and profits of market gardening in Virginia, adding that from "all we hear, it would seem . . . a better place for market gardening than Kings County." Unfortunately, it never published any replies to its request to readers for similar data from Kings County. "Market Gardening," *KCRG*, Apr. 25, 1874, 4:3.

33. A. Oemler, "Truck Farming" 584, 583. Much of this article is based on Oemler's book, which first appeared in 1883. Oemler, *Truck-Farming at the South*.

34. William N. White, *Gardening for the South* 99 (quote); USCO, *Census Reports*, vol. VI, *Twelfth Census*, pt. II, tab. 22, at 306 (quote).

35. Henderson, *Gardening for Profit* 18–19, 23 (1890 ed.) (quotes). The issue of whether Dutch farmers' competitive cost position was strengthened by the absence of land costs is distinct from the question of whether they at some point considered the present value of their land in order to calculate the opportunity cost of farming as opposed to selling the land; see part II below. On the few Dutch farmers still farming in the 1880s, see chapter 9 below.

36. Oemler, "Truck Farming" 609–10 (quote); Earle, "Development of the Trucking Interests" 439 (quote). Shortly after World War I, the FTC stated that: "A distant producer is on a footing almost equal to that of one near by who drives to market by reason of the low railroad rate. . . . It is estimated that a ton of freight can be sent by rail nearly 700 miles for the amount it costs to carry it 20 miles by horse-drawn conveyance." FTC, *Food Investigation* 124.

37. "Farm Notes," *KCRG*, Mar. 8, 1873, 6:1.

38. Oemler, "Truck Farming" 584–85. Shannon, *Farmers' Last Frontier* 123, noted that "the bountiful supply of labor to be exploited cheaply in the picking and packing season" supported nineteenth-century southern truck farming.

39. Oemler, *Truck-Farming at the South* 7.

40. Philip Bruce, *The Rise of the New South* 64. Not all southern market gardeners were white. Peter Henderson, who also operated a seed and plant business, reported that when he called on a customer in Charleston, South Carolina, he was "surprised" that the owners were "two modest-looking colored men." By 1883 they owned "75 acres of valuable land" on which they employed 75 workers. He considered the farm, generating annual profits of $20,000 to $30,000, a model and technologically more advanced than those in Hudson County. Henderson, "Market Gardening" 161–62.

41. USCO, *Census Reports*, vol. VI, *Twelfth Census*, pt. II at 307 (quote); Andrew Soule, "Vegetable, Fruit and Nursery Products and Truck Farming in the South" 128 (quote); USDA, Div. of Statistics, *Wages of Farm Labor in the United States* 22 (quote). The data were calculated according to CO, *Report on the Statistics of Agriculture in the United States at the Eleventh Census* 597, 593, 596, which must be used with caution since it omitted vegetables grown in market gardens. Ibid. at 595.

42. Corbett, *Intensive Farming* 14; Thomas Wertenbaker, *Norfolk* 313–14; Thomas Parramore, *Norfolk* 172; USDA, Div. of Statistics, *Rates of Charge for Transporting Garden Truck* 23, 9 (quote), 15 (quote), 14. "Small Farms," *KCRG*, July 29, 1882, 2:3 (quote). The transplanted New Jersey farmers, who specialized in tomatoes, secured "fabulous prices" by shipping them north two weeks ahead of their New Jersey competitors, thus making "fortunes." [Edmund Morris], *Ten Acres Enough* 118–19.

43. Sherman, *Merchandising Fruits and Vegetables* 36–37; Jeremiah Johnson, "Recollections of Old Roads, Residents and Their Occupations" 5, 15 (quote); USCO, *Census Reports*, vol. VI, *Twelfth Census*, pt. II at 323 (quote). Sherman, *Merchandising Fruits and Vegetables* 36–37, argued that southern competition had the further impact of causing commission men (the farmers' agents) to become indifferent to local producers' interests because, being paid a percentage of gross sales, they "made much more money" from selling the higher-priced southern produce, in which they had frequently invested their own money.

44. USCO, *Census Reports*, vol. VI, *Twelfth Census*, pt. II at 304; Hedden, *How Great Cities Are Fed* xiii, xiv, 101 (quotes). On Norfolk truck farms as model farms, see Petr Kropotkin, *Fields, Factories and Workshops* 101, 135.

45. USDA, *Rates of Charge for Transporting Garden Truck* 22 (quote); James Mc-

Corkle Jr., "Moving Perishables to Market" 48–50, 60; John Lloyd, "Truck-Growing" 654, 653 (quotes).

46. Landreth, *Market Gardening and Farm Notes* 3–4. On Florida, see Carolyn Lewis, "Agricultural Evolution on Secondary Frontiers."

47. Landreth, *Market Gardening and Farm Notes* 8–9 (quote); "Potatoes from Abroad," *KCRBG*, Feb. 18, 1882 (quote).

48. Oemler, *Truck-Farming at the South* 170 (quote); Landreth, *Market Gardening and Farm Notes* 9–11 (quote); "New York Vegetable Market," *KCRG*, May 30, 1874, 7:2 (quote); Bruce, *Rise of the New South* 67 (quote). By 1906, the Long Island Railroad's special service trains "placed vegetables in the hands of city consumers inside of four hours after they were packed and shipped from a distance of nearly seventy miles" in Suffolk County. Edith Loring Fullerton, *The Lure of the Land* 75–76.

49. Oemler, *Truck-Farming at the South* 140. Truck farmers in Concord, Massachusetts, began specializing in asparagus in the 1870s. When California farmers began underselling them in Boston markets in the mid-1920s, local farmers turned to noncompeting crops such as cabbage, cauliflower, and squash, "which are so heavy and low-valued that they cannot stand the freight from points outside the state," and vegetables such as sweet corn and string beans, which "do not keep well in transit." Edward Ackerman, "Sequent Occupance of a Boston Suburban Community" 68–69.

50. Quinn, *Money in the Garden* 137–39; Henderson, *Gardening for Profit* at 81 (quote).

51. Oemler, *Truck-Farming at the South* 140 (quote); Henderson, *Gardening for Profit* 23, 312, 67 (quote). Kings County's next biggest vegetable crop in monetary terms, tomatoes, was only one-sixth as large, but accounted for 54 percent of the state's total output. Calculated according to SC, *CSNY, for 1865* at 405, 327, 409. Queens accounted for 30 percent of the state's cabbage harvest and 22 percent of tomatoes.

52. Prince, "Sketch of the Agricultural History of Queens County" 278 (quote); B. Galloway, "Progress of Commercial Growing of Plants Under Glass" 583, 586 (quotes); USCO, *Census Reports*, vol. VI, *Twelfth Census*, pt. II, tab. I at 774 (prices); *History of the Massachusetts Horticultural Society* 448; Howard Russell, *A Long, Deep Furrow* 374–76, 451. Because the Boston area was the center of East Coast under-glass vegetable production, capital investment, involving hothouses, irrigation, and heating, may have been higher than in the New York area. Regional specialization may have been linked to the fact that there were longer winters, less sun, and colder air and soil in the Boston area than on Long Island — which experienced less exteme winters and summers than the mainland — which made forcing a more rational and even pressing response to southern competition. Bonsteel et al., "Soil Survey of the Long Island Area" 94. Scale increased from 1860, when 200 hotbed sashes "was a large number for one market gardener to have," to 1900, when 2,000 was not. Market gardening, according to Rawson, "will not produce millionaires, but it has laid the foundation of fortunes, though this was largely from the rise in the value of land; but

this applies only to the vicinity of Boston and other cities." Rawson, "Discussion" 73–74.

53. "Long Island Market Gardening," *Newtown Register*, May 5, 1893. Vincent Seyfried furnished a copy of this clipping, which lacks a source but which he identified as taken from this newspaper. Telephone interview with Seyfried, Oct. 7, 1997.

54. "The Farmers' Market in New York City," *KCRG*, Jan. 3, 1880, 2:2 (quote); "For the Farmers," *KCRG*, Nov. 27, 1880, 2:1; "Market Men Agitated," *NYH*, Jan. 18, 1880, 12:1 (quote); "New Utrecht," *KCRG*, Apr. 10, 1875, 8:1 (William Sieger "has one of the finest side-hills to raise hot-bed truck that we have seen for some time"); *KCRG*, Nov. 27, 1875, 3:6 (quote); *KCG*, Oct. 31, 1885, 2:6 (notice of auction sale of the farm stock of W. J. and A. J. Cropsey in New Utrecht including 30 hotbed sashes and shutters); "Flatlands," *KCRG*, May 23, 1874, 1:1 (quote). W. I. Kouwenhoven maintained large hotbeds of early productions in Flatlands, while the auction sale of Court Van Sicklen's Coney Island farm included 200 hotbed sashes. "Flatlands," *KCRG*, Mar. 29, 1879, 2:4; ibid., Feb. 1, 1879, 3:7 (advertisement). The auction of Benjamin Hitchings' farm in Gravesend also included hotbed sash and covers. Ibid., Dec. 20, 1879, 2:8. The *Rural Gazette* also frequently included advertisements for hotbed sash glazed at $2.25; e.g., *KCRG*, May 20, 1876, 5:5.

55. USCO, *Census Reports*, vol. VI, *Twelfth Census*, pt. II at 360–99. In 1899 Kings County also ranked eighth in terms of square feet of surface in florists' establishments and fifth in amount of sales of flowers and plants. USCO, *Census Reports*, vol. VI, *Twelfth Census*, pt. II, tab. 4 at 785–89.

56. Landreth, *Market Gardening and Farm Notes* 6 (quote); Sullivan, "The Advancement of Market Gardening in the Past Twenty-Five Years" 68; Rawson, *Success in Market Gardening* 75–76 (data).

57. Henderson, *Gardening for Profit* xi (1890 ed.) (quote); Charles Baltet, *L'Horticulture dans les cinq parties du monde* 261; USDA, *Rates of Charge for Transporting Garden Truck* 21, 22 (quote).

58. Sullivan, "The Advancement of Market Gardening in the Past Twenty-Five Years" at 68. See also W. Massey, "The Developing of Market Gardening Southward and its Lesson to the Northern Trucker."

59. Corbett, *Garden Farming* 2, 144.

60. USCO, *Census Reports*, vol. VI, *Twelfth Census*, pt. II at 321 (quotes); Landreth, *Market Gardening and Farm Notes* 6, 5 (quotes); Quinn, *Money in the Garden* 13 (quotes).

61. Rawson, *Success in Market Gardening* 163, 213 (quotes); *Thirteenth Annual Report of the Commissioner of Labor* 1:24–25, 87, 90–91, 93; 2:436–39, 448–55, 468–69. One advantage that southern farmers did not grasp was artificially powered machinery that only plantation-size farms would have justified financially. But in the nineteenth century, such equipment was little used anywhere in the United States, let alone in the South, where the valuation of farm equipment in 1900 was still only half of its level in 1860. Vegetable operations "were

only slightly affected by machinery even in the 1890's." Shannon, *Farmer's Last Frontier* 128–44 (quote at 144).

62. William Crozier and Peter Henderson, *How the Farm Pays* 302 (quote); Henderson, *Gardening for Profit* 78–79. Henderson operated a business on Cortlandt Street in Manhattan.

63. Peter Henderson, *Gardening for Profit* 16 (1867) (quote); Henderson, *Gardening for Profit* 20 (1890) (quote); "Gardening for Profit," *KCRBG*, Oct. 30, 1880, 2:3 (quote). More than 100,000 copies in 41 editions purportedly made Henderson's book at the time the best-selling horticultural work ever. Crozier and Henderson, *How the Farm Pays* 7 and advertisement following final page 400; Carl Woodward, *The Development of Agriculture in New Jersey 1640–1880* at 239–40. The cost-profit data that Henderson gave for the 10 years preceding publication of this edition were the same as in the second edition. Ibid. at 18. These data put in a different light his assertion in 1884 that early vegetables had been less profitable in the New York vicinity during the previous 10 years than at any time during the previous half century. Henderson, "Market Gardening" 160. Two cost components that Henderson did not include were insurance and pesticides. From frequent accounts in the *Rural Gazette* of fire damage, especially to barns and their contents, caused by lightning, insurance may have been widespread. Evert Suydam of New Utrecht was insured for $500 with the Dutchess County Mutural Insurance Co. when his barn burned down, resulting in a loss of more than $1,000. "New Utrecht, Bath and Unionville," *KCRG*, July 7, 1877, 2:7. But when the barn of Jacobus Lake in Gravesend burned down with $3,000 worth of implements, wagons, and 500 bushels of potatoes, it was uninsured. "Gravesend," *KCRBG*, Oct. 25, 1884, 2:5. The barn of Richard Berry, who for years rented the Martense farm, was also struck by lightning and burned, but insurance was not mentioned. "Struck by Lightning," *KCRBG*, July 17, 1881, 3:3. The cost of insurance is unknown, but the *Rural Gazette* estimated repairing fences, building, and insurance at $4 per acre per year. "Taxation," *KCRG*, Oct. 9, 1875, 2:1. In several years the *Rural Gazette* reported on potato bugs and the efforts to eliminate them, including the use of pesticides such as Paris Green. "Flatlands," *KCRG*, May 19, 1877, 2:4. There were also reports of army worm infestations. "Gravesend," *KCRBG*, June 12, 1880, 2:6, and ibid. at 3:1 (untitled). William Bennett bought considerable amounts of Paris Green (e.g., 128 lb. for $23.04 in 1885) as well as Paris Green machines in 1889 ($40) and as late as November 1897 ($51), the next-to-last year of his farm. William Bennett & Son, Farm Accounts.

64. Bailey, *Principles of Vegetable-Gardening* 338; Rawson, *Success in Market Gardening* 99–100; Quinn, *Money in the Garden* 89; Rawson, *Success in Market Gardening* 163.

65. William Bennett & Son, Farm Accounts; Ross, *History of Long Island* 1:793. During the first four years covered by Bennett's ledgers, 1883–86, potato prices fluctuated between $1.56 and $2.58 per barrel; in 1895–96, the range fell to $0.87 to $1.96; but by 1897–98, the farm's last years, the price range recovered to $1.55 to $2.49. A roughly similar price pattern prevailed for cabbages, which were as high

as 4.3 cents in 1884 and fell to 0.8 cents in 1894–95. The prices of potatoes and cabbages were about the same in 1854. See the journal of Williamson Rapalje.

66. A. Demaree, "The Farm Journals"; A. Demaree, *The American Agricultural Press*; Donald Marti, "Agricultural Journalism and the Diffusion of Knowledge"; Sally McMurry, "Who Read the Agricultural Journals?"

67. John C. Vanderveer was the president and Jeremiah Johnson the first vice president of the county society. Kings County Society for Promoting Agriculture, *Constitution of the Kings County Society for Promoting Agriculture* 2. The state society's conclusion that it could not "reasonably be supposed that there is any lack of liberality in sustaining the County Agricultural Society" proved as untenable as its prediction that: "If it were possible that the practical farmers in that quarter should prove negligent of their own interests in this matter, could it be doubted that there would be found in the city of Brooklyn alone numerous citizens sufficiently imbued with the love of agriculture and horticulture to render efficient aid in sustaining any society judiciously organized for promoting improvement in those essential branches of industry?" *TNYSAS* 3:654–55.

68. "Farm Notes," *KCRG*, May 10, 1873, 6:1 (quote); "Local Pride," *KCRG*, Aug. 9, 1873, 4:1 (quote); "Queens County Fair," *KCRG*, Oct. 13, 1877, 2:3; "Fair Notes," *KCRG*, Oct. 5, 1878, 2:2; "County Fairs," *KCRBG*, Oct. 4, 1884, 2:1 (quote).

69. L. H. Bailey, "An Outlook on Vegetable Gardening" 45.

4. Labor Supply: Agricultural Workers and Labor Relations

1. Eric Wolf, *Europe and the People Without History* 364.

2. "Index Showing the names of the owners of those slaves to whom Children were born after the 4th day of July 1799," in TRKC, Flatlands; CP, 1810, Schedules, NYS, KC; CP, 1820, Schedules, NYS, KC; "Ancestral Brooklynites: How the Predecessors of Our Local Millionaires Disposed of Their Property," *BDE*, Jan. 17, 1873, 2:8.

3. Boughton, "Old Flatbush" 9 n., quoted the diary according to the manuscript, which one of Baxter's descendants made available to him. This entry is lacking in the typescript at the Holland Society, which is a copy of the typescript at the BHS, which also houses an original. Since the typescript is titled "Extracts from the Journal of John Baxter of Flatlands, Long Island," perhaps Boughton read a longer version.

4. Henry Stiles, *Civil . . . History* 1:49. Because the farming season did not last all year, in order to make slaves' labor economical, owners also gave them nonagricultural productive work. Richard Moss, *Slavery on Long Island* 75.

5. 1799 N.Y. Laws, ch. 62 at 721.

6. An Act concerning Slaves and Servants, 1801 N.Y. Laws, ch. 188, sect. 1 at 612.

7. Robert Fogel and Stanley Engerman, "Philanthropy at Bargain Prices" 378–79 (quote), 392; 1817 N.Y. Laws, ch. 137, sect. 31 at 136, 144; 1799 N.Y. Laws, ch. 62 at 721–23; TRKC, UD, Flatbush, Board of Health-Manumitted and Abandoned Slaves (quote). The slaveowner's only financial obligation was to support the child during his or her first year. Slaveowners who failed to file the notice were

"answerable for the maintenance of every such child until the arrival of the . . . periods of servitude specified in . . . this act." 1799 N.Y. Laws, ch. 62 at 723. For examples of indentures, see indenture of Bill to Dominicus Vanderveer, Apr. 29, 1807, in TRKC, UD, Flatbush, Board of Health-Manumitted and Abandoned Slaves. Some older slaves when manumitted became immediately "entitled to all the rights and privileges of a free Citizen of the State of New York." Adrian Vanderveer and Jacob Rapelje, the overseers of the poor, certified this entitlement on behalf of Tone and his wife Sarah, slaves whom John Lott manumitted on August 16, 1819. TRKC, UD, Flatbush, Overseers of Poor; Slave Indentures; Slave Manumissions, 1805–1820.

8. Agreement dated Nov. 6, 1802, in Benson Papers, box V, fifth folder. For an example of the earlier trade in slaves, see an agreement, dated April 22, 1753, and witnessed, inter alia, by Gerret Couwenhoven, in which Garret Verdoon of New Ootrecht purchased for 60 pounds "one Negro winch named Dine," "to HAVE and to HOLD the said Negro winch Dine . . . for ever." Copy furnished by Catharine Weber Scarborough, a descendant of the Cowenhovens.

9. Shane White, *Somewhat More Independent* 16–18, 51–53 (quotes); Edward Bergman and Thomas Pohl, *A Geography of the New York Metropolitan Region* 12 (quote). White's figure combines data for Kings and Richmond counties, but since slavery was even more prevalent in the former, it is likely that the 90 percent figure is an understatement. On the extent of slavery in New Utrecht a century earlier, see B-Ann Moorhouse, "A 1698 Census New Utrecht." Dutch farmers also used slaves as personal servants. When Peter Kouwenhoven of Flatlands died in 1787, his will provided that if his wife did not remarry, his sons "shall allow her out of my estate a negro wench to wait upon her." "Funeral Clothes Willed to Slaves: Old Kings County Testaments Made Provision for Negroes" (copy of undated newspaper clipping provided by Catharine Weber Scarsborough).

10. Alice Kenney, *Stubborn for Liberty* 214 (quote); USBC, *A Century of Population Growth*, tab. 113 at 275; Arthur Zilversmit, *The First Emancipation* 148 (quote); White, *Somewhat More Independent* 55; Henry Hazelton, *The Boroughs of Brooklyn and Queens* 2:1087. For further evidence that "Dutch . . . owners of small, subsistence farms . . . were perhaps the largest and most dedicated slave owners throughout the eighteenth century," see *"Pretends to Be Free"* xvii.

11. USBC, *A Century of Population Growth*, tab. 114 at 282, tab. 115 at 293. In Westchester County and New York City slaves accounted for 6 and 7 percent, respectively, of the population. Ibid., tab. 104 at 194–95.

12. USBC, *Heads of Families at the First Census: New York* 96–98; Peter Ross, *A History of Long Island* 1:122–24.

13. *Census for 1820* [no pagination].

14. USBC, *Heads of Families at the First Census: New York* at 98; Journal of John Baxter (entry for Aug. 12, 1791), in Protestant Dutch Reformed Church of Flatlands, *Tercentary Anniversary* 54 (printing extracts from the journal) (quote); USBC, *Heads of Families at the First Census: New York* at 97–98; PS of the Third [*sic*; should be Second] Census 1800; CP, 1810, Schedules; CP, 1820, Schedules;

A. Leon Higginbotham Jr., *In the Matter of Color* 143 (quote). For an effort at re-
constructing slave life in one of the Lefferts families, see Firth Fabend, "Black
Roots on Brooklyn Farms" (unpub. ms.). The published census count for slaves
in Flatbush for 1820 is in error: the actual number of slaves returned in the manuscript schedules was 224 and not 211; as a result, the number actually rose
somewhat from 1810. The totals for Kings County and Flatbush for 1820 deviate
slightly from the figures in table 18, which are taken from the totals as they appeared in the census for that year (and reproduced in a secondary source cited
in that table), but which were added incorrectly. The figure of 258 free colored
persons for Flatbush for 1850 should be 257: one Irishman was presumably erroneously designated black by the census enumerator. PS of the Seventh Census, 1850 at 2. The CP did not publish race data for the Kings County towns in
1880 and 1890. The figure for Flatbush in 1880 was calculated from the manuscript schedules and includes 29 people in various Kings County institutions located in Flatbush. The schedules for 1890 were destroyed by the fire at the Department of Commerce building in 1921 and disposed of. NA, *Federal Population
Census 1790–1890* at 177.

15. 1799 N.Y. Laws, ch. 62 at 721; TRKC, Flatbush, Slave Holders, 1799–1826 at 7,
37–41 (quote); TRKC, Translations/Transliterations, Flatbush, Court Minutes,
1679–1681, Town Meeting Minutes, 1762–1818, Birth and Manumissions of
Slaves, 1799–1819 at 309 (quote); TRKC, UD, Flatbush, Overseers of Poor; Slave
Manumissions; Reports, 1818–1821 (quote); TRKC, Flatlands, "Index Showing
the names of the owners of those slaves to whom Children were born." Slaveowners who failed to file birth certificates in a timely fashion did not forfeit their
statutory entitlement to enslave the child for 25 or 28 years, but were merely subject to late fees. John Lefferts, for example, filed certificates as late as 1818 for children born in 1805 and 1807. TRKC, Flatbush, Slave Holders, 1799–1826 at 40.
John Blake, who filed the certificate in 1826, had been returned at the 1820 census as owning seven slaves.

16. Edgar McManus, *A History of Negro Slavery in New York* 172–73, 193–94
(quote); Edgar McManus, *Black Bondage in the North* 176–77. A Lott family genealogist inadvertently hinted at Dutch slaveholders' attachment to their slaves
when he wrote that Joris Lott, one of Flatlands' largest farmers, "was an owner
of slaves, but, owing to this Manumission Act, slaves were freed prior to [his
death] in 1835." A. V. Phillips, *The Lott Family in America* 58. Slaveholding patterns in Kings County resemble those in New York State as a whole and New Jersey and Delaware, where the absolute numbers of slaves increased through 1790
or 1800, but differ markedly from the course of emancipation in Pennsylvania,
Connecticut, and Rhode Island, where slavery fell rapidly throughout the postrevolutionary period. Gary Nash and Jean Soderlund, *Freedom by Degrees* 5, 7.
The data for the towns are taken from the same sources underlying table 9. The
slave figures for 1738 assume that all those listed as "Blacks" were slaves. The
decline in slaves in the various towns between 1800 and 1820 may be over- and
understated: according to White, *Somewhat More Independent* xxv, the totals
tabulated in the published census of 1800 overcounted the number of slaves in

Flatbush by 10 and undercounted those in New Utrecht by 30; for the county as a whole, 1,506 (rather than 1,479) slaves were enumerated on the manuscript schedules. For Flatbush, the manuscript schedules support the published count rather than White. The data for 1814 may not be consistent with the earlier and later census figures because they derive from a "Return of Electors (and other Inhabitants)," which contained inaccuracies and may have been conducted in a different manner.

17. Ralph Weld, *Brooklyn Is America* 159; PS of the Fifth Census, 1830, NY, KC; calculated according to Sixth Census, 1840, NY, KC, Flatbush. The allegedly 113-year-old "colored" woman, whom the census enumerator met in 1840 at the Gravesend residence of Maria Stilwell, who could milk cows "as readily as she could a hundred years ago" was presumably an ex-slave. "An Old Colored Woman," *Iowa Sun*, Oct. 3, 1840, 1:5 (photocopy furnished by Merle Davis).

18. PS of the Seventh Census, 1850; PS of the Eighth Census, 1860, NY, KC.

19. Gertrude Lefferts Vanderbilt, *The Social History of Flatbush* 6; "Mrs. Gertrude L. Vanderbilt," *NYT*, Jan. 7, 1902, 7:5 (obituary). Lefferts Vanderbilt's parents and the family into which she married manumitted slaves in 1822. Vanderbilt, *Social History of Flatbush* 257. It had been less than fifty years since Pieter Lefferts had bequeathed to his children, individually, a "negro wench" or "negro boy." Teunis G. Bergen, *Genealogy of the Lefferts Family 1650–1878* at 27.

20. Vanderbilt, *Social History of Flatbush* 263–64, 266, 267–68.

21. Teunis G. Bergen, *The Bergen Family* 248–49. The *Kings County Rural Gazette* was replete with derisive reports about "darkeys." E.g., "Gravesend," *KCRG*, Aug. 9, 1873, 1:4. Peter Wyckoff (1828–1910), by the 1890s reputedly the only farmer in Brooklyn and a director of two banks, an insurance company, a railroad, and a plate glass company in Brooklyn, reminisced that in the wake of the breakup of slavery, his father (who had died in 1883) had asked the oldest of the farm's 14 slaves "what they had done with the corn[:] the Hoges eat up the corn and nigers eat the Hogs." *The Eagle and Brooklyn* 258–59; "Reminiscences of Peter Wyckoff of Bushwick, L. I." 4 (typescript in BHS) (quote).

22. "'Uncle Sammy' Anderson: The Last Flatbush Slave," in John J. Snyder, *Tales of Old Flatbush* 177; Sixth Census, 1840, NY, KC, Flatbush; U.S. CP, 1870, Flatbush, MS at 70; U.S. CP, 1880, Flatbush, MS, SD no. 2, ED no. 252 at 62. Anderson first appeared on the Flatbush assessment roll as a property owner in 1870, when his house was valued at $125 and taxed $2.50. ARTF 1870 at 8–9. Anderson appeared with an interracial group of property owners before the Flatbush Board of Improvement to oppose a proposal to open Malbone Street on the grounds that they would not be sufficiently compensated for the damage that they expected would result. The Board members, including John A. Lott, did not allude to the presence of black citizens. "Board of Improvement [*sic*]," *KCRG*, Mar. 29, 1873, 4:1, 2.

23. Adriance Van Brunt, Diary, June 9, 10, 12, 19, 1828.

24. A. Oemler, "Truck Farming" 584–85. By the mid-nineteenth century, the black population as a proportion of the whole population of Kings County had dropped to the 1–3 percent range from 34 percent in 1790. The absolute num-

ber of free blacks began rising by the 1820s, but this increment was concentrated in Brooklyn; in Flatbush, the total black population declined steadily from 390 in 1790 to 222 in 1880; their share of the population plummeted from 41 percent to 3 percent as the total population of Flatbush increased almost sevenfold. In rural Kings County, the "colored" population of 1,058 and 1,046 in 1880 and 1890, respectively, accounted for only 3 percent of the population. Table 9.

25. At the turn of the century, "flat cars, loaded with people, and especially with women and children, run out from Chicago, Detroit, and other large cities every morning, and back every night during the berry season. Steamboat lines carry thousands of berry pickers from Chicago to the strawberry fields about St. Joseph and Benton Harbor, Mich.; and Baltimore every year sends thousands of berry pickers out into Anne Arundel and other strawberry counties of Maryland." USCO, *Census Reports*, vol. VI, *Twelfth Census*, pt. II at 306–307.

26. "Flatlands," *KCRG*, May 13, 1876, 2:4 (quote); "The 'Truck' Gardens and Market," *Frank Leslie's Illustrated Newspaper*, Nov. 17, 1888, at 218, 219 (quotes).

27. The creator of the quasi-official sets of estimates of employment for the nineteenth and early-twentieth century observed that: "The bourne from which no traveler has ever returned unscathed is the region where lie the Censuses of 1870–1900, with their indefinite estimation of 'laborers.' . . . [T]he inability, and/or unwillingness of respondents, enumerators, and coders to classify laborers with adequate precision left a large group of 'laborers, not specified.' An unknown portion of these belong in agriculture. The group is so substantial that we can have no reliable figure for agriculture without estimating them. The proper method for estimating them, however, is hard to discover." Stanley Lebergott, "Labor Force and Employment, 1800–1960" at 156–57. Census nomenclature was not uniform in 1860 among the towns of Kings County: in Flatbush, Flatlands, and New Lots, "farm laborers" was used, whereas in Gravesend "laborer" was used, and in New Utrecht both. Where "farm laborer" was not used, only a "laborer" living in a farmer's household was counted as a farm laborer; this conservative procedure necessarily understates the total number of farm laborers by omitting farm laborers who lived independently.

28. Calculated according to CP, 1860, MS; a very large proportion of servants were Irish. One hired farm woman was Mary Jane Anderson, an Irish Protestant, who worked on the Bergen family farm in Flatlands together with her brother-in-law in 1853–54, and John Johnson "coloured known as old Dad," who had lived there 28 years. John C. Bergen, Diary, Mar. 1, 1854, in John C. Bergen Papers.

29. "'Gone Home,'" *KCRG*, July 19, 1879, 2:5. In connection with a murder, the *Rural Gazette* mentioned at least one black farm laborer who did not appear in the census. "Horrible Murder!!" *KCRG*, June 22, 1872, 1:1–4.

30. Merle Curti, *The Making of an American Community* 145–46. Curti noted in his study of one Wisconsin county: "In some cases, of two sons in the same family both of working age, the older was recorded as farmer, the younger as agricultural laborer. This suggests that sometimes the older son was considered to be in line for operation of the farm when the father's working days were over." Ibid.

at 60. The 1880 data are calculated from Tenth Census, 1880, NY, vol. 37, Kings, pt. 9, 10.

31. Robert Ernst, *Immigrant Life in New York City 1826−1863* at 70, 62 (quotes). Irish-born numbered 2,555, 2,301, 4,235, 4,189, 4,564, and 4,984 at the censuses of 1855, 1865, 1870, 1875, 1880, and 1890, respectively. Calculated according to SC, *CSNY, for 1855* at 103−104; SC, *CSNY, for 1865* at 116−17; SI, Ninth Census, vol. 1 at 317, 366, 386−91; SC, *CSNY for 1875*, tab. 18 at 36; CO, *Statistics of the Population . . . Tenth Census*, tab. XIV at 521, tab. XV at 536−41; CO, *Compendium of the Eleventh Census*, pt. II, tab. 2 at 604−605, tab. 3 at 655.

32. The 1860 census asked only each individual's birthplace; the 1870 census asked whether the parents were of foreign birth, but not where they had been born. The 1880 census also returned 139 farm laborers living in the city of Brooklyn, of whom 21 were Irish and 33 German, although it is unknown where they worked; 221 farmers and planters also lived in Brooklyn, of whom 28 were Irish and 55 German, but, again, the location of their farms is unknown. CO, *Statistics of the Population . . . Tenth Census*, tab. XXXVI at 865.

33. Based on tables 9 and 10 and sources mentioned therein. The 1880 census did not break out the data for race for the towns of rural Kings County.

34. The small figure for Flatbush in 1880 is implausible, but since farm laborers were enumerated by residence, some residing in neighboring towns, all of which bordered on Flatbush, may have worked on farms in Flatbush.

35. John T. Ridge, *The Flatbush Irish* 9; calculated according to PS of the Seventh Census, 1850; calculated according to PS of the Eighth Census. The published CP for 1860 did not present county-level ethnic data. The other groups in 1850 in descending order were Germans (13), blacks (10), U.S.-born whites (8), English (2), and Danish (1).

36. Arthur Gilbert, *The Potato* 226−27; Cindy Hahamovitch, *The Fruits of Their Labor* 14−54; Friedrich Kapp, *Immigration and the Commissioners of Emigration of the State of New York* 115−17 (quote); "Facts for Farmers," *KCRG*, May 2, 1874, 3:2.

37. Calculated according to CO, *Statistics of the Population . . . Tenth Census*, tab. XIV at 521, tab. XVI at 541; *KCRG*, Apr. 12, 1873, 4:4 (quote); "Washington Cemetery," *KCRG*, Oct. 24, 1874, 1:1; "Parkville," *KCRG*, May 22, 1875, 4:3 (150 Italian workers); "Bay Ridge," *KCRG*, Mar. 18, 1876, 2:7 (Italian workers refused to work for $1 per day, but then agreed to $1.21 building the Bay Ridge R.R.). On the number of Italian immigrants, see USBC, *Historical Statistics of the United States*, pt. 1, ser. C-100 at 106; on the failed attempts to organize agricultural settlements for Italian immigrants in the South, see Humbert Nelli, *Italians in Chicago 1880−1930* at 3−5, 15−19. No evidence has been found that any significant number of Polish peasant immigrants, such as those working as farm laborers in Queens in the 1870s and 1880s, was employed on Kings County farms. Vincent Seyfried, "Truck Gardening" at 1 (unpub. paper).

38. *Reports of the Immigration Commission: Immigrants in Industries*, pt. 24, *Recent Immigrants in Agriculture*, vol. I; USDA, Bureau of Statistics, *Wages of Farm La-*

bor in the United States: Results of Nine Statistical Investigations, from 1866 to 1892 at 22 (quote); Donna Garbaccia, From Sicily to Elizabeth Street 63; Donna Garbaccia, Militants and Migrants 91–92, 127–48; USDA, Bureau of Statistics, Wages of Farm Labor in the United States: Results of Twelve Statistical Investigations, 1866–1902 at 31 (quote); Alberto Pecorini, "The Italian as an Agricultural Laborer" 383 (quote), 384–85; Kate Claghorn, "Agricultural Distribution of Immigrants" 495–506; Jay Bonsteel et al., "Soil Survey of the Long Island Area" 123–24; W. Nissley, "Vegetable Growing on Long Island" 1224; Bolton Hall, Three Acres and Liberty 72 (quote); "Farm Land Valuations Increased $42.000,000," BDE, Mar. 10, 1912, Theaters, sect. 6:3 (quote).

39. Tenth Annual Report of the Bureau of Statistics of Labor of the State of New York, for the Year 1892, pt. I at 220 (quote); Bonsteel et al., "Soil Survey of the Long Island Area" 124 (quote). On the occupational distribution of Italian immigrants to New York, see Thomas Kessner, The Golden Door.

40. E.g., Weld, Brooklyn Is America; Harold Connolly, A Ghetto Grows in Brooklyn 8–9, 33–35; U.S. CP, 1870 and 1880, KC, MS; Leon Litwack, North of Slavery 162–67, 175 (quote). Abraham Lavender and Clarence Steinberg, Jewish Farmers of the Catskills 31, mention one Jewish family that briefly had a farm on Pitkin Avenue in Brooklyn in the 1890s before joining other Jews who farmed in upstate New York, but they do not mention any who had been farm laborers in Kings County.

41. Henderson, Gardening for Profit 361 (1890 ed.).

42. "Canarsie," KCRG, June 24, 1876, 2:6. An anecdote indicates one farmer's problem recruiting workers — or his speculation as to how to take advantage of a lumpenproletarian's desire to avoid incarceration. In November — presumably a nonpeak period — 1873, Johannes Kouwenhoven of Gravesend caught a "German tramp" in a neighbor's cellar, whom he was in the process of hauling off to the village for commitment as a vagrant when he instead gave the man to a German farmer, William Willkomm, who said he would hire his landsman. Willkomm later made a bargain with the man, who, however, after three days broke into the house and fled. "Gravesend," KCRG, Nov. 15, 1873, 1:1–2.

43. "Potatoes," KCRG, July 27, 1872, 6:1.

44. "Gravesend," KCRG, July 19, 1879, 2:6. The horse epidemic was so severe that it impelled two Gravesend farmers to charter Lefferts Vanderbilt's yacht Gertrude to transport their cauliflower to Manhattan. "Coney Island," KCRG, Dec. 14, 1872, 5:1.

45. In 1870, 1874, 1879, the potato harvest amounted to 547,000, 420,000, and 772,000 bushels, respectively. Using 30 and 100 bushels as the minimum and maximum output per worker-day, respectively, the maximum and minimum number of worker-days would have been in 1870: 18,233/5,470; 1874: 14,000/4,200; 1879: 25,733/7,720. Hand diggers could harvest one-eighth to one-half an acre per day; with yields of 200 bushels per acre, these estimates are reconcilable with the productivity estimates in the text. Gilbert, The Potato at 234; chap. 2 above. For another estimate of one-half acre as the upper limit, see Samuel Fraser, The Potato 144. The agricultural censuses did not distinguish among var-

ious kinds of potatoes, but Kings County farmers grew several varieties, which, at least on some farms, prolonged the season. On John C. Bergen's farm in Flatlands in 1865, Jackson white potatoes were harvested from June 29 to July 13, Dikeman potatoes from July 13 to Aug. 13, and bucks from Sept. 2 to 12. John C. Bergen papers. To the extent that the use of mechanical potato diggers spread, it could also have diminished the demand for workers. See *KCRG*, July 12, 1873, 5:1 (advertisement for potato digger). On the increase in productivity in potato production, including the introduction of potato diggers, between 1866 and 1895, see *Thirteenth Annual Report of the Commissioner of Labor* 1:24–25; 2:452–55.

46. E.g., "Gravesend," *KCRG*, Jan. 31, 1874, 8:2 (William Willkomm, who at the 1870 census was returned as having three German laborers living in his household); Gertrude Ryder Bennett, *Living in a Landmark* 51 (slaves' quarters). In 1877, John D. Van Pelt of New Utrecht tore down a cottage that had been built forty years earlier to accommodate his farm laborers. "New Utrecht, Bath and Unionville," *KCRG*, May 12, 1877, 2:6. Laborers residing on farms were calculated according to manuscript schedules of the CP, 1860, 1870, and 1880, KC. These calculations assume that persons listed as farm laborers and residing in the household of a farmer worked for that farmer. The percentages actually understate the proportion of hired laborers living on the farm because they exclude relatives (especially sons) of the farmers listed as working on the farm from the numerator but not the denominator. The percentage for 1860 is estimated because enumerators that year did not uniformly use the occupation "farm laborer"; where, as in Gravesend, "laborer" was used, only laborers living in a farm household could be counted as farm laborers. Excluding Gravesend, 65 percent of farm laborers lived in the farm family's household, ranging from 51 percent in Flatbush to 83 percent in New Utrecht, where the enumerator did not use the term "farm laborer" consistently. In 1870, the proportion of farm laborers living on farms was relatively uniform across the five rural towns, ranging from 42 percent in New Utrecht to 58 percent in Gravesend. By 1880 the dispersion had increased, varying from 0 percent in Flatbush to 40 percent in Gravesend.

47. Kings County data calculated according to manuscript schedules of the CP and CA, 1860, 1870, and 1880; national calculated according to data in Paul Gates, *The Farmer's Age* 273.

48. Wage data calculated from the U.S. Census, 1880, Agriculture, KC; other data calculated according to CO, *Report on the Productions of Agriculture*, tab. VII at 127. It is unclear why the wage data were not published. Another set of data not published was labeled, "Weeks hired labor in 1879 upon farm (and dairy) excluding housework." This information was frequently omitted even where wages were entered; the figures bear no uniform relation to wages, and it is unclear what they refer to.

49. See also Lawanda Cox, "The American Agricultural Wage Earner, 1865–1900" at 96–97.

50. The two labor-intensive vegetable producing counties whose average per farm wage costs were next highest, New York ($784) and Hudson ($753), were also the

only counties in which market garden production formed a higher proportion of total output. Norfolk is only a seeming exception: its market garden production as a share of total output was about as high as Kings County's, yet its wage bill was only 27 percent as large. This disproportion is in large part explained by its lower wage level (it was the only southern county on the list). Nevertheless, the fact that wage expenditures in Philadelphia, where market gardening was almost as important as in Kings County, were less than two-thirds as large gives pause. Of these 19 counties, 8 were in Louisiana, 4 in Georgia, 2 in Alabama and Mississippi, and 1 in Florida, Maryland, and North Carolina. The highest per farm wages were recorded in Washington County, Mississippi ($4,746).

51. Williamson Rapalje's father of the same name and Henry Wyckoff also employed foremen; two others were enumerated in 1870 who did not live on the farm. The largest vegetable farm in 1870 was owned by W. Bennett & Brothers in New Utrecht, whose 75-acre farm produced $16,000 worth of market garden produce. U.S. CP, 1870, KC, MS; U.S. CP, 1870, KC, MS; U.S. CA, 1870, KC, MS.

52. Since enough rich nonfarmers lived in the rural towns to employ more than a few gardeners, the assumption here and throughout has been that those returned as "gardener" by the census were not part of the agricultural labor force.

53. Tracing individuals through successive censuses is difficult because census enumerators did not always spell names correctly and people themselves did not always spell their names consistently. See Stephanie Wolf, *Urban Village* 79 n.50. The limited number of names among the Dutch and the concentration of names among the Irish and blacks exacerbated this problem. A further source of possible error is the failure to report accurately and consistently the ages of all household members. If all other data indicate that it is the same person, the fact that someone was only six (rather than ten) years older at the next census did not operate to disqualify him. The procedure erred on the side of exclusion, which here affected a total of only three people.

54. The four were Michael Aljohn, Edward Coleman, John Crooke, and Edward Tully.

55. Alexander Keyssar, *Out of Work* 343; U.S. CP, NY, KC, MS. It is plausible that farm laborers living on the farm were more likely to be employed year round, but there was no uniformity: about three-fifths of farm laborers living on the farm in Gravesend experienced unemployment compared with only one-quarter in Flatlands.

56. Willard Thorp, *Business Annals* 133; *IA*, Feb. 14, 1880, at 5, col. 3.

57. William Bennett & Son, Farm Accounts; TRKC, UD, Flatbush, Highway Commissioners — Crosswalks; Railroad Petitions; Gas Lamps; Labor Reports; Proposals: 1874–1883; Henderson, *Gardening for Profit* 218 (1890 ed.) (in 1874 the labor of three men for six months cost $750, or $41.66 per person per month); W. W. Rawson, *Success in Market Gardening*; Burnet Landreth, *Market Gardening and Farm Notes* 124 (planting, hoeing, and banking celery cost $1.50 per worker-day). These calculated wages are somewhat higher than the monthly farm wages without board for all of New York State that the USDA collected for the period. USDA, Div. of Statistics, *Wages of Farm Labor in the United States: Re-*

sults of Nine Statistical Investigations 16. The data for the city of Brooklyn are neglected here because it is assumed that farm laborers returned as living in rural Kings County by the CP also worked there. Although some farm laborers were returned as living in Brooklyn, the figure was not verified because the Brooklyn census manuscript schedules were too voluminous to process. The average wage mentioned in the text may also be overstated because the Census of Population presumably did not enumerate as farm laborers those who worked only seasonally in farming; migratory farm laborers who were not residing in Kings County at the time of enumeration in June would also have been excluded. Finally, the relationship between residence on the farm, as enumerated by the Census of Population, and wages paid by the farm operator, as calculated by the Census of Agriculture, may also be a source of confusion. For example, Williamson Rapalje, whose household included 11 farm laborers in 1870, paid only $2,500 in wages, which amounts to only $227 per worker. His neighbor, Ferdinand Wyckoff, in whose household seven farm workers lived, paid $2,700, which works out to $386 per worker. Since the two groups of workers were all German-born and of a similar age, such a large difference seems implausible. One possible explanation is that Rapalje's laborers worked fewer months. U.S. CP, 1870, KC, Town of NL, MS; U.S. CA, 1870, KC, Town of NL, MS.

58. "Farm Hands to Strike," *KCRG*, Apr. 21, 1877, 3:1 (quote); "Flatlands," *KCRBG*, Mar. 25, 1882, 2:3; "'Pretty Jack' Sues for a Years [sic] Wages," *KCRBG*, June 10, 1882, 2:3; "A Novel Case from Flatlands," *KCRBG*, June 10, 1882, 2:1; "Flatlands and Canarsie," *KCG*, Oct. 17, 1885, 2:5; "A Noted Case," *KCRBG*, Aug. 5, 1882, 2:2 (quotes); "A Novel Case from Flatlands" (quote). The case is of further interest because the farm worker was represented from trial to the state's highest court by William J. Gaynor, who in 1910 became mayor of Greater New York. Before becoming a judge in the 1890s, Gaynor lived in Flatbush, where he was counsel to the Board of Health and the elite Law and Order Association of the Town of Flatbush, and had close business ties to politicians in various Kings County towns, especially John Y. McKane, the so-called czar of Gravesend. Why Gaynor represented Turner is unclear. He maintained a large and varied practice and did take cases without a fee, but he also represented a defendant who had been "sued by a servant girl for wages." Gaynor, who accumulated a fortune from his legal practice, which brought him an annual income of more than $50,000, derived considerable income from real estate speculation in Flatbush. *Lain's Business Directory of Brooklyn . . . 1886/87* at 363; Louis Pink, *Gaynor* 36, 40–41, 43 (quote), 46; *The Eagle and Brooklyn* 484. Gaynor speculated in the Flatbush land boom; in 1882, he was the second-largest buyer (10 lots) at an auction of a large and valuable property, which was in a district in which the greatest improvements in Flatbush in the previous 14 years had been made. "A Great Sale of Property," *KCRBG*, Jan. 21, 1882; "Bargains: Sale of the Robinson Estate," *KCRBG*, Feb. 4, 1882 (quote). By 1890 he had "augmented his lucrative practice by large real estate holdings." Mortimer Smith, *William Jay Gaynor* 21. Gaynor was sufficiently prominent in 1876 for the *Rural Gazette* to announce that he was moving to Flatbush. *KCRG*, May 6, 1876, 2:2.

59. U.S. CP, 1880, KC, Flatlands, ED no. 254 at 40, 42, 47, 48, 51; U.S. Census, 1880, Agriculture, reel 18, KC, Flatlands, ED no. 254, SD no. 2 at 5. Duley's name was really spelled "Dooley." New York Court of Appeals, John Turner, Respondent, against William W. Kouvenhoven, Appellant, *Appeal Book* 21.

60. Turner v. Kouwenhoven, testimony, in *Appeal Book* at 21; Brief for Appellant at 3, in *Appeal Book* (quotes); Turner v. Kouwenhoven, testimony, in *Appeal Book* at 46; Brief for Appellant at 6, in *Appeal Book*. Such annual wage arrangements were common in some regions in nineteenth-century agriculture; e.g., Britton v. Turner, 6 N.H. 481 (1834).

61. Turner v. Kouwenhoven, testimony, in *Appeal Book* 22, 24, 49.

62. CP, 1880, MS; CA, 1880, MS; Turner v. Kouwenhoven, testimony, in *Appeal Book* 49–50 (quote). Turner too testified that Kouwenhoven was known in Flatlands as "Stingy Bill." Turner v. Kouwenhoven, testimony, in *Appeal Book* 68. This testimony was taken at a previous trial on March 17, 1882. Alone in the small town of Flatlands, no fewer than 12 Kouwenhoven's were farming in 1880, including five named William, three of whom were William W.

63. Turner v. Kouwenhoven, testimony, in *Appeal Book* 85, 33, 46, 23 (quote); Turner v. Kouwenhoven, testimony of W. Kouwenhoven, in *Appeal Book* 22–29; Exhibits 1 and 2, in ibid. at 65–67; testimony of John Turner (Mar. 17, 1882), in *Appeal Book* 86. The fact that this investment was arranged through the same New York City law firm that represented Kouwenhoven in this litigation suggests that it may have had a conflict of interest. Turner v. Kouwenhoven, testimony of W. Kouwenhoven, in *Appeal Book* 46.

64. Turner v. Kouwenhoven, testimony, in *Appeal Book* 21, 24, 30, 32, 42 (W. Kouwenhoven), 50 (Ryder), 51 (C. B. Kouwenhoven).

65. Turner v. Kouwenhoven, Complaint, County Court of KC, Jan. 3, 1882, in *Appeal Book* 4. Turner v. Kouwenhoven, testimony, in *Appeal Book* 32. Turner v. Kouwenhoven, testimony, in *Appeal Book* 41 (question to which Kouwenhoven responded affirmatively) (quote). This delegation of marketing may not have been common. The USDA official in charge of the vegetable division of the Bureau of Agricultural Economics, in a historical retrospective, noted that among urban truck farmers who sold assorted vegetables chiefly at retail: "Almost invariably a member of the family drove to market and did the selling. Retail marketing was not a hired man's job. It involved handling the entire family income." Wells Sherman, *Merchandising Fruits and Vegetables* 15.

66. Kouwenhoven defended on the grounds that Turner had failed to perform his contract fully because he had not paid over to the farmer the full proceeds from the sales at market, instead having kept some of this money for himself. Despite the fact that Turner had served out his full term and that the employer had no complaints concerning Turner's work on the farm proper, he argued that Turner's failures legally disentitled him to any recovery at all. Kouwenhoven filed a counterclaim for the money Turner had allegedly retained not only in 1881 but during the two preceding years. Turner v. Kouwenhoven, 29 Hun 232, 233 (N.Y. A.D. 1883), *aff'd*, 100 N.Y. 115, 118 (1885). At trial in County Court in Kings County, the chief question for the jury was whether Turner had in fact re-

tained and converted any money belonging to the farmer. The trial judge, who agreed with both counsel that the case was one of first impression in New York State, rejected the defendant's request to charge the jury that any failure by the laborer to pay over proceeds must result in forfeiture of all his compensation for the year, but did instruct the jurors that they could deduct from an award to Turner any amounts that they found he owed. Turner v. Kouwenhoven, *Appeal Book* 54–60. Before the case went to the jury, Turner agreed that the number of loads that he had transported for Kouwenhoven was 201 rather than 398. Turner v. Kouwenhoven, *Appeal Book* 60. Kouwenhoven appealed to the intermediate appeals court the trial judge's refusal to issue the aforementioned jury instruction. Two of the three appellate judges rejected the farmer's argument that any delinquency by a laborer during a year's term should bar him from receiving any compensation whatsoever. A discharge for cause during the term could bring about such a result, but even if a farm laborer who served his entire term had injured his employer, forfeiture of his whole salary would be inappropriate where the farmer could be indemnified. Turner v. Kouwenhoven, 29 Hun 233–36.

67. Turner v. Kouwenhoven, Brief for Appellant 39–40, in *Appeal Book.*
68. Turner v. Kouwenhoven, Brief for Appellant 4, in *Appeal Book* (quote). The Court of Appeals unanimously affirmed the lower courts on essentially the same grounds. Turner v. Kouwenhoven, 100 N.Y. 120–21.

5. Comparative Demographic and Economic Development in Brooklyn and Rural Kings County

1. "Westchester Annexation," *NYT*, Nov. 1, 1873, 4:4.
2. "Suburban Homes," *NYT*, May 31, 1874, 4:1.
3. Ibid.
4. "New Utrecht Topics Local and General," *KCRG*, Feb. 27, 1875, 8:1; "New Utrecht Topics Local and General," *KCRG*, Feb. 6, 1875, 8:1 (quote); "Steam," *KCRG*, Feb. 13, 1875, 4:1 (editorial) (quote).
5. Ira Rosenwaike, *Population History of New York City* 30; 1834 N.Y. Laws, ch. 92 at 90; Ralph Weld, *Brooklyn Village* 25–26 (quote); *Appleton's Dictionary of New York and Vicinity* 39 (quote); Henry Stiles, *A History of the City of Brooklyn* 3:586.
6. Nathaniel Prime, *History of Long Island* 377–78; "Theodore Cocheu Tells About Old Williamsburgh," *BDE*, Jan. 18, 1914, 12:1.
7. *Census for 1820* [no pagination].
8. Weld, *Brooklyn Village* 47.
9. Ibid. 6–7.
10. Ibid. 47 (quote); *The Diary of Philip Hone* 1:147–48 (entry for Jan. 14, 1835) (quote).
11. David Johnson, *Planning the Great Metropolis* 14; Edward Pessen, *Riches, Class, and Power Before the Civil War* 36–38 (quote at 36).
12. Calculated according to *CSNY, for 1845.* The low one to one ratio in Flatlands may be explained by the fertilizer industry on Barren Island. The Flatbush fig-

ures were skewed by the fact that almost 30 percent of all persons returned as employed were inmates of the Kings County Poor House, which happened to be located in Flatbush, but most of whose residents came from the city of Brooklyn. PS of the Sixth Census, 1840. As early as 1830, Kings County bought 64 acres from the Martense heirs for the county farm, which that year produced 750 bushels of potatoes, 107 bushels of turnips, 13 bushels of onions, four tons of hay, and manufactured goods worth $244.36. Stiles, *Civil . . . History* 1:464–92.

13. J. T. Bailey, *An Historical Sketch of the City Brooklyn* 31, 34 (quote); calculated according to TRKC, UD, Flatbush, Jurors — List of, 1815–1847.

14. Calculated according to Enrollment of Persons Liable to Military Duty, in TRKC, Gravesend, Enrollment — Persons Liable to Military Duty, 1862; CP, 1860 and 1870, KC, MS.

15. Calculated according to Enrollment of Persons Liable to Military Duty, in TRKC, NU, Troops — Persons Liable to Military Duty; "New Utrecht," *KCRG*, June 6, 1874, 8:1.

16. Prime, *History of Long Island* 67.

17. Teunis G. Bergen, *The Bergen Family* 108–9.

18. Jeremiah Johnson, "Recollections of Old Roads, Residents and Their Occupations" 9, 5.

19. SC, *CSNY, for 1865* at 322. This was the last NYS census to break out separate data for Brooklyn.

20. Pessen, *Riches, Class, and Power Before the Civil War* 46–52 (quote at 48).

21. 1827 N.Y. Laws, ch. 260 at 270; 1840 N.Y. Laws, ch. 51 at 35; 1854 N.Y. Laws, ch. 384 at 829; "The Greater New York," *RERBG*, 53 (1355):326 (Mar. 3, 1894). Williamsburgh was incorporated as a city in 1851. 1851 N.Y. Laws, ch. 91 at 110.

22. *LDLI: For 1878–9* at 267–68, 242, 276, 279, 282; "Brooklyn Annexation Projects," *NYDT*, Apr. 6, 1894, 6:4 (editorial) (quote); "Annex Them All at Once," *BDE*, Mar. 8, 1894, 4:1 (quote); "A Great Work Well Done," *BDE*, Apr. 27, 1894, 4:1 (editorial) (quote); *NYT*, Nov. 8, 1894, 4:1 (editorial) (quote); Harold Syrett, *The City of Brooklyn, 1865–1898* at 38, 159–93, 222–27. Just the previous year, the *Eagle* had written that McKane's entire career had "revealed him to be a man of thoroughly democratic instincts, a literal believer in the equal rights of men and in fair play for all." In addition to being supervisor, chief of police, and president of the town, health, police, and water boards in Gravesend, McKane as building contractor built most of the hotels and houses on Coney Island. *The Eagle and Brooklyn* 453. McKane was also one of the Comissioners of Common Lands of Gravesend, which let lots of barren land on Coney Island which freeholders held in common. "Coney Island Lands at Auction," *BDE*, Aug. 19, 1873, 1:1 (advertisement); "The Progress of the Consolidation Commission," *BDE*, Aug. 28, 1873, 2:2. (editorial); "Gravesend Common Lands," *KCRG*, Feb. 15, 1879, 2:1 (editorial). See generally Edo McCullough, *Good Old Coney Island* 15–113. On the legislature's effort to deal with the corruption surrounding these leases, see 1880 N.Y. Laws, ch. 92 at 204. The county's budget was considerably smaller than that of the city of Brooklyn; in 1888, the two were $1.4 and $8.1 million, respectively. The interest paid on Brooklyn's debt in 1888, for example, was larger than the

county's entire budget. The county budget's largest items were, in descending order, the Department of Charities and Corrections, interest on funded debt, county wards, county jail, city court, jurors' fees, Supreme Court, Board of Supervisors, principal of funded debt, County Court, and National Guard, which accounted for more than three-fourths of total expenditures. *BDEA: 1888* at 119.

23. "Consolidation and Rapid Transit," *NYT*, Oct. 17, 1894, 4:4, 5 (quote); "Greater New-York in Doubt," *NYT*, Nov. 8, 1894, 1:3 (quote).

24. Thomas Adams, Harold Lewis, and Theodore McCrosky, *Population, Land Values and Government*, fig. 14 at 68.

25. J. J. Stilwell, "Annexation: Supervisor Stilwell Argues Against It," *BDE*, Apr. 5, 1873, 1:8 (letter to editor) (asking rhetorically who fills the county institutions in order to refute claims that rural towns did not pay their fair share of county expenses); PS of the Ninth Census, 1870. "Annexation: City and County Union," *BDE*, Mar. 3, 1873, 2:6, 7, noted that the population of 6,000 included 2,000 institutionalized inmates. The *East New York Sentinel* also noted that the population of New Lots was more than double that of Flatbush. "Who's Doing this Annexing?" *KCRG*, Jan. 11, 1873, 4:1 (reprinting article of Jan. 4). These institutions date back to the 1830s, but were expanded in the 1850s; to overcome overcrowding in Flatbush, the county in 1884 purchased 750 acres of small adjoining farms at St. Johnsland, 60 miles away on Long Island. "St. Johnsland," *KCRBG*, Aug. 22, 1885, 2:3; *Annual Report of the State Board of Charities for the Year Ending September 30, 1886*, at 38; "The Sick Poor: Shall They Be Sent to Flatbush or St. Johnland?" *BDE*, Feb. 26, 1887, 6:7; David Schneider, *The History of Public Welfare in New York State* 361. By 1892, about one thousand people were received at the Long Island location, which was renamed King's Park. *The Eagle and Brooklyn* 379. The statutory basis of the farm work requirement is set forth in 1871 N.Y. Laws, ch. 491, sect. 3 and 8 at 1030, 1031, 1033; 1874 N.Y. Laws, ch. 114, sect. 1 and 6 at 127, 130. The farm's output is documented in U.S. Census, 1860, Agriculture. The county farm was not returned at the 1850 or 1870 CA. In 1887, the products of the 70-acre Flatbush poor farm operated by the Kings County Commissioners of Charities were valued at $5,000. *BDEA: 1888* at 125. The institutional population was calculated according to PS of the Seventh Census, 1850; PS of the Eighth Census, 1860. In January 1873, the KC Commissioners of Charities reported 387 persons in the nursery, 444 inmates, 1,007 persons in the almshouse, and 745 persons in the lunatic asylum for a total of 2,583. *KCRG*, Jan. 25, 1873, 4:4. At the time of the NYS census of 1875, about 30 percent of the town's population was returned as residing in the county buildings. "The Census," *KCRG*, July 17, 1875, 2:1.

26. "Board of Health," *KCRG*, Sept. 12, 1874, 4:1, 3 (report of Dr. H. Bartlett, Flatbush health officer) (quote); "Improving Flatbush and Removing the County Buildings," *KCRBG*, Mar. 5, 1881, 2:1 (editorial) (quote); "The Paupers Turned Loose," *KCRG*, May 9, 1874, 4:1; "The New County Farm," *KCG*, Oct. 17, 1885, 2:2; "Pauper Voting," *KCRG*, Apr. 28, 1877, 2:1 (editorial).

27. *BDEA: 1893* at 97; "Enlarging Brooklyn," *NYDT*, Mar. 12, 1894, 6:3–4 (editorial); *Report of the Jamaica Bay Improvement Commission*, tab. 2 at 72, 54 (H. Doc.).

28. *Robinson's Atlas of Kings County New York.*
29. The juxtaposition between farming and manufacturing appears in one of the very few backward glances at agriculture in historical works. In a section titled, "Farming Country in 1880," a historian noted: "A sidelight on the immense growth of Brooklyn since 1880 is the fact of record that in that year Kings County contained four hundred and eighty-six farms, comprising 9,075 acres, valued, with buildings, at $4,872,055. Five years later, in 1885, Brooklyn was credited with having 85,000 buildings." Henry Hazelton, *The Boroughs of Brooklyn and Queens* 3:1590.
30. Calculated according to CO, *Report on Wealth* at 391, 393.
31. *BDEA: 1888* at 124; *BDEA: 1894* at 228. The years from 1855 to 1885 are used here because Brooklyn and rural Kings County remained territorially unchanged during this period (Williamsburgh and New Lots having joined Brooklyn in 1854 and 1886, respectively).
32. Edmund Fisher, *Flatbush Past and Present* 64.

6. The Prehistory of the Conversion of Rural Kings County Farms into Suburban Real Estate

1. Peter Ross, *History of Long Island* 1:369 (quote). Because the NYS census stopped collecting the relevant agricultural information in 1875 and the 1890 federal census manuscript schedules were destroyed by fire, shifts during the crucial decade of the 1880s can no longer be reconstructed, although it is known that aggregate county farm acreage did not decrease. The vast decline in Flatbush acreage from 1850 to 1855 resulted exclusively from the detachment of New Lots and its formation as a new town in 1852; the loss during the 1860s may have resulted in part from the creation of Prospect Park. The sharp increase in acreage in Flatlands between 1845 and 1855 resulted from the introduction in 1855 by the NYS census of data on unimproved acreage. The huge decline and increase in New Utrecht's acreage before and after the 1870 census is anomalous, resulting in all likelihood from tabulators' failure to process one schedule sheet.
2. Alter Landesman, *A History of New Lots, Brooklyn to 1887* at 91–93 (quotes); "Old County Towns"; "Annexation of New-Lots to Brooklyn," *NYDT*, May 15, 1886, 8:2 (quote).
3. "Old County Towns," in Brooklyn Daily Eagle, *Consolidation Number* 47 (quote); "Flatbush," in *The Towns that Became Brooklyn* 23; "Brooklyn Real Estate," in Brooklyn Daily Eagle, *Consolidation Number* 62 (quote); Ross, *History of Long Island* 1:325 (quote).
4. Andrew Dolkart, "Historical Introduction" 3 (quote); "'Old Flatbush,'" in Snyder, *Tales of Old Flatbush* 79–80; R. G. Strong, "History of the Town of Flatbush," in Stiles, *Civil . . . History* 1:231.
5. J. T. Bailey, *An Historical Sketch of the City of Brooklyn* 34, 33.
6. Thomas Strong, *The History of the Town of Flatbush* 71–72, 177–78.
7. Strong, "History of the Town of Flatbush" 232; *The Eagle and Brooklyn* 1136; ARTF, 1866 at 20; ARTF 1867, at 36; Teunis G. Bergen, *The Bergen Family* 333–

36. The United Freemen's Association was a division of the Sons of Temperance. *KCRG*, Jan. 18, 1873, 2:1. According to Bennett, *Living in a Landmark* 81, many of the laborers on William Bennett's Gravesend farm in the 1880s and 1890s "came from Greenfield, a small settlement of Irish emigrants."

8. Eleonora Schoenebaum, "Emerging Neighborhoods" 30–33, 91, 94–95, 100 (quotation), 97 (quotation), 101 (quotation), 104 (quotation), 178–82. For specific examples of residential gentrification of farms, see Lefferts Vanderbilt, *Social History of Flatbush* 193, 219, 230.

9. Vanderbilt, *Social History of Flatbush* 220 (quote); John A. Lott was not the owner of this farm. Oddly, a contemporaneous article characterized Suffolk as a "strickly [*sic*] farming county," Queens as "in great measure a land of market gardens," and rural Kings County as "largely taken up by the city of Brooklyn and the suburban residences of wealthy gentlemen" despite noting Kings County's large market garden production. "Long Island Agricultural Society," *KCRG*, Oct. 19, 1872, 6:1. On New York merchants living in rural Kings County, see chapter 10–11 below.

10. "The Progress of the Consolidation Commission," *BDE*, Aug. 28, 1873, 2:2 (editorial) (quote); 1835 N.Y. Laws, ch. 137, sect. 2, 5, 6 at 148, 149–50 (quote); 1853 N.Y. Laws, ch. 535, sect. 4 at 1043, 1044; 1848 N.Y. Laws, ch. 360, sect. 2 at 480; "The History of Our Toll Gate," *KCRBG*, May 5, 1883, 2:1–3; Strong, "History of the Town of Flatbush" 231. From 1850 to 1875, Lefferts, together with John Vanderbilt and others, also owned the so-called shell road to Coney Island, which they sold to Andrew Culver, the owner of the first steam railroad to Coney Island. "The Gravesend and Coney Island Bridge and Road Company," *KCRG*, Nov. 27, 1875, 2:2.

11. Strong, "History of the Town of Flatbush," in Stiles, *Civil . . . History* 1:230–32 (quotations); Fisher, *Flatbush Past and Present* 81; 1854 N.Y. Laws, ch. 370 at 776; 1857 N.Y. Laws, ch. 137, sect. 1 at 217; "In Twenty Years: From Stages to Horses — the Flatbush Avenue Railroad — Its Origins and Present Condition," *KCRBG*, May 29, 1880, 2:3; "Flatbush Rapid Transit in 1870 (From an Old Newsprint)," in Snyder, *Tales of Old Flatbush* 127–28 (quote).

12. Fisher, *Flatbush Past and Present* 41, 43–45 (quote); CP, 1870, KC, Flatbush, MS at 66; CP, 1880, KC, Flatbush, MS, SD no. 2, ED no. 252 at 45; ALFBIR, 1869–70 (Williamson Rapalja, a large New Lots farmer, was the president of the Union Gas Co.); Teunis G. Bergen, *Genealogy of the Lefferts Family* 89, 90, 131; A. V. Phillips, *The Lott Family in America* 1, 5; Bergen, *Genealogy of the Lefferts Family* 7; TRKC, Flatbush, Translations/Transliterations, Court Minutes, 1679–1681, Town Meeting Minutes, 1762–1818 at 108; "Public Meeting at Town Hall," *KCRBG*, Mar. 31, 1883, 2:2 (quote).

13. 1871 N.Y. Laws, ch. 567, sect. 1, 8, 10 at 1203, 1205, 1210; Strong, "Modern History of Flatbush" 236. At the end of the 1870s, the membership of the Flatbush Board of Improvement was virtually unchanged; the only addition was Lefferts Vanderbilt as clerk. *LDLI: For 1878–79* at 269. Philip Crooke took John A. Lott's place as president after the latter's death in 1878.

14. TRKC, Flatbush, Improvement Board–Minutes, 1872–1885 at 3, 6, 31, 47–50,

158, 178 (NYCMA). The board met at Lott's house from May 4, 1872, to January 11, 1876; it met there even when he was absent (e.g., Sept. 27, 1873). For a list of the Erasmus Hall trustees, see *KCRG*, Aug. 5, 1876, 4:7.

15. "Aroused at Last — A Delegation of the Principal Property Owners Wait on the Excise Board," *KCRBG*, May 22, 1880, 2:2; "William Matthews Is Dead," *NYDT*, Apr. 16, 1896, 14:1; "William Matthews," *NYT*, Apr. 16, 1896, 5:4; *DAB* 6:420–21. Born in Scotland, he learned the bookbinding trade in London, and emigrated to the United States in 1843; the turning point in his life was a strike in 1841 at one of London's largest binderies, when he "remained faithful to his employers and advanced rapidly to a responsible position." Ibid. Matthews also laid out Waverly Avenue and projected a development later called Matthews Park. Fisher, *Flatbush Past & Present* 83. The fact that Flatbush resident and Manhattan dry goods merchant Jonathan Longmire, whose total income of $115,191.29 in 1863, 1864, and 1865 made him the richest person in rural Kings County, was exempt from military duty during the Civil War on the grounds that he was an active fireman doing duty in Flatbush, suggests that New York merchants residing in the rural towns may have participated in civic affairs. Longmire's sworn statement, notarized by John Z. Lott and dated August 13, 1864, is in TRKC, UD, Flatbush, Military Exemptions 1862–1864.

16. Strong, "Modern History of Flatbush" at 237; "Flatbush: Telegraphic Communication Established Between It and Brooklyn," *BDE*, June 13, 1873, 4:2 (quote); "More Rapid Transit," *BDE*, Nov. 19, 1875, 3:2. "Dummy" derived from the fact that the machinery was "concealed inside the car body." John H. White Jr., "Steam in the Streets" 107.

17. 1869 N.Y. Laws, ch. 670, sect. 1, 4, 5 at 1590–91 (quote); "Our Town Improvements," *KCRG*, Jan. 18, 1873, 4:1, 2 (editorial) (quote).

18. "Town Survey Commission of Kings County," *KCRG*, Jan. 30, 1875, 4:1 (quote); "Town Survey Commission of Kings County," *KCRG*, Feb. 6, 1875, 7:1 (quote); "Town Survey Commission of Kings County," *KCRG*, Mar. 20, 1875, 7:1 (quote).

19. McElroy, "Town Survey of Kings County" 411–13 (apparently quoting from the commission's report).

20. The literature on Olmsted is huge. The discussion here is based primarily on Irving D. Fisher, *Frederick Law Olmsted and the City Planning Movement in the United States*; *Civilizing American Cities*; and the first six volumes of *The Papers of Frederick Law Olmsted*.

21. Stanley K. Schultz, *Constructing Urban Culture* 18–21.

22. Alexander Garvin, *The American City* 315–19; Spiro Kostof, *The City Shaped* 68–75.

23. Olmsted, Vaux & Co., *Observations on the Progress of Improvements in Street Plans* 22.

24. Olmsted, Vaux & Co., *Observations on the Progress of Improvements* at 23. The meaning of the phrase, "and only through the most perverse neglect of the landowners of their own interests is it [the slope] likely to be built upon for other purposes," referring to those habitations, is ambiguous. Id. at 22.

25. "Report to the President of the Board of Commissioners of Prospect Park, Brooklyn [January 1, 1867]," in *The Papers of Frederick Law Olmsted* 6:150–162.

26. Olmsted, Vaux & Co., *Observations on the Progress of Improvements in Street Plans* 23 (quote); "Report to the Brooklyn Park Commission [January 1, 1869]," in *The Papers of Frederick Law Olmsted* 6:318–349 at 329.

27. For a summary of the objections of the planners and designers who followed Olmsted, see Thomas Adams, "Modern City Planning: Its Meaning and Methods" 172.

28. Fisher, *Flatbush Past and Present* 81–83; *Papers of Frederick Law Olmsted* 6:319–40; 1860 N.Y. Laws, ch. 488, sect. 3 at 964, 965; Donald Simon, "The Public Park Movement in Brooklyn, 1824–1873" at 193 (Ph.D. diss.) (quote); "Four Years," *KCRG*, Mar. 1, 1873, 4:1 (editorial) (quote); "Development," *KCRG*, Feb. 22, 1873, 4:1, 2 (editorial) (quote). These owners included Deidrich Westfall and William Matthews in addition to John Lefferts and Abby (Lott) Zabriskie.

29. "How Water Works Benefit Real Estate," *KCRBG*, Sept. 27, 1884, 2:1 (editorial) (quote); "A Union Growl," *KCRBG*, June 30, 1883, 2:1 (editorial) (quote); "Strong Arguments Against Increased Assessments," *KCRG*, Oct. 16, 1875, 2:1 (editorial); "Kings Co. Real Estate," *KCRBG*, Aug. 28, 1880, 2:1 (editorial). Lefferts's holdings declined from 163 acres and seven houses in 1868 to 87 acres and four houses in 1870. ARTF, 1868 at 20; ARTF, 1870 at 8. The church entered into an agreement to sell three acres west of Coney Island Plank Road to John Monsell for $4,000 per acre on February 11, 1869. Reformed Protestant Dutch Church of Flatbush Archives.

30. "Annexation: City and County Union" *BDE*, Mar. 3, 1873, 2:7 (quotes); "A Week of Snow," *KCRG*, Jan. 4, 1873, 4:1; "Why Not?" *KCRG*, Feb. 8, 1873, 4:1 (editorial) (quote). Philip Crooke and other leading Flatbush residents financed the newspaper; *KCRG*, May 4, 1878, 2:1 (reprinting article from the *Brooklyn Times*).

31. "What Others Say of Us," *KCRG*, Feb. 22, 1873, 3:2–3 (quote); "Real Estate and Cheap Living," *KCRG*, Apr. 3, 1875, 4:1 (editorial) (quote); "What Others Say of Us," *KCRG*, Feb. 22, 1873, 3:2, 3; "Moving into the City," *KCRG*, Sept. 20, 1873, 4:1, 2 (quotes). Nevertheless, the paper reported that the $500,000 stock for the rapid transit scheme had all been taken so that "we may look for a large advance in real estate this coming spring in our town." *KCRG*, Feb. 22, 1873, 4:4.

32. Schoenebaum, "Emerging Neighborhoods" 304.

33. "Sewers," *KCRG*, June 8, 1872, 2:1 (editorial). A week later, the newspaper predicted "the growth of a palatial city." "Prospect Park: Its Material and Aesthetic Influence," *KCRG*, June 15, 1872, 2:1–2. These predictions provoked a reader to opine that "a mighty sewer" would be needed "to carry off the filth" that would populate the police station, jail, and penitentiary in an urbanized Flatbush. Samuel Weston, "Forebodings," *KCRG*, July 13, 1872, 8:1–2.

34. An Act to lay out, open, construct, and keep in repair Ocean Avenue, in the county of Kings, 1871 N.Y. Laws, ch. 579 at 1256; Ross, *History of Long Island* 1:368; "Rail Road Consolidation," *KCRBG*, July 8, 1882, 2:1 (editorial) (quote); 1869 N.Y. Laws, ch. 861 at 2072; 1874 N.Y. Laws, ch. 583 at 781; ARTNU, 1880 at 257

(John A. Lott's assessment for interest for the years 1874 to 1880 was $5,296.38); "Board of Supervisors," *KCRBG*, May 20, 1882, 2:4 (quote); "Taxation," *KCRG*, Oct. 9, 1875, 2:1 (editorial) (quote); 1882 N.Y. Laws, ch. 247 at 299; "Farmers Cannot Drive Loaded Wagons on the Parkway Boulevard," *KCRBG*, Mar. 10, 1883, 2:2. The *Rural Gazette* charged that Brooklyn had "run out long and expensive avenues through valuable farming lands, and . . . levied taxes on it, equal to its highest market value." "City Greed and Country Rights," *KCRG*, Mar. 16, 1878, 2:1 (editorial). From the published list of the amounts due for the construction of Ocean Parkway it is clear that the largest taxpayers were not farmers, but other large landowners, some of whose families had once farmed, such as Lott and Martense, whereas others were longtime merchant residents, such as Henry Johnson (or his heirs), or speculators such as Robert Turner. "Assessment Notice," *KCRBG*, Aug. 12, 1881, 2:7–8.

35. "Flatbush: Town Meeting," *BDE*, Mar. 27, 1873, 1:9 (reprinted from *KCRG*) (quote); "Summer Talk About Real Estate," *KCRG*, June 28, 1873, 7:2, 3 (quote); "Has Real Estate Reached the Lowest Point?" *KCRG*, Aug. 11, 1877, 2:2 (editorial); "Justice for Flatbush," *KCRG*, Feb. 21, 1874, 4:1, 2 (editorial) (quote); "The Park Tax Decision," *KCRG*, Dec. 26, 1874, 4:1, 2 (editorial); "Real Estate and Cheap Living," *KCRG*, Apr. 3, 1875, 4:1 (editorial) (quote); *KCRG*, Nov. 14, 1874, 5:3 (quote); "The Railroad Fever," *KCRG*, Sept. 16, 1876, 2:1; Seyfried, *The Long Island Rail Road* 146 (stating that Turner was a banker); "The Great Real Estate Sale," *KCRG*, Nov. 21, 1874, 4:3–4 (quote). Half a year later, however, Turner postponed a further sale when bidders refrained from buying lots at prices 50 percent lower. "A Rare Chance Lost," *KCRG*, May 22, 1875, 4:2.

36. McElroy, "Town Survey of Kings County" 411. For background, see Kings County, Minutes of Commissioners for Mapping Towns, 1869–1874.

37. "New York, Bay Ridge & Jamaica Railroad: Prospectus," *KCRG*, May 6, 1876, 1:2.

38. "Bay Ridge and Hempstead: The Railroad Now Building," *BDE*, Mar. 26, 1873, 2:5. On high farmland prices paid by railroads: According to "Bay Ridge," *KCRG*, Mar. 22, 1873, 3:2, Abram Wakeman, a director of the New York and Hempstead R.R., bought the Bergen farm for $210,000, which gave the company the right of way and access to "an exceedingly valuable water front and ferry." Earlier the newspaper had reported that the railroad had bought 110 acres for $3,000 [*sic*] per acre for a total of $220,000 in order to gain the right of way to the waterfront. "Bay Ridge," *KCRG*, Nov. 30, 1872, 5:1. The Bergen in question was Michael Bergen (1809–1875), a 60-year-old retired farmer at the time of the 1870 Census of Population, who had farmed 100 acres according to the 1860 Census of Agriculture. In 1873 the railroad became owner of 24.39 acres that had until then been owned by Bergen and were assessed at $10,780. It also appeared as the owner of an additional three properties for a grand total of 87.52 acres, none of which it had owned the previous year. In 1874, the railroad disappeared from the roll and Abram Wakeman was entered as the owner of six properties totalling 79.86 acres. Bergen had owned 105.7 acres in 1872 but only 2.3 in 1873 and 1874. ARTNU, 1872 at 28, 31–33, 54, in TRKC, vol. 2145, MR 45; ARTNU, 1873 at 33, 37, 39, 61, in TRKC, vol. 2146, MR 45; ARTNU, 1874 at 35, 49–51, 65, 67, in

TRKC, vol. 2147, MR 45. Bergen died in 1875 at the age of 66. "Died," *KCRG*, Jan. 16, 1875, 5:3. If the railroad and/or Wakeman bought all 80 acres from Bergen, the per acre price of about $2,400 was higher than the prices farmers received during the 1889 boom. See chapter 10 below. According to Seyfried, *The Long Island Rail Road* 3, the total cost to the New York and Hempstead for the 110 acres was $330,000, of which $60,000 was paid in cash, the balance remaining on bond mortgage to Bergen. In 1878, Bergen's executors, Jacob L. Bergen and Theodore V. H. Bergen, sued Wakeman, Austin Corbin, the New York, Bay Ridge, and Jamaica R.R., and the Manhattan Beach R.R. Co. to foreclose a $165,000 mortgage, which was created when Bergen gave back $165,000 of the purchase money. The state supreme court granted a decree of foreclosure, ordering a sale of the 111 acres that included the Bay Ridge depot and dock. "New Utrecht, Bath and Unionville," *KCRG*, Jan. 26, 1878, 2:5; "Bay Ridge," *KCRG*, Apr. 27, 1878, 2:6. A discrepancy in the newspaper account is that it asserted that Bergen had bought the Jacobus Cropsey farm in 1820 — at a time when Bergen would have been only 10 years old. According to the doubtless more accurate account by genealogist Teunis G. Bergen, in 1835 Michael Bergen's father, Jacob Bergen, bought 70.5 acres from John T. Bergen for $30,000 and an adjoining 17.5 acres from William Kelly for $4,000; Michael Bergen sold all but 1.5 acres to Wakeman for upwards of $200,000, and moved to a house on 2 acres that he bought from Ann Hendricksen in New Utrecht near the city line. Bergen, *Bergen Family* 345–47 (2d ed.). In 1882, a company of New York and Boston capitalists bought 26 acres of the old Michael Bergen farm on 2nd Avenue near 66th Street extending 365 feet along the shore to establish a new shipyard; the $125,000 price amounted to almost $5,000 per acre — a very high price. "Bay Ridge," *KCRBG*, July 15, 1882, 2:6. The assessed value of an 18.44-acre plot of land that the estate of Michael Bergen owned at that location was only $340 per acre in 1880. ARTNU, 1880 at 83, in TRKC, vol. 2153, MR 48.

39. "Bay Ridge and Hempstead: The Railroad Now Building," *BDE*, Mar. 26, 1873, 2:5.

40. "What Next?" *KCRG*, Nov. 15, 1873, 4:1 (editorial); "Light Dawning on Rapid Transit?" *KCRBG*, May 13, 1882, 2:1 (editorial) (quote); "Under or Over?" *KCRBG*, June 25, 1881, 2:1 (editorial) (quote); 1862 N.Y. Laws, ch. 407 at 737; *ARSESSNY for the Year Ending September 30, 1864* at 108, 175–76; "Ex-Mayor Gunther Dead," *NYH*, Jan. 23, 1885, 8:1 (quote); "A Cool Resort in Hot Weather," *NYT*, July 10, 1866, 5:2; William Fausser, *The Brooklyn and Rockaway Beach Railroad*. In 1879 the Brooklyn, Bath, and Coney Island R.R. carried 337,569 passengers, while the Brooklyn, Flatbush, and Coney Island R.R. and Prospect Park and Coney Island R.R. carried 2.5 and 11 times as many, respectively. "New Utrecht, Bath and Unionville," *KCRG*, Dec. 27, 1879, 2:5; "Railroad Notes," *KCRG*, Dec. 13, 1879, 2:5–6.

41. "Steam at Last," *KCRG*, June 12, 1875, 2:1 (quote); "Andrew N. Culver Dead," *NYT*, July 11, 1906, 1:4; Seyfried, *The Long Island Rail Road* 148; "Gravesend's Trouble," *KCRG*, Aug. 12, 1876, 2:1 (editorial) (quote); "Brooklyn's Debt," *KCRG*, Feb. 22, 1879, 2:1 (editorial); "The Annexation Scheme," *KCRG*, Feb. 22,

1879, 2:1 (editorial). The 18-minute trip from the Brooklyn city line to Coney Island cost 23 cents. "Gravesend," *KCRG*, July 3, 1875, 2:6. Some landowners protested the substitution of steam for horse power because it was more dangerous and devalued property along the route. John A. Lott advised them that they were at least entitled to greater compensation. "A Public Meeting Against Steam on the Coney Island Road," *KCRG*, Feb. 5, 1876, 2:2. The Culver line also transported freight, including building materials for the hotels and amusement centers, to Coney Island. Seyfried, *The Long Island Rail Road* 152. The year-round service particularly benefited Parkville, a section straddling several towns, which in 1881 proposed to incorporate itself as a village. "A Step Forward: Incorporation of Parkville," *KCRBG*, Sept. 10, 1881, 2:3.

42. "A Steam Railroad Sure to Pay," *KCRG*, July 21, 1877, 2:7; *ARSESSNY for the year Ending Sept. 30, 1878*, at 53–59; "Another Coney Island Railroad," *NYT*, July 2, 1878, 5:6; "The Grand Centre of Railroads for Coney Island," *KCRG*, July 6, 1878, 2:1 (editorial); "Brooklyn, Flatbush and Coney Island Rail Road Company," *KCRG*, June 15, 1878, 2:1. See also "Railroad Notes," *KCRG*, Dec. 7, 1878, 2:1; "What Brighton Did," *KCRG*, Oct. 19, 1878, 2:3; *IA*, Dec. 14, 1878, 5:2. Stiles, *Civil... History* 1:unpaginated (tab. between pp. 424 and 425), contains a comprehensive list of Kings County railroads. The railway's president, John A. Lott, on April 19, 1878, requested that the Flatbush highway commissioners permit the company to extend the road to Atlantic Avenue in Brooklyn from its then termination at the Willink entrance to Prospect Park. TRKC, UD, Flatbush, Highway Commissioners — Crosswalks; Railroad Petitions; Gas Lamps; Labor Reports; Proposals: 1874–1883. The Kings County Central R.R. opened a few days before the Brooklyn, Flatbush, and Coney Island R.R., which competed it out of existence by the end of its first season. The Kings County Central, on its way to Coney Island, made stops on the east side of Flatbush including the county buildings, but John L. Bergen, a large landowner in Flatbush and Flatlands, who was among the new owners in late 1878, had no interest in such local traffic. Seyfried, *The Long Island Rail Road* 47–59. The Manhattan Beach R.R. transported twice as many passengers that season. "Railroad Notes," *KCRG*, Oct. 12, 1878, 2:3. Like Lott, John Lefferts also resigned his position as treasurer of the railroad — not on account of infirmity, but because it demanded too much of his time, which he had to divide among his far-flung economic and political interests. "Local," *KCRBG*, Mar. 25, 1882, 3:1. Elizabeth Rawson, "Flatbush," in *The Encyclopedia of New York City* 416, ascribes a key role to this line, arguing that Flatbush remained rural until the 1880s when it was made ripe for development by the Brooklyn, Flatbush, and Coney Island R.R. and the impending annexation to Brooklyn. See also Daniel Bluestone et al., *Flatbush* 8.

43. "Active Rail Road Work," *KCRG*, Nov. 17, 1877, 2:2; "A Railroad: And Where," *KCRG*, Mar. 10, 1877, 2:1 (editorial) (quote); "Embargoes," *KCRG*, Feb. 17, 1877, 2:1; "Railroad Embargoes," *KCRG*; "Consolidating Rail Roads," *KCRG*, Aug. 18, 1877, 2:1 (editorial) (quote); "The Big Dig," *KCRG*, Jan. 26, 1878, 2:1 (editorial) (quote).

44. "Coney Island Real Estate," *RERBG*, 22 (551):813 (Oct. 5, 1878).

45. "For Local Travel," *KCRG*, Aug. 24, 1878, 2:1 (editorial) (quote); "Winter Trains in the County Towns," *KCRG*, Oct. 5, 1878, 2:1 (editorial). 1882 was the first year in which the Brooklyn, Flatbush, and Coney Island R.R. ran all winter. "A Busy Winter for the Brighton Beach Railroad," *KCRBG*, Apr. 1, 1882, 2:1.

46. "Gridironing the County Towns with Railroads," *KCRG*, Mar. 24, 1877, 2:1 (editorial); "The Great Railroad Hub!" *KCRG*, Oct. 7, 1876, 2:1 (editorial); "A New Era in Our Future," *KCRG*, Aug. 17, 1878, 2:1 (editorial) (quote); *KCRG*, July 6, 1878, 1:6, 8 (railroad schedules); "The Grand Centre of Railroads for Coney Island," 2:2; Henry M. Wells, "Tales of Old Flatbush" 13 (quote); "The Cattle Law," *KCRBG*, Sept. 2, 1882, 2:2 (editorial); *Appleton's Dictionary of New York and Vicinity* 83. Also emblematic of the end of an era was the destruction by fire in 1879 of the Flatbush Vanderveer farm mill. Built in 1804, it was being used as a storehouse for hay. At the time of the draft riots in 1863, it served as a refuge for blacks in Flatbush. "Destroyed by Fire: Vanderveer's Mill Vanishes in Flames," *KCRG*, Mar. 8, 1879, 2:3. The account in the *IA*, Mar. 15, 1879, 5:3, contained several errors.

47. "Struck at Last," *KCRG*, Oct. 13, 1877, 2:1. An acre is 43,560 square feet.

48. Seyfried, *The Long Island Rail Road* 1–12.

49. "The Bay Ridge Railroad," *KCRG*, June 13, 1874, 4:2 (quote); "A Steam Railroad," *KCRG*, June 6, 1874, 4:1; "The Bay Ridge Railroad," *KCRG*, Oct. 24, 1874, 4:1; "The Bay Ridge Steam Railroad and Ferry Company Route," *KCRG*, Feb. 27, 1875, 4:1 (editorial); "East New York," *KCRG*, Mar. 13, 1875, 1:3; "Bay Ridge Rail Road," *KCRG*, Dec. 25, 1875, 2:3.

50. Seyfried, *The Long Island Rail Road* 20 (quote); "Railroad Development," *KCRG*, Nov. 25, 1876, 2:1; "The Grand Opening of the Bay Ridge & Manhattan Railroad," *KCRG*, July 21, 1877, 2:3–6. On the acquisition of the Long Island R.R. by Corbin and a syndicate of Boston capitalists, see "Sale of Long Island Railroad," *KCRBG*, Dec. 4, 1880, 2:1.

51. David McCullough, *The Great Bridge* 26; "Annexation," *KCRG*, July 27, 1872, 4:1–2 (quote); "Around the Circle," *KCRG*, Nov. 28, 1874, 4:1 (quote); "The Bay Ridge Steam Railroad and Ferry Company Route," *KCRG*, Feb. 27, 1875, 4:1, 2 (quote); "Flatlands," *KCRG*, Jan. 5, 1878, 2:3; *KCRG*, Feb. 17, 1877, 2:1 (untitled); letter from New York and Manhattan Beach Railway Co. to Highway Commissioners of the Town of Flatbush, Jan. 7, 1878, in TRKC, UD, Flatbush, Highway Commissioners — Crosswalks; Railroad Petitions; Gas Lamps; Labor Reports; Proposals: 1874–1883 (quote). Flatlands farmers also made arrangements with the railroad to convey manure from New York according to a Long Island R.R. plan. "Flatlands," *KCRG*, Oct. 27, 1877, 3:1. Later trains that ran over the Flatlands branch road carried manure for two farmers, Jackson Ryder and George Schenck, thanks to the "kindness" of the railroad president, John Bergen. "Flatlands," *KCRG*, Feb. 1, 1879, 2:6. These trips were apparently the last run over the Kings County Central line. John L. Bergen, the president and receiver of the railroad, listed himself as residing in Flatlands (as well as Flatbush). *ARSESSNY For the Year Ending Sept. 30, 1878*, at 262–63; *ARSESSNY For the Year Ending Sept. 30, 1879*, at 504. Bergen was apparently the son of Tunis J. Bergen of Flatbush; born

in 1835, he married a daughter of the large Flatlands farmer Peter Lott, and like his father, he too was a real-estate broker. Bergen, *Bergen Family* 336 (2d ed.). See also Seyfried, *The Long Island Rail Road* 146.

52. "The Future Which Overlooks Us," *KCRG*, Apr. 19, 1873, 2:1 (editorial); "World's Fair in Flatbush," *KCRG*, Apr. 19, 1873, 2:2 (editorial); "An Effort," *KCRG*, May 10, 1873, 2:1 (editorial); "The World's Fair," *KCRG*, July 5, 1879, 2:1 (editorial) (quote).

53. 1878 N.Y. Laws, ch. 409, sect. 1–3, 4 at 486, 487; 1876 N.Y. Laws, ch. 305 at 295 (Gravesend and New Utrecht); 1893 N.Y. Laws, ch. 353 at 698 (Flatlands); E.g., "Gravesend," *KCRG*, Oct. 17, 1874, 1:1 (third burglary in the house of Edward Ridley); 4:2. "Our Police Bill," *KCRG*, June 15, 1878, 2:1 (editorial) (quotes). A shoot-out that ended in the deaths of two burglars at the house of one of the Van Brunt family in New Utrecht elicited an editorial cheer and was even reported in the British press. "Death to Burglars," *KCRG*, Dec. 19, 1874, 4:2; "A Romance of Crime," *Times* (London), Jan. 14, 1875, 3:4.

54. Strong, "Modern History of Flatbush" 239–40; "Slightly Corned," *KCRG*, Aug. 1, 1874, 4:3; "The Police Commission," *KCRG*, June 22, 1878, 2:1 (editorial) (quote); "Local," *KCRBG*, Jan. 17, 1885, 3:1; "Our Police Bill" (quote); "Public Opening & Formal Transfer of the New Town Hall," *KCRG*, Feb. 12, 1876, 2:1, 3. Henry S. Ditmas may have been content with the efficiency of the existing law enforcement system: a chicken thief who had been caught in his outhouse was sentenced to six months of hard labor. "Caught at Last," *KCRG*, May 25, 1872, 2:3.

55. 1864 N.Y. Laws, ch. 443 and 444 at 1057, 1058; Strong, "Modern History of Flatbush" at 235 (quote); "Knocked Down and Robbed," *KCRG*, July 1, 1876, 3:2; "Real Estate," *KCRG*, Mar. 15, 1873, 4:1 (quote); "Our Gas Company," *KCRG*, May 3, 1873, 4:1 (editorial) (quote); "Gas and Police," *KCRBG*, Feb. 11, 1882, 2:1 (editorial); "Darkness and Light," *KCRBG*, Feb. 18, 1882, 2:1 (editorial). For an example of the solicitation of funds for the gas company within the extended farming community, see letter from John A. Lott to Elizabeth Ludlow, Mar. 16, 1864, Cruikshank Coll., box A. Ludlow was Willink's sister-in-law and inherited his estate upon his wife's death. On the Willink family, who were not among the original Dutch settlers of Flatbush, see *The Eagle and Brooklyn* at 84. The contract with the town provided that: "The lamps are to be lighted and kept lighted during each part of the night as there is no moon light excepting those nights when the moon shall set after twelve o'clock at night." Agreement of Feb. 11, 1880, between Flatbush Gas Co. and Commissioners of Highways of the Town of Flatbush, in TRKC, UD, Flatbush, Highway Commissioners — Crosswalks; Railroad Petitions; Gas Lamps; Labor Reports; Proposals: 1874–1883.

56. Strong, "Modern History of Flatbush" 240–41; "The Romance of the Flatbush Water Works," in Snyder, *Tales of Old Flatbush* 145 (quote); "Improving Flatbush and Removing the County Buildings" (quote); "The Late General Crooke's Successor," *KCRBG*, Apr. 30, 1881, 2:1 (editorial) (quote); Proposal for Water Works (May 14, 1881), Town meetings (May 27 & June 3, 1881) (quote), Agreement (June 6, 1885), in TRKC, UD, Flatbush, Town Board, 1878–1890, Bundle no. 9, MR 18. On a dispute that erupted over Lefferts's probity in connection

with his appointment as a commissioner to appraise the value of land to be taken by a railroad to which he himself had also sold land, see "Communications," *KCRG*, Jan. 22, 1876, 3:1; John H. Bergen, letter to editor, ibid.; Jacques J. Stillwell, letter to editor, *KCRG*, Jan. 29, 1876, 2:6.

57. Gertrude Ryder Bennett, "The Farmer's Wife in the Towns of Kings County," in Snyder, *Tales of Old Flatbush* 189, 194 (quote); "Flatbush Water Works," *KCRBG*, June 11, 1881, 2:2 (quote); "The Water Question," *KCRBG*, June 13, 1885, 2:1 (editorial) (quote); "Our Water Works," *KCRBG*, Nov. 26, 1881, 2:1 (quote) (leaving unclear whom the newspaper meant in referring to nonresident capitalists as owning the great bulk of the water company's capital). William Matthews had already built a number of "reasonably priced modern style cottages" on the west side of town. "Encouraging Signs," *KCRBG*, June 11, 1881, 2:1 (editorial).

58. "Growth," *KCRBG*, Feb. 4, 1882.

59. "Growth," "Fertility," *KCRBG*, Feb. 4, 1882 (quote); *KCRBG*, Jan. 28, 1882 (quote); *KCRBG*, Apr. 12, 1884, 2:2.

60. "The Brooklyn Bridge and New York Realty," *RERBG*, 29 (730):213 (Mar. 11, 1882) (quote); Thomas Bender, "Metropolitan Culture"; Alan Trachtenberg, *Brooklyn Bridge* 23–24, 29–36, 110–13; McCullough, *The Great Bridge* 103–19; "The Brooklyn Bridge," *Railroad Gaz.* 15:348 (1883) (quote); Rufus Wilson, *Historic Long Island* 271.

61. "The Real Estate Boom in Flatbush," *KCRBG*, Nov. 17, 1883 (quote); "Night Cars to Flatbush," *KCRBG*, Mar. 15, 1884, 2:1; A. P. Stockwell, "History of the Town of Gravesend" 173 (quote).

62. Teunis G. Bergen, "History of the Town of New Utrecht" 263 (quote); Syrett, *The City of Brooklyn* 241 (quote); "Brooklyn Real Estate" (quote).

63. Syrett, *The City of Brooklyn* 241 (quote); Henry Hazelton, *The Boroughs of Brooklyn and Queens* 2:1143 (quote).

64. *Appleton's Dictionary of New York City and Vicinity* 58 (quote); *Coney Island and the Jews* 8 (quote); "Sea-Side Edition," *KCRBG*, June 19, 1880, 1:1 (steam railroads alone could accommodate 100,000 passengers daily); "Old Country Towns"; *IA*, Dec. 6, 1879, 5:3 (the Manhattan Beach Improvement Co. bought 108 acres, adjacent to the proposed Coney Island Jockey Club, from Voorhies and Vanderveer, at $600 per acre, to be laid out in streets); "Large Sales of Real Estate: The Coney Island Jockey Club," *KCRG*, Nov. 29, 1879, 2:1. Ross, *History of Long Island* 1:369 (quote).

65. "Jobbery in Coney Island Land," *KCRG*, Aug. 3, 1878, 2:1 (editorial) (quote); "Gravesend Common Lands," *KCRG*, Feb. 15, 1879, 2:1 (editorial) (quote); Gravesend," *KCRBG*, Sept. 30, 1882, 3:2 (quote).

7. Modernizers Thwarted: The Great Annexation Debate of 1873

1. 1873 N.Y. Laws, ch. 861 at 1287.

2. H., "Brooklyn and New York: An Argument in Favor of Annexation and Rapid Transit," *BDE* Jan. 29, 1873, 3:9 (letter to editor).

3. "Consolidation: Lone Meeting at New Lots Last Night," *BDE*, Oct. 22, 1873, 2:7;

1869 N.J. Laws, ch. 501 at 1225; *Report of the Commissioners to Revise the Laws for the Assessment and Collection of Taxes* 17 (quote).

4. "County and City," *BDE*, Mar. 4, 1873, 2:3 (editorial) (quote); "The Committee of One Hundred Resolve in Favor of the Annexation of the County Towns," *KCRG*, Dec. 28, 1872, 4:3.

5. Jacques J. Stillwell, letter to editor, *KCRG*, Oct. 4, 1873, 8:3.

6. H., "Annexation," *KCRG*, Oct. 4, 1873, 8:1, 2.

7. "Annexation: City and County Union," *BDE*, Mar. 3, 1873, 2:6, 8.

8. Edgar Bergen, "Annexation: A Townsman of Flatlands Opposes It," *BDE*, Mar. 19, 1873, 2:8 (letter to editor) (quote); "Annexation Hearing," *BDE*, Mar. 9, 1894, 5:5 (quote); Ten petitions to the Town Board (Dec. 22, 1893), in TRKC, UD, Flatlands, Town Board: Railroads, Lighting Cos., 1893–1894 (quote); 1893 N.Y. Laws, ch. 79 at 122. On Bergen, see the CP, 1870, KC, Flatlands, MS at 27; CA, 1870, Flatlands. By 1880, Bergen had apparently tired of remote Flatlands and moved to Flatbush. CP, 1880, KC, Flatbush, MS, SD no. 2, ED no. 252 at 37.

9. "Annexation: City and County Union," *BDE*, Mar. 3, 1873, 2:8. Flatlands' "well to do farmers" were not, however, above taking a day to party "in the surf" at Coney Island before it became a resort. "Flatlands," *KCRG*, Aug. 9, 1873, 1:3.

10. Edgar Bergen, "The Annexation Plan," *KCRG*, Oct. 11, 1873, 8:1, 2.

11. "Annexation: City and County Union," *BDE*, Mar. 3, 1873, 2:8. The obituary of George Kouwenhoven, who died at 73 in 1880 and owned a 99-acre farm in Flatlands at the 1870 census, stated that he had cultivated his large farm so successfully that he became "a wealthy man." "Flatlands," *KCRBG*, Dec. 4, 1880, 2:2.

12. A Flatlander, "Plea For (?) Annexation," *KCRG*, Jan. 11, 1873, 1:2–3.

13. "Annexation: City and County Union," *BDE*, Mar. 3, 1873, 2:8 (quote); Bergen, "Annexation: A Townsman of Flatlands Opposes It," *BDE*, Mar. 19, 1873, 2:8 (quote); Jacques J. Stilwell, "Annexation: Jacques J. Stilwell Opposes the Union of the County Towns with the City," *BDE*, Mar. 26, 1873, 1:8 (letter to editor) (quote); "County Annexation," *BDE*, Feb. 14, 1873, 2:2; "Annexation: Public Sentiment in the County Towns," *BDE*, Mar. 28, 1873, 4:2; "City and County," *BDE*, Apr. 8, 1873, 2:3 (editorial) (quote). The agricultural tax preference for Bushwick was not mentioned in the consolidation statute of 1853.

14. "Annexation: The Proposed New Twenty-third Ward," *BDE*, Feb. 20, 1873, 2:6 (quotes); "Albany: New Lots Legislation," *BDE*, Mar. 7, 1873, 2:6. See also "Annexing New Lots: Meeting at the Town Hall Last Night," *BDE*, Feb. 10, 1873, 4:3, on the drafting of an annexation bill, which provided for approval by popular vote, by a local committee. On early efforts to draft an annexation bill, see "East New York," *KCRG*, Oct. 26, 1872, 1:1–2; *JASNY at the Ninety-Sixth Session* 1:226.

15. "East New York: Reminiscences of a Resident," *BDE*, Oct. 18, 1873, 8:6 (quotes); "East New York," *KCRG*, May 24, 1873, 1:1 (quote).

16. *JASNY at the Ninety-Sixth Session* 1:284; 1873 N.Y. Laws, ch. 861, sect. 1, 7–12 at 1287–88 (quote); "The Eagle and Annexation," *BDE*, Apr. 15, 1873, 2:1 (editorial); "The City of Brooklyn," *KCRG*, Aug. 23, 1873, 4:1 (editorial); "Our Need," *KCRG*, Jan. 25, 1873, 4:1, 2 (editorial quoting the *BDE*) (quote).

17. "City and County," *BDE*, Apr. 8, 1873, 2:3 (editorial).

18. Strong, "Modern History of Flatbush" 237; CP and CA, 1870, MS; Pessen, *Riches, Class, and Power Before the Civil War* 55 (quote); Stiles, *Civil . . . History* 1:352–54; "The Legislature's Work," *NYT*, Mar. 15, 1881, 1:6; "Hon. John A. Lott," *KCRG*, July 11, 1874, 4:1. Peter Lott (1815–1879), was a successful market gardener, his 70 acres, the products of which he sold at Washington market, yielding him "a handsome yearly income" until his retirement in 1874. A. V. Phillips, *The Lott Family in America* 84. Peter Lott and John A. Lott were distant relatives, both being descendants of the common ancestor of the entire Lott family of Long Island, Peter Lott, who settled in Flatbush in 1652. Ibid. at 1, 5–6, 84, 101. William Bennett (1823–1903) was a large potato farmer, who did not sell his 100-acre farm until the turn of the century; his account books from the 1880s and 1890s are cited in this book. Gertrude Ryder Bennett, *Living in a Landmark*.

19. O. W. Holmes, "Murphy, Henry Cruse," *DAB* 13:350 (referring to the 1830s) (quote); Phillips, *The Lott Family in America* 101 (quote); *LDLI: For 1878–79* at 269; "Brooklyn Riches," *KCRG*, May 29, 1875, 4:1 (quote); *NYT*, Aug. 9, 1878, 8:5 (though "one of the most methodical of business men," Lott left no will). On Lott's landholdings, see U.S. Census, 1850, Agriculture; PS of the Seventh Census, 1850, Flatbush 20. In 1873 Lott stated at a conference of the New York State Board of Assessors and the Brooklyn assessors and supervisors that personal property was taxed "a great deal more than it ought to be" — in Flatbush, where he lived, it was taxed at its full value. "County Affairs: View of Judge Lott on the Equalization of State Taxes," *BDE*, June 30, 1873, 4:2. Despite his great wealth and the extensive landholdings that he reported and paid taxes on, Lott consistently reported to the Flatbush tax assessor that he owned no taxable personal property; in contrast, John Lefferts consistently reported and paid taxes on more than $100,000 in personal property. E.g., ARTF, 1872 at 10–11, 24–25. In declaring that he had no taxable personalty, Lott may have been taking advantage of a statutory provision permitting taxpayers to deduct their just debts from the value of their personal property. See chapter 8 below. Lott, who had been born in Flatlands and still owned land there, continued to pay taxes there too. "The Consolidation Commission: Another Report on Consolidation by Judge Lott," *KCRG*, Sept. 13, 1873, 4:2, 4. Van Brunt and Adrianna Magaw were the grantors of the land that Abraham Lott bought; the date of recording was September 20, 1821. The conveyance is to be found in Kings County real property records, Liber 13, page 65. This title was abstracted from the property records for section 16, block 5240, Brooklyn City Hall. Van Brunt Magaw was the son of Robert Magaw and Marritie Van Brunt, the daughter of Rutgert Van Brunt and Altie Cortelyou; the Van Brunt and Cortelyou families both owned considerable amounts of land. Van Brunt Magaw (1783–1831) married Adrianna Voorhees, whose family appears to have acquired this land in the first part of the eighteenth century. Bergen, *The Bergen Family* 371–73 n.1. John A. Lott's extensive landholdings may in part have been a function of his unusual status, among the Kings County Dutch, as an only child. Phillips, *The Lott Family in America* 73.

20. Pessen, *Riches, Class, and Power Before the Civil War* 109.

21. Gertrude Lefferts Vanderbilt, *The Social History of Flatbush* 205; "Protection

Against Fire," *KCRG*, Aug. 10, 1872, 4:1–2 (editorial); *NYTrib*, July 22, 1878, 5:5; "The Death of Judge Lott," *KCRG*, July 27, 1878; "Two Noted Jurists Dead: Judge Lott Stricken Down Without Warning," *NYT*, July 21, 1878, 12:1 (quotations).

22. Indenture, John A. Lott to George Sprague, for land in Huntington, Long Island (Apr. 9, 1873), [Anita Lott] Cruikshank Collection, box 1. On Willink's land transactions in New Jersey and Texas, see Cruikshank Collection (box A, John A Willink).

23. "The Consolidation Commission: Another Report on Consolidation by Judge Lott," *KCRG*, Sept. 13, 1873, 4:2, at 5:1 (quote); Snyder, *Tales of Old Flatbush* iii (quote).

24. "The Progress of the Consolidation Commission," *BDE*, Aug. 28, 1873, 2 (editorial) (quote); "Our Need," *KCRG*, Jan. 25, 1873, at 4:1, at 2 (editorial) (quote). A dummy was a locomotive whose steam whistle was muffled. Lott's judicious evenhandedness was amply on display at the commission's first meeting when he likened Brooklyn's building of Prospect Park partly in Flatbush "to a rich man building a house of his own volition — a noble mansion in the vicinity of the residences of his poorer neighbors, and then calling upon them to pay part of the expense which he had voluntarily incurred." "Organization of the Annexation Commission," *BDE*, Aug. 12, 1873, 4:2.

25. "Manifest Destiny," *KCRG*, Jan. 10, 1873, 4:1 (editorial) (Lott as largest landowner). John A. Lott's farmland straddled Flatbush, Flatlands, Gravesend, and New Utrecht. M. Dripps, *Map of Kings County* (1868); *Robinson's Atlas of Kings County New York*, plate 6. The 1850 CA recorded that John A. Lott also owned a 41-acre farm in Flatlands and a 45-acre farm in Gravesend. That his name disappeared from later Censuses of Agriculture suggests that tenant farmers were operating them. In 1870, he was listed as owning 100 acres in Flatlands with an assessed valuation of $16,500. ARTFl, 1870 at 15, TRKC, vol. 4036, roll 77. In the mid-1870s, he was still one of the biggest taxpayers in Flatlands. "Flatlands," *KCRG*, Aug. 5, 1876, 2:4. Lott appeared as the owner of 20 acres of tillable land on the New Utrecht assessment roll for the first time in 1863, although he was not listed as a nonresident. He was assessed property tax on the 20 acres he owned along Ocean Parkway in New Utrecht in 1870, as was his estate in 1880. NUAR, 1863 at 30, TRKC, vol. 2136, roll 44; ARTNU [for 1870] 61, TRKC, vols. NU, AR, 1870, vol. 2143, MR 45; ARTNU, 1880 at 166, 170, TRKC, vols. NU, AR, 1880, vol. 2153, MR 48. Lott also owned 24 acres in Gravesend. AR, Town of Gravesend at 14, in TRKC, vol. 3066, roll 69.

26. Samuel Purple, "A Brief Memoir of the Life and Writings of Hon. Teunis G. Bergen" 152 (quote); Stiles, *Civil . . . History* 1:268; *JASNY at the Ninety-Sixth Session* 1:368.

27. "Annexation: Payment of a Political Obligation — Ode to Uncle Tune Bergen. — How Gravesend Became the Last Ditch," *BDE*, Apr. 4, 1873, 2:8.

28. "The Consolidation Commission," *BDE*, Aug. 12, 1873, 2:1, 2 (editorial) (quote); Strong, "Modern History of Flatbush" at 231–32; ARTF, 1867 at 40; "A Steam Railroad Sure to Pay," *KCRG*, July 21, 1877, 2:7; "The Great Railroad Hub!" *KCRG*, Oct. 7, 1876, 2:1 (editorial); "Supervisors," *KCRG*, Aug. 12, 1876, 2:2. Sev-

eral other residents, including farmers, supported Bergen. "New Utrecht," *KCRG*, Aug. 19, 1876, 2:2. Although Bergen succeeded in securing a temporary injunction against Supervisor Gubner's construction of a new town hall, it was eventually built. "New Utrecht, Bath and Unionville," *KCRG*, Oct. 7, 1876, 2:4; "New Utrecht, Bath and Unionville," *KCRG*, Jan. 20, 1877, 2:6.

29. "Kings County Annexation," *NYT*, Aug. 13, 1873, 3:1.

30. "Brooklyn's Greater Issues," *NYDT*, Aug. 13, 1873, 8:1 (quotes); "County Consolidation," *BDE*, Aug. 19, 1873, 2:8. The report in the *Times* stated that the vote was 8 to 2. "Kings County Annexation." Three days later the commissioners rejected the view that they were empowered to draft a new charter for consolidated Brooklyn. "The Annexation Movement," *NYDT*, Aug. 16, 1873, 8:1. Bayliss attended only one meeting before resigning because of illness, and was replaced by Thomas Kinsella, editor of the *Eagle*. Commissioners were paid $10 per day not to exceed a total of $300. "The Annexation Commission," *KCRG*, Aug. 30, 1873, 4:4; "Consolidation: The Last Meeting of the Commission," *BDE*, Dec. 1, 1873, 3:2.

31. "Communications," *KCRG*, Jan. 15, 1876, 2:6; Vincent Seyfried, *The Long Island Rail Road* 21.

32. "County Consolidation: Decided Progress Made Toward Settling the Terms of Union," *BDE*, Aug. 20, 1873, 4:5 (quotes); "Consolidation: The Consideration of Judge Lott's Plan," *BDE*, Sept. 10, 1873, 2:7, 8. One of the Brooklyn commissioners also stated that farmland assessments would be considerably lower than those on ordinary property. "Brooklyn Annexation Casuistry," *NYDT*, Aug. 19, 1873, 8:2. Gowanus became Brooklyn's Eighth Ward when Brooklyn became a city in 1834. 1834 N.Y. Laws, ch. 92, sect. 2 at 90–91. An opponent of annexation claimed that in Gowanus (and Wallabout) landowners "could not sell it for enough to pay taxes and assessments, and those who were thought to be rich were made comparatively poor." "Awake," *KCRG*, Mar. 15, 1873, 2:2.

33. "Brooklyn Consolidation," *NYT*, Aug. 21, 1873, 8:2 (quote); "Kings County Consolidation," *NYDT*, Aug. 28, 1873, 8:3 (quote).

34. "Kings County Consolidation," *NYDT*, Sept. 2, 1873, 8:4; "County Consolidation: Meeting of the Commissioners and Discussion of the Proposed Union," *BDE*, Aug. 27, 1873, 4:3; "Plundered Brooklyn," *NYDT*, Aug. 30, 1873, 1:1; "Brooklyn Annexation," *NYT*, Sept. 2, 1873, 8:1 (quotes). See also "Annexation Difficulties," *BDE*, Sept. 2, 1873, 2:1.

35. "Brooklyn Consolidation," *NYT*, Sept. 14, 1873, 8:4 (quotes). See also *NYDT*, Sept. 9, 1873, 8:3; "Kings County Consolidation," *NYDT*, Sept. 15, 1873, 12:4. On judicial exemption of Flatbush property owners from assessments for benefits resulting from the park, see "The Park Assessment Decision," *BDE*, Nov. 29, 1873, 2:2 (editorial); "The Vacation of the Park Assessment on Flatbush," *BDE*, Dec. 4, 1873, 2:2 (editorial); "Prospect Park: Judge Gilbert's Opinion on the Assessment Question," *BDE*, Dec. 6, 1873, 4:5.

36. "Improvement: A General Survey of Brooklyn and Vicinity," *BDE*, Oct. 11, 1873, 2:4, 5 (quote); "Flatbush and East New York," *BDE*, Jan. 23, 1873, 2:8 (quote); "The Terms of Consolidation," *BDE*, Sept. 15, 1873, 2:1 (editorial); "The Con-

solidation Commission — The Plan Agreed To," *BDE*, Sept. 11, 1873, 2:1 (editorial); "County Consolidation — Judge Lott's New Section to the Plan," Sept. 15, 1873, 2:5 (quote). Those parts of Flatbush that did specially benefit from the park were to be assessed.

37. Plan for the Consolidation of the Towns of New Lots, Flatbush, New Utrecht, Gravesend and Flatbush with the City of Brooklyn, art. II, sect. 1, 2, in "Annexation: Shall the City of Brooklyn and the Five County Towns Be United?" *BDE*, Nov. 3, 1873, 2:8, 9.

38. "County Consolidation — Judge Lott's New Section to the Plan," *BDE*, Sept. 15, 1873, 2:6–7 (quote); "New Utrecht," *KCRG*, June 20, 1874, 8:1 (quote).

39. "County Consolidation: Judge Lott's New Section to the Plan," *BDE*, Sept. 15, 1873, 2:5, 7. It was far more eloquent than the quasi-minority report that Bergen, Peter Lott, and William Bennett published in pamphlet form, which focused almost exclusively on budget items such as piers, docks, and truant homes, for which the annexed towns would be taxed, and never even alluded to the demise of farming. "Consolidation: Address by Hon. Tunis G. Bergen Against the Proposition," *BDE*, Oct. 27, 1873, 2:6. John A. Lott's response was confined to correcting errors in the items and amounts that might be taxed. Ibid.; "Consolidation: The Issue Succinctly Stated by the Honorable Judge Lott," *BDE*, Oct. 29, 1873, 2:9.

40. "Ald. Scholes on the Issue Between the Consolidation Commissioners," *BDE*, Sept. 5, 1873, 2:3 (editorial) (quote); "County Consolidation: Judge Lott's New Section to the Plan," *BDE*, Sept. 15, 1873, 2:7 (quote); "Consolidation: The Consideration of Judge Lott's Plan," *BDE*, Sept. 10, 1873, 2:7, 8 (quotes). For Prospect Park Bergen also refused to pay on the grounds that people from New Utrecht rarely visited it: "If I want to see curiosities, I'd take my friends to Greenwood cemetery." "Consolidation: The Consideration of Judge Lott's Plan," ibid., 2:7.

41. "Ald. Scholes on the Issue Between the Consolidation Commissioners," *BDE*, Sept. 5, 1873, 2:4; "New Utrecht, Bath and Unionville," *KCRG*, Feb. 1, 1879, 2:7–8.

42. This interpretation was supported by a resident of New Lots who claimed that for fifteen or twenty years "the farming interest" had stymied his efforts to open streets: farmers refused to sell their land but wanted their neighbors to improve theirs so that the farmers could enhance the value of their property without incurring any expenses. "Anti-Annexation: Mr. Joseph F. Bridges to the People in General and the Voters of New Lots in Particular, on the Consolidation Question," *BDE*, Oct. 3, 1873, 2:6, 7 (letter to editor).

43. "Consolidation: Lone Meeting at New Lots Last Night," *BDE*, Oct. 22, 1873, 2:7.

44. Plan for the Consolidation of the Towns, art. I, sect. 9, in "Annexation," *BDE*, Nov. 3, 1873, 2:9 (quote); "The Consolidation of the Towns and the City — The Vote Tomorrow," *BDE*, Nov. 3, 1873, 2:1 (quote).

45. "The Consolidation of the Towns and the City," ibid. (quotes). After the commissioners had voted on September 13 to submit the annexation proposal to the electorate, they also voted to print 150,000 copies of it in pamphlet form for distribution to the voters. Just as Bergen's motion to reduce that number to 100,000

lost, so, too, the commissioners rejected his argument that they lacked authority to provide 400,000 ballots (one-half for each side). "County Consolidation: Judge Lott's New Section to the Plan," *BDE*, Sept. 15, 1873, 2:7; "Annexation: The Work of the Commissioners on Consolidation Practically Finished," *BDE*, Sept. 30, 1873, 2:2.

46. "The Consolidation of the Towns and the City," *BDE*, Nov. 3, 1873, 2:1. In fact, all of the towns, according to the population data in table 18, had grown significantly between 1860 and 1870.

47. "The Candidates," *KCRG*, Nov. 1, 1873, 4:1, 2.

48. "The Defeat of Consolidation," *BDE*, Nov. 6, 1873, 2:3 (editorial); "Consolidation: What an East New Yorker Has to Say on the Defeat of the Scheme," *BDE*, Nov. 12, 1873, 4:6; "Annexation: Enthusiastic Meeting at East New York," *BDE*, Nov. 18, 1873, 4:2 (78 votes); "Consolidation: The Closing Meeting of the Commissioners," *BDE*, Nov. 25, 1873, 4:3; "Consolidation Defeated: Official Announcement of the Vote," *KCRG*, Dec. 6, 1873, 1:2; Strong, "Modern History of Flatbush" 237–38. The *Times*, *Tribune*, and *Eagle*, after extensive reporting on the commission's proceedings, failed to publish the vote count. Strong's mention of a 1,568 majority against annexation in the towns may have been taken from the report in the *KCRG*, which used this aggregate number despite the fact that the sum of the majorities in the towns was 1,478. The *Gazette* projected a final majority in Brooklyn in favor of annexation of 20,000 once all the districts had been heard from, although at the time the majority was only 16,197. The Consolidation Commission's final official tally, which omitted five election districts, stated that in Brooklyn 23,665 voted for and 4,056 against consolidation. This official tally, as reported in the *Rural Gazette*, differs somewhat from the data in table 22. The total vote in the five rural towns was 2,284 against and 902 in favor; in addition, 147 ballots were endorsed "no" and 10 left blank. "Consolidation Defeated: Official Announcement of the Vote," *KCRG*, Dec. 6, 1873, 1:2. In boasting of its rapid publication of general election results from the rural towns, one Brooklyn paper noted that despite the vote against consolidation, "in matters of news, and all the advantages flowing from its gathering and publication, they shall be a part of the city in spite of themselves." "The Union's Election Returns," *BDU*, Nov. 5, 1873.

49. "The Election," *KCRG*, Nov. 8, 1873.

50. "The Defeat of Consolidation," *BDE*, Nov. 6, 1873, 2:3 (quotes); "Annexation Defeated in New Lots," *BDE*, Nov. 26, 1873, 2:3, 4 (editorial) (quotes).

51. "Sunday Prowlers," *KCRG*, Nov. 8, 1873 (editorial) (quotes); "The Supervisors of the County Towns, and the Annexation Act," *KCRG*, July 26, 1873, 4:1–3 at 2 (quotes).

52. "Anti-Annexation: Meeting at New Lots Last Night," *BDE*, Nov. 25, 1873, 3:8; 1873 N.Y. Laws, ch. 853, sect. 15 at 1275, 1277–78; *NYT*, Nov. 26, 1873, 8:4; "Annexation Defeated in New Lots"; "East New York: The Anti-Annexationists Successful at Polls," *BDE*, Nov. 28, 1873, 4:5; "East New York," *KCRG*, Apr. 17, 1875, 2:5; 1875 N.Y. Laws, ch. 53 at 49 (providing for yet another annexation vote); "East New York," *KCRG*, Feb. 24, 1877, 2:7 (quote); Peter Rapelje, "The Rapelje

Farm at New Lots" (quote). In 1883, another annexation bill was filed in the state legislature providing for a vote in New Lots and Brooklyn and tax preferences for agricultural land. "New Lots," *KCRBG*, Mar. 10, 1883, 2:5.

53. "Brooklyn or New-Jersey," *NYT*, Nov. 15, 1873, 6:6; "Local," *KCRBG*, Mar. 24, 1883, 3:1.

54. 1874 N.Y. Laws, ch. 465, sect. 1 at 607 (authorizing Flatbush to borrow $40,000 payable within 30 years); Daniel Bluestone et al., *Flatbush* 4; "The Grand Opening of the Bay Ridge & Manhattan Railroad," *KCRG*, July 21, 1877, 2:3, 5 (quote).

55. "Our Town Supervisors to the Front," *KCRBG*, May 20, 1882, 2:1 (editorial); "Eleven Years Old," *KCRBG*, Apr. 21, 1883, 2:1 (editorial) (quote).

56. David Hammack, *Power and Society* 185 (quote), 203–14; 1894 N.Y. Laws, ch. 64 at 146; *Report of the Commissioners Appointed Pursuant to Chapter 311* at 2; *BDEA: 1895* at 298; "Brooklyn Favors Consolidation," *NYDT*, Nov. 9, 1894, 3:4, reported Flatlands voting in favor of consolidation; "Greater New-York in Doubt," *NYT*, Nov. 8, 1894, 1:3, 4, published preliminary figures 958 to 708. Neither "Brooklyn for Consolidation," *NYT*, Nov. 9, 1894, 1:3, nor "For Consolidation," *NYT*, Nov. 10, 1894, 1:6, nor the *BDEA* mentioned Flatlands, which was annexed January 1, 1896, was a part of the 31st Ward (Gravesend) in 1894, and became the 32nd Ward in 1895. 1895 N.Y. Laws, ch. 313 at 428.

8. The Impact of Property Tax Laws on Deagriculturalization

1. Pranay Gupte, "Hunger for Land Is Turning a Region of Choice Farms into One of Houses," *NYT*, Feb. 8, 1976, sect. 8 at 1:1, 4:1, 1:2. Wendell Berry, *The Unsettling of America* 65, used "journal fodder" to describe a *National Geographic* report on a Long Island farm that had been owned by one family since 1737 and would be driven out by competition and high taxes unless it mechanized and expanded. For evidence that urbanization, soil productivity, and retirement are more important determinants of loss of farmland than property taxes, see Thomas Plaut, "Urban Growth and Agricultural Decline" 274–87.

2. Ellen Snyder-Grenier, *Brooklyn!* 104, 106. Snyder-Grenier cited no source in support of this claim; in a telephone interview in October 1996 she was also unable to cite any source. Daniel Bluestone et al., *Flatbush* 32–36, 56, assert that after annexation, "tax laws for Flatbush changed. Instead of a tax on farm property, land was taxed by town lots which had already been plotted along Flatbush Avenue on the east side. Taxes made it too expensive to own land within the city limits. . . . Farmers could not afford to pay the taxes on their many lots and were forced to begin selling off their farms." This undocumented claim is at odds with the fact that tax rates in fact did not increase. For a documented example of Queens farmers "forced to sell" by higher taxes based on full market value assessments at the turn of the century, see Jeffrey Kroessler, "Building Queens" 347–48 (Ph.D. diss.). Gertrude Ryder Bennett, *Living in a Landmark* 43, asserted with respect to Gravesend that: "Around the turn of the century, taxes forced farmers to sell their farms."

3. Lott was jocularly referring to Teunis Bergen's motion to remove the parks and

other assets of Brooklyn from among the properties that would accrue to the consolidated city and for which the rural towns would then have had to accept financial responsibility.

4. J. Peter De Braal, *Taxes on U.S. Agricultural Real Estate*, tab. 1 at 6; Thomas Adams, Harold Lewis, and Theodore McCrosky, *Population, Land Values and Government* 264; *BDEA: 1887* at 103; *BDEA: 1900* at 448; *BDEA: 1893* at 201; *BDEA: 1895* at 240; *BDEA: 1896* at 250; *BDEA: 1897* at 352; *BDEA: 1898* at 413. From 1895 to 1896 the average rate in Brooklyn declined from $34 to $29 per $1,000 of valuation. "Now Get Your Tax Bills," *NYDT*, Nov. 20, 1896, 10:2. An anonymous author asserted in 1920 that "taxes rose in leaps and bounds and the man who had a fifty acre farm threw up his hands when it came to be assessed, not as agricultural land, but as a city plot. Consolidation of Brooklyn with New York further increased the tax burden." Few 50-acre farms — and certainly no "great areas where corn . . . had been grown up to the time of their [the developers'] acquisition of the land" — remained by the 1890s in Flatbush, the only town whose annexation statute lacked a special tax privilege for owners of farmland. "Old Flatbush," in Snyder, *Tales of Old Flatbush* 79.

5. *Report of the Industrial Commission on Agriculture and on Taxation in Various States* 36 (quote); *Report of the Joint Select Committee Appointed at the Last Session to Revise and Amend the Assessment Laws of the State* 2 (quote).

6. "The Taxes," *KCRG*, Aug. 5, 1876, 2:3; "Flatlands," ibid., 2:4. Oddly, the lists omitted John A. Lott from Flatbush, but did correctly list him for Flatlands.

7. Chap. XIII: Of the Assessment and Collection of Taxes, tit. I, sect. 3, in *Part of the Revised Statutes* 223 (quote); Chap. XIII: Of the Assessment and Collection of Taxes, tit. I, sect. 4(9) at 225 (exemption from execution); Chap. XIII: Of the Assessment and Collection of Taxes, tit. II, sect. 9(4) at 227 (quote). The personalty tax also included "such portions of the capital of incorporated companies, liable to taxation on their capital, as shall not be invested in real estate." The ban on "double taxation" of corporate income was in fact complete because a later section provided that: "The owner . . . of stock in any incorporated company liable to taxation on its capital shall not be taxed as an individual for such stock." Chap. XIII: Of the Assessment and Collection of Taxes, tit. I, sect. 7, in *Part of the Revised Statutes* 224, 225. State law exempted from execution ten sheep, one cow, two swine, the family's food and fuel, all necessary wearing apparel, beds and bedding, necessary cooking utensils, one table, six chairs, six plates, teacups, and saucers, a mechanic's tools and implements necessary to carrying on his trade up to $25 in value, a householder's necessary household furniture and working tools, and team up to a value of $150 (excluding execution issued on a demand for the purchase money of such items), and the lot and buildings of a homestead up to $1,000. *Revised Statutes of the State of New York*, vol. 3, tit. v, pt. iii, ch. vi, sect. 22, 23, 28 at 644, 645–47. Abraham I. Ditmas on Aug. 3, 1867, filed a preprinted form, sworn to before the assessor, Jacob V. B. Martense, stating that "after deducting his just debts and property invested in the stock of incorporated Companies, liable to taxation, . . . the value of the Personal Estate owned by him does not exceed the sum of five thousand five hun-

dred dollars. And that he has not in any way disposed of his Personal Property, or created any indebtedness with a view to avoid being assessed for such property, or to enable him to make this affidavit." On July 27, 1863, John A. Lott filed the same form, swearing that after making the same deductions he had no personal estate liable to taxation. These figures then appeared on the assessment rolls for those years. TRKC, UD, Flatbush, Taxes; Personal Property Oaths; Assessors' Notices; Internal Revenue 1870–1895.

8. *Report of the Comptroller* 3 (quote); *Annual Report of the Comptroller* 35 (1859) (quote); *First Annual Report of the State Assessors* 22 (quote); *Report of the Commissioners to Revise the Laws for the Assessment and Collection of Taxes* 62–63 (quote); "Assessed Value in Flatbush," *KCRG*, Sept. 21, 1878, 2:3. Tax officials almost unanimously observed that "oaths as a matter of restraint, or as a guarantee of truth in respect to official statements, have, in great measure, ceased to be effectual; or in other words, that perjury has become so common as to almost cease to occasion notice." *Report of the Commissioners to Revise the Laws for the Assessment and Collection of Taxes* 69. Despite continuing complaints over many years from high-ranking state officials — even Governor Grover Cleveland urged treating both kinds of property equally by abolishing deductions for debt — it continued to be set off against personal property throughout the nineteenth century. *Annual Report of the Comptroller* 18–19 (1868); "Away with Unjust Taxation," *KCRBG*, Jan. 19, 1884, 2:1. The provision was again included in the tax code enacted at the end of the century. 1896 N.Y. Laws, ch. 908, art. II, sect. 21(4) at 796, 805.

9. Nevertheless, at the end of the century, when it became clear that "escape of personal property from taxation . . . must be accepted as a basic fact," the state comptroller reported that personal property was more fully assessed in rural counties because "[n]early all of the personal property of the farmer is tangible, open to view, and easily reached by the assessor." *Annual Report of the Comptroller of the State of New York* xv.

10. *Annual Report of the State Assessors of New York for the Year 1889* at 16 (quote); ARTF, 1873 at 28–29; ARTF, 1874 at 24–25; ARTF, 1876 at 24–25; ARTF, 1877 at 10–11. Often the largest proportion of tax revenue was assigned to the towns. In 1889, two-thirds of property taxes in Flatbush were designated for the town. *Annual Report of the State Assessors of New York for the Year 1889* at 53. Towns, however, did not always receive the bulk of the tax receipts. In New Utrecht in 1852, for example, the county received 78 percent of the total revenue. NUAR, 1852, TRKC, vol. 2125, roll 43. The New York State legislature imposed certain rates of property taxation to be levied by the counties for specified state purposes. See, e.g., 1872 N.Y. Laws, ch. 736 at 1782; 1873 N.Y. Laws, ch. 765 at 1161; "Brooklyn and the State Tax," *BDE*, Oct. 11, 1873, 4:2.

11. Letter from John Lefferts to the Commissioners of Highways of the Town of Flatbush, Jan. 21, 1880, TRKC, UD, Flatbush, Highway Commissioners — Crosswalks; Railroad Petitions; Gas Lamps: 1874–1883 (quote); ARTF, 1880 at 3; CA, 1880, KC, Flatbush, MS; "The Cost of Health," *KCRG*, Sept. 19, 1874, 4:1 (editorial). For earlier years, tax rates in New Utrecht — where for the years af-

ter 1858 the tax rate was often identical to that in Flatbush's nongas district — show how minimal taxation was. It was 0.25 percent in 1831, falling to a low of 0.13 percent in 1841, and reaching a high of 0.65 percent in 1857. In 1840, for example, Evert Suydam was assessed $18.33 in tax on his 100-acre farm (valued at $10,000) and $1,000 personal estate. Calculated according to NUAR, 1831–1869, roll 43–44; NUAR, 1840 at 1, vol. 2050, roll 43. The fact that the legislature did not even authorize the establishment of gas districts in New Utrecht until 1888, more than two decades after their creation in Flatbush, points to the earlier suburbanization of Flatbush despite the considerable contingent of wealthy Manhattan merchants residing in New Utrecht since before the Civil War. 1888 N.Y. Laws, ch. 576, sect. 8–20 at 932, 933–35.

12. ARTF [1853] at 8, 7 (typed copy of original ms. at BHS). The 1860 CA listed each as farming 80 acres. On the relation between property taxes and profits, see chapter 10 below and table 36.

13. The tax on real estate in New York State encompassed land and buildings as well as trees, mines, and minerals. Chapter XIII: Of the Assessment and Collection of Taxes, tit. I, sect. 2 at 224. Because there is no unambiguous correlation between jumps in the assessed value and the appearance of another house, it is not possible to draw conclusions as to the relative weight to be attributed to the houses. Nevertheless, it seems plausible to conclude that, since the amount of land, which was more or less identical with the extent of his farm acreage, remained relatively unchanged, the additional houses may have contributed disproportionately to the rising assessments. Williamson was no exception to the general pattern: the opening of Prospect Park caused assessed values to rise sharply after 1868; the depression that began in 1873 deflated them. See chapter 6 above. Williamson reported to the CA in 1870 and 1880 that the value of his farm was $25,000 and $28,000.

14. ALFBIR, 1864, NY, CD 2, div. 8 at 162; ALFBIR, 1865, NY, CD 2, div. 8 at 394; ALFBIR, 1866, NY, CD 2, div. 8 at 36; ALFBIR, 1870–71, NY, CD 2, div. 8, at 362; ALFBIR, 1869–70, NY, CD 2, div. 8 at 362.

15. ARTF, 1894 at 482, 484.

16. The data in this paragraph are based on the tables discussed in chapter 2 above.

17. The group of Flatlands farmers is composed of John C. Bergen, Asher Hubbard, Cornelius B. Kouwenhoven, George Lott, Robert Magaw, Richard Remsen, Jeremiah Ryder, James Schenck, and Jeffrey Van Wyck. John A. Lott's land is also included. Not all of these farmers appeared in all the assessment rolls; by the 1890s, several had died and their heirs were listed instead. The Flatlands AR for 1860, 1870, 1880, 1890, and 1892 are found in the TRKC, vol. 4057, roll 80; vol. 4036, roll 77; vol. 4043, roll 78; vol. 4050, roll 79; and vol. 4052, roll 80, respectively. The NYCMA appears to lack the assessment rolls for Flatlands after 1892. The averages for Gravesend are based on the taxes of Benjamin Hitchings, William Bennett, David Jones, Philip Leib, Daniel Stillwell, Barnardus, Voorhees, and James Williamson. The Gravesend AR for 1860, 1870, 1880, 1890, and 1883–1893 are found in the TRKC, vol. 3056, 3066, and 3076, roll 69; vol. 3079–3082, roll 70; vol. 3083–3085, roll 71; 3086–3087, roll 72; and vol. 3083

and 3089, roll 73. 1893 is the last year for which the NYCMA has the assessment rolls. Bennett's profits are calculated from William Bennett & Sons, Farm Accounts. Bennett's taxes as a proportion of his profits reached their low point of 4.3 percent in 1886 and their high point of 22.6 percent in 1893, averaging 10.8 percent. These proportions may, however, be overstated: at the 1880 Census of Agriculture, Bennett's son Elias was returned as renting half the farmland on which his father paid taxes; the annual receipts that William recorded in his account books between 1883 and 1898 were strikingly uniform and about the same as the $6,000 in total production he reported to the census in 1879, when his son reported an additional $3,000. The taxes would, then, amount to a considerably smaller proportion of total profits for both farms. In New Lots, which was industrialized and incorporated into Brooklyn earlier than the other towns, the trend in farmland taxes did not deviate significantly from that in the other towns. For example, Abraham Linington, one of the county's largest farmers, paid $0.98 in real property tax per acre in 1860, $4.42 in 1870, and $4.34 in 1880. The New Lots AR for 1860, 1870, and 1880 are located in the TRKC, vol. 14, roll 28; vol. 24, roll 30; and vol. 34, roll 33.

18. Warren W. Rawson, "Discussion" 73.

19. Michael Sullivan, "The Advancement of Market Gardening in the Past Twenty-Five Years" 69.

20. 1956 Md. Laws, ch. 9, sect. 1 at 10 (quote); A. M. Woodruff, "City Land and Farmland" 33 (quote). After the statute was held unconstitutional, the state constitution was amended to permit the legislature to tax farmland at a different rate. State Tax Comm'n v. Gales, 161 A.2d 676 (Md. 1960); 1960 Md. Laws, ch. 65 at 186. John Mackenzie and Gerald Cole, "Use-Value Assessment as a Farmland Preservation Policy" 252, also claimed: "Maryland enacted the first use-value tax assessment law in the United States in 1957." See also Raleigh Barlowe, "Taxation of Agriculture" 98; William Whyte, The Last Landscape 121; Henry J. Aaron, Who Pays the Property Tax? 85; John Opie, The Law of the Land 164; Lockeretz, "New Life for Metro Farming" 83; Nelson Bills, "Urban Agriculture in the United States" 15. For evidence that preferential taxation cannot stop urban expansion but can prevent discontinuation of farming before urbanites are willing to make high offers, see Howard Conklin and William Lesher, "Farm-Value Assessment as a Means for Reducing Premature and Excessive Agricultural Disinvestment in Urban Fringes." A very late and ambiguous example of a farmer who sold out was John B. Kouwenhoven, a descendant of the original Dutch settlers of Flatlands, who died at the age of 82 in 1926 after having owned a farm for years. His obituary stated that: "The realty development of the section forced him to dispose of it a few years ago." NYT, Jan. 28, 1926, 23:3.

21. In incorporating the city of Brooklyn in 1834, the New York State legislature provided that the two new (agricultural) wards could not be included in the fire and watch district without the written assent of two-thirds of the resident householders and owners and lessees of land (or an act of the legislature). 1834 N.Y. Laws, ch. 92, sect. 37 at 90, 103–104. Two years later, the legislature amended the incorporation act to extend the fire and watch district provisions to the whole

city. 1836 N.Y. Laws, ch. 76, sect. 1 at 101. In 1853, the legislature empowered the consolidation commission preparing the union of Brooklyn, Bushwick, and Williamsburgh to set the relative rates of taxation in the various wards. 1853 N.Y. Laws, ch. 577, sect. 7 at 1057, 1058. The commission's general plan (art. 1, sect. 2) provided that the agricultural wards (part of Bushwick, Gowanus, and Bedford) would not be subject to taxation for the fire department, police, and street lighting. "County Consolidation," *BDE*, Aug. 20, 1873, 4:5, 6. A similar provision was then written into the consolidation statute, whereby the common council was authorized to include the wards by a two-thirds vote. 1854 N.Y. Laws, ch. 384, sect. 23, 25 at 829, 846, 847.

22. 1856 Pa. Laws, sect. 6 at 567, 568; 1868 Pa. Laws, no. 407, sect. 1 at 443, 444, *repealed by* 1939 Pa. Laws, no. 404, sect. 22 at 1199, 1205; 1870 Pa. Laws, no. 234, sect. 9 at 242, 243 (quote); sect. 1, 1859 Conn. Spec. Acts 27–28. The Pennsylvania legislature enacted the two-thirds agricultural tax rate for cities of the second class (Pittsburgh and Scranton) in 1867, reducing it to one-half in 1876 and one-third of the highest rate in 1897. 1867 Pa. Laws, no. 775, sect. 6 at 846, 850; 1876 Pa. Laws, no. 91, sect. 3 at 124, 125; 1897 Pa. Laws, no. 182, sect. 3 at 219, 220–21; *repealed by* 1911 Pa. Laws, 273; 1913 Pa. Laws, no. 147 at 209, 210. Despite the repeal, the 1897 statute remains on the books. Pa. Stat. Ann., tit. 53, sect. 25900 (Purdon 1957). See generally, Simen's Appeal, 41 Pitts. 13 (1893). The year after it extended Erie's city limits, the legislature supplemented the statute to deprive any tract that was laid out into city lots and sold as such of its farmland assessment. 1871 Pa. Laws, no. 743 at 811. See also City of Erie v. Reed, 6 A. 679 (Pa. 1886). That knowledge of this statutory agricultural tax preference was not totally lost, was shown by the reference to it by Frederick Law Olmsted Jr., "Introductory Address on City Planning" 28. Because the tax preference was applied to large estates of wealthy families in Pittsburgh that were adorned with the trappings of pseudofarms, it created distributional injustices. Shelby Harrison, "The Distribution of Taxation in Pittsburgh."

23. 1833 Ky. Acts, ch. 204, sect. 17 at 211, 217; 1836 Ky. Acts, ch. 257, sect. 28 at 280, 289–90; 1851 Ky. Acts, ch. 373 at 682; 1876 Iowa Acts, ch. 47, sect. 4 at 38, 39 (quote), *repealed by* 1972 Iowa Acts, ch. 1088, sect. 199 at 219, 289; Leicht v. City of Burlington, 34 N.W. 494, 495 (Iowa 1887) (quote); Fulton v. City of Davenport, 17 Iowa 404, 407 (1864) (quote). Plaintiffs in *Leicht* were farmers growing vegetables on farms whose size fell below the statutory threshold, which the legislature had in the meantime reduced to 10 acres. 1878 Iowa Acts, ch. 169, sect. 5 at 156.

24. Several state supreme courts agreed with farmers that bringing farmlands within a city's limits for the sole purpose of taxing them "without the pretext of extending the protection of the city over them" was an unlawful taking of private property without compensation — even where the incorporation statute prescribed assessment of the land by the acre according to its value for agricultural purposes and the farmland in question was taxed at only one dollar per acre. Morford v. Unger, 8 Iowa 82, 85, 92–93 (1859); 1856 Iowa Acts, ch. 18, sect. 5 at 49, 51 (city of Muscatine). See also City of Covington v. Southgate, 54 Ky. 491

(15 B. Mon.) (1854). The foremost nineteenth-century treatise writer favoring this position was John F. Dillon, *Treatise on the Law of Corporations*, sect. 633–34 at 597–600. At the same time Dillon, who had been a justice on the Supreme Court of Iowa, was writing on this subject, he appeared as a pro se litigant before that court, unsuccessfully suing the city of Davenport, Iowa, to restrain it from levying taxes on the 16 acres that he used as a residence and improved with gardens, orchards, and vineyards. Dillon continued to cite the decision at great length in all editions of his treatise without mentioning that he had been a plaintiff in the case that his former colleagues had decided against him. Durant v. Kauffman, 34 Iowa 194, 201–202 (1872). See also John F. Dillon, *Commentaries on the Law of Municipal Corporations* 2:973 n.1 (1890); ibid., 4:2429–30 n.2 (1911). Other courts in effect gave legislatures a free hand to tax such farms on the grounds that burdens and benefits could not be calibrated and that farmland owners presumptively benefited from whatever promotes the interests of the larger community of which they had become part. Kelly v. Pittsburgh, 104 U.S. 78 (1881); J. Hare, *American Constitutional Law* 1:299–300.

25. Kelly v. City of Pittsburgh, 85 Pa. 170, 170–71 (1877). The $10 per acre income was rent that Kelly received for letting his land for dairy purposes; the valuation of his land was increased 50-fold from 1873 to 1874. Master's Report 12, Kelly v. Pittsburgh, 104 U.S. 78; Argument for Plaintiff in Error 3, Kelly v. Pittsburgh.

26. Kelly v. City of Pittsburgh, 85 Pa. 173.

27. Kelly v. City of Pittsburgh, 85 Pa. 176, 178, 179 (quotes); Kelly v. Pittsburgh, 104 U.S. at 82 (quotes). Even state supreme courts that vindicated complaining farmers seemed to harbor a suspicion that the plaintiffs operated with a hidden agenda: "There is little reason to apprehend, that when the city actually grows up to the land now in question, the proprietor, whoever he may be, will withhold it from the necessities of a growing population." City of Covington v. Southgate, 54 Ky. 496.

28. 1873 N.Y. Laws, ch. 853, sect. 14 (quote), 15 at 1275, 1277; 1886 N.Y. Laws, ch. 335, sect. 11 at 544, 546 (quote). On annexation, see chapter 7 above. At the same time that annexation was under discussion, amendments to the city charter for Brooklyn were also being debated. Although this provision was ultimately not adopted when the legislature amended the charter in 1873, one proposal with regard to newly admitted wards read: "The valuation for the lands actually used for agricultural purposes . . . shall be based upon the value of said lands . . . for agricultural purposes only." "The One Hundred: Meeting Last Night — Valuation of County Towns Lands," *BDE*, Jan. 28, 1873, 3:8. Between enacting the two New Lots statutes, the legislature in 1877 amended an 1870 statute authorizing Albany to annex parts of two towns to prohibit the assessment of farmland used exclusively for such purpose at a valuation greater than that of similar farmland in the adjoining town. 1877 N.Y. Laws, ch. 402, sect. 2 at 416.

29. People ex rel. Vanderveer v. Wilson, 26 N.E. 454 (N.Y. 1891).

30. "Enlarging Brooklyn," *NYDT*, Mar. 12, 1894, 6:3–4 (editorial) (quote); 1895 N.Y. Laws, ch. 954 at 1992; 1894 N.Y. Laws, ch. 449, sect. 13 at 911, 918; ch. 450, sect. 10 at 918, 924; "Old County Towns," Brooklyn Daily Eagle, *Consolidation Number*

47 (quote); *The Citizen Guide to Brooklyn and Long Island* at 183 (quote). The *Times* highlighted the agricultural provision in the Gravesend statute. "County Towns as City Wards," *NYT*, Apr. 28, 1894, 9:5.

31. 1894 N.Y. Laws, ch. 451, sect. 9 at 925, 929–30 (quote); "Anxious to Be Taken In," *BDE*, Mar. 10, 1894, 5:3; "All Ready for Annexation," *BDE*, Mar. 11, 1894, 24:3; "Work for Good Government in New Utrecht," *BDE*, Mar. 30, 1894, 4:4 (editorial) (quote). A provision similar to that for New Utrecht was enacted about the same time on behalf of other market gardeners along the East Coast. In 1888, when the Maryland legislature extended the limits of Baltimore to parts of Baltimore County, another leading vegetable producer, it prohibited any increase in the tax rate or the assessment of property in the annexed areas until the year 1900. 1888 Md. Laws, ch. 98, sect. 19 at 113, 127. In upholding the provision, the state's highest court opined that, since the annexed territory largely consisted of vacant lots and farming lands, "the plainest principles of justice would seem to require a qualified exemption of such property, for a limited period, at least, from the heavy burden of city taxation. It must be some time before such property can be available for building or business purposes, or can enjoy the full benefits and privileges of city government." Daly v. Morgan, 16 A. 287, 289 (Md. 1888).

32. Jeremiah Johnson, "Recollections of Old Roads, Residents and Their Occupations" 7.

33. 1894 N.Y. Laws, ch. 356 at 692 (Flatbush statute); "Annexation Hearing," *BDE*, Mar. 9, 1894, 5:5 (sewers); 2. "Twenty-ninth Ward of Brooklyn," *BDE*, Apr. 26, 1894, 4:1 (quote); *The Citizen Guide to Brooklyn and Long Island* 183 (quote). Perhaps the most detailed contemporary newspaper article on the subject of assessments in Brooklyn, which quoted the statutory provisions on agricultural land taxes, did not explain why the legislature had treated Flatbush differently, but noted that with the exception of Flatbush, property in the newly annexed towns was assessed at 25 to 50 percent of its value. "Unequal Assessments," *NYDT*, June 27, 1896, 14:1, 2. On a group of Flatbush residents who opposed annexation on the ground that it would compel small landowners to pay increased taxes without any benefit, see "Flatbush Citizens Protest," *NYT*, Mar. 17, 1894, 9:2. Justice Edward Sweeney, a Flatbush Democrat, contended that "a large majority of the people in the town were against the bill, and that it will only benefit land speculators and the water and lighting companies, while the small householder will get the worst of it." "Flatbush Enters as a Ward," *BDE*, Apr. 26, 1894, 12:1.

34. Brief for Appellant at 28, People of the State of New York ex rel. Coney Island Jockey Club v. Purdy, 137 N.Y.S. 1136 (1912). The census of 1910 recorded 110 farms, only 8 of which were fifty acres or more in all of Kings County. USBC, *Thirteenth Census of the United States*, vol. VII at 200. Of the two farms enumerated as encompassing 100 to 174 acres, the Jockey Club stated that it owned one, the 100-acre Vanderveer farm, which for some years it had been renting to a farmer for $700. Petition for Writ of Certiorari, in Papers on Appeal from Order of Reversal at 7–25 at 15, People of the State of New York ex rel. Coney Island Jockey Club v. Purdy, 137 N.Y.S. 1136 (1912). The Jockey Club still argued in 1912 that

Gravesend "is and always has been a rural town, there are large farms there and a great quantity of land tilled for truck and garden farming." Brief for Appellant at 24, People of the State of New York ex rel. Coney Island Jockey Club v. Purdy, 137 N.Y.S. 1136 (1912).

35. "Annexation Hearing," *BDE*, Mar. 9, 1894, 5:5 (quote). *The Real Estate Record and Builders' Guide* was exceptional in not reporting on the course of legislative proceedings. After annexation it published a brief piece speculating that the "cordon of beer gardens, with dance hall attachments, the vilest and most demoralizing of all evils," which were located just outside the city limits would "have to sneak away beyond the new frontiers, or go out of business." *RERBG*, 53 (1363):685 (Apr. 28, 1894). The magazine's preoccupation resurfaced when it complained that Brooklyn's "superabundance of the tough and vulgar element" seriously affected property values. "The Leaven of Morality in Brooklyn," *RERBG*, 54 (1383):351 (Sept. 15, 1894).

36. "The Single Tax Agitation," *RERBG*, 43 (1096):346 (Mar. 16, 1889).

37. "Unequal Assessments" 14:1 (quoting George Case).

38. "Unequal Assessments" 14:2.

39. "Unequal Assessments" 14:3.

40. Bennett, *Turning Back the Clock* 33–34 (quotation). In a case involving property that the Board of Assessors of the City of Brooklyn conceded had always been used exclusively for farming purposes, it took the position that the legislature had intended "to exclude from the exemption (i.e., from the privilege of having his property assessed as agricultural lands)" all owners whose property had been divided up into building lots before the statute was enacted regardless of whether a map had been filed with the board or whether any of the land had been sold. The court rejected this interpretation, instead viewing the provision "as prescribing a general rule of taxation to be applied to the acquired territory, rather than as a provision for the exemption of property there situated." Consequently, the statute required all real estate in Gravesend "to be assessed at the value of the land for agricultural purposes" unless it had been sold or used as a building lot. Since the owner clearly did not fall into either exception, he prevailed. People of the State of New York ex rel. Ferguson v. Neff, 16 A.D. 107, 109, 110 (1897).

41. People of the State of New York ex rel. The Coney Island Jockey Club v. Purdy, 136 N.Y.S. 667, 668–69 (App. Div., 1912), *aff'd*, 137 N.Y.S. 1136 (1912). On the acquisition of 125 acres near Sheepshead Bay by the Jockey Club in 1880, Ross, *History of Long Island* 1:369. See also Rufus Jarman, "The Great Racetrack Caper."

9. Were All Kings County Farmers Descendants of the Original Dutch Settlers? The Farm-Tenure Structure

1. "New Utrecht," *KCRBG*, Apr. 21, 1883, 2:6; John A. Kouwenhoven, "Brooklyn Before the Bridge" 12 (quote); Lefferts Vanderbilt, *The Social History of Flatbush* 175 (quote). When Rutgert van Brunt's farm was offered for sale in 1879, it, too, had been in the family for more than two centuries. "New Utrecht, Bath and

Unionville," *KCRG*, Mar. 29, 1879, 2:7. Tunis Kouwenhoven, who died in 1935, operated until its sale in 1925 part of the farm that his ancestor, William Gerrit Kouwenhoven, had established in 1636. "Tunis G. B. Kouwenhoven," *NYT*, July 6, 1935, 14:1.

2. Phillips, *The Lott Family in America* 58 (quote), 85.

3. *The Eagle and Brooklyn* 258; "Annexation: City and County Union," *BDE*, Mar. 3, 1873, 2:6, 7 (quote); ARTF, 1873 at 28–29. The church owned a large tract west of the church at what is now Flatbush and Church Avenues. F. W. Beers, *Atlas of Long Island*. The church began selling off the farmland in the 1860s when it was no longer needed to support the minister. Joseph Berg, "The Flatbush Church in the Last 50 Years" 10; Charles Livingston Jr., "Background and History of the Church" 22. The agreements with Heaslip (Feb. 17, 1885, and Mar. 1, 1886) and Kennedy (Feb. 27, 1886) ran one year, and those with Garnin (Mar. 15, 1882, and Feb. 1885) for a term of three years. Reformed Protestant Dutch Church of Flatbush Archives. For the basic data on these tenant farmers at the 1880 CA, see table 27.

4. Bergen, *The Bergen Family* 366; "Original Deeds," *KCRG*, May 19, 1877, 2:1; Bergen, *Genealogy of the Lefferts Family 1650–1878*, passim and at 132–33. Ditmas was apparently née Suydam, from which family her title stemmed.

5. Charles Andrew Ditmas, *Historic Homesteads of Kings County* 51–52; CA, 1850 and 1860, KC, Flatlands, MS.

6. [Anita Lott] Cruikshank Collection (quote); ARTF, 1860 at 22–23; Ditmas, *Historic Homesteads of Kings County* 67. The 1860 Census of Agriculture returned a Thomas Barnett(e) as farming 10 acres in Flatbush, but no Thomas Bennett; the value of his production of market garden produce on 10 acres ($1,000) was equal to Lott's on 80 acres (Lott did produce more potatoes). The 1860 Census of Population returned two farmers named Thomas Bennett but no Barnett(e). It is unclear whether Bennett and Barnett were the same person. At his death in 1861, part of Jeremiah Lott's farmland passed to his daughters Catharine, who married her first cousin, Judge John A. Lott, and Abby Lefferts, who married John Zabriskie. In 1862, they are listed in the Flatbush assessment rolls as owning 80 and 35 acres, respectively. Phillips, *The Lott Family in America* 50, 70, 101; ARTF, 1862 at 16–17, 20–21.

7. W. H. Stillwell, "Local Emigration from Kings County," *KCRG*, Nov. 30, 1872, 6:2–3. Bizarrely, Stillwell, an antiquarian in Gravesend, exemplified the disadvantage of higher rental, manure, and wages over the advantage of lower transportation costs by reference to Kings County farmers' inability to grow wheat profitably.

8. "Flatlands," *KCRBG*, Dec. 11, 1880, 2:6 (quote); "New Lots," *KCRBG*, Mar. 5, 1881, 2:4.

9. William Williamson, who at 35 farmed 41 acres in Flatlands in 1870, ten years later was forced by failing health to let out the remaining acres of his farm. "Flatlands," *KCRBG*, July 17, 1880, 3:3. Langley's ad appeared in *KCRG*, Oct. 28, 1876, 3:6. The last year in which Langley owned 44 acres designated as a farm was 1870, but he continued to own almost as much land into the 1880s. NUAR, 1870

at 21, TRKC, vol. 2143, MR 45; NUAR, 1871 at 28, in TRKC, vol. 2144, MR 45; NUAR, 1876 at 66, in TRKC, vol. 2149. On Bergen, see "Flatlands," *KCRBG*, Mar. 21, 1885, 2:4; *KCRG*, Nov. 15, 1873, 8:3; *KCRG*, Jan. 31, 1874, 8:2; *KCRG*, Oct. 5, 1878, 3:7. Bergen was not returned as living in Flatlands at the 1880 census. He did not sell the Bergen Island until 1892, when his name was crossed out of the assessment roll and those of Thomas Adams Jr. and Perry J. Williams inserted. As of 1890, Bergen was listed as owning 80 acres of land and 25 acres of meadow valued at $13,100. In 1891 his holdings rose to 90 and 150 acres, respectively, valued at $14,000. In 1892, the holdings of the new owners were 90 and 122 acres, respectively, valued at $30,000. The property tax on the land remained virtually unchanged between 1870, when a tax of $201.50 was imposed on land valued at $11,865, to 1891, when a tax of $204.55 was imposed. ARTFl, 1870 at 1, TRKC, vol. 4036, roll 70; ARTFl, 1890 at 14, TRKC, vol. 4050, roll 79; ARTFl, 1891 at 14, TRKC, vol. 4051, roll 80; ARTFl, 1892 at 13, TRKC, vol. 4052, roll 80.

10. "Flatlands," *KCRG*, Oct. 16, 1875, 2:5 (Irish farmers). Included here are only persons whom the census schedules returned as "farmers"; sons of farmers whose occupation was listed as "farming" have been included among farm laborers. The category "farming" was not used in the 1860 census schedules: sons were all returned as "farmer." The following Dutch family farmers appeared in the 1860 Census of Population: Allgeo (1), Antonides (1), Bennett (25), Bergen (16), Cozine (4), Cropsey (6), Degroff (1), Denyse (5), Ditmas (4), Duryea (7), Emmons (6), Hegeman (8), Hendrickson (7), Hubbard (6), Lake (4), Linington (1), Lott (29), Kowenhoven (22), Magaw (3), Neufus (3), Remsen (10), Repalje (4), Ryder (15), Ryerson (2), Schenck (10), Schoonmaker (3), Snediker (2), Suydam (9), Stillwell (23), Stoothoff (5), Stryker (9), Van Brunt (13),Van Cleef (2), Vanderveer (9), Van Duyne (1), Van Dyke (5), Van Pelt (6), Van Sicklen (14), Van Sinderen (2), Van Wyck (6), Voorhees (25), Williamson (18), and Wyckoff (25). The 1870 CP returned the following number of farmers from Dutch families: Allgeo (1), Antonides (1), Bennett (21), Bergen (14), Cozine (5), Cropsey (6), Degroff (4), Denyse (5), Ditmas (6), Duryea (4), Eldert (3), Emmons (4), Hegeman (4), Hendrickson (4), Hubbard (4), Lake (7), Linington (2), Lott (20), Kowenhoven (18), Magaw (3), Neufus (2), Remsen (7), Repalje (6), Ryder (15), Ryerson (3), Schenck (7), Schoonmaker (4), Suydam (4), Stillwell (13), Stoothoff (4), Stryker (7), Van Brunt (8),Van Cleef (4), Vanderveer (12), Van Dyke (5), Van Pelt (4), Van Sicklen (12), Van Sinderen (2), Van Wyck (4), Voorhees (16), Williamson (10), and Wyckoff (15). In 1880 the enumerated farmers were: Bennett (18), Bergen (10), Cortelyou (1), Cropsey (4), Degroff (3), Denyse (5), Ditmas (3), Dittmars (3), Eldert (2), Emmons (6), Hegeman (6), Hendrickson (1), Hubbard (3), Lake (5), Lefferts (1), Lott (10), Kowenhoven (15), Linington (3), Magaw (1), Monfort (3), Neufus (1), Remsen (6), Repalje (6), Ryder (10), Schenck (6), SchooInnmaker (3), Suydam (3), Stillwell (7), Stoothoff (2), Stryker (5), Van Brunt (6),Van Cleef (2), Vanderbilt (1), Vanderveer (9), Van Dyke (2), Van Pelt (1), Van Sicklen (7), Van Wyck (2), Voorhees (7), Williamson (5), and Wyckoff (8). Inclusion is based in large part on the account given by Teunis G. Bergen, *Register in Alphabetical Order, of the Early Settlers of Kings County*; Vanderbilt,

Social History of Flatbush 175–248. Orthography has been made uniform for names that families and enumerators spelled differently. On the multiple spellings of one family name, see Lincoln Cocheu, "The Von Kouwenhoven–Conover Family." English-sounding names may also have been corruptions of Dutch names; in some cases, for example, Johnson was a corruption of Jansen. Kouwenhoven, "Brooklyn Before the Bridge" 15. This masking of Dutch names may well have led to an undercount of Dutch families, which, however, should not have affected the trend over time. On the origins of one prominent Dutch farm family, see Morton Wagman, "The Rise of Pieter Claessen Wyckoff." Because the enumerator's handwriting was poor in 1850, it is possible that additional illegible names in the CA were also Dutch; 1850, 1860, 1870, and 1880 CA, KC, MS.

11. Pessen, *Riches, Class, and Power Before the Civil War* 207, 209. Pessen erroneously stated that Jeremiah and John Lott were cousins.

12. Ditmas, *Historic Homesteads of Kings County* 103–105; Teunis G. Bergen, *Genealogy of the Van Brunt Family* 23–24; Snyder, *Tales of Old Flatbush* 160, iii (quotes). Because many people shared the same first and last names (with some families' last names becoming other people's first names), it is difficult to trace farmers from one census or assessment roll to the next.

13. Some Dutch farmers may have been exposed to such economic pressures. When the New Utrecht farm of the recently deceased John Bennett was sold at auction to his brother-in-law, the $17,000 price just sufficed to cover the mortgage to the Long Island Savings Bank. Yet a few years earlier, New York "capitalists" had offered $50,000 for the farm. *KCRG*, Feb. 1, 1879, 2:7–8. Murphy and Phillips were the only farmers in that landed property group in Flatbush and Gravesend, respectively. Unclear is not only how Murphy and Phillips acquired their land, but also what they did with it. Murphy reported to the CA in 1870 that his 37 acres were worth $120,000 — which would have worked out to a wholly fantastic $3,243 per acre — but that his farm produced only 2,500 bushels of potatoes, no market garden produce, and a total value of only $2,500. The William Murphy listed as a farmer in Flatbush in 1880 was returned as retired. Phillips reported that his 75 acres were worth $48,000 — this $640 per acre was quite high for the time — but yielded only 1,500 bushels of potatoes, no market garden produce, and only $2,000 worth of total production. The data for both of these wealthy Irish farmers thus seem suspect. The other 11 farmers with property valued at more than $100,000 resided in New Lots: Abraham Linington ($100,000), 53 years old; Christopher Lott ($150,000), 43 years old and retired; Williamson Rapalje ($100,000), 67 years old and retired; Isaac Schenck ($130,000), 66 years old and retired; Abraham Vanderveer ($100,000), 52 years old; John Vanderveer ($100,000), 51 years old; Stephen Vanderveer ($133,000), 44 years old; Ulpine Vansinderen ($100,000), 40 years old; and New Utrecht: J. R. Bennett ($100,000), 56 years old, retired, and also reporting $60,000 in personal estate; Daniel Van Brunt ($100,000), 44 years old; and Ralph Van Brunt ($100,000), 44 years old. U.S. CA, 1870, KC, MS; U.S. CP, 1870, KC, MS; U.S. CP, 1880, KC, MS.

14. John T. Ridge, *The Flatbush Irish* 7.

15. PS of the Seventh Census, 1850; PS of the Ninth Census, 1870, Flatbush at 73; Tenth Census, 1880, Flatbush 50 (Anderson). In 1900, a single tenant was "colored." *Twelfth Census . . . Agriculture*, tab. 10 at 106–7. In 1860, Francis Anderson, whose family members identify him as the same person returned as F. Anderson in 1870, was listed as a mulatto farm laborer. PS of the Eighth Census, 1860, Flatbush 89. In contrast, a contemporary source stated that by the end of the 1850s, blacks owned $276,000 in unencumbered real estate in Brooklyn and $151,000 in Williamsburgh. James Freeman Clarke, "Conditions of the Free Colored People of the United States" 254. A historian of the Midwest concluded that the "'farmer' without a farm . . . seems to have worked on a farm much as the farm laborer did. But since a different name was used in reporting occupation, we adhered to the census classification in considering these as separation occupational groups. We thought the census takers would hardly have classified so many men as 'farmers' and so many others on farms simply as agricultural laborers unless there had been in their minds a definite difference." Merle Curti, *The Making of an American Community* 60. Some relatives of owners may have been jointly operating farms but would have been excluded from the Census of Agriculture, which listed only one person per farm (though in rare cases it included an entry such as "Cropsey Brothers"), but these instances cannot account for the large discrepancy. Some farmless "farmers" may simply have called themselves such when they in fact occupied more subordinate positions on farms. 1870 CA for New Utrecht. The data for 1860, 1870, and 1880: PS of the Eighth Census, 1860, KC; PS of the Ninth Census, 1870, Flatbush; Tenth Census 1880, Flatbush; U.S. Census, 1880, Agriculture, reel 5, KC; U.S. Census, 1880, Agriculture, reel 18, KC. Farmers in the city of Brooklyn have been excluded from the counts although it is possible that some rural Kings County residents operated farms in Brooklyn.

16. *KCRG*, July 17, 1875, 2:3.

17. James Bennett, Edward Kennedy, and James Leary are examples of Irish immigrants who were tenants in 1880 and had been farm laborers in 1870 in Flatbush, while Patrick Fitzpatrick, Patrick Maher, and John Whalen had been general laborers, and John Heaslip the son of a (tenant) farmer. John Keenan may have been a farm laborer in 1860, but the identification in the Census of Population is not unambiguous.

18. CP and CA, 1870, MS; ARTF, 1870; Vanderbilt, *Social History of Flatbush* 175–248; CA, 1880, KC, Flatbush, SD no. 2, ED 251 at 2 (quote). John A. Lott's farm in Flatlands was also let. By 1885, the farm, which the Van Wyck brothers had been occupying, was let in parcels to three men for farming purposes. "Flatlands," *KCRBG*, Mar. 21, 1885, 2:4.

19. CA, 1860; ARTF, 1860. The 1860 Census of Agriculture also marked the last appearance of several old farming families, such as Voorhies and Stoothoff, which later also no longer figured as landlords. 1860 was the last census at which certain families, such as Suydam, Neefus, Vanderveer, and Lott were represented by several members; others, such as Vanderbilt, disappeared after the 1850 Census of Agriculture.

20. "Annexation: City and County Union," *BDE*, Mar. 3, 1873, 2:7.

21. On methodological problems related to tenancy data, see Allan Bogue, *From Prairie to Corn Belt* 62–64.

22. "Annexation: City and County Union," *BDE*, Mar. 3, 1873, 2:7.

23. ARTF, 1872 at 10–11. The almost $2,000 per acre land value may have been so high — about three times higher than that for many farms in the assessment rolls — because the homestead itself was expensive. The value of John Lefferts' real property was almost as high, but the value included several houses.

24. The Martense farms derived from Martin Adriaence (1668–1754), Jacob Martense's great-great-great-great-grandfather, whose Flatbush estate encompassed 500 acres and was divided among his three sons, Rem (1695–1760), Gerrit (1697–1732), and Adriaen (1707–1784). Rem's male lineage died out by the end of the eighteenth century (one of his great-granddaughters married Philip Crooke), but Adriaen's great-grandson, George (1791–1835), Jacob Martense's father, and Gerrit's great-great grandson, Judge Gerrit L. (1793–1860), operated the farms in the first half of the nineteenth century. After the death of his surviving brothers in the early 1860s, Jacob Martense presumably controlled his father's farm. After Judge Martense's death in 1860, only one son, Leffert, who died without issue, survived; although he was returned as a farmer living in his father's household at the 1850 Census of Population, the 1860 Census of Agriculture returned Jacob Martense as the only Martense left farming. In 1870, 54-year-old Leffert was returned as living together with his sister in his 80-year-old mother's household; like them, he was listed as owning $25,000 of real property, but had no occupation and the Flatbush assessment roll did not list him as a property owner; Lefferts died two days after his mother in 1875. Jacob Martense was one of the heirs of his father, George Martense, whose land continued to appear under this name on the Flatbush assessment rolls (its 84 acres and house were valued at $44,282 and taxed $616.45 in 1872), but may not have been an heir of the estate of his fourth cousin, G. L. Martense, which continued to appear under this name on the Flatbush assessment rolls. However, Jacob Martense may still have effectively administered both farms — he was listed as the administrator of his father's estate in 1862 — which were contiguous on the west side of Coney Island Avenue, thus prompting his remarks about it in the *Eagle*. Albert Ryerson, *The Ryerson Genealogy* 301–8; *NYT*, Dec. 14, 1875, 5:6; *NYT*, Dec. 17, 1875, 5:5; PS of the Seventh Census, Flatbush 23; CP, 1870, Flatbush, MS 65; ARTF, 1862 at 12. On the incomes of Martense and Prince, see tab. 37–38.

25. *BDE*, Dec. 16, 1881, 4:2 (obituary) (quote); *NYT*, Dec. 17, 1881, 8:3 (obituary); Stiles, *Civil . . . History* 1:412–13. The *Eagle* obituary called Martense a farmer; John Lefferts and other prominent Dutch farm family heads attended the funeral. "At Rest: Interment of the Remains of Ex-Supervisor Martense," *BDE*, Dec. 20, 1881, 4:2. T. G. Bergen, "The Martense Family" 66, characterized Martense as a "retired farmer." Possibly the sciatic rheumatism from which he had suffered for a long time prompted his retirement. *KCRBG*, Dec. 24, 1881, 2:1–2.

26. CA, 1870 and 1880, MS; Ditmas, *Historic Homesteads of Kings County* 67–69.

27. "An Agreement of Lease," Oct. 14, 1864, in Benson Family Papers, box V, first

folder; Agreement, Egbert Benson with Otto Gubner, Oct. 8, 1862, in ibid., sixth folder; calculated according to NUAR, 1864 to 1869, TRKC, vol. 2137–42, MR 44.

28. "Annexation: City and County Union," *BDE*, Mar. 3, 1873, 2:7.

29. Ibid. 2:7–8.

30. ARTF, 1873 at 187–202; Ditmas, *Historic Homesteads of Kings County* 67–68.

31. "No Annexation," *KCRBG*, Jan. 20, 1883, 2:1.

32. "Convincing Figures," *KCRBG*, Oct. 22, 1881, 2:1 (editorial).

33. "Public Opening & Formal Opening of the New Town Hall," *KCRG*, Feb. 12, 1876, 2:1, 4.

34. Calculated according to ARTF, 1870 at 8, 11, 23; ARTF, 1880 at 3, 11. After Lott died in 1878, his estate was listed as the owner. Assessments declined between 1870 and 1880 because they had been inflated during the "speculative excitement, in and about the year 1868" in the mistaken expectation that the opening of Prospect Park would trigger a residential building boom; the long depression beginning in 1873 then reduced prices significantly. "Strong Arguments Against Increased Assessments," *KCRG*, Oct. 16, 1875, 2:1.

35. Calculated according to ARTF, 1880 at 13, 46; see chapter 10 below.

36. In 1883, 32.5 acres were assessed at $52,000 and taxed $777.43 ($23.92/acre); another 24 acres were assessed at $15,600 and taxed $233.23 ($9.72/acre). ARTF, 1883 at 12. In 1885, the 32.5 acres were taxed $1,025.90 ($31.57/acre). ARTF, 1885 at 53. All the extant agreements in the church archive, running from 1882 to 1888, provided for $20 per acre rent.

37. CP, 1870, KC, Flatbush, MS 63; CP, 1880, KC, Flatbush, MS, SD no. 2, ED no. 252 at 37. In 1870, Martense declared that he owned a personal estate worth $18,000 but no real estate at all.

38. USBC, *United States Census of Agriculture: 1925*, pt. I, county tab. I at 192–93; *Thirteenth Census*, vol. VII, tab. 2 at 206. In the two categories in which Kings County ranked second lowest, it was surpassed only by Manhattan, which had literally only a handful of farms. In the category in which it ranked fourth highest, two of the other three were Staten Island and Suffolk, which were only 2–3 percentage points higher. During the Depression, tenancy declined as owners, presumably, seized an opportunity to supply themselves with food. By 1935, only 3 of 35 farms were tenant-operated. USBC, *United States Census of Agriculture: 1935*, vol. I, pt. 1, county tab. I at 54.

39. CO, *Report on Farms and Homes*, tab. 103 at 405, tab. 108 at 452; calculated according to data in CO, *Report on . . . Agriculture . . . Eleventh Census*, tab. 6 at 220.

10. What Was the Dutch Farmers' Price?
Profits, Taxes, Land Prices, and Incomes

1. Thomas Plaut, "Urban Growth and Agricultural Decline" 36 (Ph.D. diss.); Marion Clawson, *Suburban Land Conversion in the United States* 103, 122 (quote).

2. As late as 1895, an authority on horticulture confirmed that Long Island vegetable farms were still profitable: "While this competitive factor has certainly lessened their profits, even at the lower prices that prevail to-day there is still a

fair profit in the business for them, certainly more than in ordinary farm crops." Alford Henderson, "American Horticulture" 254.

3. Kenneth Jackson, *Crabgrass Frontier* 129–30.

4. William Lockeretz, "New Life for Metro Farming" 82.

5. William Heffernan and Susan Elder, "Quality of Life for Farm Families in Metropolitan and Nonmetropolitan Counties" 91–92 (quote). David Cohen, "Dutch-American Farming: Crops, Livestock, and Equipment, 1623–1900" at 185, notes that "in the countryside a distinct Dutch-American culture area survived through the end of the nineteenth century." See also David Cohen, *The Dutch-American Farm* 4–5, 131. In his dissertation, William McLaughlin, "Dutch Rural New York: Community, Economy, and Family in Colonial Flatbush" 30, 54–55, 90, 93–94, 101, 138, 170–71, argues that their individualism, at least during the colonial period, had been egalitarian and not accumulation oriented.

6. Timothy Dwight, *Travels in New England and New York* 233–35.

7. "Developing Long Island," *BDE*, Dec. 19, 1881, 2:1 (editorial).

8. Karl Marx, *Das Kapital* 3:631.

9. Daniel M. Tredwell, "Flatbush" 44.

10. Moreau de Saint-Méry, *Voyage aux États-Unis de L'Amérique, 1793–1798* at 189. A poignant portrayal of the premodern way of life appears in Traven's novelistic description of the early twentieth-century attempt by a U.S. oil company to buy a hacienda in Mexico. The owner, when offered $400 per acre for land that the company claims is otherwise worth less than one dollar, pleads that he cannot sell the land because he does not own it: he is merely its current custodian, administering it as did his ancestors and passing it along to the generations that will succeed him including the descendants of the hacienda's workers. The notion that he could just as well take the money and buy land elsewhere overlooks the hacienda's cultural uniqueness: it had been fertilized with the blood, sweat, hopes, sorrow, and joy of their fathers and mothers. The oil company president, who regards the owner as insane, takes as his matrix the early-twentieth-century U.S. farm, to which the farmer is no more emotionally attached than to any other object of commerce: a farmer builds up the farm not to create a home, but to make a profit by selling it and buying another farm to start the process all over. B. Traven, *Die weisse Rose* 23, 153, 173, 178–79.

11. "Notebook on the History of Brooklyn and Long Island, NY, including Jeremiah Johnson's Reminiscences," [unpaginated at ca. 40] (NYPL, [after 1862]). The word "plutonic" is difficult to decipher and has been guessed at. On the elder Johnson, see "Death of General Jeremiah Johnson," *NYT*, Oct. 23, 1852, 6:4–5.

12. Karl Marx and Friedrich Engels, *Manifest der Kommunistischen Partei* 466 (quote); John Thompson, "The Primary Sector" 203 (quote).

13. *Farm Real Estate Values in the United States by Counties* 24; USBEA, *Long Term Economic Growth, 1860–1970*, ser. B73 and B75 at 224; Paul Douglas, *Real Wages in the United States 1890–1926*, tab. 231 at 646; chap. 2 above; DI, CO, *Report on . . . Agriculture in the United States at the Eleventh Census*, tab. 6 at 198–235, tab. 24 at 500–537. Manhattan real-estate mortgage rates at the time were about 1.6 percentage points higher. USBEA, *Long Term Economic Growth*, ser. B77. Ac-

cording to Richard Hurd, *Principles of City Land Values* 133: "At the outer circumference of cities land is held as acreage, the prices per acre advancing from the normal value of farm land near cities, $50 to $150 per acre, up to market garden land, which may earn interest on $300 to $1,000 per acre, and, finally to speculative tracts held at $500 to $5,000 per acre." According to A. Oemler, "Truck Farming" 607, a good truck farmer could net $100 per acre on a farm with costs up to harvest time of $125 per acre on a farm two miles from a city. In contrast, the census data for 1880 show that no county produced even $125, let alone $225, per acre.

14. $100 \div 72.5 = 137.9$; $100 \div 77 = 129.9$. Neither the agricultural nor the population census for 1880 listed four of the names; several of the other names are found in the 1880 agricultural census but only as tenants, while still other names are listed more than once.

15. PS of the Third [*sic*; should read Second] Census 1800, NY, KC, NU 9; NUAR, 1830, TRKC, vol. 2043, roll 43; NUAR, 1837, TRKC, vol. 2114, roll 43; NUAR, 1848, TRKC, vol. 2058, roll 43. On Jacques Cortelyou, see *Brooklyn Before the Bridge* 64. Although what was called the 130-acre Cortelyou farm roughly matched the acreage owned by Peter Cortelyou, it passed through so many hands and had been split up so many times into smaller holdings, that by the 1880s no one was cultivating such a large farm. This account is strengthened by the fact that the developer bought the Cortelyou farm from Edward Egolf. "A Land Boom in New Utrecht." The farm associated with the Vechte-Cortelyou house on Fifth Avenue and Third to Fourth Streets was sold in 1850 for real-estate development to Edward Litchfield. Maud Dilliard, *Old Dutch Houses of Brooklyn*, no. 28. A farmline map from about 1872 shows farms owned by Sieger, E. Suydam, and A. Lott. *Map of Kings County*. By 1870, the only Cortelyous listed as owning land on the 1870 assessment roll for New Utrecht were the nonresident heirs of Isaac Cortelyou, who owned 13 acres of salt meadows on the beach. Nonresidents Solomon Sharp and V. K. Stevenson were listed as owning 24 acres and 64 acres, respectively, of farmland and meadowland (and many lots) in 1880. ARTNU [for 1870] at 20, TRKC, vols., NUAR, 1870, vol. 2143, MR 45; ARTNU, 1880 at 40–58, in TRKC, vols., NUAR, 1880, vol. 2153, MR 48.

16. CP, 1850, NU, MS at 35; CP, 1860, NU, MS at 44. Gelston, who was not of an old-line Kings County Dutch farming family, having been born in Connecticut, is oddly listed in 1860 as only 40 years old. Later it was reported that: "Apparently the greater part of the village [Ft. Hamilton] belongs to Mr. G. S. Gelston, whose notices of sale are spread all about." "Fort Hamilton," *KCRG*, May 4, 1878, 2:6.

17. Otto, Walter, and Adolph Gubener (ages 27, 26, and 21), all listed as farmers, arrived in New York on October 28, 1850, from Antwerp aboard the Westminster. *Germans to America* 341. According to his obituary in the *NYDT*, Nov. 22, 1887, 3:3, Gubner arrived in 1852. The 1880 census returned him as 57, but at the 1860 census he was 32, which is consistent with the age according to the passenger list. Otto Gubner was also a farmer in New Utrecht, renting 40 acres in the 1860s from Egbert Benson. Agreement of Lease, Oct. 8, 1862, in Benson Family Papers,

box V, sixth folder. Frederick Gubner was killed in 1881 (at age 22) when he was struck by a train while driving his farm wagon in New Utrecht. He was reported as having managed, on his own account, one of his father's farms. The father won a verdict of the "handsome sum" of $4,000. "New Utrecht," *KCRBG*, Sept. 10, 1881, 3:2; "New Utrecht," *KCRBG*, Sept. 24, 1881, 2:5; "A Verdict of $4,000," *KCRBG*, Dec. 3, 1881, 2:2. On Gubner's officeholding, see *BDEA: 1886* at 121; *BDEA: 1887* at 97; *Lain's Business Directory of Brooklyn, Kings County . . . 1886/87* at 372; *KCRG*, Dec. 6, 1879, 2:7 (election to justice of sessions). Gubner's assets sufficed to permit him to bid on leases for the common lands in Gravesend. "Gravesend," *KCRBG*, Mar. 19, 1881, 2:4. Gubner was "rewarded" with his interpreter's job for having merely fined rather than sentenced to imprisonment a man accused of brutally assaulting an ex-judge. *NYDT*, Nov. 22, 1887, 3:3 (obit); Stiles, *Civil . . . History* 412–13.

18. "New Utrecht," *KCRG*, Apr. 10, 1875, 8:1 (quote); Douglas, *Real Wages in the United States*, tab. 62 at 186; *BDEA: 1888* at 121 (in 1887, weekly wages of skilled building trades workers ranged between $12 and $30); Ronald Karr, "The Transformation of Agriculture in Brookline" 41 (quote). Sieger first appeared as owner of a 43-acre farm on the 1860 New Utrecht assessment roll; the next year and for several years thereafter Sieger and Gubner appeared as "occupant" of a 37-acre farm owned by the estate of John Deleplaine, which adjoined Sieger's land; in 1867 Gubner appeared as the owner of a 17-acre farm. NUAR, 1860 at 5, TRKC, vol. 2133, roll 44; NUAR, 1861 at 5, TRKC, vol. 2134, roll 44; NUAR, 1862 at 5, TRKC, vol. 2135, roll 44; NUAR, 1867 at 4, TRKC, vol. 2140, roll 44. They appeared as "Sieger & Gubner" on an 1873 farmline map and in the Kings County Business Notices in that atlas: "Sieger & Gubner . . Farmers, State Road, New Utrecht." F. W. Beers, *Atlas of Long Island* 24, 63. In addition, according to the 1865 and 1866 federal tax assessors' lists, Gubner and Sieger had, to the penny, precisely identical taxable incomes — $1,008.34 and $285.60, respectively. ALFBIR, 1862–66, M603, NY, dist. 2, Annual List 1865, roll T-45 1865 at 301, 319; ALFBIR, 1862–66, M603, NY, dist. 2, Annual List 1866, roll T-46 1866 at 312, 331. Sieger and Gubner appeared for the first time in the 1860 and 1870 Censuses of Agriculture, respectively. Sieger was not listed in the 1870 Census of Agriculture, but this omission may be the result of the loss of the census schedule before it was tabulated.

19. The fact that Suydam sold 47 acres in 1889 while owning only 12 in 1880 suggests that he had bought additional land in the interim or that part of his land had been farmed by tenants in 1880. In fact, in early 1880 Suydam did advertise to let 25 acres of land for farming in New Utrecht. *KCRG*, Jan. 10, 1880, 3:7. Since he was only 21 years old in 1880, the Evart Suydam returned as farming 45 and 100 acres in 1860 and 1850, respectively, was presumably his father. No other Suydam was returned as a farmer by the 1870 or 1880 Census of Population and no other Suydam was returned as operating a farm in New Utrecht by the 1850 Census of Agriculture; a Cornelius Suydam was enumerated in the 1860 Census of Agriculture. The three Cropseys owned more than they sold, but the ambi-

guity here lies more in identifying which one was the seller. The great-great-grandfathers of Aaron Lott and John A. Lott were brothers. Like the latter, he married a Lott family cousin. Phillips, *The Lott Family in America* 69, 98.

20. "The Reason Why," *KCRG*, Oct. 11, 1873, 4:1 (editorial).

21. The reason that no tax data are displayed for the Cropseys is that they are not listed as owning any acreage on the assessment roll for 1879 (or 1880), although the census returned them as farming and owning considerable acreage (and renting none). The assessments for three of the other five farmers are shaped by a similar inconsistency: Gubner, Sieger, and Martin were all assessed for fewer acres than they farmed — 15, 23, and 35 acres, respectively. Whereas Suydam owned 45 acres more than he farmed, only Lott farmed and owned the same acreage. Despite these discrepancies, the taxes that they actually paid underscore the constraints under which they operated farms and presumably reinforced their decisions to sell their land.

22. "A Handsome Suburb," *NYT*, Nov. 9, 1890, 16:2 (quote); "Bay Ridge Real Estate Sold," *NYT*, Nov. 14, 1890, 8:4; "Good Prices for Bay Ridge Lots," *NYT*, Mar. 5, 1891, 8:4 (quote). Extensive descriptive advertisements by the Bay Ridge Park Improvement Co. appeared in the opening (unpaginated) pages of *BDEA: 1891*. None of the officers or trustees of the company had a Dutch name.

23. All the land owned by Gubner, Lott, and Suydam was listed as taxed either to their estate or heirs. ARTNU, 1886, 1888, 1889, and 1890. One of the male Cropseys was a lawyer; "Seek an Accounting of Cropsey Estate," *NYT*, Nov. 25, 1915, 18:1. Both farmers (William Williamson and John Garnin) reported as giving up farming for reasons of ill health were only in their thirties. "Flatlands," *KCRBG*, July 17, 1880, 3:3; "Local," *KCRBG*, Dec. 12, 1881, 3:1.

24. Calculated according to U.S. CA, 1880, KC, NU, MS 3, 8. In conformity with the preceding examples, the farmer's fertilizer and wage costs were multiplied by 1.3.

25. Calculated according to U.S. CA, 1860, KC, NU, MS; U.S. CA, 1870, KC, NU, MS.

26. As early as 1872, Vanderveer sold 31 acres for $21,700. "Real Estate," *KCRG*, May 25, 1872, 2:3. This relatively high price may have been a function of the post-Prospect Park real-estate boom, which came to an end the following year. Vanderveer may have been motivated to sell by the fact that at the 1870 census, his farm, which he valued at $80,000, was returned as having only $2,620 worth of production, only $400 of which was market garden produce. U.S. Census, 1870, Agriculture, KC, Flatbush.

27. U.S. CA, 1860, MS; U.S. CA, 1880, MS.

28. ARTF, 1893 at 243 (Williamson); ARTF, 1894 at 482 (Williamson); ARTF, 1874 at 204 (Neefus); ARTF, 1893 at 214 (Neefus); ARTF, 1894 at 424, 427–28, 437–39 (Neefus); "Death of John Neefus," *KCRG*, Oct. 9, 1875, 2:2; ARTF, 1893 at 250 (47 acres owned by Suydam); ARTF, 1894 at 468 (total of 53.31 acres subdivided by Suydam), at 482–84, 487 (Schenck); TRKC, UD, Town Board, 1878–1890, Bundle No. 10: Town Board 1892–1894, MR 18 (franchise).

29. The taxes reported in the assessment roll have been adjusted by taking two factors into consideration. First, for Williamson and Vanderveer that part of the tax has been deducted which was accounted for by their personal property as

contradistinguished from their real estate; and second, since the Schencks and Vanderveer reported to the census that their farms encompassed more land than the assessment roll recorded, their taxes have been increased by the appropriate percentage. William Bennett, the large Gravesend farmer, also illustrates the light burden of property taxes at the time of the 1879–80 Census of Agriculture. The $88.56 tax on his 94 acres amounted to only 2.6 percent of his calculated profit of $3,465. Since he was returned as farming 45 acres and his son Elias was returned as a tenant on the other 45 acres, the tax should in fact be set in relation to the total profit of both farms; it amounted to only 1.8 percent of that sum of $5,035. Gravesend AR, 1879 at 1, in TRKC, vol. 3075, roll 69; U.S. CA, 1880, KC, Gravesend, MS at 3.

30. Henderson, *Gardening for Profit* 216, 218 (1890).

31. Further light is cast on the potential profitability of these farms by data on vegetable farms at a slightly later time. The 1900 Census of Agriculture reported that whereas a cereal field yielding $8–10/acre was doing unusually well, truck gardens yielded $80 to $200. The additional labor and capital costs did not offset these higher yields, thus leaving "a very considerable margin . . . for higher wages and for profits." USCO, *Twelfth Census*, pt. II at 307. The census conceded that inexact data on the acreage devoted to vegetables made derivative calculations "somewhat uncertain." Ibid. In 1913, when the USDA conducted a study of the analogous set of processes forcing farmers outside Louisville, Kentucky, to adapt their operations to generate interest on the increased capitalized value of their land plus a profit, it published data showing that on small intensive potato-truck farms (under 80 acres) near the city, the average farmer derived net income of $23 per acre on $96 per acre of gross receipts, which amounted to 7 percent profit on invested capital (in addition to $1,000 in imputed labor income included in the operating expenses). USDA, *Influence of a City on Farming*, tab. VIII at 12.

32. These invaluable lists, which scholars have rarely if ever used to study any part of the United States, are available on microfilm only for tax years 1862 through 1865 — yet no library appears to hold any for New York City or Brooklyn. The original lists for the last years of the tax are preserved at the New York Regional Office of the National Archives, where they have languished virtually untouched. At the time of the War of 1812, Congress levied direct internal taxes on houses, land, slaves, and certain articles. The Dutch farmers of Kings County were well represented on the list of these taxpayers and of the tax they paid, although they were not among those paying the highest amounts. "Statement of the Amount of Internal Duties . . . during the year one thousand eight hundred and fifteen," and "Statement of the Amount of Internal Duties . . . during the year one thousand eight hundred and sixteen." TRKC, UD, Flatbush, Taxes; Personal Property Oaths; Assessors' Notices; Internal Revenue: 1870–1895. During and after the Civil War, Congress revised progressive tax rates as follows: 3 percent on income between $600 and $10,000, and 5 percent on more than $10,000 (1862); 5 percent on income between $600 and $5,000, 7.5 percent on $5,000 to $10,000, and 10% on more than $10,000 (1864); 5 percent on $600 to

$5,000, and 10 percent on more than $5,000 (1865). As taxpayers' complaints began to mount after the war, Congress raised the exemption level, lowered the rate, and eliminated progressivity: in 1867 the rate became 5 percent on all income above $1,000, and in 1870 it was 2.5 percent on all income above $2,000. Act of July 1, 1862, ch. 119, sect. 90, 12 Stat. 432, 473; Act of June 30, 1864, ch. 173, sect. 116, 13 Stat. 223, 281; Act of Mar. 3, 1865, ch. 77, 13 Stat. 468, 479; Act of Mar. 2, 1867, ch. 169, sect. 13, 14 Stat. 471, 478; Act of July 14, 1870, ch. 255, sect. 6 & 13, 16 Stat. 256, 257, 260. See generally, Frederic Howe, *Taxation and Taxes in the United States* 90–102; Harry Smith, *The United States Federal Internal Tax History* 45–97. On the publicness of the assessment lists, see Marc Linder, "Tax Glasnost' for Millionaires" 962.

33. John C. Bergen papers. The Brooklyn Historical Society does not appear to hold any other farm account books from the Civil War forward.

34. *Trow's New York City Directory for the Year Ending May 1, 1869* at 6 (quote). The occupational data are taken from the CP, 1870, KC, MS. Schaffer was returned as living in Flatlands; it is assumed that Garvin was E. L. Garvin, the only Garvin returned in Flatbush. CP, 1870, KC, Flatbush, MS at 24. George Hope, though president of an insurance company, personally supervised the management of his small acre farm and boasted of the town's earliest vegetables in 1879. "Bay Ridge," *KCRG*, Oct. 11, 1879, 2:7. His eight-acre farm was returned at the 1860 Census of Agriculture, but not thereafter.

35. The speculation that Ryerson must have had other sources of income is strengthened by the fact that in 1870 his personal property was valued at $18,000 — the second highest amount in Flatlands and four times greater than that of his land. ARFl, 1870 at 9, TRKC, vol. 4036, roll 77. Because the 1870 Census of Agriculture listed operations of the Bennett, Cropsey, and Van Brunt Brothers without specifying the names of the brothers, it is not possible to determine the cost-revenue structure of the farms of several farmers such as Adolphus Bennett and Daniel von Brunt whose taxable incomes were somewhat higher than Linington's. Because one sheet from the 1870 Census of Agriculture for New Utrecht was apparently lost, it is not possible to determine the revenues and costs of a number of farmers. Larzelere married into the Lott family, having married Catharine Aletta Lott, daughter of Charles Lott, in 1858. Phillips, *The Lott Family in America* 97.

36. Act of Mar. 2, 1867, ch. 169, 14 Stat. 478. Laborers' subsistence was deductible, but no deduction was permitted for labor or services furnished or produce consumed by the farmer or his family. Commissioner of Internal Revenue, Regulations for the Assessment of the Income-Tax, May 1, 1863, printed in George Boutwell, *A Manual of the Direct and Excise Tax System of the United States* 196–98 at 197. Nevertheless, complaints were voiced that farmers' consumption of their own produce was not taxed. "The Income Tax," *NYTrib*, Dec. 10, 1869, 4:4, 5. Although the statute did not expressly permit deductions for fertilizer expenditures, the Commissioner ruled that: "Fertilizers purchased by farmers to maintain their land in present productive condition will be considered as 'repairs' in estimating income." Decision no. 110, May 1863, printed in Boutwell,

Manual of the Direct and Excise Tax System of the United States 273–75. For a fac-
simile of the Civil War–era income tax form, see ibid. at 156; IRS, *Income Taxes
1862–1962* at 7–10. In publishing the incomes for the Boston area in book form,
a newspaper noted that "some names are wanting, and among those are persons
having large incomes. Most of these parties declined or neglected to make their
returns, and have been or will be 'doomed' by the Assessors." Boston Traveller,
Incomes of the Citizens of Boston n.p. [iii]. David Wells issued his report as Special Commissioner of the Revenue in 1869 in which he recommended that the
uniform 5 percent tax be reduced to 3 percent because it would "bring within
reach of the tax great numbers who now either avoid giving in lists at all, or,
while doing so, force the constituents of their income so as to escape contribu-
tion entirely." *Report of Special Commissioner of the Revenue* LXIX.

37. Roberts, whose name in censuses and tax records was also spelled "Robert" and
"Robarts," was not listed in the various lawyers' directories of the period. A legal notice that appeared in a newspaper after the death of his wife, Jane, spelled
the family's name as "Robert." *KCG*, Oct. 31, 1885, 2:6. Roberts, who first appeared as living in New Utrecht at the 1840 census, may have been the son of a
very wealthy physician who acquired a fortune in the West Indies. In 1845 a
Daniel Roberts was an attorney in Manhattan with wealth estimated at $100,000.
Sixth Census, 1840, NY, KC, NU at 818; *Wealth and Biography of the Wealthy Citizens of New York City* 25. Roberts's high annual incomes as recorded in the federal tax assessor's lists may have stemmed from bonds or other investments. He
first appeared on the New Utrecht assessment roll in 1836 as the owner of a
160-acre farm which until then had been owned by Garret Stoothoff. NUAR,
1836 at 1, TRKC, vol. 2047, roll 43. This genesis, however, conflicts with the account given by Teunis Bergen, who stated that in 1827 "Daniel Robarts" married
Jane Cowenhoven, who inherited a farm that ultimately derived from the Van
Brunt family. Bergen, *Genealogy of the Van Brunt Family* 25. In addition to the
119-acre farm, Roberts owned another 42 acres (with five houses) in 1870.
ARTNU, 1870 at 1, 45, TRKC, vol. 2143, MR 45.

38. Two of the largest farms in New Utrecht and all of Kings County — two dairies
in Bushwick with output of $20,000 were larger — the production of which was
valued at $17,000 and $13,500, were returned by the Census of Agriculture as
owned by Van Brunt & Brothers and W. Bennett & Brothers, respectively. Given
the large number of Bennetts and moderate number of Van Brunts farming at
that time, identifying the partners is beset with difficulties. The same problem
affects the Cropsey Brothers. The Van Brunts reputedly could trace their property holdings back farther than any other family in New Utrecht. "The Bi-
Centennial of New Utrecht," *KCRG*, Oct. 27, 1877, 2:3, 6.

39. Whether these low or nonpayments actually reflected flagging profitability or
merely placed "the honest tax-payer at a disadvantage in comparison with his
neighbor or business competitor who escapes," might be determined if researchers could compare the income tax returns themselves, which included entries for such deductions as amounts paid for hired labor, repairs, and interest,
with the data in the 1870 Census of Agriculture manuscript schedules. *Report of*

Special Commissioner of the Revenue LXIX. Unfortunately, they may have been destroyed a century ago. In any event, the National Archives believes that they were destroyed, does not have them, and reports that even if they were at the Archives, the IRS takes the position that the confidentiality conferred on post-1913 tax returns retroactively applies to the Civil War–era tax returns and would prohibit their use. Telephone interview with Cynthia Fox, Branch Chief, Textual Reports, NA (Apr. 15–17, 1997). Fox asserts that the returns were burned because Congress, after the U.S. Supreme Court had held the 1894 income tax unconstitutional, ordered all income tax returns in the possession of the Treasury Department destroyed. Cynthia Fox, "Income Tax Records of the Civil War Years" 144. In fact, Congress directed the Secretary of the Treasury to "cause the immediate destruction of all income tax returns and any copies thereof, with all statements and records relative thereto, now in possession of the Treasury Department, by reason of 'An Act to reduce taxation,' and so forth, in effect August eighth, eighteen hundred and ninety-four." H.R.J. 42, 54th Cong., 1st sess., 29 Stat. 470 (1896). Fox concedes that this resolution did not pertain to the Civil War–era tax returns, but speculates that the Treasury Department might have destroyed them without specific authorization. The Commissioner of Internal Revenue did request Congress to authorize the destruction of all income tax records in the custody of the Internal Revenue's office. *Annual Report of the Secretary of Treasury on the State of the Finances for the Year 1895* at 482. Fox could offer no source for her claim that the returns were burned, but refers to a congressional report in which the Treasury Department recommended destruction of all Forms 22 from 1863 through 1869. Fox contends that Form 22 was the tax return, but the list expressly characterized it as "Collector's monthly abstract of amount collected on each article or occupation." *Useless Papers in the Treasury Department* 6. However, even if the returns had been preserved, since taxpayers were permitted simply to affirm that their income was lower than the exemption level in lieu of filing a return, it might still be impossible to scrutinize many farmers' economic condition. Act of June 30, 1864, sect. 118, 13 U.S. Stat. 223, 282. The accuracy of the returns may have deteriorated over time as the federal income tax came "to be regarded by the better class of citizens with more and more disfavor from year to year." *Income Tax* 1.

40. Boston Traveller, *Incomes of the Citizens of Boston* 28–29; *Annual Report of the Commissioner of Internal Revenue* VI (nationally, 272,843 persons were assessed for federal income tax in 1869 compared with 266,135 in 1867). The $1,000 exemption was in effect during both years. Brookline was, to be sure, more of a metropolitan suburb, home to wealthy Boston businessmen, and less of a farming community, than rural Kings County. See generally, Karr, "The Transformation of Agriculture in Brookline" 41.

41. Phillips, *The Lott Family in America* 101; CP, 1880, KC, Flatbush, SD no. 2, ED 251 at 32.

42. Bergen, *Genealogy of the Lefferts Family* 42; "Flatbush" at 7 in *The Towns that Became Brooklyn* (quote); Lockeretz, "New Life for Metro Farming" at 84 (quote).

On the sale of Flushing farms to larger Dutch farming families from Kings County in the nineteenth century, see Tony Hiss, *The Experience of Place* 110. At least one of the Flatlands Kouwenhoven farming families moved to Queens in the early nineteenth century, buying an estate of several hundred acres. The property was "worth millions of dollars" by the early twentieth century when a descendant, Luke Kouwenhoven, who had been born in 1829, died at age 85. Half a century before his death, he had been able to retire from farming to "manage his financial affairs." "Obituary: Luke Kouwenhoven" (undated newspaper clipping furnished by Catharine Weber Scarborough). Gottmann offered this stereotype of the farmer who sold out in the post–World War II period: "The capital gain that comes when a farmer surrenders to the city is a handsome reward. He naturally feels much better about the deal than the suburbanite who follows him with a split-level on an eighty-foot lot and thirty-year mortgage. The 'poor farmer' can grieve at his leisure on Miami Beach while the 'rich city slicker' works the rest of his able lifetime to pay for taking his land." Gottmann, *Megalopolis* 333.

43. *KCRG*, Apr. 12, 1873, 6:3 (quote); *BDE*, Apr. 16, 1873, 3:8 (quote); *KCRG*, Apr. 12, 1873, 6:3. In 1872 John S. Ryder of Gravesend bought an 80-acre farm in Smithstown, Long Island, and was to move there. "Gravesend," *KCRG*, Sept. 21, 1872, 5:2; *KCRG*, Oct. 12, 1872, 5:1. The 1870 Census of Population and Census of Agriculture included several people with this name, one of whom was a butcher and another an operator of a small farm. In 1873 Henry J. Van Sicklen of Gravesend bought a 100-acre farm in Bellport, Long Island. "Gravesend," *KCRG*, May 10, 1873, 5:2. It is unclear whether he was the 65-year-old restaurant owner or 34-year-old farmer of a six-acre farm at the 1870 census. Within a week of each other in 1874, A. Stryker and Samuel Stryker of Gravesend were reported to have moved to Rockville Center, Long Island, and Long Island (without town), respectively. "Gravesend," *KCRG*, Nov. 7, 1874, 1:3; "Island Items," *KCRG*, Nov. 14, 1874, 7:1. Neither item mentioned that the residents had bought a farm; two persons with each name, one of each of whom was a small farmer, were returned at the 1870 census. Only one destination lay outside the New York metropolitan area: two brothers from a prominent Gravesend Dutch farming family who were, however, apparently themselves not farmers, bought a large farm in Wisconsin. James Van Sicklen, a carpenter in his 40s, explained that carpentry in Kings County was "too poor . . . to get along." "Gravesend," *KCRG*, Nov. 14, 1874, 1:3 (quote); "Gravesend," *KCRG*, Nov. 28, 1874, 1:3. At the 1870 Census of Population, James was returned as a 39-year-old carpenter, while Lawrence was not listed. On the Van Wycks, see "Flatlands and Canarsie," *KCRBG*, Mar. 14, 1885, 2:3. The father, Z. B. Van Wyck, appeared in the 1870 and 1880 Census of Population as 50 and 54 years old, respectively, while his son Franklin was 17 and 27; by 1880, four of his sons worked on the farm. Although the 1870 Census of Agriculture returned him as operating a 100-acre farm and producing $10,000 worth of product, Van Wyck did not appear at all in the 1880 Census of Agriculture. At the same time that the Van Wycks were auctioning off their stock, the

newspaper reported that (the deceased) Judge Lott's farm in Flatlands, which had recently been occupied by the Van Wyck brothers, was being let in parcels to three persons to farm. "Flatlands," *KCRBG*, Mar. 21, 1885, 2:4. It is unclear whether Van Wyck also owned his own land or had merely rented Lott's farm for many years. Van Wyck did not appear on the Dripps farmline maps for 1868 or 1872.

44. Bergen, *Bergen Family* 353–61, 343–44. By the mid-1870s, one of the brothers had already moved from Mattituck to Brooklyn.

45. "Bay Ridge," *KCRG*, Feb. 2, 1878, 2:6 (the buyer was George Bergen, who was not a farmer in 1870, and the seller J. V. P. Wyckoff) (quote); One of Them, "About Long Island Wild Lands," *KCRBG*, Jan. 15, 1881, 2:1–2 (quote).

46. "Farm Lands in Demand," *Long Island Farmer*, Feb. 10, 1899, 1:2; Gertrude Ryder Bennett, *Turning Back the Clock* 42.

47. Pessen, *Riches, Class, and Power Before the Civil War* 38 (quote); "John Z. Lott Dies at 76," *NYT*, Oct. 25, 1914, sect. 3 at 3:4; *Flatbush of To-Day* 132 (quote); "John Z. Lott Left $281,355," *NYT*, Dec. 13, 1914, sect. II at 12:1; Phillips, *The Lott Family in America* 101–2; Ditmas, *Historic Homesteads of Kings County* 51–52. In Gravesend, Edward Bennett, who had farmed with his father William, became involved in Brooklyn real estate but continued to live in the old farmhouse after the farm was sold at the turn of the century. Papers in Wyckoff-Bennett homestead.

48. *Flatbush of To-Day* 137, 138, 149, 142 (quote); Phillips, *Lott Family in America* 120.

49. "Death of John Lefferts," *NYT*, Apr. 19, 1893, 2:3 (quote); ARTNU, 1870 at 5, TRKC, vol. 2143, MR 45; ARTNU, for the Year 1880 at 6, 38, TRKC, vol. 2153, MR 48; *KCRG*, May 18, 1872, 4:3 (advertisement); "James Lefferts Dead," *NYT*, Nov. 6, 1915, 11:7 (quote borrowing much verbatim from *Flatbush of To-Day* 144); Thompson, *History of Long Island* 3:239; ARTNU, 1880 at 6, 38, TRKC, vols., NUAR, 1880, vol. 2153, MR 48; "Local," *KCRBG*, Sept. 30, 1882, 3:1 (quote); "A Happy Union," *KCRG*, June 17, 1876, 2:3. For the location of Lefferts' farm in New Utrecht, see *Map of Kings County* (1872?). In his will, signed in December 1892, a few months before his death, John Lefferts bequeathed to his five sons $51,000, which represented the proceeds from the sale of his farm at New Utrecht. Kings County Surrogate Court.

50. "The Estate of Henry Clay Ditmas," *NYT*, Mar. 28, 1895, 16:5 (quote); "John H. Ditmas," *NYT*, June 11, 1914, 11:6; "J. H. Ditmas Left $177,326," *NYT*, Nov. 28, 1914, 15:6; Ditmas, *Historic Homesteads of Kings County* 59–60; LBDBKC . . . *1890* at 355; TRKC, UD, Flatbush, Town Board 1892–1894, Bundle No. 10; TRKC, UD, Flatbush, Jurors — List of; Justices — Drawing of Terms — Report; Knickerbocker Electric; Light and Power Co. Agreement, 1815–1847, 1890, 1893.

51. *Atlas of the Townships of New Utrecht, Gravesend, Flatbush, Flatlands and New Lots*; ARTNU, 1888 at 321; ARTNU, 1889 at 369–70; ARTNU, 1890 at 1:550; *BDE*, Aug. 28, 1892 (quote). Some biographical data are taken from a letter to the author from Garret Cowenhoven's granddaughter, Catharine Weber Scarborough (April 16, 1997), as well as from material prepared by her and published as "Some

Cowenhovens of Borough Park in New Utrecht," in *The Van Kouwenhoven-Conover Family Association Tidings* 30–35 (undated); and the obituary in *NYT*, Aug. 31, 1927, 21:3.

52. "May Accuse Captain Worth," *BDE*, Jan. 24, 1898 (quote); "News from the Suburbs: The Kouwenhoven Barn Looks Like a Club House," *BDE*, Jan. 30, 1898, at 11 (quote). Cowenhoven's granddaughter, who was born after his death — he did not marry until he was about 50 years old — though amused by the report of his status as millionaire, does not doubt the possibility based on the lifestyle of her mother as a child; she thinks it likely that Garret Cowenhoven no longer worked by the mid-1890s when his children were born. Telephone interview with Catharine Weber Scarborough, Wilmington, Delaware (Apr. 27, 1997). Apparently even after the sale of the farmland, Cowenhoven continued to own land that he inherited from John Van Duyne (the mother of Cowenhoven's mother, Ann Denyse, was Catherine Van Duyne). A letter from September 1897 states that the Scholl Bros. had paid Cowenhoven $5 for hay cut from the meadowland inherited from Van Duyne. Copy of letter provided by Catharine Weber Scarborough; letter from Catharine Weber Scarborough to author (Apr. 30, 1997).

53. "R. G. Cowenhoven Dead," *NYT*, Mar. 5, 1890, 9:4.

54. "Death of Abram Van Sicklen," *NYT*, Feb. 22, 1898, 7:5; U.S. Census, 1870, Agriculture, KC, Gravesend, MS. Insularity may have run in the Van Sicklen family: in 1873 Court J. Van Sicklen of Gravesend, "who has not been absent from home over night during the last thirty years, recently went to Bellport, L. I., and remained there two or three days." *KCRG*, May 17, 1873, 4:4. Provinciality was not a two-way street for the *Times*, which opined at the opening of the Brooklyn Bridge that "not one in one thousand of them [New Yorkers] will be likely ever to have occasion to use the new structure except from curiosity." "The Opening of the Bridge," *NYT*, May 29, 1883, 4:2 (editorial).

55. "Personal," *NYT*, Feb. 23, 1898, 6:5.

56. Tredwell, "Flatbush" 41.

11. Case Studies in Suburbanization

1. "Kings Co. Real Estate," *KCRBG*, Aug. 28, 1880, 2:1 (editorial); "Property in Flatbush," *KCRBG*, Dec. 10, 1881, 2:2 (quote); Jesse Williams, "Rural New York City" 179 (quote); "Fruit Thieves," *KCRG*, Aug. 22, 1874, 5:2.

2. Williams, "Rural New York City" 180.

3. Stephanie Wolf, *Urban Village* 70–73. Daniel Bluestone et al., *Flatbush* 8, fail to capture the essence of the differentiation process by arguing that the "'Old Guard' . . . balanced in an unsteady position. While they were powerful people who wished to maintain all the goodness of Flatbush they were also the landholders, and development meant opportunity for furthering their economic position. Many were soon to join the ranks of the capitalists — the prodevelopment citizenry." This position is inadequate because it fails to see that the old guard, who as employing farmers had already been capitalists for de-

cades, were making a choice between their traditional role as agrarian capitalists and a future role as real-estate speculators or, once (sub)urbanization had gained ground, more diversified investment fields.

4. TRKC, Flatbush Improvement Board-Minutes, Oct. 11, 1875, at 150–53; Lefferts Vanderbilt, *Social History of Flatbush* 236–37 (quote).

5. Jay Bonsteel et al., "Soil Survey of the Long Island Area" 125 (quote); *Map of Kings County* (1868); *Map of Kings County* (1872?); calculated according to Assessments for Drainage, &c., in the Northern Drainage District, of the Town of NU; Teunis G. Bergen, *The Bergen Family* 110–11; ARTNU, [1870], TRKC, vols., NUAR, 1870, vol. 2143, MR 45; ARTNU, 1880, TRKC, vols., NUAR, 1880, vol. 2153, MR 48.

6. ARTNU, 1846, TRKC, vol. 2056, roll 43; ARTNU, 1852, TRKC, vol. 2125, roll 43. Although Murphy, an important Brooklyn lawyer, appeared on the assessment rolls as a nonresident residing in Brooklyn until 1862, the 1850 Census of Population returned him as living in New Utrecht. CP, 1850, KC, NU, MS at 58.

7. See generally, Lefferts Vanderbilt, *The Social History of Flatbush* 175–248. On Langley: CP, 1860, NU, MS at 74; "Obituary: William C. Langley," *NYT*, Dec. 11, 1890, 2:2 (quote); "William C. Langley's Will," *NYT*, Dec. 17, 1890, 9:4. Langley was also one of the incorporators in 1855 of the Brooklyn Hunt Botanical and Horticultural Garden of the County of Kings, to which he donated considerable land in New Utrecht although the project never came to fruition. 1855 N.Y. Laws, ch. 224 at 332; Gager, "The Four Botanic Gardens of Brooklyn" 8–10 (Jan. 1940). Langley and Henry C. Murphy, a Brooklyn lawyer who lived in New Utrecht, were also vice presidents of the Brooklyn Horticultural Society. *HJRART* 4:148 (1854); *HJRART* 7:199 (1857). On Fox: Lefferts Vanderbilt, *The Social History of Flatbush* 178. Fox appeared as early as 1858 in the Flatbush assessment roll as owning eight acres. ARTF, 1860 at 18–19. The 1860 Census of Agriculture returned Fox as owning a 15-acre farm, but he did not list himself as a farmer in the 1860 Census of Population. Fox died in 1872. "Long Island News," *KCRG*, Nov. 2, 1872, 3:1. Fox's elegant eight-acre estate, "the cream of suburban property," was sold at an executor's sale in 1874 for $18,750 to Hubert Giroux, president of a Brooklyn insurance company. The surmise that just a short time previously it could have been sold for $30,000 was an index of the "dullness" of the real estate market following a period of "[e]xtravagance." "Real Estate," *KCRG*, June 20, 1874, 4:4. On Longmire: Lefferts Vanderbilt, *The Social History of Flatbush* 219; Catherine Nelson & Theo. Nelson, "The Village of Flatbush as It Was in the Year 1870" (map). By 1879, however, his history of "living luxuriously and not paying his debts" caught up with him as he succumbed to his creditors and was arrested for defrauding his creditors. "Jonathan Longmire's Methods," *NYT*, Mar. 25, 1880, 3:1; "A Verdict Against Longmire," *NYT*, Mar. 26, 1880, 3:3 (quote); "Longmire's Assignment," *NYT*, Aug. 5, 1880, 3:3; Smith v. Longmire, 24 Hun 257 (1881). As early as 1861, Longmire appeared in the Flatbush assessment roll as owning 16 lots. ARTF, 1861 at 22–23.

8. "Fatal Dive into Gravesend Bay," *NYT*, July 12, 1895, 1:6 (obituary of Young's son). The obituary in the *Times* stated merely that Young was "reported to be

quite wealthy." *NYT*, Oct. 24, 1895, 8:2. Young's interest in an enlarged population to increase the value of his real estate conflicted with his aversion to trespasses on his land associated with thicker settlement. "New Utrecht," *KCRBG*, Dec. 3, 1881, 2:5.

9. "Archibald Young," *NYDT*, Oct. 24, 1895, 7:5 (obituary). Curiously, the New Utrecht assessment rolls do not confirm this account: Young was not listed as owning any land until 1854, when as a nonresident (39 Broadway, New York), he bought four acres, "late of J. Cropsey." Not until 1875, when he acquired two tracts totaling 113 acres, did Young appear as owning significant acreage. ARTNU, 1854 at 7, TRKC, NUAR, 1854, vol. 2127, MR 43. ARTNU, 1875 at 105, TRKC, vols., NUAR, 1880, vol. 2148, MR 46. In 1874 Young (together with Barney Williams) bought the old Post farm at Fort Hamilton, paying $39,000 for 130 acres. "Real Estate," *KCRG*, May 16, 1874, 4:2. Two months later he was being praised as a "public spirited gentleman" for having built 100 bathhouses and a five-acre park at Bath. "New Utrecht," *KCRG*, July 4, 1874, 8:1. In 1859 Young appeared as a resident of New Utrecht. ARTNU, 1859 at 8, TRKC, NUAR, 1859, vol. 2132, MR 44.

10. "Railroad Notes," *KCRG*, Feb. 15, 1879, 2:2; ARTNU, 1886 at 77, 190–91; "New Utrecht, Bath and Unionville," *KCRBG*, July 4, 1885, 2:6.

11. 1871 N.Y. Laws, ch. 564, sect. 1 at 1199 (quote); Enrollment of Persons Liable to Military Duty, TRKC, NU. The town's cosmopolitan bona fides was called into question in the 1870s when an attempt was made to prohibit a "foreigner" from teaching, even German, in its schools. "New Utrecht Topics, Local and General," *KCRG*, Oct. 31, 1874, 8:1. The incident prompted a German-American in Canarsie to doubt whether New Utrecht would ever "produce anything but cabbages, etc." "New Utrecht Science and Progress," *KCRG*, Nov. 7, 1874, 8:1, 2.

12. "Appleton's Bindery," *KCRG*, Dec. 2, 1876, 2:5–6; "Local," *KCRBG*, Mar. 24, 1883, 3:1. Matthews was atypical of the mercantile elite of rural Kings County in that he was not the owner, but a partner in the Appleton firm (and manager of the Appleton bindery). Stiles, *Civil . . . History* 2:740. Johnson, who died in 1872, was of the publishing firm Johnson, Fry & Co. on Beekman Street in New York. "Gravesend," *KCRG*, Nov. 30, 1872, 4:4.

13. The occupational data are taken from: 1850 CP, KC, Brooklyn, MS at 41 (Fox); 1860 CP, KC, NL, MS at 23 (Hoag); NU at 93 (Spedding); 1870 CP; 1880 CP, Flatbush, SD No. 2, ED No. 252 at 39 (Westfall); *TNYCD for the Year Ending May 1, 1869* (Ceballos, Keyser, and Kattenhorn); *TNYCD for the Year Ending May 1, 1861* (Hoag); Beers, *Atlas of Long Island* 63; *LDLI: For 1878–79*. The 1860 Census of Agriculture returned Robert Fox as operating a 15-acre farm, but its outputs were small. According to Lefferts Vanderbilt, *The Social History of Flatbush* 193–94, Lyles was a bank president. On the wealth of the Willink and Ludlow families, see ibid. at 238–46. In addition to the incomes reported in table 38, in October 1871 a 4 percent tax amounting to $17,176.17 was paid on the $429,404.32 estate of Elizabeth Ludlow paid out to her first cousin Charles Livingston; in October 1872, a 2 percent succession tax of $8,500 was paid by the heirs and executors of Daniel and Wilhelm Willink on the $175,000 estate of John Willink. Since

Teunis Bergen was also a surveyor, farming may not have accounted for all this income; the next highest ranked farmer in 1863 was Winant Bennett of New Utrecht, 21st, with an income of $4,713.47. Daniel Roberts, who was listed as having the fourth-highest income in rural Kings County in 1870, was returned by the 1870 Census of Agriculture as operating a 119-acre farm the value of the output of which was $5,000, but he reported himself as a lawyer to the Census of Population. Since Jacob Ryerson's farm's output in 1870 was only a fraction of his taxable income, he presumably had another source of income. The next highest-income farmer in 1870 was Abraham Linington, whose $3,223.01 income put him in 18th place and was plausibly generated solely on his farm given the size of his output. Like Jacob Ryerson, John Ryerson produced on his farm only a small fraction of the taxable income he reported; the source of his other income is unknown. That he had other sources is supported by the fact that the value of his personal property was exceptionally high for Flatlands and more than twice as high as that of his real property. ARTFl, 1870 at 9, in TRKC, vol. 4036, roll 77. The farmer with the next highest income, in 20th place, was Asher Hubbard of Flatlands whose $2,332.29 income could plausibly have been produced from his farm. Although J. Remsen Bennett was important enough to merit two obituaries in the *Rural Gazette*, including one seven column-inches long, the paper provided no information on his business life or even mentioned that he had been a farmer. "Sudden Death of J. R. Bennett," *KCRG*, Jan. 24, 1880, 3:1; "Death of J. Remsen Bennett," *KCRG*, Jan. 31, 1880, 2:7. The papers on file relating to Bennett's will, of which his son William R. was the executor, do not include any mention of his assets. KC Surrogate's Court.

14. CP, 1870, KC, Town of Gravesend, MS at 49; *KCRG*, May 17, 1873, 4:4 (quote, adding that Ridley was building a new barn); "Obituary: Eduard Ridley," *NYT*, Aug. 1, 1883, 5:4; "Death of Edward Ridley," *KCRBG*, Aug. 4, 1883, 2:1; Stiles, *Civil . . . History* 1:211. For an advertisement for Ridley's store, see *NYDT*, Nov. 3, 1873, 6:3. For years, Ridley advertised in every issue of the *KCRG*. He also owned a five-acre residence at Pleasantville, Westchester. "Gravesend," *KCRG*, July 7, 1877, 2:6.

15. "Gravesend," *KCRG*, May 8, 1875, 4:6; Stiles, *Civil . . . History* 1:211; "Gravesend," *KCRBG*, Feb. 19, 1881, 2:5. See also "New Utrecht," *KCRG*, Nov. 8, 1873, 1:2. Ridley's house was located near the corner of King's Highway and Coney Island Avenue. Catherine Nelson and Theodore Nelson, "The Village of Gravesend As It Was in 1870."

16. TRKC, Minutes of Flatbush Board of Health, Meeting of Sept. 7, 1874, Rules and Regulations, sect. 7 at 2, 6, and Meeting of Aug. 7, 1879; TRKC, Minutes of Flatbush Board of Health, Meeting of May 4, 1875, at 24, and Meeting of Dec. 7, 1876, at 42 (quote). The unbidden dumping of manure even on farms was also unlawful; for a false report that someone had dumped manure on the Martense farm, see Minutes of Meeting of Jan. 4, 1877, in ibid. at 43.

17. "The Excise Law," *KCRG*, July 12, 1873, 4:2–3; "Our Excise Board," *KCRG*, Jan. 10, 1880, 2:2; "Aroused at Last — A Delegation of the Principal Property

Owners Wait on the Excise Board," *KCRBG*, May 22, 1880, 2:2; "To the Citizens of Flatbush," ibid.

18. "Law and Order," *KCRBG*, May 14, 1881, 2:2; "Just Verdict," *KCRBG*, Oct. 23, 1880, 2:2–3; *KCRBG*, Oct. 9, 1880, 3:1 (Lefferts' farm in Vermont). For other efforts by the association to combat sales of liquor and sex, see "Law and Order," *KCRBG*, Aug. 14, 1880, 3:1; "Our Excise Board," *KCRBG*, Nov. 6, 1880, 3:1–2.

19. "Healthful Action," *KCRG*, Sept. 12, 1874, 4:1 (quote); "Board of Health," *KCRG*, Sept. 12, 1874, 4:1–3 (quotes). Convictions for keeping piggeries also antedated the creation of the Flatbush board of health. E.g., *KCRG*, July 20, 1872, 4:3 (untitled).

20. "Board of Health," *KCRG*, Sept. 19, 1874, 4:2–3.

21. "Board of Health," *KCRG*, Sept. 26, 1874, 4:2–3.

22. For possible insight into the political machinations against which Bartlett warned, see "Piggeries," *KCRG*, July 17, 1875, 2:6; "Piggeries," *KCRG*, July 24, 1875, 3:1.

23. TRKC, Minutes of Flatbush Board of Health, Meeting of Sept. 23, 1874, Rules and Regulations 18 (quotes); "Enlarging Brooklyn," *KCRG*, Jan. 16, 1875, 4:1 (editorial).

24. TRKC, Minutes of Flatbush Board of Health, Meeting of May 4, 1875, Rules and Regulations 25; TRKC, Minutes of Flatbush Board of Health, Meetings of July 6, 1875, at 27–28, June 23, 1877, at 48–50; "A Raid on the Piggeries," *KCRG*, July 28, 1877, 2:5 (quote).

25. TRKC, Minutes of Flatbush Board of Health, Meetings of Aug. 1, 1878, at 67–68, Nov. 7, 1878, at 70–71; "The Health Board and the Piggeries," *KCRG*, Aug. 24, 1878, 2:2; "Abolishing the Piggeries," *KCRG*, Aug. 24, 1878, 2:1 (editorial); "Our Supervisor," ibid. (editorial) (quote). In an act of marital wealth consolidation reminiscent of the habits of the Dutch farmers, Matthews's son William married Prince's daughter Gertrude. "William Matthews Is Dead," *NYDT*, Apr. 16, 1896, 14:1.

26. "At Last," *KCRBG*, Sept. 17, 1881, 2:2–3 (quote); TRKC, Minutes of Flatbush Board of Health, Sept. 22, 1881, at 135–36 (quote); "Decided Action," *KCRBG*, Sept. 24, 1881, 2:2.

27. "Flatbush Health Board," *KCRBG*, Jan. 14, 1882, 2:2; "We Must Dissent," *KCRBG*, Jan. 28, 1882, 2:1; "The Piggeries," *KCRBG*, Mar. 3, 1883, 2:3; "The Piggeries," *KCRBG*, Aug. 25, 1883, 2:1 (quote); "The Piggeries," *KCRBG*, Aug. 2, 1884, 2:1; "The Hog Cholera and the Piggeries to Be Abolished," *KCRBG*, Dec. 13, 1884, 2:1 (editorial); "The Piggeries Abolished," *KCRBG*, Dec. 20, 1884, 2:1; "Local," *KCRBG*, May 2, 1885, 3:1 (quote); "Local," *KCRBG*, May 30, 1885, 3:1. In 1884, swill milk was "still produced largely in the suburbs of Brooklyn; but that industry is by common consent ruled out as an agricultural pursuit." Stiles, *Civil . . . History* 1:39a.

28. Frederick Law Olmsted, "The Future of New York," *NYDT*, Dec. 28, 1879, 5:1, 2.

29. "Two Great Cities United," *NYT*, May 25, 1883, 1:6, 2:2 (address of Rev. Dr. Richard Storrs) (quote); Senate, Sub-Committee of the Joint Committee on the

Affairs of Cities, *In the Matter of the Hearing in Relation to "The Greater New York"* 65 (quote). On Abraham, see Weld, *Brooklyn Is America* 106–7.

30. Ellsworth Huntington, "The Water Barriers of New York City" 172.

31. "Brooklyn, a City of Homes," *RERBG*, 53 (1355):350 (Mar. 3, 1894).

32. David Hammack, *Power and Society* 361 n.86 (quote); "A Greater New York," *RERBG*, 52 (1323):102 (July 22, 1893) (quotes); *RERBG* 52 (1344):755 (Dec. 16, 1893); "Consolidation and Taxes," *RERBG* 53 (1161):596 (Apr. 14, 1894) (quote); "To Develop Long Island," *BDE*, Apr. 17, 1894, 4:5 (quote). In 1892 the *New York Times* editorially characterized consolidation as in the interest of Brooklyn property owners because interborough tax equalization would lead to lower taxes in Kings County and thus encourage housing construction on unimproved land. "The Consolidation Scheme," *NYT*, Jan. 19, 1892, 4:2–3. See also "An Issue for Brooklyn," *NYT*, July 17, 1892, 16:1; "Brooklyn's Alternative," *NYDT*, Apr. 3, 1891, 4:1 (gap between New York and Brooklyn property tax rates widened between 1880 and 1890).

33. *The Eagle and Brooklyn* 1135.

34. *The Eagle and Brooklyn* 1137.

35. Vanderbilt, *The Social History of Flatbush* 175–76. On Vanderbilt and Lefferts, see Charles Ditmas, *Historic Homesteads of Kings County* 79; "Death List of a Day: Mrs. Gertrude L. Vanderbilt," *NYT*, Jan. 7, 1902, 7:5; "Died While Driving: Sudden End of John Lefferts," *NYDT*, Apr. 19, 1893, 2:4; "Obituary: John Vanderbilt," *KCRG*, May 19, 1877, 2:3. Margaret Latimer, *New York and Brooklyn the Year the Great Bridge Opened* 17–18, in her snapshot of Brooklyn in 1883, offers no inkling of the trend, instead characterizing the five towns of Kings County in general as "largely . . . small, quiet communities," and Flatbush in particular as "a lovely suburban town . . . known for its gracious tree-lined lanes as well as for its fussiness about who lived within its borders." More curious is the *New York Times* review of a later edition of Vanderbilt's book from 1909, which, in a vast understatement, observed that "even since the book was written (1880) there has been a notable divergence from the older habits of life." "Social History of Old Flatbush," *NYT*, Aug. 14, 1909, pt. 2 at 488:3. The book must have resonated with contemporaries: by 1883 a second edition appeared. *KCRBG*, Mar. 10, 1883, 3:2. For a sense of the appreciation accorded the book at the time, see, "Mrs. Vanderbilt's 'Social History of Flatbush,'" *KCRBG*, Jan. 29, 1881, 2:2–3. The publisher D. Appleton (the wealthy Flatbush resident William Matthews was a member of the firm) appointed Egleston, the editor of the *Rural Gazette*, sole sales agent in the rural Kings County towns. Ibid. at 3:3.

36. Letter from Gertrude Lefferts Vanderbilt to Elizabeth Ludlow (undated but ca. 1865–66), Cruikshank Coll. Ludlow inherited part of the estate of her brother-in-law, John A. Willink.

37. "Rowdyism in Brooklyn — Forty Roughs Arrested," *NYT*, Apr. 27, 1874, 8:4.

38. "New Utrecht Topics, Local and General," *KCRG*, Aug. 22, 1874, 8:1–2; 1874 N.Y. Laws, ch. 511, sect. 1 at 701; 1871 N.Y. Laws, ch. 721, sect. 1 at 1669; "Bay Ridge," *KCRG*, June 16, 1877, 3:2; *The Citizen Guide to Brooklyn and Long Island* 180, 183 (quote); "Delight in Flatbush," *BDE*, May 21, 1894, 6:3 (editorial) (quote).

39. "General Principles," *KCRBG*, Oct. 1, 1881, 2:1 (quote); "Life in a Brooklyn Suburb," *NYDT*, Nov. 29, 1884, 3:5 (quote). The *Tribune*'s failure to mention the longstanding conflict over piggeries suggests that the article was an infomercial.

40. "Some Suburbs of New York" 124–25.

41. "Flatbush Avenue Improvements," *NYDT*, Apr. 21, 1889, 21:5 (quote);Vincent Seyfried, *The Long Island Rail Road* 51–52 (objection to steam railroad); "The History of Our Toll-Gate," *KCRBG*, May 5, 1883, 2:1–3 (quotes); 1889 N.Y. Laws, ch. 161, sect. 2 at 186, 187. In January 1870, the Flatbush Plank Road Co. paid $39.47 federal tax on $789.47 of dividends. ALFBIR, 1869–70.

42. "Opening Streets," *KCRBG*, Feb. 16, 1884, 2:1 (editorial) (quote); "The Real Estate Boom in Flatbush," *KCRBG*, Nov. 17, 1883, 2:1 (editorial) (quote).

43. "D. R. [sic; should be "M."] Tredwell Dies at 95," *NYT*, Nov. 12, 1921, 13:5. See also Daniel Tredwell, *Personal Reminiscences of Men and Things on Long Island*. The *Rural Gazette* reported that he moved to Flatbush from Brooklyn in 1882, at which time John Lefferts sold him land 75 feet by 505 feet on East New York Avenue for $10,000. "Local," *KCRBG*, Apr. 1, 1882, 3:1; "Real Estate," *KCRBG*, May 6, 1882, 2:5.

44. Daniel Tredwell, "Flatbush" 41–42 (1964). Tredwell's reliability can be gauged by the fact that according to the Census of Agriculture, John's 25-year-old son, James Lefferts, who managed his farms, harvested 7,500 bushels of potatoes in 1879 on 31 acres. U.S. Census, 1880, Agriculture, KC, Flatbush, MS, ED no. 252, SD no. 2 at 3. Lefferts, one of the county's biggest potato growers — in late March 1882 he was "busy . . . with all hands ploughing lands and planting potatoes" — produced no market garden produce, and was returned as a tenant. James Lefferts also advertised repeatedly seed potatoes for sale. U.S. CP, 1880, KC, Flatbush, MS 45; "Local," *KCRBG*, Apr. 1, 1882, 3:1 (quote); "Death of John Lefferts," *NYT*, Apr. 19, 1893, 2:3; *KCRG*, Mar. 15, 1879, 3:7 (advertisement).

45. Tredwell, "Flatbush" 44 (quote); "'Old Flatbush,'" in Snyder, *Tales of Old Flatbush* 78–85 (quote).

46. Ditmas, *Historic Homesteads of Kings County* 67. Before this time "several farms had been divided and offered for sale in building lots, with indifferent success. As far back as 1885 . . . John Reis established a real estate brokerage business in Flatbush, and was followed, before the larger development of the section took place, by other brokers, who negotiated occasional transfers of farm land." *Flatbush of To-Day* 112.

47. "Ex-Dock Official Drowned Up-State," *NYT*, Aug. 21, 1940, 21:3; *The Eagle and Brooklyn* 464–65 (quote); Henry Meyer, *Vanderveer Park* 56 (quote).

48. Meyer, *Looking Through Life's Window* 101, 105–8. Puffery may explain the assertion by a Flatbush bank that the deed covering a 133-acre plot (on which one of its offices was located) sold for $199,766.85 (or about $1,500/acre) on March 1, 1899, "might be called the 'Historic Deed of Modern Flatbush.'" Green Point Savings Bank, *Historic Flatbush* 22–23.

49. Meyer, *Looking Through Life's Window* 112. See also *Flatbush of To-Day* 96.

50. John Heffernan, *Brooklyn Times*, May 31, 1931, Henry A. Meyer, pkg. 139A, box 1, BHS. One of the reasons for their success, despite having been the "laughing butt

of their competitors," was their policy of returning deposits to customers who were not perfectly satisfied. Review of Meyer, "Looking Through Life's Window," *Canarsie Civic*, Nov. 12, 1932, Henry A. Meyer, pkg. 139A, box 1.

51. Meyer, *Looking Through Life's Window* 116–21 (quotes); ARTF, 1892 at 141, 252–53; ARTF, 1893 at 136, 252–53; Meyer, *Looking Through Life's Window* at 119 (the $1,250 per acre was an average cost including 15 acres of another Vanderveer farm; an additional 15 acres of land owned by the Cortelyou family was also crossed out, but it is unclear who acquired it); TRKC, UD, Flatbush, Town Board, 1878–1890, Bundle No. 10, Town Board 1892–1894. John Z. Lott was not a distinterested observer: just four days after the contract was signed, he arranged to buy, at Meyer's cost, 16 acres of the Cortelyou farm on behalf of the Flatbush Water Company, which, in order to protect its plant, agreed to lay the land out as a park and to cooperate with Germania by laying water mains as Germania improved its property. Meyer, *Looking Through Life's Window* 120–21. Ironically, in the midst of this hectic sell-off, *Harper's* published a hopelessly obsolete article on Greater Brooklyn asserting that although farms had been changing into city blocks for decades, "the prevailing rule of the place, marked by littleness in financial operations, affected the transformation. The process was slow. The farmers sold a little now and a little later, to middle-men, ahead of the actual demands of the inrushing tide of humanity." Julian Ralph, "The City of Brooklyn" 656.

52. Meyer, *Looking Through Life's Window* 121–24; ARTF, 1894 at 382. That land at this time was commonly sold subject to a lease for agricultural purposes is confirmed by a deal gone awry, by which John Suydam would have sold the 50-acre Flatbush farm of Cornelius Suydam in 1893 for $2,500 an acre to the stock promoter Cyrus E. Staples through the real-estate office of Adrian Vanderveer. This price was about five times as high as the value that 77-year-old Cornelius Suydam had declared to the census enumerator in 1880 and four times its assessed value in 1893. Vanderveer v. Suydam, 83 Hun 116 (A.D. 1894); Louis Pink, *Gaynor* 49; 1880 CP and CA, KC, Flatbush, MS; ARTF, 1893 at 250 (47 acres and house valued at $29,600).

53. Meyer, *Looking Through Life's Window* 124–40. Later critics presumably were not referring to such fertile farmland when they wrote: "Some lands in New York have been taken from farming use and held idle during the transition. But the aggregate produce of such land is relatively unimportant. In the case of New York City large areas are useless for any but urban purposes. The rocky hills of the west side were good for nothing but goat pasture." *Report of the Commission on Housing and Regional Planning* 50. According to *Flatbush of To-Day* 121, after buying John Vanderveer's 150-acre farm, Germania bought five more farms totalling 1,000 acres; later, Charles Osborn, a real-estate broker, sold a 90-acre John Vanderveer farm. Peter McNulty and others bought 70.65 acres from John A. Lott's heirs. ARTFl, 1892 at 1, TRKC, vol. 4052, roll 80. To illustrate the course of development of the Lott farm: that part of the Lott estate that is today bounded by Ocean Avenue, Foster Avenue, East 19th Street, and Glenwood Road was first

conveyed by John A. Lott's children to Germania on July 29, 1899. John Z. Lott continued to convey parts of the same block to Germania in 1900, 1902, 1903, 1904, and 1905. In 1907 Germania began conveying land on this block to the John R. Corbin Co., which built houses there. These entries are taken from the abstract of title for section 16, block 5240, Kings County, at Brooklyn City Hall.

54. ARTF, 1867 at 35, 36, 40, 50, 54, 56; ARTF, 1867 at 8; ARTF, 1870 at 162, 1; Lefferts Vanderbilt, *Social History of Flatbush* 236–37. On Philip S. Crooke (1810–1881), a politically well-connected Brooklyn lawyer who acquired by marriage farmland in Flatbush that had once been owned by the Martense family and held several offices in Flatbush, see "Death of General Philip S. Crooke," *KCRBG*, Mar. 19, 1881, 2:2–3; Crooke v. County of Kings, 97 N.Y. 421 (1884).

55. "The Annexation of Flatbush," *NYDT*, Feb. 2, 1890, 20:6; "Flatbush Enters as a Ward," *BDE*, Apr. 26, 1894, 12:1–2 (quote); Pink, *Gaynor* 46 (quote). For an 1890 petition circulated by proannexation forces including John Lefferts and John Lott, see Bluestone et al., *Flatbush* 11.

56. *The Eagle and Brooklyn* 244 (quote); *KCRG*, Feb. 19, 1876, 3:6. ARTF, 1893 at 38; "Death of John Lefferts," *NYT*, Apr. 19, 1893, 2:3; *KCRBG*, Mar. 21, 1885, 3:3 (Lefferts offered 14.5 acres in Flatbush suitable for market gardening); Bluestone et al., *Flatbush* 41–44; ARTF, 1887 at 35; ARTF, 1880 at 3. John Lefferts had been selling his houses for decades. In 1872, it was announced that he would build several residences in Flatbush. *KCRG*, Apr. 20, 1872, 4:3. The next year he advertised to sell a house and eight lots near Prospect Park. *BDE*, Apr. 3, 1873, 3:8. Three years later he advertised lots for sale on Lefferts Avenue.

57. *BDE*, Feb. 21, 1894, 7:7; *BDE*, Mar. 17, 1894, 8:3; *BDE*, Apr. 24, 1894, 7:7; *BDE*, Apr. 29, 1894, 19:4. Meyer had at first considered naming it "Homestead," "but because of the riots at Homestead, Pa. . . . we decided this would not do, since we felt public sentiment was against the strikes." Meyer, *Looking Through Life's Window* 110.

58. *BDEA: 1896* at 446 (advertisement) (quote); Bluestone et al., *Flatbush* 20.

59. Pessen, *Riches, Class, and Power Before the Civil War* 284 (quote); "Jere Johnson, Jr., Dead," *NYT*, Feb. 16, 1898, 2:4; "Death of General Jeremiah Johnson," *NYT*, Oct. 23, 1852, 6:4–5; "The David Dudley Field Sale," *RERBG*, 47 (1208):738 (May 9, 1891) (quote); *The Eagle and Brooklyn* 1108 (quote).

60. *BDE*, Feb. 10, 1894, 7:5; "Jere Johnson, Jr., Dead"; *BDE*, Mar. 21, 1894, 7:3 (quote); *BDE*, Apr. 27, 1894, 7:2 (quote); *BDE*, Apr. 29, 1894, 19:4 (quote).

61. Meyer, *Looking Through Life's Window* 114–15; *RERBG* 47 (1211):III (May 30, 1891) (quote). The property was located on Ocean Avenue, East 11th to 22nd Streets, Avenues C and D, Flatbush Avenue, and Coney Island Road or Avenue.

62. "Old County Towns," Brooklyn Daily Eagle, *Consolidation Number* (quote); "Brooklyn Real Estate," Brooklyn Daily Eagle, *Consolidation Number* 62 (quote); Meyer, *Looking Through Life's Window* 110 (quote), 129–31; Fisher, *Flatbush Past and Present* 84–86 ("restricted"); Richard Dutton, "This Was Flatbush" 10; John R. Corbin Co. Houses ("substantial"); *Flatbush of To-Day* 131(quote); *BDEA: 1900* at 630 (quote).

63. Jackson, *Crabgrass Frontier* 176 (quote); Tredwell, "Flatbush" 41 (quote). Jackson's empirical assertion about Brooklyn — namely, that "the biggest gainers were usually those who owned close-in farms" — is not supported by his source.

64. "'Old Flatbush'" 83–84. The successful struggle over annexation in Kings County differed in one vital respect from a similar conflict in another market garden suburb in the Northeast: timing. In Brookline, farmers were among the strongest supporters of annexation to Boston in 1873 because suburbanization had already taken a firm grip on the town, quadrupling the population during the previous three decades. This accomplished fact produced a twofold polarized result. First, the reduced number of farmers, working smaller farms, faced a radically altered economic situation despite the continued profitability of their operations. Second, the chief obstacle to the farmers' efforts to treat their land as the mere commodity it had become in their plans was a group that scarcely existed in the Kings County towns: the already resident commuter suburbanites, who "wanted the town to retain its rural atmosphere" and to slow the very pace of development that would increase the price of land that the market gardeners wanted to sell. With Brookline already providing a level of services that towns like Flatbush lacked, the nonagrarian middle class was able to put an end to Boston's annexationist strivings altogether. Karr, "The Transformation of Agriculture in Brookline" 41–42 (quote); Ronald Karr, "Brookline Rejects Annexation, 1873."

65. See also "A Hint to Capitalists," *RERBG*, 2 (29):3 (Oct. 3, 1868) (editorial).

66. *Appleton's Dictionary of New York and Vicinity* 19 (quote); Teunis G. Bergen, "History of the Town of New Utrecht" 1:254 (quote).

67. Hazelton, *The Boroughs of Brooklyn and Queens* 2:1088.

68. "A Unique Suburb," *RERBG*, 44 (1118):1132–33 (Aug. 17, 1889); U.S. Census, 1860, Agriculture, NYS, reel 4, KC, NU at 11; CP, 1810, Schedules, NYS, KC, NU at 98; Fifth Census, 1830, PS, NY, vol. 29, KC, NU at 393. No Benson was recorded as farming by the 1850 Census of Agriculture. George Martense Benson was born in 1826 and died in 1867. "Inscriptions on Tombstones in the Cemetery of the Reformed Dutch Church, New Utrecht, L.I."

69. Indenture between Egbert Benson Jr. Esq. of Town of New Utrecht and Maria Cowenhoven, his wife, parties of the first part, and Jane Cowenhoven of Flatbush, Aug. 31, 1826, in Benson Family Papers, box V, sixth folder; TRKC, NUAR, 1830, vol. 2043, roll 43; TRKC, NUAR, 1842, vol. 2117, roll 43; TRKC, NUAR, 1849, vol. 2123, roll 43; TRKC, NUAR, 1855, vol. 2128, roll 43; TRKC, NUAR, 1856, vol. 2129, roll 43. The Van Brunt, Wyckoff, Gifford, and Voorhees conveyances are found in ibid., first folder. Egbert Benson was the son of Robert Benson (1739–1823), the secretary of the convention adopting the New York State constitution, who was the brother of Egbert Benson (1746–1833), an important figure in the Revolution and later a federal judge. Robert married Dinah, the daughter of John Kouwenhoven. Their children included Robert (1785–1872), Catherine (who married John Lefferts), Maria (who married Judge Leffert Lefferts), and Egbert, who married Maria, the daughter of John Kouwenhoven. This Egbert, a personal friend of Henry Clay and other "great men" of his time,

acquired the New Utrecht farmland from his wife's family. Martha J. Lamb, *History of the City of New York* 2:509–10 n.1 (quote); Bergen, *Genealogy of the Van Brunt Family* 25; "Inscriptions on Tombstones in the Cemetery of the Reformed Dutch Church, New Utrecht, L.I."; *The Papers of Henry Clay* 10:623–24. Some of the land that the Bensons acquired from the Cowenhovens originally stemmed from Lady Deborah Moody, who had received the original patent for Gravesend. The total acreage of the farms was about 400. Mrs. Bleeker [Charlotte] Bangs, *Reminiscences of Old New Utrecht and Gowanus* 161–62; Hazelton, *The Boroughs of Brooklyn and Queens* 2:1086–87.

70. *KCRG*, Nov. 27, 1875, 3:1; "An Agreement of Lease," Oct. 14, 1864, in Benson Family Papers, box V, first folder. An "Agreement," dated September 13, 1864, between Egbert Benson and Cornelius Doyle and Robert Waters, running during the same three-year period did not specify the acreage. Benson Family Papers, box V, first folder. A similar lease with Otto Gubner ran from March 1, 1863 to March 1, 1866, obligating the tenant to pay $450 annually for 40 acres. Ibid. sixth folder.

71. U.S. CP, 1870, NY, KC, NU at 56; U.S. CP, 1880, NY, KC, NU, SD no. 2, ED no. 262 at 5; "Railroad Notes," *KCRG*, Feb. 15, 1879, 2:2; TRKC, ARTNU, [1870] at 13, vols., NUAR, 1870, vol. 2143, MR 45; TRKC, ARTNU, 1880 at 37–38, 100, 113, vols., NUAR, 1880, vol. 2153, MR 48. TRKC, ARTNU, 1887 at 52; TRKC, ARTNU, 1888 at 48. In 1870 a black farm laborer also lived with the family.

72. "A Unique Suburb," *RERBG*, 44 (1118):1132–33 (Aug. 17, 1889).

73. Hazelton, *The Boroughs of Brooklyn and Queens* 2:1089. Lynch was sufficiently influential that in 1889 he prevailed upon the county Board of Supervisors to alter the boundary lines between Gravesend and New Utrecht in both of which towns he was a property owner. Board of Supervisors of Kings County, Resolution No. 1, in 1889 N.Y. Laws at 799. Lynch, who also developed New London, Connecticut, as a summer resort, died in 1917, leaving an estate in excess of $300,000. *NYT*, May 12, 1917, 11:6; *NYT*, May 1, 1919, 21:3. Contrary to the claim of the architectural critic of the *New York Times*, neither was Bensonhurst named for or developed by Arthur Benson, nor did it even exist in the 1870s. Paul Goldberger, "The Once and Future Montauk," *NYT*, Sept. 15, 1994, C1:3 (Lexis). The same erroneous account appeared in Thomas Clavin, "Battle over Beach Waged in Montauk," *NYT*, Feb. 10, 1985, sect. 11LI at 11:1 (Lexis). But the *Times* has also gotten the story right: Lynette Holloway, "Change Turns a Neighborhood's Eyes Toward the Past," *NYT*, Feb. 20, 1994, sect. 13 at 10:3; Rosalie Radomsky, "If You're Thinking of Living in Bensonhurst," *NYT*, Aug. 26, 1984, sect. 8 at 9:1 (Lexis).

74. "Better Offerings Awaited," *NYT*, Sept. 27, 1891, 20:3 (quote); *The Eagle and Brooklyn* 1150 (quote).

75. "Bensonhurst-by-the-Sea," *RERBG*, 44 (1114):1017 (July 20, 1889) (quotes); "A Unique Suburb: Where a Large Part of New York's Population Gravitates to — Thoughts for Real Estate Investors," *RERBG*, 44 (1118):1132–33 (Aug. 17, 1889) (quotes). Depending on the number of lots sold at a time, lots were soon selling for $200–500. *RERBG*, 44 (1121):1211 (Sept. 7, 1889); *RERBG*, 44 (1126):1372

(Oct. 12, 1889); *RERBG*, 44 (1127):1409 (Oct. 19, 1889). A half-year earlier Lynch sold lots publicly at prices 25 percent lower than had been anticipated. *RERBG*, 43 (1093):237 (Feb. 23, 1889). For still earlier transactions, see *RERBG*, 42 (1062):929 (July 21, 1888); *RERBG*, 42 (1068):1071 (Sept. 1, 1888).

76. "A Unique Suburb."

77. *The Eagle and Brooklyn* 1151–52. On the contemporaneous formation of Blythe-bourne (later Boro Park), a New Utrecht suburb for "the thrifty wage-earner and the careful husbander of a limited income," see *The Eagle and Brooklyn* 1152–53. See also Norman Litchfield, "Blythebourne."

78. "Suburban New York — I," *RERBG*, 46 (1166):73 (July 19, 1890) (quote); "Suburban New York — III: Bensonhurst-by-the-Sea," *RERBG* 46 (1171):243−44 (Aug. 23, 1890) (quotes).

12. Conclusion: Is Urban Agriculture Oxymoronic?

1. *Report of the Jamaica Bay Improvement Commission* 29.

2. Robert Haig and Roswell McCrea, *Major Economic Factors in Metropolitan Growth and Arrangement* 43 (quote); "Farms Near New York," *RERBG* 3 (15):4 (June 26, 1869) (quote). According to the *Real Estate Record*: "The small farm-ers east of the Mississippi are dying out and their properties are falling into the hands of large holders of landed estates. . . . [S]ome small holdings still obtain near the large cities, but they are only truck or vegetable farms. . . . To farm economically — that is, to use labor saving machinery with advantage — large farms are indispensable. The small farmers cannot compete on equal terms with the owner of machinery, hence he must go to the wall, that is, he must sell out. Rich farmers are getting richer not only in money but in land." The *New York Times* comes close to making the "Times Square into a potato patch" charge when it bemoans the uses to which vacant lots on which tenements once stood in Manhattan have been put: "Some have been planted with rows of corn. In the middle of America's most densely populated city . . . prime residential real estate has been converted to . . . farmland. Those cornstalks, not the Empire State Building, are the symbol of modern New York." John Tierney, "At the Intersec-tion of Supply and Demand," *NYT Mag.*, May 4, 1997, at 38–52 at 41. Wendell Berry, *The Unsettling of America* 41, argues that the "only difference" between agricultural modernization in the United States, which "involved the forcible displacement of millions of people," and "the forced removal of the populations of villages in communist countries" is that the latter used military force and "with us, it has been economic — a 'free market' in which the freest were the richest."

3. Henry George, *Social Problems* 229, 235, 236, 238–39. Despite Marx's low opin-ion of him as an economic theorist, George's denunciation of the mutually harmful relationship between the modern city and countryside was reminiscent of Marx's critique of the mutually destructive impact of the capitalist city and countryside. For Marx's views of George, see letters from Marx to John Swinton, June 2, 1881, and to Friedrich Sorge, June 20, 1881, in Karl Marx [and] Friedrich

Engels, *Werke* 35:191, 199–201. Marx moved from a philosophical view that the abolition of the antagonism between city and country was one of the first conditions of the creation of a higher-order community to the political-economic conclusion that by piling up population in cities, "capitalist production disturbs the metabolism between humans and the earth, i.e., the return to the soil of the components of the soil that humans have used up in the form of food and clothing, the eternal natural condition of lasting fertility of the soil." Karl Marx and Friedrich Engels, *Die deutsche Ideologie* 50; Karl Marx, *Das Kapital* 1:494.

4. George, *Social Problems* 239 (quote); *Henry George's 1886 Campaign* 26, 78 (speeches of Oct. 5 and Oct. 22, 1886) (quotes).

5. Edward Pratt, *Industrial Causes of Congestion of Population in New York City* 201(quote); *Report of the Jamaica Bay Improvement Commission* 5 (quote). For a contemporaneous suggestion that while more than 300,000 aliens settled in cities in New York State in fiscal year 1904–5, 50,000 agricultural laborers could find employment at good wages on farms in the state, see Bolton Hall, *Three Acres and Liberty* 303. The Jamaica Bay commission believed that Bronx's congestion could have been avoided if suitable railway lines had been built to make the growth of Brooklyn and Queens even more "marvelous" than it was.

6. E. H. Bennett, "Report on General Plan for the Borough of Brooklyn" 21 (quote), 115–16; "Houses for Homemakers," *NYT*, May 14, 1898, 14:1 (quote). Bennett conceded that "for a long time to come Long Island will furnish a great deal of the market and other perishable produce which will be consumed within the Borough." Bennett, "Report on General Plan for the Borough of Brooklyn" 33–34. For the background on this report, see David Johnson, "The Emergence of Metropolitan Regionalism" 68–73 (Ph.D. thesis). On the background of the plan and the committee, see "Brooklyn City Plan," *BDE*, Jan. 18, 1914, City Plan Section. The masses of Jews and Italians who moved from Manhattan to Brooklyn after the construction of the Brooklyn Bridge did not, for several decades, settle in the recently deagriculturalized rural towns, but in the wards closer to Manhattan. Only later, as rapid transit began to reach those former towns between 1908 and 1920, were workers able to trade off longer commutes for cheaper land and rents. Moses Rischin, *The Promised City* 93; Thomas Kessner, *The Golden Door* 144–58; Daniel Bluestone et al., *Flatbush* 37–40; Donna Gabaccia, "Little Italy's Decline"; Deborah Moore, "On the Fringes of the City." The *Kings County Rural and Brooklyn Gazette*'s boosterism at the opening of the Brooklyn Bridge must also have quickly become an embarrassment: "one must imagine a completed system of Rapid Transit routes, radiating from the common center in every direction across the entire County of Kings, upon which millions of energetic thriving busy people are daily enjoying the bright sunshine and pure ocean air that comes so freely to all parts." "The Bridge," *KCRBG*, May 26, 1883, 1:1.

7. "The Greater Brooklyn," *BDE*, Jan. 18, 1914, 4:2–3.

8. Quoting a food scout for a restaurant in San Francisco, which relies for its fresh vegetables and fruits on the midcity San Francisco Garden Project, an offshoot of the city jail farm. See generally, H. Patricia Hynes, *A Patch of Eden*.

9. "Frederic B. Platt Outlines Next Steps in City Plan Movement," *BDE*, Jan. 18, 1914, Mag. sect., 2:2, 4–5; Harry Brearley, *The Problem of Greater New York and Its Solution* 50, 48 (under the auspices of the Committee on Industrial Advancement of the Brooklyn League).

10. FTC, *Food Investigation* 204, 201, 233.

11. J. W. Sullivan, *Markets for the People* 1, 4–5, 46, 47. Sullivan was later a representative of the AFL and a Federal Food Administration official during World War I. *Who's Who in America* 14:1841–42 (1926–27).

12. National Municipal League, *The Relations of the City to Its Food Supply* 3–4; FTC, *Food Investigation* 197 (quote); William Ogburn, "A Study of Food Costs in Various Cities" tab. 9 at 22; Charles Artman, *Food Costs and City Consumers* 12–17; Harlean James, *Land Planning in the United States* 404 (quotes).

13. Milton Whitney, "Rich Acres Nearby," *NYT*, Feb. 5, 1913, 10:6 (letter to editor).

14. Sullivan, *Markets for the People* 102, 86. Since Sullivan by this time had been living on Stillwell Avenue for at least a decade, it seems unlikely that he would have been unaware of the history of market gardening in Kings County. *Who's Who in America* 3:1443 (1903–5).

15. Corbett et al., "Fruit and Vegetable Production" 314, 321.

16. Wells Sherman, *Merchandising Fruits and Vegetables* 441–42, 444. That it was the pull of high land prices rather than the push of bankruptcy that prompted local farmers' exit from vegetable production would have simplified market-transcending measures that the state could have taken to maintain local market gardeners. If nearby farmers could hold their own with regard to cost, price, and profitability, there would have been no need to intervene in consumer markets or to provide subsidies to producers. Only land prices would have been relevant to retaining land in production.

17. Sherman, *Merchandising Fruits and Vegetables* 451–52, 456, 442–43.

18. Edwin Spengler, *Land Values in New York in Relation to Transit Facilities* 104–7, tab. 7 at 166 (quote); *Report of the Mayor's Market Commission of New York City* 11 (quotes).

19. *BDEA: 1896* at 127–28; *Report of the Mayor's Market Commission of New York City* 16–17, 22.

20. L. Weld, *The Marketing of Farm Products* 394, 393, 392, 390, 393, 239–40.

21. Clyde King, "Trolley Freight" 129, 134 (quote); National Municipal League, *The Relations of the City to Its Food Supply* 14; William Smythe, *City Homes on Country Lanes* 219–21 (quote).

22. Edward B. Voorhees, "Annual Address of the President" 55 (quote); C. Woody Thompson and Wendell Smith, *Public Utility Economics* 53, 524–44 (quote).

23. Thomas Adams, "The Development of the Plan" 144–45.

24. Thomas Adams, *Outline of Town and City Planning* 222; Robert Fishman, "The Regional Plan and the Transformation of the Industrial Metropolis" 106 (quote); David Johnson, *Planning the Great Metropolis* 1; Thomas Adams, *The Building of the City* 34 (quote); Staff of the Regional Plan of New York and Its Environs. Vol. 1 at 173 (quote). See generally, Michael Simpson, *Thomas Adams and the Modern Planning Movement* 119–67.

25. Thomas Adams, Edward Bassett, and Robert Whitten, "Problems of Planning Unbuilt Areas" 216, 220. The policy horizon of the *New York Times* editorial board extended no further than that of the average New Yorker: by 1931 it could imagine agriculture in Queens only as "amateur 'farms'. . . already valued as suburban developments." "Agricultural New York," *NYT*, June 19, 1931, 22:4 (editorial). The newspaper was echoing the views of a Queens developer: "In 1909, when the project of Jackson Heights was first conceived, the present area of development was occupied by some six farms, about 325 acres of space. A rustic place it was, with all the characteristic slowness, sparsity and informality of farms. Then as now, it was geographically near the heart of Manhattan. But it appeared to many a contemporary that the farms were destined to go on for years and years, supplying the needs of the City of New York by means of transportation that consisted chiefly of horses and the ferries to 34th Street." Franklin Sherman, *Building Up Greater Queens Borough* 64.

26. Adams, Bassett, and Whitten, "Problems of Planning Unbuilt Areas" 217.

27. Staff of the Regional Plan, *Graphic Regional Plan* 384, 386–87; Frederick Law Olmsted Jr., "Appendix A — Laws of Planning Unbuilt Areas" 324. The Plan's positive evaluation of urban farming stands out as even more extraordinary in light of the critique that the Plan accepted urban aggrandizement as automatic and inevitable and acquiesced in the push to centralize and fill in empty spaces. Lewis Mumford, "The Plan of New York." This judgment is corroborated by the fact that Adams, the Plan's coordinator, though a leader of the garden city movement in England at the beginning of the century, had become "a bland proponent of 'practical,' business-oriented planning," forcefully opposed to back-to-the-land sentimentalism. Thomas Adams, *Garden City and Agriculture*; Simpson, *Thomas Adams and the Modern Planning Movement* 9–39, 79–80; Fishman, "The Regional Plan" 111 (quote).

28. Land Planning Comm. of the National Resources Board, *Maladjustment in Land Use in the United States* 41 (quote); *Urban Planning and Land Policies*, fig. 45 at 225.

29. Meyer, *Vanderveer Park* 30. The same year (1901), *Scribner's* published "Rural New York City," recounting that "our great Greater New York, which is better known as having the most densely populated tenement districts in the world, can show places that are more truly rural than any other city of modern times, places where the town does not succeed in obtruding at all." Whereas urban landmarks could be seen from the bucolic sections of London and Chicago, "out in the broad, rolling farm lands of [Queens], you can walk on for hours and not find any sign of the city you are in, except the enormous tax rate, which, by the way, has the effect of discouraging farmers (many of whom did not want to become city people at all) from spending money for paint and improvements, and this only results in making the country look more primitive, and less like what is absurdly called a city." Although such sections of rurality were exceptional because the city had "stretched out its hand" without leaving "the mark of the beast," the author knew that "the end . . . will come soon enough." Jesse Williams, "Rural New York City" 180, 191.

30. Adams, Bassett, and Whitten, "Problems of Planning Unbuilt Areas" 219 (quote); Adams, Lewis, and McCrosky, *Population, Land Values and Government* 48–49 (quote).

31. 1879 N.Y. Laws, ch. 310 at 397; *BDEA*, vol. VIII, 1893 at 150; *Rules and Regulations of Green-Wood Cemetery* 5; Donald Simon, "Green-Wood Cemetery and the American Park Movement"; Percival Jackson, *The Law of Cadavers and of Burial and Burial Places* 395 (quote); Whyte, "A Case for Higher Density Cities" 71 (quote); Martha Fisher, "Cemeteries and Land Use." The original promoters of Greenwood Cemetery paid $134,675.40 for 178 acres of the Bennett, Bergen, and Wyckoff farms. *The Eagle and Brooklyn* 354. The Martense farm also once included part of the cemetery. Ditmas, *Historic Homesteads of Kings County* 67. An historian noted shortly after the cemetery's opening: "While the location, the general elevation and unevenness of the ground, all mark it as a spot unlikely to be coveted by the spirit of improvement, and therefore may reasonably be expected to remain undisturbed for ages yet to come, it is impossible to convey to the mind of a stranger, a correct idea of the . . . beauty and solemn grandeur of the place. The surface is admirably diversified by hill and dale, while every now and then, a beautiful little lake is spread out in the valley. The greater part of the area is deeply shaded with dense forest trees." Prime, *A History of Long Island* 367.

32. R.C., "Greenwood," *KCRG*, July 25, 1874, 1:1, 2 (quote); "Washington Cemetery," *KCRG*, Oct. 24, 1874, 1:1; R.C., "About Cemeteries," *KCRG*, June 28, 1873, at 2:2, 3 (quote). See also "A Grand Offer at the Washington Cemetery," *KCRG*, Oct. 30, 1875, 2:2; Bennett v. Culver, 97 N.Y. 250 (1884). When Bennett first laid out his 100 acres as a cemetery, other farmers ridiculed him, "but the farm in a Cemetery has proved to be worth more than 10 times as much as it would have been in a farm." "Parkville," *KCRBG*, Jan. 26, 1884, 2:2. To be sure, in its advertisements, Washington Cemetery management did not predict its own demise. E.g., *KCRG*, May 6, 1876, 3:2.

33. Florence Kelley, "Congestion and Sweated Labor" 50.

34. Sam Bass Warner Jr., *The Urban Wilderness* 27 (quote); Frederick Howe, "The Municipal Real Estate Policies of German Cities" 14, 15, 18 (quote); Dawson, *Municipal Life and Government in Germany* 123 (quote). See generally, Frederick Howe, *European Cities at Work*; Dawson, *Municipal Life and Government in Germany* 141–60.

35. Howe, "The Municipal Real Estate Policies of German Cities" 19 (quote); Dawson, *Municipal Life and Government in Germany* 129.

36. Göran Sidenbladh, "Stockholm" 82 (quote); Shirley Passow, "Land Reserves and Teamwork in Planning Stockholm" 180; David Pass, *Vällingby and Farsta — from Idea to Reality* 29–33; *Urban Planning and Land Policies* 312–13; "Wythenshawe Rehouses More Than 6,000 Families from Manchester's Insanitary Area." On Wythenshawe's later fate, see Peter Hall, *Cities of Tomorrow* 109–11.

37. *Urban Planning and Land Policies* 228; *Statistisches Jahrbuch deutscher Gemeinden*, vol. 30 at 31; Mel Scott, *American City Plan Since 1890* at 341–42.

38. Ebenezer Howard, *Garden Cities of To-Morrow* 45–65. On the movement in

general and Howard's considerable and influential following in the United States, see Kostof, *The City Shaped* 75–89; Garvin, *The American City* 315–20; Cliff Moughtin, *Urban Design* 99–109; Arnold, *The New Deal in the Suburbs* 5–19.

39. Garvin, *The American City* 319–20 (quote); Arnold, *The New Deal in the Suburbs* 8 (quote); Kostof, *The City Shaped* 78–79 (quote).

40. Adams, "Modern City Planning: Its Meaning and Methods" 172–73 (quote); Arnold, *The New Deal in the Suburbs* 243 (quote).

41. H. Roger Grant, *Self-Help in the 1890s Depression* 23–40; Sam Bass Warner Jr., *To Dwell Is to Garden* 13–17; *BDEA: 1898* at 497; *BDEA: 1898* at 144. A similar movement reemerged during the depression of the 1930s; Joanna Colcord and Mary Johnston, *Community Programs for Subsistence Gardens*. In New York City, the Society for the Improvement of the Condition of the Poor set up quarter-acre farms in Queens to grow potatoes. *NYDT*, Apr. 12, 1895, 10:3. Vacant city lot cultivation survived the depression: in Philadelphia, over 200 acres were cultivated by more than 800 families, who produced more than $40,000 worth of produce in 1906 Bolton Hall, *Three Acres and Liberty* 42–63, 179–81.

42. William H. Whyte Jr., "Urban Sprawl" 143 (quote); Lockeretz, "New Life for Metro Farming" 83 (quote); N.Y. Constitution, art. XIV, sect. 4 (1996) (quote).

43. 1971 N.Y. Laws, ch. 479, sect. 300 at 1370, 1371.

44. 1971 N.Y. Laws, ch. 479, sect. 301(2) at 1371 (quote), sect. 303–306 at 1372–80; Nelson Bills and Richard Boisvert, "New York's Experience in Farmland Retention" 231; William Lockeretz, Julia Freedgood, and Katherine Coon, "Farmers' Views of the Prospects of Agriculture in a Metropolitan Area" 58 (quote).

45. Nelson Bills, "Urban Agriculture in the United States" 17; Thomas Plaut, "Urban Growth and Agricultural Decline" 367–71 (Ph.D. diss.).

46. "Maryland Farmers See Suburban Neighbors as a Means of Survival," *NYT*, Feb. 2, 1997, sect. 1 at 11:2 (nat. ed.); USDA, Natural Resources Conservation Service, *America's Private Land* 22; Barnaby Feder, "Sowing Preservation: Towns Are Slowing Invasion of Farms by Bulldozers," *NYT*, Mar. 20, 1997, C1:2, C19:2 (nat. ed.) (quote). On the first statewide program for the purchase of development rights, begun in Massachusetts in 1977, see Scott Merzbach, "Celebrating the Rich Soil," *Daily Hampshire Gaz.*, Sept. 15, 1997, 9:1; Meredith Passa, "20 Years of Protecting Farms," *The Recorder* (Franklin County), Sept. 1, 1997, 1:1.

47. Jac Smit et al., *Urban Agriculture: Food, Jobs and Sustainable Cities; Sustaining Agriculture Near Cities* 65–74; William Lockeretz, "New Life for Metro Farming" 82. Alternatively: "As rising property and labor costs make it more difficult to compete with large commercial operations, an increasing number of family farms, primarily those growing fruit and vegetables along the restless edges of suburbia, are abandoning the conventional notions of farming and cranking up the show biz" — in the form of various kinds of amusements such as corn mazes. Julie Iovine, "A New Cash Crop: The Farm as Theme Park," *NYT*, Nov. 2, 1997, sect. 1 at 1:1 (Lexis).

48. Thomas Adams, *Outline of Town and City Planning* 275; Gerrit Knaap and Arthur Nelson, *The Regulated Landscape* 39–68; Timothy Egan, "Drawing the

Hard Line on Urban Sprawl," *NYT*, Dec. 30, 1996, A1:2–3 (nat. ed.) (quote); Timothy Egan, "Seattle and Portland in Struggle to Avert Another Paradise Lost," *NYT*, Nov. 1, 1997, 1:2 (nat. ed.) (quote). In 1997, for the first time since 1979, the Portland Metro Council voted to open up the urban area — by 4,500 acres. R. Gregory Nokes, "Metro Oks Modest Expansion," *Portland Oregonian*, Oct. 24, 1997, at A1 (Westlaw). The long debate between farmers and developers and among farmers, reminiscent in some ways of that in nineteenth-century Kings County, can be tracked in the *Portland Oregonian*. According to George Ford, "What Is Regional Planning?" 17, cities of 100,000 and 1,000,000 inhabitants would require an encircling farm belt of 18 and 60 miles in radius, respectively, to produce their food needs: "Of course, in practice these belts are vastly smaller as most of our foodstuffs must come from elsewhere."

49. Regine Levitan, "Urban Agriculture" 1, 42–46, 92 (M.A. thesis).
50. Jean Gottmann, *Megalopolis* 272.
51. USDA, ERS, *Farming in the City's Shadow* 12–13 (quote); USDA, *America's Private Land* 28.
52. Harriet Friedmann, "After Midas's Feast"; Ann Crittenden, "The Regional Farm Resurgence," *NYT*, Dec. 25, 1980, sect. 2 at 35:3 (Lexis) (quote).
53. Lydia Herman et al., "The New York Metropolitan Area Produce Market."
54. Anna Robaton, "Can You Dig It?" *Brooklyn Bridge*, May 1997, at 18. Even in Buffalo, the oil-soaked remains of a steel mill in Buffalo were converted in 1997 into an 18-acre computer-controlled greenhouse sheltering 170,000 tomato plants growing in artificial soil. Andrew Revkin, "For Urban Wastelands, Tomatoes and Other Life," *NYT*, Mar. 3, 1998, A1:3 (nat. ed.).
55. Lewis Mumford, *The Highway and the City* 228.

BIBLIOGRAPHY

The bibliography is comprehensive except for newspaper articles, cases, and statutes, which are cited in full in the notes and are not included at all here. All U.S. government publications were, unless otherwise indicated, published in Washington, D.C., by the Government Printing Office; all New York State documents were, unless otherwise indicated, published in Albany.

MANUSCRIPTS AND PERSONAL PAPERS

Baxter, John. Extracts from the Journal of John Baxter of Flatlands, Long Island. Commenced January 1, 1790. Copied from the original by Garret Bergen and Presented by Strycker Bergen to the Long Island Historical Society. Typescript. Holland Society of New York.

Bennett, William, & Son. Farm Accounts, 1883–1909. Wyckoff-Bennett Homestead.

Benson Family Papers. Box V, NYHS.

Bergen, John C. Papers. Account Book. BHS, 1974.114.

[Anita Lott] Cruikshank Collection. Box 1. BHS, 1974.215.

Cruikshank Collection (Box A, John A Willink). BHS, 1977.284A.

Land Sale and Lease Agreements. Reformed Protestant Dutch Church of the Town of Flatbush.

Lefferts, John. Last Will and Testament, Dec. 17, 1892. Kings County Surrogate's Court.

Meyer, Henry A. Pkg 139A, Box 1, BHS.

"Notebook on the History of Brooklyn and Long Island, NY, including Jeremiah Johnson's Reminiscences." NYPL, Ms. Div. (undated [after 1862]).

Rapalje, Williamson. Journal, 1853–60. In possession of Peter Rapelje.

Rapelje, Peter. "The Rapelje Farm at New Lots," 1948. In possession of Peter Rapelje.

"Reminiscences of Peter Wyckoff of Bushwick, L. I." Typescript. BHS.

Tredwell, Daniel M. "Kings County in Fact, Legend and Tradition." BHS, 1974.65, 67–70 (vault package 2), 1917.

Van Brunt, Adriance. Diary, June 8, 1828–March 20, 1830. NYPL, Ms. Div.

UNPUBLISHED ARTICLES AND BOOKS

Fabend, Firth. "Black Roots on Brooklyn Farms: Lefferts Homestead, 1790–1840." April 1, 1989.

Mandel, Harvey. "The Sequent Pattern of Agriculture on Long Island, New York." Department of Geography, Columbia University, March 1956. Typescript. BHS, Pamphlets, Vol. 27, No. 8.

Meyer, Henry. *Vanderveer Park*. 1901.

Seyfried, Vincent. "Truck Gardening." April 15, 1988.

"Some Cowenhovens of Borough Park in New Utrecht." In *The Van Kouwenhoven-Conover Family Association Tidings*, 30–35. Undated.

Wells, Henry M. "Tales of Old Flatbush" March 14, 1933. Reformed Protestant Dutch Church of Flatbush.

UNPUBLISHED CENSUS OF POPULATION SCHEDULES

Population Schedules of the Third [*sic*; should read Second] Census of the United States 1800. Roll 23: NY. Microcopy No. 32. RG 29. Washington: NA, 1959.

Census of Population. 1810. Schedules. NYS, KC. Roll 28. NA, RG 28, M252.

Census of Population. 1820. Schedules. NYS, KC. Roll 64. NA, RG 28, M33.

Fifth Census of the United States. 1830. Roll 112. PS: NY. Vol. 29. Washington: NA, 1955.

Sixth Census of the United States. 1840. PS: NY, KC. Roll 92. M704.

Population Schedules of the Seventh Census of the United States. 1850. Roll 521. NY, KC (pt.). Microcopy No. 432. Washington: NA, 1963.

Population Schedules of the Eighth Census of the United States. 1860. M653, Roll 776. NY, KC. Washington: NA, 1967.

Population Schedules of the Ninth Census of the United States. 1870. Roll 963. NY, Vol. 30 (1–306), KC. Washington: NA, 1965.

Tenth Census. 1880. NY, Vol. 37: Kings, pt. 9.

UNPUBLISHED CENSUS OF AGRICULTURE SCHEDULES (NYS LIBRARY)

U.S. Census. 1850. Agriculture. Reel 4. KC.

U.S. Census. 1860. Agriculture. Reel 4. KC.

U.S. Census. 1870. Agriculture. Reel 5. KC.

U.S. Census. 1880. Agriculture. Reel 18. KC.

UNPUBLISHED U.S. GOVERNMENT DOCUMENTS (NA)

Assessment Lists of the Federal Bureau of Internal Revenue. NY, Dist. 2, Div. 7–8. Annual Lists. 1863–64. M603. Roll T-44. Washington: NA, 1965.

Assessment Lists of the Federal Bureau of Internal Revenue. NY, Dist. 2, Div. 5, 8. Annual Lists. 1865. M603. Roll T-45. Washington: NA, 1965.

Assessment Lists of the Federal Bureau of Internal Revenue. NY, Dist. 2, Div. 5, 8. Annual Lists. 1866. M603. Roll T-46. Washington: NA, 1965.

Assessment Lists of the Federal Bureau of Internal Revenue. NY, Dist. 2, Div. 5, 8. Monthly and Special Lists. March–December 1865. M603. Roll T-47. Washington: NA, 1965.

Assessment Lists of the Federal Bureau of Internal Revenue. NY, Dist. 2, Div. 5, 8. Annual Lists and Monthly Lists. 1869, 1870, and 1871. RG 58. NA, NYRO.

UNPUBLISHED NEW YORK STATE CENSUS

State of New York. Census for the Year 1845. Town of Flatbush, County of Kings.
In TRKC, Translations/Transliterations. Flatbush. State Census, 1845. Vol. 136–
137. MR 123. NYCMA.

UNPUBLISHED KINGS COUNTY DOCUMENTS

Assessment Roll of the Town of Flatbush. [1853]. Typed copy of original Ms. BHS,
file no. 240.
Kings County Real Property Records. Brooklyn City Hall.
Minutes of Commissioners for Mapping Towns, 1869–74. NYPL, Ms. Div.
"Statement of the Amount of Internal Duties, imposed by the United States
(excepting those on Household Furniture, on Watches, and on Stamps,)
paid by each Person, in the First Collection District of New-York, during the
year one thousand eight hundred and fifteen." TRKC. UD. Flatbush. Taxes;
Personal Property Oaths; Assessors' Notices; Internal Revenue: 1870–1895.
Bundle No. 16. MR 18. NYCMA.
"Statement of the Amount of Internal Duties, imposed by the United States
(excepting those on Household Furniture, on Watches, and on Stamps,) paid
by each Person, in the First Collection District of New-York, during the year
one thousand eight hundred and sixteen." TRKC. UD. Flatbush. Taxes;
Personal Property Oaths; Assessors' Notices; Internal Revenue: 1870–1895.
Bundle No. 16. MR 18. NYCMA.
Wills. KC Surrogate's Court.

UNPUBLISHED TOWN OF FLATBUSH DOCUMENTS (NYCMA)

Assessment Roll. 1853–1894.
Improvement Board, Minutes. 1872–1885. Vol. 1060. MR 7.
Minutes of Flatbush Board of Health. TRKC. Translation/Transliterations.
Flatbush. Board of Health Minutes, 1874–1886. Vol. 132. MR 122.
Slave Holders. 1799–1826. MR 8.
Translations/Transliterations. Court Minutes, 1679–1681. Town Meeting Minutes,
1762–1818. Birth and Manumissions of Slaves, 1799–1819. Vol. 107. MR 120.
Unbound Documents. Board of Health-Manumitted and Abandoned Slaves,
1800–1814. Bundle No. 1. MR 17.
———. Highway Commissioners — Crosswalks; Railroad Petitions; Gas Lamps;
Labor Reports; Proposals, 1874–1883. Bundle No. 25. MR 20.
———. Jurors, List of; Justices, Drawing of Terms, Report; Knickerbocker Electric;
Light and Power Co. Agreement, 1815–1847, 1890, 1893. Bundle No. 47. MR 23.
———. Military Exemptions, 1862–1864. Bundle No. 48. MR 23.
———. Overseers of Poor; Slave Indentures; Slave Manumissions, 1805–1820.
Bundle No. 2. MR 17.
———. Overseers of Poor; Slave Manumissions; Reports, 1818–1821. Bundle
No. 3. MR 17.

————. Taxes; Personal Property Oaths; Assessors' Notices; Internal Revenue, 1870–1895. Bundle No. 16. MR 18.
————. Town Board, 1878–1890. Bundle No. 9. MR 18.
————. Town Board, 1878–1890. Bundle No. 10. Town Board, 1892–1894. MR 18.

UNPUBLISHED TOWN OF FLATLANDS DOCUMENTS (NYCMA)

Assessment Rolls. 1849–1892.
"Index Showing the names of the owners of those slaves to whom Children were born after the 4th day of July 1799." Slaves Register and Records of Personal Mortgages, 1799. Vol. 4054. MR 80.
Unbound Documents. Flatlands. Town Board. Railroads, Lighting Cos., 1893–1894. Bundle No. 7. MR 100.

UNPUBLISHED TOWN OF GRAVESEND DOCUMENTS (NYCMA)

Assessment Rolls. 1860–1893.
Enrollment of Persons Liable to Military Duty. In TRKC. Gravesend. Enrollment — Persons Liable to Military Duty, 1862. Vol. 3020. MR 63.

UNPUBLISHED TOWN OF NEW LOTS DOCUMENTS (NYCMA)

Assessment Rolls. 1860–1880.

UNPUBLISHED TOWN OF NEW UTRECHT DOCUMENTS (NYCMA)

Assessment Rolls. 1830–1894.
Enrollment of Persons Liable to Military Duty. In TRKC. NU. Troops — Persons Liable to Military Duty, 186_. Vol. 2035. MR 39.
Northern Drainage District, of the Town of New Utrecht. In TRKC. NU. Health Board — Assessors' Record, Drainage Assessments, Northerly District, 1871. Vol. 2027. MR 39.

U.S. GOVERNMENT DOCUMENTS

Annual Report of the Commissioner of Internal Revenue on the Operations of the Internal Revenue System for the Year 1872. 42d Cong., 3d sess., 1872. House Exec. Doc. 4.
Annual Report of the Secretary of Treasury on the State of the Finances for the Year 1895. 1896.
Bonsteel, Jay, et al. "Soil Survey of the Long Island Area, New York." In U.S. Bureau of Soils, *Field Operations of the Bureau of Soils, 1903,* 91–128. 58th Cong., 2d sess., 1904. House Doc. 746.

Bureau of the Census. *A Century of Population Growth: From the First Census of the United States to the Twelfth 1790–1900.* 1909.

————. *Heads of Families at the First Census of the United States Taken in the Year 1790: New York.* 1908.

————. *Historical Statistics of the United States: Colonial Times to 1970.* Bicentennial ed. 1975.

Bureau of Economic Analysis. *Long Term Economic Growth, 1860–1970.* 1973.

Campbell, George. "Horticulture." In *Reports of the United States Commissioners to the Paris Universal Exposition 1878.* Vol. V, *Agricultural Implements, Agricultural Products, Live Stock, Horticulture, Pisciculture,* 343–418. 46th Cong., 3d sess., 1880. House Exec. Doc. 42, pt. 5.

Census Office. *Report on Wealth, Debt, and Taxation at the Eleventh Census: 1890.* Pt. II, *Valuation and Taxation.* 1895.

————. *Tenth Census.* Vol. 18, *Report on the Social Statistics of Cities.* Pt. I: *The New England and Middle States.* 1886.

Claghorn, Kate. "Agricultural Distribution of Immigrants." In *Reports of the Industrial Commission on Immigration.* 15:492–646. 57th Cong., 1st sess., 1901. House Doc. 184.

Congressional Globe. 39th Cong., 1st and 2d sess., 1866–1867.

Corbett, L. C. *The Potato as a Truck Crop.* USDA Farmers' Bull. 407. 1910.

Corbett, Lee, et al. "Fruit and Vegetable Production." In USDA, *Agriculture Yearbook 1925,* 151–452. 1926.

De Braal, J. Peter. *Taxes on U.S. Agricultural Real Estate, 1890–1991, and Methods of Estimation.* USDA, ERS, Statistical Bull. 866. 1993.

Department of Agriculture. *Farming in the City's Shadow: Urbanization of Land and Changes in Farm Output in Standard Metropolitan Statistical Areas, 1960–70.* Agric. Economics Rep. 250. 1974.

————. *The Fertilizing Value of Street Sweepings.* Bull. 55. 1898.

————. *Influence of a City on Farming.* Bull. 678. 1918. Written by J. Arnold and Frank Montgomery.

————. *Yearbook of Agriculture 1931.* 1931.

————. Bureau of Statistics. *Wages of Farm Labor in the United States: Results of Twelve Statistical Investigations, 1866–1902.* Misc. Ser. — Bull. 26. 1903. By James Blodgett.

————. Division of Statistics. *Rates of Charge for Transporting Garden Truck, with Notes on the Growth of the Industry.* Misc. Ser. — Bull. 21. 1901. Written by Edward Ward Jr. and Edwin Holmes Jr.

————. Division of Statistics. *Wages of Farm Labor in the United States: Results of Nine Statistical Investigations, from 1866 to 1892, with Extensive Inquiries Concerning Wages from 1840 to 1865.* Misc. Ser. Rep. 4. 1892.

————. Economic Research Service. *Urbanization of Land in the Northeastern United States.* ERS 485. 1971.

————. Forest Service. *Wood Paving in the United States.* Circular 141. 1908.

————. Natural Resources Conservation Service. *America's Private Land: A Geography of Hope.* N.p., 1996.

————. Office of Experiment Stations. *Dietary Studies in New York City in 1895 and 1896*. Bull. 46. 1898. Written by W. O. Atwater and Charles Woods.

Earle, F. "Development of the Trucking Interests." In *Yearbook of the United States Department of Agriculture 1900*, 437–52. 1901.

Federal Trade Commission. *Food Investigation: Report of the Federal Trade Commission on the Wholesale Marketing of Food, June 30, 1919*. 1920.

Fox, Cynthia. "Income Tax Records of the Civil War Years." In *Our Family, Our Town: Essays on Family and Local History Sources in the National Archives*, 141–46. Timothy Walch, comp. National Archives and Records Administration. 1987.

Galloway, B. "Progress of Commercial Growing of Plants Under Glass." In *Yearbook of the United States Department of Agriculture: 1899*, 575–90. 1900.

Goode, G. Brown. "The Sea Fisheries (A History of the Menhaden)." In U.S. Commissioner of Fish and Fisheries, *Report of the Commissioner for 1877*, appendix A. 45th Cong., 2d sess., 1879. Sen. Misc. Doc. 49.

Income Tax: Letter from the Commissioner of Internal Revenue. 41st Cong., 3d sess., 1871. House Misc. Doc. 51.

IRS. *Income Taxes 1862–1962: A History of the Internal Revenue Service*. Pub. 447. 1962.

Land Planning Committee of the National Resources Board. *Agricultural Land Requirements and Resources*. Pt. III of *Report on Land Planning*. 1935.

————. *Maladjustment in Land Use in the United States*. Pt. VI of *Report on Land Planning*. 1935.

National Archives. *Federal Population Census 1790–1890: A Price List of Microfilm Copies of the Schedules*. 1969.

Oemler, A. "Truck Farming" In *Report of the Commissioner of Agriculture: 1885*, 583–627. 1885.

Report of Special Commissioner of the Revenue. 41st Cong., 2d sess., 1869. House Exec. Doc. 27.

Report of the Commissioner of Agriculture for the Year 1872. 1874.

Report of the Industrial Commission on Agriculture and on Taxation in Various States. Vol. 11, pt. VII. 1901.

Report of the Jamaica Bay Improvement Commission. 60th Cong., 2d sess., 1909 [1907]. House Doc. 1506.

Reports of the Immigration Commission: Immigrants in Industries. Pt. 24: *Recent Immigrants in Agriculture*. Vol. I. 61st Cong., 2d sess., 1911. Senate Doc. 633.

Thirteenth Annual Report of the Commissioner of Labor: 1898: Hand and Machine Labor. 1899.

Urban Planning and Land Policies. Vol. II of *Supplementary Report of the Urbanism Committee to the National Resources Committee*. 1939.

Useless Papers in the Treasury Department. 53d Cong., 3d sess., 1895. House Rep. 1993.

Wright, Carroll. *The History and Growth of the United States Census*. 56th Cong., 1st sess., 1900. Senate Doc. 194.

PUBLISHED CENSUS OF AGRICULTURAL MATERIALS

Census for 1820. Washington: Gales & Seaton, 1821.

Journal of the Senate of the State of New-York at Their Forty-Fifth Session. Cantine & Leake, 1822.

Journal of the Senate of the State of New-York at Their Forty-Ninth Session. Croswell, 1826.

Census of the State of New-York, for 1835. Groswell, Van Benthuysen & Burt, 1836.

Department of State. *Sixth Census of Enumeration of the Inhabitants of the United States in 1840.* Blair & Rives, 1841.

————. *Compendium of the Enumeration of the Inhabitants and Statistics of the United States, as Obtained at the Department of State, from the Returns of the Sixth Census.* Thomas Allen, 1841.

Census of the State of New-York, for 1845. Carroll & Cook, 1846.

Superintendent of the United States Census. *The Seventh Census of the United States: 1850.* 1853.

Superintendent of the Census. *Census of the State of New-York, for 1855.* Van Benthuysen, 1857.

Secretary of the Interior. *Agriculture of the United States in 1860: Compiled from the Original Returns of the Eighth Census.* 1864.

Superintendent of the Census. *Census of the State of New York, for 1865.* Van Benthuysen, 1867.

Secretary of the Interior. *Ninth Census.* Vol. III, *The Statistics of the Wealth and Industry of the United States.* 1872.

Superintendent of the Census. *Census of the State of New York for 1875.* Weed, Parsons, 1877.

Department of Interior, Census Office. *Report on the Productions of Agriculture as Returned at the Tenth Census (June 1, 1880) Embracing General Statistics.* 1883.

————. *Report on the Statistics of Agriculture in the United States at the Eleventh Census: 1890.* 1895.

U.S. Census Office. *Census Reports.* Vol. V, *Twelfth Census of the United States, Taken in the Year 1900, Agriculture.* Pt. I, *Farms, Live Stock, and Animal Products.* 1902.

————. *Census Reports.* Vol. VI, *Twelfth Census of the United States, Taken in the Year 1900, Agriculture.* Pt. II, *Crops and Irrigation.* 1902.

U.S. Bureau of the Census. *Thirteenth Census of the United States Taken in the Year 1910.* Vol. V, *Agriculture 1909 and 1910: General Report and Analysis.* 1913.

————. *Thirteenth Census of the United States Taken in the Year 1910.* Vol. VII, *Agriculture 1909 and 1910: Reports by States, with Statistics for Counties: Nebraska-Wyoming.* 1913.

————. *Fourteenth Census of the United States Taken in the Year 1920.* Vol. VI, pt. 1, *Agriculture: Reports for States with Statistics for Counties: The Northern States.* 1922.

————. *United States Census of Agriculture 1925.* Pt. I, *The Northern States.* 1927.

————. *Fifteenth Census of the United States: 1930: Agriculture.* Vol. II, pt. 1, *The Northern States.* 1932.

————. *Fifteenth Census of the United States: 1930: Agriculture.* Vol. III, *Type of Farm.* Pt. 1, *The Northern States.* 1932.

————. *United States Census of Agriculture: 1935.* Vol. I, *Reports for States with Statistics for Counties and a Summary for the United States.* Pt. 1, *The Northern States.* 1936.

————. *United States Census of Agriculture: 1935.* Vol. II, *Reports for States with Statistics for Counties and a Summary for the United States,* second series. Pt. 1, *The Northern States.* 1936.

————. *Sixteenth Census of the United States: 1940, Agriculture.* Vol. I, first and second series, *State Reports.* Pt. 1, *Statistics for Counties.* 1942.

————. *Sixteenth Census of the United States: 1940, Agriculture.* Vol. II, third series, *State Reports.* Pt. 1, *Statistics for Counties.* 1942.

————. *United States Census of Agriculture: 1945.* Vol. 1, pt. 2, *Middle Atlantic States: Statistics for Counties.* 1946.

————. *United States Census of Agriculture: 1950.* Vol. 1, *Counties and State Economic Areas.* Pt. 2, *Middle Atlantic States.* 1952.

————. *United States Census of Agriculture: 1954.* Vol. 1, *Counties and State Economic Areas.* Pt. 2, *Middle Atlantic States.* 1956.

————. *U.S. Census of Agriculture: 1959, Final Report.* Vol. I, pt. 7, *Counties: New York.* 1961.

————. *Census of Agriculture, 1964.* Vol. I, *Statistics for the States and Counties.* Pt. 7, *New York.* 1966.

————. *1969 Census of Agriculture.* Vol. I, *Area Reports.* Pt. 7, *New York.* Sect. 1, *Summary Data.* 1972.

————. *1974 Census of Agriculture.* Vol. 1, pt. 32, *New York: State and County Data.* 1977.

————. *1978 Census of Agriculture.* Vol. 1, *State and County Data.* Pt. 32, *New York.* 1981.

————. *1982 Census of Agriculture.* Vol. 1, *Geographic Area Series.* Pt. 32, *New York.* 1984.

————. *1987 Census of Agriculture.* Vol. 1, *Geographic Area Series.* Pt. 32, *New York: State and County Data.* 1989.

————. *1992 Census of Agriculture.* Vol. 1, *Geographic Area Series.* Pt. 32, *New York: State and County Data.* 1994.

PUBLISHED CENSUS OF POPULATION DOCUMENTS

Department of State. *Return of the Whole Number of Persons Within the Several Districts of the United States.* 1801.

Aggregate Amount of Each Description of Persons Within the United States of America, and Territories Thereof, Agreeably to Actual Enumeration Made According to Law, in the Year 1810. 1811.

Journal of the Senate of the State of New-York. Southwick, 1814.

Census for 1820. Washington: Gates & Seaton, 1821.

Fifth Census; or, Enumeration of the Inhabitants of the United States. 1830. Duff Green, 1832.

Department of State. *Sixth Census or Enumeration of the Inhabitants of the United States in 1840*. Blair and Rives, 1841.

U.S. Census. *The Seventh Census of the United States: 1850*. Armstrong, 1853.

Department of the Interior. *Population of the United States in 1860: Compiled from the Original Returns of the Eighth Census*. 1864.

————. *A Compendium of the Ninth Census* (June 1, 1870). 1872.

Secretary of Interior. *Ninth Census*. Vol. 1, *The Statistics of the Population of the United States*. 1872.

Census Office. *Statistics of the Population of the United States at the Tenth Census* (June 1, 1880). 1883.

————. *Compendium of the Tenth Census* (June 1, 1880). 1883.

————. *Report on the Population of the United States at the Eleventh Census: 1890*. Pt. I. 1895.

————. *Compendium of the Eleventh Census: 1890*. Pt. II. 1894.

NEW YORK STATE GOVERNMENT DOCUMENTS

Annual Report of the Comptroller. New York State Assembly, Doc. 4. 1859.

Annual Report of the Comptroller. New York State Assembly, Doc. 3. 1868.

Annual Report of the Comptroller of the State of New York. Wynkoop Hallenbeck Crawford, 1899.

Annual Report of the State Assessors of New York for the Year 1889. Sen. Doc. 45. 1890.

Annual Report of the State Board of Charities for the Year Ending September 30, 1886. Argus, 1887.

Annual Report of the State Board of Tax Commissioners of the State of New York, 1898. Sen. Doc. 9. Wynkoop Hallenbeck Crawford, 1899.

Annual Report of the State Engineer and Surveyor of the State of New York for the Year Ending September 1863. Assembly Doc. 125. Weed, Parsons, 1864.

Annual Report of the State Engineer and Surveyor of the State of New York For the Year Ending Sept. 30, 1878. Assembly Doc. 80. Van Benthuysen, 1879.

Annual Report of the State Engineer and Surveyor of the State of New York For the Year Ending Sept. 30, 1879. Assembly Doc. 75. Van Benthuysen, 1880.

Fiftieth Annual Report of the New York State Agricultural Society: For the Year 1890. Assembly Doc. 72. Lyon, 1891.

First Annual Report of the State Assessors. Assembly Doc. 11. 1860.

Forty-Ninth Annual Report of the New York State Agricultural Society: For the Year 1889. Assembly Doc. 93. Lyon, 1890.

Fourth Annual Report of State Assessors. Assembly Doc. 40. 1863.

Journal of the Assembly of the State of New York at the Ninety-Sixth Session. Argus, 1873.

N.Y.S. College of Agriculture, Dept. of Agricultural Economics. *Changes in New*

York State Agriculture 1850–1950: As Indicated by State and Federal Censuses. No. 917. Ithaca: Cornell U, 1954.

New York Court of Appeals. John Turner, Respondent, against William W. Kouvenhoven, Appellant. *Appeal Book.* New York: Burgoyne, 1883.

Nissley, W. "Vegetable Growing on Long Island." In NYSDA, *The Vegetable Industry in New York State,* 1222–29. Bull. 70. 1915.

Part of the Revised Statutes, Passed at the Second Meeting of the Fiftieth Session of the Legislature of the State of New-York. Croswell, 1827.

Peters, Theodore. *A Report on the Agricultural and Other Resources of the State of New York. TNYSAS* 23:234–379 (1863). Assembly Doc. 203. Comstock & Cassidy, 1864.

Prince, L. Bradford. "Sketch of the Agricultural History of Queens County." *TNYSAS* 21:269–79 (1861). Assembly Doc. 252. Van Benthuysen, 1862.

Report of the Commission on Housing and Regional Planning. Legis. Doc. 91 (1925). Lyon, 1925.

Report of the Commissioners Appointed Pursuant to Chapter 311, Laws 1890, relative to the Consolidation of Certain Areas about the Port of New York into One Municipality. Sen. Doc. 7. 1895.

Report of the Commissioners to Revise the Laws for the Assessment and Collection of Taxes. Assembly Doc. 39 (1871). Argus, 1871.

Report of the Comptroller, in Compliance with a Resolution of the Senate, Relative to the Assessment Laws. Senate Doc. 95. 1858.

Report of the Joint Select Committee Appointed at the Last Session to Revise and Amend the Assessment Laws of the State. Senate Doc. 30. 1863.

Revised Statutes of the State of New York. Banks, 1859.

Second Annual Report of the Board of Railroad Commissioners of the State of New York, for the Fiscal Year Ending September 30, 1884. Senate Doc. 8. Weed, Parsons, 1885.

Secretary of State. *Instructions for the Taking of the Census of the State of New York in the Year 1875.* Weed, Parsons, 1875.

Senate, Sub-Committee of the Joint Committee on the Affairs of Cities. *In the Matter of the Hearing in Relation to "The Greater New York."* Senate Doc. 44. Wynkoop Hallenbeck Crawford, 1896.

Tenth Annual Report of the Bureau of Statistics of Labor of the State of New York, for the Year 1892. Pt. I. Lyon, 1893.

Wilkinson, A. "Market Gardening in New York State." In NYSDA, *Vegetable Industry in New York State,* 1215–21.

NEW YORK CITY GOVERNMENT DOCUMENTS

Dolkart, Andrew. "Historical Introduction." In Landmarks Preservation Commission, *Prospect Park South Historic District Designation Report,* 2–13. NY: City of New York, 1979.

King, Clyde. "Trolley Freight — A Promising Agency for Local Distribution." In *Report of the Mayor's Market Commission of New York City,* 129–34. 1913.

Report of the Mayor's Market Commission of New York City. NY: Little & Ives, 1913.

NEWSPAPERS

Brooklyn Daily Eagle
Brooklyn Daily Union
Irish-American
Kings County Gazette
Kings County Rural Gazette
Kings County Rural and Brighton Gazette
Kings County Rural and Brooklyn Gazette
New York Daily Tribune
New York Herald
New York Times
New York Tribune
Real Estate Record and Builders' Guide

MAPS

Atlas of the Townships of New Utrecht, Gravesend, Flatbush, Flatlands and New Lots: Kings County, New York. NY: Dripps, 1877.
Beers, F. W. *Atlas of Long Island, New York: From Recent and Actual Surveys and Records*. NY: Beers, Comstock & Cline, 1873.
Dripps, M. "Map of Kings County N.Y." NY: Dripps, 1868.
Map of Kings County, with Parts of Westchester, Queens, New York & Richmond Counties: Showing Farm Lines, Soundings &c. NY: Dripps, n.d. [ca. 1872].
Nelson, Catherine, and E. Theo. Nelson. "The Village of Flatbush As It Was in the Year 1870." Brooklyn: Clark, 1943.
Nelson, Catherine, and E. Theodore Nelson. "The Village of Flatlands As It Was in the Year 1870." Brooklyn: Clark, 1944.
———. "The Village of Gravesend As It Was in the Year 1870." Brooklyn: Clark, 1943.
———. "The Villages of Fort Hamilton and Bay Ridge As They Were in the Year 1870." Brooklyn: Clark, 1943.
Robinson's Atlas of Kings County New York. NY: Robinson, 1890.
Soil Map No. 5. New York, Hempstead Sheet. In U.S. Bureau of Soils, *Field Operations of the Bureau of Soils, 1903*. 58th Cong., 2d sess. House Doc. 746. Washington: GPO, 1904.
U.S. Geological Survey. Topographic Sheet, New York, Brooklyn Quadrant. December 1898 (originally surveyed 1888–89).

THESES AND DISSERTATIONS

Emerson, Frederick. "A Geographic Interpetation of New York City." Ph.D. diss., U of Chicago, 1909.

Johnson, David. "The Emergence of Metropolitan Regionalism: An Analysis of the 1929 Regional Plan of New York and Its Environs." Ph.D. thesis, Cornell U, 1974.

Kroessler, Jeffrey. "Building Queens: The Urbanization of New York's Largest Borough." Ph.D. diss., City U of New York, 1991.

Levitan, Regine. "Urban Agriculture: An Argument for Alternative Land Use in Urban Areas: A Case Study in Philadelphia." M.A. thesis, Temple U, 1986.

McLaughlin, William. "Dutch Rural New York: Community, Economy, and Family in Colonial Flatbush." Ph.D. diss., Columbia U, 1981.

Plaut, Thomas Plaut. "Urban Growth and Agricultural Decline: Problems and Policies." Ph.D. diss., U of Pennsylvania, 1978.

Schoenebaum, Eleonora. "Emerging Neighborhoods: The Development of Brooklyn's Fringe Areas, 1850–1930." Ph.D. diss., Columbia U, 1976.

Simon, Donald. "The Public Park Movement in Brooklyn, 1824–1873." Ph.D. diss., New York U, 1972.

GENEALOGIES

Bergen, T. G. "The Martense Family." *NYGBR* 8 (1):62–67 (Jan. 1877).

Bergen, Teunis G. *The Bergen Family: Or the Descendants of Hans Hansen Bergen, One of the Early Settlers of New York and Brooklyn, L. I.* NY: Bergen & Tripp, 1866.

———. *The Bergen Family: Or the Descendants of Hans Hansen Bergen, One of the Early Settlers of New York and Brooklyn, L. I.* 2d ed. Albany: Munsell, 1876.

———. *Genealogy of the Lefferts Family 1650–1878.* Albany: Munsell, 1878.

———. *Genealogy of the Van Brunt Family, 1653–1867.* Albany: Munsell, 1867.

Phillips, A. V. *The Lott Family in America.* Ann Arbor, Mich.: Edwards Brothers, 1942.

Ryerson, Albert. *The Ryerson Genealogy: Genealogy and History of the Knickerbocker Families of Ryerson, Ryerse, Ryerss; also Adriance and Martense Families.* Chicago: Ryerson, 1916.

Schenck, P[eter]. L[awrence]. *Memoir of Johannes Schenck, the Progenitor of the Bushwick, L.I., Family of Schenck.* Flatbush: 1876.

BOOKS AND ARTICLES

Aaron, Henry. *Who Pays the Property Tax? A New View.* Washington, D.C.: Brookings, 1975.

Abbott, Richard H. "The Agricultural Press Views the Yeoman: 1819–1859." *AH* 42 (1): 35–48 (Jan. 1968).

Ackerman, Edward. "Sequent Occupance of a Boston Suburban Community." *EG* 17 (1):61–74 (Jan. 1941).

Adams, Thomas. *The Building of the City.* Vol. 2 of *Regional Plan.* NY: Regional Plan of New York and Its Environs, 1931.

———. "The Development of the Plan." In *Proceedings of the Ninth National Conference on City Planning*, 141–54. NY: 1917.

———. *Garden City and Agriculture: How to Solve the Problem of Rural Depopulation*. London: Simpkin, 1905.

———. "Modern City Planning: Its Meaning and Methods." *National Municipal Rev.* 11 (6):157–76 (June 1922).

———. *Outline of Town and City Planning: A Review of Past Efforts and Modern Aims*. NY: Russell Sage Foundation, 1935.

———. "Preface to the Regional Survey." In *Regional Survey of New York and Its Environs*. 1, viii. NY: Regional Plan of New York and Its Environs, 1927.

Adams, Thomas, Edward Bassett, and Robert Whitten. "Problems of Planning Unbuilt Areas." In *Regional Survey: Neighborhood and Community Planning*. 7:211–355. NY: Regional Plan of New York and Its Environs, 1929.

Adams, Thomas, Harold Lewis, and Theodore McCrosky. *Population, Land Values and Government: Studies of the Growth and Distribution of Population and Land Values, and of Problems of Government. Regional Survey*. Vol. 2. NY: Regional Plan of New York and Its Environs, 1929.

Agee, James. "Brooklyn Is." *Esquire* 70:180, 181 (Dec. 1968).

Albion, Robert. *The Rise of New York Port: 1815–1860*. NY: Scribner's, 1939.

Andrews, Charles. *The Colonial Period of American History*. Vol. 3, *The Settlements*. New Haven: Yale UP, 1964 [1937].

Appleton's Dictionary of New York and Vicinity. NY: D. Appleton, 1883.

Armbruster, Eugene. *Brooklyn's Eastern District*. Brooklyn: n.p., 1942 (written 1928).

Arnold, Joseph L. *The New Deal in the Suburbs: A History of the Greenbelt Town Program 1935–1954*. Columbus: Ohio State UP, 1971.

Artman, Charles. *Food Costs and City Consumers: Significant Factors in Metropolitan Distribution of Perishables*. NY: Columbia UP, 1926.

Baden, John. "Regulating Agricultural Land Use." In *The Vanishing Farmland Crisis: Critical Views of the Movement to Preserve Agricultural Land*, 145–60. John Baden, ed. Lawrence, Kans.: UP of Kansas, 1984.

Bailey, J. T. *An Historical Sketch of the City Brooklyn*. Brooklyn: Author, 1840.

Bailey, L. H. "An Outlook on Vegetable Gardening." In *The New York State Vegetable Growers' Association: Report for 1911–12, 1912–13*, 45. Geneva, N.Y.: 1913.

———. *The Principles of Vegetable-Gardening*. 11th ed. NY: Macmillan, 1911 [1901].

Baker, M. "The Utilization of City Wastes on the Farm." In *Cyclopedia of American Agriculture*. 5th ed. 1:510–13. L. H. Bailey, ed. NY: Macmillan, 1917 [1907].

Baker, Theodore. "Market Gardening." In State of New Jersey. *Twelfth Annual Report of the New Jersey Board of Agriculture: 1884–1885*, 215–24. Trenton, N.J.: Murphy, 1885.

Baltet, Charles. *L'Horticulture dans les cinq parties du monde*. Paris: Société Nationale d'Horticulture, 1895.

Bangs, Bleeker [Charlotte]. *Reminiscences of Old New Utrecht and Gowanus*. N.p., 1912.

Barlowe, Raleigh. "Taxation of Agriculture." In *Property Taxation: USA*, 83–102. Richard Lindholm, ed. Madison: U of Wisconsin P, 1967.

Bartlett, Fredk. *The History of Wallabout Market Established in 1884: The Largest Market in the World*. Brooklyn: Brooklyn Eagle, 1902.

Bastedo, Russell. "Introduction." In *Brooklyn Before the Bridge: American Paintings from the Long Island Historical Society*, 7. Brooklyn: Brooklyn Museum, 1982.

Beecher, Henry Ward. *Pleasant Talk about Fruits, Flowers and Farming*. New ed. NY: Ford, 1874.

Bender, Thomas. "Metropolitan Culture: Brooklyn Bridge and the Transformation of New York." In *Bridge to the Future: A Centennial Celebration of the Brooklyn Bridge*, 325–32. Margaret Latimer et al., eds. NY: New York Academy of Sciences, 1984.

Bennett, E. H. "Report on General Plan for the Borough of Brooklyn." Chicago: n.p., 1914 (typescript at Cornell U Library).

Bennett, Gertrude Ryder. "The Farmer's Wife in the Towns of Kings County." In Snyder, *Tales of Old Flatbush*, 189–95. NY: n.p., 1945.

———. *Living in a Landmark*. Francestown, N.H.: Marshall Jones, 1980.

———. *Turning Back the Clock in Gravesend: Background of the Wyckoff-Bennett Homestead*. Francestown, N.H.: Marshall Jones, 1982.

Berg, Joseph. "The Flatbush Church in the Last 50 Years." In *Tercentenary of the Reformed Protestant Dutch Church of the Town of Flatbush in Kings County*, 9–13.

Bergen, Teunis G. "History of the Town of New Utrecht." In Stiles, *Civil . . . History*, 1:255–69. NY: Munsell, 1884.

———. *Register in Alphabetical Order, of the Early Settlers of Kings County, Long Island, N.Y., from Its First Settlement by Europeans to 1700*. NY: Green's Son, 1881.

Bergman, Edward, and Thomas Pohl. *A Geography of the New York Metropolitan Region*. Dubuque, Iowa: Kendall/Hunt, 1975.

Berry, Wendell. *The Unsettling of America: Culture and Agriculture*. NY: Avon, 1978.

———. "Where Cities and Farms Come Together." In *Radical Agriculture*, 14–25. NY: Harper & Row, 1976 [1972].

Bidwell, Percy, and John Falconer. *History of Agriculture in the Northern United States 1620–1860*. Washington, D.C.: Carnegie Institution, 1925.

Biemer, Linda. "Lady Deborah Moody and the Founding of Gravesend." *JLIH* 17 (2):24–42 (1981).

Bills, Nelson. "Urban Agriculture in the United States." Cornell Agric. Econ. Staff Paper 91-21. Aug. 1991.

Bills, Nelson, and Richard Boisvert. "New York's Experience in Farmland Retention Through Agricultural Districts and Use-Value Assessment." In *Sustaining Agriculture Near Cities*, 231–50. William Lockeretz, ed. Ankeny, Iowa: Social and Water Conservation Society, 1987.

Biographical Directory of the American Congress 1774–1996. Alexandria, Va.: Congressional Quarterly, 1997.

Bluestone, Daniel, et al. *Flatbush: Architecture and Urban Development from Dutch Settlement to Commercial Strip*. NY: Columbia U Grad. School of Architecture, Planning and Preservation, 1990.

Bogue, Allan. *From Prairie to Corn Belt: Farming on the Illinois and Iowa Prairies in the Nineteenth Centuries*. Chicago: U of Chicago P, 1963.

Bogue, Donald. *Metropolitan Growth and the Conversion of Land to Nonagricultural Uses*. Scripps Foundation for Research in Population Problems, Studies in Population Distribution No. 11. Oxford, Ohio: n.p., 1956.

Boston Traveller. *Incomes of the Citizens of Boston and Other Cities and Towns in Massachusetts*. Boston: Worthington, Flanders, 1867.

Boughton, Willis. "Old Flatbush." In *Flatbush of To-Day: The Realm of Light and Air*, 7–14. Herbert Gunnison, ed. Brooklyn: n.p., 1908.

Boutwell, George. *A Manual of the Direct and Excise Tax System of the United States*. Boston: Little, Brown, 1863.

Brearley, Harry. *The Problem of Greater New York and Its Solution*. NY: Search-Light Book, 1914.

Bridenbaugh, Carl. *Cities in the Wilderness: The First Century of Urban Life in America, 1625–1742*. London: Oxford UP, 1971 [1938].

Brooklyn Before the Bridge: American Paintings from the Long Island Historical Society. Brooklyn: Brooklyn Museum, 1982.

Brooklyn Daily Eagle. *Consolidation Number*. In Eagle Library, No. 22, 13 (22):47 (Jan. 1898).

Brooklyn Daily Eagle Almanac: 1886–1900. Brooklyn: Brooklyn Daily Eagle, 1886–1900.

Bruce, Philip. *The Rise of the New South*. Philadelphia: G. Barrie & Sons, 1905.

Calhoun, W. "The World's Largest Produce Market," *Agricultural Situation* 24 (1):22–24 (Jan. 1940).

Caro, Robert. *The Power Broker: Robert Moses and the Fall of New York*. NY: Vintage, 1975 [1974].

Child, L[ydia]. Maria. *Letters from New York*. 11th ed. NY: Francis, 1852 [1844].

Chinitz, Benjamin. "New York: A Metropolitan Region." In *Cities: A Scientific American Book*, 105–21. NY: Knopf, 1965.

The Citizen Guide to Brooklyn and Long Island. Brooklyn, 1893.

Civilizing American Cities: A Selection of Frederick Law Olmsted's Writings on City Landscapes. S. B. Sutton, ed. Cambridge, Mass.: MIT Press, 1971.

Clarke, James Freeman. "Conditions of the Free Colored People of the United States." *Christian Examiner*, March 1859, 246–65. Reprinted in *The Free People of Color*. NY: Arno, 1969.

Clawson, Marion. *Suburban Land Conversion in the United States: An Economic and Governmental Process*. Baltimore: Johns Hopkins UP, 1971.

Clawson, Marion, and Peter Hall. *Planning and Urban Growth: An Anglo-American Comparison*. Baltimore: Johns Hopkins UP, 1973.

Cleveland, H. "Notes on the Market Gardening of New Jersey." *HJRART* 1:403–6 (1847).

Cocheu, Lincoln. "The Von Kouwenhoven–Conover Family." *NYGBR* 70 (3):230–35 (July 1939).

Cohen, David. *The Dutch-American Farm*. NY: New York UP, 1992.

———. "Dutch-American Farming: Crops, Livestock, and Equipment, 1623–1900." In *New World Dutch Studies: Dutch Arts and Culture in Colonial America 1609–1776*, 185–200. Roderic Blackburn and Nancy Kelley, eds. Albany, N.Y.: Albany Institute of History and Art, 1987.

Colcord, Joanna, and Mary Johnston. *Community Programs for Subsistence Gardens*. NY: Russell Sage, 1933.

Coney Island and the Jews: A History of the Development and Success of this Famous Seaside Resort. NY: Carleton, 1879.

Conklin, Howard, and William Lesher. "Farm-Value Assessment as a Means for Reducing Premature and Excessive Agricultural Disinvestment in Urban Fringes." *Am. J. of Agric. Economics* 59 (4):755–59 (Nov. 1977).

Connolly, Harold. *A Ghetto Grows in Brooklyn*. NY: New York UP, 1977.

Corbett, Lee. *Garden Farming*. Boston: Ginn, 1913.

———. *Intensive Farming*. NY: Outing, 1913.

Cox, Lawanda. "The American Agricultural Wage Earner, 1865–1900." *AH* 22 (2):95–114 (Apr. 1948).

Crozier, William, and Peter Henderson. *How the Farm Pays: The Experiences of Forty Years of Successful Farming and Gardening*. NY: Peter Henderson, 1902 [1884].

Cummings, Richard. *The American and His Food*. NY: Arno, 1970 [1941].

Curti, Merle. *The Making of an American Community: A Case Study of Democracy in a Frontier Community*. Stanford: Stanford UP, 1969 [1959].

Danhof, Clarence. *Change in Agriculture: The Northern United States, 1820–1870*. Cambridge, Mass.: Harvard UP, 1969.

Dasmann, Raymond. *The Destruction of California*. NY: Macmillan, 1965.

Dawson, William. *Municipal Life and Government in Germany*. London: Longmans, Green, 1914.

De Voe, Thomas. *The Market Book: Containing a Historical Account of the Public Markets in the Cities of New York Boston Philadelphia and Brooklyn*. Vol. 1. NY: Franklin, 1969 [1862].

Demaree, A. L. *The American Agricultural Press, 1819–1860*. NY: Columbia UP, 1941.

———. "The Farm Journals, Their Editors, and Their Public, 1830–1860." *AH* 15 (4):182–88 (Oct. 1941).

The Diary of Philip Hone, 1828–1851. Vol. 1. Allan Nevins, ed. NY: Dodd, Mead, 1927.

Dickens, Charles. *American Notes*. London: Nelson, n.d. [1st ed. 1842].

Dilliard, Maud. "A Village Called Midwout." *JLIH* 11:6–24 (1972).

Dillon, John F. *Commentaries on the Law of Municipal Corporations*. 4th ed. Boston: Little, Brown, 1890.

———. *Commentaries on the Law of Municipal Corporations.* 5th ed. Boston: Little, Brown, 1911.

———. *Treatise on the Law of Corporations.* Chicago: Cockroft, 1872.

Ditmas, Charles Andrew. *Brooklyn's Garden: Views of Picturesque Flatbush.* Brooklyn: Ditmas, 1908.

———. *Historic Homesteads of Kings County.* Brooklyn: Compiler, 1909.

Douglas, Paul. *Real Wages in the United States 1890–1926.* Boston: Houghton Mifflin, 1930.

Douglass, Harlan. *The Suburban Trend.* NY: Century, 1925.

Dunn Jr., Edgar. *The Location of Agricultural Production.* Gainesville: U of Florida P, 1954.

Dutton, Richard. "This Was Flatbush." N.p.: n.d.

Dwight, Timothy. *Travels in New England and New York.* Cambridge, Mass.: Harvard UP, 1969 [1822].

The Eagle and Brooklyn: The Record of the Progress of the Brooklyn Daily Eagle. Henry Howard, ed. Brooklyn: Brooklyn Daily Eagle, 1893.

"The Economic Garden." *BBGR* 2:101 (1913).

The Encyclopedia of New York City. Kenneth Jackson, ed. New Haven: Yale UP, 1995.

Ernst, Robert. *Immigrant Life in New York City 1825–1863.* NY: Octagon, 1979 [1949].

Farm Real Estate Values in the United States by Counties, 1850–1959. Thomas Pressly and William Scofield, eds. Seattle: U of Washington P, 1965.

"Farming and Market Gardening." *The Working Farmer* 13 (9):193 (Sept. 1, 1861).

Fausser, William. *The Brooklyn and Rockaway Beach Railroad: The Old Canarsie Line.* N.p., 1976.

Fischel, William. "Urban Development and Agricultural Land Markets." In *Vanishing Farmland Crisis,* 79–98. John Baden, ed. Lawrence, Kans.: UP of Kansas, 1984.

Fisher, Edmund. *Flatbush Past and Present.* Brooklyn: Flatbush Trust Co., 1901.

Fisher, F. J. "The Development of the London Food Market, 1540–1640." *EHR* 5 (2):46–64 (Apr. 1935).

Fisher, Irving D. *Frederick Law Olmsted and the City Planning Movement in the United States.* Ann Arbor, Mich.: UMI Research Press, 1986 [1976].

Fisher, Martha. "Cemeteries and Land Use." In *Land Use in the United States: Exploitation or Conservation,* 93–98. Grant McClellan, ed. NY: Wilson, 1971 [1968].

Fishman, Robert. "The Regional Plan and the Transformation of the Industrial Metropolis." In *The Landscape of Modernity,* 106–25. David Ward and Oliver Zunz, eds. NY: Russell Sage, 1992.

Flatbush of To-day: The Realm of Light and Air. Herbert Gunnison, ed. Brooklyn: n.p., 1908.

"Flatbush Rapid Transit in 1870 (From an Old Newsprint)." In Snyder, *Tales of Old Flatbush,* 127–28. NY: n.p., 1945.

Fogel, Robert, and Stanley Engerman. "Philanthropy at Bargain Prices: Notes on the Economics of Gradual Emancipation." *J. of Legal Studies* 3 (2):377–401 (June 1974).

Fogelson, Robert. *The Fragmented Metropolis: Los Angeles, 1850–1930*. Berkeley: U of California P, 1993 [1967].

Ford, George. "What Is Regional Planning?" *Proceedings of the Fifteenth National Conference on City Planning*, 1–32. Baltimore: 1923.

Fraser, Samuel. *The Potato*. NY: Orange Judd, 1915 [1905].

Freund, Ernst. "Discussion." *Proceedings of the Fifth National Conference on City Planning*, 62–63. Boston: 1913.

Friedmann, Harriet. "After Midas's Feast: Alternative Food Regimes for the Future." In *Food for the Future: Conditions and Contradictions of Sustainability*, 213–33. Pat Allen, ed. NY: Wiley, 1993.

Fullerton, Edith Loring. *The Lure of the Land: The History of a Market-Garden and Dairy Plot*. 3d ed. Long Island: Long Island Railroad, 1911 [1906].

Futterman, Wendy. "Which Came First: The Transit Line or the Neighborhood? The Relationship Between Transportation and Neighborhood Settlement in Brooklyn." *LIHJ* 5 (1):91–100 (1992).

Gabaccia, Donna. *From Sicily to Elizabeth Street: Housing and Social Change Among Italian Immigrants, 1880–1930*. Albany: SUNY Press, 1984.

———. "Little Italy's Decline: Immigrant Renters and Investors in a Changing City." In *The Landscape of Modernity*, 235–51. David Ward and Oliver Zunz, eds. NY: Russell Sage, 1992.

———. *Militants and Migrants: Rural Sicilians Become American Workers*. New Brunswick, N.J.: Rutgers UP, 1988.

Gabriel, Ralph. *The Evolution of Long Island: A Story of Land and Sea*. New Haven, Conn.: Yale UP, 1921.

Gager, C. Stuart. "The Four Botanic Gardens of Brooklyn." *LIHSQ* 2 (1):5–19 (Jan. 1940).

Garvin, Alexander. *The American City: What Works, What Doesn't*. NY: McGraw-Hill, 1996.

Gates, Paul. *The Farmer's Age: Agriculture, 1815–1860*. NY: Harper Torchbooks, 1968 [1960].

George, Henry. *Social Problems*. In *The Complete Works of Henry George*. Vol. 2. Garden City, N.Y.: Doubleday, Page, 1911 [1883].

Germans to America: Lists of Passengers Arriving at U.S. Ports, 1850–1855. Vol. I, *January 1850–May 1851*. Ira Glazier and P. William Filby, eds. Wilmington, Del.: Scholarly Resources, 1988.

Gilbert, Arthur. *The Potato*. NY: Macmillan, 1917.

Goodwyn, Lawrence. *Democratic Promise: The Populist Moment in America*. NY: Oxford UP, 1976.

Gottmann, Jean. *Megalopolis: The Urbanized Northeastern Seaboard of the United States*. NY: Twentieth Century Fund, 1969 [1961].

Grant, H. Roger. *Self-Help in the 1890s Depression*. Ames: Iowa State UP, 1983.

Green Point Savings Bank. *Historic Flatbush: A Brief Review of Pioneer Days*. Brooklyn: Green Point Savings Bank, 1937.

Greene, Evarts, and Virginia Harrington. *American Population Before the Federal Census of 1790*. Gloucester, Mass.: Smith, 1966 [1932].

Greiner, T. *The Young Market Gardener: Beginner's Guide*. Buffalo: Klein, 1896.

Hahamovitch, Cindy. *The Fruits of Their Labor: Atlantic Coast Farmworkers and the Making of Migrant Poverty, 1870–1945*. Chapel Hill, U of North Carolina P, 1997.

Haig, Robert, and Roswell McCrea. *Major Economic Factors in Metropolitan Growth and Arrangement: A Study of Trends and Tendencies in the Economic Activities Within the Region of New York and Its Environs*. NY: Regional Plan of New York and Its Environs, 1927.

Hall, Bolton. *Three Acres and Liberty*. NY: Macmillan, 1914 [1907].

Hall, Peter. *Cities of Tomorrow: An Intellectual History of Urban Planning and Design in the Twentieth Century*. Oxford: Blackwell, 1988.

Hamilton, G. Warren. "History of the Town of New Lots." In Henry Stiles, *Civil . . . History*, 1:306–26. New York: Munsell, 1884.

Hammack, David. *Power and Society: Greater New York at the Turn of the Century*. NY: Columbia UP, 1987 [1982].

Hare, J. *American Constitutional Law*. Boston: Little, Brown, 1889.

Harrison, Shelby. "The Distribution of Taxation in Pittsburgh." In *The Pittsburgh Survey: The Pittsburgh District: Civic Frontage*. 5:156–213. Paul Kellogg, ed. NY: Survey Associates, 1914.

Harriss, C. Lowell. "Free Market Allocation of Resources." In American Assembly, *Farm and the City: Rival or Allies*, 123–44. Englewood Cliffs, N.J.: Prentice-Hall, 1980.

Hazelton, Henry. *The Boroughs of Brooklyn and Queens, Counties of Nassau and Suffolk, Long Island, New York 1609–1924*. Vol. 2–3. NY: Lewis Historical, 1925.

Hedden, W. P. *How Great Cities Are Fed*. Boston: D. C. Heath, 1929.

Hedrick, U. P. *A History of Horticulture in America to 1860*. NY: Oxford UP, 1950.

Heffernan, William, and Susan Elder. "Quality of Life for Farm Families in Metropolitan and Nonmetropolitan Counties." In *Sustaining Agriculture Near Cities*, 91–101. William Lockeretz, ed. Ankeny, Iowa: Soil and Water Conservation Society, 1987.

Henderson, Alford. "American Horticulture." In *1795–1895: One Hundred Years of American Commerce*, 1:248–56. Chauncey Depew, ed. NY: Greenwood, 1968 [1895].

Henderson, Peter. *Gardening for Profit: A Guide to the Successful Cultivation of the Market and Family Garden*. NY: Orange Judd, 1867.

———. *Gardening for Profit: A Guide to the Successful Cultivation of the Market and Family Garden*. Entirely new & greatly enlarged ed. NY: Orange Judd, 1890 [1867].

———. "Market Gardening." In State of New Jersey. *Eleventh Annual Report of the New Jersey State Board of Agriculture: 1883–84*, 159–63. Newton: Bunnell, 1884.

———. "Market Gardening in the Vicinity of New York" In *Report of the Commissioner of Agriculture for the Year 1865*, 243–49. Washington: GPO, 1866.

Henry George's 1886 Campaign: An Account of the George-Hewitt Campaign in the New York Municipal Election of 1886. Louis Post and Fred Leubuscher, eds. NY: Henry George School, 1961 [1887].

Herman, Lydia, et al. "The New York Metropolitan Area Produce Market: A New Opportunity to Preserve Long Island Farmland." Flushing, N.Y.: Center for the Biology of Natural Systems, 1982.

Higginbotham Jr., A. Leon. *In the Matter of Color: Race and the American Legal Process: The Colonial Period.* NY: Oxford, 1978.

Hiss, Tony. *The Experience of Place.* NY: Knopf, 1990.

History of the Massachusetts Horticultural Society: 1829–1878. Boston: For the Society, 1880.

Holmes, O. W. "Murphy, Henry Cruse." In *Dictionary of American Biography.* 13:350. NY: Scribner's, 1943.

Hoover, Edgar, and Raymond Vernon. *Anatomy of a Metropolis: The Changing Distribution of People and Jobs Within the New York Metropolitan Region.* Cambridge, Mass: Harvard UP, 1959.

"How New York Is Fed." *SM* 14 (6):729–43 (Oct. 1877).

Howard, Ebenezer. *Garden Cities of To-Morrow.* F. J. Osborn, ed. Cambridge, Mass.: M.I.T. Press, 1966 [1898].

Howe, Frederic. *The City: The Hope of Democracy.* Seattle: U of Washington P, 1967 [1905].

———. *European Cities at Work.* NY: Scribner's, 1913.

———. "The Municipal Real Estate Policies of German Cities." In *Proceedings of the Third National Conference on City Planning,* 14–26. Boston: 1911.

———. *Taxation and Taxes in the United States under the Internal Revenue System 1791–1895.* NY: Crowell, 1896.

Huntington, Ellsworth. "The Water Barriers of New York City." *GR* 2 (3):169–83 (Sept. 1916).

Hurd, Richard. *Principles of City Land Values.* NY: Record and Guide, 1924 [1903].

Hynes, H. Patricia. *A Patch of Eden: America's Inner-City Gardeners.* White River Junction, Vt.: Chelsea Green, 1996.

Ierardi, Eric. *Gravesend: The Home of Coney Island.* NY: Vantage, 1975.

"Inscriptions on Tombstones in the Cemetery of the Reformed Dutch Church, New Utrecht, L.I." *Kings County Genealogical Club Collections* 1 (1):3 (June 1, 1882).

Jackson, Kenneth. *Crabgrass Frontier: The Suburbanization of the United States.* NY: Oxford UP, 1985.

Jackson, Percival. *The Law of Cadavers and of Burial and Burial Places.* 2d ed. NY: Prentice-Hall, 1950 [1936].

James, Harlean. *Land Planning in the United States for the City, State and Nation.* NY: Macmillan, 1926.

Jarman, Rufus. "The Great Racetrack Caper." *Am. Heritage* 19 (5):24–27, 92–94 (Aug. 1968).

John R. Corbin Co. Houses. N.p.: 1909.

Johns, Elizabeth. "The Farmer in the Works of William Sidney Mount." *J. Interdisciplinary Hist.* 17 (1):257–81 (Summer 1986).

Johnson, David. *Planning the Great Metropolis: The 1929 Regional Plan of New York and Its Environs.* London: Spon, 1996.

Johnson, Jeremiah. "Kings County Agricultural Society: Report of the Committee on Farms and Grain." *TNYSAS for the Year 1842* 2:345–46. Albany: Mack, 1843.

———. "Recollections of Old Roads, Residents and Their Occupations." Brooklyn: Society of Old Brooklynites, 1894.

Josephson, Matthew. *The Robber Barons: The Great American Capitalists 1861–1901.* NY: Harcourt, Brace & World, 1962 [1934].

Kapp, Friedrich Kapp. *Immigration and the Commissioners of Emigration of the State of New York.* NY: Arno, 1969 [1870].

Karr, Ronald. "Brookline Rejects Annexation, 1873." In *Suburbia Re-Examined*, 103–10. Barbara Kelly, ed. NY: Greenwood, 1989.

———. "The Transformation of Agriculture in Brookline, 1770–1885." *Hist. J. of Massachusetts* 15 (1):33–49 (Jan. 1987).

Kelley, Florence. "Congestion and Sweated Labor." *Charities and the Commons* 20 (1):48–50 (Apr. 4, 1908).

Kenney, Alice. *Stubborn for Liberty: The Dutch in New York.* Syracuse: Syracuse UP, 1975.

Kessner, Thomas. *The Golden Door: Italian and Jewish Immigrant Mobility in New York City 1880–1915.* NY: Oxford UP, 1977.

Ketcham, William. "The Manures Used Upon Long Island." *TNYSAS* 3 (1843):462–66. Albany: Carroll & Cook, 1844.

Keyssar, Alexander. *Out of Work: The First Century of Unemployment in Massachusetts.* Cambridge: Cambridge UP, 1986.

"Kings County Agricultural Society: Report of the Committee on Farms and Grain." *TNYSAS* 2:345–46. Albany: Mack, 1843.

Kings County Society for Promoting Agriculture and Domestic Manufactures. *Constitution of the Kings County Society for Promoting Agriculture and Domestic Manufactures.* Brooklyn: Worthington, 1819.

Knaap, Gerrit, and Arthur Nelson. *The Regulated Landscape: Lessons on State Land Use Planning from Oregon.* Cambridge, Mass.: Lincoln Institute of Land Policy, 1992.

Kostof, Spiro. *The City Shaped: Urban Patterns and Meanings Through History.* Boston: Little, Brown, 1991.

Kouwenhoven, John A. "Brooklyn Before the Bridge." In *Brooklyn Before the Bridge: American Paintings from the Long Island Historical Society*, 8–15. Brooklyn: Brooklyn Museum, 1982.

Kropotkin, Petr. *Fields, Factories and Workshops.* Boston: Houghton, Mifflin, 1899.

Lain's Business Directory of Brooklyn . . . 1886/87. N.p., 1887.

Lain's Business Directory of Brooklyn, Kings County . . . 1890. Brooklyn: Lain, 1890.

Lain's Directory of Long Island: For 1878–9. Geo. Lain, comp. Brooklyn: Lain, 1878.

Lamb, Martha J. *History of the City of New York: Its Origin, Rise and Progress*. Vol. 2. NY: Barnes, 1880.

Landesman, Alter. *A History of New Lots, Brooklyn to 1887: Including the Villages of East New York, Cypress Hills, and Brownsville*. Port Washington, N.Y.: Kennikat, 1977.

Landreth, Burnet. *Market Gardening and Farm Notes: Experiences and Observations in the Garden and Field of Interest to the Amateur Gardener, Trucker and Farmer*. NY: Orange Judd, 1903 [1892].

The Landscape of Modernity: Essays on New York City, 1900–1940. David Ward and Olivier Zunz, eds. NY: Russell Sage, 1992.

Lanier, Henry. *A Century of Banking in New York, 1822–1922: The Farmers' Loan and Trust Company Edition*. NY: Gilliss, 1922.

Latimer, Margaret. *New York and Brooklyn the Year the Great Bridge Opened*. Brooklyn: Brooklyn Educational & Cultural Alliance, 1983.

Lavender, Abraham, and Clarence Steinberg. *Jewish Farmers of the Catskills: A Century of Survival*. Gainesville: UP of Florida, 1995.

Lebergott, Stanley. "Labor Force and Employment, 1800–1960." In Conference on Research in Income and Wealth, *Output, Employment, and Productivity in the United States After 1800*, 117–204. NY: National Bureau of Economic Research, 1966.

Lewis, Carolyn. "Agricultural Evolution on Secondary Frontiers." In *The Frontier: Comparative Studies*. 2:205–33. William Savage Jr. and Stephen Thompson, eds. Norman: U of Oklahoma P, 1979.

Linder, Marc. "Tax Glasnost' for Millionaires: Peeking Behind the Veil of Ignorance Along the Publicity-Privacy Continuum," *N.Y.U. Rev. of Law and Social Change* 18 (4):951–86 (1990–91).

Litchfield, Norman. "Blythebourne: A Community that Was Swallowed Up." *JLIHy* 4 (3):28–39 (Summer 1964).

Litwack, Leon. *North of Slavery: The Negro in the Free States, 1790–1860*. Chicago: U of Chicago P, 1967 [1961].

Livingston Jr., Charles. "Background and History of the Church." In *Tercentenary of the Reformed Protestant Dutch Church of the Town of Flatbush in Kings County*, 19–38. N.p., [1954].

Lloyd, John. "Truck-Growing." In *Cyclopedia of American Agriculture*. 5th ed. 2:653–56. L. H. Bailey, ed. NY: Macmillan, 1917 [1907].

Lockeretz, William. "New Life for Metro Farming." *Issues in Science and Technology* 4 (4):81–86 (Summer 1988).

Lockeretz, William, Julia Freedgood, and Katherine Coon. "Farmers' Views of the Prospects of Agriculture in a Metropolitan Area." *Agricultural Systems* 23:43–61 (1987).

Luck, Herbert. *Zur ökonomischen Lehre des J. J. Von Thünen: Zur Entstehung der kapitalistischen Junkerwirtschaft in Mecklenburg*. Berlin: Die Wirtschaft, 1956.

Mackenzie, John, and Gerald Cole. "Use-Value Assessment as a Farmland Preservation Policy." In *Sustaining Agriculture Near Cities*, 251–62.

Makielski Jr., S. *The Politics of Zoning: The New York Experience.* NY: Columbia UP, 1966.

Marti, Donald B. "Agricultural Journalism and the Diffusion of Knowledge: The First Half-Century in America." *AH* 54 (1):28–37 (Jan. 1980).

Marx, Karl. *Das Kapital: Kritik der politischen Oekonomie.* Vol. 1, *Der Produktionsprocess des Kapitals.* Hamburg: Meissner, 1867; photomechanical reprint.

———. *Das Kapital: Kritik der politischen Ökonomie.* Vol. 3, *Der Gesamtprozeß der kapitalistischen Produktion.* In Karl Marx [and] Friedrich Engels, *Werke.* Vol. 25. Berlin: Dietz, 1964 [1894].

Marx, Karl, and Friedrich Engels. *Die deutsche Ideologie.* In Marx and Engels, *Werke.* Vol. 3. Berlin: Dietz, 1958 [1845–46].

———. *Manifest der Kommunistischen Partei.* In Marx and Engels, *Werke.* 4:459–93. Berlin: Dietz, 1959 [1848].

———. *Werke.* Vol. 35. Berlin: Dietz, 1967.

Massey, W. F. "The Developing of Market Gardening Southward and its Lesson to the Northern Trucker." In State of New Jersey. *Thirty-Second Annual Report of the State Board of Agriculture: 1904,* 139–59. Trenton: MacCrellish and Quigley, 1905.

McCorkle Jr., James. "Moving Perishables to Market: Southern Railroads and the Nineteenth-Century Origins of Southern Truck Farming." *AH* 66 (1):42–62 (Winter 1992).

McCullough, David. *The Great Bridge.* NY: Simon & Schuster, 1972.

McCullough, Edo. *Good Old Coney Island: A Sentimental Journey into the Past.* NY: Scribner's, 1957.

McElroy, Samuel. "Town Survey of Kings County." *Van Nostrand's Eclectic Engineering Mag.* 12 (77):140–44 (May 1875).

McKenzie, R. D. "The Rise of Metropolitan Communities." In *Recent Social Trends in the United States: Report of the President's Research Committee on Social Trends,* 443–96. NY: McGraw-Hill, 1933.

McManus, Edgar. *Black Bondage in the North.* Syracuse: Syracuse UP, 1973.

———. *A History of Negro Slavery in New York.* Syracuse: Syracuse UP, 1970 [1966].

McMurry, Sally. "Who Read the Agricultural Journals? Evidence from Chenango County, New York, 1839–1865." *AH* 63 (4):1–18 (Fall 1989).

McWilliams, Carey. *Southern California Country: An Island on the Land.* NY: Duell, Sloan and Pearce, 1946.

Meinig, D. "Geography of Expansion, 1785–1855." In *Geography of New York State,* 140–71. John Thompson, ed. Syracuse: Syracuse UP, 1966.

Merriman, John M. *The Margins of City Life: Explorations on the French Frontier, 1815–1851.* NY: Oxford UP, 1991.

Meyer, Henry A. *Looking Through Life's Window: Personal Reminiscences.* NY: Coward-McCann, 1930.

Moore, Deborah. "On the Fringes of the City: Jewish Neighborhoods in Three

Boroughs." In *Landscape of Modernity*, 252–72. David Ward and Oliver Zunz, eds. NY: Russell Sage, 1992.

Moorhouse, B-Ann. "A 1698 Census New Utrecht." *JLIH* 14(1):54–57 (1977).

[Morris, Edmund]. *Ten Acres Enough: A Practical Experience*. 3d ed. NY: Miller, 1864.

Moss, Richard. *Slavery on Long Island: A Study of Local Institutional and Early African-American Communal Life*. NY: Garland, 1993.

Moughtin, Cliff. *Urban Design: Green Dimensions*. Oxford: Butterworth-Heinemann, 1996.

Mumford, Lewis. *The City in History: Its Origins, Its Transformations, and Its Prospects*. NY: Harcourt, Brace and World, 1961.

———. *The Highway and the City*. NY: New American Library, 1964.

———. "The Plan of New York." *New Republic* 71:121–26, 146–54 (1932).

Nash, Gary, and Jean Soderlund. *Freedom by Degrees: Emancipation in Pennsylvania and Its Aftermath*. NY: Oxford UP, 1991.

National Municipal League. *The Relations of the City to Its Food Supply: Report of a Committee of the National Municipal League*. Philadelphia: National Municipal League, 1915.

Nelli, Humbert Nelli. *Italians in Chicago 1880–1930: A Study in Ethnic Mobility*. NY: Oxford UP, 1975 [1970].

O'Callaghan, E. B. *The Documentary History of the State of New-York*. Vol. 1, 3, 4. Albany, N.Y.: Weed, Parsons, 1849–51.

Ödman, Ella, and Gun-Britt Dahlberg. *Urbanization in Sweden: Means and Methods for the Planning*. Victor Braxton, trans. Government Publishing House, 1970.

Oemler, A. *Truck-Farming at the South: A Guide to the Raising of Vegetables for Northern Markets*. New and rev. ed. NY: Orange Judd, 1894 [1883].

Ogburn, William. "A Study of Food Costs in Various Cities." *Monthly Labor Rev.* 9 (2):1–25 (Aug. 1919).

"'Old Flatbush.'" In John J. Snyder, *Tales of Old Flatbush*, 78–85. Brooklyn: n.p., 1945.

Olmsted, Vaux & Co. *Observations on the Progress of Improvements in Street Plans with Special Reference to the Park-Way Proposed to be Laid Out in Brooklyn, 1868*. Brooklyn: I. Van Anden's Print, 1868.

Olmsted, Frederick Law. "The Future of New York." *NYDT*, Dec. 28, 1879, 5:1.

———. *Papers of Frederick Law Olmsted*. Vol. 6, *The Years of Olmsted, Vaux & Company, 1865–1874*. David Schuyler and Jane Censer, eds. Baltimore: Johns Hopkins UP, 1992.

———. "Report to the Brooklyn Park Commission [January 1, 1869]." In *The Papers of Frederick Law Olmsted*. 6:318–49.

———. "Report to the President of the Board of Commissioners of Prospect Park, Brooklyn [January 1, 1867]." In *The Papers of Frederick Law Olmsted*. 6:150–162.

Olmsted Jr., Frederick Law. "Appendix A — Laws of Planning Unbuilt Areas:

Open-Development Zoning." In *Regional Plan: Neighborhood and Community Planning.* 7:320–25. NY: Regional Plan of New York and Its Environs, 1929.

Olmsted [Jr.], Frederick Law. "Introductory Address on City Planning." In *Proceedings of the Second National Conference on City Planning and the Problems of Congestion,* 15–32. Boston: University Press, 1910.

Opie, John. *The Law of the Land: Two Hundred Years of American Farmland Policy.* Lincoln: U of Nebraska P, 1987.

The Papers of Henry Clay. Vol. 10. Melba Hay, ed. Lexington: UP of Kentucky, 1991.

Parramore, Thomas. *Norfolk: The First Four Centuries.* Charlottesville: UP of Virginia, 1994.

Pass, David. *Vällingby and Farsta — from Idea to Reality: The New Community Development Process in Stockholm.* Cambridge, Mass.: MIT Press, 1973 [1969].

Passow, Shirley. "Land Reserves and Teamwork in Planning Stockholm." *J. of the Am. Institute of Planners* 36 (2):179–88 (Mar. 1970).

Pecorini, Alberto. "The Italian as an Agricultural Laborer." *AAAPSS* 33: 380–90 (1909).

Pessen, Edward. *Riches, Class, and Power Before the Civil War.* Lexington, Mass.: Heath, 1973.

Pink, Louis. *Gaynor: The Tammany Mayor Who Swallowed the Tiger.* Freeport, N.Y.: Books for Libraries Press, 1970 [1931].

Politics of Land: Ralph Nader's Study Group Report on Land Use in California. Robert Fellmeth, ed. NY: Grossman, 1973.

Pratt, Edward. *Industrial Causes of Congestion of Population in New York City.* NY: Columbia U, 1911.

Pred, Allan. *The External Relations of Cities During 'Industrial Revolution': With a Case Study of Göteborg, Sweden: 1868–1890.* U of Chicago, Department of Geography, Research Paper 76. Chicago: 1962.

"Pretends to Be Free": Runaway Slave Advertisements from Colonial and Revolutionary New York and New Jersey. Graham Hodges and Alan Brown, eds. NY: Garland, 1994.

Prime, Nathaniel Prime. *A History of Long Island: From Its First Settlement by Europeans to the Year 1845.* NY: Carter, 1845.

Protestant Dutch Reformed Church of Flatlands. *Tercentary Anniversary: 1654–1954.* Brooklyn: Protestant Dutch Reformed Church of Flatlands, n.d. [1954].

Purple, Samuel. "A Brief Memoir of the Life and Writings of Hon. Teunis G. Bergen of New Utrecht." *NYGBR* 12(4):149–54 (Oct. 1881).

Quinn, P. T. *Money in the Garden: A Vegetable Manual, Prepared with a View to Economy and Profit.* NY: Orange Judd, 1891 [1871].

Ralph, Julian. "The City of Brooklyn." *Harper's New Monthly Mag.* 86:651–71 (Apr. 1893).

Rawson, W. W. *Success in Market Gardening: A New Vegetable Growers' Manual.* Boston: Author, 1892.

Rawson, Warren W. "Discussion." In *TMHS for the Year 1901.* Pt. 1, 73 (1902).

Relis, Paul. "Land Disputes and the Urban-Rural Border." In *Radical Agriculture*, 171–87. Richard Merrill, ed. NY: Harper & Row, 1976.

Reynells, M. "Urban Sprawl as It Affects the Southern California Poultry Industry." In *Sustaining Agriculture Near Cities*, 65–74. William Lockeretz, ed. Ankeny, Iowa: Soil and Water Conservation Society, 1987.

Ridge, John T. *The Flatbush Irish*. Brooklyn: Division 35 Ancient Order of Hibernians, 1983.

Rischin, Moses. *The Promised City: New York's Jews, 1870–1914*. Cambridge: Harvard UP, 1977 [1962].

Robbins, Catherine Chapman. *David Hosack: Citizen of New York*. Philadelphia: Am. Philosophical Society, 1964.

"The Romance of the Flatbush Water Works." In Snyder, *Tales of Old Flatbush*, 145–48. Brooklyn: n.p., 1945.

Rosenwaike, Ira. *Population History of New York City*. Syracuse: Syracuse UP, 1972.

Ross, Peter. *A History of Long Island: From Its Earliest Settlement to the Present Time*. Vol. 1. NY: Lewis, 1903.

Rules and Regulations of Green-Wood Cemetery. New York: 1849.

Russell, Howard. *A Long, Deep Furrow: Three Centuries of Farming in New England*. UP of New England, 1976.

Saint-Méry, Moreau de. *Voyage aux États-Unis de l'Amérique, 1793–1798*. Stewart Mims, ed. 1913.

"Sanitary Notes — Sewerage and Sewage." *Scientific American* 28 (26) (n.s.): 405 (June 28, 1873).

Schneider, David. *The History of Public Welfare in New York State*. Montclair, N.J.: Patterson Smith, 1969 [1938].

Schultz, Stanley K. *Constructing Urban Culture: American Cities and City Planning, 1800–1920*. Philadelphia: Temple UP, 1989.

Scott, Mel. *American City Planing Since 1890: A History Commemorating the Fiftieth Anniversary of the American Institute of Planners*. Berkeley: U California P, 1969.

Seyfried, Vincent. *Corona: From Farmland to City Suburb 1650–1935*. N.p., 1986.

———. *The Long Island Rail Road: A Comprehensive History*. Pt. Four, *The Bay Ridge and Manhattan Beach Divisions*. Garden City, N.Y.: Seyfried, 1966.

Shannon, Fred. *The Farmer's Last Frontier: Agriculture, 1860–1897*. NY: Harper, 1968 [1945].

Sherman, Franklin J. *Building Up Greater Queens Borough: An Estimate of Its Development and the Outlook*. NY: Brooklyn Biographical Society, 1929.

Sherman, Wells. *Merchandising Fruits and Vegetables: A New Billion Dollar Industry*. NY: McGraw-Hill, 1930.

Sidenbladh, Göran. "Stockholm: A Planned City." In *Cities: A Scientific American Book*, 75–87. NY: Knopf, 1965.

Simon, Donald. "Green-Wood Cemetery and the American Park Movement." In *Essays in the History of New York City: A Memorial to Sidney Pomerantz*, 61–77. Irwin Yellowitz, ed. Port Washington, N.Y.: Kennikat, 1978.

Simpson, Michael. *Thomas Adams and the Modern Planning Movement: Britain, Canada and the United States, 1900–1940*. London: Mansell, 1985.

Sinclair, Robert. "Von Thünen and Urban Sprawl." *Annals of the Assoc. of Am. Geographers* 57 (1):72–87 (Mar. 1967).

Smit, Jac, et al. *Urban Agriculture: Food, Jobs and Sustainable Cities*. NY: U.N. Development Programme, 1996.

Smith, Harry. *The United States Federal Internal Tax History from 1861 to 1871*. Boston: Houghton, Mifflin, 1914.

Smith, Kathleen. "*Moore's Rural New Yorker*: A Farm Program for the 1850s." *AH* 45 (1):39–46 (Jan. 1971).

Smith, Mortimer. *William Jay Gaynor: Mayor of New York*. Chicago: Henry Regenery, 1951.

Smythe, William. *City Homes on Country Lanes: Philosophy and Practice of the Home-in-a-Garden*. NY: Macmillan, 1921.

Snyder, John J. *Tales of Old Flatbush*. NY: n.p., 1945.

Snyder-Grenier, Ellen. *Brooklyn! An Illustrated History*. Philadelphia: Temple UP, 1996.

"Some Suburbs of New York: II. — Westchester and Long Island." *Lippincott's Mag.* 8 (new ser.):113–28 (Aug. 1884).

Soule, Andrew. "Vegetable, Fruit and Nursery Products and Truck Farming in the South." In *The South in the Building of the Nation: Economic History, 1865–1909*. 6:127–35. James Ballagh, ed. Richmond, Va.: Southern Historical Publication Society, 1909.

Spann, Edward. *The New Metropolis: New York City, 1840–1857*. NY: Columbia UP, 1981.

Spengler, Edwin. *Land Values in New York in Relation to Transit Facilities*. NY: Columbia UP, 1930.

Staff of the Regional Plan of New York and Its Environs. Vol. 1, *Regional Plan: The Graphic Regional Plan: Atlas and Description*. NY: Regional Plan of New York and Its Environs, 1929.

Stanhill, G. "An Urban Agro-Ecosystem: The Example of Nineteenth-Century Paris." *Agro-Economics* 3:269–84 (1977).

Statistisches Jahrbuch deutscher Gemeinden. Vol. 30. Jena: Fischer, 1935.

Stiles, Henry. *The Civil, Political, Professional and Ecclesiastical History and Commercial and Industrial Record of the County of Kings and the City of Brooklyn, N.Y. from 1683 to 1884*. 2 vols. NY: Munsell, 1884.

———. *A History of the City of Brooklyn: Including the Old Town and Village of Brooklyn, the Town of Bushwick, and the Village and City of Williamsburgh*. Vol. 3. Brooklyn: n.p., 1870.

Stockwell, A. P. "History of the Town of Gravesend." In Stiles, *Civil . . . History*. 1:156–79. NY: Munsell, 1884.

Straubenmüller, Gustave. *A Home Geography of New York City*. Boston: Ginn, 1905.

Strickland, William. *Journal of a Tour in the United States of America 1794–1795*. J. E. Strickland, ed. [New York]: New-York Historical Society, 1971.

Strong, R. G. "History of the Town of Flatbush." In Stiles, *Civil . . . History*. 1:212–54. NY: Munsell, 1884.

Strong, Thomas. *The History of the Town of Flatbush in Kings County, Long-Island.* NY: Thomas R. Mercein Jr., 1842.

Sullivan, J. W. *Markets for the People: The Consumer's Part.* NY: Macmillan, 1913.

Sullivan, Michael. "The Advancement of Market Gardening in the Past Twenty-Five Years." *TMHS for the Year 1901.* Pt. I, 63–71 (1902).

Sundquist, James. *Dispersing Population: What America Can Learn from Europe.* Washington, D.C.: Brookings Institution, 1975.

Sustaining Agriculture Near Cities. William Lockeretz, ed. Ankeny, Iowa: Soil and Water Conservation Society, 1987.

Syrett, Harold. *The City of Brooklyn, 1865–1898: A Political History.* NY: Columbia UP, 1944.

Tarr, Joel. "From City to Farm: Urban Wastes and the American Farmer." *AH* 49 (4):598–612 (Oct. 1975).

———. "Urban Pollution: Many Long Years Ago." *Am. Heritage* 22 (6):65–69, 106 (Oct. 1971).

Tercentenary of the Reformed Protestant Dutch Church of the Town of Flatbush in Kings County 1654–1954. N.p.: n.d. [1954].

Thick, Malcolm. "Market Gardening in England and Wales." In *The Agrarian History of England and Wales.* V, pt. II, *1640–1750: Agrarian Change,* 503–32. Joan Thirsk, ed. Cambridge: Cambridge UP, 1985.

Thompson, Benjamin. *History of Long Island from Its Discovery and Settlement to the Present Time.* 3d ed. Vol. 3. Port Washington, N.Y.: Friedman, 1962 [1839].

Thompson, C. Woody, and Wendell Smith. *Public Utility Economics.* NY: McGraw-Hill, 1941.

Thompson, John. "The Primary Sector." In *Geography of New York State,* 201–31. John Thompson, ed. Syracuse: Syracuse UP, 1966.

Thorp, Willard. *Business Annals.* NY: National Bureau of Economic Research, 1926.

The Towns That Became Brooklyn. Brooklyn: Brooklyn Eagle Press, 1946.

Trachtenberg, Alan. *Brooklyn Bridge: Fact and Symbol.* Chicago: U of Chicago P, 1979.

Transactions of the New York State Agricultural Society. 3:654–55. Albany: Carroll & Cook, 1844.

———. 12 (1852):535–36. Albany: Benthuysen, 1853.

Traven, B. *Die weisse Rose.* Frankfurt a.M.: Diogenes, 1983 [1929].

Tredwell, Daniel. "Flatbush." *JLIH* 4 (4):40–47 (1964 [1914]).

———. *Personal Reminiscences of Men and Things on Long Island.* Brooklyn: Charles Andrew Ditmas, 1912.

Trow's New York City Directory for the Year Ending May 1, 1861. Vol. 74. H. Wilson, comp. NY: Trow, 1860.

Trow's New York City Directory for the Year Ending May 1, 1869. Vol. 82. H. Wilson, comp. NY: Trow, 1868.

"The 'Truck' Gardens and Market." *Frank Leslie's Illustrated Newspaper.* Nov. 17, 1888, 218–19.

"'Uncle Sammy' Anderson: The Last Flatbush Slave." In John J. Snyder, *Tales of Old Flatbush* 176–77. NY: n.p., 1945.

Vanderbilt, Gertrude Lefferts. *The Social History of Flatbush, and Manners and Customs of the Dutch Settlers in Kings County.* Brooklyn: Loeser, 1909 [1880].

Van Zanden, J. L. *The Tranformation of European Agriculture in the Nineteenth Century: The Case of the Netherlands.* Amsterdam: VU Uitgiverij, 1994.

von Thünen, Johann Heinrich. *Der isolierte Staat in Beziehung auf Landwirtschaft und Nationalökonomie.* 3d ed. Jena: Gustav Fischer, 1930 [1826].

Voorhees, Edward B. "Annual Address of the President." In State of New Jersey. *Thirty-Third Annual Report of the State Board of Agriculture: 1905,* 39–57. Paterson: News Printing, 1906.

Wagman, Morton. "The Rise of Pieter Claessen Wyckoff: Social Mobility on the Colonial Frontier." *New York History* 53 (1):5–24 (1972).

Walker, James. *Fifty Years of Rapid Transit 1864–1917.* NY: Arno, 1970 [1918].

Wallace, David, et al. *Metropolitan Open Space and Natural Process.* Philadelphia: U of Pennsylvania, 1970.

Ward, David, and Olivier Zunz. "Between Rationalism and Pluralism: Creating the Modern City." In *The Landscape of Modernity,* 3–15. NY: Russell Sage, 1992.

Warner Jr., Sam Bass. *The Private City: Philadelphia in Three Periods of Its Growth.* Philadelphia: U of Pennsylvania P, 1968.

———. *To Dwell Is to Garden: A History of Boston's Community Gardens.* Boston: Northeastern UP, 1987.

———. *The Urban Wilderness: A History of the American City.* NY: Harper & Row, 1972.

Watts, Ralph, and Gilbert Watts, *The Vegetable Growing Business.* NY: Orange Judd, 1940 [1939].

Wealth and Biography of the Wealthy Citizens of New York City. 6th ed. NY: Sun, 1845. Reprinted in Henry Lanier. *A Century of Banking in New York, 1822–1922: The Farmers' Loan and Trust Company Edition.* NY: Gilliss, 1922.

Webber, Ronald. *Market Gardening: The History of Commercial Flower, Fruit and Vegetable Growing.* Newton Abbot: David & Charles, 1972.

Weber, Adna. *The Growth of Cities in the Nineteenth Century: A Study in Statistics.* NY: Macmillan, 1899.

Weld, L. D. H. *The Marketing of Farm Products.* NY: Macmillan, 1928.

Weld, Ralph. *Brooklyn Is America.* NY: Columbia UP, 1950.

———. *Brooklyn Village: 1816–1834.* NY: Columbia UP, 1938.

Wertenbaker, Thomas. *Norfolk: Historic Southern Port.* Durham: Duke UP, 1931.

White, Shane. *Somewhat More Independent: The End of Slavery in New York City, 1770–1810.* Athens: UP of Georgia, 1991.

White, William N. *Gardening for the South; or, How to Grow Vegetables and Fruits.* 3d ed., rev. and enl. by P. H. Mell. Richmond, Va.: B. F. Johnson, 1901.

Whitman, Walt. "Brooklyniana." In *The Uncollected Poetry and Prose of Walt Whitman* 2:222–321. Emory Holloway, ed. Garden City, N.Y.: Doubleday, Page, 1921 [1862].

————. "The Future of Brooklyn." In *I Sit and Look Out: Editorials from the Brooklyn Daily Times*, 146–47. Emory Holloway and Vernolian Schwarz, eds. NY: Columbia UP, 1932 [July 14, 1858].

Who's Who in America. Vol. 3, 14. Albert Marquis, ed. Chicago: Marquis, 1903–1905, 1926–1927.

Whyte, William. "A Case for Higher Density Cities." In *Land Use in the United States: Exploitation or Conservation*, 62–74. Grant McClellan, ed. NY: Wilson, 1971 [1968].

————. *The Last Landscape*. Garden City: Doubleday, 1970 [1968].

Whyte, William H., Jr. "Urban Sprawl." In *The Exploding Metropolis*, 133–56. Garden City, N.Y.: Doubleday, 1958.

Willensky, Elliott. *When Brooklyn Was the World: 1920–1957*. NY: Harmony Books, 1986.

Williams, Jesse. "Rural New York City." *Scribner's* 30:178–91 (Aug. 1901).

Wilson, Rufus. *Historic Long Island*. NY: Berkeley Press, 1902.

Wines, Richard. *Fertilizer in America: From Waste Recycling to Resource Exploitation*. Philadelphia: Temple UP, 1985.

Wolf, Eric. *Europe and the People Without History*. Berkeley: U of California P, 1982.

Wolf, Stephanie. *Urban Village: Population, Community, and Family Structure in Germantown, Pennsylvania, 1683–1800*. Princeton: Princeton UP, 1980 [1976].

Wolfe, Thomas. "Only the Dead Know Brooklyn." In *The Complete Short Stories of Thomas Wolfe* 260–64. Francis Skipp, ed. NY: Scribner, 1987 [1935].

Woodruff, A. M. "City Land and Farmland." In American Assembly, *Farm and the City: Rival or Allies* 11–35. Englewood Cliffs, N.J.: Prentice-Hall, 1980.

Woodruff, A. M., and Charles Frink. "Introduction." In American Assembly, *The Farm and the City: Rivals or Allies?* 1–10. Englewood Cliffs, N.J.: Prentice-Hall, 1980.

Woodward, Carl. *The Development of Agriculture in New Jersey 1640–1880: A Monographic Study in Agricultural History*. New Brunswick, N.J.: Agricultural Experiment Station, 1927.

Wooldridge, Charles. *Perfecting the Earth*. NY: Arno Press, 1971 [1902].

The WPA Guide to New York City: The Federal Writers' Project Guide to 1930s New York. NY: New Press, 1992 [1939].

"Wythenshawe Rehouses More Than 6,000 Families from Manchester's Insanitary Area." *American City*, Nov. 1936, 46–49.

Younger, William. *Old Brooklyn in Early Photographs, 1865–1929: 157 Prints from the Collection of the Long Island Historical Society*. NY: Dover, 1978.

Zilversmit, Arthur. *The First Emancipation: The Abolition of Slavery in the North*. Chicago: U of Chicago P, 1967.

INDEX